ADVANCES IN TAGMEMICS

NORTH-HOLLAND
LINGUISTIC SERIES 9
Edited by S. C. DIK and J. G. KOOIJ

ADVANCES IN TAGMEMICS

Editor:

RUTH M. BREND

Michigan State University

1974

NORTH-HOLLAND PUBLISHING COMPANY - AMSTERDAM · LONDON
AMERICAN ELSEVIER PUBLISHING COMPANY, INC. - NEW YORK

Library of Congress Catalog Number 73-81526

North-Holland ISBN for this series 0 7204 6180 4
North-Holland ISBN for this volume 0 7204 6190 1
American Elsevier ISBN 0 444 10534 4

Publishers:
NORTH-HOLLAND PUBLISHING COMPANY – AMSTERDAM
NORTH-HOLLAND PUBLISHING COMPANY, LTD. – LONDON

Sole distributors for the U.S.A.:
AMERICAN ELSEVIER PUBLISHING COMPANY,
52 VANDERBILT AVENUE
NEW YORK, N.Y. 10017

PRINTED IN THE NETHERLANDS

PREFACE

This collection is designed to supplement the major texts of tag-memics (*Language in Relation to a Unified Theory of the Structure of Human Behavior*, by K.L. Pike; *An Introduction to Morphology and Syntax*, by Ben F. Elson and Velma B. Pickett; and *Grammar Discovery Procedures*, by Robert E. Longacre), which appeared several years ago. I have endeavored to show changes and developments in the theory since their appearance and have included one tagmemically-based study in an area other than pure linguistic analysis.

The tagmemic literature to date is large. For annotated listings of ap-proximately 400 publications, see Kenneth L. Pike, 'A Guide to Publica-tions Related to Tagmemic Theory', *Current Trends in Linguistics, III: Theoretical Foundations*, ed. T.A. Sebeok, The Hague: Mouton and Co., 1966, pp. 365–394; and my 'Tagmemic Theory: an Annotated Biblio-graphy', with one Appendix, *Journal of English Linguistics*, 4.7–45, 1970, and 6.1–16, 1972.

Throughout the excerpts and articles included here a few major de-velopments can be seen: (1) Use of a "Matrix type analysis" (first intro-duced by Pike in his 'Dimensions of Grammatical Constructions', *Lan-guage*, 38.221–244, 1962) to specify relationships between construc-tions and to reveal patterning below the morpheme level; (2) the addi-tion of "roles" (i.e., case relationships) to the previously-delineated grammatical functions (the possibility of such roles first seen in the pre-liminary edition of Pike's *Language ...*, in 1954, with his postulation of subject-as-actor, subject-as-goal, and later elaborated by him in selection 17 of this volume, and by others). These studies, together with the addi-tion of "reading rules" to tagmemic formulas – see especially selection 13 – have helped make tagmemic formulas become more generative; (3) sentence, paragraph and discourse levels, not looked at in early tag-memic writings, but currently being carefully studied by Robert Long-acre and others; and (4) the interrelationship of grammar and lexicon (see especially selections by Becker, Wise, and Ballard, Conrad and Long-acre.

The number of phonological selections has been kept purposively small since it is anticipated that a companion volume, entitled *Readings in Tone and Intonation by Members of the Summer Institute of Linguistics,* will appear shortly as a volume of *Bibliotheca Phonetica.* In it, one may find both pre-tagmemic and tagmemic articles which are illustrative of theory and of pitch systems from various areas of the world. I have also endeavored to include articles included in Kenneth L. Pike: *Selected Writings* (The Hague: Mouton and Co., 1972), and to include a number of articles which have not been published before, or were published in a language other than English. Of the former, the two articles co-authored by Eunice Pike (selections 7 and 8) are of interest, since they describe a tonal system not previously encountered in the Americas. The article on the English Verb Phrase, by K.L. Pike (selection 12) should also be of special interest since it is a demonstration of the application of tagmemic theory to an area which has been of interest to scholars in other theories.

Ruth M. Brend

INTRODUCTION

In 1954 I asked the question: (1) Can an analogue of the phoneme be found for grammar? By the next year I was asking: (2) Since the tagmeme (resultant from question one) is in a hierarchy, can the syllable be fitted into linguistic theory (instead of being kept out, as in the then current climate) in a comparable hierarchy? By 1952 I wished to know: (3) How can I treat the obvious parallels between language and non-verbal behavior — especially since there are instances where both must be included, interwoven, substitutably in a single event — an event as unified as a wedding or a party game? These questions, and others growing out of them, occupied me for a decade and the result could be seen in my basic monograph, *Language in Relation to a Unified Theory of the Structure of Human Behavior* (preliminary edition: Vol. 1, 1954, Vol. 2, 1955; Vol. 3, 1960—revised, second edition, The Hague: Mouton and Co., 1967). By 1960, I was asking: (4) Can a chart for grammar be found, analogous to a chart of phones or phonemes? By 1963, I wished to know: (5) Can the subject-as-actor, versus subject-as-goal tagmemes (cf. volume 1 of my basic monograph, 1954) be generalized for all types of grammatical roles versus situational roles (the latter since called 'case' by many scholars) — and could this factor be generalized for all levels of the hierarchy? (See my 'Discourse Analysis and Tag- ; meme Matrices', selection 17). Specifically, here, the question draws in all kinds of semantic problems, many of which were anticipated in the early volumes, but which are now being developed much more fully and explicitly. For example, there is the attempt to retain the initial commitment to language (and to various units of language) as a form—meaning composite. That is, my variety of tagmemics at least (though R.E. Longacre and W. Merrifield are slightly less rigid in this assumption than I appear to be some of my colleagues) does not find it congenial to allow contrastive features of meanings to be sharply divided from organizational aspects, and placed in a remote place in the theory or its axioms. That is, in current terms, 'deep' and 'surface' must be handled not only in practical heuristic but in theoretical development also as close together, and separated only for brief analytical moments, for tentative abstraction, before being brought together into theoretical units. It is such an approach, perhaps, which leads tagmemic theory in all its varieties, I think, to emphasize the necessity of units, not merely features, as essential to language and to other forms of behavior.

Still later in the decade of the sixties I wished to know: (6) Can standard mathematics of some type – not mathematics developed ad hoc for some particular linguistic phenomenon – be utilized to describe – or even discover – some generalizations which have otherwise evaded us? And, going back to work sporadically of interest, and intermingled with efforts to answer the earlier questions: (7) How can these same insights be brought to bear to integrate our knowledge of various disciplines – from the study of poetry or rhetoric to our talks with the physicists or psychologists?

Thus, central to tagmemics is the insistence on the possibility and necessity on both theoretical and practical levels, of keeping units as prime constructs in the theory and also to the internal linguistic structure of the speakers. Thus, from this approach, there can be seen an implicit philosophy of the nature of man. Man is not, in this view, a box with compartments only connected by lines of communication, but rather, man is a unitized creature. Universal to the languages of the world, these units can be such only when high-level generalized conditions are met – a unit must have contrastive-identificational features, a range of variability, with physical (including as all or part – neurological element), and distribution in class, sequence, and system. No theory which omits such high-level generalizations can satisfy anyone who has once seen these facts of the nature of man, since their loss eventually divorces man's consciousness of himself from the nature of himself, his language from the matrix of experience within which it can alone be learned. Without such controls on all possible theories, one ends up with language conditioning concepts (rather than the two learned together), with language as a mathematics (rather than as behavior, designed to do a work in a society, having an impact on understanding and on behavior). These goals, no less, are in front of our vision as we try to find and describe the configurations of abstractions (in part incomplete and with residues) from that experience called language.

The articles reprinted in this collection give some answers to the above questions, and explication of the above theoretical outlook, beyond that which was available in the early material. Numerous other scholars have by now taken up these concerns, added others of their own, and developed beyond our early starting points. Robert Longacre has added notably to studies of discourse (note selections 16, 18, and 19). Alton Becker and Mary Ruth Wise have made large contributions to the study of situational role in its relation to the larger structures (selections 14 and 21). Klammer and others have studied the relation of linguistics and literature (see selection 20). For some of these materials, see the tagmeme bibliographies[1] – a collection of this size cannot include them all.[2] Rather, the editor has chosen a selection to show the varied kinds of output, rather than developing any one in detail. She has attempted to choose so as to show crucial new developments in the theory, and the varied applications of the theory to areas which are not strictly linguistic in nature.

Kenneth L. Pike
University of Michigan

[1] Kenneth L. Pike, 'A Guide to Publications Related to Tagmemic Theory', *Current Trends in Linguistics, III: Theoretical Foundations,* Ed. T.A. Sebeok, The Hague: Mouton and Co., 1966, pp. 365–94; Ruth M. Brend, 'Tagmemic Theory: an Annotated Bibliography', *Journal of English Linguistics,* 1970, 4.1–45; Ruth M. Brend, 'Tagmemic Theory: An Annotated Bibliography, Appendix I', *Journal of English Linguistics,* 1972, 6.1–16.

[2] In addition, duplication was avoided between this volume, and the volume, which is to appear shortly, *Studies in Tone and Intonation by Members of the Summer Institute of Linguistics,* Bibliotheca Phonetica, 1973. For this reason, also, the phonology section here is rather small.

ACKNOWLEDGEMENT

Various articles contained in this volume were earlier published elsewhere. References to these sources are given in the Table of Contents.

The editor wishes to thank all publishers, editors and authors for granting permission to reprint these articles.

TABLE OF CONTENTS

Preface V
Introduction VII

General theory

1 John Algeo, Tagmemics: a brief overview 1
                                     J. Engl. Linguist, vol. 4, 1–6, 1970
2 Robert E. Longacre, Some fundamental insights
   of tagmemics 11
                                   Language, vol. 41, no. 1,65–76, 1965
3 Peter H. Fries, Some fundamental insights of
   tagmemics revisited 23
4 Kenneth L. Pike, Crucial questions in the development of tagmemics: the Sixties and Seventies 35
        Monogr. Ser. Languages Linguist., no. 24, 79–98, Georgetown University, 1971
5 Austin Hale, On the systematization of Box 4 55

Phonology

6 Robert D. Olson, The syllable in Chipaya 75
                 Int. J. Amer. Linguist., vol 33, no. 4, 300–304, 1967
7 Eunice V. Pike and Kent Wistrand, Step-up terrace
   tone in Acatlan Mixtec (Mexico) 81
8 Eunice V. Pike and Priscilla Small, Downstepping
   terrace tone in Coatzospan Mixtec 105

Morphology

9 Kenneth L. Pike and Barbara Erickson, Conflated
   field structures in Potawatomi and in Arabic 135
               Int. J. Amer. Linguist, vol. 30, no. 3, 201–212, 1964
10 Janette Forster and Myra L. Barnard, A classification
    of Dibabawon active verbs 147
                      Lingua, vol. 20, 265–278, 1968

11   John C. Callow, A hierarchical study of neutralization
      in Kasem   161
                                    J. Linguist., vol. 4, 33–45, 1968

Syntax – below the sentence

12   Kenneth L. Pike and Evelyn G. Pike, Rules as com-
      ponents of tagmemics in the English verb phrase   175
13   Kenneth Jacobs and Robert E. Longacre, Patterns and
      rules in Tzotzil grammar   205
                                    Found. Language, vol. 3, 325–389, 1967
14   Alton L. Becker, Conjoining in a tagmemic grammar
      of English   223
         Monograph. Ser. Languages Linguist., no. 20, 109–20, Georgetown University, 1967
15   Kenneth L. Pike, A syntactic paradigm   235
                                    Language, vol. 39, no. 2, 216–230, 1963

Syntax – sentence level

16   Robert E. Longacre, Sentence structure as statement
      calculus   251
                                    Language, vol. 46, no. 4, 783–815, 1970

Syntax – above the sentence

17   Kenneth L. Pike, Discourse analysis and tagmeme matrices   285
                                    Oceanic Linguist., vol. 3, no. 1, 5–25, 1964
18   D. Lee Ballard, Robert J. Conrad and Robert E. Longacre,
      The deep and surface grammar of interclausal relations   307
                                    Found. Language, vol. 7, 70–118, 1971
19   Robert E. Longacre, Narrative versus other discourse
      genre   357
                                    From Soundstream to Discourse, 167–185, 1972
20   Thomas P. Klammer and Carol J. Compton, Some recent
      contributions to tagmemic analysis of discourse   377
                                    Glossa, vol. 4, no. 2, 212–222, 1970
21   Mary Ruth Wise, Social roles, plot roles, and focal roles
      in a Nomatsiguenga Campa myth   389
                                    Actas y Memorias del 19em Congr. Int. de Americanistas
22   Helen Larsen, Some grammatical features of legendary
      narrative in Ancash Quechua   419
                                    Actas y Memorias del 19em Congr. Int. de Americanistas

Analysis of society

23   Philip K. Bock, Social structure and language structure   441
Southwest. J. Anthropol., vol. 20, no. 4, 393–403, 1964

Index   453

General theory

TAGMEMICS: A BRIEF OVERVIEW

John ALGEO

At a time when linguistic theorizing is a glamorous enterprise that outdazzles the drabber efforts of mere description and taxonomy, the tagmemic theory of Kenneth Pike has one clear distinction. Pike and his associates have not scrupled to dirty their hands with the commoner forms of linguistic labor. Willie Stark, in Robert Penn Warren's *All the King's Men*, observed that you cannot build hospitals without bricks and that "somebody has to paddle in the mud to make 'em". Willie was talking about morality in politics, but the metaphor is applicable also to field work in linguistics, and as such, can be taken (without any further equation of linguistics and populism) as a fair representation of the stance that tagmemicists have assumed: you cannot build theories without facts and somebody has to paddle in the empirical mud to find them. The tagmemic school has indeed sought to develop theory and praxis to an equal degree. It is thus no accident that Pike's *Language in Relation to a Unified Theory* ... should be balanced (symbolically, not in weight) by Longacre's *Grammar Discovery Procedures* as comprehensive statements of tagmemic theory and practice. To be sure, all theoreticians must occasionally soil themselves with data, but the tendency has been to take readily available facts about well-known languages and to redescribe them according to the favorite theory. The distinction of the tagmemicists is that they have gone on collecting new data about ill-known languages, with unconcern for the low prestige of data-gathering in our time.

In addition to a strongly empirical and pragmatic orientation, tagmemics has a number of characteristics that help to differentiate it from other current forms of linguistics. The most significant of these is indicated by the full title of Pike's major work: *Language in Relation to a*

Unified Theory of the Structure of Human Behavior. Pike aims at accounting for language, not as a *sui generis* phenomenon, but as an integral part of the whole of man's life. Language is to be studied, not as an isolated structure, but as a system set off only by indeterminate bounds from a context that expands in time and space and complexity to include ultimately whatever forms a part of man's experience. Pike's aim in the study of behavior is analogous to Einstein's in physics. His linguistic theory is not specifically a theory of language, but is rather a special case of a general, unified theory that accounts for all cultural behavior, of which language is itself only a special case.

There is in this tagmemic insistence that language can be adequately studied only as a part of man's total behavior, an apparent contradiction with much of post-Saussurian linguistics, for example, Hjelmslev's view that "linguistics must attempt to grasp language, not as a conglomerate of non-linguistic (e.g., physics, physiological, psychological, logical, sociological) phenomena, but as a self-sufficient totality, a structure *sui generis*" (*Prolegomena to a Theory of Language*, tr. F.J. Whitfield, Madison, 1963, pp. 5-6). The contradiction is, however, more apparent than real. Hjelmslev's concern was to assert the right of the linguist to consider language as an end of investigation, not merely a means. Pike's concern is to affirm that language cannot be adequately investigated apart from the rest of human behavior. Thus their positions are not really in conflict, Hjelmslev being concerned with ends and Pike with scope.

The tagmemic insistence that language be viewed as part of the whole of human behavior and that there be a unified theory to account for the whole can be seen clearly in two ideas: that behavior, including language, can be described from both emic and etic standpoints, and that behavior, again including language, is trimodally structured.

First, the difference between an etic description and an emic one is the difference between what we might expect an alien observer to see and what we would expect of a native. A noncardplayer observing a game of bridge will see different things than a bridge-player will. The noncardplayer, who is an "alien" in this situation, may notice that the cards are handled and passed around, that the players pick up the cards in front of them and carry on a short conversation in cryptic phrases, that one player then puts all of his cards on the table while the other three put theirs down one by one as this player or that pulls little piles of cards in front of him, that a conversation goes on sporadically during

the play, and finally that the cards are put together again before the
process is repeated. What the bridge-player sees as a "native" to the game
is a distinct unit called a "hand", consisting of the deal, the bidding, the
play, and the scoring. The noncardplayer observes a number of etic
facts, some of which fit into the emic categories of the bridge-player
and some of which are irrelevant. Furthermore, the etic observer may
have altogether missed some emically significant events, like the scoring.
To know which events at the card table are significant for the game,
which are not, and how the significant events are related to one another,
one must know the rules of the game — that is, one must know the events
emically.

The etic and emic standpoints are alternate ways of viewing the same
reality. The etic standpoint is a view from outside, either random in its
selectivity or with a set of presuppositions that have only a chance relationship to the scene being described. The emic standpoint is a view
from within that notices just those features of the scene that are marked
as significant by internal criteria.

For speech, a sound spectrogram is a good example of etic description. So is a narrow phonetic recording of a language the transcriber has
never heard before. In both cases, some things that are emically relevant
to the phonology of the language will almost certainly be missed, whereas a good many quite irrelevant features will be recorded. Such a record
of English speech may show the irrelevant voicelessness and friction of
the *r* in *try*, but fail to record the emically significant differences between a colorless 3-1 intonation contour and a 2-2 pattern that means,
when given to the isolated word *try*, 'but you probably won't succeed'.
On the other hand, a phonemic transcription, whether it consists of
"autonomous" or of "systematic" phonemes, is an emic description of
speech. So also, an etic description would note the variation in sequence
between *He put the book up* and *He put up the book* although it is of no
emic relevance to the grammar. The distinction is a familiar one, but
Pike was the coiner of the terms and the one who has most clearly
pointed out that the concepts are applicable to all of man's activities.

The belief that human behavior is structured in three modes is
another aspect of tagmemic theory which emphasizes the continuity of
language and non-linguistic culture. Every unit of behavior can be described in three ways, first according to those features that identify it as
a distinct unit and that contrast it with all other distinct units of behavior (feature mode). Second, the unit can be described according to

the range of variations by which it is manifested (manifestation mode). And third, the unit can be described according to its distribution relative to other units: whether as a member of a class, a component of a combination, or a cell in a matrix (distribution mode).

For example, in a bridge game a given bid relates to the whole game through all three modes. In its feature mode, a bid of "three clubs" is identified and contrasted with other possible bids by two features – the suit ("clubs") and the number of tricks ("three"). In the manifestation mode, the bid can have a number of variations: "Three clubs", "I bid three clubs", "Well, well, well, thr-r-ree clubby-dubs", "Three clubs?" – although the last especially lacks propriety. In the distribution mode, the bid is an opener, an overcall, or a raise; a free bid, a forced bid, or a jump bid; a preemptive bid, a cue bid, or a normal bid; and so forth, depending on its relationship to the preceding bids in the hand.

The three modes are reflected in language as a whole by its three hierarchies: the feature mode in the lexicon, the manifestation mode in the phonology, and the distribution mode in the grammar. In a general way lexical units are the features of language, phonology its manifestation, and grammar its distribution. But each of the hierarchies can also be analyzed according to the three modes. For example, in the feature mode of phonology, the phoneme unit /m/ is identified and contrasted with all other units by the features of labiality and nasality. In the manifestation mode, /m/ can be bilabial as in *empire* or labiodental as in *emphasize*, and it can be fully voiced as in *mile* or partially devoiced as in *smile*. In the distribution mode, /m/ belongs to the classes of segments that can occur initially (like /h/), finally (like /ŋ/), and as a syllabic (like /ə/).

So also in the feature mode of the lexicon, the morpheme unit *wife* is identified and contrasted with other units by its morphophonemic features /wif/, its syntactic feature 'noun', and its semantic features 'female spouse'. In the manifestation mode it can be /waif/ or /waiv/ (as in *wives*) or /waːf/ (as in some parts of the South). In the distribution mode, *wife* has its place in the system of kinship terms and belongs to the class of items that can occur as subject of *hope* and as antecedent of *who* and *she*.

In the grammatical hierarchy, there is a basic unit called the tagmeme. The concept of the tagmeme, from which the entire theory is named, was evolved by Pike to fill the need he felt for a basic grammatical unit parallel to the phoneme as a phonological unit and the morpheme as a lexical one. The term comes from Bloomfield's *Language*, where it was used, however, in quite a different sense. Nowhere other than in linguistics is T.S. Eliot's observation truer that words "slip, slide ... will not stay in place, will not stay still", so we must make do with technical terms that change their meaning with almost every user. As Pike has defined *tagmeme*, it refers to the correlation between a "slot", or grammatical function, and the class of items that can fill that slot. Thus in the clause construction *Men talk*, there is a functional slot of actor-subject with the filler class of nouns represented by *men* and a functional slot of action-predicator with the filler class of intransitive verbs represented by *talk*. The two categories of functional slot and of filler class are defined correlatively, each by the other, together making up the grammatical unit of the tagmeme. In the feature mode of the grammar, the tagmemic unit "noun as actor-subject" contrasts with other units by the features of its functional slot "actor-subject" and its filler class "noun". In the manifestation mode, it can be a large number of morphemes (*men, parrots, money*). In the distribution mode, the tagmeme has a place in various clause structures.

Each of the modes can be seen as reflecting a dominant characteristic: particle, wave, or field theories of structure. Thus the feature mode tends to reflect the unit as a discrete particle with its own identity and contrasting with all other discrete particles — phonemes, morphemes, or tagmemes. The manifestation mode tends to reflect the unit as a continuous wave of activity, without discrete boundaries. For example, allophones in the pronunciation of *woe* overlap and blend into one another in a way that makes segmentation partly arbitrary; similarly there is wavelike overlapping of allomorphs in *whacha want* in which it is difficult to segment neatly the morphemes *what, do,* and *you*; and there is an overlapping of tagmemes in *He saw Xanthippe emptying her pot*, in which *Xanthippe* represents both the object tagmeme after *saw* and the subject tagmeme before *emptying*. The distribution mode tends to reflect the unit as a position in a field or a cell in a matrix. So a phoneme can be located in the traditional articulation chart; psychologists like Osgood can plot morphemes on a graph as they are measured by a semantic differential scale; and tagmemes can be located in a field in which they are transformationally related. Language, and indeed all human behavior can be viewed as particle, wave, or field, as a part of its general trimodal structure.

Once the principle of trimodality is accepted, it begins to expand its applications. Everything can be seen as consisting of contrastive features, with variant manifestations and distributional relations. Lexicon, phonology, and grammar analogize not only with particle, wave, and field; but also with segment, hierarchy, and matrix; with item, process, and relation; with stasis, dynamics, and function; with point, line, and space; with science, art, and philosophy; and even with the true, the beautiful, and the good. We tremble on the verge of a Father-feature, Son-manifestation, and Holy Ghost-distribution that would make proto-tagmemicists out of the conciliar fathers of Nicaea.

We may begin to wonder whether this world and the next are really trimodally structured or whether tagmemics has not slipped a pair of trifocals on us. Are all these triplicities objectively present in the material being studied, or are they a product of the theory on which the study is based? The foregoing question is merely a special case of that dichotomy named by Fred Householder "God's-Truth" versus "Hocus Pocus". A God's-Truth man believes that language has a pattern which it is the task of the linguist to discover and account for. The Hocus-Pocus man, on the contrary, holds that language has a pattern which is not directly amenable to description, so that the linguist must invent systems to stand for the data, though these systems can never be uniquely correct representations of the data.

There are no rational grounds for choosing between these two positions. One or the other must be accepted on faith. On the whole, Pike is a God's-Truther who talks about "the discovery of the phoneme", somewhat ironically in view of the attitude of some other proponents of God's-Truth, iike Noam Chomsky. Yet it is not altogether fair to align Pike wholly with either party in the quarrel. In his usual ecumenical fashion, Pike has attempted to provide for both sides of the dichotomy. For him, etic descriptions are Hocus Pocus because invented and imposed upon the data by the observer; emic descriptions are God's-Truth — or at least aim at it — because they are discovered within the data itself. Trimodality for the tagmemicist falls in the latter category; it is an emic fact about the nature of human things and thus represents a significant statement about the universe. Of all modern linguistic theories, it is perhaps only tagmemics that opens its scientific windows onto such mystical landscapes.

Pike, playing upon the etymology of the word *theory*, through which it is connected with the Greek verb *theasthai* 'look at, contemplate', has likened theories to windows through which we view reality, the view we get depending on the kind of window we look through (*Language*, p. 70). Put so, tagmemics is less a single window than a bank of them, differing in shape, size, and quality. Of all modern theories, tagmemics is probably the most open to influences from outside, the most eclectic. Furthermore, the eclecticism would appear to be by design rather than accident. A God's-Truther, unless he is of one of the more intolerant persuasions, must conclude that whatever light some other theory is capable of shedding on the linguistic data must be the light of God's own sun and thus must be accepted and somehow incorporated into the larger theory. Consequently, what Pike has aimed at is a "unified theory" not only in the sense that it unifies the treatment of language and nonlinguistic behavior, but also in the sense that it tries to unify whatever is useful in other theories. "Whatsoever things are true, whatsoever things are honorable, whatsoever things are just, whatsoever things are pure, whatsoever things are lovely, whatsoever things are of good report; if there be any virtue, and if there be any praise, think on these things", the apostle Paul wrote to the Philippians, but the tagmemicists heard him.

One of the reasons tagmemics can absorb notions from other theories with relative ease is that it is itself not very tight-knit. It is less pure theory than a combination of some theoretical ideas about language in general and a set of procedures for analyzing particular languages. Its strongly heuristic orientation helps it to remain open to influences from other theories, the only requirement being that new approaches must help in the description of a language. In spite of its God's-Truth orientation, tagmemics is on the whole a more tolerant theory than most.

It is possible to see in tagmemics broad correlations with other current approaches to language study. Thus, the tagmemic postulate of three simultaneous and parallel hierarchies in language — the phonological, lexical, and grammatical — has strong affinities with the stratificational view of language as comprising three main kinds of structure. The earlier kind of meaningful transformation, found for example in Chomsky's *Syntactic Structures*, is rejected by tagmemics in favor of its own concept of the matrix, which relates structures with formal and semantic parallels, such as active and passive clauses or statements and questions. The later kind of transformation, however, which serves to derive one level of structure from another in the generative process, does appear in Longacre's tagmemics as "rewrite operations" (*Grammar Discovery Procedures*, pp. 24–34).

The theory with which tagmemics has the greatest affinities, however, is the systemic or scale-and-category grammar of M.A.K. Halliday. On a very general level, Halliday's concern with the situational context of language is reminiscent of Pike's desire to relate language to the totality of human behavior; and Halliday's three levels of phonology, lexis, and grammar parallel quite closely Pike's three hierarchies. More specifically, Halliday's four grammatical categories can be identified in tagmemics: Halliday's unit can be identified with Pike's constructional level (in both theories there are five – sentence, clause, phrase, word, and morpheme). Halliday's elements, which are organized into the category of structure, can be identified with Pike's tagmemes, which are organized into constructions, or syntagmemes. Halliday's classes are identical with Pike's distributional classes; and Halliday's system is essentially what Pike seeks to describe with his concept of matrix – a closed set of items that can be related to one another along various dimensions. Furthermore Halliday's three scales have their tagmemic correspondences: rank scale appears as hierarchical level; delicacy corresponds to etic continuum or variable focus; and exponence has been borrowed by Longacre from Halliday (*Grammar Discovery Procedures*, pp. 27–28).

Some believe that there is no possibility of a synthesis among the linguistic theories that compete for our attention today, since they believe that these theories, or some of them, are incompatible in their basic assumptions and aims. It may be so, but to the extent that a synthesis can be made, tagmemicists would appear to have made more progress on the way than any other group. One thing is certain – if the internecine warfare that characterizes much of current linguistics is ever to give way to an age of peace, the insights of tagmemic theory will have to find their place in the new age. But tagmemics will have, perhaps, a better claim on the attention of the next generation of linguists than its mere presence on the field of battle.

Dwight Bolinger has suggested in *Aspects of Language* (New York, 1968; pp. 208–212) that each new movement in linguistics has tended to emphasize most what was most neglected by the preceding movement. It seems clear, as Bolinger points out and as this paper began by assuming, that what is most neglected today is the collection and analysis of raw data. But that is exactly the area in which tagmemicists are most effective. It has been widely assumed among theoretical linguists that data-gathering is a form of arrested development and that those who do it are much like a tribe of food-gatherers living on the edges of a technologically advanced culture, But what if data-gatherers should turn out to be, not a remnant of the past, but instead a wave of the future?

University of Florida

SOME FUNDAMENTAL INSIGHTS OF TAGMEMICS *

Summer Institute of Linguistics

Four fundamental insights of tagmemics[1] are the correlativity of function and set, the search for constructions of maximum relevance, the emphasis on explicit, systemic hierarchy, and the concept of relatedness in logical space (with transformation only one of the possible parameters which relate constructions). Developing these points gives an indirect answer to certain recent criticisms.[2]

1. Tagmemics makes grammatical functions focal, but associates such functions with sets of items and constructions. A function may be considered to be a defining property of a set while the set may be said to manifest a function.[3] Functions are formally demonstrable. Sets may be described and operated on as prescribed by set theory.

By function is meant the peculiar office or role of one formally distinguishable part of a construction type in relation to other parts of the same construction.[4] Thus, a predication clause may be considered to pose a drama in miniature. The verb gives the PLOT. Such functional segments as subjects, objects, and indirect

* Language, 41. 65-76, 1965. Reprinted by permission.

[1] These four insights, which are here considered only in relation to grammar, are also applicable to phonology and lexicon; cf. Longacre, 'Prolegomena to lexical structure', *Linguistics* 5.5–24 (1964). Two basic assumptions of tagmemics are (a) that language is trimodally structured into the semiautonomous but interlocking modes—phonology, grammar, and lexicon; and (b) that language must be viewed from several perspectives, of which three are particle, wave, and field (Kenneth L. Pike, 'Language as particle, wave, and field', *The Texas quarterly* 2.37–54, 1959).

Until recently transformational grammar has not been much interested in the distinction of phonology, grammar, and lexicon. Lees in 1960 ('A multiply ambiguous adjectival construction in English', *Lg.* 36.207-21) expressly rejected Pike's trimodalism. Phonology has been treated as simply the last section of rules in a transformational grammar, with no attention to higher-leveled phonological units such as syllables and stress groups. Lexicon has been treated by running a lexical sample into the phrase-structure rules. More recently, however, transformational grammar has been awakening to the necessity of treating both phonology and lexicon more thoroughly. Witness the excellent book of Saporta and Contreras, *A phonological grammar of Spanish*, (Seattle, 1962), as well as the article of Katz and Fodor, 'The structure of a semantic theory', *Lg.* 39.170–210 (1963).

[2] Point 1 above has been criticized by Paul M. Postal, 'Constituent structure: A study of contemporary models of syntactic description' 34–6 (*IJAL* 30:1, part III), and Emmon Bach, *An introduction to transformational grammars* 42 (New York, 1964). Points 2–4 may be considered an answer to Postal's query: '... it is important to ask why the formulators of tagmemics believe that in a rather deep sense they have succeeded in formulating a new theory which is above and beyond immediate constituent analysis of the ordinary Bloch-Wells-Harris-Hockett sort' (34).

[3] 'Function-set' has been referred to as 'slot-class'. The 'slot' is not a physical slot but a functional entity. On the other hand, the 'class' is not necessarily a grammatical class of any great relevance. For this reason I suggest 'function-set' as preferable to the older term.

[4] FUNCTION as used here is not a recent importation from mathematics but is at least as old as Bloomfield (185). In writing of positions and the forms that could occur in those positions, he said, 'The positions in which a form can appear are its *functions* or, collectively, its *function*.'

objects give the DRAMATIS PERSONAE. Further functional segments indicating manner, time, place, instrument, etc. give us SETTING and STAGE PROPS. A few of these are exemplified in the short one-clause sentence *John went downtown yesterday*, where each word is a separate functional segment: subject, predicate, locational, temporal. As subject, *John* is in a quaternary relation to the other three words of its clause; as predicate, *went* is in a similar quaternary relation; as are also *downtown* and *yesterday*. Thus the four segments of the clause manifest grammatical functions which are at the same time relations within the clause. The goal of tagmemic analysis is not simply to isolate constituents but to reveal relations.[5]

Each grammatical function is associated with a set of items or constructions or both. In making functions the defining properties of sets, we are not reverting to semantic analysis as practiced by traditional grammar. The correlation of an isolable (though not necessarily closed or finite) set with each function provides a formal base for the function. Nevertheless, since the validity of the set depends to a high degree on the function, formal justification is also sought for the function-set as a unit. Typically, a function-set is demonstrable in reference to more than one parameter. Thus, while word order is of crucial importance to recognizing subject, predicate, and object in the English clause, word order is by no means the only significant parameter. Other relevant parameters are (1) the structure of the noun phrases (which manifest subject and object) versus that of the verb phrases (which manifest predicate); (2) case of pronouns; (3) lexical probability; and (4) phonological clues—including intonation. Thus, in *John ran the home* we have a sequence subject, predicate, object in one-to-one correspondence with noun phrase, verb phrase, noun phrase; *the home* is commutable with such items as *the show*, *the machinery*, and *the whole affair*. But *John ran home* is different in that *home* here manifests a locational tagmeme, as seen by its commutability with other members of its set such as *away*, *to the house*, and *towards the dog*. In the permutation *home ran John* we have neither subject, predicate, object, nor subject, predicate, locational; but rather locational, predicate, subject. Here the further parameters of lexical probability and set membership (and possibly intonation as well) combine to overrule the parameter of word order— which would normally cause us to interpret the first noun as subject.

In fact, in spite of the importance of word order in English, the productive potential of the language permits permutations which 'violate' the more frequent word order. Violation of normal word order, whether in daily conversation or in works of literature, alerts us to the fact that further parameters are involved— since the utterances remain intelligible in spite of the violation. Thus, both the order object, subject, predicate, and the order subject, object, predicate are heard in animated informal discourse: *But the massive spread into various fields of research one has to feel to appreciate | She, undismayed, his onslaught withstood; I capitulated.* In Milton's poetry the order object, subject, predicate is not uncommon: *Him the Almighty Power/Hurled headlong flaming from th' ethereal sky*

---

[5] Cf. Postal's misunderstanding (37–8): 'The tagmemic characterization thus seems to miss the relational aspect of grammatical features like "subject", "object", "predicate", and confuses these with constituents.'

(*Paradise lost* 1.44–5); *Such place eternal justice had prepared/For those rebellious* (id. 1.70–1). But Milton also used the order subject, (locational), object, predicate: *... he from Heaven's height/All these our motions vain sees and derides* (id. 2.190–1). He even used the order object, predicate, subject, which is still unambiguous since *he* manifests subject: *Created thing nought valued he ...* (id. 2.679).

Thus, in English—considering the whole set of possible utterances—grammatical function is not reducible either (a) to the parameter of word order alone (1, 2, 3 = subject, predicate, object) nor (b) to the parameters of word order plus indication of word class (NP, VP, NP = subject, predicate, object). Rather, function is a high-level abstraction in *n* parameters.

In languages other than English, case endings (Latin and Greek), or function-indicating particles (Malayo-Polynesian), or cross reference to affixes in the verb (Totonac and other Mexican Indian languages) are parameters considerably more important than word order in distinguishing clause-level functions.

Tagmemics is frankly and unapologetically interested in functional relations in the internal structure of words, phrases, clauses, and sentences as well as in such relations and contrasts among constructions. By bringing together function and set in the tagmeme, function is at once kept in focus and made amenable to formal analysis. Traditional grammar talked much of functions—subject, object, modifier, etc.—but did not pay sufficient attention to form to bring such functions into clear focus. Earlier American structuralism, with adolescent enthusiasm, all but tossed out function in its zeal for form. Tagmemics is a reaffirmation of function in a structuralist context.

The set of items manifesting a function may range from a set composed of but one member, through listable sets with closed membership, to open-ended sets whose properties can be stated but whose members cannot be exhaustively listed. Thus, the identifier tagmeme in Trique noun phrases is manifested by a unit set containing the morpheme ne^3h 'identified plural'. The deictic tagmeme in Trique noun phrases is manifested by a set of three morphemes: nq^3h 'here (in sight)', mq^3h 'there (out of sight)', dq^3h 'a certain one'. By contrast, clause-level subject and object tagmemes are manifested by lexically open sets of nouns (although by a closed set of noun phrase types).

2. Tagmemics is not content with the various concepts of construction posited by earlier American structuralism. The construction type, or SYNTAGMEME, as posited in tagmemics, is different in kind from these earlier concepts. I propose to substantiate this claim by examining a well-written representative American structuralist grammar, Jorden's *Syntax of modern colloquial Japanese.*[6] My thesis is that from the standpoint of tagmemic theory this grammar is characterized by functional overdifferentiation, functional underdifferentiation, and functional fragmentation. By the first I mean the distinguishing of constructions that are functionally identical. Functional underdifferentiation is the converse: failure to distinguish constructions that are functionally different. And functional fragmentation is the horizontal dissection of what is properly one construction into separate (so-called) constructions.

[6] Eleanor Harz Jorden, *The syntax of modern colloquial Japanese* (*Language dissertation* no. 52; 1955).

By a modified immediate-constituent analysis Jorden arrives at 39 major constituent types in Japanese. Seven of these are single-symbol types (Verb, Adjective, Copula, Noun, Particle, Demonstrative, Confirmative); the remaining 32 are binomial symbol types such as VV, AV, CV, NV, VA, AA. Multiple-constituent types are discussed briefly (about one page, 70–1) toward the end of the grammar—as is typical in grammars based on immediate-constituent analysis, where it is assumed that progressive dichotomous cutting is the normal procedure. The 32 binomial symbol types are further divided into a variety of subtypes, a grand total of 82.

Several observations are relevant here: (1) This seems to be a piece of orthodox American structuralism of the era beginning with Harris's article 'From morpheme to utterance' (1946)[7] and Wells's 'Immediate constituents' (1947).[8] Note that constructions are obtained by a species of immediate-constituent cutting and then are labelled and described as sequences of classes.[9] (2) However we may criticize its theoretical base, the grammar is well written and profusely exemplified. (3) On first examination the descriptive apparatus seems to be quite adequate: 82 binomial-symbol subtypes grouped under 32 binomial-symbol major types and seven single-symbol types, with a few further elements—pseudo-constitutes (68–9), multiple constitutes (69–70), and quotatives (70–2).

Nevertheless, in spite of the care and organization evident in the grammar, functional overdifferentiation is seen among the binomial subtypes. Notice e.g. Jorden's description of VV-pro.1 (36): 'The first constituent ends with a provisional form and expresses the stipulation by which the action or state of the second constituent is realized.' Thus *isóide* : *ikéba* VV/ *ma ni* : *aimasu* PV 'you'll be on time provided you hurry.' This construction is considered to be a VV (verb-verb) construction because its first immediate constituent (which is also VV) ends in a verb, as does also the second immediate constituent (which is PV, particle-verb). In that the last verb of the first immediate constituent is inflected for the provisional, the whole construction is labelled VV-pro.1. Well and good. Turning to page 38 of the grammar we find, however, AV-pro.1: *suŋu* : *yomitákereba* NA/# *íma* : *kaimasu* NV 'if you want to read it right away, I'll buy it now.' The construction is regarded as an AV construction since its first constituent NA (noun-adjective) ends with A while its second constituent NV (noun-verb) ends with verb. Again, because the first constituent ends with a word inflected for the provisional, the whole construction is labelled AV-pro.1. The parallelism of VV-pro.1 and AV-pro.1 is such that Jorden does not comment further on the latter than to say 'See VV-pro.1.' Similarly homologous are CV-pro.1 (copula-verb, 39), VA-pro.1 (42), AA-pro.1 (44), CA-pro.1 (45), VC-pro.1 (48), AC-pro.1 (49), CC-pro.1 (51), VN-pro. 1 (54), AN-pro.1 (56), and CN-pro.1 (57). These various 'constructions' are cross-referenced to each other: (a) AV-pro.1, CV-pro.1, VA-pro.1, AA-pro.1, CA-pro.1, AC-pro.1, and CC-pro.1 are all

---

[7] Zellig S. Harris, 'From morpheme to utterance', *Lg.* 22.161–83 (1946).

[8] Rulon S. Wells, 'Immediate constituents', *Lg.* 23.81–117 (1947).

[9] The phrase-structure sections of present-day generative grammars reflect the same technique. They share, therefore, the inherent weakness of such an approach and require wholesale correction by means of grammatical transformations in the following sections of such grammars.

followed by 'See VV-pro.1'; (b) VN-pro.1 requires the additional explanation that 'the second constituent ends with a verbal noun' but this is followed by 'For the relation between the two constituents, see VV-pro.1'; (c) AN-pro.1 and CN-pro.1 are followed by the comment 'See VN-pro.1'. Here, in terms of functional relations, we have—by Jorden's admission—the same unit; nevertheless, the device of dichotomous cutting into constituents ending in words of differing classes distributes varying exponents of this unit into a dozen 'constructions' whose description is scattered over 21 pages of the grammar. VV-pro.2 heads a chain of similarly functionally equivalent 'constructions', as does also VV-c.

In such a situation, the tagmemic distinction of function and set is highly strategic. All the constructions labelled pro.1 are treated as a single syntagmeme with two functional parts (in this case linearly ordered): protasis tagmeme manifested by $x \mid x = $ Cl č (V, A, C)-pro (i.e. the set of all x such that x is a clause containing a verb, adjective, or copula inflected for the provisional), and apodosis manifested by $y \mid y = $ Cl č V, A, C, N' (where N' is a verbal noun).[10]

By positing tagmemes (which at the same time distinguish but associate function and set), it is possible to obtain constructions of high relevance. Thus, the Japanese construction above, which we might call STIPULATORY PROVISIONAL contrasts with another construction (VV-pro.2, AV-pro.2, etc.) which might be termed COORDINATE PROVISIONAL.[11] The latter is described by Jorden (for VV-pro.2) as follows (37): 'The first constituent ends with a provisional form and expresses an action or state coordinate with the action or state of the second constituent. The subjects of both constituents are followed by the particle *mo* "also" '. Thus, *áme mo* : *húreba* PV/# *kaze mo* : *huku* PV 'not only does it rain, it's windy too'. This construction likewise has two linearly ordered units: protasis' manifested by $q \mid q = $ Cl č S + *mo*, (V, A, C) + pro.; and apodosis' manifested by $r \mid r = $ Cl č S + *mo*, (V, A, C, N').

Description in terms of word classes linearly ordered without regard to function leads not only to functional overdifferentiation (as just illustrated) but also to functional underdifferentiation. Thus, on page 40 of her grammar Jorden describes NV-1 as follows: 'The first constituent ends with a noun and is in construction with the second; it indicates extent, point in time, manner, coordination, condition, concession, the person addressed in an imperative expression, etc.' Evidently a variety of clause-level functions is subsumed here, and the list (notice the 'etc.') does not claim to be exhaustive. Furthermore, 'condition' and 'concession' probably refer to sentence-level functions. Note also PV-1 (41): 'The first constituent ends with a particle other than *no* "pertaining to", and is

---

[10] Tagmemic grammars employ a more succinct notation than that of set theory. The colon which occurs between the symbol for a function and the symbol (or symbols) of a set means 'preceding function defines following set'. Thus, S:NP may be read 'subject function defines set of noun phrases'. Often the set is specified by reference to subsets or to a collection of sets, e.g. S:NP, pr., nom. cl., 'Subject function defines a set composed of the following subsets: noun phrases, pronouns, nominal clauses'.

[11] The exact structural level on which these two contrasting Japanese constructions occur is not easily deduced from the Jorden grammar. They appear to be on the sentence level. If they are sentence types, then the final particles which must terminate the constructions constitute one or more further sentence-level tagmemes.

in construction with the second constituent; depending upon the particle, the first constituent may indicate a concessive, a coordinate, the sentence topic, a direct or indirect object, a point in time, manner, destination, origin, agent, etc. PV-1 constitutes are among the most common.' Here again a variety of clause-level functions (the so-called sentence topic, a direct or indirect object, a point in time, manner, destination, origin) and of sentence-level functions (possibly concessive and coordinate) are indicated with the comment that the list is not exhaustive. Tagmemic analysis, in that it is functionally oriented, would carefully analyze such constructions as NV-1 and PV-1. The verbs would be found to manifest predicates in various clause types. The nouns and particles would take their place as manifestations of various clause-level and sentence-level tagmemes. The open-ended listing of function ('... etc.') would be replaced by a discrete inventory of clause-level and sentence-level tagmemes shown to be formally contrastive.

Finally, the approach exemplified in this grammar parcels out among various pseudo-constructions (obtained by dichotomous cutting into parts labeled by word class) elements that properly belong in the same horizontal array. In a grammar so written it is difficult for the reader to get the parts of such arrays back together. Inevitably portions of varying constructions which are relevant on phrase, clause, and sentence levels come to be indiscriminately lumped together according to parameters that are functionally trivial. An array like the following, for one type of Trique noun phrase, is difficult to obtain within the procedures and assumptions underlying a grammar like Jorden's:

$\pm$ i:{ne^3h 'the'} $\pm$ q:{numerals} $\pm$ H:noun phrase $\pm$ A:{adjectives}

$\pm$ d:{nq^3h 'here', mq^3h 'there', dq^3h 'a certain one'}

where i = identifier, q = quantifier, H = head, A = attributive, d = deictic; lower-case letters symbolize tagmemes manifested by closed sets, upper-case letters tagmemes manifested by open classes. An analysis like Jorden's would lead rather to these constructions: a N (article-noun), num N (numeral-noun), N A (noun-adjective), N d (noun-deictic). Other readings of the tagmemic formula, such as i q H (or: a num N) and H A d, find no ready place in such a system—though H A d might be considered to be layered as (H A) d and thus a variety of H d.

Tagmemics replaces these functionally unoriented concepts with that of the syntagmeme. Simply conceived, a syntagmeme is a structurally contrastive type on a given level of hierarchical structuring, e.g. a word type (in terms of internal structure), a phrase type, a clause type, a sentence type, a paragraph type, a discourse type. More explicitly: a syntagmeme, as a functionally contrastive string on a given level, has (1) closure and internal coherence; (2) a minimal structure (a nucleus at least part of which is obligatory) and usually an expanded structure (the entire nucleus plus the optional periphery); and (3) contrast, variants, and distribution. It may also be characterized by internal layering or grouping and by multiple nesting. Requirement 1 reminds us that any structured string must be bounded (it starts and stops), and must have parts which are in functional relation with each other (hence patterned and restricted as to the choice and structure of each part). Requirement 2 allows for varying degrees of structural elaboration while at the same time it allows us to connect functionally a minimal structure (say a single noun) and its expansion (say the noun with various qualifiers) so that both manifest the same syntagmeme. The distinction of nucleus versus periphery is furthermore useful in that nuclear tagmemes are especially characteristic of the syntagmemes where they occur. Nuclear tagmemes also tend to be in sharper structural contrast than do peripheral tagmemes.[12] Requirement 3 is basic not only to the syntagmeme but to any linguistic unit. Pike has argued that without identifying-contrastive features, variants (allo-units, whether phonological, grammatical, or semantic), and distribution (in strings and in a system) no linguistic unit can be posited.[13]

Internal layering and multiple nesting characterize many syntagmemes. While the tagmemes of some syntagmemes occur in straightforward linear array like beads on a string, those of other syntagmemes are arranged in groups, or are layered as assumed in immediate constituent analysis. Furthermore, some syntagmemes permit multiple nesting of other syntagmemes on the same level, as in *the real study of that two-thirds of the surface of the earth*. Such structures are recursively expandable without systemic limitation.

A syntagmeme is represented by a formula which can be operated on so as to yield readings, permutations, and exponential combinations,[14] and which (with proper exit to phonology and lexicon) yields terminal constructions. Such formulas commonly use a plus sign before obligatory and a plus-or-minus sign before optional tagmemes. Alternatively, parentheses could be used to enclose optional items, as in transformational grammar. Tagmemics, however, has other uses for parentheses (and brackets and braces) in the formulas. Thus, parentheses are used to enclose the nucleus of a syntagmeme. A dual notation can be used for function-set, as i:ne^3h for identifier function manifested by the set of items (of but one member) ne^3h 'the'. When specification of a set is lengthy, this information can be given in a separate rule following the formula.

DIAGRAM 1   DIAGRAM 2

---

[12] Tagmemic contrast is, therefore, a CLINE. Cf. M. A. K. Halliday 'Categories of the theory of grammar', *Word* 17.254 (1961).

[13] The tagmeme and syntagmeme concepts are not necessarily associated with use of these terms as such nor with a particular variety of symbolism. For an example of a tagmemic article without use of either term, see Doris Cox, 'Candoshi verb inflection', *IJAL* 23.129–40 (1957).

[14] A reading of a formula is any possible sequence of symbols which may be deduced from it (as permitted by the signs and superscripts of the formula). Thus, the formula $+ P + S \pm L^2 \pm T^2$ has a reading PSLL. Exponents refer to the syntagmemes or morphemes which may manifest a tagmeme. Barring special constraints, there are as many exponential combinations of a syntagmeme as the product of the exponents of all its tagmemes. Permutation is used in its usual mathematical sense. For a detailed discussion of readings, permutations and exponential combinations, see *Grammar discovery procedures* 23 ff. For a more elegant mathematical presentation of the same, see Walter A. Cook, S.J., *On tagmemes and transforms* 53–6 (Washington, 1960).

Permutations are handled in tagmemics in straightforward fashion. It is not necessary to assume, as in transformational grammar, that a permutation changes the structure of a sentence tree.[15] The necessity of such a change in performing a permutation in transformational grammars underscores the clumsiness and ad-hoc nature of the apparatus of sentence trees as 'phrase markers' (P-markers). Consider the simple tree diagram of elements X, Y, Z in diagram 1. When Y is permuted to first position by means of a transformational rule, the result is a new tree, as in diagram 2. It seems counterintuitive that a mere change of word order within a syntagmeme (especially in a language with free ordering) must entail a change of structure beyond the permutation itself. Are we to believe that these Latin clauses—*puer amat puellam, amat puer puellam, puellam amat puer, puer puellam amat, amat puellam puer, puellam puer amat*—have different structures over and above the obvious fact of different orderings? Rather, we have six permutations of the reading SOP (subject, object, predicate) for Latin transitive clause. The permutations themselves are the sole and sufficient structural distinction among the six.

Different in kind are permutations that transform one syntagmeme to another, e.g. *John did come* versus *Did John come?*, where the permutation is a feature of the interrogative transformation. Compare also the Jacaltec *no? wakax* 'the cow' (*no?* classifier for 'animal', *wakax* 'cow'), a phrase, versus *wakax no?* 'it (is) a cow', an equative clause.[15a] It is evident that not all permutations have the same structural significance. Specifically, permutations within the same syntagmeme are distinct from permutations across syntagmemes (and even across structural levels). Absence or presence of syntagmemic contrast is the crucial factor in evaluating permutations.

3. The notion of structural levels arranged in explicit systemic hierarchy is another basic concept of tagmemics. Syntagmeme and level are correlative concepts: the former is defined (as already noted) as a functionally contrastive string on a given level of hierarchical structuring. This correlativity of syntagmeme and level must be added to the correlativity of function and set (within the tagmeme) and the correlativity of tagmeme and syntagmeme.

Only by positing systemic levels in the structure of a given language can

[15] Cf. Bach 79, from which these tree diagrams are taken. Cf. also Noam Chomsky and George A. Miller, 'Introduction to the formal analysis of natural languages', *Handbook of mathematical psychology* 2.304: 'The general principle of derived constituent structure in this case is simply that the minimal change is made in the P-marker of the underlying string, consistent with the requirement that the resulting P-marker again be representable in tree form.' This 'minimal principle' coupled with use of tree structure diagrams necessitated Chomsky's considering that *turn out some of the lights* has a different structure from *turn some of the lights out*. Tagmemics would interpret the latter sentence as consisting of a sequence of predicate, manner, object with permutation to predicate, object, manner in the former sentence. Since tree diagrams are not employed, no structural change need be assumed beyond the mere fact of the permutation itself. In brief it appears to practitioners of tagmemics that tree diagrams involve layerings which are incidental to particular word orders and which are therefore structurally trivial.

[15a] Clarence and Katherine Church, 'The Jacaltec noun phrase', *Mayan studies* 1.163-4 (Norman, Okla., 1960).

constructions of maximum relevance be obtained. Immediate-constituent analysis
of sentences is uninformed by semantic hierarchy. The resultant ad-hoc dissection of sentences fails to distinguish important breaks (where constructions
on a higher level divide into constituents of a lower level) from less important
layerings (on the same level) and from recursive nestings.

Note the English sentence *A great big green frog is sitting on the bump on the
back of a log on the bank of the pond.* Tagmemic analysis divides this one-clause
sentence into three clause-level tagmemes: subject (S) manifested by *A great big
green frog*, predicate (P) manifested by *is sitting*, and locational (L) manifested
by the rest of the sentence. The cuts above are considered to be important—
although in terms of layering tendencies P and L may be more closely related
than S and P (and certainly more closely than S and L).[16] The noun phrase which
manifests subject may be regarded as a string consisting of identifier tagmeme,
manifested here by *a*; several attributive tagmemes not here distinguished,[17]
manifested by *great, big, green*; and head tagmeme manifested by *frog*. It seems
trivial to raise questions about layering within such a linear string—although
one could, for example, assume that *green* is more closely related to *frog* than is
big; that *big* goes with *green frog*, *great* with *big green frog*; and *a* with all that
follows. Locational tagmeme in the clause is manifested by a Chinese-box
arrangement of phrase-within-phrase; analysis of this multiple nesting is non-
trivial in that the nested structures are phrase types which are in clear structural
contrast in the language.[18]

Hierarchical structuring as commonly conceived involves distribution of
lower-level units into higher-level units. Thus, in English, morphemes build into
words which build into phrases ... into clauses ... into sentences ... into paragraphs ... into discourses. Recursive layerings may occur on the same level: word
within word ('compounds'), phrase within phrase (as illustrated above), clause
within clause, etc. There may be backlooping from higher levels. Occurrence
of a subordinate clause which manifests a phrase-level tagmeme *(the boy who came
yesterday)*, or of a sentence within a clause *(when heads-I-win-tails-you-lose is the*

[16] Witness the sentence *He's sitting on the log and gazing at the pond*, where *on the log*
layers with *sitting* and *at the pond* with *gazing*, as seen in the fact that but one subject occurs
with both. Notice, however, that in permutations to the order object, subject, verb (see §1)
the element normally postverbal is farther removed from the verb than the subject.

It is by no means a cultural universal that objects, complements and the like are more
closely related to the predicate than is the subject. In Trique, Isthmus Zapotec, and certain
other languages of Mexico, certain clause types have the preferred ordering predicate,
subject, object, (and nothing may be inserted between predicate and subject); in such
clause types predicate and subject seem to be more intimately related than predicate and
object.

[17] Cf. Longacre, *Grammar discovery procedures* 97–8, and Harris, *String analysis of sentence
structure* 36 (Papers on formal linguistics; The Hague, 1962).

[18] Thus the whole string is a relator-axis phrase of which *on* manifests relator and the
rest manifests axis. The included phrases *on the back of a log on the bank of the pond* and
on the bank of the pond are also relator-axis, as are *of a log* and *of the pond*. The phrases *the
bump on a log on the bank of the pond* and *a log on the bank of the pond* are head-modifier
phrases in which *the bump* and *a log* manifest head. Finally, *the back of a log on the bank of
the pond* and *the bank of the pond* are item-possessor phrases (as witnessed by the possible
transformation to *a log's back* and *the pond's bank*).

order of the day) exemplify first-order backlooping. Occurrence of a sentence
within a phrase (*his heads-I-win-tails-you-lose attitude*) exemplifies second-order
backlooping.[19] Level-skipping may also occur: a sentence-level tagmeme manifested by a phrase or a clause-level tagmeme by a word exemplifies first-order
level-skipping, while a sentence-level tagmeme manifested by a word exemplifies
second-order level-skipping.[20]

Ascending from one hierarchical level to another does not necessarily mean
expansion of the linear string. In some languages (with extensive verb inflection)
a minimal word may manifest a minimal phrase which manifests a minimal
clause, a minimal sentence, and a minimal discourse. But expansion possibilities
are markedly different on different hierarchical levels. In general, a minimal
word expands by adding further affixes; a minimal phrase expands by adding
further words in the same phrase or by imbedding further phrases; a minimal
clause expands by adding further phrases or by imbedding clauses; a minimal
sentence expands by adding further unimbedded clauses with or without conjunctions and particles, or by imbedding sentences.

A geometric analogy is convenient here by way of summary and transition.
Let tagmeme be compared to a point, syntagmeme to a line, level to a broken
line, and hierarchy to a set of broken lines (diagram 3). As a function set, the
tagmeme may be considered simply a pattern point. We are not now interested
in the internal structure of sequences which manifest the tagmeme (except for
what we need to know to distinguish it from other tagmemes). Syntagmeme, by
contrast, is a string or sequence.[21] A level, as a disjoint collection of syntagmemes,
is represented as a broken line with a separate segment for each syntagmeme on
the level. Hierarchy is represented as a set of parallel broken lines. In such a set,
the segments of the lines are not in any one-to-one correspondence, nor are the

tagmeme	syntagmeme	level	hierarchy
		— — —	— — —
		– — —	— — — —
			— — — – –
.	————	– – – –	– – – – – –

DIAGRAM 3. GEOMETRIC ANALOGY OF BASIC CONCEPTS IN TAGMEMICS

[19] Such imbedding of sentence within a phrase has special phonological characteristics
(level, run-on intonation, and lack of pause before termination of the imbedding phrase).
These phonological features signal 'phrase still unterminated'.

[20] Non-Bloomfieldian definitions of word, phrase, and sentence are assumed. A word is
not simply 'a minimum free form' (Bloomfield 178), but is required to have syntagmemic
structure (although a single morpheme may be a minimal word provided that it also occurs
with affixes). A phrase is not required to be a group of two or more words; rather a minimal
phrase may be manifested by a single word provided it also occurs with other words in a
phrase. A sentence is not altogether an 'independent linguistic form' (Bloomfield 170), for
it may figure in the structure of a paragraph. Furthermore, sentence and clause may be
fruitfully distinguished, even though there are many one-clause sentences.

[21] The analogy is imperfect, however, on two scores. Chord structures may occur—
tagmemes occurring simultaneously (tone replacives, simulfixes); and certain features of a
syntagmeme are analogous to a wave. Cf. 'Prolegomena to lexical structure' 12.

broken lines of the set necessarily of the same length.[22] Trique shows four hierarchical levels: word, phrase, clause, sentence.[23] The number of syntagmemes
found on each level is 9 for words, 29 for phrases, 5 for clauses, 28 for sentences.
This would indicate that phrase and sentence are the most elaborated hierarchical levels in Trique; but many more readings and permutations characterize
clause structure than other levels. Taking into account the number of readings
and permutations possible per level, the clause emerges as bearing almost three
times the functional load of the phrase in Trique; while the relative functional
load of the other two levels is not greatly affected.

4. A further concept of tagmemics is the matrix whose model is space in n
dimensions (one-dimensional matrices are trivial unless in a system of matrices
with further dimensions). In grammar[24] this develops the notion of relatedness
in logical space by arranging syntagmemes or tagmemes in a system of co-
ordinates. Like items are made contiguous; unlike items are separated. Transformation relations take their place among parameters which relate constructions.
In the following matrix for Zoque clause types (diagram 4)[25] one parameter is
that of transitivity, grading from nontransitive (descriptive clause) to intransitive
to transitive to ditransitive; a second parameter is that of transformational
relation, grading from indicative (kernel structures) to subordinate, interrogative,
and imperative.

		transformational parameter			
		INDICATIVE	SUBORDINATE	INTERROGATIVE	IMPERATIVE
	NONTRANSITIVE	X	X	X	
	INTRANSITIVE	X	X	X	X
	TRANSITIVE	X	X	X	X
	DITRANSITIVE	X	X	X	X

DIAGRAM 4. PARAMETERS OF ZOQUE CLAUSE STRUCTURE

[22] Hierarchy is in no sense comparable to a sentence tree, which is necessarily ad hoc to a
given sentence and in which units become fewer at each higher rank of nodes.

[23] Trique has a well defined system of close-knit sentences which I formerly considered
to constitute a further hierarchical level intermediate between clause and sentence (called
the COLON level in *Grammar discovery procedures* 132 ff.). I no longer consider these structures to constitute a level, since (1) imbedding of what I formerly called sentence in colon
is so frequent that it is more plausible to consider this to be recursive structuring on the
same level than backlooping from a higher level; and (2) sentence and colon occur with the
same introductory particles. The close-knit sentence types (or colons) and the loose-knit
sentences are indeed strikingly different in certain respects; but so are noun and verb
phrases in many languages—even though both are admittedly on the phrase level.

[24] Matrices are also useful in phonology (e.g. a chart of the phonemes of a language) and
in the lexicon (a plotting of semantic oppositions in a specific lexical domain). Pike and
Erickson's work on Potawatomi, 'Conflated field structures in Potawatomi and in Arabic'
IJAL 30.201–12 (1964), studies the field structures of certain lexical oppositions within
given orders of Potawatomi verb affixes. An earlier work of Pike's, 'Dimensions of grammatical constructions', *Lg.* 38.221–44 (1962), uses matrices to relate grammatical constructions.

[25] This diagram is adapted from Engel and Longacre, 'Syntactic matrices in Ostuacan
Zoque', *IJAL* 29.331–44 (1962).

R.E. Longacre

	LEVEL-SKIPPING[3]	LEVEL-SKIPPING[2]	LEVEL-SKIPPING[1]	HIERARCHICAL	RECURSIVE	BACK-LOOPING[1]	BACK-LOOPING[2]
$T_{\P}$	W	P	C	S	¶	D	
T_S	M	W	P	C	S	¶	D
T_C		M	W	P	C	S	¶
T_P			M	W	P	C	S
T_W				M	W	P	C

DIAGRAM 5. FIELD STRUCTURE OF HIERARCHY

As a means of conceptualizing field structure the matrix is a versatile and useful tool. To conclude this paper, I illustrate the usefulness of both hierarchy and matrix by presenting the FIELD STRUCTURE OF HIERARCHY. In diagram 5, T symbolizes tagmemes identified by subscripts ¶, S, C, P, and W as paragraph level, sentence level, clause level, phrase level, and word level. D and M symbolize discourse and morpheme as top and bottom points of reference. These six hierarchical levels (and morpheme, which is not a level) comprise the vertical coordinate of the chart. There is a central column labelled HIERARCHICAL, with successive columns to the right and left. Cells are filled with symbols for levels. Thus, the intersection of T_C and HIERARCHICAL is cell P; we read: 'Clause-level tagmeme manifested by a set of phrase-level syntagmemes'.

The field structure represented above has the following characteristics. (1) Every row is displaced one cell to the right in respect to the row above it and one cell to the left in respect to the row below it. (2) Every column is displaced one cell upwards in respect to the next column to the right, and one cell downwards in respect to the next column to the left. (3) All left-to-right descending diagonals have the same cells.

Columns further removed from the center are less likely to be actualized in languages. Thus, while English is rich in backlooping devices, some languages do not use backlooping so extensively. In general, the types of recursiveness, backlooping, and level-skipping are characteristic of the structure of each language and are necessarily less frequent than regular hierarchical structuring.[26] Notice, however, that all varieties of mutual imbedding of constructions from various levels find their place in a periodic matrix like that in diagram 5 and none need be considered aberrant or extrasystemic. Rather, the apparent exceptions to hierarchy (recursiveness, backlooping, and level-skipping) are part of a field structure in which hierarchy finds its ultimate justification. The relative spacing—which is possibly the fundamental notion in hierarchy—is preserved regardless of the horizontal or vertical shifting of rows and columns.

[26] Probably backlooping is comparatively rare in phonological hierarchy.

SOME FUNDAMENTAL INSIGHTS OF
TAGMEMICS REVISITED*

Peter H. FRIES

In its development over the past two decades, tagmemic theory has been strongest in dealing with relations which hold on or near the surface[1]. But even on this level tagmemicists have had difficulty in integrating their insights into a coherent system. Longacre (1965), for example, attempts to present some of the fundamental insights of tagmemics in the realm of grammar. He deals in particular with the concepts tagmeme, syntagmeme, level, hierarchy, and field[2]. In spite of his efforts, however, the concept of hierarchy remains weakly motivated and the concept of field is not really integrated within the system. This paper is an attempt to integrate these two concepts into tagmemic theory in a theoretically well motivated way and in a way which is consistent with

---

* In honor of the retirement of A.A. Hill from the University of Texas.

[1] Actually it can be shown that tagmemics has no level of analysis which is identical to the level called surface structure by transformational grammarians; specifically through the use of double function, tagmemicists may deal with some of the elements transformationists analyze as being deleted from the string. The level of structure tagmemics does deal with is so shallow, however, (especially in comparison to the analysis of Ross and Lakoff or the case grammar of Fillmore) that we in this paper will use the term surface structure for the level of analysis that tagmemics treats.

[2] Longacre (1965) uses the term *matrix* instead of *field*. I prefer *field* or *system* for two reasons. First of all, *matrix* refers to a visual n-dimensional array which may be used to represent a system of a language (each dimension of the array representing a parameter of the system). Since I believe the things said here have some relevance for a language system, not merely its visual representation, I prefer to use *system* and *field* which directly refer to the objects being described. My second objection to the use of the term *matrix* is that on a number of occasions within tagmemic literature matrices have been used to represent objects other than systems. Pike (1970:38) presents a 'Co-Occurrence Matrix of Bimoba Clauses in Clusters'. This matrix is no more than a chart of the various clause types which may co-occur within a clause cluster. No attempt is made to state that this chart represents a system of the language. Neither *field* nor *system* has, to my knowledge, been applied to such a representation. I prefer to use the terms which exclude such charts, hence I will restrict myself to the terms *field* and *system*.

the actual practice of tagmemicists. I attempt this topic in the hope that a more coherent and explicit theory of surface grammar will make it easier to develop useful theories of deep structure and semantic structure, as well as to relate these structures to the surface structure.

Since the portion of tagmemic theory I am trying to formalize deals with surface structure, each of the elements, relations, and contrasts discussed in this paper are (unless otherwise noted) elements, relations, and contrasts of the surface structure. In other words, it is not necessary to refer to deep structure relations in order to motivate surface structure grammar. It is true that a large number of contrasts which obtain on a surface level do correlate with contrasts on a deeper level as well. Thus, an interrogative clause differs from a declarative clause on both the surface and the deep levels of structure. But other surface level contrasts (say the difference between *John saw the dog* and *what John saw was the dog*) do not correlate with a difference on the deep structure level of analysis.

1. Tagmeme

A tagmeme is an association of a grammatical function with the set of items which may fill that function. As Longacre has said, 'Tagmemics makes grammatical functions focal, but associates such functions with sets of items and constructions' (1965:65). The primacy of grammatical function arises because the various functions contribute a type of meaning. Thus the subject of a clause is the topic of the clause. *John saw Bill* is a statement about John, while *Bill was seen by John* is a statement about Bill. Similarly, *the dented fender* is not an exact paraphrase of *the fender dented.* (*The dented fender was the left one. The fender dented was the left one.*) When the participle occurs before the noun it characterizes the noun in a relatively permanent way. When the participle follows the noun it modifies no such permanence is implied[3]. The difference in the relationship between modifier and head in the two examples above is a result of the difference in the grammatical functions the two modifiers fill.

Differences in functional relationships are formally demonstrable in that they correlate with differences in form: e.g. different filler classes,

[3] See Bolinger (1967) for a detailed discussion with many examples.

permutability, transformation potential, agreement, etc. It is important to note, however, that these formal correlates do not define the function but only correlate with the function. A grammatical function is a relationship between a constituent and the construction of which it is a part. The formal correlates of a grammatical function are not the relationship itself, but a result of such a relationship.

2. Syntagmeme and field

Since a grammatical function is a relationship between a constituent of a construction and the construction itself, to speak of a grammatical function implies the existence of some unit which contains the function. Such units are called syntagmemes. But the units of language are contrastive units, thus syntagmemes are contrastive construction types. Now it is well known in phonology that the way to show contrast is to find examples of minimal pairs, or, if these cannot be found, examples showing contrast in analogous environments. But neither of these situations is a necessary condition for saying that two phones contrast and therefore belong to different phonemes. [h] and [ŋ] are in complementary distribution in English, yet few linguists (and no tagmemicists) have seriously considered them to be allophones of the same phoneme. Similarly, it is impossible to find good examples of contrast between consonants and vowels, yet [a] and [p] are not considered to be allophones of the same phoneme in any language. In other words, contrast in identical environments and contrast in analogous environments are merely manifestations of a more basic kind of contrast; contrast in field. The English phonemes /h/ and /ŋ/, and, for that matter, /p/ and /b/, are considered to be different phonemes primarily because they play different roles within the system of English phonemes. Contrast in field usually (but not always) correlates with contrast in identical or analogous environments.

Contrast within the grammatical hierarchy has been difficult to define as long as linguists searched for an analog in grammar to the minimal pair in phonology. Once one realizes that the basic contrast is contrast in field, then the inability to find an analog for minimal pairs is no longer so disturbing. A field, in the sense being used here, is a set of language units which differ from each other along a certain finite set of parameters. In the grammatical hierarchy, the units are syntagmemes and the

parameters of each field are expressible in terms of grammatical functions.

Though this last statement is not made overtly in statements of tagmemic theory, it can be shown to be consistent with the practice of tagmemicists. On the one hand, no tagmemic grammar, as far as I know,
has posited two contrasting syntagmemes solely on the basis of differences in form. While it is true in a number of cases that the differences
in form may be the most obvious differences, tagmemicists have always
intuitively felt that a difference in grammatical relationship also existed.
Thus one might find in the description of a language two clause syntagmemes described as follows[4]:

(A)   Transitive clause = + Subject: NP + Predicate: VP_{-be} + Object: NP

(B)   Equative clause = + Topic: NP + $Predicate_{link}$: VP_{be} + Comp: NP

The primary formal difference between (A) and (B) lies in the fact that
the filler of the predicate in (A) is all verbs other than *be*, while the
filler of the predicate in (B) is the verb *be*. But this is not the only difference posited between the two clauses. Differences in functions are
posited as well. The second NP in (A), for example, fills the object function while the second NP in (B) fills the complement function. Such a
situation is typical of tagmemic practice.

A second bit of evidence that the parameters of grammatical fields are
grammatical functions arises from the fact that in all cases which I have
examined in which an author has attempted to present a system of contrasting syntagmemes, differences in the component functions are the
parameters of the field[5]. A typical case in point is the following matrix
adapted from Liem (1966) showing a portion of the system of English
clauses. Each cell in every row has some set of functions (or absence of
functions) in common and each cell in every column has some set of
functions (or absence of functions) in common. We can now make an

---

[4] While this example does not pretend to describe any actual language, examples similar to the
one presented here may be found in Trique (Longacre, 1966:244), Lamani (Trail, 1970:38,
50–51), and Totonac (Reid, Bishop, Button and Longacre, 1968:31,34,44).

[5] In personal conversations Pike has indicated that the theory allows differences in distribution
to be possible parameters of systems. In searching the literature, I have not found any cases
in which this possibility has been used. I believe that should such cases occur, the differences
in distribution will probably correlate with differences in grammatical function. Hence, it will
not be necessary to use distribution as a parameter of a grammatical system.

Independent Clauses

	Declarative Clause	Imperative Clause	Yes-No Interrogative Clause
Intransitive	+ S + Act Intr Decl Pr He ran.	+ Act Intr Imp Pr Run!	+ S + Act Intr Inter Pr Did he run?
Single Transitive	+ S + Act Sg Tr Decl Pr + DO She guided the tourists.	+ Act Sg Tr Imp Pr + DO Guide the tourists!	+ S + Act Sg Tr Inter Pr + DO Did she guide the tourists?
Double Transitive	+ S + Act Db Tr Decl Pr + IO + DO They gave John a book.	+ Act Db Tr Imp Pr + IO + DO Give John a book!	+ S + Act Db Tr Inter Pr + IO + DO Did they give John a book?
Attributive Transitive	+ S + Act At Tr Decl Pr + DO + At They elected him chairman.	+ Act At Tr Imp Pr + DO + At Elect him chairman!	+ S + Act Att Tr Inter Pr + DO + At Did they elect him chairman?
Equational	+ S + Eq Decl Pr + Eq Co She was kind.	+ Eq Imp Pr + Eq Co Be kind!	+ S + Eq Inter Pr + Eq Co Is she kind?

analogy with phonology. If we consider each cell in the field to be a unit — analogous to a phoneme — the distinctive features of that unit are the surface level grammatical functions which compose it. One might predict a possible difference of opinion as to what the real linguistic unit is, the occupant of the cell (the phoneme or syntagmeme) or the set of features defining each cell (the phonological distinctive feature or surface grammatical functions. This last is usually verbalized as transitive intransitive, or declarative—imperative, etc.). It is our belief that both unit and feature are relevant.

Once we see that the contrast involved when we say 'a syntagmeme is a contrastive construction type' is contrast within field and when we realize that the variables of the field are largely functional variables, we see some of the reasons for the heuristics used by tagmemicists. First of all, the heuristics on a syntagmeme level are necessary in order to distinguish differences in function which constitute variables of the system of syntagmemes from those differences in function which do not. Thus, on a clause level, any clause may be modified for time. Thus the presence or absence of a time modifier cannot distinguish one clause from another. And secondly, Longacre's dual criterion[6] for contrasting syntagmemes is merely an affirmation that an 'important' difference (an emic difference) between two clause types should correlate with more than one formal difference.

From the foregoing discussion of system it can be seen that Longacre (1968:xiii) is being largely repetitious when he says:

> syntagmemic contrast is, then, in reference to three considerations: (1) the internal tagmemic structure of the syntagmeme; (2) the distribution of the syntagmeme (as an exponent of tagmemes) in other (usually higher level) syntagmemes; and (3) the distribution of the syntagmeme within a system of syntagmemes. (1968:xiii)

The past few pages have shown that (1) and (3) are, to all intents and purposes one basic factor — role in system — looked at from two points of view: (1) from the point of view of distinctive features of the system, and (3) from the point of view of system as a whole. Some aspects of (2) are accounted for by the fact that certain tagmemes directly affect

---

[6] Longacre's dual criterion unfortunately was initially heralded as a major theoretical advance. Pike (1962:231) calls it a 'crucial theoretical advance'. In reality, the dual criterion is a very useful heuristic which derives from a theoretical advance which in the early sixties remained unexpressed.

the distributional properties of the including syntagmemes. Questions do not have the same distribution as the corresponding declarative or imperative clauses. It remains to be seen, however, whether all significant differences in distribution correlate with differences in the component functions of the contrasting syntagmemes.

3. Level and hierarchy

A level is a system of contrasting syntagmemes. A hierarchy is a system of contrasting levels. These two definitions in conjunction with what has already been said about system (in particular that the parameters of a system are definable in terms of surface structure function) imply that the various levels within a hierarchy are to be contrasted and identified by the various functional relations posited for the syntagmemes with each level.

That is, roughly, a clause is a clause because it contains a predicate or predicate-like tagmeme while a phrase is a phrase because it contains tagmemes such as head, modifier, etc. It is worth noting here that in saying this I am merely emphasizing one aspect of the definition of levels, especially the clause and phrase levels, already used by tagmemicists. Thus, in Elson and Picket, the definition of clause included the statement 'A clause construction is any string of tagmemes which consists of or includes one and only one predicate or predicate-like tagmeme among the constituent tagmemes of the string...' (1962:64). Similarly Longacre included the following sentence in his definition of phrase. '[A phrase] may be single centered, double centered, or relator-axis; and expresses such relationships as head-modifier, linkage of elements, or relation of an element to the clause by means of an overt relator' (1964: 74).

These two statements are examples of the type of statement advocated here. The difficulties with them lie in the fact that the first statement is over-simple, since there are constructions which we may want to call clauses, but which do not contain predicate or predicate-like constructions. Note, for instance, the following examples:
(a) *(I don't like) John playing near the railing*
(b) *With the king safely out of the way (the barons quickly distributed among themselves the wealth of the commoners)*
(c) *(I wanted) John to come*
The second statement is more complete, but does not seem to be unified

by any underlying principle. One could justifiably ask whether these relations have anything in common which contrasts them as a group with
relations which are typical of clauses or words. As far as I can tell, Longacre has no answer to such a question other than 'that's the way things
are'. I believe this lack of motivation stems from his emphasis on descending exponence in the definition of hierarchy. Longacre includes,
for example, a statement that phrases are 'a class of syntagmemes of a
hierarchical order ranking above such syntagmemes as the word and/or
stem and below such syntagmemes as the clause and sentence' (1964:74).
The definition of each level; sentence, clause, phrase and word, in
Longacre (1964) contains a similar statement locating it within the hierarchy of levels. In this context saying that clause level ranks just above
phrase level implies, among other things, that phrases typically manifest
clause level tagmemes.

It is clear from the pervasiveness of statements locating construction
types within the hierarchy that descending exponence plays an important
role in Longacre's definition of hierarchy. He admits, however, that

>Attempts to define hierarchy overly rigidly in terms of exclusively
>descending exponence can only lead to complete jettisoning of the
>notion of hierarchy. The exceptions are too glaring to rationalize
>away successfully for very long. (1970:185)

However, we should note that Longacre clearly regards counter examples
to this general rule that higher ranking constructions have constituents
which belong to the next lower rank, as nothing more than temporary
exceptions to the general rule.

>... without the downward thrust of constituent structure [from dis-
>course level to morpheme level – PHF] there could not be hierarchy.
>Descending hierarchy and level skipping are but different instances
>here of the same tendency. Furthermore, both recursion and back
>looping must, eventually, terminate and give way to the downward
>thrust. (1970:186)

Within this model of hierarchy Longacre has no means of explaining why
the exceptions to the 'downward thrust' of hierarchy occur when and
where they do. Why, for example, do relative clauses fill noun phrase
tagmemes but not the tagmemes of a prepositional phrase?

It seems to me that such questions can be answered only if we focus
away from descending exponence as a defining feature of hierarchy and
search for a more basic defining feature. A good candidate for such a
basic defining feature is the kind of function each unit has in a connected discourse.

If we look at the use of language in connected discourse we find certain things assumed, certain things asserted[7], and relations between assertions expressed. In a clause such as *the old man walked home* the assertion is made that a given individual walked to a particular location. In addition to this assertion, however, the information is given that the individual involved is a man and is old (and probably that he has been mentioned before). The information that he is old and is a man, however, has a different status within the clause from the information which is asserted: it is not asserted. It is brought in in order to supply enough information to the listener so that he can identify the participant in the action. Information which is not asserted takes on roughly the status of features describing the participant[8]. These features may be used to contrast the actual participant with other potential participants (the old man instead of the young one, the old man instead of the old woman) or they may be used to more fully describe a participant in order to explain a further action (and its implications). It can be shown that the clause *the old man walked home* is true whether or not the listener agrees that the man is old. The clause is true if a particular individual (whom I described as old) walked home. It is true that conversations such as (A) *The old man walked home*, (B) *He's not old* may occur but the participants realize that such a sequence of sentences is strange.

Noun phrases are semantically complexes of features even if they contain restrictive relative clauses. Thus, *I found out that those men I met at the party yesterday are bank presidents,* and *Beware of men you meet at parties* both contain noun phrases (with *men* as head) which contain relative clauses. The function of the first relative clause is to contrast one individual with others, while the function of the second is to describe the relevant feature of a given class of *men*. In both instances, however, the semantic interpretation of the noun phrases will be in terms of a set of semantic features. Thus, when they are considered from the

---

[7] While the term *assert* normally refers only to one function of a speech act, one which is closely related to declarative clauses, my use of the term here is to be understood as including other functions of speech acts such as questioning and commanding. These, of course, are closely related to interrogative and imperative clauses.

[8] The distinction between the information which is asserted and the information which is used as descriptive or identificational features of a participant of an assertion is roughly similar to the distinction Leech (1970:25–28) makes between the including predication, rank-shifted predications, and downgraded predications. Downgarded predications take on the status of features, while the including predications and rank-shifted predications are asserted.

standpoint of the including clause, restrictive relative clauses are to be interpreted as merely adding descriptive/identificational features within the noun phrase. Functions of speech acts and portions of speech acts, such as assertion, and description or identification of participants in an assertion may be called discourse functions. These functions are signalled in the surface structure and hence may be called surface grammatical meaning.

If we look at the way these discourse functions are distributed throughout the hierarchy, we see that the various hierarchical levels correlate generally with different discourse functions. Clauses typically express assertions (cf. Longacre, 1964: 35), phrases typically indicate participants in the assertions (*the man*), features of the participants (*the very old man*), or restrictions on the assertion such as limitations as to time, place, manner, etc. Within participants of an assertion I must include the action itself (e.g. *will have been completed*) and any modalities and conditions imposed on the action such as aspect, and tense. Relations between assertions such as cause, conjunction, antithesis, and relations between a participant in an assertion and the assertion itself (*I gave the book to Harry*) are expressed by single words.

With such a correlation we are now not only prepared to find a general trend of descending exponence (phrases typically manifest clause level tagmemes, words typically express phrase level tagmemes, etc.) but we are also prepared to find exceptions to this general trend. Exceptions occur, for instance, when a relation between two assertions is overtly expressed; e.g. in *John came downstairs because he wanted some milk* the word *because* fills a sentence level tagmeme. If, on the other hand, a participant in an assertion is itself an assertion, we expect to find a clause filling a grammatical function within another clause (*That he came early surprised me.*). Similarly, if we wish to identify a participant in one assertion by noting that he also is a participant in a second, the theory would predict that a clause would fill a phrase level tagmeme. Thus, if a given individual both shot a guard and led a gang, then one could find either *the one who shot the guard led the gang,* or *the one who led the gang shot the guard.* The choice of one or the other alternative depends on what is already known by the listener.

Now if we accept discourse function as the underlying motivation for hierarchy, it seems to me we must ask where the source for discourse functions such as assertion, identification of participants, etc. lies. My answer is that it lies largely in the functional aspect of the component tagmemes of the syntagmemes. That is, clauses predicate because they have tagmemes which interact in such a way as to predicate (*The dog is barking*). Noun phrases do not predicate (*the barking dog, the dog barking in the street*) because they have no tagmemes which interact to make a predication[9]. I do not deny here that the same information is conveyed in *the dog is barking* and *the barking dog*. The two constructions differ in that, in the first, barking is asserted with respect to the dog, while in the second, the fact that the dog is barking is used as an identifying or descriptive feature of the dog.

In summary we now have a system of five terms: tagmeme, syntagmeme, level, hierarchy and field (=system) which are inter-related largely via the concept of surface structure grammatical function. But this means that functional relations are of crucial importance within this theory of grammar. That is, if we lable the functions of *head down* in *Head down, the bull charged* as Subject-Predicate, we imply that this construction is some sort of clause, while if we call these functions Head-Modifier, we imply that the construction belongs on the phrase level.

But basing this aspect of tagmemic theory on surface level grammatical functions offers a direct challenge to tagmemicists. If surface structure grammatical relations are so important to the theory, then tagmemicists ought to develop a coherent theory of surface structure grammatical relationships. What does it mean when we say that X is the subject or object of a clause? What similarities must subjects in language (A) share with subjects in a language (B)? How may subjects differ? In short, what is needed is a kind of etics of surface level grammatical functions. Tagmemicists have implicitly operated with such a theory for a long time. Velma Pickett for example has told me of long conversations about how best to label certain grammatical functions in her dissertation. It seems to me that it is time for tagmemicists to make such a theory explicit.

Central Michigan University

---

[9] The approach I am suggesting here may also provide a criterion for treating certain clause-like and phrase-like constructions as clauses rather than phrases, e.g.

With John gone (there were only six of us to feed).
Head down (the bull charged).
(John came home) tired.

Each of the above examples has neither a typical clause level structure nor a typical phrase level structure; thus, internal formal criteria are indecisive. All three express assertions which are independent of the 'including' assertion. As a result they may be considered clauses, though their lack of a typical clause structure indicates that they are marginal to the clause system.

Bibliography

Bolinger, D. (1967) "Adjectives in English: Attribution and Predication." *Lingua*. Vol. 18, No. 1:1–34.

Elson, Benjamine and Velma Pickett. (1962) *An Introduction to Morphology and Syntax*. Summer Institute of Linguistics, Santa Ana.

Longacre, Robert E. (1964) *Grammar Discovery Procedures*. Mouton and Co. The Hague. Janua Linguarum Series Minor 33.

Longacre, Robert E. (1965) "Some Fundamental Insights of Tagmemics." *Language*. Vol. 41: 65–76.

Longacre, Robert E. (1966) "Trique Clause and Sentence: A Study in Contrast, Variation, and Distribution". *IJAL*. Vol. 32:242–252.

Longacre, Robert E. (1968) *Philipine Languages: Discourse, Paragraph and Sentence Structure*. Summer Institute of Linguistics, Santa Ana.

Longacre, Robert E. (1970) "Hierarchy in Language" in Paul Garvin (ed.). *Method and Theory in Linguistics*. Mouton and Co. Janua Linguarum Series Maior 40:173–195.

Leech, Geoffry N. (1970) *Towards a Semantic Description of English*. Indiana University Press.

Liem, Nguyen Dang. (1966) *English Grammar: A combined Tagmemics and Transformational Approach*. Linguistic Circle of Canberra Publications. Vol. 1. Series C. Canberra, Australia.

Pike, K.L. (1970) *Tagmemic and Matrix Linguistics Applied to Selected African Languages*. Summer Institute of Linguistics, Santa Ana.

Reid, Aileen, Ruth G. Bishop, Ella M. Button and Robert Longacre. (1968) *Totonac: From Clause to Discourse*. Summer Institute of Linguistics, Santa Ana.

Trail, Ronald. (1970) *The Grammar of Lamani*. Summer Institute of Linguistics, Santa Ana.

CRUCIAL QUESTIONS IN THE DEVELOPMENT OF
TAGMEMICS--THE SIXTIES AND SEVENTIES

KENNETH L. PIKE

University of Michigan

Abstract. The sixties began, for tagmemics, with publications
answering the question: What kind of high-level generalization can
be made to characterize all units of human behavior or knowledge?
A large number of studies of grammatical pattern and of phonological
hierarchy grew out of this approach during the sixties.
  By 1961, a crucial new question under attention was: Can there
be a grammatical chart (a grammatical feature matrix) comparable
to a phonetic one, and which is itself a unit? This first led to studies
in the relationship between clauses, and then to integrating them with
morphology, and morphology to some principles of historical change.
  In 1963, a further question arose: Can matrices be developed to
show the relation between situational role (case) and grammatical role?
And can these be related to discourse structure? Becker and Wise,
after the middle of the decade, worked on these questions, studying
also the work of Fillmore which was beginning to contribute heavily
to case analysis. Wise carried the underlying question further, to
the study of the lexemic structure of discourse, while Longacre con-
tributed vigorously to the study of grammatical constructions at that
level.
  By 1964, questions concerning the generativeness of tagmemic
formulas, under the stimulus of transformational grammar, had been
discussed by Longacre, and later followed up by Cook.
  By 1968, a new question arose: Could group theory, from mathematics, aid in the description of pronominal sequences in embedded
quotations, and in discourse structure itself? Pike and Lowe joined
in this endeavor.
  For the seventies: (a) How continue the mathematizing of discourse
structure (Lowe, Wise, Grimes, Hale, Pike)? (b) How relate hierarchies (Longacre, Wise, Pike)? How show the relation between various

current theories? (c) How continue studying 500 languages so as to gather data to set up, inductively, substantive universals, and to test the validity of those guessed at deductively?

A theory can be characterized by the questions which it chooses to ask.

The first crucial question:

(1a) Who was Mr. John Doe III, born August 14, 1938, on Evans Way, Boston--have I ever met him?

This question is normal, rational, reasonable. Its validity is a presupposition of all rational discourse. If the question is in principle not answerable, then all human behavior as we know it must cease, all intuitive tests for validity are lost, and knowledge itself evaporates into skepticism.

This affirmation may be viewed as the epistemological starting point of tagmemic theory--a theory which in 1960 reached a crucial point in its development with the appearance of the last volume of the first edition of my Language in Relation to a Unified Theory of the Structure of Human Behavior. Tagmemic theory staked its claims on the belief that essential to the description of human behavior as we live it must be the ability to recognize a friend even though he has just had Wheaties for breakfast, cut his long hair, and replaced his necktie. Most of us do not know the shape of the molecules inside our friend's liver, nor even the length in millimeters of his small intestine. But lack of complete knowledge does not prevent us from knowing John Doe III.

We are able to recognize some objects in spite of the fact that we do not know everything about them. Similarly, and by direct epistemological parallelism, we must be able to recognize events, and we must be able to discuss rationally whether or not two particular utterances are or are not instances of the same poem, or of the same clause, or of the same word, in spite of changes in them over time, variability in context, and similarity to other--but contrastive--forms All of this, then, leads to Question (1b), treated in the volume already mentioned:

(1b) What kind of high-level generalization can be made to characterize all units of human behavior or knowledge?

What is it, that is, about any person, event, situation, object, concept, which allows us to call it a unit, and to describe it adequately? By 1960, tagmemics (in the volume referred to) had finished answering this question in general terms: (a) A unit--any unit--in order to be well described must have had specified those characteristics which differentiate it from every other (and these same features allow it to be identified in further contexts); (b) its range of variability and its necessary physical components must have been given; and (c) the range of contexts in which it may appropriately occur (its distribution in class, in sequence, and in system) must be stated. (Or, its feature mode, manifestation mode, and distribution mode must have been specified.)

But it was from a related question, which I first asked in 1948 and for which provisional answers began to emerge in 1949, that I date the beginning of tagmemics:

(1c) Is there a unit of grammar which would be as important to us-- if we could find it--as the phoneme (or--rephrased for some scholars in the 1970's, perhaps--as the phone)?

Late in the Spring of 1949 an affirmative answer began to emerge-- developed as tagmeme-in-syntagmeme by the 1960 third volume. The sixties, however, were a drab climate within which to continue this affirmation. As the decade began, constituents--as units needing mutual relating by means of a generalization about units as such-- were in general repudiated or ignored by theory, even while cropping up as undefined terms in practice. Fortunately, as the decade closed, however, attention to the validity of constituents, and to some other units, began to receive more explicit attention. At the beginning of the sixties, however, tagmemics--on the theoretical front--stood alone in any attempt to capture the generalization directly; but by tagmemi- cists the concept was being heavily and usefully exploited. (See anno- tated bibliographies of Pike 1966b, and Brend 1970, for monographs and articles by--among others--Pickett, Waterhouse, Blansitt, and Brend for grammar; Eunice Pike, Scott, West, and others for phonol- ogy of upper hierarchical levels; Grimes for some early incorporation of both tagmemic and transformational views.)

These studies involve another question, however:

(1d) How are these different elements hierarchically related?

Once the concept of unit had been firmly accepted by the theory, the hierarchical nature of some of these units proved inevitable, and was heavily developed in the 1960 volume.

The relationship between the hierarchies received initial attention, so that by this third volume specific sections were beginning to explore the relationships: phonology to grammar, phonology to lexicon, gram- mar to lexicon. Specific studies, also, were developed. Among them, for example, was one on Auca (Pike 1964b) in which a most elegant pattern showed a chain of alternating stresses on a verb beginning from the first syllable of the stem, moving towards the end of the stem, and a second chain of stresses beginning from the end of the suffix chain working back towards the stem; the addition of another syllable (another morpheme) affected the place of stress. Elegant rules led to adjacent stresses when the stress chains clashed at the juncture of stem with suffix.

In spite of some such studies, however, the question of the interlocking of the hierarchies was in general given only minor attention.
It was left to other theories during the sixties to focus heavily on this
point (such that transformational grammar attempted to cross over
the hierarchies--in our view--by way of rules, and stratificational
grammar did so by networks). Their contributions pose further questions of tagmemics for the seventies: Can tagmemics utilize the extensive results of the two mentioned theories to refine the limited statements of the early tagmemic approach, while retaining its own unit
contribution?

While other theorists were dealing with these matters, however,
the attention of the tagmemic theoretical front moved to a different
question--our leading theoretical question for the first half of the
sixties. It was this question which opened my Presidential address
to the Linguistic Society of America in 1961 (see Pike 1962a):

(2a) Is it possible that there is some kind of grammatical chart (or
'matrix') comparable to a phonetic chart, with contrastive features for
rows and columns, but with grammatical units in the cells?

This question had as a pair of presuppositions both the presence of
grammatical units (just as a phonetic chart has a presupposition of
some kind of phone, whether or not one grants the phoneme as a unit)
and the relevance of contrastive features of grammatical constructions
(analogous to distinctive features of voicing, aspiration, and so on,
of phones).

By 1961, in a workshop in Peru, this question was solved in a preliminary form. Mildred Larson provided us with a contrastive chart
of Aguaruna clause types, with imperative versus stative, active, and
equative as features of one parameter, and transitive, intransitive,
nominative as features of the other (in Pike 1962a:222). This development opened up a whole new area for effective presentation of total
structure in a simple, easily graphable fashion. Relations between
clauses (or between sentences, phrases, etc.) could be easily seen
as a function of the change of one or more sets of features. It opened
the door, furthermore, to an easy way of specifying a relation between
one whole set of grammatical constructions and a different set of constructions merely by the addition or subtraction of a set of features.
Thus, one could start with a set of kernel constructions, and (a) show
derivation of a second set from such a kernel (if one wished to use
derivational terminology, which for some purposes continued to prove
valuable) or (b) one could specify the two sets as mutually related by
having comparable cells for many of the same contrastive features of
their respective charts (without specifying a derivational base).
Regardless, that is to say, of the theoretical statement of the relationships, this display of the relationships is clear and helpful.

In addition, the matrices themselves can themselves be units which are hierarchically related, such that a matrix of verb stems may involve some of the contrastive-feature sets which later differentiate the clauses--as in Larson's situation. A series of such charts at various levels of the grammatical hierarchy is helpful if one wishes to take advantage of the theory in order to get a quick insight into a total pattern. For example, just as in the Bloomfieldian era various scholars, including Bloomfield himself, would utilize or publish phonetic charts even while repudiating their theoretical relevance, so today a matrix of grammatical constructions is an extremely useful tool for insight into a system even for those people who ignore or repudiate the validity of the analysis of the grammatical matrix as a unit.

(2b) Can a system of grammatical constructions, seen as a matrix of units, itself be a unit?

The tagmemic answer is a firm yes. It is not only actual behavioral events which can be units (along with physical objects or John Doe III himself), but systems as well. If we ask: A unit for whom? Then one may answer, if one chooses: A unit in the output of the analyst (rather than in the behavior of the speaker). At this point, tagmemics is quite ready to grant that there may be units in the behavior of the analyst which are not necessarily in the behavior of the non-analytical speaker. We merely add that an analyst is human--and, if one of his features is a matrix-creating capacity, then it is a human capacity of interest to our theory. Here tagmemics does not commit the epistemological fallacy in which a theory covers all statements about the world except the statment about the statements.

(2c) Can such feature-matrices of various types be extended profitably to nonverbal situations?

The matrices of Bock (1962; see also 1964, 1967, annotated in Brend 1970), developed independently of ours, shows this to be feasible, with space-time-role arrays (discussion in Pike 1967:667-78, 673-74).

The feature-times-feature matrix, however, was not the only one which gave positive results. There was also the one of unit-times-sequential components, which led to various kinds of syntactic paradigms. Here, the question of the matrix was:

(2d) Can redundancy be utilized to display illustrations of a syntactic system in a compact form, such that illustrative material will vary only when the structure demands it?

The result was a paradigm in syntax comparable to paradigms in morphology, but integrated with them: successive paradigms moving down from the clause into morphological structure were helpful. (See, for example, Pike 1962b on Kanite, and 1966a on African languages.) Out of these matrix materials, however, a third major questions arose in the first of the sixties:

(3a) How can we handle relations of form to meaning in a morphological system when the relationship of form to meaning is not one-to-one?

Here a technique was made explicit which, when used at all by other scholars, had been used intuitively but without an explicit heuristic which could be generalized and taught in the classroom (see Pike and Jacobs 1968). The device was to record the affixed forms of ordinary paradigms in some kind of a feature matrix. Having done so, one by one, rows were permuted so that, for example, row two might become row four, while four became two; columns were similarly permuted, with the goal of bringing into a connected solid block all those segments (called 'formatives') in the cells which were phonologically alike.

The resultant formative blocks turned out to have considerable importance. On the one hand, they represented the logical intersection of features from two or more parameters (instead of semantic features being represented through a single row, consistently, by some phonological trait). A formative block would represent only those places at which certain specific features from the rows intersect with specific features from the columns. As a result, the classical morpheme (containing a form and its meaning), became a special instance of a matrix formative--a formative in the shape of a single row. Morphophonemics, on the other hand, turned out to be a device--seen from this perspective--to make a row appear to be uniform when, in fact, it was not. That is, by the replacement of certain formatives with another formative from the same row, the row itself appeared symbolically uniform--i.e. was morphophonemically written--so that the morpheme itself then had a single phonological representation in the morphophonemic formula.

But the extreme opposite to the classical morpheme was the formative which occurred in one cell only. In this instance the formative signalled two (or more) semantic features simultaneously--one from the row and one from the column. The formative was multisystemic. If the whole matrix were of this type--which I called an 'ideal' type as over against the 'simple' one of classical morphemics--every formative would have more than one meaning, and no simple morphemes would occur.

When we tried to understand, however, how such patterns of formative blocks could come about, other questions arose:

(3b) How does change in a morphological set of affixes appear over time, seen from the perspective of morphological matrices?

The answer here was that there must exist two driving mechanisms: the one is a drive towards phonological fusion in a high-level phonological unit pronounced at high speed; i.e. smearing of phonemes and phones in a high-level phonological wave. As the smearing continues, classical morphemes begin to smear and fuse into single-celled formatives. If this were the only driving mechanism, language would end up as completely unintelligible, made up of a million (plus) separate items. There has to be a mechanism which induces a 'counter-flow' toward re-establishing some degree of morphemic simplicity of the classical type. This counter-flow can be seen as working through matrix analogy, which brings to bear various kinds of systemic pressures. If rows and columns of formatives which were incomplete or irregular were to be extended and made uniform, there would be re-established the simpler kind of system. Thus, the historical principle involves phonological fusion leading to the loss of classical morphemes, combined with matrix regularization leading toward the reestablishment of classical morphemes. (See Pike and Scott 1963, Pike 1965, and bibliographies.)

At the same time, agreement irregularities within a system had to be described, which led to the following question:

(3c) How could concord be handled simply in a way which avoids listing all the details every time--whether the detail be of a feature specification or of a phonological-context specification?

Here our answer again was in terms of the morphological matrices. (a) If there were two units in a sequence in which some or all of the same contrastive features were used, comparable matrices should be developed at those points, with features lined up in the same order. (b) Then, to show concord, it would not be necessary to list details-- nor even rules of detail--but it would be only necessary to list the number-index of the matrices involved, with a rule saying that one must pick from each matrix indexed in the relevant string the topo-logically equivalent cell--i. e. a cell from the same numbered row and column. Thus a high degree of concord could be handled by a simple indexing of matrices. (See, for German, Pike 1965.)

Such a use of various kinds of charts led to the attempt to classify tagmemes themselves in a systematic way. From the first tagmeme publication, I had had subject tagmemes contrasting by elements such as agent versus goal. This led, specifically, to a 'distribution class of tagmemes' which included the subject-as-actor tagmeme in contrast to the subject-as-recipient tagmeme in active and passive clauses respectively. (See Pike 1954:Sections 7.3, 7.321, 7.43, 7.6; or see revised edition 1967, same sections, pp. 196, 219, 231, 246-48.) In the early sixties, however, I wished to develop some kind of array in which we would have the 'logical' or 'structural-meaning' component as one parameter, and the grammatical elements as another. This led to one of the most important tagmemic questions of the sixties: ·

(4) How are the 'situational' roles such as agent or goal related to 'grammatical' roles such as subject and object--and how are these related to discourse structure?

The question was answered programmatically in a paper on discourse analysis presented to the Linguistic Society of America in the summer of 1963, and published a year later (Pike 1964a). In it, on the one hand, were several kinds of matrices, including one with situational role (now, since Fillmore, usually called 'case') versus grammatical role and, on the other hand, there were tagmemes made up of combined situational and grammatical role, as one parameter, over against certain kinds of observer involvement (focus, emphasis, surprise), over against a grammatical hierarchical level. This article developed in a workshop in the Philippines where I was struggling with problems of topic (focus) and its rearrangements in clause structure pointed out by my colleagues of the Summer Institute of Linguistics. In this article I also pointed out that if the same event were reported from several points of view--with different people telling the same story--the situations would be constant, but the grammatical roles relative to the narrator-participant would vary. Within the tagmemic literature, three more-or-less independent approaches have attempted to grapple with this kind of data, and have carried these programmatic suggestions much further.

In the Philippines itself, Myra Lou Barnard developed an elaborate tree diagram of a narrative (from discourse to morpheme), with a black-outlined tree giving grammatical structure and a red-outlined, printed overlay giving the tree structure of the lexemic pattern (see Longacre 1968, volume 3, inserted folded appendix). In addition, she co-authored with Longacre a section of his report (1968, now printed in Vol. 1, Part 3, of Longacre 1970) discussing details of the interlocking of grammar and lexicon--or that which I now call lexemics--on levels of discourse, paragraph, and sentence.

A second development, on a more restricted topic, the subject of English clause, occurred in a dissertation by Becker (1967) who discussed four components of a tagmeme: a grammatical form (subject); grammatical meaning (agent); lexical form (noun phrase); and lexical meaning (single male human). Before completion of his work, however, he had access to Fillmore's early work on case (1966), and was able to discuss some of the similarities between the approaches. The need for further study of the relation between the implications of tagmemics and of case grammar comprises a major topic of concern for the seventies; at this point, tagmemics should benefit greatly from the work of the case grammarians. (See also Cook 1971.)

A third stage in the development of a tagmemic view of the situational versus grammatical role material, however, was given in the dissertation of Wise (1968). She had gathered material in Peru in order to check on my suggestion about permutations of participant relations (in situational versus grammatical roles) in the multiple tellings of a story from different viewpoints. The size of the problem became so large,

however, that she had to limit her first goals, so that some of her discourse material was delayed. (See Question (7b) where I return to her
more recent work.) She made a major advance, however, by insisting
(a) on the retention of form-meaning relations in setting up these
lexemic units, so that certain lexemic elements were not treated
merely as abstract semantic components; and (b) that lexemic constructions occurred at all hierarchical levels, from word to discourse.
This was crucial, since it allowed us to insist again on the necessity of
form-meaning composites, hierarchically structured, which had been
basic to tagmemics from the beginning. The alternative of abstracting
the semantic component away from any necessary form, so that one
had some kind of deep abstraction versus surface objectification, was
unacceptable to us both. The view which Wise developed appeared to
me to tie into the epistemological outlook of tagmemics which keeps us
always in touch with both physical and psychological reality at every
stage in the generative or representational process. (The minimum
physical component of every unit--including that of a false concept--
would be some kind of neurological one.) At the same time, Wise carried further the relation of meaning to the observer viewpoint, to the
plot, and to the social setting. For the seventies, I have already begun
to explore the extension of this approach in various directions. (For
a related view, with less hierarchical emphasis on the lexemic component, see now Ballard, Conrad, and Longacre 1971.)

The linguistic climate of the early sixties faced the question:

(5a) Is a tagmemic formulaic representation generative?

Longacre (1964) demonstrated that it indeed was so, implicitly,
but that its generative power could--and should--be made explicit.
Considerable study on generativeness of tagmemic formulas has also
been handled since then by Cook (1967). The presence of this generative implication of tagmemics should not be unexpected by anyone who
reflects for a moment on the fact that tagmemics grew up in a context
where translation theory and practice was in view. Most people working on tagmemic material were expecting to use these formulas as a
formal aid towards idiomatic translations. If the formulas were not,
in fact, productive in this sense, they would eventually prove to be
worthless for these purposes. The future survival value of tagmemics
can, therefore, in part be measured by the degree to which this generative aspect helps nonnative speakers to cross language boundaries
for translation purposes. It should be clear, then, that Longacre's
insistence was not an ad hoc defense of an armchair theory, but rather
an explicit component in the answer of the following question:

(5b) How is translation possible--and how is it related to tagmemic
formulas?

It should appear that the grammatical formulas of tagmemics pose
grammatical constraints on all possible sequences in a particular

language, and that the lexemic formulas of Wise impose various kinds
of situational constraints. For the seventies, also, it should be clear
that translation interest continues for many of us dealing with tagmemics, but that the focus has shifted to the higher levels of discourse
structure. (Considerable hybridization of tagmemics with stratificational theory is occurring here--especially with the work of Gleason
(cf. Gleason 1968)--e. g. Grimes and Glock 1970.) That is, we may
ask:

(5c) What kind of discourse formulas can be generative of the
grammar of narrative, or of dialogue, or of hortatory presentations,
and the like ?

In the last years of the sixties, major advance in the grammatical
phase of discourse analysis came from Longacre on the basis of work
on a couple of dozen Philippine languages (1968), and he is carrying
on in the early seventies by his work on languages of New Guinea.
Emphasis on the difference between grammatical construction and
lexemic construction on the discourse level, however, has been largely
the contribution of Wise (1968), as we have indicated.

Such materials, in combination with a tagmemic emphasis on unit
and on perspectives of particle, wave, and field, were built into an
approach to the teaching of composition through tagmemic theory
(Young, Becker, and Pike 1970). This suggests the development of
further applications to the study of literature in the seventies.

We turn back now to discuss one other crucial idea extended during
the second half of the sixties:

(6a) Can grammar be viewed as a 'wave', profitably, much as high-
level phonological units and stress groups were sometimes viewed by
tagmemics as waves, and sometimes as particles?

In the sixties, the development of phonology as wave was extended.
There was an attempt to exhaust, as an underlying general principle,
the kinds of things that could happen to any high-level phonological unit
(Pike 1962b); and numerous studies on phonological hierarchy were
related to this (see bibliographies cited--especially works by Eunice
Pike). For a long time, furthermore, I had been interested in the way
that phonological fusions led to grammatical problems (see, for example, discussion above about fusion in morphological matrices). On the
basis of experience in Africa it was clear that it was not merely phonological units which changed relative to their place in the nucleus or
margin of a phonological wave, but that grammatical units could change
according to their place in reference to their closeness to the nucleus
of the grammatical construction--viewed-as-a-wave. The closer to the
nucleus the unit under attention came, the fuller and more contrastive
and greater the set of freedoms the unit might enjoy, including modifi-
ability by other tagmemes. The farther from the nucleus, the more
the unit might be abbreviated or lose its freedom of distribution and of

semantic variability. (This material was presented when I was last at Georgetown--see Pike 1968.) There were sharp differences between phonological fusion, where the phones themselves could be modified, and grammatical fusion, where it was degrees of constraint on freedom of membership of morphemes in classes, presence or absence of additional modifying tagmemes, special phonological rules, and special semantic elements which were in general involved.

This material still awaits extensive development; it is difficult to handle since it requires simultaneously a theoretical commitment (a) to the presence of units and (b) to indeterminacies between them or their changing manifestations. This question has lain dormant, therefore, for half a decade. In the meantime, however, it fills in a major point in the speculative pattern of the tagmemics of the sixties--and conceivably could develop into a major point of interest in the seventies.

(6b) To what extent is it useful to view language and other human behavior via perspectives of particle, wave, field?

It should be clear that, in the fifties, ending with the publication of Pike 1960, the emphasis of tagmemics was clearly on defining the unit, which in this context we may call a particle. On the other hand, it should be equally clear that with the development of the matrix material in the sixties, an alternative view could be held--a view which I called 'field', or a matrix of relational, grammatical characteristics. With the development of the viewpoint of grammar as wave--supplementing the earlier phonological materials--this third possible perspective joins the other two for language and behavior as a whole.

It has proved impossible to handle all the materials of interest to me from any one of these three perspectives. Nor is it possible for me to integrate them all into a single statement. Rather the differences represent differences in observer standpoint; and as the analyst-observer changes his stance, he sees things from a different perspective, and describes them differently. It is this observer stance which allows representation of the same materials either as a set of particles (with variants), or as a set of waves, or as a point or points in a set of intersecting features (as a field).

This multiple viewpoint has proved extremely useful. I do not know of any more exciting set of relationships which I have ever studied. Again and again it has proved fruitful in driving me to look in profitable directions. Nevertheless, the metaphor has been troublesome. To a theoretical physicist and mathematician such as Ivan Lowe, for example, the metaphor of field seems misplaced. He and Peter Fries have urged me to define the terms 'wave', 'field', and 'particle' in reference to other terms, so that the metaphor could be in principle dropped. So that one of our tasks for the seventies (already under way) is to answer the question:

(6c)   How can the terms particle, wave, and field be defined in multiple sets of postulates by nonmetaphorical terms, such that the resemblances (or identities) between them can be seen, the terms themselves
can be avoided, and the alternative viewpoints formally exploited?

Since the areas covered by the terms overlap (inasmuch as any element can be viewed as particle or as wave or as point in a field), there
are redundancies in the system. Unless these are formally specified,
we may end with confusion. In addition to refining my first postulate
set, however, I hope to be able to show that with alternate sets of postulates we can begin from other viewpoints and retain all of the contributions of wave and field without certain of the difficulties currently involved in them.

But a radically different question arose toward the end of the sixties:

(7a)   Is it possible to use standard mathematical group theory, with
its standard axioms, to apply to some phases of natural language; and
to develop mathematical theorems from them which are mappable on to
natural language?

Specifically, I became interested in the problem of the use of pronouns in direct quotations, on the basis of certain problems arising in
African languages (Pike 1966a:86-92, where, for example, in a story a
chief will be quoted directly but a commoner indirectly, to give status
to the former. It occurred to me that the relationship between three
persons Abe, Bill, and Charlie, in their relationship to the pronouns I,
you, and he, appeared as if in some kind of game of 'musical chairs'--
with three chairs named ', you, he', in which A, B, C found seats in
various arrangements. Closure occurred (since the number of arrangements was limited and recurring), so that group theory of mathematics
might conceivably apply. Eventually, a mathematician--Ivan Lowe--
teamed up with me in preparing a paper (Pike and Lowe 1969) in which
not only is group theory used (with its standard axioms as I had hoped),
but also the development was carried by Lowe to the point where he
could set forth an interesting theorem which he proved by standard
mathematical procedures of induction. This theorem can be used to
generate to the nth embedded direct quotation the relationships between
cast (Abe, Bill, Charlie), person (I, you, he), and case (agent, goal, un-
defined--or particular grammatical subject-object relationships). In a
further paper, Lowe (1969) extended the theorem to include inclusive
and exclusive plurals.

This material has led directly to one of our major questions for the
seventies:

(7b)   Can components of discourse structure be mathematized?

While I was working on the early stages of this material, I had wondered if the same kind of mathematical group theory might somehow be
brought to bear upon the changes of relation of dramatis personae to

the narrative, when different participants told the 'same' story--see Question (4). Wise now took the data gathered in a Peruvian language for the purposes of the earlier question, and studied it with Lowe to see if together they could arrive at its mathematical description in terms of group theory. Certain phases of this work were completed successfully in 1970. Various scholars (Wise, Lowe, Grimes, Hale) are working to extend the area of application of this approach.

I am myself working intensively to show that the pronominal structures referred to can be used to define not only sequences of quotations within sentences, but to define certain characteristics of conversations as wholes--the structured order in which different persons are allowed to speak to other persons. Yet one serious difficulty plagued me early: there were different ways to represent each of the six speaker-addressee axes (each representing a monologue) which were possible when three people were involved in the conversation (A-B, i. e. A speaks to B; B-A; A-C; C-A; B-C; C-B). But if each of these axes were treated as a terminal of some kind, then it followed that we had multiple ways--twenty-four of them--to generate this set of six terminal strings. In some cases the mathematics was quite different (non-communicative versus communicative groups which were abstractly different--having different multiplication tables). In other cases, the mathematics was similar (abstractly same) but concretely different (having same multiplication tables but different Cayley diagrams). And some groups were completely the same mathematically (both abstractly and concretely same), but different in terms of the sociological assignments of the mathematical symbols. Of these various groups some were totally alien to any normal conversational constraints which I have been able to imagine; others specified certain constraints which were present in some degree in different styles or conditions of normal conversation. This led to a further question:

(7c) Granted a large number of alternative mathematical models for a simple linguistic situation, what kind of sociolinguistic evaluative measure could be found to aid in the choice of the appropriate model or appropriate models?

In this particular instance my evaluation of the alternative models is made in the following way: (a) Each model grants to each individual in the set of three individuals, starting from an initial axis arbitrarily chosen, a set of 'rights': He may be allowed to speak or may not be allowed to speak; to reply or not to reply; to shift attention to someone else or not to shift. In addition, (b) there may be general negative constraints which grow out of the sum of the rights of all individuals in the system. A person may be told: 'Don't speak until you're spoken to', or, on the contrary, he may be chided: 'Answer the gentleman--didn't you hear him speak to you?' On the other hand, (c) one may study the characteristics of a conversational 'system'--that is, the total set of

all possible sequences of conversational interchange which may be
allowed within the pattern of initial rights granted to individuals.

These different patterns vary to an astonishing degree: By the
most restricted pattern which I have generated, after twelve conversational monologues (i. e. after there have been twelve stages of the
conversation, each stage being a different axis from the preceding
one) the total system has exactly one path which may be followed; this
results from the fact that at each change of speaker-addressee axis
there is exactly one choice available to the system as a whole.   This
is in contrast to a different pattern which generates precisely the
same six axes, but which allows 531, 441 alternative paths to reach
the six axes of the 12th stage, varying from 89, 939 to 87, 891 paths
to each axis.

In addition, at each stage of the generative system various alternative patterns may emerge. Under one model at one stage only half of
the axes are available, whereas at the succeeding stage the other half
is available to the system; this alternation continues permanently.
Under any other system, after the fifth stage, all six axes are available at each stage.   These different patterns allow us to specify something about the 'flexibility' of a system and its social relevance.   For
example, in a conversation, where there are rights for more than one
person to speak (providing he can get the floor by shouting louder),
there are more paths than in a system in which the presence of the
prior axis determines strictly the only one person allowed to choose
to speak at the next stage.

The explication of alternate sets of these sociological rules, following up the work of Pike and Lowe (1969) and Lowe (1969), is much
too extensive to be given here, but is in preparation elsewhere (Pike
1971).   I shall, however, try to let the audience 'hear'--not merely
see--the formalism of a few of these patterns, by representing them
as condensed formal abstractions in a different medium.   The way I
shall do this is to replace the members of the cast--Abe, Bill, Charlie--
each by a note on the piano. A pair of notes in sequence then represents a monologue (of any duration) in a conversation in which one
member of the cast is speaking to another--i. e. it establishes a speaker-
addressee axis.   A second pair of notes shows that the axis has shifted
to involve the third member of the cast in some way, as speaker or as
addressee.   Symbols of the mathematical representation are 'generators' of the group elements. (The multiplication tables and Cayley diagrams that justify certain of these operations are found in the articles
referred to.)

Figure 1 illustrates[1] the musical abstraction when the starting point
(the mathematical 'identity') is chosen as the relation 'A, calling himself I or me, is speaking to B, whom he calls you'.   The operation of
_r[eply] reverses the speaker-addressee axis, so that B becomes the

FIGURES 1 - 9

FIGURES 10 - 12

speaker and A becomes the addressee; a second application of the $\underline{r}$ generator flips the axis and gets us back to the same axis we began with (i.e. $\underline{rr} = \underline{r^2} = \underline{I}$). This can go on indefinitely, with the alternation forming the basis of a representation of a 'dialogue' between Abe and Bill.

In Figure 2, the generator $\underline{s}$[hift] allows the speaker to shift away from his starting addressee in order to address the third member of the cast. If this operation is applied again, it--like $\underline{r}$-- brings us back to the starting point (i.e. $\underline{ss} = \underline{s^2} = \underline{I}$). Similarly, if the addressee is retained, but the speaker is shifted, then we see (and hear) the result of this in Figure 3 (with $\underline{t^2} = \underline{I}$).

When $\underline{r}$ and $\underline{s}$ are both used, and when $\underline{r^2} = \underline{s^2} = \underline{(rs)^3} = \underline{I}$, six elements will be generated ($\underline{I}$, $\underline{r}$, $\underline{s}$, $\underline{rs}$, $\underline{sr}$, $\underline{rsr}$) which can be mapped against the six axes A-B, B-A, A-C, C-A, B-C, C-B. See Figure 4. (But on the figures, I give below each axis only the particular generator which is being applied to the preceding axis, which in turn has had a generator affect the preceding state, and so on; I am not listing here the cumulative products of these elements.)

When $\underline{r}$ and $\underline{s}$ but not $\underline{t}$ are combined, the 'right' of the speaker is to shift addressee, the right of addressee is to reply--upon which, having become speaker, he may himself at the next monolog-stage shift addressee--but the listener has no speech rights (but can listen in without being rude), being under the interdict of 'don't speak unless spoken to'. Nevertheless, a substantial number of possible sequences of tone paths result from this combination.

In Figure 5, the $\underline{t}$ is given again, but is applied to $\underline{r}$ after $\underline{r}$ has been applied to $\underline{I}$; in Figure 6, $\underline{t}$ is applied to $\underline{s}$ for a slightly different result. Then in Figure 7, $\underline{r}$, $\underline{s}$, and $\underline{t}$ are all given, but with the choice of sequence determined by the flip of a coin.

In Figure 8, however, a much more restricted pattern is given, in which it takes six stages--six monologs--for the initial axis to reappear. Exactly this one path is allowed, where $\underline{g}^6 = \underline{I}$, and where $\underline{g}$ is defined in turn as the effect of the double operation of the $\underline{r}$ followed by the $\underline{w}$ seen in Figure 10.

In the latter, note that $\underline{w}$ leads to a cycle of A-B, B-C, C-A, A-B, but that when $\underline{r}$ reverses any one of these axes, the cycle direction continues with the same pairs of the cast involved, but with their axes reversed to B-A, C-B, A-C. (Here, $\underline{w}^3 = \underline{r}^2 = \underline{(rw)}^2\underline{w} = \underline{I}$, and $\underline{rw} = \underline{wr}$.) In Figure 9, on the other hand, $\underline{m}^3 = \underline{r}^2 = \underline{(rm)}^2 = \underline{I}$ (but $\underline{rm} \neq \underline{mr}$). As a result, the cycle starts just as it does for $\underline{w}$, but when $\underline{r}$ enters the sequence, the reversal of the one axis simultaneously reverses the direction of the cycle for $\underline{m}$.

Even though the patterns sound different, with different generators (or different sequences of application of the same generators), they have one thing in common: each of these mathematical groups generates precisely the same six terminal points--the same six relations between A, B, C. The difference between them, then, lies not in their ability to generate different 'terminal strings' of such a small unit as a monolog, but in their output of different monolog-sequence types as characterizing different conversation structures. Each of the formalisms of these sets is equivalent in being able to generate all and only the correct terminal strings of monolog size, with respect to those pronominal features under study (but not treating, here, gender, for example).

On the other hand, the groups differ radically in the degree to which the structures which they generate approximate natural conversations. Any of the groups which lack an $\underline{r}$, for example, do not reflect a characteristic which is basic to every dialog--the ability of some addressee under some circumstances to reply to the speaker. Natural conversation includes the right to reply, and the mathematics chosen to map natural conversation must reflect that fact.

It should be clear in the seventies, therefore, that sheer formalism is not enough. The fact that one has a mathematically-firm mapping of his results is not enough--nor even the fact that it maps all and only the correct linguistic sentence elements without contradiction. There

must also be a cultural evaluation of the results to see if, in fact, the
social situation presupposed by the mapping is represented naturally.

Similarly, it should be clear that a conversation is not merely a
string of sentences joined together by man or by any simple coordinating device. Rather a conversation may of itself be a highly structured
element, in which each monolog is controlled in its relation to the next
monolog by a tight sequence of sociological rules determining linguistic
rules--and the formalization of the linguistic changes as the social situation changes. Conversations between king and commoner follow different rules from a conversation between pals.

But the speaker not only speaks to John Doe III of Evans Way, Boston. He turns to speak to him.

Query:

(7d) How can the formalisms of our pronominal axes be paralleled
by kinesic formalisms, so that a mathematical approach to gesture can
bring it, too, under more rigid control?

This question, just beginning to be studied, might conceivably open
the door of the seventies to the study of language-speaking human
beings--or language formally studied in a context of the formal study
of a unified theory of the structure of human behavior as a whole.

Finally, I might mention that the Summer Institute of Linguistics
has now begun the analysis of the 500th language in its study program.
It expects to continue the study of these languages in order to gather
data which can be used to set up, inductively, substantive universals,
and to test those guessed at inductively. The theoretical notions of tagmemics continue their heuristic impact in this area, and should be
heightened in their coverage during the seventies by coming more
closely into relation with other theories by sociological means such as
those represented by this Round Table.

NOTE

[1]I am indebted to Stephen Pike for selecting the particular notes
used to identify Abe, Bill, Charlie--occasionally varied arbitrarily
from Figure to Figure for interest--and for the drawing of the Figures.

REFERENCES

Ballard, D. Lee, Robert J. Conrad, and Robert E. Longacre. 1971.
    The deep and surface grammar of interclausal relations. Founda-
    tions of Language 7:70-118.
Becker, Alton L. 1965. A tagmemic approach to paragraph analysis.
    College composition and communication 16:237-42.
___ ___. 1967. A generative description of the English subject tagmeme.
    Unpublished Ph.D. dissertation, University of Michigan.

Bock, Philip K. 1962. The social structure of a Canadian Indian reserve. Ph. D. dissertation, Harvard University.
_____. 1964. Social structure and language structure. Southwestern journal of anthropology 20:393-403.
_____. 1967. Three descriptive models of social structure. Philosophy of science 34. 168-74.
Brend, Ruth M. 1970. Tagmemic theory: an annotated bibliography. Journal of English linguistics 4. 7-46.
Cook, Walter A. 1967. The generative power of a tagmemic grammar. Monograph series on languages and linguistics, Georgetown University (Proceedings of the 18th Annual Georgetown University Round Table on Languages and Linguistics) 20. 27-41.
_____. 1971. Case grammar as a deep structure in tagmemic analysis. Languages and linguistics: Working papers, number 2. 1-9. Washington, D. C. , Georgetown University Press.
Fillmore, Charles J. [1966] 1968. The case for case. Universals in linguistic theory, Emmon Bach and R. T. Harms (eds.). New York, Holt, Rinehart, and Winston, Inc. , 1-88.
Gleason, H. A. , Jr. 1968. Contrastive analysis in discourse structure. Monograph series on languages and linguistics, Georgetown University (Proceedings of the 19th Annual Georgetown University Round Table on Languages and Linguistics) 21. 39-64.
Grimes, Joseph E. and Naomi Glock. 1970. A Saramaccan narrative pattern. Language 46. 408-25.
Koen, Frank M. , Alton L. Becker, and Richard E. Young. 1968. The psychological reality of the paragraph. Proceedings of the conference on language and language behavior, Eric M. Zale (ed.). New York, Appleton-Century Crofts, 174-87.
Longacre, Robert E. 1964. Grammar discovery procedures: a field manual. The Hague, Mouton and Co.
_____. 1968 [1970]. Discourse, paragraph, and sentence structure in selected Philippine languages, Vol. 1, Discourse and paragraph structure; Vol. 2, Sentence Structure; Vol. 3, Text material [with inserted foldouts of tree structures of discourse length]. Vols. 1 and 2 issued in 1970 as No. 21 of Summer Institute of Linguistics Publications in Linguistics and Related Fields.
Lowe, Ivan. 1969. An algebraic theory of English pronominal reference. Semiotica 1. 397-421.
Pike, Kenneth L. [1954, 1955, 1960] 1967. Language in relation to a unified theory of the structure of human behavior, [first and] second edition. The Hague, Mouton and Co.
_____. 1962a. Dimensions of grammatical constructions. Language 38. 221-44.
_____. 1962b. Practical phonetics of rhythm waves. Phonetica 8. 9-30.

_____. 1963. Theoretical implications of matrix permutation in Fore (New Guinea). Anthropological linguistics 5.8, 1-23.

_____. 1964a. Discourse structure and tagmeme matrices. Oceanic linguistics 3.5-25.

_____. 1964b. Stress trains in Auca. In honor of Daniel Jones, D. Abercrombie and others (eds.), 425-31.

_____. 1964c. On systems of grammatical structure. Proceedings of the ninth International Congress of Linguistics [1962], H.G. Lunt (ed.), 145-54.

_____. 1965. Non-linear order and anti-redundancy in German morphological matrices. Zeitschrift für Mundartforschung 32.193-220.

_____. 1966a. Tagmemic and matrix linguistics applied to selected African languages. Report to U.S. Office of Education. In press with the Summer Institute of Linguistics.

_____. 1966b. A guide to publications related to tagmemic theory. Current trends in linguistics, T. A. Sebeok (ed.), 3.365-94.

_____. 1967. Grammar as wave. Monograph series on languages and linguistics, Georgetown University (Proceedings of the 18th Annual Georgetown University Round Table on Languages and Linguistics) 20.1-14.

_____ and Gill Jacobs. 1968. Matrix permutation as a heuristic device in the analysis of the Bimoba verb. Lingua 21.321-45.

_____ and Ivan Lowe. 1969. Pronominal reference in English conversation and discourse: a group theoretical treatment. Folia linguistica 3.68-106.

_____. 1971. Sociolinguistic evaluation of alternative mathematical models in linguistics--English pronouns in conversation structure. Presented to the Linguistics Club of the University of Michigan, March 23, 1971.

Wise, Mary Ruth. 1968. Identification of participants in discourse: a study of aspects of form and meaning in Nomatsiguenga. Ph.D. dissertation, University of Michigan. In press.

_____ and Ivan Lowe. 1970. Permutation groups in discourse. Languages and linguistics working papers, number 3. Washington, D.C., Georgetown University Press.

Young, Richard E., Alton L. Becker, and Kenneth L. Pike. 1970. Rhetoric: discovery and change. New York, Harcourt, Brace and World, Inc.

ON THE SYSTEMATIZATION OF BOX 4*

Austin HALE

It is at present quite possible to be a tagmemicist in good standing without subscribing to any particular doctrine regarding the form of grammar. To one who received a good portion of his linguistic up-bringing within the tradition of transformational generative grammar, this realization comes as a shock and a revelation[1].

To the extent that this is true, critiques of tagmemics dealing with the mechanisms which have been used to represent analyses within tagmemics have failed to attack the heart of the matter. Formalisms exist for the sake of analytic and descriptive convenience. To the extent that they represent analyses directly and clearly, are pedagogically useful in the training of linguistic technicians, have heuristic value in the search for linguistic regularities, and are in consonance with the basic assertions which define tagmemics, they are acceptable tools for the tagmemicist.

This may help explain why relatively little effort has been expended on the study of the form of grammar within tagmemics, and why so little has been published within tagmemics that was recognizable to a transformational grammarian as having to do with the theory of grammar. It may also help explain the fact that tagmemicists do not typically

* The research leading to this paper was sponsored in part by the Institute of International Studies, U.S. Department of Health, Education and Welfare under contract No. OEC-0-9-097721-2778(014). The paper is a revised and expanded version of a paper presented at the IXth International Congress of Linguists, August 28, 1972, in Bologna, Italy.
[1] This first came to the writer's attention during a conversation with Pike. What defines Tagmemics is not any particular formalism or set of rule types or schema for a grammar complete with specifications of components and their input-output relationships. What defines Tagmemics is rather a set of twelve assertions about the characteristics of rational human communication. One may consider himself a Tagmemicist in good standing to the extent that he accepts all twelve of these assertions. How these assertions are to be translated into formal representations appears to be quite open to discussion and investigation. For a brief discussion of the twelve assertions that define Tagmemics, see Kenneth L. Pike (1964).

show undue concern for the redundancies required by their formulaic representations, and tend to shrug off such searching critiques of basic working concepts as that of Huddleston (1971). The formulaic representations themselves are not proposed as a crucial measure of the adequacy of the theory in any serious sense. More important than the apparent relative simplicity of the representation is the analytic stability of a system built around types and levels. A change in one formula in the grammar usually has rather limited ramifications for the rest of the grammar. By contrast, if one changes a rule within the tight and economical framework of virtually any one of the notational variations of transformational grammar, one may well find himself picking up the pieces for a long time thereafter. The practical advantages of this stability to the ordinary working linguist in a field situation whose dedication to abstract formalism falls somewhat short of the fanatical should be obvious − the stable system provides a better basis for setting up one's files.

In a day in which there is a bewildering array of theories which may be viewed by certain linguists as notational variations of a standard theory (as in Chomsky, 1971) yet by others as radically superior departures from the standard theory, it is comforting to know that one need not renounce his interest in and admiration for these developments within transformational grammar in order to pursue what seems to be an interesting development within tagmemics. Indeed, unless one enjoys the kind of acrid debate that currently accompanies disputes over such things as whether one can motivate a level such as deep structure within the grammar or not, or whether semantics is best viewed as generative or interpretive, one is sorely tempted to see what would happen if one attempted to systematize in some principled way certain of the inventories of concepts tagmemicists are so successfully utilizing in achieving the practical linguistic goals that interest them. Eventually it might even be possible to identify a variant of the standard theory which also meets the requirements of tagmemics.

The line of inquiry that led to the writing of this paper grew out of two kinds of interests: (1) an interest in the notion of clause type, and (2) an interest in the kinds of subcategorizing relationships between nouns and verbs that have become known as role relations or cases[2]. The result of this inquiry constitutes an embryonic contribution to the theoretical structure of what we shall refer to as Box 4 of the nine box tagmeme.

[2] For footnote, see next page.

1. Box 4 and other boxes

What do we mean by Box 4? Recent work in Tagmemics[3] has led to the development of what might be viewed as a feature analysis of syntactic constructions. There are some nine kinds of information potentially relevant to any analysis of linguistic structure. A tagmeme can now be viewed as a complex symbol in which features of various kinds are used to specify the information relevant to a given analysis. These nine kinds of information are defined by a dimensional array in which the three hierarchies (grammatical, sememic, and phonological) are placed along one axis, and the three notions, function, systemic class, and item are placed along the other axis. The cells so formed are conventionally numbered one through nine.

	Function	Systemic class	Item
Grammatical	1. Focus	2. Category	3. Citation
Sememic	4. Role	5. Concept	6. Gloss
Phonological	7.	8.	9.

Fig. 1. The nine-box tagmeme.

Each of the boxes lays claim to an independent status within tagmemics. The degree to which any given tagmeme shows redundancy among its cells is currently taken as a measure of the peripherality of

[2] This paper grows out of a workshop held in Nepal during the academic year 1971–72 under the project direction of Kenneth L. Pike. Had it not been for the stimulation and encouragement of Kenneth and Evelyn Pike, the development which this paper sketches out would never have taken place. It should not be assumed, however, that they would agree with everything presented in this paper. The writer also wishes to express his appreciation to the following individuals for stimulating comments and supporting data: David Watters (Kham), Burkhard Schottelndreyer (Sherpa), Ross Caughley (Chepang), Dora Bieri and Marlene Schulze (Sunwar), Doreen Taylor (Tamang), Gary Shephard (Magar), Chura Mani Bandhu (Nepali), Thakurlal Manandhar (Newari), Uwe Gustafsson (Kotia), Jennifer Williams (Maithili), Esther Strahm (Jirel), Kent Gordon (Dhangar), and Ronald L. Trail. A report of this workshop is due to appear in 1973 (Trail. forthcoming and Hale, forthcoming). Of these languages, Kotia is a language of India. All the other languages referred to here are spoken in Nepal.
[3] See especially Pike, 1972, Klammer, 1971, and Wise, 1971. Our presentation of the nine-box tagmeme grows out of recent work of Pike.

the tagmeme[4]. This claim to independence can be rather simply illustrated. We will limit our discussion to the first six boxes.

(1) John read a book to Sammy.

(2) A book was read to Sammy by John.

(3) Sammy was read to by John.

In example (1), the grammatical function of *John* may be viewed as
complex. It is at least the subject of the sentence. It is probably also
theme of the sentence. This same grammatical function is performed in
example (2) by *a book*, and in example (3) by *Sammy*. While *John* in
(1), *a book* in (2), and *Sammy* in (3) share the same grammatical function, they differ in sememic function, *John* being an actor, *a book* being
what we will call an undergoer, and *Sammy* being what we shall refer to
as a site.

Examples of this sort are quite common in the literature on case grammar and tend to support the view, in whatever way it may be stated, that
grammatical function and sememic function are to some extent indepen-

---

[4] This can be illustrated in terms of a tentative analysis of *yesterday* in the following two examples.

(a) Yesterday, he went to find his brother.

(b) Yesterday was a rainy day.

In (a) *yesterday* is peripheral, does not subcategorize the verb, and shows considerable redundancy among the representations in boxes 1, 2 and 5.

Time Adjunct	Time Expression	Yesterday
	+ abstract + time	

(Note that in (a) we have left box 4 blank, since we have not yet approached the problem of
box 4 entries for peripheral items in any systematic way. Presumably its function is to mark
time setting. It may well be that peripheral items are derived by sentence demotion. Example
(a) may come from a sequence something like (c).

(c) It was yesterday. He went to find his brother.

If such derivations can be maintained, we will need to come to some explicit understanding of
how such derivations assign values to the resultant derived tagmemes. It may be that the re-
dundance which is characteristic of peripheral tagmemes is a result of the operation of demotion rules that have applied in their derivation.) In (b), *yesterday* is nuclear and shows much
less redundancy.

Subject Theme	Noun	Yesterday
Undergoer	+ abstract + time	

dent. Given only the grammatical function of an item, it is not in general possible to determine the sememic function and vice versa. Boxes 1 and 4 are thus independent. Both need to be specified in some way by the grammar.

(4) The noise bothered me.

(5) He makes a lot of noise when he sleeps.

(6) The cave gave a hollow resonance to the noise.

Given only a particular grammatical item such as *noise* in examples (4) through (6), it is not in general possible to predict either the grammatical function or the sememic function that it performs. Neither grammatical nor sememic function are in general predictable strictly in terms of the identification of a citation form. Box 3 is thus independent both of box 1 and of box 4.

(7) The cobbler used a steel last to make that shoe.

(8) He came in last in the 100 yard dash.

(9) How long did it last?

Given only a particular grammatical item it is not always possible to make a unique specification of grammatical system and class or even of the gloss of the citation form. In example (7), *last* is a noun; in (8) it is some kind of adverb; and in (9) it is a verb. In each instance it has a different gloss. Box 3 is thus in principle independent of boxes 2 and 6.

(10) The ship was all decked out for her maiden voyage.

(11) The pants were well pressed.

(12) More than one of his students comes here to bowl.

Examples (10) through (12) illustrate reasons for distinguishing grammatical gender and number from their sememic counterparts. In general the semantic class or domain of a word is independent of its role in a clause, of the particular grammatical class or category that it belongs to, and does not uniquely predict its gloss. Thus there is a noun, *heat* and a verb, *heat* which share a great deal with one another within box 5. In box 2, however, they share relatively little, since derivations are probably best treated elsewhere.

Examples of this kind lead one to conclude that box 4 is in principle independent of the other six semantico-syntactic boxes. It consists of a set of functional or relational notions relevant to the sememic interpretation of the tagmeme. On clause level, box 4 relates to those case-like relations in terms of which verbs are subcategorized.

2. Box 4 and case

A chronic practical problem for the tagmemic field worker has been that of inventing appropriate labels for slots and for fillers. Now that we have sememic slots (box 4) as well as grammatical slots (box 1), and sememic filler classes (box 5) as well as grammatical ones (box 2), this problem promises to become increasingly acute in the absence of some kind of etic framework. Our pursuit of system within box 4 started with a query. Will it eventually be possible to specify an exhaustive inventory of possible sememic relations? Could all the labels be supplied in advance? It should in principle be possible to enumerate for all languages the possible range of sememic functions on the clause level and this inventory should provide a principled basis for the selection of feature values for box 4. A linguist who was trained from such a point of view would be able to *recognize* predefined box 4 relations in any language under study and label-making would become a venture for the theorist who sought to argue for the theoretical status of a new relation rather than an ad hoc occupation of the field analyst.

A further hope was that it would be possible to relate each box 4 entry in a clause to all other possible entries in such a way as to show its place in a coherent closed system and to make clear the range of phenomena covered by each possible entry.

Our earliest candidates for the features of box 4 on clause level were Fillmorian cases. We moved away from this starting point rather early and it may be useful to give some indication of the reasons for and direction of this move. Fillmorian cases appeared to incorporate a great deal which is, from our point of view, non-relational. The feature of animateness was a part of the definition of certain cases[5]. From our point of view the specification of animateness belonged to box 5, and we did not wish to treat it again as part of the definition of a sememic relationship. We wished, for example, to be able to show parallelisms between the sememic relationships of subject to verb (or clause) in examples such as the following.

---

[5] See Fillmore (1968:24). Animateness is typical of Agentive and Dative. Inanimateness is typical of Instrumental. In Fillmore (1971:251) there is a hint that Fillmore has somewhat revised his own views of the relevance of animateness specifications for cases, though the continued existence of cases like Experiencer seems to indicate that we still have cases typically marked for animateness within case grammar.

(13) The river washed the boulder away with a sudden torrent of water.

(14) John scrubbed the dirt away with a brush.

(15) The locomotive cleared the snow away with a snowplough.

(16) The tree supported the blind with three of its branches.

In some sense, *the river, John,* and *the locomotive* are all actors and are in some sense all capable of the actions named by their accompanying verbs. Yet neither the river nor the locomotive is animate in the sense of a volitional responsible initiator and neither is personified in these instances. If these could not be agents by virtue of their inanimateness, then we would need another case, say, inanimate agent.

We wished to distinguish between the properties of particular words or sets of words on the one hand and relationships on the other. Pike noted that one way to approach this would be to look at the total range of relations a given noun could enter into with respect to its verb. We would expect that if we had the right system, most nouns would occur in most relationships at one time or another, otherwise our set of relations might be accused of incorporating elements which should actually be analyzed as parts of the meanings of individual lexical items.

In Fillmore's case system it appears that most lexical items do not enter into the full range of case relationships. There are also rather severe apparent restrictions on the occurrent subsets of the set of cases. Nothing approaching the full set of cases occurs with any given verb in any given clause in a subcategorizing relationship to the verb. The following examples taken from Fillmore (1971:249) may be used to illustrate how our thinking was moving relative to Fillmore's analysis.

(17) I am warm.

(18) This jacket is warm.

(19) Summer is warm.

(20) The room is warm.

In (17) *I* is Experiencer. In (18) *this jacket* is Instrument. In (19) *summer* is Time. In (20) *the room* is Location. It should be noted that in each instance in which the noun is concrete the sentence is ambiguous. In (17) we thus have at least two interpretations: (1) the person speaking feels warm (Experiencer) or (2) the person speaking has had his temperature taken and *is* warm (Object?). (I'm warm according to that thermometer, but I sure *feel* cold.) The first person pronoun apparently lacks Instrumental, Temporal, and Locative interpretations. In (18) we find a slightly wider range of interpretations. One may use a jacket to get warm (Instrument), one may determine by using a thermometer that the jacket *is* warm (Object), and it may be warm *in* the jacket (Locative), but the jacket lacks the Experiencer relationship and the temporal relationship. It might be suggested that the reason that the jacket cannot be an Experiencer is that it is insentient, and the reason that it cannot occur in a Time case is that it is a concrete noun, thus it is neither abstract nor temporal. We began to get the impression that restrictions on the set of cases that a given noun can occur in may be traced to domains of meaning that we would prefer to deal with in box 5. Consider, by way of comparison, the following:

(21) The water is warm.
         It's warm in the water, come on in!

Water in example (21) may be an Object, a Location, and possibly an Instrument. It fails as an Experiencer because it is insentient. It fails as a Time since it is concrete and non-temporal. Restrictions on the case relations a given word can enter into seem to have a great deal to do with what a given word means. This we found uncomfortable.

3. Role features and the transitivity system

We propose to explore another possible approach at this point. Suppose we say that there is an attributive relationship between the subject and the predicate adjective in each of the examples (17) through (21). Suppose we call this relationship *undergoer*. By reference to features available in box 5 we can then reconstruct the experiencer relationship as that which holds between a predicate which names a sensation and a sentient noun which is its undergoer. The ambiguity is captured by the fact that *warm* may name a sensation or a relative temperature. Both are permitted as the meaning of the word. The ambiguity is then interpreted as lexical, not syntactic.

We have moved two steps away from a Fillmorian case system. The first step involved factoring box 5 notions out of the case system. The desirability of doing this came first to our attention in terms of the animate—inanimate distinction that existed between various cases, but later became much more general as illustrated above. The second step was to draw a line between nuclear and peripheral items that would allow only non-predictable items within the clause nucleus. Constituents that were optional and whose optional occurrence possibility could be predicted in terms of other items in the clause were tentatively excluded from the clause nucleus. These steps led us to the following eight branch tree which we propose as a candidate system for box 4.

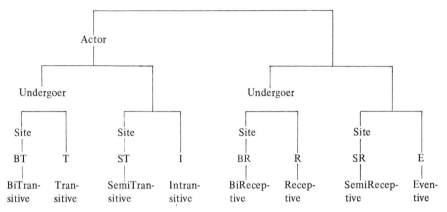

Fig. 2. The transitivity system as defined by role features.

Our preliminary approach derives from the fact that with each cell in the nine-box tagmeme there is associated a system expressible as a tree or a matrix. Within this approach we posit a limited inventory of putative universal roles in terms of which languages may be comparably described and rather directly compared. We conceive of this as a conceptual space defined by role features such as actor, undergoer, and site.

The tree in fig. 2 explicity links features to the notion of relative transitivity. It also entails the view that the most basic and central of the transitivity types are the BiTransitive and the Transitive. The tree explictly exhausts its conceptual universe in terms of binary choices. The features in terms of which it is constructed are symmetrical to the system and independent of one another, allowing us to represent the same system in terms of a dimensional array to which we will refer as the transitivity matrix. Our standard matrix representation of the tree given in fig. 2 is that given in fig. 3.

The relation of the role system to transitivity may be viewed informally in the following way. The highest degree of transitivity usually attributed to a clause is that of BiTransitive. Taking BiTransitive as basic to the system, we observe that BiTransitive may be defined as having three role features: actor, undergoer, and site. The rest of the system is then arrived at by establishing one transitivity type for each possible

	Und + Sit	Und	Sit	
Actor	BT	T	ST	I
	BR	R	SR	E

Fig. 3. The transitivity system as a dimensional array.

combination of the unordered subsets of the features which define
BiTransitive. It now appears that one of the functions of embedding in
natural language is that of preventing the formation of a clause with a
higher degree of transitivity than BiTransitive. The transitivity types obtained in this way may be illustrated for Newari as follows: (Evt stands
for 'event'.)

 (22) BT: Waą jitaa saphuu bila.
      Act Sit Und   Evt
      He gave me a book.
 (23) T: Waą lāsā dāla
      Act Und Evt
      He beat the matress.
 (24) ST: Wa cheą cwana.
      Act Sit   Evt
      He stayed home.
 (25) I: Wa dana.
      Act Evt
      He stood up.
 (26) BR: Jitaa wa lākāą jila.
      Sit   Und   Evt
      Those shoes came to fit me.
 (27) R: Rām khwāę jula.
      Und Evt
      Ram became deaf.
 (28) SR: Mirāyā tyānhula.
      Sit   Evt
      Myra came to feel tired.

The English gloss for example (28) is not SemiReceptive. An English
example of SemiReceptive might be
 (29) It got hot in the room.
The eventive pattern is not an inherent contrastive type in Newari. The
following might be an example for English:

(30) It rained.

where *it* is an empty subject fulfilling no particular role.

4. Inherent patterns and their derived variants

A contrastive clause pattern may be thought of as a set of verbs together with a common role frame which they govern. Since the roles in
a role frame are not always obligatory, we often have a wide range of
derived variants within a single clause pattern. Take as an example the
BiTransitive clause,

(31) He   read   the book   to his son.
     Act   Und   Sit

By omission of a role we may have the Transitive variant,

(32) He   read   the book.
     Act   Und

or the SemiTransitive variant,

(33) He   read   to his son.
     Act   Sit

or even the Intransitive variant,

(34) He   read.
     Act

In addition to this, the passive derivation allows the set of Receptive
variants: the BiReceptive,

(35) The book   was read   to his son.
     Und   Sit

the Receptive,

(36) The book   was read.
     Und

and the SemiReceptive,

(37) His son   was read to.
     Sit

Lacking is only the Eventive, since the verb *read* appears to disallow the
empty *it* as its subject. For our purposes we wish to distinguish between
derived variants and *inherent contrastive patterns*. A verb will be assigned
to the inherent contrastive pattern which corresponds to that defined by
its full complement of roles. *Read,* in the sense just illustrated, is thus
BiTransitive, and each of the derived variants illustrated is viewed as a
variant of the BiTransitive pattern. The derived variant BiReceptive

clause in example (35) is thus viewed as contrasting with the inherently
contrastive BiReceptive clause,

(38) The book was difficult for him.
      Und   Sit

since *difficult* does not control a frame which includes an actor.

5. Some role marker systems: an embryonic typology

We assume that the roles of actor, undergoer, and site are universal
and that each language has ways of marking these roles in surface structure. Working under these assumptions, we have undertaken to make a
preliminary study of role markers in a number of the languages of Nepal.
We have found that the way in which a given role is marked differs from
cell to cell of the transitivity matrix. Thus, the actor of the Intransitive
clause will in general be marked differently from an actor in a Transitive clause. As it often turns out, the actor marker not only marks a
given noun phrase as an actor, but also signals the presence of an undergoer elsewhere in the pattern.

The most surprising result of the preliminary study was the close similarity of distribution and function of role markers across the languages
investigated, in spite of the fact that the phonological shapes of the
markers involved were quite diverse. The syntactic similarities led to an
impression of a relatedness that the phonological forms themselves
would not have suggested.

Actor Markers. Three basic patterns for the actor marker have
emerged. In one pattern, Transitive and BiTransitive actors are marked
by an agentive suffix, whereas the Intransitive and SemiTransitive actors
are unmarked. Furthermore, the agentive suffix marks the underlying
pattern, not just the surface variant. Actor is agent marked in the
BiTransitive and Transitive even when the Undergoer is omitted.

The agentive affixes involved are relatively diverse. Nepali has *−le*,
Kham has *−e*, Magar has *−e* in alternation with *−i*, Chepang has *−ʔi*,
Jirel has *−ki*, Sherpa has *−ki* in alternation with *−i*, Newari has *−naɋ* in
alternation with lengthening and nasalization of the stem-final vowel,
and Sunwar has *−m*.

In a second pattern, Intransitive actors are optionally marked with
the agentive affix, while the BiTransitive, Transitive, and SemiTransitive
actors are obligatorily marked. In this pattern, the agentive marking of

BT	T	ST	I
Actor is Agent Marked		Actor is Unmarked	
BR	R	SR	E

Fig. 4. Pattern I actor markers.

BT	T	ST	I
Actor is obligatorily Agent Marked			Actor Optionally Marked
BR	R	SR	E

Fig. 5. Pattern II actor markers.

the Intransitive actor appears to serve also as an ancillary focus device. This pattern may be represented as in fig. 5. The second pattern is represented by Western Tamang. The agentive suffix in Western Tamang is $-ce$[6].

In a third pattern, the actor is everywhere unmarked, but is distinguished from other roles by verbal concord. To this pattern belongs Kotia. According to early reports, a number of other vernaculars spoken in the Terai of Nepal also conform to this pattern. This pattern may be represented as in fig. 6.

BT	T	ST	I
Actor is Unmarked, has verbal concord			
BR	R	SR	E̅

Fig.6. Pattern III actor markers

Undergoer Markers. Undergoer marking in the languages surveyed typically shows involvement with focus and concept. If we specify that the undergoer is animate, and is in some sense in focus, and that if there is a site, the site is not an animate-goal site, then we find two patterns of undergoer marking.

---

[6] M. Mazaudon reports that Eastern Tamag conforms to the first pattern.

BT T	ST	I
Undergoer is Goal-Marked		
BR R	SR	E
Undergoer is Unmarked		

Fig. 7. Pattern I undergoer markers.

There is one pattern in which the undergoer is goal-marked in the BiTransitive and Transitive patterns, but unmarked in the BiReceptive and Receptive patterns. Goal marking in these languages indicate the simultaneous presence of an actor and an undergoer in the pattern. Furthermore, the goal marker marks the underlying pattern, and not just the surface representation. The undergoer is goal marked in BiTransitive clauses even when the actor is omitted from the surface structure. The undergoer markers in this set of languages also show some diversity. Nepali has *−lai*, Kham has *−lay*, Jirel has *−la*, Sunwar has *−kali*, Chepang has *−kaay*, Magar has *−ke*, and Newari has *yāta* in alternation with *−taa*.

There is a second kind of undergoer marking pattern in which the undergoer is goal-marked only in the Transitive clause pattern. In the Bi-Transitive, BiReceptive, and Receptive patterns it is unmarked. To this group belong Tamang and Sherpa. Tamang has *−ta* as its goal-marker; Sherpa has *−laa*.

BT Under- goer	T Under- goer is Goal-Marked	ST	I
BR is	R Unmarked	SR	E

Fig. 8. Pattern II undergoer markers.

Site Markers. Under the heading of site are grouped three kinds of locative expressions that subcategorize the verb: goal to which, source from which, and place in which. Animate sites of the goal-to-which variety are obligatorily marked with the same goal markers used for animate undergoers occurring in clauses that have no animate site. Animate sites of the goal-to-which variety are classified as indirect objects within the focus system. Since site marking is considerably more complex than actor or undergoer marking, and since that complexity adds little to this discussion, we will not consider it further in this paper.

6. Clause-type patterning: toward a typology

Languages will differ widely in the number and type of basic contrastive clause patterns that they have. Since the analysis of clause patterns in the languages of Nepal is still in its early stages, it is not yet possible to make a typological classification of any great number of languages from this point of view. Tentative results now available do, however, make it possible to indicate the direction that such a typological study might take.

There is one additional classificatory feature which has been found relevant to the clause systems of the languages of Nepal, namely that of *state versus event*. This feature just doubles the transitivity matrix developed in section 3.

		Und + Sit	Und	Sit	
Event	Act	BiTransitive	Transitive	SemiTransitive	Intransitive
		BiReceptive	Receptive	SemiReceptive	Eventive
State	Act	BiStative	Stative	SemiStative	Descriptive
		BiAttributive	Attributive	SemiAttributive	Circumstantial

Fig. 9. A fuller transitivity matrix.

In terms of this sixteen-cell matrix it is possible to make certain tentative typological observations. The current analysis of clause patterns in Sherpa (Schottelndreyer, 1972) views Sherpa as having thirteen contrastive clause patterns, as shown in fig. 10. The missing cells, BiStative, Eventive, and Circumstantial can be filled by clauses derived from other cells, but no verbs have yet been found which are inherently BiStative, Eventive, or Circumstantial.

BT	T	ST	I
BR	R	SR	
	S	SS	D
BA	A	SA	

Fig. 10. Clause-type patterning in Sherpa.

BT	T		I
	R		
	A		

Fig. 11. Clause-type patterning in Chepang.

In contrast with the Sherpa system is the Chepang system in which only five contrastive clause patterns are posited (Caughley, 1972). Current indications are that Newari and Jirel will have clause-type patterning similar to that of Sherpa.

7. Rule patterning in derived variants

A contrastive clause pattern is defined primarily in terms of its potential role structure. The variants are defined in terms of the rules applied to the basic patterns. Both clause-type patterning and rule patterning are necessary for a balanced typology. Languages in Nepal already show strong evidence in support of the contention that languages differ widely in the extent to which derived variants may differ from their parent contrastive patterns. Although the analyses of languages of Nepal are still quite tentative, it is possible to illustrate the differences among rule patternings that are currently coming to light.

With each cell in the transitivity matrix that corresponds to a basic contrastive pattern for a given language there will be associated a tree diagram which specifies the possible derivational variants for that basic contrastive pattern. Allowance will be made for recycling from cell to cell within the derivational matrix, thus the tree diagram associated with a given cell gives only a partial picture of the derivational possibilities. Some idea of relative derivational complexity, however, can be gained from the following derivational trees. We have selected the tree for the Attributive clause pattern from Kham, Sherpa, and Chepang for this‚ purpose.

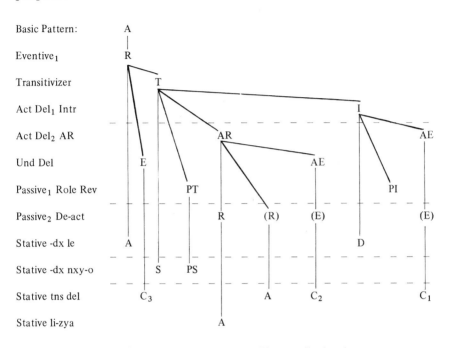

Fig. 12. Derivational patterning in Kham attributive clauses.

The left-hand column in fig. 12 lists the rules which apply in the derivation of variants from the basic Attributive clause pattern. All rules apply optionally with one exception: wherever a node on the tree is parenthesized, some following rule must apply. Parenthesized variants are deviant, and are given as intermediate points in a derivation. Non-parenthesized variants are well-formed. The prefixes A (as in AR, AE) and P (as in PT, PS) stand for active and passive respectively. Otherwise, the letters which form nodes in the tree are simply abbreviations for the transitivity types listed in fig. 9. Cycling information was omitted from fig. 12. A sampling of cycling is included in fig. 13.

Nodes enclosed between slashes are used to indicate that a derived clause at that point in the derivation can be admitted to the derivational

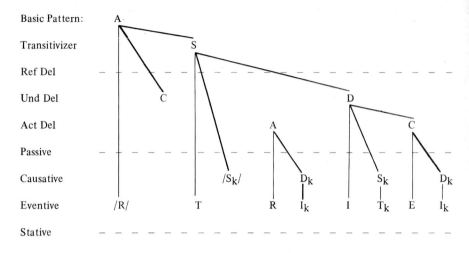

Fig. 13. Derivational patterning in Sherpa Attributive clauses.

tree of the corresponding basic pattern. Thus /R/ indicates that the particular Receptive derivational variant of the Attributive clause can now be treated as a Receptive clause for the purposes of further derivation. The subscript k marks derived variants which have undergone causative embedding.

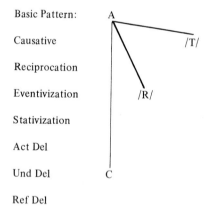

Fig. 14. Derivational patterning in Chepang Attributive clauses.

Relative derivational complexity can be more easily seen in terms of transitivity matrices of derived variants. In figs. 15 through 17 we give

	T, PT		I, PI
	R, AR		E, AE
	S, PS		D
	A		C

Fig. 15. Relative derivational complexity: Kham Attributive.

	T, T_k		I, I_k
	/R/		E
	S, /S_k/		D, D_k
	A		C

Fig. 16. Relative derivational complexity: Sherpa Attributive.

	/T/		(/I/)
	/R/		(E)
	(/S/)		(D)
	(/A/)		C

Fig. 17. Relative derivational complexity: Chepang Attributive. (Elements which are parenthesized represent types derivable only by recycling through /T/ and /R/.)

the derivational variants for Kham, Sherpa, and Chepang Attributive clauses.

Clearly, a great deal of work remains to be done. What we have presented in this paper should serve to indicate how we have begun to envision the systematization of box 4 in a display grammar. We have only mentioned rules. The rule grammar presupposed by the mention of rules constitutes an important part of the work that remains to be done. It is also true, of course, that our hypotheses regarding box 4 can never be adequately tested apart from a compatible systematization of boxes 1, 2, and 5 as should be clear from our discussion of case. In addition, we are reminded that this paper dealt only with box 4 at clause level. Our eventual systematization must include all other levels as well.

Summer Institute of Linguistics

Bibliography

Caughley, Ross. (forthcoming) Clause patterns in Chepang. To appear in Hale, forthcoming.
Chomsky, Noam. (1971) Deep structure, surface structure, and semantic interpretation, in D.D. Steinberg and L.A. Jakobovits (Eds.). Semantics, an interdisciplinary reader in philosophy, linguistics, and psychology. Cambridge: Cambridge University Press, pp. 183–216.
Fillmore, Charles J. (1968) The case for case, in E. Bach and R.T. Harms (Eds.). Universals in linguistic theory. New York: Holt, Rinehart, and Winston pp. 1–90.
Fillmore, Charles J. (1971) Some problems for case grammar, in C.J. Fillmore (Ed.). Working papers in linguistics No. 10, August 1971. Columbus: Department of Linguistics, The Ohio State University, pp. 245–265.
Hale, Austin. (forthcoming) Clause, sentence, and discourse patterns in selected languages of Nepal. Summer Institute of Linguistics publications in linguistics and related fields, 40.
Huddleston, Rodney. (1971) The syntagmeme, IJAL 37:39–44.
Klammer, Thomas P. (1971) The structure of dialogue paragraphs in written English dramatic and narrative discourse. University of Michigan dissertation.
Pike, Kenneth L. (1964) Beyond the sentence, CCC15:129–35.
Pike, Kenneth L. (1972) Recent developments in Tagmemics. Paper presented at the XIth International Congress of Linguists, Bologna, 28th August, 1972.
Schöttelndreyer, Burkhard. (1972) Clause patterns in Sherpa. To appear in Hale, forthcoming. Kathmandu: S.I.L. mimeographed.
Trail, Ronald L. (forthcoming) Patterns in clause, sentence, and discourse in selected languages of India and Nepal. Summer Institute of Linguistics publications in linguistics and related fields, 41.
Wise, Mary Ruth. (1971) Identification of participants in discourse: a study of aspects of form and meaning in Nomatsiguenga. Summer Institute of Linguistics publications in linguistics and related fields, 28.

Phonology

THE SYLLABLE IN CHIPAYA*

Ronald D. Olson

SUMMER INSTITUTE OF LINGUISTICS

1.0. Introduction
1.1. Consonants
1.2. Vowels
2.0. Syllables
2.1. Phonemic syllables
2.2. Sibilant nucleus syllable
3.0. Syllable structure
3.1. As field
3.2. As wave
3.3. As particle

1.0 The Chipaya language is spoken by about 800 Indians who live on the high Bolivian plateau, 125 miles southwest of Oruro, just above the Salt Lake of Coipasa. This group forms a small linguistic island in the midst of the Aymara Indians. Chipaya is grouped with Uru as Uru-Chipaya. The author has proposed that Chipaya is also genetically related to the Mayan language family.[1]

This paper presents the Chipaya syllable as a structural unit in terms of Pike's theoretical framework of particle, wave, and field.[2] A sketch of the phonemes of Chipaya is presented as necessary background to discussion of the syllable.

*International Journal of American Linguistics, 33. 300-304, reprinted by permission.

[1] Mayan Affinities with Chipaya of Bolivia I: Correspondences, IJAL 30.313-24 (1964), and II: Cognates, IJAL 31.29-38 (1965).

The data for this paper were gathered on field trips from August, 1961, to April, 1963, under the auspices of the Summer Institute of Linguistics. The author gratefully acknowledges the careful reading of the manuscript and suggestions of Irvine Davis, Barbara Erickson, and Eunice Pike.

[2] Kenneth L. Pike, Language in Relation to a Unified Theory of the Structure of Human Behavior, 3.38-39 (Glendale, now Santa·Ana, Calif., 1960); Pike, Language as Particle, Wave, and Field, Texas Quarterly 2.2.37-54 (1959). For a discussion of language as a field in relation to grammatical description, see: Pike, Dimensions of Grammatical Constructions, Lang. 38.221-44 1962).

1.1. There are six groups of consonant phonemes: stops and affricates, fricatives, nasals, laterals, flap, and semivowels.[3]

p	t	c	č	ç̌	k	kʷ	ḳ	ḳʷ
p′	t′	c′	č′	ç̌′	k′		ḳ′	
		s	ṣ	š	h	hʷ	x	xʷ
m		n	ñ		ŋ			
		l	lʸ					
		r						
w			y					

Voiceless stops are at the following points of articulation: bilabial, alveolar, velar, and backed velar. The velar stops occur both simple and labialized. Voiceless affricates are at the following points of articulation: alveolar, alveopalatal, and retroflexed alveopalatal. Stops and affricates group in pairs of simple versus glottalized at the same point of articulation, except for the labialized velars, which occur only simple. Since the vast majority of glottalized stops occur in Aymara and Quechua loan words, this lack of symmetry is explained by the fact that both Aymara and Quechua lack labialized velars. With more Aymara and Quechua data, perhaps all instances of glottalized stops would be found to occur in such loan words. In the present data the rare phonemes c′ and ç̌′, and often č′, occur in words not suspect of being loans. This may indicate that although glottalization of stops from an earlier stage of the language was

[3] When women speak together ? occurs in place of ç̌ in the final morpheme. oḳača *I am going (man speaking)*, oḳaʔa *I am going (woman speaking to woman)*. The glottal stop also occurs in word final position on kinship-greeting terms with a meaning of gratitude: mama *mother*; mamaʔ *thank you, mother*. However, these uses of glottal stop are slowly disappearing from the language, and the younger generation occasionally derides the usage of glottal stop. Because of this restricted use, ? is not included in the phoneme inventory.

lost completely, the glottalization of affricates remained in some obscure environments.

The simple stops have allophones with a slight aspirated release in word final, in syllable final before a stop or affricate at a different point of articulation, and occasionally in syllable final before a fricative. The glottalized stops and all affricates are restricted in their distribution to syllable initial position.

t and k have palatalized allophones immediately preceding alveopalatals, and slightly backed allophones immediately preceding ç, ḳ, and ṣ.

The stops and affricates contrast as in: pata *small hill*, p'ata *full*; tirça *he offers*, t'irça *he mends*; c'irḳa *a fish without scales*, čiyança *he moans*, č'iyança *he takes out little by little*; tarṣ *hips*, carṣ *metal sheet for toasting grain*, čara *hair*, č'arança *he wets (with urine)*, çara *rock*, ç'atça *he bites*; čutu *twisted*, č'utu *hill*, ç'utu *foam*; ḳara *wide*, k'ara *barren land*, ḳara *comb*, ḳ'ara *salty*; koñi *ground toasted quinoa*, k'olta *gully, ravine*, ḳoña *soft*, ḳ'oñi *lukewarm*, thekça *he tramples, kicks*, thekʷça *she chants (girl), it rises (sun)*, thaḳça *he augments*, thaḳʷça *he rears (animals, persons)*.

The fricatives, s, ṣ, š, h, hʷ, x, xʷ, occur at the following points of articulation: fronted alveolar, backed alveolar, retroflexed alveopalatal, lenis velar (simple and labialized), and fortis velar (simple and labialized).

ṣ has two allophones: [š] which occurs only after high vowels, and [ṣ] which occurs elsewhere. h has two allophones: [h] which occurs contiguous to a consonant within the syllable, and [x] which occurs elsewhere. The fricatives contrast as in: sḳara *crotch*, ṣḳara *left*, šḳara *hawk*; usa *an ancient custom*, uṣa *boy*, uša *north*; hihtça *he moves by inching along the ground*, hʷihtça *he rubs*; ahça *he argues (one against several)*, axça *he harvests*, ahʷça *he washes*; tha·ça *he gives*, txa·ça *he laughs*; thʷatça ∼ thatça *he forgets, swallows*, txʷatança ∼ txatança *he has (something) stolen*.

The nasals are m, n, ñ, ŋ. They contrast as in: neḳs(i) *there*, ñeḳça *he presses (with the body)*; ḳhança *he illuminates*, ḳhañça *he takes away*; thami *wind*, txança *he makes cry*, thaŋça *he robs*, tomça *he borrows*, thonça *he comes*, toñi *navel*, toŋça *he receives a gift*.

The laterals and the flap are l, lʸ, r. The laterals and the flap have voiceless allophones contiguous to a velar fricative. The flap has a word initial allophone, [ẓ] voiced alveopalatal retroflexed grooved fricative, which is an approximation of the Bolivian Spanish word initial r (Chipaya r occurs word initially only in loan words). The laterals and the flap contrast as in: ḳala *tight*, ḳalʸa *start!*, ḳara *comb*; ali *small plant*, alʸpi *muddy water*, ari *sharp*.

The semivowels are w and y. w has two allophones: [b] which occurs before front vowels, [w] which occurs elsewhere. we·n *night*, wata *year, foot (of animal)*, ewu *new*, šew *widow*; yoḳa *ground*, uyi *ice*, thončamḳay *have you come?*

1.2. The vowels are i, i·, e, e·, a, a·, o, o·, u, u·. The short vowels have voiceless allophones when they occur between velar fricatives. Before velar fricative within the syllable, the short vowels have allophones which fade into voicelessness and which have a breathy quality. i and e have slightly lowered allophones when they occur word initially before a velar, between front velars, or in an unstressed syllable contiguous to a front velar. a has a close allophone [ə] in unstressed open syllables. a, o, and u have allophones with a palatal offglide before alveopalatals. a, e, and i have allophones with a labiovelar offglide before labialized velars or w. The vowels contrast as in: siñi *egg*, si·ñi *translucent*; č'iṣ *fish*, či·ça *he talks*; hiks *road*, hekça *he appears*; tikça *he dies*, tekunça *he carries to the country*; thekça *he tramples, kicks*, the·ḳça *he holds with the pressure of a finger*, çhetça *it is left over*, çhe·tça *he stretches out*, paṣsa *he loses*, pa·ṣ *money*, ḳaṣsa *he converses*, ḳa·ṣsa *he cries*; hoči *ranch*, ho·či *hung up*; ḳohč *rope*, ḳo·či *thin*; uwa *a food*, owa *knee*; oṣa *nose, beak*, uṣa *boy*, u·ṣa *sheep*; txuṣṣa *he carries away*, thu·ča *it swells up*, txo·ṣṣa *he lines out (by dragging)*; lusa *enamelware*, lu·ṣ *a big water-jar*.

2.0 The Chipaya syllable is the unit on the next level of the phonological hierarchy above the phoneme. Its slots are filled by phonemes, and it, in turn, fills slots in the word, the next higher phonological level.

2.1. Three phonemic syllable types occur in Chipaya: (1) with short vowel nucleus, (2) with long vowel nucleus, and (3) with sibilant nucleus. The phonemic syllable is marked by features of timing, peak of sonority, and juncture. A syllable may have one to three moras of length. Syllables with a long vowel nucleus and a final consonant have three moras of length. Syllables with a long vowel nucleus or syllables with a short vowel nucleus and a final consonant have two moras of length. All other syllables have one mora of length. A peak of sonority occurs on the nucleus of the syllable. Juncture occurs at the margins.

2.2. The sibilant nucleus syllable (Sn) has a rudimentary internal structure (no onset, and coda limited to a stop). It is postulated for the following reasons: (a) the timing of Sn follows the same pattern as vowel-nucleus syllables;[4] (b) there is a peak of sonority on Sn; (c) Sn is preceded by juncture and receives an audible attack. A stop preceding Sn may be slightly aspirated. Following Sn, juncture and an audible attack on the next syllable occur. If Sn occurs word initially, the following juncture is especially pronounced and is marked by a slight voiceless transitional vowel.

ap.ṣt.ḳal.ča[5] *he has surely followed*, caht.

[4] The rhythmic timing is the same for: a.ta.ki.ča *he is going to be able, they say*, at.ñi.ki.ča *he is habitually able, they say*, at.ṣ.ki.ča *he is able, they say*. The phonetic data concerning the sibilant nucleus syllable are readily observed by recording the Chipaya forms and playing them back at a slower speed.

[5] In this paper a dot below the line signifies retroflexion or backing; a dot above the line

ṣt.ḳal.ča *he has surely danced*, thoht.st.ḳal.ča *he has surely fallen*, tik.ṣt.ḳal.ča *he has surely died*, ap.ṣ.ki.ča *he is following, they say*, ma.khat.ṣ.ki.ča *he is approaching, they say*, ahk.ṣ.ki.ča *he is rounding up, they say*, tar.ṣ *hips*, kit.s *hair ornament*, ik.ṣ *womb*, ṣ.pekʷ. či.ča *he asked (him)*,[6] ṣ.tha·.či.ča *he gave (him)*, ṣ.kahl.či.ča *he pulled (it) out*, ṣ.ahk. či.ča *he rounded (them) up*, ṣ.cuk.ča *he is afraid (of him)*.

A sibilant may also occur as the margin of a syllable. In this position it does not have a mora of length, but is phonetically short; the peak of sonority occurs on the vowel nucleus; and there is no juncture between the sibilant and the contiguous phoneme within the syllable. ṣima *lunch*, ṣeṣi *afternoon, evening*, las *tongue*, maṣ *stone*.

3.0. The contrastive syllable types in Chipaya will be discussed in terms of Pike's theoretical framework of particle, wave, and field, beginning with the syllable as field.[2]

3.1. The basic field structure of the three syllable types is most easily grasped by means of matrix charts with onset and coda as the dimensional axes. A matrix of the short vowel nucleus syllable is:

coda → onset ↓	#	C	CC	CCC
#	V	VC	VCC	VCCC
C	CV	CVC	CVCC	CVCCC
CC	CCV	CCVC	CCVCC	CCVCCC
CCC	*CCCV	CCCVC	CCCVCC	CCCVCCC

C is consonant, and V is short vowel. The above matrix illustrates two relevant facts of the short vowel nucleus syllable type. First, the structure is symmetrical. With the exception of *CCCV, the cells of the matrix find their expression in the actual constructions of the language: a.ri *sharp*, am *you*,

signifies length; and a dot on the line signifies syllable division. Syllable division is indicated only in those examples where it is pertinent.

[6] The initial sibilant nucleus syllable appears ·to manifest the vestige of an older object referent series. Today the use of this prefix is idiolectical. It is not commonly used by the younger generation.

ehp *father*, ahkt.ḳal.ča *he had surely rounded up*; ḳa.ṣa *duck*, wit *stove*, maht *daughter*, kahlt.ḳal.ča *he had surely pulled (it) out*; ḳha.ra *hand*, phit *straw*, thoht.ñi.ča *he habitually falls*, ṣhihkt.ḳal.ča *he had surely brought*; škhuh.ku *narrow, confining*, ṣḳxexp.la *brain*, škhahḳt.ḳal.ča *he had surely opened (the door) a bit*. The *CCCV gap in the Chipaya data reflects no apparent structural restriction; with further data examples will presumably be found.

Second, the extremes of the matrix represent those syllable patterns which are less frequently encountered. The matrix may be viewed as a point (the upper left-hand cell) which spreads down and out in successive waves. The extremes are the first wave, embracing syllable patterns without any onset or coda, and the last wave, embracing syllable patterns with the most complex onset and/or coda.

The field structure of the long vowel nucleus syllable is:

coda → onset ↓	#	C	CC
#	V·	V·C	V·CC
C	CV·	VC·C	CV·CC
CC	CCV·	CCV·C	CCV·CC

C is consonant, and V· is long vowel. This matrix chart is also symmetrical and the extremes represent patterns less frequently encountered in the Chipaya language data. u·.ṣa *sheep*, e·k.ṣa *he hungers, thirsts*, e·kt.ḳal.ča *he surely had hungered, thirsted*; ma· *mother*, lu·ṣ *big water-jar*, po·kt.ḳal.ča *he had surely produced*; thu· *name*, txa·n.ča *he makes cry*, tha·ht.ḳal.ča *he had surely taught*.

The sibilant nucleus syllable has a simple field structure, as is shown below.

coda → onset ↓	#	t
#	sb	sbt

sb is sibilant, and t is alveolar stop. There are only two patterns of this syllable type, the sibilant and the sibilant plus t. The pattern without a coda is the most frequent. For examples, cf. **2.2.**

3.2. The syllable as a wave structure is presented by means of phonotagmemic formulas which are generative.[7] While the field structure clearly shows the overall syllable pattern, it does not give the specific detail which enables one to generate actual syllables. There is a maximum of three phonotagmemes in the syllable string: onset, nucleus, and coda. The nucleus is always manifested by a single phoneme; both onset and coda may be manifested by phoneme clusters generated by the following formulas.[8] Onset clusters are:

$$Cl_1 = \pm S_1{:}s/\underset{.}{s} + C_1{:}p + F_1{:}h$$
$$Cl_2 = \pm S_2{:}s/\underset{.}{s}/\check{s} + C_2{:}k/\underset{.}{k} + F_2{:}h/x$$
$$Cl_3 = \pm S_1{:}s/\underset{.}{s} + C_3{:}p/k/k^w/\underset{.}{k}^w/h/h^w/m/n$$
$$Cl_4 = \qquad\quad + C_4{:}t + F_3{:}h/h^w/x/x^w$$
$$Cl_5 = \qquad\quad + C_5{:}c/\check{c}/\underset{.}{\check{c}}/l + F_1{:}h$$

Coda clusters are:

$$Cl_6 = +F_2{:}h/x + C_6{:}p/t/k/\underset{.}{k}/1/1^y/r \pm C_4{:}t$$
$$Cl_7 = +F_4{:}h^w/x^w + C_2{:}k/\underset{.}{k} \pm C_4{:}t$$
$$Cl_8 = \qquad\quad + S_2{:}s/\underset{.}{s}/\check{s} + C_7{:}t/k/\underset{.}{k}$$
$$Cl_9 = \qquad\quad + C_8{:}100 + C_4{:}t$$

Cl is cluster; S is sibilant slot; C is consonant slot; and F is velar fricative slot. Class 100 comprises simple stops, fricatives, nasals, laterals, flap, and semivowels. Cl_8 only occurs when a final vowel has been elided.

The formulas for the three phonemic syllable types are:

$$Syl_1 = \pm O_1{:}Cl_{1-5}/200 + N_1{:}v \pm Cd_1{:}Cl_{6-9}/300$$
$$Syl_2 = \pm O_2{:}Cl_{1-5}/400 + N_2{:}v\cdot \pm Cd_2{:}Cl_9/500$$
$$Syl_3 = \qquad\quad + N_3{:}sb \pm Cd_3{:}t$$

Syl is syllable type; O is onset; N is nucleus; Cd is coda; v is short vowel; v· is long vowel;

[7] For a more extensive discussion of phonology in terms of phonotagmemics, cf. John C. Crawford, Totontepec Mixe Phonotagmemics, 55–64 (Norman, Okla., 1963).

[8] Two syllables occur which the above formulas do not generate. The present Chipaya data contain ilḳ.ča *he grazes*, and isḳ.ča *he fears*. It is not known whether or not these are loans. Chipaya forms are approximately 33% loans from Aymara, Quechua, and Spanish in a dictionary listing. In text the percentage of loans actually used in much lower.

and sb is sibilant. Class 200 comprises all consonants except ŋ. Class 300 comprises all consonants except affricates and glottalized stops. Class 400 comprises all consonants except velar fricatives and glottalized stops and affricates. Class 500 comprises simple stops, grooved fricatives, nasals, laterals, and flap.

Although not all possible combinations of onset, nucleus, and coda occur in the present data, structurally determined co-occurrence restrictions are not clearly revealed. The rare consonant phonemes ŋ, lʸ, kʷ, ·k̓ʷ, and the less frequent vowel phonemes e and o, account for a majority of the gaps. Any vowel may co-occur with any combination of onset and coda clusters.

3.3. The syllable functions as a particle, a single unit, as it fills a slot in the word, the next higher level of the phonological hierarchy. The scope of this paper being limited, only a few generalized structural patterns will be stated.

Syl₁ patterns of CV and CVC may occur in any slot within the word. The more complex Syl₁ patterns, those with consonant clusters, almost always fill a word initial slot, the exceptions generally occurring in loan words. They very rarely fill contiguous slots in the word. Syl₁ patterns with glottalized consonants or labialized velars fill a word initial slot, except in a few rare loan words. Syl₂ patterns usually fill a word initial slot. Syl₃ occurs in any word slot, although the pattern with a coda only occurs in a word medial slot. The nuclear slot of a word is always filled by Syl₁ or Syl₂. The nuclear slot is characterized by primary stress in normal speech.

Certain consonants occur with greater frequency in clusters across Syl₁ and Syl₂ boundaries. A stop, fricative, or semivowel occurs most frequently as the first member of a CC cluster across syllable boundaries. A stop or affricate occurs most frequently as the second member of a CC cluster across syllable boundaries.

STEP-UP TERRACE TONE IN ACATLÁN MIXTEC (MEXICO)

Eunice V. PIKE and Kent WISTRAND

1. Introduction

The tone system of the Acatlán dialect of Mixtec[1] (Mexico) is of special interest in that in a sequence of syllables, there may be a step-up of tone which suggests, in reverse, the 'terrace' downstep of tone described for Africa by Welmers[2]. The step-up of tone is all the more startling since another dialect of Mixtec (San Juan Coatzospan) has a system of downstepping terrace tone[3].

In the Acatlán dialect, the sequence of tones which step up is in conflict with the intonation downdrift which may occur when there is a sequence of low tones.

The contrast of the three tones high, mid, and low is as commonly defined, but there is a fourth tone which we call 'step-up' which is higher than any contiguously preceding syllable. A sequence of step-up tones is a sequence of successively higher tones. A high tone which follows the

---

[1] The data in this paper were gathered during the period from 1962 to 1967 on field trips to a town about nine miles from Acatlán de Osorio in the state of Puebla, México. The principal informant was Teófilo Martínez, a 47-year-old bilingual from the town of Xayacatlán de Bravo. Three towns, Xayacatlán de Bravo, San Jerónimo Xayacatlán, and Gabino Barreda, with a total of approximately 5,000 inhabitants, speak essentially the same dialect. They are approximately eight miles from each other. In general, Kent Wistrand provided the language data and is responsible for the analysis of the segmental phonemes; Eunice V. Pike is responsible for the tone analysis and presentation of the material. We wish to acknowledge our indebtedness to Miss Muriel Perkins, and Mr. and Mrs. Melvin Carson, for the use of their field notes.

[2] W.E. Welmers, Tonemic, Morphotonemics, and Tonal Morphemes, General Linguistics, 4.1–9 (1959). See also Paul Schachter, Phonetic Similarity in Tonemic Analysis with Notes on the Tone System of Akwapim Twi, Language, 37.231–38 (1961), and J.M. Stewart, The Typology of the Twi Tone System, (with comments by P. Schachter and W.E. Welmers), Bulletin of the Institute of African Studies 1.1–67 (1964).

[3] Chapter 8, of this volume.

step-up tone is level with it, but higher than a high which precedes the step-up tone.

The step-up tone is rare in basic allomorphs, but is frequent in non-basic allomorphs. It has a limited distribution in that it never occurs postpause; it follows only high tone or another step-up tone. (As a part of basic allomorphs, it occurs only in verbs of Class A, see 4.1, with the tone sequence high, step-up.)

Acatlán Mixtec has an intricate system of tone sandhi which we have divided into five subsystems. The tone sandhi which causes the step-up tone is part of two subsystems. The sequence of step-up tones which occurs when basic high tones change to step-up tones (see 5.5) is restricted for the most part to Class A morphemes. There is also a sequence of step-up tones which is caused for the most part by Class C morphemes (see 5.7).

In looking for a historical cause for the step-up tone, we note with interest that most Class C Acatlán morphemes which are followed by allomorphs of a higher level are cognate with morphemes of Ayutla[4] Mixtec whose basic allomorphs end in /ʔ/, and that it is these morphemes which (in the Ayutla dialect) cause changes in the tone of following morphemes. Since, however, in Acatlán Mixtec, a sequence of Class A morphemes may have step-up tones, and since some Class B morphemes are occasionally followed by step-up tones, we have not as yet determined with certainty the historical cause of all of the rises.

A summary of the literature and the theoretical implications of a downstep tone (and by implication of a step-up) are discussed by K.L. Pike[5]. Gleason also gives a summary of various treatments of downstep[6].

[4] Leo Pankratz and Eunice V. Pike, Phonology and Morphotonemics of Ayutla Mixtec, IJAL, 33.287–99 (1967).

[5] Kenneth L. Pike, Tagmemic and Matrix Linguistics Applied to Selected African Languages, Final Report Contract No. OE-5-14-065, U.S. Department of Health, Education, and Welfare, Office of Education, Bureau of Research, Nov. 1966, pp. vi-288, esp. pp. 133–144. (Reprinted, minus Appendix, Summer Institute of Linguistics Publications in Languages and Linguistics, Norman, Oklahoma, 1970.)

[6] H.A. Gleason Jr., Review of Malcolm Guthrie, Ed. African Language Studies I, London, 1960, and I. Richardson, The role of Tone in the Structure of Sukúma, London, 1959, Language, 37.294–308 (1961).

kʷí̱^{L}ta^{H}ni^U *you will be weak*. HH: kú^{L}mi^L (C I) *four* + yá^{M}vi^M (A I) (rule 14) *gravehole* > kú^{L}mi^L yá^{H}vi^H *four graveholes*. UL: tí̱^{M}i̱^{M} (B) *will grab* + ni^H (A) *you sing. polite* + tó^{H}ʔo^L (A) (rule 16) *stranger* > tí̱^{M}i̱^{M}ni^H tó^{U}ʔo^L *grab the stranger*. UH: ^{n}dú^{M}ku^M (C I) *will look for* + te^M (C) (rule 12) *third pers. masc. fam.* + yá^{M}vi^M (A I) (rule 15) *gravehole* > ^{n}dú^{M}ku^{M}te^H yá^{U}vi^H *he'll look for the gravehole*. UU: da^M (C) *causative* + čá^{L}ʔma^L (C I) (rule 6) *will be crushed* + si^M (C) (rule 12) *animal pronoun* + ^{m}bé^{M}lu^H (A) (rule 16) *hat* > da^{M}čá^{H}ʔma^{L}si^H ^{m}bé^{U}lu^U *the animal will crush the hat*.

Class A allomorphs with tones H, MH, HL, or HU are sometimes basic and sometimes nonbasic.

Class B morphemes (except for verbs with HM) are either level in tone or have a tone pattern in which the second syllable is higher than the first. Basic allomorphs occur with M, LM, LH, MM, or HM. Examples: tu^M *again*; ví^{L}ši̱^{M} *cold*, ^{n}zí^{L}ʔi̱^{M} *will enter*; ší^{L}ka^H *walking*, ká^{L}ʔnu^H *large*; vé^{M}ʔe^M *house*, ká^{M}ka^M *will walk*; ^{n}zí^{H}ʔi̱^{M} *entering*.

Nonbasic Class B allomorphs occur with H, U, MH, HH, HU, UH, or UM. They occur as a result of tone sandhi as in the following examples. H: dú^{M}ka̱^{H} (B III) *thus* + ni^M (B) (rule 14) *just* > dú^{M}ka̱^{H}ni^H *just thus*. U: né^{L}či^L (C I) *person* + ʔi^{L}kú^{H}mi^H (C) *has* + tu^M (B) (rule 15) *again* > né^{L}či^L ʔi^{L}kú^{H}mi^{H}tu^U *the person who has (it) again*. MH: na^M (B) *as* + ká^{L}ʔnu^H (B II) (rule 10) *large* > na^{M}ká^{M}ʔnu^H *as large as*. HH: kú^{L}mi^L (C I) *four* + vé^{M}ʔe^M (B I) (rule 14) *house* > kú^{L}mi^L vé^{H}ʔe^H *four houses*. UH: né^{L}či^L (C I) *person* + ʔi^{L}kú^{H}mi^H (C) *has* + ví^{M}či^M (B I) (rule 15) *now* > né^{L}či^L ʔi^{L}kú^{H}mi^H ví^{U}či^H *the person who has (it) now*. UM: ni^L (A) *past tense marker* + ší^{M}ni^M (A I) (rule 1) *see* + te^M (C) *third pers. masc. fam.* + ʔí̱^{M}i̱^{M} (C I) (rule 14) *hail* + ví^{L}ši̱^{M} (B) (rule 9) *cold* > ni^{L}ši^{M}ni^{L}te^M ʔí̱^{H}i̱^{H} ví^{U}ši̱^{M} *he saw the cold hail*.

The pattern HM when part of Class B morphemes is sometimes with basic and sometimes with nonbasic allomorphs.

Basic allomorphs of Class C morphemes occur with L, M, LL, ML, MM, or HL. Examples: ši^L *with*; na^M *when*; yú^{L}u^L *stone*, dí^{L}ta^L *tortilla*; ^{n}zí^{M}ki̱^{L} *seed*, dí^{M}ko^L *to sell*; yú^{M}u^M *hard*, sá^{M}a^M *new*; čó^{H}ʔo^L *being boiled*, ^{n}zí^{H}i̱^{L} *being scorched*.

Nonbasic Class C allomorphs occur with H, U, HH, UL, UM, or UH. They occur as a result of tone sandhi as in the following examples. H: te^L (A) *personifier* + ʔi^{L}kú^{H}mi^H (C) *has* + ši^L (C) (rule 11) *with* > te^{L}ʔi^{L}kú^{H}mi^{H}ši^L *the one who has (a thing)*. U: ʔi^{L}kú^{H}mi^H (C) (rule 2) *has* + te^M (C) (rule 12) *third pers. masc. fam.* > ʔi^{M}kú^{H}mi^{H}te^U *he has*.

HH: ma^L (C) *negative* + $kó^Mko^M$ (C I) (rule 14) *will swallow* + te^M (C) (rule 12) *third pers. masc. fam.* + $ña^L$ (A) (rule 7) *thing pronoun* > $ma^Lkó^Hko^Hte^Uña^U$ *he will not swallow it.* UL: $ní^{H?}i^L$ (C) *succeeds in* + te^M (C) (rule 12) *third pers. masc. fam.* + $k^wá^{H?}a^L$ (C) (rule 16) *fits in* + te^M (C) (rule 12) *third pers. masc. fam.* > $ní^{H?}i^Lte^H$ $k^wá^U?a^Lte^H$ *he succeeds in fitting in.* UM: $?i^Lkú^Hmi^H$ (C) (rule 2) *has* + $^nda^L$ (C) (rule 11) *we incl.* + $^nzí^Mki^L$ (C) (rule 15) *seed* > $?i^Mkú^Hmi^Hnda^H$ $^nzí^Uki_{\cdot}^M$ *we have seed.* UH: $?i^Lkú^Hmi^H$ (C) (rule 2) *has* + $^nda^L$ (C) (rule 11) *we incl.* + $dí^M?i^M$ (C I) (rule 15) *mother* > $?i^Mkú^Hmi^Hnda^H$ $dí^U?i^H$ *we have a mother.*

Class C allomorphs with tones L, M, LL, or HL are sometimes basic and sometimes nonbasic.

4.2. There is another classification (Classes I, II, III) which cuts across Classes A, B, and C, but which affects only those morphemes whose basic allomorphs have the tone patterns LL, MM, or LH.

Morphemes which in the basic allomorph have the tone pattern LL are divided again into Class I versus II. They are divided in accordance with the tone patterns which occur in the nonbasic allomorphs. A morpheme with LL (I) has nonbasic allomorphs with ML, HL, or UL (see chart 2, col. 2), whereas a morpheme with LL (II) has nonbasic allomorphs with MM or HH (see col. 6). Some morphemes with LL (I) are Class A, and some are Class C, but morphemes with LL (II) are all Class C.

A morpheme MM (I) has nonbasic allomorphs with HH or UH (see col. 12), whereas a morpheme MM (II) has nonbasic allomorphs with HH or LL (see col. 9). Some morphemes with MM (I) are Class A, some Class B, and some Class C, but MM (II) morphemes are all Class C.

Morphemes with the tone pattern LH in the basic allomorph are divided into three classes. Class LH (I) – all Class A – is separated from LH (II or III) by the type of allomorph. Specifically LH (I) has nonbasic allomorphs with HU or UU (see col. 4). LH (II or III) have nonbasic allomorphs with LL, MM, HH, MH, or HU (see chart 1, and chart 2, col. 7).

In a sequence of two morphemes, the Class I versus II is divided into classes in accordance with the allomorph of the second morpheme, whereas the Class II versus III is divided into classes in accordance with the allomorphs of the first morpheme.

Morphemes with LH (II) differ from those with LH (III) in that a LH (III), but not LH (II), is changed to LL, MM, or HH when preceding

Chart 1
SUBSYSTEM 3, Regressive Change.

First Morpheme, basic or nonbasic allomorph	Second Morpheme, basic allomorph	
	L (C), H (A), LH (III)	LH (II), HL(verb), HM, HU
LH (II)	LL	LH
(III)	LL	LL
MH (II)	MM	MH
(III)	MM	MM
HU (II)	HH	HU
(III)	HH	HH
Covered by rules	3	4

The pertinent class and tones of the first morpheme (nonbasic as well as basic allomorphs) are listed in the rows at the left. The tones, and class if pertinent, of the second morpheme (basic allomorphs only) are listed in the columns at the top. The cells contain the sandhi tones of the first morpheme which occur when preceding a morpheme of the type specified for that column.

LL (II), LH (II), HL, H, M, or HU (see rule 4). Morphemes with LH (I) are all Class A; morphemes with LH (II) and LH (III) are all Class B.

4.3. There is an overlap between phonological and grammatical classification. In our data, basic allomorphs with the tone sequence MH are all Class A nouns. Those with the tone sequences HM are all Class B verbs. Those with HU are all Class A verbs. Except for LH, modifiers are composed of tone sequences whose basic allomorphs have only the tones L or M.

In monosyllabic basic allomorphs, no pronoun is Class B. Any pronoun or particle which has H is Class A.

Nouns are never Class II or III (they are only Class I), but verbs and modifiers may also be Class I. All MM (II) and LH (III) are modifiers. All LL (II) are verbs.

Other tone patterns do not seem to be restricted to any particular grammatical class.

Chart 2

SUBSYSTEM 4, Progressive Change.

First Morpheme, basic or nonbasic allomorph	Second Morpheme, basic allomorph												
	1	2	3	4	5	6	7	8	9	10	11	12	13
	(A)	(I)		(I)	(C)	(II)	(II,III)	(C)	(II)	(B)		(I)	
	L	LL	LM	LH	L	LL	LH	M	MM	M	ML	MM	MH
Final M (B)	M*	ML			M	MM	MH	L		H	HM	HH	HU
Final H or U (B)	H*	HL			H	HH	HU		HH	H	HM	HH	HU
Final L (C)	H	HL	HM	HU				H	LL	H	HM	HH	HU
Final M (C)	H	HL	HM	HU	M	MM	MH	H		H	HM	HH	HU
LH or HM (C)	H*	HL			M	MM	MH						
H or U (C) or combination	U	UL	UM	UU	H	HH	HU	U	HH	U	UM	UH	UU
Covered by rules	5,6,7		8,9		10,11			12	13			14,15	

The pertinent class and tones of the first morpheme (nonbasic as well as basic allomorphs) are listed in the rows at the left. The tones, and class if pertinent, of the second morpheme (basic allomorphs only) are listed in the numbered columns at the top. The cells contain the sandhi tones of the second morpheme which occur when following a morpheme of the type specified for that row. If the cell is blank, the basic allomorph occurs there.

* If the second morpheme is not followed by M or H.

5. Tone sandhi

There is a system of tone sandhi whereby the tones of one morpheme affect the tones of another morpheme[11]. The domain of influence of one tone upon another is restricted to contiguous morphemes, but it is not restricted to contiguous syllables. The domain of the influence is the same when the two morphemes are parts of one word, as it is when they are parts of two words, but the domain of influence does not extend beyond pause.

There are five subsystems of tone sandhi: (1) A subsystem (5.1) in which a following morpheme affects a preceding Class A morpheme. (2) A subsystem (5.2) in which the tone of the allomorph is dependent upon its place postpause versus nonpostpause. This subsystem is restricted to morphemes with LL (II), and LH (II,III). (3) A subsystem (5.3) in which Class B morphemes with basic LH (II,III) are affected by a following morpheme. (4) A subsystem (5.4) in which Class B and Class C morphemes cause the tones of following morphemes to change. This is the most extensive subsystem. (5) A subsystem (5.5) in which a morpheme-initial H becomes U when contiguously following a morpheme-final H or U.

In an utterance, the tone-sandhi influence of one morpheme upon another progresses from left to right morpheme by morpheme. Descriptively, however, when two contiguous morphemes are under consideration, a regressive change (5.1, 5.3) takes place first, then a progressive change takes place. If the first morpheme is changed either regressively (5.1, 5.3), or progressively (5.2, 5.4), it is the allomorph which occurs as a result of that change which has influence upon the second morpheme (5.4, 5.5).

5.1. Class A morphemes may be changed by regressive sandhi.

Rule 1. When a disyllabic Class A allomorphic with a level pitch sequence precedes tones M or H, the second tone of the morpheme becomes L. That is, MM, HH, UH become ML, HL, UL respectively. ví^{M}u^M

---

[11] In this paper, we have not discussed three-syllable morphemes. For example, ka^{L}nú^{H}u^H (C) *on purpose*, ?á^{M}n$_{zi}$^{M}vi^M (C) *heaven*, sa^{M}k^{w}á^{M}a^M (C) *deer*. We have not discussed tone sandhi changes within certain frozen combinations of morphemes, for example: di^{L}ni^{L}ñú^{L}u^H *Totoltepec*, di^{L}ta^{L}ndú^{L}či^H *bean tamale*, ka^M?a^{L}yú^{L}i^H *mouth of a river branch*. Nor have we discussed numerous complex verb stems such as či^{M}ndú^M?u^M (C) *to cause to lie*, da^{M}na^{M}k^{w}í^{M}tya^L (A) *to disperse*, ku^{M}si^{M}kí^{M}di^L (A) *to become infested*. Furthermore, the sandhi which occurs between a few of the verb prefixes and following stems needs additional study, e.g., nu^H *conditional marker*, ni^L *hortatory marker*, di^L *specifier*, ši^H *pluralizer*.

(A I) (rule 1) *corn plant* + k^{w}á^{M}ti^M (C II) *small pl.* > ví^{M}u^L k^{w}á^{M}ti^M *small corn plants*; sá^{M}ku^M (A I) (rule 1) *few* + te^M (C) *third pers. masc. fam.* > sá^{M}ku^{L}te^M *few of them*; ʔí^{M}tu^M (A I) (rule 1) *cornfield* + ni^H (A) *you sing. polite* > ʔí^{M}tu^{L}ni^H *your cornfield*; ma^L (C) *negative* + kú^{M}ni^M (A I) (rule 14 then rule 1) *will see* + ña^M *third pers. fam.* > ma^{L}kú^{H}ni^{L}ña^M *she will not see*; ma^{L}di^L (C I) *negative specifier* + ʔi^M ni^M (C I) (rule 14) *all over* + kú^{M}tu^M (C II) (rule 13) *just* + ñú^{M}u^M (A I) (rule 15 then rule 1) *town* + k^{w}á^{M}ti^M (C II) *small pl.* > ma^{L}di^L ʔi^{H}ni^H kú^{H}tu^H ñú^{U}u^L k^{w}á^{M}ti^M *not all over the small towns.*

5.2. The tone sequences LL and LH may change when postpause.
Rule 2. Basic LL (II) morphemes (all Class C) become MM when postpause. Basic LH (II, III) – but not LH (I) – become MH when postpause. ña^L (A) *thing* + ^{n}dá^{L}ta^L (C II) (remains unchanged) *tears* + si^M (C) (rule 12) *animal pronoun* > na^L^{n}da^{L}ta^{L}si^M *what the animal tears*, but ^{n}dá^{L}ta^L (C II) (rule 2) *tears* + si^M (C) (rule 12) *animal pronoun* + a^L (A) (rule 7) *thing pronoun* > ^{n}dá^{M}ta^{M}si^{H}a^U *the animal tears it*; te^L (A) *he* + sá^{L}ʔnu^H (B II) (remains unchanged) *old* > te^{L}sá^{L}ʔnu^H *the old man*, but sá^{L}ʔnu^H (B II) (rule 2) *old* + te^M (C) *third pers. masc. fam.* > śa^{M}ʔnu^{H}te^M *he is old.*

5.3. Morphemes with a basic LH (II or III) are changed regressively in certain environments. The way the allomorphs are changed and the environments in which they change are depicted on chart 1.
Rule 3. The allomorphs LH (basic), MH (nonbasic), and HU (nonbasic) of Classes II and III become LL, MM, HH respectively when preceding L (C), H (A), or LH (III). See chart 1, col. 1.
Examples: ^{n}dá^{M}ʔa^L (C) *hand* + ká^{L}ʔnu^H (B II) (rule 3) *large* + ni^H (A) *you sing. polite* > ^{n}dá^{M}ʔa^L ká^{L}ʔnu^{L}ni^H *your large hand*; kí^{M}si^L (C) *animal* + ká^{L}ni^H (B II) (rule 3) *beating* + ^{n}da^L (C) *we incl.* > kí^{M}si^L ká^{L}ni^L^{n}da^L *the animal that we are beating*; tú^{M}u^M (A I) *lane* + ká^{L}ni^H (B II) (rule 3) *long* + yú^{L}ka^H (B III) *that* > tú^{M}u^M ká^{L}ni^L yú^{L}ka^H *that long lane*; yó^{L}ʔo^H (B III) *this, here* + yú^{L}ka^H (B III) (rule 10) *that, there* > yó^{M}ʔo^M yú^{M}ka^H *here and there*; dá^M^{n}du^M (C I) *then* + vé^{M}ʔe^M (B I) (rule 14) *house* + ná^{L}ʔnu^H (B II) (rule 11 then rule 3) *large pl.* + ma^L (C) (rule 11) *previously referred to* > dá^M^{n}du^M vé^{H}ʔe^H ná^{H}ʔnu^{H}ma^H *then those large houses* ... (In the last example, the change in the tones of ná^{L}ʔnu^H *large pl.* from LH to HU, rule 11, is obscured by the regressive lowering of the final syllable to H when preceding ma^L (C) *previously referred to*, rule 3.)

Rule 4. Allomorphs of Class III (but not Class II) with tone patterns LH (basic), MH (nonbasic), and HU (nonbasic) become LL[12], MM, and HH respectively when preceding LH (II) HL (verb but not noun), HM, or HU. See chart 1, col. 2.

Examples: ña^L(A) *thing* + yú^{L}ką^H (III) (rule 4) *there* + ^{n}dú^{L}u^H (B II) *is* + a^L (A) (rule 6) *thing* > ña^{L}yú^{L}ką^L ^{n}dú^{L}a^H [13] *that's it*; ma^{L}di^L (C I) *negative specifier* + dó^{L}ʔo^H (B III) (rule 4) *thus* + ką^{H}ʔą^L (A) *speaks* + te^M (C) *third pers. masc. fam.* > ma^{L}di^{L}dó^{L}ʔo^L ką^{H}ʔą^{L}te^M *he doesn't speak thus*; ma^{L}di^L (C I) *negative specifier* + k^{w}į^{M}si^L (C) (rule 14) *only* + ni^M (B) (rule 14) *just* + dó^{L}ʔo^H (B III) (rule 11 then rule 4) *thus* + ^{n}dó^{H}o^M (B) (rule 16) *remains* + te^M (C) (rule 12) *third pers. masc. fam.* > ma^{L}di^{L}k^{w}į^{H}si^{M}ni^H dó^{H}ʔo^H ^{n}dó^{U}o^{M}te^L *he doesn't just remain thus*.

5.4. The way in which Class B and Class C morphemes cause certain morphemes which follow them contiguously to change is depicted on chart 2. The specific rules by which the first of two morphemes causes the second to change are stated below. To make the examples easier to follow, beside each morpheme which changes is placed the number of the rule which applies to the change.

Rule 5. When following a Class B with a final tone M, then L (A), if not followed by M or H, and an LL (I) become M and ML respectively. See chart 2, col. 1 and 2.

Examples: ʔį^{M}į^M (B I) *one* + dí^{L}ta^L (C I) (rule 5) *tortilla* > ʔį^{M}į^M dí^{M}ta^L *one tortilla*; kú^{L}di^M (B) *will get dirty* + ve^L (A) (rule 5) *infant pronoun* > kú^{L}di^{M}ve^M *the baby will get dirty*, but kú^{L}di^M (B) *will get dirty* + ve^L (A) (does not change, rule 5) *infant pronoun* + tą^{M}ą^M (A I) *tomorrow* > kú^{L}di^{M}ve^L tą^{M}ą^M *the baby will get dirty tomorrow*.

Rule 6. When following a Class B with final tone H or U, or when following a Class C allomorph which has an L or M for at least one of its tones, then LL (I) becomes HL. In the same environment, L (A) becomes H, but after a Class B morpheme, or a Class C with LH or MH, it

---

[12] Sequences LHH, MHH, HUH when the final H is part of the morpheme ni^M (B) *quite* or te^M (B) *and* become LLL, MMM‘ HHH in these environments. For example, dú^{L}ką^H (B III) (rule 2 then rule 4) *thus* + ni^M (B) (footnote 12) *quite* + ki^{L}da^H (B II) (rule 10) *does* > dú^{M}ką^{M}ni^M kí^{M}da^H *doing quite thus*.

[13] Fusion of the verb stem with a following pronoun subject which has canonical shape V, or of a pronoun subject with a following pronoun object which has canonical shape V, is prevalent but not discussed in this paper.

comes H, but after a Class B morpheme, or a Class C with LH or MH, it becomes H only if not followed by M or H. See chart 2, col. 1 and 2.

Examples: ká^{L}ni^H (B II) (rule 2) *beats* + ne^L (A) (rule 6) *third pers. polite* > ká^{M}ni^{H}ne^H *he beats* (but in the following example, ne^L (A) does not change: ká^{M}ni^{H}ne^{L}te^M *he beats him*); ʔį̃^{L}į̃^{H} (B II) (rule 2) *stands* + ⁿdá^{L}a^L (A I) (rule 6) *straight* > ʔį̃^{M}į̃^{H} ⁿdá^{H}a^L *stands straight*; kʷá^{L}ʔa^L (C I) *many* + kú^{L}ʔi^L (A I) (rule 6) *sister* > kʷá^{L}ʔa^L kú^{H}ʔi^L *many sisters.*

Rule 7. When following a Class C which has no tone lower than H, then L (A) and an LL (I) become U and UL respectively. See chart 2, col. 1 and 2.

Examples: ma^L (C) *negative* + čį̃^{M}tu^M (C II) (rule 13, footnote 14) *will be filled* + kó^{L}ʔo^L (C I) (rule 7) *plate* > ma^{L}čį̃^{H}tu^H kó^{U}ʔo^L *the plate will not be filled*; ʔa^M (C) *interrogative* + dá^{M}ña^M (C I) (rule 14) *will loose* + ka^L (A) (rule 7) *more* + te^M (C) *third pers. masc. fam.* + si^M (C) (rule 12) *animal pronoun* > ʔa^{M}dá^{H}ña^{H}ka^{U}te^{M}si^H *will he loose the animal any more?*

Rule 8. When following a Class C allomorph which has an L or M for its final tone, then LM becomes HM, and an LH (I) becomes HU. See chart 2, col. 3 and 4.

Examples: kʷá^{L}ʔa^L (C I) *many* + dé^{L}ʔe^M (B) (rule 8) *child* > kʷá^{L}ʔa^L dé^{H}ʔe^M *many children*; dí^{M}ʔi^M (C I) *mother* + ⁿzí^{L}ku^M (B) (rule 8) *will sew* > dí^{M}ʔi^M ⁿzí^{H}ku^M *the mother who will sew*; kó^{L}o^L (C I) *there is not* + yá^{L}a^H (A I) (rule 8) *tongue* + si^M (C) *animal pronoun* > kó^{L}o^L yá^{H}a^{U}si^M *the animal has no tongue*; ⁿdyá^{M}či^M (C I) *will blow away* + yá^{L}ka^H (A I) (rule 8) *dust* > ⁿdyá^{M}či^M yá^{H}ka^U *the dust will blow away.*

Rule 9. When following a Class C allomorph which has no tone lower than H, then LM becomes UM, and an LH (I) becomes UU. See chart 2, col. 3 and 4.

Examples: na^M (C) *when* + kí^{M}ni^M (C I) (rule 14) *will shoot* + dé^{L}ʔe^M (B) (rule 9) *son* > na^{M}kí^{H}ni^H dé^{U}ʔe^M *when the son will shoot*; ʔa^M (C) *interrogative* + ví^{M}da^M (C I) (rule 14) *wet* + yá^{L}a^H (A I) (rule 9) *tongue* + ña^M (C) *third pers. fem. fam.* > ʔa^{M}ví^{H}da^H yá^{U}a^{U}ña^M *is the girl's tongue wet?*

Rule 10. When following a final tone M of Class B or Class C, or when following a Class C with LH or MH, then an L (C) becomes M, an LL (II) becomes MM, and an LH (II, III) becomes MH. See chart 2, col. 5, 6, 7.

Examples: ʔá^{M}na^M (A I) (rule 1) *who* + ⁿdá^{M}ši^M (B I) *will loose* + ši^L (C) (rule 10) *with* + ⁿda^L (C) (rule 10) *we incl.* > ʔá^{M}na^L ⁿdá^{M}ši^{M}ši^{M}ⁿda^M

the person who will loose us; kʷí^{M}ko^M (C I) *will carry* + ⁿda^L (C) (rule 10) *we incl.* > kʷí^{M}ko^{Mn}da^M *we will carry*; dó^{M}ko^M (B I) *but* + tá$^{L?}$vi^L (C II) (rule 10) *breaking* + te^M (C) (rule 12) *third pers. masc. fam.* + a^L (A) (rule 7) *thing pronoun* > dó^{M}ko^M tá$^{M?}$vi^{M}te^{H}a^U *but he is breaking it*; dí$^{M?}$i^M (C I) *mother* + ší^{L}ši^H (B II) (rule 10) *eating* > dí$^{M?}$i^M ší^{M}ši^H *the mother who is eating*; te^M (B) *and* + dó$^{L?}$o^H (B III) (rule 10 then rule 3) *thus* + kú^{L}nu^H (B II) (rule 10) *deep* + ña^L (A) (rule 6) *thing pronoun* > te^{M}dó$^{M?}$o^M kú^{M}nu^{H}ña^H *and it is this deep*.

Rule 11. When following a Class B with a final tone H or U, or a Class C allomorph which has no tone lower than H, then L (C) becomes H, an LL (II) becomes HH, and an LH (II, III) becomes HU. See chart 2, col. 5, 6, 7.

Examples: ña$^{M?}$a^L (C) *woman* + ká^{M}ka^M (B I) (rule 14) *will walk* + yó$^{L?}$o^H (B III) (rule 11 then rule 3) *here* + ši^L (C) (rule 11) *with* + yú^{L}ka̰^{H} (B III) (rule 11) *there* > ña$^{M?}$a^L ká^{H}ka^H yó$^{H?}$o^H ši^{H}yú^{H}ka̰^{U} *the woman who will walk from here to there*; né^{L}či^L (C I) *person* + ší^{L}nu^H (B II) *running* + ší^{L}ko^L (C II) (rule 11) *carrying* > né^{L}či^L ší^{L}nu^H ší^{H}ko^H *the person who carries (something) on the run*; ⁿdá$^{M?}$a^L (C) *hand* + nu^M (C) (rule 12) *tree pronoun* + ná^{L}ni^H (B II) (rule 11) *long pl.* > ⁿdá$^{M?}$a^{L}nu^H ná^{H}ni^U *its long leaves*; né^{L}či^L (C I) *person* + ʔį́^{L}į^H (B II) *standing* + ší^{L}ši^H (B II) (rule 11) *eating* > né^{L}či^L ʔį́^{L}į^H ší^{H}ši̧^{U} *the person who eats standing up*; te^L (A) *personifier* + kí^{L}da^H (B II) *doing* + ká$^{L?}$nu^H (B II) (rule 11 then rule 3) *large* + dú^{L}ka̰^{H} (B III) (rule 11) *thus* > te^{L}kí^{L}da^H ká$^{H?}$nu^H dú^{H}ka̰^{U} *the one who celebrates thus*.

Rule 12. A monosyllabic M (C) is sometimes L, sometimes H, and at times U. It becomes L when following M (B); it becomes H when following L or M (C); it becomes U when following an allomorph (C) which has no tone lower than H. See chart 2, col. 8.

Examples: má^{L}ni^L (C I) *loved* + te^M (C) (rule 12) *third pers. masc. fam.* > má^{L}ni^{L}te^H *he is loved*; dí$^{M?}$i^M (C I) *mother* + te^M (C) (rule 12) *third pers. masc. fam.* > dí$^{M?}$i^{M}te^M *his mother*; má^{L}ni^L (C I) *loved* + te^M (C) (rule 12) *third pers. masc. fam.* + nú^{L}u^L (C I) (rule 7) *by* + dí$^{M?}$i^M (C I) (rule 14) *mother* + te^M (C) (rule 12) *third pers. masc. fam.* > má^{L}ni^{L}te^H nú^{U}u^L dí$^{H?}$i^{H}te^U *he is loved by his mother*.

Rule 13. When following a Class C allomorph which ends in L, then MM (II)[14] becomes LL. When following a Class B allomorph which ends in H or U, or a Class C allomorph which has no tone lower than H, then MM (II) becomes HH. See chart 2, col. 9.

[14] For footnote, see next page.

Examples: túᴹtʉᴸ (C) *firewood* + kʷáᴹtiᴹ (C II) (rule 13) *small pl.* > túᴹtʉᴸ kʷáᴸtiᴸ *small firewood*; šíᴸkaᴴ (B II) (rule 2) *walks* + ⁿdéᴹeᴹ (C II) (rule 13) *fast* + ⁿzyaᴸ (A) (rule 7) *you pl. polite* > šíᴹkaᴴ ⁿdéᴴeᴴ ⁿzyaᵁ *you walk fast*.

Rule 14. When following any Class B with a final H or U, and when following a Class C allomorph which has L or M for at least one tone, then an M (B) becomes H, an ML becomes HM, an MM (I) becomes HH, an MH becomes HU. See chart 2, col. 10, 11, 12, 13.

Examples: kóᴸoᴸ (C I) *there is not* + niᴹ (B) (rule 14) *not even* + ʔíᴹįᴹ (B I) (rule 14) *one* + ᵐbéᴹluᴬ (A) (rule 14) *hat* > kóᴸoᴸ niᴴʔįᴴįᴴ ᵐbéᴴluᵁ *there isn't even one hat*; ⁿdóᴸʔoᴴ (B II) (rule 2) *is suffering* + čéᴹluᴸ (C) (rule 14) *calf* > ⁿdóᴹʔoᴴ čéᴴluᴹ *the calf is suffering*; sáᴹaᴹ (C II) *new* + náᴹmaᴹ (A I) (rule 14) *wall* > sáᴹaᴹ náᴴmaᴴ *the wall is new*; maᴸ (C) *negative* + náᴸniᴴ (B II) *long pl.* + čįᴹįᴹ (A) (rule 14) *fingernails* + iᴸ (A) *my* > maᴸnáᴸniᴴ čįᴴįᵁįᴸ *my fingernails are not long*.

Rule 15. When following a Class C allomorph which has no tone lower than H, then M (B) becomes U, an ML becomes UM, an MM (I) becomes UH, and MH becomes UU. See chart 2, col. 10, 11, 12, 13.

Examples: šíᴸkaᴴ (B II) (rule 2) *walks* + núᴹuᴹ (B I) (rule 14) *about* + tiᴹįᴹ (C II) (rule 13) *small* + tuᴹ (B) (rule 15) *again* > šíᴹkaᴴ núᴴuᴴ tiᴴįᴴtuᵁ *walks about awhile again*; kʷáᴸʔａᴸ (A) *goes* + míᴹįᴹ (C I) *alone* + siᴹ (C) (rule 12) *animal pronoun* + táᴹšiᴹ (C I) (rule 15) *to chase* + siᴹ (C) (rule 12) *animal pronoun* + kóᴹčiᴹ (A I) (rule 15) *pig* > kʷáᴸʔａᴸ míᴹįᴹsiᴴ táᵁšiᴴsiᵁ kóᵁčiᴴ *he chases pigs all by himself*; šíᴸoᴸ (C I) *will sour* + siᴹ (C) (rule 12) *fruit pronoun* + ʔíᴹdaᴴ (A) (rule 15) *day after tomorrow* > šíᴸoᴸsiᴴ ʔíᵁdaᵁ *the fruit will sour day after tomorrow*.

5.5. There may be a progressive change of basic H to U.

Rule 16. The initial tone H of a basic allomorph (of any morpheme class) becomes U when it contiguously follows H or U (of any morpheme class).

Examples: šíᴸniᴴ (A) (rule 2) *sees* + niᴴ (A) (rule 16) *you sing. polite* > šíᴹniᴴniᵁ *you see*; veᴹʔeᴹ (B I) *house* + niᴴ (A) *you sing. polite* + ⁿzíᴴʔįᴹ (B) (rule 16) *are entering* + niᴴ (A) *you sing. polite* > véᴹʔeᴹniᴴ ⁿzíᵁʔįᴹniᴴ *you are entering your house*; koᴴ (A) *negative* + káįᴴʔａᴸ (A) (rule 16) *speaks* + neᴸ (A) *third pers. polite* > koᴴkáᵁʔａᴸneᴸ *he does not speak*; maᴸ (C) *negative* + saᴸ (C) (meaning not determined) +

---

[14] There is an exception in that when following maᴸ (C) *negative* and ʔaᴹ *interrogative*, then MM (II) becomes HH. For example, maᴸ (C) *negative* + tiᴹįᴹ (C II) *small* > maᴸtiᴴįᴴ *not small*; ʔaᴹ (C) *interrogative* + tiᴹįᴹ (C II) *small* > ʔaᴹtiᴴįᴴ *is it small?*

ká^{M}ni^M (B I) (rule 14) *will beat* + ni^H (A) (rule 16) *you sing. polite* + mé^{H}e^L (A) (rule 16) *baby* > ma^{L}sa^{L}ká^{H}ni^{H}ni^U mé^{U}e^L *don't beat the baby*; ko^H (A) *negative* + yú^H?i^U (A) (rule 16) *fears* + ni^H (A) (rule 16) *you sing. polite* > ko^{H}yú^U?i^{U}ni^U *you do not fear.*

5.6. The tone sandhi is so extensive that some morphemes, specifically those whose basic allomorphs are LL (C), MM (A), and LH (B), have as many as six allomorphs which are differentiated by tone. Those with basic allomorph LL (A) or L (A) have four allomorphs; all the rest have three.

By way of illustration, we are giving examples of the six allomorphs of ñú^M?u^M (A I) *fire*.

MM: ñú^M?u^M *fire* + vá^L?a^M (A) *good* > ñú^M?u^M vá^L?a^M *a good fire*. ML: ñú^M?u^M (rule 1) *fire* + ní^H?i^M (B) *flaring* > ñú^M?u^L ní^H?i^M *a flaring fire*. HH: ma^{L}di^L (C I) *negative specifier* + ñú^M?u^M (rule 14) *fire* > ma^{L}di^L ñú^H?u^H *not a fire*. HL: ma^{L}di^L (C I) *negative specifier* + ñú^M?u^M (rule 14 then rule 1) *fire* + tí^{M}i^M (C II) *small* > ma^{L}di^L ñú^H?u^L tí^{M}i^M *not a small fire*. UH: ni^L (A) *completive marker* + ^{n}dú^{M}ku^M (C I) *to seek* + ña^M (C) (rule 12) *third pers. fem. fam.* + ñú^M?u^M (rule 14) *fire* > ni^L^{n}dú^{M}ku^{M}ña^H ñú^U?u^H *she sought for a fire*. UL: ni^L (A) *completive marker* + ^{n}dú^{M}ku^M (C I) *to seek* + ña^M (C) (rule 12) *third pers. fem. fam.* + ñú^M?u^M (rule 14 then rule 1) *fire* + ní^H?i^M (B) *flaring* > ni^L^{n}dú^{M}ku^{M}ña^H ñú^U?u^L ní^H?i^M *she sought for a flaring fire*.

A Class B morpheme with the tone pattern LH has six allomorphs differentiated by tone. By way of illustration, we are giving examples of the six allomorphs of sa^L?nu^H (B II) *old*.

LH: sa^L (A) *continuative marker* + sá^L?nu^H *old* + ne^L (A) (rule 6) *third pers. polite* > sa^{L}sá^L?nu^{H}ne^H *they are old now*. MH: sá^L?nu^H (rule 2) *old* + ne^L (A) (rule 6) *third pers. polite* > sá^M?nu^{H}ne^H *they are old*. HU: mí^{M}i^M (C I) *alone* + vé^M?e^M (B I) (rule 14) *house* + sá^L?nu^H (rule 11) *old* > mí^{M}i^M vé^H?e^H sá^H?nu^U *just the old house*. LL: sa^L (A) *continuative marker* + sá^L?nu^H (rule 3) *old* + ^{n}da^L (C) *we incl.* > sa^{L}sá^L?nu^L^{n}da^L *we are now old*. MM: dó^{M}ko^M (B I) *but* + sá^L?nu^H (rule 10 then rule 3) *old* + ^{n}da^L (C) (rule 10) *we incl.* > dó^{M}ko^M sá^M?nu^{M}nda^M *but we are old*. HH: mí^{M}i^M (C I) *alone* + vé^M?e^M (B I) (rule 14) *house* + sá^L?nu^H (rule 11 then rule 3) *old* + yú^{L}ka̧^{H} (B III) (rule 11) *that* > mí^{M}i^M vé^H?e^H sá^H?nu^H yú^{H}ka̧^{U} *just that old house*.

A morpheme with L (A) has four allomorphs; they are illustrated by na^L (A) *thing pronoun*.

L: ʔú^{L}i^L (A) *two* + ña^L *thing pronoun* > ʔú^{L}i^{L}ña^L *two of them*. M: ʔį̓^{M}į^M (B) *one* + ña^L (rule 5) *thing pronoun* > ʔį̓^{M}į^{M}ña^M *one of them*. H: ká^{L}ni^H (B II) (rule 2) *long* + ña^L (rule 6) *thing pronoun* > ká^{M}ni^{H}ña^H *it is long*. U: tá^{Lʔ}vi^L (C II) (rule 2) *breaks* + te^M (C) (rule 12) *third pers. masc. fam.* + ña^L (rule 7) *thing pronoun* > tá^{Mʔ}vi^{M}te^{H}ña^U *he is breaking it*.

5.7. Since the step-up terrace tone is of interest in reference to theory of phonology, we are giving examples of the terracing as it occurs when various morpheme classes and sandhi rules are involved.

When rule 16 applies to a sequence of Class A morphemes, the tone steps up with terraces of one syllable: ko^H (A) *negative* + čí^{H}tu^U (A) (rule 16) *kisses* + wa^H (A) (rule 16) *so* + ni^H (A) (rule 16) *you sing. polite* + mé^{H}e^L (A) (rule 16) *baby* > ko^{H}čí^{U}tu^{U}wa^{U}ni^U mé^{U}e^L *you don't kiss the baby so much*. The contour is 34567 81. The sequence of five U tones is actualized as five different levels of pitch.

When rule 11 applies to a sequence of LH (B) morphemes, the tone rises with terraces of two or more syllables: ká^{L}na^H (B II) (rule 2) *coming forth* + má^{Mn}gu^M (B I) (rule 14) *mango* + ná^{Lʔ}nu^H (B II) (rule 11) *large pl.* + kú^{L}u^H (B II) (rule 11) *being seen* + tu^M (rule 14) *habitually* + yú^{L}ka^H (B III) (rule 11) *there* > ká^{M}na^H má^{Hn}gu^H ná^H?nu^U kú^{H}u^{U}tu^H yú^{H}ka̧^{U} *the large mangos usually seen there are starting to grow*. The contour is 23 33 34 45 556.

When rule 15 applies to a sequence of MM (C I) morphemes, the tone rises with terraces of two syllables: ma^L (C) *negative* + kó^{M}ko^M (C I) (rule 14) *will swallow* + yú^{M}a^M (C I) (rule 15) *father* + dí^{Mʔ}i^M (C I) (rule 15) *mother* + mí^{M}i^M (C I) (rule 15) *specifier* + te^M (C) (rule 12) *third pers. masc. fam.* + ʔį̓^{M}į^M (C I) (rule 15) *hail* > ma^{L}kó^{H}ko^H yú^{U}a^H dí^{Uʔ}i^H mí^{U}i^{H}te^U ʔį̓^{U}į^H *his parents will not swallow the hail*. The contour is 133 44 55 667 88.

When there is a mixture of MM (B or C) and LH (B) morphemes, there is a step-up of tone: ʔa^M (C) *interrogative* + tí^{M}i^M (C II) (rule 13, footnote 14) *small* + vé^{Mʔ}e^M (B I) (rule 15) *house* + šį̓^{L}į^H (B II) (rule 11) *buys* + sá^{M}a^M (C II) (rule 13) *new* + te^M (C) (rule 12) *third pers. masc. fam.* + nú^{L}u^L (C I) (rule 7) *from* + ni^H (A) (rule 6) *you sing. polite* > ʔa^{M}tí^{H}i^H vé^U?e^H šį̓^{H}į^U sá^{H}a^{H}te^U nú^{U}u^{L}ni^H *is the new house that he is buying from you small?* The contour is 233 44 45 556 713.

By way of contrast we have included a sentence with a sequence of low tones. It is made up of all basic allomorphs: ni^{L}šį̓^{M}ni^{M}ne^L ʔú^{L}i^L kú^{Lʔ}i^{L}ne^L *she saw her two sisters*. The following sentence has a sequence of mid tones; all are basic allomorphs: ni^{L}ší^{M}ni^{M}ne^L ?i̧^{M}i̧^{M} vé^M?e^M ?i̧^{M}du^M *he saw one horse house (barn)*.

The following example shows a high tone raised to the fifth level and maintained there. ko^H (A) *negative* + ší^{L}ko^L (C II) *carries* + mí^{M}i^M (C I) (rule 14) *alone* + te^M (C) (rule 12) *third pers. masc. fam.* + ni^M (B) (rule 15) *not even* + ?i̧^{M}i̧^{M} (B I) (rule 14) *one* + ña^L (A) (rule 6) *thing pronoun* > ko^{H}ší^{L}ko^L mí^{H}i^{H}te^U ni^U?i̧^{H}i̧^{H}na^H *he doesn't carry even one of them*. The contour is 311 334 5555.

6. Consonant contrasts

There are twenty-one consonant phonemes in Acatlán Mixtec. Stops: /p, t, k, k^w, ?/. Affricates: /č/. Prenasalized stops: /^{m}b, ^{n}d, ^{n}g/. Prenasalized affricates: /^{n}z, ^{n}ǰ/. Nasals: /m, n, ñ/. Voiceless fricatives: /s, š/. Voiced fricatives: /v, d/. Lateral and vibrants: /l, ř, r̃/. Semiconsonants: /w, y, h/.

The labials /p, ^{m}b, m, v (labiodental), w/ contrast as follows: pé^{Mn}ǰi^L *orphan*, ^{m}bé^{M}lu^H *hat*, mé^{H}e^L *baby*, vé^{L}i^M *I'm heavy*, ka^{M}va^L *boulder*, wé^{M}i^H *ox*. The phoneme /w/ is rare. In our data, it occurs only in: wé^{M}i^H *ox*, wá$^{L?}$a^M (alternating with vá$^{L?}$a^M) *good*, ?á^{M}wa^M *last year*, and in words with the morpheme wa^H *so*.

The dentals /t, d (interdental), ^{n}d, ^{n}z, s, n, l, ř(flap), r̃(trill)/ contrast as follows: té$^{L?}$e^L *plant runner*, dé$^{L?}$e^M *son*, ^{n}dé$^{L?}$i^H *dark*, ^{n}zí$^{L?}$i^M *to enter*, sí^{M}vi^M *to blow*, ne$^{L?}$í^{M}vi^L *people*, lé^M?e^M *rooster*, lí^{M}tu^H *a kid*, ní^{L}nu^M *up-river*, dí^{L}i^L *to singe*, r̃í^{M}i^L *sheep*, vá^{M}ve^{M}řu^H *apron*, ^{m}bá^{M}r̃u^M *bridge (of the nose)*. Both /ř/ and /r̃/ are rare; for the most part, they occur in loan words.

The alveopalatals /č, ^{n}ǰ, š, ñ, y/ contrast as follows: čí^M?i^M *to plant*, ^{n}ǰi^{M}či^M *green bean*, ší^M?i^M *young locust*, ñá$^{L?}$ma^L *spongy tissue*, ñú^{M}ñu^M *marrow*, yú^{M}yu^M *a drop, dew*.

The alveopalatals /č, š/ also contrast with the sequences /sy, ty/ as in: šá^{L}vi^H *to get tired*, sya^{M}ka^M *fish*, čá^{M}a^M *naked*, tyá^{L}a^M *man*.

The contrast between /^{n}ǰ/ and /^{n}dy/ is elusive, since /^{n}ǰ/ occurs preceding /i/ and /e/, whereas /^{n}dy/ does not precede these vowels (ku^{Mn}ǰí^{M}i^L *to shine*, ?i^{M}tu^{Mn}dyá^{M}a^M *to lean back on*). We have considered them to be in contrast because of the analogy with /č/ and /ty/.

The velars /k, k^w, ^{n}g, h/ and glottal stop contrast as follows: ká^{H}a^L *it is excavated*, k^{w}á^{L}a^M *yellow*, há^{M}a^M *yes*, ?á^{M}na^M *who*; ví^{M}ko^L *fiesta*, šá^{M}k^{w}a^M *crooked*, ló^{Mn}go^M *vulture*, k^{w}á$^{L?}$a^M *to give*. The phoneme /h/

is rare. In our data, it occurs only in the words: há^{M}a̧^{M} *yes*, há^{M}a̧^{L} *there, that*, hó^{M}ʔlo^M *carnival*, hú^{M}u̧^{L} *O.K., yes*.

7. Consonant variants

The stop or affricate of the prenasalized stops and affricates /^{m}b, ^{n}d, ^{n}z, ^{n}ǰ, ^{n}g/ is usually lightly voiced, but it may fluctuate to voicelessness: ^{m}bé^{M}lu^H *hat*, ^{n}dó^{L}ʔo^M *adobe*, ^{n}zí^{H}ku^M *sewing*, ^{n}ǰé^{M}ʔle^M *cucumber*, ló^{Mn}go^M *vulture*.

All consonants except /ř/ are lengthened when contiguously following a stressed syllable: čé^{M}lu^L [tšé^{M}l·u^L] *calf*, yá^{L}ka^H [žá^{L}k·a^H] *dust*, ʔí^{Hn}du^L [ʔí^{Hn}·tu^L] *where*, pé^{Mn}či^L [pé^{Mn}·tši^L] *orphan*.

The voiceless stops /t, k/ may become lenis fricatives with light voicing, and /s/ may become voiced when following word-stress noncontiguously: ší^{M}ka^H[s/z]i^M *the animal walks*, ni^{L}sá^{M}te^L[t/đ]e^M *the boy spits out*, ʔú^{L}i^L[k/g]a^L *two more*. (This allophone of /t/ differs from that of /d/ in that the allophone of /t/ is lenis and dental; the allophone of /d/ is fortis and interdental.)

The voiceless stop /t/ has a nasal release when preceding nasalized vowels: tá^{M}a̧^{M} [tná^{M}a̧^{M}] *tomorrow*.

The semiconsonant /y/ varies from very light to heavy friction when it is initial in a syllable, but when it contiguously follows a consonant, it is resonant: [y/ž]á^{M}a^M *song*, vá^M[y·/ž·]a^M *squash flower*, tyá^{L}a^M *man*.

8. Vowel contrasts

There are five oral and five nasal vowels: /i, e, a, o, u, i̧, ȩ, a̧, o̧, u̧/. They contrast as follows: ʔí^{M}i^M *husband*, ʔí^{M}i^L *skin*, ^{n}dú^{M}se^H *I am bad*, ku^{M}dú^{M}sȩ^{H} *I am lazy*, k^{w}á^{L}ʔa^M *to give*, k^{w}á̧^{L}ʔa̧^{L} *going*, ^{n}dí^{M}sa^M *true*, ^{n}dí^{L}sa̧^{L} *sandals*, ka^{Mn}dí^{H}so^H *you sing. fam. believe*, ku^{M}dú^{M}so̧^{M} *you sing. fam. are lazy*, sá^{L}ʔu^H *polite*, sá̧^{L}ʔu̧^{L} *fifteen*, dé^{L}ʔe^M *son*, dí^{M}ʔi^M *mother*, dó^{L}o^L *blanket*, dú^{L}u^L *to whistle*, kó^{L}ʔi^H *my plate*, kú^{M}ʔi^M *to be sick*.

There is also a contrast between a single vowel and a sequence of two, and even three like vowels: dá^{M}na^M *bad, mean*, dá^{M}ná^{H}a^L *to pay back*, kú^{M}ʔi^M *to be sick*, ku^{M}ʔí^{M}i^L *to be baptized*, ku^{M}ʔí^{H}i^{L}i^H *I am being baptized*, ʔí^{M}ʔi^H *sweat bath house*, ʔi^{M}ʔí^{M}i^M *one by one*, vé^{L}e^M *heavy*, mí^{M}i^{M}ve^H *it (baby)*, nú^{L}u^L *eye, face*, kó^{L}o^L *snake*.

9. Vowel variants

A vowel with word-stress is especially long when contiguous to a vowel without word-stress. That is, a cluster of vowels, the first of which is stressed, is considerably longer than a cluster, the first of which is nonstressed. For example, in the following words, the vowel clusters in kuᴹʔíᴴiᴸ *being baptized* and ⁿdéᴸaᴸ *will flow out* are considerably longer than the clusters in kúᴸʔiᴴiᴸ *I hurt* and táᴸʔⁿdeᴸaᴸ *it will be cut*.

A vowel is especially short when part of a sequence of three or four vowels, none of them with word-stress: díᴹkoᴴeᴴaᴸ *I'm selling it*, šíᴴkọᴸ ịᴸaᴴ *you fam. ask for it.*

The vowel /i/ may become voiceless, or it may actualize as a part of a long [š] when the sequence /ši/ occurs preword-stress: šiᴸkʷéᴹʔeᴹ [š·kʷéᴹʔ·eᴹ /šIKʷéᴹʔ·eᴹ] *worthless.*

There is no contrast of a nasal versus an oral vowel following /m, n/ or /ṇ/. A single vowel in that environment may or may not be nasalized. A sequence of two vowels following a nasal consonant is usually heavily nasalized: niᴹiᴸ [niᴹiᴸ] *corn on the cob.* Since there is no contrast, we have chosen to write them as oral vowels.

Word-final nasalized vowels are optionally followed by a lenis velar closure: ʔiᴸ[iᴸ/inᴸ] *nine*, kuᴹduᴹs[eᴴ/e ᴴ] *I am lazy*, kaᴸ[aᴹ/a ᴹ] *to get accustomed to*, cuᴹ[uᴹ/u ᴹ] *work.*

When following /k/, a word-final /i/ may actualize as a syllabic velar nasal: ʔiᴹkiᴸ [ʔiᴹk·iᴸ/ʔiᴹk· ᴸ] *squash.*

10. Distribution of phonemes

10.1. There are certain restrictions in the distribution of consonants in relation to vowels.

Except that a nasalized vowel may follow /d/, nasalized vowels do not follow voiced consonants: dáᴸʔạᴸ *language.*

Nasal vowels follow any voiceless consonant: káᴸkạᴸ *to ask*, šíᴴkẹᴸ *I am asking*, sáᴸʔạᴸ *went and returned*, šíᴹiᴴ *buying*, šáᴹạᴹ *place*, číᴹʔạᴹ *curse.*

The distribution of the alveopalatal consonants /č, y, ñ, ⁿǰ/ and the dental /ⁿz/ is nonsymmetrical in relation to a contiguously following /i/.

The alveopalatal consonants /ñ/ and /y/ only rarely precede /i/:

kú^{M}ʔñi^H *I irrigate*, kú^{M}yi^H *I am industrious*, ñá^{M}a^L *dark (as at night)*, yá^{M}a^M *song*.

But for the one word, ⁿǰé^{M}ʔle^M *wild cucumber*, in our data, /ⁿǰ/ occurs only before /i/: ⁿǰí^{M}či^M *green bean*; /ⁿz/ occurs only before /i/: ⁿzí^{L}ku^M *to sew*; /č/ usually occurs before /i/, but it also occurs before other vowels: čá^{M}a^M *naked*, čá^{L}ʔma^L *to be crushed*, čé^{M}le^H *scissors*, čé^{M}lu^L *calf*, čó^{L}ʔo^L *to be cooked*, čú^{M}u̧^{M} *job*, čú^{M}ʔu̧^{M} *to comb*.

10.2. Consonant clusters of two consonants are composed of: (1) /ʔ/ followed by a voiced consonant, (2) a consonant followed by /y/, (3) /st/.

In our data, there is one consonant cluster of three consonants, /ʔⁿdy/: ví^{L}ʔⁿdya^L *prickly pear*, dí^{L}ʔⁿdya^H *stingy*.

A consonant cluster in which the first consonant is a glottal stop occurs only stem-medial. The second consonant may be any voiced consonant but /d/: ká^{M}ʔvi^M *to read*, dá^{M}ʔma^L *sheet*, vá^{L}ʔna^H *sleep*, dá^{L}ʔⁿde^L *thick coen cake*, ᵐbé^{H}ʔla^L *big*, r̃ú^{M}ʔᵐbu^L *type of bird*, r̃ó^{L}ʔⁿgo^L *joint*, kú^{M}ʔyu^L *little owl*, kú^{M}ʔñu^M *to irrigate*, ko^{L}yá^{L}ʔⁿǰi^L *rainbow*, ká^{M}ʔⁿzi^M *to explode*.

There are the following sequences of consonant plus /y/: /ty, dy, ⁿdy, sy, ⁿzy, my/: tyá^{M}ku^M *to hear*, dyé^{M}ʔe^M *rust*, ⁿdyá^{M}a^H *is worth*, syá^{M}ka^M *fish*, ⁿzyó^{M}ʔo^H *you pl. fam.*, si^{L}myá^{M}ʔa^L *Satan*.

Consonant clusters with the sequence /st/ occur in the three morphemes stó^{M}ʔo^M *owner, lord*, stá̧^{L}ʔa̧^{H} *one another*, the morpheme sta̧^{H}a̧^{L} *also* as in yú^{L}ʔu^{L}sta̧^{H}a̧^{L} *I also*.

10.3. Vowel clusters may be composed either of geminate vowels or of diverse vowels: si^{L}kí^{L}i^H *bottle*, ké^{M}e^M *will come out of*, ká^{L}a^M *iron*, kó^{L}o^L *snake*, kú^{M}u^M *will happen*, ší̧^{M}i̧^{H} *buying*, ká̧^{L}a̧^{M} *to become accustomed to*, ñé^{M}e^M *to skin*, ñú^{M}u^M *town*, ká^{M}i^L *will cough*, dí^{L}a^M *skirt*, ʔí^{M}u^M *empty*, ⁿdé^{L}a^L *mesquite tree pod*, té^{M}i^M *burro saddle*, ⁿdú^{L}a^L *will crack*, ⁿdú^{M}i^M *daytime*, tú^{M}i^M *will sting*, yú^{M}e^H *my father*, kʷí̧^{M}u̧^{M} *swelling*.

There are clusters of three vowels: ⁿdú^{H}i^{L}a^L *both of them*, tú^{H}i^{M}a^L *she appears*, ší̧^{H}u̧^{M}a̧^{M} *it swells up*, ⁿzyá^{M}a^{H}i^L *I arrive*, kʷí̧^{M}u̧^{M}a̧^{H} *you sing. fam. will buy it*, ku^{M}ʔí̧^{H}i̧^{L}i̧^{H} *I am baptized*, dí^{M}ko^{H}e^{H}a^L *I am selling it*, da^{M}ná^{H}u^{L}a^H *you sing. fam. pay her*, ší̧^{H}ko̧^{L}u̧^{L}a̧^{H} *you sing. fam. ask for it*.

Occasionally there is a cluster of four vowels: da^{M}dá^{H}a^{L}i^{H}a^L *I heat it*, ^{n}zí^{M}da^H ví^{H}i^{M}i^{H}a^L *I repair it*, da^{M}ku^{H}ʔí^{U}i^{L}i^{H}a^M *I baptize her*.

11. Syllable

A syllable has one vowel as a nucleus. The predominant syllable type is CV, but a nucleus may also be preceded by two or three consonants: tá^{M}ta^M *seed*, stó^{M}ʔo^M *owner*, ví^{M}ʔ^{n}dya^L *prickly pear*.

The syllable type V does not occur word initially. It follows a syllable with a consonantal onset (té^{M}i^M *saddle*) or another syllable of type V (k^{w}í^{M}u̧^{M}a̧^{H} *you sing. fam. will buy it*).

An utterance may be segmented into syllables: (1) between a vowel and following consonant, lú^{M}su^M *fox*, ^{n}dá^{L}ʔvi^H *poor*, tó^{H}ʔo^L *stranger*, ší^{H}tya^L *spreading*; (2) between vowels which are of different quality, dí^{L}a^M *skirt*, ^{n}dú^{M}i^M *daytime*; (3) between a sequence of two different tones, yá^{L}a̧^{H} *tongue*, ší^{M}i̧^{H} *buying*, ku^{M}ʔí̧^{H}i^{L}i^H *I am being baptized*; (4) in the middle of a phonetically long stressed vocoid, tí^{M}i^M *little*, kó^{L}o^L *snake*.

12. Stress

There are two types of stress: word-stress and phrase-stress.

Each phonological word has a syllable with word-stress. Any consonant, except /ř/ which contiguously follows a syllable with word-stress may be lengthened. The consonant is usually lengthened when part of a prepause word; it is frequently not lengthened when not part of a prepause word. The lengthened consonant is more prominent in slow speech than it is in fast speech: dí^{M}vi^M [dí^{M}v·i^M] *that very one*, tú^{M}tu^M [tú^{M}t·u^M] *paper*, lú^{M}su^M [lú^{M}s·u^M] *fox*, ká^{M}ʔ^{n}zi^M [ká^{M}ʔ·^{n}dzi^M] *to explode*, ló^{Mn}go^M [ló^{Mn}·go^M] *vulture*.

If the syllable with word-stress is followed by a type V syllable, or by a syllable beginning with /ř/, then the vowel of the stressed syllable is lengthened: dí^{L}a^M [dí·^{L}a^M] *skirt*, ʔó^{M}řa^H [ʔó·^{M}řa^H] *sun*. Word-stress never occurs on the last syllable of a word.

There is a correlation between the phonological and grammatical hierarchies in that in two-syllable stems, it is the stem-medial consonant which is long, the first syllable which has word-stress. Because morphemes may precede and/or follow the stem, stress placement is not predictable in a phonological word.

Examples with contrastive stress placement: dá^{M}ka^{M}ni^H *you mix*, da^{M}ká^{M}ni^H *I cause to spring forth*; ná^{M}na^{M}ni^H *you go up*, na^{M}ná^{M}ni^H *when I go up*; ku^{M}ní^{M}ni^M *I will listen*, kú^{M}ni^{L}ni^H *you will want*; ke^{M}tá^{M}tu^{L}te^M *the boy will rest*, ^{n}dá^{M}ta^{M}si^{H}a^U *the animal tears it*.

Every utterance has at least two syllables, and the syllable which precedes pause has phrase-stress. Phrase-stress has about the same intensity as word-stress; therefore, when a two-syllable word is said in isolation, the two syllables have about equal intensity, since the first syllable has word-stress and the second has phrase-stress. (In the following examples, we have marked phrase-stress with ^.) ^{n}dú^{M}kû^M *create*, tá^{M}tâ^M *seed*, tú^{M}tû^M *paper*.

When a word with more than two syllables occurs prepause, it will have nonstress, word-stress, and phrase-stress: ká^{M}ni^{H}ne^{L}sî^M *they beat the animal*, či^{M}ká^{M}ni^{M}ne^{L}nû^M *they will set up the wood thing*, ni^{L}sí^{M}sâ^M *hardened*, ni^{L}ká̜^{L}?a̜^{L}ne^{L}ši^L^{n}dâ^L *they spoke to us*, k^{w}á̜^{L}?i̜^{L} ^{n}dú^{M}ki^H si^L?í̜^{M}na^{L}šî^M *I'm going to look for my dog*, dá^{Mn}du^M ?í̜^{H}ku^H ni^{L}ší̜^{L}?i̜^{L}nâ^L *then yesterday he died*.

Summer Institute of Linguistics

DOWNSTEPPING TERRACE TONE IN COATZOSPAN MIXTEC

Eunice V. PIKE and Priscilla SMALL

1. Introduction

There are four especially interesting features of the Coatzospan dialect[1] of Mixtec: (1) Within the tonal system there is a process phoneme such that when certain classes of words are in sequence, there is downstepping terrace tone. (2) The process phoneme is the key to the tone sandhi changes. That is, changes which appeared to be arbitrary are in fact regular once the presence of the process phoneme is recognized. (3) There are contrastive nuclei of the phonological word-phrase: those marked by glottal stop, and those marked by a lengthened vowel. The distribution of both consonants and vowels varies in accordance with these contrastive nuclei. (4) There are oral word-phrases versus nasal word-phrases. The nasal word-phrase always has the component of second person singular familiar, and the extent of the nasalization within the word-phrase is predictable.

[1] Coatzospan Mixtec is spoken by roughly 2,000 Mixtec Indians living in the municipality of San Juan Coatzospan in the district of Teotitlán del Camino in northern Oaxaca, Mexico. The municipality is comprised of the head town, San Juan Coatzospan, plus three surrounding villages: San Isidro Coatzospan, Agua Español and Loma de la Plaza, all within a three mile radius. There is a sharp linguistic division between Coatzospan and the surrounding towns, which speak dialects of Mazatec and Cuicatec. The nearest Mixtec town, Santa Ana Cuahtemoc, is separated from Coatzospan by a river canyon and a day's journey on foot.

The principal informant used for this analysis was 13-year-old Joaquin Mancera Castillo. Additional help was given by 23-year-old Dolores Acosta Campos. For the most part, Priscilla Small is responsible for the analysis of the segmental phonemes and for the vocabulary. Eunice V. Pike is responsible for the tone analysis and the presentation of the material.

2. Downstepping terrace tone

In all dialects of Mixtec thus far described, there have been tones
that contrast in a paradigmatic situation. The Coatzospan dialect of
Mixtec, however, has, in addition to the usual high versus low tones, a
tone which is a process phoneme[2]. The type of system of which this
process phoneme is a part has been called "terrace tone" and has usually
been reported in Africa (Welmers, 1959; Schachter, 1961; and Stewart,
1964).

This process phoneme has no specific phonetic content, but it exerts
a lowering influence on a following high tone and causes a change of
key in the sequence between that point and pause, or between that
point and another process phoneme. This lowering influence and subsequent change of key may occur more than once within the same pause
group, but even though there is a change of key, the lowered high continues to function as high, since a high following it is level with it and a
contrast between the high and low tone is still maintained.

It is the lowering influence of the process phoneme (written in this
paper as /!/) which causes the downstepping terrace tone[3].

Because the process phoneme causes a high tone to lower, a contrast
does, in fact, occur between three levels of tone: high, lowered high,
and low. This three-way contrast never occurs postpause, however, nor
following a low tone, since it occurs only as a result of a preceding /!/.
The contrast is best seen in a sequence of at least three morphemes,
since the process phoneme is recognizable only when morphemes occur
in sequence. One of the morphemes should be an unchanging frame.

Contrast between the high, lowered high, and low can be demonstrated in the following examples. In examples (1b), (2b), (3b), (4b)
and (5b), the high tone following the process phoneme /!/ has been
lowered, producing the contrast between high, lowered high, and low.

---

[2] We have based our theory of the process phoneme on that set forth by K. Pike (1967 and
1970, pp. 93–98).

[3] Less than a hundred miles away, upstepping terrace tone occurs in the Acatlán dialect of
Mixtec (see ch. 7, of this volume). The discription of that dialect, however, has a different theoretical base. Instead of a process phoneme, a step-up tone is described as always higher than
any contiguously preceding syllable, and as having extremely limited distribution – it occurs
only following high or another step-up tone.
    Perhaps Mixtec of Santa María Peñoles is a second dialect with downstepping terrace tone.
John Daly's description of it (manuscript in preparation) uses the transformational model.

In this contrastive set there is contrast of three tones on the next to the last syllable:

(1a) kú?cį̀ ka?nį̀-ð⁴ 'we will kill a pig'
(1b) kú?cį̀ lú?!kú-kð 'our crazy pig'
(1c) kú?cį̀ kú?šì-ð 'we will bury a pig'

In sets (2) and (3) note the contrast of three tones on the third from the last syllable:

(2a) kú?cį̀ kú?šì-ð 'we will bury a pig'
(2b) tú?tú! kú?šì-ð 'we will bury paper'
(2c) tú?tú kà?mį̀-ð 'we will burn paper'
(3a) díó-ñą̀ cá?kà-kð 'they want our fish'
(3b) díó-kó! cá?kà-kð 'I want our fish'
(3c) díó-kó gà?cì-kð 'I want our blanket'

In the following two sets the last two syllables are: high-high, mid-mid, low-low.

(4a) cùmę̀ vį̀dį́ ká?mį́ 'burn sweet candles'
(4b) cùmę̀ kʷì?šį́! kí?nį́! 'tie up white candles'
(4c) cùmę̀ kʷì?šį́ kà?mì̀ 'burn white candles'
(5a) ñą́túvì dù?nų́ dá?ví! 'there are no poor shirts'
(5b) ñą́túvì tù?tú! vį́dį́ 'there is no sweet paper'
(5c) ñą́túvì tù?tú cùdè 'there is no ragged paper'

The following sentences show how the process phoneme, together with tone sandhi (see 5), cause sentences to have various contours:

Level pitch: díó-ñą̀ kú?cį̀ kánį́ 'They want a long pig.'
One downstep: díó-kó! kú?cį̀ kánį́ 'I want a long pig.'
Two downsteps: díó-kó! tú?tú! lú?kú 'I want crazy paper.'
Three downsteps: díó-kó! tú?tú! ví?šį́! lú?kú 'I want crazy cold paper.'
Downstep after the first word only: díó-kó! dú?nų́ kánį́ 'I want a long shirt.'
A drop from high to low: díó-kó! tú?tú kànį̀ 'I want a long paper.'
The last three words with low tone: díó-kó šì?kɨ̀ kànį̀ kà?nų̀ 'I want a big long squash.'
Mostly high: dì?kó-ñą́ šì?kɨ̀ kánį́ ká?nų́ 'They ground a big long squash.'
Low in the center: díó-kó gà?cì dívú 'I want an ancient blanket.'
Low, high, low: gà?cì kánį́ kú?šì-ñą̀ 'They will bury a long blanket.'
Couplet-medial downstep: lú?kú tú?!tú! díó-kó! 'The paper I want is crazy.'

---

⁴ The hyphen separates the nucleus of the phonological word-phrase from the margin (see 5).

Two couplet-medial downsteps: lú?kú kú?!cį dí!ó-kó! 'The pig I want is crazy.'

Alternating tones: kɨmį cá?kà n̨ąnɨ́ kú?s̨ì-ŏ 'We will bury four long fish.'

In a sequence in which the high tones have been lowered once or twice, the pitch interval between a high-high and a low-low is narrow and difficult to hear when prepause. Sometimes it is easier to determine the emic tone by listening for relaxed downdrift, indicating emic low-low (see 4), versus sustained pitch, indicating emic high-high:

ká?dé! tú?tú kànį   'cut long paper' vs.

ká?dé! ɖú?nų́ !dívú   'cut an ancient shirt';

ká?dé s̨ɨ̃?kɨ̨ kànį   'cut a long squash' vs.

ká?dé! s̨ɨ́?kɨ̨ dívú   'cut an ancient squash'.

The basic form of certain morphemes includes a final /!/; for example: tú?tú! 'paper', ñų́ų́! 'town', kʷì?s̨į! 'white'.

The basic form of certain couplets includes an initial /!/; for example: !s̨té?nų 'tom turkey', !rkú?ú 'deer', !dívú 'ancient'. (Most of the words which have an initial /!/ appear to be a fusion of three or more syllables into two. For example, !s̨té?nų 'tom turkey' is perhaps derived from cų́ų̃ 'turkey' + té?nų 'male', !rkú?ú 'deer' from íɖú! 'horse' + kù?ú! 'wild', and !dívú 'ancient' from the three-syllable Spanish word: antiguo.)

A few morphemes both begin and end with /!/; for example: !skʷĩdú! 'spotted', !î?cí! 'dry'.

A process phoneme occurs couplet-medially only when a morpheme of class ˊˊ or !ˊˊ precedes a morpheme of class ˊˊ or ˊˊ! (see 5.1, rule 12e): kú?cį vį́!ɖį́ 'a sweet (candy) pig'.

Some enclitic variants also end with /!/: gà?cì-kó! kú?s̨ì 'bury my blanket'.

In order to know that a couplet has an initial process phoneme, we must know that it is lowered when following a high tone. Likewise, in order to know that a couplet, or enclitic, has a final process phoneme, we must know that a high tone is lowered when following it.

The process phoneme has phonetic actualization only when occurring between two high tones. We have written it, however, prepause and postpause, since the tone sandhi rules are more apparent to the reader when he is aware of the process phoneme potential. Therefore, when a couplet-initial or couplet-final /!/ is written on a variant contiguous to pause, we are asserting that we know how that couplet would affect or be affected by a preceding or following high tone.

3. Tone contrasts

In Coatzospan Mixtec there are tones (high and low, and tone clusters high-low and low-high) which are phonemes of relation, that is, they are recognizable by paradigmatic contrast within a frame. In addition tò these, there is the process phoneme, /!/, which is recognizable only in sequence (see 2).

Contrast between high and low tone can be seen in the following examples: tú?tú-kǒ 'our paper', cà?ká-kǒ 'our fish'; šɨ?kɨ-kǒ 'our squash', dú?nừ-kǒ 'our shirt'.

Contrast between high, low, and high-low tone cluster occurs: cà?ká! víˀsɨ-kò 'my cold fish', cà?ká dàˀví-kò 'my poor fish', cà?ká! skʷídú-kò 'my spotted fish'.

Contrast between high, low, and low-high cluster occurs: cà?ká dà?ví! 'poor fish', cà?ká kànì 'long fish', cà?ká vìdě 'wet fish'.

The low-high tone cluster occurs only when preceding pause: gàˀcǐ 'blanket', but gàˀcì kànɨ 'long blanket'; whereas the high-low tone cluster occurs only in the first syllable of a couplet: šɨ?kɨ skʷîdú kànɨ 'a long spotted squash', dú?nú vîˀtá-kò 'my soft shirt'.

In isolation a couplet may have one of the following tone patterns: ´´, ` ´, ` `, ´˘ ˇ˘, as in: šúˀvé 'thread', èˀmɨ 'burned', dàˀmà 'skirt', váˀǎ 'good', cùmě 'candle'.

The pattern ´` may occur when following ´, as in: !dívú víˀì 'the house is ancient' (see 5.1, chart 1, 7D).

When those with initial or final /!/ are included, five more patterns are added: ´´!, !´´, !´´!, `´!, !´`!. For example: ídú! 'horse', !skʷílú 'buzzard', !skʷíí! 'pinto', kùnú! 'deep', !îˀcí! 'dry'.

The pattern !´` and !´˘ may occur when following ´, as in: !dívú !kɨdɨ 'the pot is ancient', šúˀvé !éˀmɨ '(someone) burned thread'.

The following examples show tone contrast on otherwise homophonous words: làà 'flower', làá! 'bird'; láá-kó! 'my flower', làà-kǒ 'our flower', làá-kò 'my bird', làá-kǒ 'our bird'; ñúˀú 'fire', ñúˀú! 'earth'; víɖɨ 'sweet' !víɖí! 'warm'; tàˀšì 'give', tàˀší 'gave'; nèˀšɨ-ñá! 'they will sweep', nèˀšɨ ñá! 'they swept'; kóˀó-tú! 'she will drink', kóˀò-tú! 'her dish'.

4. Tone variants

The highest allotone of high which occurs is the first high between
lows, or the first high after a sequence of lows: cà^ʔká-kò 'my fish',
cà^ʔká kànɪ̧ 'long fish', gà^ʔcì-kó! 'my blanket', cùmɛ̧̀ tá^ʔšì '(someone)
gave candles', gà^ʔcì-kŏ 'our blanket'.

An allotone not quite as high occurs between a high and a low. That
is, in tú^ʔtú-kò 'my paper' and tú^ʔtú kànɪ̧ 'long paper', the second syllable is higher than the first, but not as high as ká in cà^ʔká-kò 'my fish'.
The last syllable of a sequence low-low-high, for example: gà^ʔcì-kó! 'my
blanket', is higher than the last syllable of the sequence high-low-high:
đú^ʔnṳ̀-kó! 'my shirt'. The low-high cluster glides to a higher pitch in
gà^ʔcì-kŏ 'our blanket' than it does in đú^ʔnṳ̀-kŏ 'our shirt'.

High tone, when in the first syllable of a nonglottalized couplet in
the nucleus of a word-phrase (see 6), has a downgliding allotone when
preceding low or a lowered high. The second from the last syllable has a
downglide in each of the following examples: ñá̧ñá̧ 'lion', kú^ʔcɪ̧ šú!šú
'glass pig', cùmɛ̧̀ íđò '(someone) carried candles'. This glide is not as deep
nor as long as the emic high-low glide which actualizes the high-low tone
cluster: !vɪ̧đɪ̧! 'warm'. The downglide does not occur when high tone
precedes low between word-phrases: nɛ̧̀^ʔšɪ̧ vì^ʔì 'to sweep the house', or
between the nucleus and the margin: cà^ʔká-ñá̧ 'their fish'.

The first syllable of the glottalized couplet has an interrupted vowel.
When that first syllable has high tone while the second has low tone or
a lowered high tone, the vocoid following the glottal stop is lower than
that preceding it: ví^ʔšɪ̧ 'cold', kú^ʔcɪ̧ lú^ʔ!kú 'crazy pig'. The vocoid following the glottal stop is not as low, however, as the vocoid which oc-
curs as part of the high-low tone cluster: đú^ʔnú̧ vɪ̧^ʔtá! 'soft shirt'.

A low tone has a slight downglide when preceding a voiced consonant
while in the first syllable of a prepause couplet: gà^ʔcì vìđĕ 'wet blanket',
kɨ̵mɪ̧̀ šǎvɪ̵ 'four holes', cùmɛ̧̀ kànɪ̧ 'long candle'.

If a prepause syllable has low tone and a voiceless consonant, it may
fluctuate to voicelessness, especially after high: ká^ʔnɪ̧ tṳ̀ 'she will kill',
tú^ʔtú-kò 'my paper'.

There is a slight downdrift in a sequence of low tones occurring prepause: kú^ʔšì-tú̧ šɨ̵^ʔkɨ̵ kànɪ̧ 'she will bury (plant) a long squash'.

In isolation a sequence of highs with no contrasting low tone is lowered, whereas a sequence of low tones with no contrasting highs is raised.
Therefore in isolation the two sequences, díó-ñá̧ tú^ʔtú! 'they want paper'
and šɨ̵^ʔkɨ̵ kànɪ̧ 'a long squash', have approximately the same pitch.

Perhaps it could be said that all sentences start on approximately the same pitch and that the emic tones of the initial syllables are indeterminate until a contrasting tone occurs. That is, the etic pitch of ší²kɨ 'squash' is perceptually the same in the following two utterances: ší²kɨ vɨ́dɨ́-kò 'my sweet squash' versus ši²kɨ vɨdè-kó! 'my wet squash'. (The morpheme ší²kɨ 'squash' was raised in the first utterance by regressive perturbation (3J, see rule 13).) If, however, the two sentences are repeated several times, and the informant knows that the contrastive utterances are being alternated, he may start one lower than the other:

ši²kɨ kànɨ kà²mɨ-ñà̀   'they will burn a long squash'
ší²kɨ kánɨ ká²mɨ-tʉ́!   'she will burn a long squash'.

5. Tone sandhi

Tone sandhi is so extensive that three classes or subclasses of couplets each have five sets of variants differentiated by the tone-process phoneme pattern, and eight other classes or subclasses each have three or four sets of variants differentiated by the tone-process phoneme pattern.

The classes with their variants are:

Class ` `: ` `, ` ´, ´ ´, ´ ` (noun), ´ ˅ (noun or adjective)
Class ` ˅: ˅ ˅, ` , ` `, ´ ˅, ´ ´! (verb), ´ ´ (noun or adjective)
Class ´ `: ´ `, ` ´, ´ ˅
Class ´ ´: ´ ´, ´!´, ` ´
  Subclass of ´ ´: ´ ´, ´ ˅, ´!´, ` ´, ´ `
Class ´ ´!: ´ ´!, ` ´!, ´!´! (noun)
  Subclass of ´ ´!: ´ ´!, ´ ˅, ` ´!, ´ ` (adjective)
Class !´ ´: !´ ´
  Subclass of !´ ´: !´ ´, ´ ˅, ´ `
Class !´ `: !´ `, ` ´, ` `
Class !´ ˅: !´ ˅, ` ´!, !´ `
Class ` ´!: ` ´!, ´ ´!, ^ ´!, ` `
Class !^ ´!: !^ ´!, !` `
Class !´ ´!: !´ ´!

5.1. *Tone sandhi between couplets*

In order to predict the tone sandhi between two couplets[5], it is nec-

---

[5] For footnote, see next page.

essary to know five things[6]: (1) the presence versus absence of a process phoneme in the isolation variant and the basic form; (2) the tones of the basic form of the second couplet, that is, the tones which occur between /!/ and pause; (3) the tones of the first couplet as it occurs in isolation, that is, the tones of the isolation variant; (4) the grammatical category (noun, adjective or verb) of the second couplet; (5) the grammatical category (noun, adjective or verb) of the first couplet if the isolation variant is ˆˇ.

The tones of the basic form of a couplet are those which occur between /!/ and pause. That is, it is the post /!/ variant. The basic form whose first tone is high has an initial /!/ if it is lowered after class ˊˊ (or when following any high tone). For example: !dívú !kídɨ 'the pot is ancient'. The couplet !kídɨ 'pot' has an initial /!/ because it is lowered after !dívú 'ancient'.

A basic form whose last tone is high is followed by /!/ if class ˊˊ (or any morpheme with an initial high tone) is lowered when following it. For example: túʔtú! lúʔkú 'crazy paper'. The couplet túʔtú! 'paper' has a final /!/ because lúʔkú 'crazy' is lowered when following it.

A class of morphemes consists of those morphemes which have the same tone-process phoneme pattern when between /!/ and pause. Most classes have the same variant when in isolation as they do when between /!/ and pause. Three classes, however, have an isolation variant which differs from that of the post /!/ variant. They are (the post /!/ variant is listed first): ˊˋ ~ ˊˋ, !ˊˇ ~ ˋˊ!, !ˊˋ ~ ˋˊ.

Three classes are subdivided since some members of the class have the same variant when post /!/ as when in isolation whereas some members of that same class have ˆˇ as an isolation variant. The classes which are subdivided are: !ˊˊ, ˊˊ! and ˊˊ.

There is a restriction in the grammatical categories which occur in the various tone classes. All three categories occur with ˋˇ and ˋˋ; only verbs occur with ˊˋ; only past tense verbs occur with !ˊˋ; only nouns occur with !ˊˇ; only adjectives occur with !ˆˊ!; only adjectives occur with the subclass of ˊˊ! whose isolation variant is ˊˇ, whereas nouns and verbs occur with the other subclass of ˊˊ!; verbs and adjectives occur

---

[5] Tone sandhi changes which occur between proclitics or prefixes and a following couplet need further study and have not been described in this paper.

[6] For the description of a Mixtec dialect in which the tone sandhi changes are in relation to a word-final glottal stop, see Pankratz and Pike, 1967: 295–298.

with ⹁′!; nouns and adjectives occur with both subclasses of ′′ ; nouns occur with the subclass of !′′ which has the isolation variant ′ˇ, while nouns and adjectives occur with the other subclass.

The tone sandhi changes which occur between classes of couplets is shown on chart 1, together with the interaction between the process phoneme and the tones. Phrase-final and phrase-initial process phonemes have been written on the chart even though a sequence of tones ending in /!/ and the same sequence of tones without a final /!/ are etically the same. We have included the phrase-final and phrase-initial process phonemes since occasionally a couplet with a final /!/ is changed in a different way than a couplet without a final /!/ would be in that environment (see 2E versus 3D, and 2K versus 3J).

The row across the top of chart 1 includes all of the basic forms (the post /!/ variant)[7] of all classes of couplets, but five classes occur under the column "Initial !". They are: !′′, !′′!, !ˆ′!, !′ˇ, !′ˋ.

The column at the left consists, not only of the isolation variants, but also of those which may occur initial and those which may occur non-initial in a sequence.

The row "Final ′!" includes classes: ′′!, ⹁′!, !ˆ′!, !′′!. It also includes a nonbasic variant ′!′!, and an enclitic variant with ′! could also be included here.

The row "Final ′" includes classes ′′, !′′. It also includes their nonbasic variants ′!′ and ⹁′, (but not the ⹁′ or ′′ variants of class ⹁⹁; see rule 16).

The only sequences of two couplets not included on the chart are those in which classes ⹁ˇ or ⹁′! would follow ⹁⹁ (7B, 7G, 7H, 7I, see rule 15), and those in which classes ⹁⹁, ′′, or ′′! would follow ′′ (7C) or ⹁′ (7B, 7G, 7H, 7I) which are variants of class ⹁⹁ (see rule 16).

Rules are given below describing the tone sandhi changes between two couplets. Each rule is in cross reference to a column, row or box in chart 1. Examples demonstrating the rules are listed together in one section, and they are cross-referenced both to the rule involved and the chart. For the sake of simplicity, the same morphemes have been used again and again in the examples but we have added additional words grouped by their classes. A reader may change the examples by substi-

---

[7] There is one word: !lúʔdǐ 'small', which has alternating post /!/ variants: ′′ ~ ′ˇ. Following ′ there are three variants: ′′ ~ ′ˇ ~ !′ˇ: kúʔcį lúʔdí ~ kúʔcį lúʔdǐ ~ kúʔcį !lúʔdǐ 'small pig'.

Chart 1
Tone sandhi between couplets.

	Post /!/ variant							
	Initial		noun, adj.	verb	verb, adj.	noun, adj.	verb	
Any variant:	ˈˇ	ˇˈ	ˈˇ	ˈˇ	ˈˈˇ	ˋ	ˇˋ	A
Final ˈ!	ˇˈ	ˈˈ	ˈˈ	ˈˇ	ˈˇ	ˈˈ	ˈˈ	B
noun !ˈˇ ~ ˈˇ ˇ	ˈˇ	ˈˇ	!ˈˇ	!ˈˇ	!ˈˇ	!ˈˇ	!ˈˈˇ	C
		verb ˈˇˈ!	noun, adj. ˈˇ ˈˈ!	verb ˈˇ ˈˇ	verb, adj. ˈˇ ˈˈˇ/ˇ	verb ˈˇ ˈˈˈ/ˇˇ	verb, adj. ˈˇ ˈˈˇ	D
Final ˈ	ˈ !ˈ	noun ˈˇ ˈˈ!	noun, adj. ˈˇ ˈˈ!			noun, adj. ˈˇ ˈˈˈ/ˇ	noun ˈˇ ˈˈˇ	E
(nonclass ˈˈ)		adj. ˈˇ ˇ			adj. ˈˇ ˈˈ!	noun, adj. ˈˇ ˈˈˇ	noun, adj. ˈˇ ˈˈˇ	F
noun ˋ ˇ	ˋˇ	ˋˇ ˈˈ!	ˋˇ	ˈˇ ˈˇ	verb ˋˇ ˈˈ!	verb ˋˇ ˈˈˇ	verb ˋˇ ˈˇ	G
ˋ ˇ	ˋˇ	ˋˇ ˈˈ!	ˋˇ	ˋˇ ˈˈˈˈˇ	ˋˇ ˈˈ!	ˋˇ ˈˈˇ	ˋˇ	H
verb. adj, ˈˇ ˇ	ˈˇ	ˈˇ ˈˈ!	ˈˇ	ˈˇ ˈˈˈˇ	ˈˇ ˈˈ!	ˈˇ ˈˇ	ˈˇ	I
ˈˇ ~ ˈˈ	ˈˇ	verb, noun ˈˇ ˈˈ!	ˈˇ	ˈˇ	ˈˇ ˈˈ!	ˈˇ ˈˇ	ˈˇ	J
(class ˈˈ)	ˈˇ	adj. ˈˇ ˈˈˇ	ˈˇ	ˈˇ	ˈˇ	ˈˇ	ˈˇ	K
	1	2	3	4	5	6	7	

tuting any word for any other word of the same class – provided the grammatical categories are the same, of course.

Rule 1. The basic tones of a couplet are those which occur between /!/ and pause (row A).

Rule 2. A process phoneme /!/ is lost when contiguous to ˋ (5A, 6A, 7A, 1B, 1G, 1H, 1I).

Rule 3. The second in a sequence of two contiguous process phonemes is lost (1A).

Rule 4. There is a change to a lower key whenever /!/ is contiguously followed by ˊ (1A, 2A, 3A, 4A, 1D, 2D, 3D).

Rule 5. The tones of any couplet whose basic form includes an initial /!/ remain unchanged when it occurs second in a sequence of two couplets (col. 1).

Rule 6. Basic tones occur when following class !ˊˇ (row B), except that class ˋˋ becomes ˋˊ (7B).

Rule 7. In a sequence of two couplets not separated by /!/, the two middle syllables have like tones (cols. 2–7, rows C–K), except when following class !ˊˇ (see rule 6, row B).

Rule 8. The upgliding tone cluster ˇ occurs only when prepause. When ˇ occurs at the end of the first couplet, it is changed to ˋ (rows B, G, H, I).

Rule 9. All couplets but class ˋˇ, and those beginning with /!/, become ˋˊ when following ˋˋ of class ˋˇ (row I) and when following the sequence ˊˋ (rows G, H) which is a variant of some class other than class !ˊˇ (row B).

Rule 10. When prepause, a class ˋˇ couplet retains its basic tones (col. 6), except that when following a ˊ it alternates from ˊˊ to ˊˇ (see rules 11, 12; 6C, 6D, 6F).

Rule 11. When an adjective or noun whose basic form begins with ˋ (cols. 5, 6, 7) follows a noun of subclass ˊˊ ~ ˊˇ (row F), the first couplet becomes ˊˊ (5F, 6F, 7F) whereas the second couplet, if it is class ˋˇ, alternates between ˊˊ and ˊˇ (6F); if it is class ˋˋ, it becomes ˊˇ (7F). If the second couplet is class ˋˊ! (col. 5), it becomes ˆˊ! (5F).

Rule 12. When the first couplet of a sequence ends with ˊ, it remains unchanged (rows C, D, E). The second couplet changes in accordance with its class (its basic form) and its grammatical category:

(a) Verbs or adjectives, class ˋˊ!, alternate from ˊˊ! to ˆˊ! (5C).

(b) Verbs, class ˋˇ, alternate from ˊˊ! to ˊˇ (6C), whereas nouns and adjectives, class ˋˇ, alternate from ˊˊ to ˊˇ (6D).

(c) Verbs or adjectives, class ``, become `´´` (7C), but a noun, class ``, becomes `´``` (7D).

(d) Nouns, class `´´`!, become `´!´`! (2D), but adjectives become `´``` (2E).

(e) Couplets of class `´´` become `´!´` (3D).

(f) Verbs, class `´´`! and `´``, remain the same (2C, 4C).

Rule 13. When a morpheme of class `` precedes `´`, the `` is changed to `´´` (2J, 3J, 4J), except that when a `` precedes an adjective of class `´´`!, the resultant sequence is `` `` ! (2K). When class `` precedes a ``, there is no change (5J, 6J, 7J).

Rule 14. When !´ follows a couplet with basic ``, first the process phoneme /!/ is lost (rule 2), then the `` is changed to `´´` (rule 13). The result is that `` + `´´` (3J) and `` + !`´´` (1J) are actualized as the same phonetic and phonemic tone sequence.

Rule 15. A couplet of class `` becomes `` ´ (see rule 9) when following any low which is non-class ``, or when following an enclitic which is not class ` (7B, 7G, 7H, 7I). The `` ´ variant of class `` is, however, changed back to `` when it in turn is followed by class `` `` or class `` ´ !: gàʔcǐ 'blanket' + kànį̀ 'long' > gàʔcì kànį́ 'long blanket'; gàʔcì kànį́ + tì̵ʔvǐ 'push' > gàʔcì kànì tì̵ʔvǐ 'push a long blanket'; gàʔcì kànį́ + nè̵ʔší̵! 'sweep' > gàʔcì kànì nè̵ʔší̵! 'sweep a long blanket'.

Rule 16. Class `` becomes `´´` when following the `` ´ or `´´` variants of class `` (but see rule 12(c)); classes `´´` and `´´`! remain the same (but see rule 12(d), (e)): gàʔcǐ 'blanket' + kànį̀ 'long' + kà̵ʔmì̵-ñá̵ 'burn-they' > gàʔcì kànį́ ká̵ʔmí̵-ñá 'they will burn a long blanket'; kúʔcį́ 'pig' + kànì 'long' + kàʔmì̵ ñà̵ 'burn-they' > kúʔcį́ kánį́ ká?mí̵-ñá 'they will burn a long pig'.

Rule 17. The class of verbs !`` has an isolation variant `` ´. When that isolation variant occurs initial in a sequence, it has the same tone changes as a class `` that is preceded by class `` ´ (see rules 2, 14, 15):

è̵ʔmį́ kúʔcį́   '(someone) burned a pig',
è̵ʔmį́ šté̵ʔnų́   '(someone) burned a turkey',
è̵ʔmį̀ gàʔcǐ   '(someone) burned a blanket'.

Rule 18. When class `` follows /!/ while preceding `´`, the `` is raised to the height of the following `´` (rule 13); then the sequence is lowered because of the preceding /!/ (rule 4): tú̵ʔtú! paper' + kànì 'long' + ká̵ʔdé! 'cut' tú̵ʔtú! kánį́ ká̵ʔdé! 'to cut long paper'.

Following is a list of examples. They are cross-referenced to chart 1 and to the rules.

1A	túˀtú!	dívú	'ancient paper'	Rules 1, 3, 4, 5
2A	túˀtú!	túˀtú!	'paper paper'	1, 4
3A	túˀtú!	lúˀkú	'crazy paper'	1, 4
4A	túˀtú!	kúˀšì	'bury paper'	1, 4
5A	túˀtú	dàˀví!	'poor paper'	1, 2
6A	túˀtú	vìdĕ	'wet paper'	1, 2
7A	túˀtú	kànį̀	'long paper'	1, 2
1B	!cáˀkà	dívú	'ancient fish'	5, 6, 8
2B	!cáˀkà	túˀtú!	'paper fish'	6, 8
3B	!cáˀkà	lúˀkú	'crazy fish'	6, 8
4B	!cáˀkà	kúˀšì	'bury fish'	6, 8
5B	!cáˀkà	dàˀví!	'poor fish'	6, 8
6B	!cáˀkà	vìdĕ	'wet fish'	6, 8
7B	!cáˀkà	kànį́	'long fish'	6, 8, 15
1D	kúˀcį́	!dívú	'ancient pig'	5
2C	kúˀcį́	káˀnį́!	'kill pig'	12(f)
2D	kúˀcį́	túˀ!tú!	'paper pig'	12(d)
2E	kúˀcį́	víˀšį̀	'cold pig'	12(d)
3D	kúˀcį́	lúˀ!kú	'crazy pig'	12(e)
4C	kúˀcį́	kúˀšì	'bury pig'	12(f)
5C	kúˀcį́	dáˀví!	'poor pig'	12(a)
or	kúˀcį́	dâˀví!	'poor pig'	12(a)
6C	kúˀcį́	tɨ̵ˀví!	'push pig'	10, 12(b)
or	kúˀcį́	tɨ̵ˀvǐ	'push pig'	10, 12(b)
6D	kúˀcį́	vídé	'wet pig'	10, 12(b)
or	kúˀcį́	vídĕ	'wet pig'	10, 12(b)
7C	kúˀcį́	kánį́	'long pig'	12(c)
7D	kúˀcį́	šíˀkɨ̵	'squash pig'	12(c)
5F	dú̵ˀnú	dâˀví!	'poor shirt'	11
6F	dú̵ˀnú	vídé	'wet shirt'	10, 11
or	dú̵ˀnú	vídĕ	'wet shirt'	10, 11
7F	dú̵ˀnú	kánį̀	'long shirt'	11
1G	dú̵ˀnù	dívú	'ancient shirt'	5, 8
2G	dú̵ˀnù	tù̵ˀtú!	'paper shirt'	8, 9
3G	dú̵ˀnù	lù̵ˀkú	'crazy shirt'	8, 9
4G	dú̵ˀnù	kù̵ˀší	'bury shirt'	8, 9
5G	dú̵ˀnù	nę̀ˀšį́!	'sweep shirt'	8, 9

6G	dú?nù	tɨ̀?vǐ	'push shirt'	8
7G	dú?nù	kà?mí̧	'burn shirt'	8, 9, 15
1H	kú?s̆ì	s̆té?nú̧	'bury turkey'	5, 8
2H	kú?s̆ì	tù?tú!	'bury paper'	8, 9
3H	kú?s̆ì	kù?cí̧	'bury pig'	8, 9
4H	kú?s̆ì	kù?s̆í	'bury bury'	8, 9
5H	kú?s̆ì	dà?ví!	'bury poor'	8, 9
6H	kú?s̆ì	gà?cǐ	'bury blanket'	8
7H	kú?s̆ì	s̆ɨ̀?kɨ̧	'bury squash'	8, 9, 15
1I	gà?cì	dívú	'ancient blanket'	5, 8
2I	gà?cì	tù?tú!	'paper blanket'	8, 9
3I	gà?cì	lù?kú	'crazy blanket'	8, 9
4I	gà?cì	kù?s̆í	'bury blanket'	8, 9
5I	gà?cì	dà?ví!	'poor blanket'	8, 9
6I	gà?cì	vìdě	'wet blanket'	8
7I	gà?cì	kàní̧	'long blanket'	8, 9, 15
1J	s̆ɨ́?kɨ̧	dívú	'ancient squash'	5, 14
2J	s̆ɨ́?kɨ̧	tú?tú!	'paper squash'	13
2K	s̆ɨ́?kɨ̧	vì?s̆í̧!	'cold squash'	13
3J	s̆ɨ́?kɨ̧	lú?kú	'crazy squash'	13
4J	s̆ɨ́?kɨ̧	kú?s̆ì	'bury squash'	13
5J	s̆ɨ́?kɨ̧	dà?ví!	'poor squash'	13
6J	s̆ɨ́?kɨ̧	vìdě	'wet squash'	13
7J	s̆ɨ́?kɨ̧	kàrì̧	'long squash'	13

Following is a list of words arranged by classes. Any word within the class (or subclass) may be substituted for any other word within the class. When two variants are listed, the first is the post /!/ variant and the second is the isolation variant:

Class `` : s̆ɨ́?kɨ̧ 'squash' dù?cì 'beans', dà?mạ̀ 'skirt, vì?ì 'house', làà 'flower'; kàní̧ 'long', kà?nù̧ 'big', rà?và 'pot-bellied', dù?ù 'fat', cùdè 'ragged'; kà?mì̧ 'burn', kà?cì̧ 'cut', dì?kò 'grind', kò?ò 'drink', kʷì̧ì 'buy'.

Class `ˇ : gà?cǐ 'blanket', jà?ǎ 'broth', cùmě 'candle', rkùnǔ 'board'; vìdě 'wet', à?tǎ 'old', lò?ǒ 'deaf'; tɨ̀?vǐ 'push'.

Class ´` ~ ´ˇ : kú?s̆ì 'bury', kɨ́?kù 'sew', kʷé?è 'give'.

Class ´´ : kú?cí̧ 'pig', s̆ú?vé 'thread'; lú?kú 'crazy'.

Subclass ´´ ~ ´ˇ : dú?nú̧ shirt', é?tú̧ 'box', kó?ó 'dish', s̆úmȩ́ 'wax'; vídí 'sweet', dí̧í̧ 'fierce'.

Class ´´! : tú?tú! 'paper', í?s̆á! 'child', ídú! 'horse', ñú̧ú̧! 'town', ká?ní̧! 'kill', kí?ní̧! 'tie' ká?dé! 'cut'.

Subclass ″! ~ ′ˇ: ví'šį̂! 'cold', vá'á! 'good', víí! 'heavy', šéé! 'new'.
Class !″: !šté'nų́ 'tom turkey', !ndí'ú 'goat', !rkú'ú 'deer', !rkʷéɨ́ 'ladder', !skʷílú 'buzzard'; !dívú 'ancient'.
Subclass !″ ~ ′ˇ: !čó'ó 'medicine', !dʸų́'ų́ 'money'.
Class !′ˋ ~ ˋ′: !dí'kò 'ground (v)', !ká'cį̀ 'cut', !é'mì 'burned', !ší'ì 'drank', !ñį̂ 'bought'.
Class !′ˇ ~ ˋ′!: !cá'kǎ 'fish', !lá'pɨ̌ 'pencil', !kɨ́dɨ̀ 'pot', !tínǎ 'dog', !láǎ 'bird'.
Class ˋ′!: dà'ví! 'poor', vì'tá! 'soft', kʷì'ší! 'white', kʷą̀ą́! 'yellow', ìá! 'sour'; nè'ší! sweep', nè'kį̂! 'comb (v)'.
Class !ˆ′!: !skʷîdú! spotted', !vįdį̂! 'warm', !î'cí! 'dry'.
Class !″!: !skʷíí! 'pinto'.

5.2. *Tone sandhi between couplet and enclitic*

There are more than 20 enclitics, but they all fall into one of three classes: ′!, ˋ, ˇ.
Class ′!: Enclitics of class ′!, for example: -tų́! ~ -tų̀ 'she, her' and -kó! ~ -kò 'me, my', have the opposite tone of the last syllable of the couplet or other enclitic which precedes them (chart 2, col. 8). According to that rule, the variant ′! is used following ˋˋ or ˋ. Then, however, the ˋˋ or ˋ is raised to ″ (rule 13), so that the resulting sequence is ″′! (8Q):
kà'mì burn' + tų́! 'she' > ká'mį́-tų́! 'she will burn';
ká'nį̂! 'kill' + tų́! 'she' > ká'nį́-tų̀ 'she will kill';
ká'nį́-tų̀ 'kill-she' + kó! 'me' > ká'nį́-tų́kó! 'she will kill me' (rule 18).
Classes ˋ and ˇ: The enclitics of classes ˋ and ˇ both have four variants: ˋ, ˇ, ′, ′!. An example of class ˋ is -ñą̀ ~ -ñą́ ~ -ñá! ~ -ñą̌ 'they, them, their'[8]. Examples of class ˇ are: -kǒ ~ -kó ~ -kó! ~ -kò 'us, our (incl.)' and -ǒ ~ -ó ~ -ó! ~ -ò 'we (incl.)'.
Both classes have high variants following ′ (cols. 9, 10, row O), except that the ′! variant occurs following a ′!ˋ variant: kú'cí 'pig' + lú'kú 'crazy' + kǒ our' + ká'nį̂! 'kill' + ñą̀ 'they' > kú'cí lú'!kú-kó! ká'nį́-ñą̀ 'they will kill our crazy pig'.

---

[8] The question marker -dù is also class ˋ, but the couplet to which the -dù is added has the same variant as it would have if following classˋˇ. Notice the following sets of examples: ví'šɨ̌ 'cold', gà'cì vì'šɨ̌! 'cold blanket'. vì'šɨ́-dù 'is it cold?'; kànɨ̀ 'long', gà'cì kànɨ̀ 'long blanket' kànɨ́-dú 'is it long?'.

The basic forms (` and ˅) occur following ` (9Q, 10Q) and following ´! (9L, 10L), except that when following classes `´! and !^´! both classes of enclitics use the ´! variant, and the preceding couplet is changed. The resultant sequences are `` ´! (9M, 10M) and !^` ´! (9N, 10N).

Class ` has ` when following ` (9Q).

Class ˅ has ˅ when following ` (10Q), and when following ˅ (10P). Class `, however, has the ˅ variant only when following a syllable which would have the ˅ cluster if the enclitic were removed (9Q versus 9P).

A ` variant which is derived from ˅ does not become ´ when preceding ´. This differs from other ` variants which do become ´ when preceding ´ (see rule 13). Note the contrasting examples:

ká?ní̧-ǒ 'kill-we' + -tú̧! 'her' > ká?ní̧-òtú̧!
        'we will kill her' versus

ká?ní̧-ņ̃à 'kill-they' + -tú̧! 'her' > ká?ní̧!-ņ̃á̧tú̧!
        'they will kill her';

ká?ní̧-ņ̃à 'kill-they' + !cá?kǎ 'fish' > ká?ní̧!-ņ̃á̧ cá?kǎ
        'they will kill fish' versus

ṯ̈?vì-ņ̃à 'push-they' + !cá?kǎ 'fish' > ṯ̈?vì-ņ̃à cá?kǎ
        'they will push fish'.

When an enclitic follows another enclitic, the changes are the same as when following a couplet (see chart 2):

ṯ̈?vì-ņ̃à 'push-they' + tú̧! 'her' > tì?vì-ņ̃àtú̧!
        'they will push her' (8P),

ṯ̈?vì-tú̧! 'push-she' + ņ̃à 'them' > ṯ̈?vì-tú̧ņ̃à
        'she will push them' (9L);

ká?ní̧-ņ̃à 'kill-they' + tú̧! 'her' > ká?ní̧!-ņ̃á̧tú̧!
        'they will kill her' (8Q),

ká?ní̧-tù̧ 'kill-she' + ņ̃à 'them' > ká?ní̧-tù̧ņ̃à
        'she will kill them' (9Q);

kà?mì̧-ǒ 'burn-we' + tú̧! 'her' > kà?mì̧-òtú̧!
        'we will burn her' (8P),

ká?mí̧-tú̧! 'burn-she' + kǒ 'us' > ká?mí̧-tú̧kǒ̧
        'she will burn us' (10L).

An enclitic causes the same changes in a following couplet as another couplet would cause (see 5.1). That is, class ` acts like class ``, class ˅ acts like class `˅, class ´! acts like a final ´!, and a ´ variant acts like a raised class `` :

Chart 2
Tone sandhi between couplet and enclitic.

Any variant:	Class ´!		Class `		Class ˘		
			Class of enclitic:				
Final ´!*	´	`	´	`	´	˘	L
verb, adj. ` ´!	` ´	`	` `	´!	` `	´!	M
! ˆ ´ !	! ˆ ´	`	! ˆ `	´!	! ˆ `	´!	N
Final ´	´	`	´	´	´	´	O
Final ˘	`	´!	`	˘	`	˘	P
Final `	´	´!	`	`	`	˘	Q
	8		9		10		

* This includes class ´´! and nouns with the ` ´! variant.

káʔnį́-ñà̰ 'kill-they' + !štéʔnų́ 'turkey' > káʔnį́-ñá̰ štéʔnų́
    'they will kill a turkey' (rule 18);
káʔdé-ñà̰ 'cut-they' + ši̜ʔki̜ 'squash' > káʔdé-ñà̰ ši̜ʔki̜
    'they will cut squash' (rule 13);
kà̰ʔmi̜-ǒ 'burn-we' + túʔtú! 'paper' > kà̰ʔmi̜-ò tùʔtú!
    'we will burn paper' (rules 8, 9);
káʔmí̜-tų́! 'burn-she' + túʔtú! 'paper' > káʔmí̜-tų́! túʔtú!
    'she will burn paper' (rule 4);
káʔmí̜-tų́! 'burn-she' + si̜ʔki̜ 'squash' > káʔmí̜-tų́ ši̜ʔki̜
    'she will burn squash' (rules 1, 2);
èʔmí̜-ñá̰ 'burned-they' + ši̜ʔki̜ 'squash' > èʔmí̜-ñá̰ ši̜ʔki̜
    'they burned squash' (rules 15, 16).

    Following is a list of examples cross-referenced to chart 2:
8L	túʔtú-tù̜	'her paper'
9L	túʔtú-nà̰	'their paper'
10L	túʔtú-kǒ	'our paper'
8M	nḛ̀ʔ ši̜-tù̜	'she will sweep'
9M	nḛ̀ʔ ši̜-ñá̰!	'they will sweep'
10M	nḛ̀ʔ ši̜-ó!	'we will sweep'

8N	!vîdî-tù	'she is warm'
9N	!vîdì-ñá!	'they are warm'
10N	!vîdì-ó!	'we are warm'
8O	kú?cî-tù	'her pig'
9O	kú?cî-ñá	'their pig'
10O	kú?cî-kó	'our pig'
8P	gà?cì-tú!	'her blanket'
9P	gà?cì-ñà	'their blanket'
10P	gà?cì-kǒ	'our blanket'
8Q	šî?kɨ-tú!	'her squash'
9Q	šî?kɨ-ñà	'their squash'
10Q	šî?kɨ-kǒ	'our squash'

Following is a list of enclitics arranged according to classes:

Class ´!: -tú! 'she, her (familiar)', -kó! 'me, my', -ú! 'I', -dɨ! 'we (excl.)', -čí! 'he, him, his (fam., women's speech)'.

Class `: -ñà 'they, them, their (polite)', -nà 'he, him, his (fam., men's speech)', -ò 'you (object), your (fam.)', -dò 'you, your (polite)', -tɨ 'it, its (animal, fruit)', -ì (indefinite person); -dù (question marker).

Class ˅: -ǒ 'we (incl.)', -kǒ 'us, our (incl.)'.

6. Phonological word-phrases

Word-phrases in Coatzospan Mixtec are strikingly different from words or phrases in other Mixtec languages in that Coatzospan word-phrases have contrastive nuclei — glottalized versus nonglottalized. In addition, the word-phrases themselves contrast — oral versus nasal.

We hesitated to call the units of this level "words", since they may include a noun plus one or two modifiers. Yet we hesitated to call them "phrases" since many of them consist of single morphemes. In addition, there is considerable fluctuation in the pronounciation of a word-phrase. In normal speech a sequence of several morphemes may be fused together into one word-phrase. It is identified as one word-phrase since it includes only one glottalized syllable (if it is a glottalized word-phrase), or only one lengthened syllable (if it is a nonglottalized word-phrase). In slower, slightly emphasized speech, the same sequence of morphemes may separate into a sequence of two or more word-phrases. That is, it may have two or more glottalized or lengthened syllables.

For the most part the morphemes which fuse into one word-phrase are made up of noun plus one or two modifiers, or noun plus noun, as in the following examples: vì²ì 'house' + šúǔ 'stone' > víšúú 'house of stone'; ɖú²nǔ 'shirt' + kʷì²ší! 'white' > ɖúnúkʷí²ší! 'white shirt'; kóǒ 'snake' + ñú²ú! 'earth' + tè²ú! 'rotten' > kóñútè²ú! 'fer de lance'.

Sequences of morphemes which seldom fuse are made up of numeral plus noun, noun plus verb, or adjective plus noun: vìdè ɖù²nú 'the shirt is wet', ká²ní! kú²cí 'kill a pig', í²šá šì²ì 'a child died', úvì cá²kǎ 'two fish'.

A minimal word-phrase consists of the nucleus which is the couplet. The couplet may be preceded or followed by one-syllable morphemes which even in slow speech do not become a separate word-phrase. The following examples show contrastive placement of the couplet in relation to some of these one-syllable morphemes. (Throughout this paper the couplet either precedes word space or hyphen. If there is no hyphen in the word-phrase, the couplet consists of the two syllables preceding word space.) Some examples are: kìdí-kò 'my cooking pot', cíkàñá 'rattle', kú²cí-ñá 'their pig', dàá-túnìkó! 'she told me', kʷè²è-kádòvènì 'okay, go along now', nàkùcídú²té-ñátú! 'he will baptize her', kànàštívà²à-ñá! 'they are putting it away'.

6.1. *Nonglottalized couplet*

In a nonglottalized couplet the first vowel of the couplet is usually lengthened: d[i·]vú 'ancient', š[ò·]ɖò 'valley', d[ù·]ɖí! 'honey'. The exceptions are: (1) When /i/ is the first vowel preceding a diverse vowel with the same tone, then that /i/ is not lengthened: díó-kó! 'I want', kúcíú 'knife'. (2) When the first vowel of the couplet has a low tone, it is not as long as an upgliding prepause vowel: cùmě 'candle', rkùnǔ 'board', ɖèdǔ 'dirty'.

When a morpheme moves from the nucleus of a word-phrase to the margin, the vowel length is lost: ɖávǐ 'rain', dávíšúǔ 'hail'; cídǐ 'earrings', !cídínání 'long earrings'.

Except for /š/, only voiced consonants occur medially in a nonglottalized couplet: kànì 'long', lùzǐ 'top', ìšǔ 'empty'.

6.2. *Glottalized couplet*

In a glottalized couplet with a medial consonant, the first vowel is interrupted by a glottal stop: d[íˀⁱ]šę̌ 'sandal', r[àˀa]và 'pot-bellied', g[àˀa]cǐ 'blanket', m[ę́ˀe]ñų̌ 'center'.

Either a voiced or a voiceless consonant may occur medially in a glottalized couplet – except that /d/ does not occur in that environment: túˀtú! 'paper', ɖúˀnų̌ 'shirt', ƚˀšɨ! 'rooster', ɖúˀmę̌ 'tail', !lúˀdǐ 'small', càˀvá! 'frog'.

The following word-phrases show contrast between a glottalized couplet versus a nonglottalized couplet: úvǐ 'two', úˀvǐ 'it hurts; dɨšɨ! 'corpse', dɨˀšɨ! 'sores'; kíní̧-ñà̧ 'they will see', kíˀní̧-ñà̧ 'they will tie'.

In a glottalized couplet without a medial consonant, the first syllable ends in a glottal stop, or, optionally, the glottal stop is followed by a vocoid which echoes the first vowel: t[ȩ̀ˀ/ȩ̀ˀᵋ]u! 'rotten' ɖíˀí 'ring', ɖì̧ˀá! 'comadre', váˀǎ 'good'.

The glottal stop is more fortis in a glottalized couplet without a medial consonant than it is when in a couplet with a medial consonant: kóˀkó! 'it will burn' versus kóˀò-kó! 'my dish'.

When a morpheme moves from the nucleus of a word-phrase to the margin, the glottal stop is lost. Glottalized couplets which were in contrast with nonglottalized couplets in isolation may become homophonous when in the margin of a word-phrase:

šɨˀšɨ 'mushroom'   šɨšɨkʷíˀšɨ! 'white mushroom';
šɨšɨ 'badger',   šɨšɨkʷíˀšɨ! 'white badger';
kóˀǒ 'dish',   kóvíɖě 'wet dish';
kóǒ 'snake',   kóvíɖě 'wet snake'.

6.3. *Nasal word-phrase*

Nasal word-phrases contrast with oral word-phrases. The nasal word-phrase (identified in this paper by a final 'n') has a contrastive feature of nasalization which starts at the end of the word-phrase and continues regressively, nasalizing each vowel until it reaches either the beginning of the word-phrase or a voiceless consonant. (The nasalization will also pass through /š/ when it is medial in a nonglottalized couplet, but not when it is medial in a glottalized couplet: kùšǔ 'diligent', kùšǔn [kù̧šų̌·] 'you (fam.) are diligent'; but, kóˀšǒ 'to fall', kóˀšǒn [kóˀošǒ·] 'you (fam.) will fall'.)

A nasal word-phrase always has the second person familiar as one of its components of meaning[9]:

---

[9] For footnote, see next page.

kàʔtà 'sing', kàʔtàn [kàʔᵃtà̰] 'you (fam.) will sing';
kàʔnį́! 'kill', káʔnín! [ká̰ʔᵃnį́] 'you (fam.) will kill';
kɨ̆ʔvɨ̆ 'be drunk', kɨ̆ʔvɨn [kɨ̰ʔⁱvɨ̰] 'you (fam.) will get drunk';
kúdįį́ 'get angry', kúdíín [kúdį́į́] 'you (fam.) will get angry';
kádáší 'diet', kádášín [ká̰dá̰·š̰į́] 'you (fam.) will diet';
kótódéé 'examine', kótódéén [kótǫ́ⁿdę́ę́] 'you (fam.) will examine';
cíkʷéʔcì 'complain', cíkʷéʔcìn [tsíkʷέ̰ʔᵋts̰į̀] 'you (fam.) will complain'.

An oral word-phrase with nasal vowels can be homophonous with a nasal word-phrase: cį̀į̀ 'fingernail', cìin [tsį̀į̀] 'you (fam.) will get wet'.

The nasal vowels in an oral word-phrase are perceptually the same as nasalized vowels in a nasal word-phrase, but we have chosen to treat the nasalization on two different levels of the phonological hierarchy.

There are various reasons for treating nasalization in two parts of the hierarchy:

(1) A morpheme which has a vowel which is nasalized on the phoneme level, /į, ę, ą, ɨ̧, ų/, remains nasalized in all environments (dḛ̀ʔę́! 'grease', dę́!kúʔcį́ 'lard'; tą̀ʔą̀ 'cousin', tą̀ʔò 'your cousin', tą̀iiʔkà-ó 'your distant cousin'), whereas a morpheme which has nasalized vowels because it is a part of a nasal word loses that nasalization in other environments: íšá!váʔán [íšá̰!bá̰ʔá̰] 'you (fam.) are a good child', íʔšá! [íʔⁱšá] 'child'.

(2) There is no phoneme */ǫ/, but /o/ can become nasalized in a nasal word: kòʔtò 'to look', kòʔtòn 'you (fam.) will look'; kòʔò 'drink', kòʔòn 'you (fam.) will drink'.

(3) There is a limited distribution of /į, ę, ą, ɨ̧, ų/ in that (a) they do not follow /b, z, g, gʷ/ in nonglottalized couplets, (b) they do not follow voiced consonants (except for /m, n, ñ/) in glottalized couplets. When in a nasal word-phrase, however, vowels can become nasalized even if they are following those consonants: ká̰ʔdén 'you (fam.) will cut', kɨ̆ʔvɨn 'you (fam.) are drunk', zòʔón! 'you (fam.) are a hummingbird', cà̰ʔbàn 'you (fam.) are fat', rà̰ʔgʷàn 'you (fam.) are huge', nàgàván 'you (fam.) let it loose'.

(4) The distribution of /į, ę, ą, ɨ̧, ų/ in an oral word-phrase is different from that of the distribution of nasalized vowels in a nasal word-phrase.

---

[9] In Tereno of Mato Grosso, Brazil, the category of first person is linked with nasalization: "The phonetic actualization is as follows: (a) the nasalization of all vowels and semi-vowels in the word up to the first stop or fricative. In words without stops or fricatives all vowels and semi-vowels are nasalized, together with (b) a nasalized consonantal sequence replacing the first stop or fricative ..." (Bendor-Samuel 1960:350). Bendor-Samuel has chosen to interpret this part of the system as "a prosody of nasalization" (p. 353).

Specifically, in an oral word-phrase the last vowel may be oral while the next to the last vowel is nasal (kèdé-ù 'I sneezed'). In a nasal word-phrase however, the last vowel is always nasalized.

7. Syllable

The nucleus of a syllable consists of one vowel (1) preceded, or not preceded, by one or two consonants, (2) with one tone, or with a cluster of two tones. That is, the segmental combinations CCV, CV, V occur with a high or low tone, or with the clusters high-low or low-high.

In the following examples the syllables have been separated by a dot. Examples of syllables in nonglottalized word-phrases: škì.nì 'last night', dè.ĕ 'black', ì.ǎ 'sour', šú.mę̆ wax', !vî̧.dí̧! 'warm'.

Examples of syllables in glottalized word-phrases: !šté'nų̃ 'tom turkey', dú'.nų̃ 'shirt', vá'.ǎ 'good', á'.vǐ 'expensive', !štâ'.mą̃! 'squatty, dù'.tè 'water', kʷì'.sí̧! 'white'.

8. Consonant contrasts

There are twenty-two consonant phonemes in native Mixtec words. (For additional phonemes introduced through Spanish loans, see 14.) There is a set of voiceless stops and affricates /p (rare), t, c, č, k, kʷ/ paralleled by a set of prenasalized voiced stops and affricates /b (rare), d, z, ǰ g, gʷ/. There are voiceless and voiced fricatives /s, š, v, d, dʸ/, nasals /m, n, ñ/, a lateral /l/ and a flap /r/.

Bilabials /p, b, v, m/: pà'á! 'baby', vá'ǎ 'good'; vì'ì 'house', mí̧'í̧ 'where'; cà'bà 'fat', cà'vá! 'frog', dà'mą̃ 'dress'.

Dentals /t, d, d/: tá'kǎ nest , dà'kà to leave', dá'ká 'to be mixed'.

Alveolars /c, z, s, n, l, r/: có'ó 'flea , zó'ò! 'hummingbird'; cà'á! gourd', sá'ǎ 'this', nà̧'ǎ 'a long time', là'à 'knot', rà'và 'pot-bellied'.

Alveopalatals /č, ǰ, š, ñ/ and palatalized dental /dʸ/: čó'ð 'medicine', ǰò'kð 'sultry', šò'kò 'steam', dʸú'ų̃ money', ñų̃'ų̃ 'fire'. (See 13 regarding palatalization in women's speech.)

Contrasting /t c, č, d, z, ǰ/: tò'ó! 'owner', có'ó 'flea', čó'ð 'medicine', dò'ó! 'adobe', zò'ó! hummingbird', tèǰò'ð 'Puebla'.

Contrasting /s/ and /š/: sá'ǎ 'this', šà'à 'chili'.

Contrasting /d/ and /l/: dá'ká 'to be mixed', lá'ká 'scarecrow'; ídú 'horse', cílú 'dragonfly'. In some morphemes /d/ and /l/ alternate: dèdǔ ~ lèdǔ 'dirty', dɨ̀ʔɨ̵̂ ~ lɨ̀ʔɨ̵̂ 'mother', dàʔkɨ̵̵ ~ làʔkɨ̵̵ 'rough'.

Contrasting /n, ñ, d, ǰ/: nǜʔú̧! 'tooth', ñú̧ʔǔ̧ 'fire', dùʔù 'fat', ǰú̧ʔú̧ 'doctrine', ǰúʔvé 'hammock'.

Since nasals /m, n, ñ/ are followed only by nasal vowels, and since /v, d, dʸ, l, d, ǰ/ occur with a following nasal vowel in only a few morphemes, we have listed these contrasts: mɪ̧nɪ̧! 'lake', vɪ́dɪ̧ 'sweet', dɪ̧dɪ̧ 'handle'; nàʔá̧ 'a long time', dà̧ʔá̧ 'Mazatec'; nùʔú! 'tooth', lùʔú! 'roadrunner'; ñúʔǔ 'fire', dʸúʔǔ 'money', ǰú̧ʔú̧ 'doctrine'; kámá̧n 'you (fam.) hurry up', kàvàn 'you (fam.) go to bed'.

Velars /k, kʷ, g, gʷ/: kàá! 'metal', kʷàá! 'late'; káʔcí 'cotton', gàʔcǐ 'blanket'; kʷìi 'green', gʷìí 'the rest'.

Contrasting /kʷ/ and /ku/: kʷàá! 'late', kùǎ (kùvì 'become' + ìǎ 'sour') 'to get sour'.

Prenasalized stops and affricates are considered to be unit phonemes, (1) because only consonant clusters of two consonants occur couplet initially (/st, št, rt/), and [sⁿd] and [šⁿd] also occur there: sdàá! 'white hair', !šdóʔó 'spider'; (2) because only single consonants occur medially in a couplet; [ᵐb], [ⁿd], [ⁿdz], and [ᵑgʷ] also occur couplet medially: càʔbà 'fat', cídɪ̀ 'earring', lùzǐ 'top', ràʔgʷà 'huge'.

In contrast, [nd] occurs as a cluster of two consonant phonemes in !ndíʔú 'goat'. It contrasts with [ⁿd] in dìʔù 'shut'.

9. Consonant variants

The prenasalized dental stop /d/ has a palatalized allophone [dʸ] when preceding /ɨ, u, u̧/ (no example has been found of /d/ preceding /ɨ̧/): [ⁿdʸ]ɨ̧ʔɨ̵̂! 'all', [ⁿdʸ]ùʔù 'fat', ùʔ[ⁿdʸ]ǔ 'short', [ⁿdʸ]u̧dɪ̧! 'honey'. The nonpalatalized allophone occurs elsewhere: [ⁿd]èǔ 'black', [ⁿd]àʔà 'hand', [ⁿd]à̧dǔ̧ 'brittle', [ⁿd]ìdì 'handle', !lúʔ[ⁿd]ǐ 'small', [ⁿd]òʔó! 'adobe'.

The voiceless dental stop /t/ likewise has a palatalized allophone [tʸ] when preceding /ɨ, ɨ̧/ and /u/, but not when preceding /u̧/: tʸ ɨ́ʔ[tʸ]ɪ̧! 'many', [tʸ]úʔ[tʸ]ú! 'paper', but [tʸ]ùʔ[t]ù̧ 'firewood', [t]ù̧ʔú! 'word'. The nonpalatalized allophone occurs elsewhere: [tʸ]ìná̧! 'dog', [tʸ]úʔ[t]é 'gruel', [t]à̧ʔ[t]á̧ 'witch-doctor', [t]òʔó! 'owner'.

The palatalized allophone of /t/ occurs preceding /u/, even when it is allophonically nasalized as part of a nasal word-phrase: kù[tʸ]ùví 'to sit down', kù[tʸù̧]vín 'you (fam.) sit down'; cìˀ[tʸù]-[tú̧]! 'she is swollen', cíˀ[tʸù]-[ⁿdʸŭ̧] 'is it swollen?, cíˀ[tʸù̧]-[ⁿdʸŭ̧]n 'are you (fam.) swollen?'.

In postcouplet syllables when preceding a nasal vowel, the voiceless velar stop /k/ occasionally varies to a lenis voiced velar fricative [g], while the alveolar fricative phoneme /s/ varies to [h]: kʷíá díˀɫkò[k/g]ą̧́ 'last year'; nį́nù̧-[s/h]ą́ 'up here', ñą̧ˀą́-nì̧[s/h]á (emphatic negative).

The alveopalatal fricative /š/ fluctuates from retroflexed to nonretro-flexed. For the most part, the retroflexed allophone precedes /ɨ/ and /u/, and the nonretroflexed allophone is more frequent preceding /i/ and /e/: šɨ́šɨ́ 'badget', išŭ 'empty', èˀş̌ì 'bowl', šíˀ̧ɨ 'door', šéé 'new', šòɖò 'valley' šàˀà 'chili'.

The alveopalatal fricative /š/ also fluctuates from voiceless [š] to voiced [ž] when it occurs medially in a nonglottalized couplet or be-tween vowels in a word-phrase margin: šú[š/ž]ú 'glass', ɫɨˀ[š/ž]ɨ! 'rooster', ɫɨ[š/ž]ɨkàˀnù̧ 'big rooster'.

The dental fricative phoneme /ɖ/ has a voiceless allophone when in a cluster following /t/: ɖúˀm̧ę̆ 'tail', t[θ]úˀmę̧́ 'scorpion'.

The alveolar flap phoneme /r/ has a voiceless allophone when in a cluster preceding a voiceless consonant: [ř]kìmą̆ 'hoe', ![ɽ]kʷéɫ 'ladder'. Elsewhere it is voiced: [ř]àˀvà 'pot-bellied', tɨ[ř]àˀú! 'peanut', t[ř]ìˀtá! 'woodpecker'.

The alveopalatal nasal phoneme /ñ/ varies to a palatal nasalized non-syllabic vocoid [y̧] medially in a word-phrase: [ñ]ą̧ˀą̧ 'people', mę̧́?[ñ/y̧]ŭ 'center', kù[ñ/y̧]ú! 'meat', ɖìvì-[ñ/y̧]ą́! 'his name'.

10. Vowel contrasts

There are six oral vowels /i, e, a, o, u, ɨ/ but only five nasal vowels /į, ę, ą, ų, ɨ̧/.

The oral vowels contrast: šíˀ̧ɨ 'door', šéˀ̆e 'gave', šà?à 'chili', šòˀ̀o 'rope', šùˀ̀ù 'mouth', šɨˀ̧ɨ 'raw'.

The nasal vowels contrast: tį́į̧́ 'perspiration', štę̧́ę̧́ 'forehead', tą́ą̧̆ 'earth-quake', tų́ų̧̆ 'charcoal', tɨ̧̀ɨ̧̀ 'to grasp'.

The front vowels /i, į, e, ę/ contrast: kʷìì 'green', kʷį̀į̧̀ 'to buy', kʷèˀé! 'red', kʷę̧́ę̧́ 'to go'.

The central vowels /ɨ, ɨ̧, a, ą/ contrast: áˀkɨ 'burnt', kàˀkɨ̧ 'to be hungry', kàˀkà 'to walk', káˀ̧ką̆ 'to beg'.

The back vowels /u, ų, o/ contrast: cùˀú! 'gopher', cùˀų́! 'chicken', cóˀó 'flea'.

The high vowels /i, į, ɨ, ɨ̨, u, ų/ contrast: kìˀì 'to take', kį̀ˀį̀ 'several', nákɨ́ˀɨ 'to be inserted', kɨ̨́ˀ 'to go', kùˀú! 'herb', kų̀ˀ ų̀ 'to be put in'.

The low vowels /e, ę, a, ą, o/ contrast: kʷèˀé! 'red', kʷę̀ˀę́ 'to go', kʷàá! 'late', kʷą̨́ą́! 'yellow'; kàá! 'metal', kóŏ 'snake'.

11. Vowel variants

Vowels are lengthened in the first syllable of the nonglottalized couplet: š[á·]vĭ 'hole', [í·]dú! 'horse', k[ù·]nų́! 'deep', š[ɨ́·]šɨ́ 'badger'. Vowels carrying tone clusters are also lengthened: !skʷ[î·]dú! 'spotted', v[ì·]d[ɛ̀·] 'wet', kóˀš[ŏ·] 'it fell'.

The high vowels /i/ and /u/ are generally shorter than the other vowels when they are followed by diverse vowels having the same tone: kʷĭá 'year', !rkʷéɨ 'ladder', šùà 'Compadre (vocative)', mą́ų́ 'aide', kàdìò 'is needed', kàdèɨ 'is upside down'.

The vowel /e/ is open [ɛ] and varies to a slightly raised [æ] when in a nonglottalized couplet preceding /n/, /ñ/ or /d/: l[ɛ́?ɛ́] 'circle', dù?š[ɛ́] 'gum', [ɛ̀ˀɛ]d[ɛ́] 'cut', [ɛ́·/ǽ·]nį́! 'brother', n[ɛ̀·/æ̀·]ñų̀ 'blackberry', d[ɛ̀·/æ·]dŭ 'dirty'.

The vowel /o/ [o] is likewise open and varies to a raised [ɔ] in the word-phrase margin prepause: kóˀ ò-k[ó/ɔ́] 'my dish', kɨ̨́ˀ[ŏ·/ɔ̌·] 'let's go', dì[ŏ·/ɔ̌·] 'let's go out'.

The nasalization of a vowel is heavier when the vowel is contiguous to another nasal vowel: ñų́ų́ 'town', versus ñų́ˀtɨ 'sand', cìñù 'work'. The degree of nasalization is also related to vowel quality: the high vowels, and particularly /ų/, are more heavily nasalized than the lower vowels, with /ą/ being the least nasalized: ñų́ˀų̆ 'fire', dɨ̨́ˀɨ̨́! 'leg', cɨ̨̀ɨ̨̀ 'fingernail', tą̀ˀą̨ 'sister', mą́ˀną́ 'sleep'.

There is no noticeable difference in the degree of nasalization of nasal vowels following nasal consonants versus nasal vowels following nonnasal consonants: nų́ų́ 'face', cų́ų̆ 'turkey hen'; nų̀ˀ ú! 'tooth', tų̀ˀ ú! 'word'; neither is there any difference in the nasalization of a nasal vowel and the nasalization which an oral vowel receives when it is nasalized in a nasal word: kį̀ˀį̀ 'several', kìˀìn 'you (fam.) take it'; kìdĭ 'sticky', kídìn 'you (fam.) slept'.

12. Distribution of phonemes

Phoneme distribution in Coatzospan Mixtec is here presented in relation to the couplet, which is the most pertinent unit of description. The
data included here are restricted to phonemes found in native Mixtec
words.

12.1. *Consonants*

Any consonant may occur initially in the couplet. Three consonants
/s, dʸ, r/ do not occur in the second syllable of the couplet except in
Spanish loans: aʔsu 'garlic (Sp. ajo)', radʸu 'radio', vuru 'burro'. The alveopalatal affricates /č/ and /ǰ/ occur in the second syllable only in
women's speech (see 13).

In addition to the above restrictions, the dental fricative /d/ does not
occur in the second syllable of glottalized couplets, and the alveopalatal
fricative /š/ is the only voiceless consonant that may occur medially in a
nonglottalized couplet: šúšǔ 'glass', ìšǔ 'empty'.

12.2. *Consonant clusters*

Consonant clusters may occur initially in a couplet but not medially
except in cases of fusion of two morphemes.

Where initial clusters occur, the first member of the cluster may be
one of the following consonants: /t, s, š, n, r/. The dental stop /t/ occurs
followed by /d/ and /r/: !tdúʔmę́ 'scorpion', tràná! 'tomato'; /s/ is followed by /k/, /d/ and /m/: !skúdí 'cricket', sdàá 'white hair', smįí!
'bumble bee'; /š/ is followed by /t, k, kʷ, d, n/: !štéʔnų 'tom turkey',
škìnį̀ 'last night', škʷíʔnǎ̧ (derogatory term), !šdóʔó 'spider', šnų̀nų́!
'toad'; /n/ is followed by /d/ in only one word: !ndíʔú 'goat'; and /r/ is
followed only by velar stops /k, kʷ/: rkìmǎ̧ 'hoe', rkʷàʔdí! 'rainbow'. (For
additional clusters introduced through Spanish loans, see 14.)

Clusters containing /š/ plus /t, k, d, n/ occur at morpheme junctures
where a vowel /i/ has been dropped: káʔštú! (káʔší-tų̀) 'she will eat',
káʔšdó (káʔší-dò) 'you will eat', úškímį̌ (úʔší 'ten' + kímį̌ 'four') 'fourteen',
dúšnų̧ų́ (duʔci 'bean' + nų̧ų̧ 'face') 'eye'.

12.3. *Vowels following consonants*

All oral vowels have been found to occur following /t, c, č, k, d, s, đ, l/. Vowels /o, u, ɨ/ do not occur following labials /p, b, v, m, kʷ, gʷ/. Front vowels /i, e/ do not follow /g/ nor (except in women's speech) /ǰ/. Vowels /e, ɨ/ do not occur following /s/; /đʸ/ may be followed by any vowel except /i/, and /r/ is followed by any vowel except /e/. The rare occurrence of /p/, /b/, and /z/, each in less than five morphemes, probably accounts for their limited distribution: /p/ occurs before /a/, /b/ before /e/ and /a/, and /z/ only before /i/ and /o/.

Nasal vowels may occur following any consonant except the prenasalized stops /b, z, g, gʷ/. They do, however, occur following two prenasalized stops, /d/ and /ǰ/: dị̌dị̌ 'handle', ǰú'ụ́ 'doctrine'. Only nasal vowels occur following nasal consonants /m, n, ñ/.

12.4. *Vowels preceding consonants*

Within a couplet, the vowel /o/ has the most restricted distribution with reference to following consonants. It does not occur preceding labials, nasals, prenasalized stops, nor before /c/. The distribution of the other vowels before consonants is not noticeably restricted, though not all possible combinations have been found to occur.

12.5. *Vowel distribution within the couplet*

In monomorphemic couplets of canonical pattern CVV, CV'V, and CVCV, if nasal vowels occur, they occur in both syllables: cụ́ụ̌ 'turkey hen', đè'ę́! 'grease', vị́đị̌ 'sweet'. In a glottalized couplet with a medial consonant, the second vowel may be nasal if the consonant is voiceless: đí'cị̌ 'nose', dí'šę̌ 'sandal'. Nasal vowels occur only in those glottalized couplets which either have no medial consonant or whose medial consonant is either voiceless or nasal /m, n, ñ/: tụ̀'ụ́! 'word', mị̌'ị̀ 'where', mą́'ną́ 'sleep', ñụ́'tɨ́ 'sand', mị̌'dé 'prickly pear', đú'nụ̌ 'shirt', mị̌'cị̌! 'fan'.

When nasal vowels are contiguous in the couplet, they are normally identical: đị́ị̌ 'fierce', tą̀'ą̌ 'sister'. Only a few examples of CVV/CV'V couplets containing diverse nasal vowels have been found, and these are usually morphemically complex: látákʷą́ị́ 'marigold', šę́ų̌ 'other one', šę̌'ụ̌ (ú?šɨ 'ten' + ụ́'ụ̌ 'five') 'fifteen'.

When /o/ is present as the first vowel of a monomorphemic couplet, it is usually repeated in the second syllable: kóʔŏ 'dish', ǰòʔkŏ 'sultry', šòdò 'valley'. There are at least three exceptions to this rule: róî 'you there (vocative)', tèkòʔɨ (name of a spring in San Juan), đòʔtá 'tortilla cloth' (probably a fusion of đóŏ 'cloth' and íʔtǎ 'tortilla'). When /o/ is the second vowel in a couplet, it is commonly preceded by /i/ and rarely by /e/ and /u/: cìdó! 'rabbit', šàlèʔdò (kind of chili), đókúdó 'Tuxtepec'.

The other oral vowels occur preceding and following each other in all possible combinations in couplets in which they are separated by a consonant.

12.6. *Vowel clusters*

In CVʔV couplets the two vowels are usually identical, but where diverse vowels appear, /i/ may be followed by /a, o, u/: đìʔá! 'comadre', cíʔŏ 'cooked', díʔǔ 'beard'; /e/ may be followed by /a, u/: déʔǎ 'peach', tèʔú! 'rotten'; and /a/ may be followed by /u/: tàʔǔ 'tight'. The vowels /u/ and /ɨ/ are followed only by identical vowels: dùʔù 'fat', dɨʔɨ 'mother'.

Where vowels are contiguous in CVV couplets, geminate clusters are most frequent: šíî 'delicate', šéě 'new', šáǎ 'ashes', šóŏ 'moon', šúǔ 'stone', šɨɨ 'husband'. However, in clusters of diverse vowels, /i/ may be followed by /a, o/: ìǎ 'sour', šíŏ 'comal'; /e/ may be followed by /u, ɨ/: dèù 'gravy', dèɨ 'noose'; /a/ may be followed by /u, ɨ/: cau 'cough', rkaɨ 'burnt'; and /u/ by /a/: šùà 'compadre (vocative)'. The vowel /ɨ/ is followed only by itself.

Since there is frequent vowel loss or change when vowel clusters occur across morpheme borders, the above restrictions are not pertinent to bimorphemic clusters.

13. Women's speech

In women's speech the dental stops /t/ and /d/ never occur before front vowels /i/ and /e/. They are replaced by the alveopalatal affricates /č/ and /ǰ/ respectively. In the following pairs of words, the first of the pair is men's speech and the second is women's speech: tìná! ~ čìná! 'dog', dùʔtè ~ dùʔčè 'water', !lúʔdì ~ !lúʔǰì 'small', dèě ~ ǰèě 'black'.

When preceding other vowels the phonemes /t, č/ and /d, ǰ/ contrast in both men's and women's speech: tòʔó! 'owner', čóʔŏ 'medicine', dàʔà 'hand', ǰàʔǎ 'broth'.

The sequences /či/ and /če/ do occur in men's speech, but only rarely: čìí! 'rifle', čèʔtų̌ 'cedar'.

14. Spanish loans

In addition to the 22 consonant phonemes described in 8, there are 17 more consonants which occur only in Spanish loans. These are fricatives /f, x, ǥ/: fòʔkó 'lightbulb (foco)', spéʔxú 'mirror (espejo)', ǥáʔstú 'expense (gasto)'; labialized phonemes /xʷ, đʷ, ǥʷ, mʷ, nʷ, lʷ, rʷ/: xʷą̌ą́ 'Juan', đʷárđú 'Eduardo', ǥʷérǔ 'pale (güero)', sámʷéé 'Samuel', mą́nʷéé 'Manuel', lʷíí 'Luis', rʷíí 'Ruiz'; palatalized phonemes /sʸ, xʸ, vʸ, mʸ, lʸ, rʸ/: sʸédú 'hundred (ciento)', lòʔxʸú 'Elogio', vʸérné̦ 'Friday (viernes)', mʸą̌nų́! 'Maximillano', xúlʸá 'Julia', kùrʸá! 'Gregoria'; and the palatal phoneme /y/: ǥáyéʔtá 'cookie (galleta)'.

A number of consonant clusters occur in Spanish loans which are not found in native words (see 12.2). The majority of these involve /s/ plus a stop or nasal consonant: skʷélá 'school (escuela)', óvíʔskú 'bishop (obispo)', sną́đų́ 'soldier (soldado)'; or some combination involving /r/, either preceding or following another consonant: préférú 'February (febrero)', ságríʔstá 'sacristan', kʷéʔrká 'filthy pig (puerco)', vártúmą́ 'steward (Mayordomo)'. The lateral /l/ does not occur in native Mixtec clusters and is generally replaced by /r/ when loan words are assimilated: vróʔsá 'bag (bolsa)', àrmą́! 'soul (alma)'.

A cluster of three consonants /str/ has been found to occur both initially and medially in Spanish loans: strámé̦dú 'sacrament (sacramento)', púʔstrú 'apostle (apóstol)'.

Summer Institute of Linguistics

Bibliography

Bendor-Samuel, John T. (1960) "Some Problems of Segmentation in the Phonological Analysis of Tereno", Word 16.348-55.
Pankratz, Leo and E.V. Pike. (1967) "Phonology and Morphotonemics of Ayutla Mixtec", IJAL 33.287-99.
Pike, Eunice V. and K. Wistrand. (1972) "Step-up Terrace Tone in Acatlán Mixtec (Mexico)", Studies in Tone and Intonation by Members of the S. I. of L. Bloomington: Indiana Univ. Press, forthcoming. (See also ch.7 of this volume.)

Pike, Kenneth L. (1967) "Suprasegmentals in Reference to Phonemes of Item, of Process, and of Relation", To Honor Roman Jakobson: Essays on the Occasion of His Seventieth Birthday (The Hague, Mouton) 1545–1554.

Pike, Kenneth L. (1970) Tagmemic and Matrix Linguistics Applied to Selected African Languages (Summer Institute of Linguistics Publications in Linguistics and Related Fields: Publication Number 23) (Norman, Oklahoma, Summer Institute of Linguistics).

Schachter, Paul. (1961) "Phonetic Similarity in Tonemic Analysis with Notes on the Tone System of Akwapim Twi", Language 37.231-38.

Stewart, J.M. (1964) "The Typology of the Twi Tone System" (with comments by P. Schachter and W.E. Welmers), Bulletin of the Institute of African Studies 1.1-67.

Welmers, W.E. (1959) "Tonemics, Morphotonemics, and Tonal Morphemes", General Linguistics 4.1-9.

Morphology

CONFLATED FIELD STRUCTURES IN POTAWATOMI AND IN ARABIC*

KENNETH L. PIKE
UNIVERSITY OF MICHIGAN

BARBARA ERICKSON
SUMMER INSTITUTE OF LINGUISTICS

1. Ranking within matrix patterns in Potawatomi
1.1. Major-person ranking of formatives
1.2. Minor-person ranking
1.3. Subject-object ranking, and zero block
1.4. Plurality
1.5. Field structure
1.6. Alloformatives
2. Conflated prefix and suffix in Arabic
2.1. Prefix-suffix matrix patterns
2.2. Category
2.3. Field structure
3. Summary

1. In a previous paper[1] one of the authors (Pike) presented theory and technique for handling morphological fusion of extraordinary complexity in a language of New Guinea. He hoped that the approach would also illuminate some of the perplexing[2] morphological data which had been published concerning various Algonquian languages of North America. He asked Barbara Erickson, a colleague of the Summer Institute of Linguistics, to try to draw from Hockett's Potawatomi data[3] material for

testing this hunch. She found that Hockett's citations and analysis were sufficiently detailed to allow for various sets of matrices to be abstracted.[4] Matrices (6–9), for example, are part of this work, reflecting the structure of the pronominal affixes of the transitive independent verb.

The technology involved helps in the search for pattern. A matrix is first set up with rows and columns determined by some arbitrary arrangement of semantic categories, or units, or components of various types. Then one column is moved to right or left so as to bring together—or closer together—similar formatives (phonological intersects in the cells); this operation is repeated as often as is desired. Similarly—or alternately, with a column change—a row can be moved up or down to bring formatives together. The goal: (a) to get the most compact blocks of formatives together, and then (b) to study semantic or formal characteristics of these blocks.

---

*International Journal of American Linguistics, 30. 201-212, reprinted by permission.

[1] Presented to the Linguistic Society of America in New York, December, 1962; appeared as Kenneth L. Pike, Theoretical Implications of Matrix Permutation in Fore (New Guinea) in AL5:8.1–23 (1963).

[2] H. A. Gleason, in An Introduction to Descriptive Linguistics, Revised edition (New York, 1961), says of Cree, an Algonquian language, "The Cree endings cannot be neatly dissected into morphemes" (p. 119), "Certainly no simplification can be achieved"; "The recurrent resemblances . . . show such complications as to defy analysis. The paradigms as they stand are unanalyzable" (p. 119).

[3] Charles F. Hockett, Potawatomi I: phonemics,

morphophonemics, and morphological survey; II: derivation, personal prefixes, and nouns; III: the verb complex; IV: particles and sample texts; IJAL, 14.1–10, 63–73, 139–49, 213–25 (1948).

For a quite different presentation of Algonquian structure see A. E. Meeusen, Tabulation of the independent indicative in Algonquian, SIL, 15.19–23 (1960).

[4] Her matrices showing the relation between the possessive pronouns and the verbal pronominal affixes cannot be given here.

A few changes from Hockett's symbolism have been introduced: 4, for Hockett's 3'; 1p, 2p, for his 15, 25. The symbols 1, 2, 3, represent first, second, and third persons; p is plural; 1p is first person plural exclusive of hearer, 12 is first person plural inclusive; 4 represents a further—or extra—'third' person, the 'obviative'.

The value of the technique can be illustrated by matrix (1). The rows show the prefix formatives which are used when the subject person is 1, 2, 3, 4, 12, 1p, 2p, 3p. Columns show the same persons, but serving as object. The formatives are, therefore, a composite signal of one person as subject with another person as object. Empty cells occur where the desired semantic combinations are not permitted in this type of verb form.

(1) Potawatomi Person Prefix

	1	2	3	4	12	1p	2p	3p
1		k	n	n			k	n
2	k		k	k		k		k
3	n	k		w	k	n	k	
4	n	k	w		k	n	k	w
12			k	k				k
1p		k	n	n			k	n
2p	k		k	k		k		k
3p	n	k		w	k	n	k	

One—of many—possible sequences of permutations which will bring us to this goal is the following: Since column 2 is like column 2p, moving them together starts grouping the formatives. Similarly, 3p is like 3, and can be placed after it. This gives matrix (2).

(2 = a column permutation of 1)

	1	2	2p	3	3p	4	12	1p
1		k	k	n	n	n		
2	k			k	k	k		k
3	n	k	k			w	k	n
4	n	k	k	w	w		k	n
12				k	k	k		
1p		k	k	n	n	n		
2p	k			k	k	k		k
3p	n	k	k			w	k	n

Cursory study of (1)—note that parentheses always enclose matrix numbers, but not numbers referring to persons—reveals that formatives k, n, and w occur in that order of frequency (and that tremendous ambiguity is present, since each formative represents various semantic combinations). The formatives are, however, scattered—and

we would like to see them grouped in rows, columns, or blocks of some kind.

An isolated w is on the bottom row. By moving it up to a place below row 3, it would leave the w set grouped together (except for the neighboring empty cells of the matrices). If, however, row 3p is best treated like column 3p, presumably row 2p might be moved as was column 2p. This is done in matrix (3).

(3 = a row permutation of 2)

	1	2	2p	3	3p	4	12	1p
1		k	k	n	n	n		
2	k			k	k	k		k
2p	k			k	k	k		k
3	n	k	k			w	k	n
3p	n	k	k			w	k	n
4	n	k	k	w	w		k	n
12				k	k	k		
1p		k	k	n	n	n		

We continue to be troubled about the discontiguous n blocks. They occur on each frontier of the matrix, but never in the center. Note the abstraction of this box-shaped pattern in (4).

(4 = n abstracted from 3)

	1	2	2p	3	3p	4	12	1p
1				n	n	n		
2								
2p								
3	n							n
3p	n							n
4	n							n
12								
1p				n	n	n		

In order to pull these into a block, we might move column 1 and row 1 to a place in between 12 and 1p, as in (5).

(5 = permutation of 4)

	2	2p	3	3p	4	12	1	1p
2			k	k	k		k	k
2p			k	k	k		k	k
3	k	k			w	k	n	n
3p	k	k			w	k	n	n

```
4    k  k  w  w        k        n  n
12         k  k  k
1    k  k  n  n  n
1p   k  k  n  n  n
```

Here (5) is close to what we seek. Only the split k formative (where some of its occurrences come after the central w block, but most precede or are above it) is inelegant. By moving the columns containing the w block to the right we leave the vertical k sets together. By moving the rows with w to the bottom, the block with w stays intact—we do not lose this gain—and the k block (ignoring, as above, the empty cells) is solid. This we see in (6).

(6–9) Potawatomi Pronominal Affixes for Transitive Animate Independent Verb

(6) Prefix for Major Person Ranking

Object

Subject	2	2p	12	1p	1	3	3p	4
2				k	k	k	k	k
2p				k	k	k	k	k
12						k	k	k
1p	k	k				n	n	n
1	k	k				n	n	n
3	k	k	k	n	n			w
3p	k	k	k	n	n			w
4	k	k	k	n	n	w	w	

(7) Suffix for Subject-Object Ranking

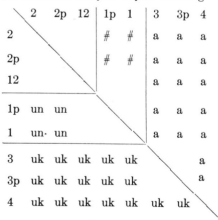

(8) Suffix for Plurality Ranking

	2	2p	12	1p	1	3	3p	4
2				mun	—	—	—	—
2p				mun	wa	wa	wa	wa
12						mun	mun	mun
1p	mun	mun				mun	mun	mun
1	—	wa				—	—	—
3	—	wa	mun	mun	—			
3p	—	wa	mun	mun	—			wa
4	—	wa	mun	mun	—	—	wa	—

(9) Suffix for Minor Person Ranking

	2	2p	12	1p	1	3	3p	4
2				—	—	—	k	n
2p				—	—	—	k	n
12						—	—	—
1p	—	—				—	—	—
1	—	—				—	k	n
3	—	—	—	—	—			n
3p	k	k	k	k	k			n
4	—	—	—	—	—	—	n	n

1.1 We first treat the Potawatomi major-person ranking of formatives. The empty cells in matrix (6) occur at points (and only at those points) where reflexiveness is involved. No inflectional forms are found in this part of the language system if both subject and object refer to the same person. For example, a subject containing 2, whether singular 2 or plural 2, or 12 inclusive, cannot enter the same cell. Nor can ambivalent 12 as subject occur with 1 as object.

The one-phoneme formatives in the cells have simultaneous composite reference to categories of person, of plurality, and of subject versus object. Contrast between the categories shows as neutralized within any one part of a matrix when the formatives there are homophonous.

For each cell in the upper right corner of (6) there is an identical cell in the lower left corner: an upper-right cell is the mirror image of the cell which would be on top of it if the matrix were folded on the upper-left to lower-right diagonal. This symmetric matrix (6) results from the neutralization of subject-object contrast for the entire matrix. For example, n would be the formative whether 1p is subject or object, if 3 is its companion object or subject. (For object-subject contrast, see (7).)

Neutralization of the singular-plural contrast leads to further ambiguities of formative in (6).

Matrix (6) provides an important ranking between persons 2, 1, 3, and 4: whenever the *2* set[5] of categories is involved, k occurs in any nonreflexive cell (whether *1* is subject or *1* is object). Presence of *2* outranks presence of *1*; and *1* outranks *3* or *4*; this produces the multiple-ranking L pattern of (6).

This relationship, for diagrammatic purposes, is by no means self-evident in (1). It shows up in display only after matrix permutation highlights the pattern which otherwise may elude us. Most of us have a deepseated bias in favor of listing the persons as 1, 2, 3, 1 incl., 1 excl., 2p, 3p, etc., which can blind us to any other pattern. The permutation of 2 in (6) to a priority over 1, and of grouping 2 with 2p, 1 with 1p, are necessary before the display highlights the underlying symmetry of the system. (A further permutation presents 1, 1p as 1p, 1—and 12 between 2p and 1p—in order that symmetries of (8) shared by 12 and 1p may emerge without destroying symmetries shared by 12 with 2 and 2p in (6).) A comparison of the simplicity of the matrix forms presented here with the bewildering complexity of the more conventional arrays given by Hockett and Gleason lets one see the power of matrix permutation as a tool.

When the rows and columns of *1* were permuted to the lower right-hand corner in (5) the *1* L pattern opened to the upper left, stopped and enclosed by the larger L pattern of *2*. The placing of the L in (6), however, gives faster insight into the rank-

ing, by displaying it as downward steps toward the lower right.

This downward stepping—or successive inclusion of L blocks—indicates a ranking of inclusion. If *2* is involved either as subject or as object, formative k appears as the prefix. If *2* is not involved, but *1* is involved either as subject or as object, formative n appears as prefix. When neither *2* nor *1* is involved, then prefixal formative w shows that *3* and *4* are involved.

The ranking of these nonreflexive formatives of (6) can also be symbolized as in (10). The formula applies only to the filled—i.e., nonreflexive—cells. The ∩ is to be read 'and'; ∪ to be read as 'or'; prime as 'not'. (If one omits the primed classes of (10), leaving the remaining lined up vertically as before, the diagonal pattern is the analogue of the downstepping L sets of (6).)

$$(10) \quad \begin{array}{l} \text{k of (6)} = 2 \cap (1 \cup 3 \cup 4) \\ \text{n of (6)} = 2' \cap 1 \cap (3 \cup 4) \\ \text{w of (6)} = 2' \cap 1' \cap 3 \cap 4 \end{array}$$

Whereas matrix (6) represents a prefix set (i.e., a prefix tagmeme manifested by the formatives of the matrix), matrices (7), (8) and (9) represent three suffix sets. Each prefixal or suffixal set provides one crucial ranking[6] of relations. It is the union and intersection of the blocks of formatives produced by these ranked sets within the matrices that develops the total effective form-meaning signal. When one matrix is superimposed upon several others made up of intersects of the same categories, so that their combination gives the total number of contrasts relative to the categorical sets, we may call the combined matrix set the conflated field structure. (See (12) for detail and discussion.)

The extensive ambiguities of (6) will be cut only when matrices (7–9) are conflated

[6] The term dichotomy might have been preferable (a) if only two major subgroups were involved in the matrices, (b) if these did not overlap in (6) versus (9), for example, and (c) if ranking relations were not so important.

with it to show the resulting field structure. The possibility of effective Algonquian communication in the pronominal system can be understood only in reference to total field structure.

Although in conventional treatment (cf. Gleason (230) the formatives of (6) are given semantic reference, with k of (6)—for example—as 'hearer involved,' n as 'speaker but not hearer involved,' w as 'neither hearer nor speaker involved,' this does not cover the k and n in (9). More striking: it does not provide a morpheme for subject, or for object, or for plural, or inclusive in (6); or 3 versus 4; etc. It is only when one searches futilely for pronominal morpheme affixes in one-to-one relationships between single category and single formative (or for one category manifested by a list of non-overlapping allomorphs) that the deep strangeness appears of a formative-meaning relation such as 'hearer involved'. The semantic component labelled as 'involved' represents a ranking of (10) as an included property of the intricate nonconventional conflated field structure of (12).

1.2. Turning now to the minor-person ranking of (9) we see a double L—but with its point toward the lower right corner. Ranking is involved in (9) in the opposite direction from (6). It would take a 180° rotation to show the L facing in the same direction as (6). Since the arms of *4*, n, extend (with gaps) to one or both edges of the matrix, it implies a ranking priority; the k of 3p, engulfed by n has second rank. (The gaps for n may leave one uneasy with this judgment. If, however, we interchange vectors of 3p with vectors of 4, a cross pattern develops for n but not for k. This, in spite of the gaps, provides evidence that n, not k, must be on the outside if we wish to display the L rank pattern.)

In (9) the formatives have only two distinct overt ranks (versus three for (6)), and cover only 3p and 4, not 3, nor *2* nor *1*. This less extensive coverage allows us to treat (9) as a minor person referent, but (6) as the

major referent (with terms taken from Hockett 141, after Bloomfield; and cf. fn. 13, below). (Note, also, that k of (9) has no simple semantic relation to k of (6).)

The minor sets of (9) now contrast category 4 with category 3p—not accomplished by (6)—and 3p from 3. The conflated field structure of (12) will later reflect these person and plurality contrasts. Part of the ambiguity of (6) disappears when conflated with (9) at the intersection of their reverse-direction L patterns. For example, (6) with k says that *2* is involved; (9) with k says 3p is involved; but neither specify which is subject nor which is object nor whether from *2* we are to choose 2, 2p, or 12. For these decisions we must have further formatives from (7) and (8).

In (9) hyphens mark cells which though empty in (9) were filled in (6), and are part of the conflated field structure of (12). The empty cells of (6), due to reflexity, persist throughout the field structure and are unmarked in the matrices.

Hyphens of (9) in vectors for 3p and 4 represent gaps in mirror-image and L patterns. From the viewpoint of this L structure the gaps are unexpected and arbitrary but empirically determined.[7] They lead, as we shall see presently, to homonymy in some full word forms of (13), and leave ambiguities in the conflated field structure of (12).

1.3. Contrast between subject and object categories is introduced into the total field by (7):—but a block of zero formatives must be postulated to maintain the relevant structure of the matrix. Symmetry is retained in cell placement, but not a mirror image of identical formatives (the matrix is skew symmetric). For every uk in lower left we see a present in the comparable cell in upper right; un corresponds to #. The presence of one of these formatives in this

[7] Deduced from Hockett's statement concerning homonymy, 143, end of §7.211; also top of 142a, concerning these formatives with plural. See, also, our discussion of (13) below.

suffix slot of the verb signals the subject or object function of the person represented by them. The combination of k prefix of (6) with uk suffix of (7), for example, cuts the ambiguity until only 3, 3p, or 4—by (7)—can be subject, and 2, 2p, or 12 must therefore be object—since 2 by (6) must somehow be involved as subject or object.

In (7), as in (9), there is a double L shape with its point toward lower right; the ranking, as in (9), therefore, begins with 4; but (7) differs from (9) by grouping 4, 3p, 3 (i.e., 4, 3) and separating 1 from 2 as does (6). Note, also, that because of this inverse ranking that 3, 4 here outrank 1, and 1 outranks 2.

The # of (7) is structurally different from the reflexive empty cells since the # set is the image of the un block. Therefore by its absence # signals the object function for 1 in contrast to subject. Here, then, we have a zero formative block[8] definable only in reference to the total pattern of the combined matrices of (6–9), where the absence of phonemic content is as significant at this point in the total work of field signalling as would be a phonemically manifested block.

1.4. By (8), contrasts of singular with plural which were not accounted for by (6) intersecting with (9) are now introduced by means of a further suffix matrix of ranked formatives. The 1p mun contrasts with the 12 empty; 1p mun also contrasts with 1 empty, and with 1 as wa, in intersection with 2, 2p respectively—whether subject or

object; but 1p has the same formative mun as 12, contrasting with 1 empty, when intersecting with 3, 3p, 4. The 2p wa contrasts with 2 empty in intersection with 1, 3, 3p, 4. The 3p wa contrasts with empty 3 when intersecting with 4.

This matrix implies that vectors of 1p—whether subject or object—are contrasted with 12 by formative mun versus empty cells, respectively. Vectors of 1p contrast with 1 by mun versus wa provided these are intersecting with 2 or 2p respectively. Yet 1p is noncontrastive with 12—having the same emic formative[9] mun—but contrastive with 1 as empty, provided that 1p, 12 are intersecting with vectors of 3, 3p, 4. The 2p wa contrasts with 2 empty provided it is intersecting with 1, 3, 3p, 4; 3p wa contrasts with 3 empty when intersecting with 4. Note also that the lower left corner is in (8) a mirror image of the upper right.[10]

[8] If the reader were dealing exclusively with the material presented here and in matrix (13), he might prefer an alternative segmentation which leads to # being replaced by uy ~ u. (Compare discussion in fn. 14.) The field structure, however, would not be affected. (See also reference in fn. 1, for alternate segmentations as sometimes irrelevant to field structure.) For the analysis with #, however, Erickson follows Hockett. This also allows us to illustrate the techniques by which zero alloformatives can be handled. In (9), on the other hand, random—nonblock—empty cells marked for 3p, 4 by hyphen are due to irregular absence of formative, not to a systematic and contrastive zero block.

[9] The data of (8) have had applied to them a prior analysis. In object 12 with subject 3, 4, mun occurs as nan. For either subject or object 1, intersecting with 2p, wa occurs as um. These alloformatives will be displayed in (11) of fn. 10.

[10] The structure and differential role of (8) is difficult to grasp quickly, in spite of its importance for eliminating ambiguity of person and number. Is matrix (8) as arbitrary as it appears on the surface? If so, it will be awkward to remember and the linguist will find it difficult to understand how the system of overlapping matrices could in fact work efficiently.

In order to search for a deeper regularity we try on (8) a set of permutations according to the general technique (see also reference in fn. 1) for bringing like formatives into a solid block together and for moving the arms of a cross into an L pattern. We add (11), achieved after trial and error, to meet these conditions.

(11 = permuted 8) Ranking in Plurality Polarity

	1p	12	2p	3p	4	1	2	3
1p			mun	mun	mun		mun	mun
12				mun	mun			mun
2p	mun			wa	wa	um		wa
3p	mun	nan	wa		wa	—	—	
4	mun	nan	wa	wa		—	—	—
1			um	—	—			—
2	mun			—	—			—
3	mun	nan	wa			—	—	—

1.5. Now, however, we ask the question: What is the full field structure of the four combined person matrices? And does the combination in fact eliminate all ambiguities?

The total signal of person, plurality, and subject-object function is obtained by

In (11), 1p, 12 come together into a top-ranking L block (with alloformative nan replacing mun at 12 object—see fn. 9, and **1.6**). A second-ranking L block contains wa (with alloformative um at intersection of 1 with 2p).

Hyphens in (11) represent nonreflexive cells which are empty here, but which are filled in (6)— and in the full field structure (11). This permutation of (11) brings the hyphens into a minimum-ranking empty L block—the nonreflexive intersections of any two of the singulars 4, 1, 2, 3—and intersection of 3p with 1, 2.

These results were startling: the double L pattern proved that plurality, like major person and minor person and subjectivity, is arranged in a polarity ranking. Mirror image symmetry, also, is preserved from lower left to upper right, as in (6, 7, 9). This symmetry is present in (8) but much harder to see there.

The groupings of sets *2, 1, 3, 4* are very much interrupted. Plural members of the sets all rank higher than singular members. (This is the fact that makes it convenient to label the group as a plurality polarity.)

The first-person groups in (8)—versus those in (6)—outrank the second person groups. The formative for 12 takes its ambivalent cue in (8) from highest ranking 1p, as before in (6) it did from highest ranking set *2*. Ranking after 1p, 12 come the plurals 2p, 3p; then the singulars 4, 1, 2, 3— with 4 placing at the top of the singular list instead of at the bottom.

One further question arises: Does not nan in (8) appear to be contrastive with cells with mun? Why conceal this overt difference in an alloformative treatment? The answer: Since nan occurs only after k of (7) and mun does not, there is never any ambiguity of the combined signal of the two matrices. (As, for English, one may treat sol as an allomorph of the stem sell, conditioned by d in sold; avoidance of some such segmentation requires treatment in higher-level matrices (see reference in fn. 1.) No further cells of the conflated field of (12) would be differentiated by treating nan as a formative in its own right. (This differs, therefore, from the contrastive treatment of uk as image of a in (7) where subject-object contrast depends on the differentiation. It will not do, to treat a as a variant of uk in (7).)

conflating the ranking sets of the person formatives of (6), with the reversed ranking sets of (9), with the differently-divided and reversed person ranking plus subject-object skewed symmetric of (7), with the sharply-distinct ranking of the plurality set of formatives of (8).

In (12) we conflate these four matrices.[11] In order to bring out the differential contribution of each of the matrices, we use for (6) a continuous line ———; for (7) a dotted line · · · · ; for (8) a broken line -----; and for (9) a slashed line. In order that the separate overt (nonzero) formatives from any one matrix be kept distinct, all instances of a particular formative in a particular matrix are enclosed in a continuous line; from (6), for example, the k is included within one solid contour line, n in another, w in a third. A hyphen occurs in any cell where a formative occurs in any one of the matrices. The cells which by reflexivity are empty in all the matrices have no hyphen. Whenever two hyphens are unseparated by one of the field lines ambiguity occurs for those cells on the level of the word (but could be resolved on a syntax level).

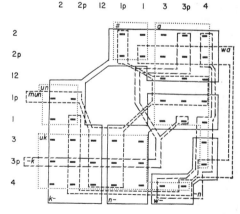

(12=conflated 6,7,8,9) Field Structure for Potawatomi; Subject-Object Affixes

Note that hyphens for subject 1p with

[11] Matrix (8) is used in its nonpermuted form— not as in (11), or the cells would not be comparable or conflatable.

(13) Potawatomi Transitive Animate Independent Verb

Object	2	2p	12	1p
Subject				
2				k--#-mun-E kwapmuymun
2p				k--#-mun-E kwapmuymun
12				
1p	k--un-mun-E kwapmunmun	k--un-mun-E kwapmunmun		
1	k--un-E-E kwapmun	k--un-wa-E kwapmunum		
3	k--uk-E-E kwapmuk	k--uk-wa-E kwapmukwa	k--uk-mun-E kwapmuknan	n--uk-mun-E nwapmuknan
3p	k--uk-E-k kwapmukok	k--uk-wa-k kwapmukwak	k--uk-mun-k kwapmuknanuk	n--uk-mun-k nwapmuknanuk
4	k--uk-E-I kwapmuk	k--uk-wa-I kwapmukwa	k--uk-mun-I kwapmuknan	n--uk-mun-I nwapmuknan

object 2 or with object 2p, or its image of subject 2 or 2p with object 1p, indicate a pair of ambiguities; the hyphens are not separated by a vertical or a horizontal line.

In addition, objects 3, 3p, and 4 are ambiguous when they intersect with subject 12 or when they intersect with subject 1p. These particular ambiguities are due to the irregular lack of n and k in the object columns for 4 and 3p in (9).

Similarly, the lack of n in the subject row for 4 in (9) leaves ambiguities between words with subject 3 or 4 when intersecting with sets *2* or *1*, as can be seen in the word data of (13). This particular ambiguity does not show up directly in (12) because the choice of row sequence places 3p between the partially homophonous rows 3 and 4. Permuting 3 next to 4 in order to get that block together, however, would introduce more extensive problems into the display. The present order more accurately reflects the general system. Only the irregular lack of n for part of subject 4 brings this difficulty.

Otherwise every nonreflexive cell (every cell containing a hyphen) is separated from every other cell by either a horizontal or a vertical line. Ambiguity is nearly zero. The presence of multiple lines between cells indicates multiple features of contrast. The large number of cells separated by just one line indicates how subtly delicate[12] is the contrastive system as a whole—i.e., how dependent the hearer is on interweaving data from all four matrices.

1.6. There remain in the Potawatomi data some further formatives which are of the conventional conditioned type; these variants of cell manifestations may be called alloformatives. They are variants of a wave type, however, since affected phonologically by their neighbors in larger sequences.

[12] A conclusion strongly reinforced by the fact, however, that a small irregularity at one point in the system—the lacking n and k formatives of (9)—has repercussions for the field structure as a whole.

1	3	3p	4
k--#-E-E	k--a-E-E	k--a-E-k	k--a-E-n
kwapum	kwapma	kwapmak	kwapman
k--#-iwa-E	k--a-wa-E	k--a-wa-k	k--a-wa-n
kwapmum	kwapmawa	kwapmawak	kwapmawan
	k--a-mun-E	k--a-mun-I	k--a-mun-I
	kwapmamun	kwapmamun	kwapmamun
	n--a-mun-E	n--a-mun-I	n--a-mun-I
	nwapmamun	nwapmamun	nwapmamun
	n--a-E-E	n--a-E-k	n--a-E-n
	nwapma	nwapmak	nwapman
n--uk-E-E			w--a-E-n
nwapmuk			wapman
n--uk-E-k			w--a-wa-n
nwapmukok			wapmawan
n--uk-E-I	w--uk-E-n	w--uk-wa-n	
nwapmuk	wapmukon	wapmukwan	

In order that the reader may more easily check the degree of difference between the basic cell formatives and the alloformatives as seen in context, matrix (13) (based on one provided by Erickson) gives word forms containing the stem wapm *to see* with formatives from the four person matrices (6–9).

Directly above each cited form the basic alloformatives are given; one hyphen separates formative from formative or stem; two represent the stem; E warns the reader that the affixal person cell of the appropriate matrix is empty in that formula (but the reflexive totally-empty word cells are left entirely blank); an I indicates that a cell from (24) is (nonreflexively) empty, but irregularly so from the viewpoint of what it would be were the cells of the L pattern filled. Sequence of the order of persons (2, 2p, 12, and so on) follows Erickson's arrangement[13] from (6).

Certain formative wave variants Erickson has eliminated before listing the basic formatives in the cells.[14] Further fusions order, reflecting priorities of singular over plural, and of 1 over 2, 2 over 3. His arrangement of the tables reflects a further priority of words with the formative a, in the upper diagonal of our (7), all of which are called 'direct' following Bloomfield (see Hockett 141, fn. 5); the words with uk, from the lower diagonal of our (7), are then called 'inverse'. (Forms with un from the same matrix (7) get unrelated treatment on Hockett 143b.) The subject involved with a, and object with uk, is called 'major'—apparently reflecting the priority of person rankings seen in our (6), since high-ranking subject 2 may be involved with a but not uk; low-ranking subject 4 may be involved with uk but not a. The different priorities of Hockett and Erickson lead to strikingly different displays.

The data in (13) are drawn directly from Hockett's tables on 142, 144; and indirectly, for certain cells (subject 12 with object 3p/4, subject 1p with object 3p/4, subject 4 with object 2s/2p/12/1p/s), from his homonymy statement on 143, end of §7.211.

[13] Which differs from that of Hockett's tables on 142. Hockett uses a more conventional person

[14] This, of course, is one possible source of difference in judgment between analysts—but varying results of this type should be mechanically

and irregularities occur in those animate transitive verb affixes when a negative morpheme s'i (with some alternates) occurs in the verb between (7) and (8), or when a

convertible. The reader is referred to Hockett 140–7, for extensive morphophonemic discussion which is relevant to these judgments. Note, also, his morphophonemic stem formula wapUm *to see*, on 144.

I list, in (14), the alloformatives as they appear to grow out of (13) without reference to more widely applicable morphophonemic rules (see Hockett §2.23), with the number of the matrix in which their basic formative is seen; and the phonological environment, also with matrix number of the relevant conditioning formative. Citation references such as 3p2s are to be read: 'third person plural subject intersecting with second singular object'.

(14) uk (7) ∼ uko before k (9) [see 3p2s; 3p1s]; and before n (9) [see 4s3s];
   k (9) ∼ uk after mun (8) ∼ nan (11) [see 3p1p; 3p12];
   mun (8) ∼ nan (11) after uk (7) [3s12; 3p12; 4s12; 3s1p; 3p1p; 4s1p];
   w (6) plus w of wapm (stem) ∼ w [see 3s4; 3p4];
   wa (8) ∼ um (11) after # (7) [see 2p1s];
   wa (8) ∼ um (11) after un (8) [see 1s2p];
   wapm (stem) ∼ wapum before # (7) [see 2s1s];
   mun (8) ∼ uymun after # (7) [see 2s1p; 2p1p].

Although the last alternation of this set attempts to follow Hockett's form yUmUn (p. 143, §7.212) (and his statement concerning zero, in the same paragraph, leads to our # in (7)), his conclusion leaves me uneasy. If kwapmuymun were rather segmented into k-wapm-uy-mun instead of into k-wapm-#-uyman, the uy would replace the # alloformative in two of the four # slots in (7)— 2s1p and 2p1p. (See, above, fn. 8.) If, further, the wapum of the wapm ∼ wapum alternation could then be interpreted as wap . . . m plus infixed u of subject-object (7), all the nonreflexive # cells of (7) would disappear; un would contrast with and be in image symmetry with uy ∼ u. The infix vowel, however, Erickson would feel has been covered by Hockett's morphophonemic rules (see his §2.23) and hence the infix solution for u as 2s1s, 2p1s is not an attractive alternative here; the # must be retained. It is not clear to me yet, however, how uy can be eliminated as an alternative segment for 2s1p, 2p1p; note also the u segment in 2s1p, 2p1p in indicative preterit and negative indicative preterit in Hockett (§7.212, under 2(5)– 15).

preterit morpheme pun ∼ punin occurs between (8) and (9), or when stems other than wapm are studied.

In spite of the large number of such fusions and irregularities we are nevertheless puzzled by the extensive regularities of a system which involves such intricate interplay of matrices. Would not such a system sometimes break down? And, if so, what would be the effect on analysis? We predicted (see reference in fn. 1) that this change would move in the direction of an ideal matrix with single-cell formatives (and no subgroupings of those formatives).

Fortunately, for Potawatomi, we can see a result far advanced in this direction, through the conjunct suffixes. Hockett (p. 148) lists them in tabular form (which we will not reproduce here). Almost total irregularity of matrix pattern has developed,[15] yet the categories of the field continue to contrast.

2. Turning from languages little known, where our theory has developed, we now suggest that conflation of prefix and suffix sets of formatives might be of some interest applied to a small problem in modern

In reference to possible matrix reconstruction (cf. reference in fn. 1) Erickson had already noted before this set of alternative possibilities arose, that matrices from Eastern Ojibwa (based on Leonard Bloomfield pp. 46–9, Ann Arbor, 1956), would show yi in some of the spots corresponding to Potawatomi # (7) (or the suggested alternative uy ∼ u) as the image of Ojibwa iNi corresponding to Potawatomi un of (7).

For impact of alloformative nan on matrix display, see (11). For implications of stem fused to affix, leading to high-level particles in a larger matrix, see reference in fn. 1.

[15] All the mirror images of (6–9) are lacking. Of the characteristics of the field structure of (12) only the following remain: The reflexive cells continue to be empty. Homonymity of 1p2s with 1p2p continues, as does its contrastive image 2s1p and 2p1p. All categories continue to be contrastive; none are totally neutralized, even though the contrast occasionally is found in only one cell of one row or column. (Thus 3, 3p of subject would reach neutralization except for the wa with 3p2s, 3p1s and aw with 3p4.)

literary Arabic. We choose the indicative imperfect strong verb stem ktub *to write*, of a stem type which may be accompanied[16] by certain prefixes and suffixes.

2.1. The co-occurrence restrictions of prefix with suffix, and the formative-categorical relations lead to matrix patterns[17] of considerable interest. For the indicative[18] prefix matrix, see (16a); for the suffix matrix see (16b).

(16) Modern Literary Arabic Indicative Affixes

(16a) Prefix

	s	d	p
3m	y	y	y
3f	t	t	y
2m	t	t	t
2f	t	t	t
1m/f	ʔ	n	n

(16b) Suffix

	s	d	p
3m	u	aani	uuna
3f	u	aani	na
2m	u	aani	uuna
2f	iina	aani	na
1m/f	u	u	u

[16] The paradigmatic data are found in G. W. Thatcher, Arabic grammar of the written language,[5] p. 72 (London, 1956; reprinted 1958). In (15) we give Thatcher's paradigmatic data; we use f for feminine, m masculine; s singular, d dual, p plural; 1, 2, 3, for persons; we respell his vowel plus macron with vowel doublets, and his initial zero with /ʔ/.

(15)

	s	d	p
3m	yaktubu	yaktubaani	yaktubuuna
3f	taktubu	taktubaani	yaktubna
2m	taktubu	taktubaani	taktubuuna
2f	taktubüna	taktubaani	taktubna
1m/f	ʔaktubu	[naktubu]	naktubu

[17] Provided for us by James H. Snow, University of Michigan.

[18] This prefix set also occurs with the subjunctive and the jussive form. The suffix set co-occurs with strong stems taking prefix set (16a).

2.2. If we try to find category meanings for the prefixes y, t, ʔ and n, note that we have,

for y: 3ms, d, p; 3fp;
for t: 3fs, d; 2ms, d, p; 2fs, d, p;
for n: 1md, p; 1fd, p;
for ʔ: 1ms, 1fs.

Few clear category meanings emerge for any of these formatives; the ʔ versus n is first singular versus nonsingular, but the categorical plurality versus singularity contrast is not paralleled for the other persons.

Similarly, for the suffixes, we have:

for u: 3ms; 3fs; 2ms; 1ms, d, p; 1fs, d, p;
for aani: 3md; 3fd; 2md; 2fd;
for uuna: 3mp, 2mp;
for na: 3fp, 2fp;
for iina: 2fs.

Here, for category meanings, one might abstract aani as dual, uuna as third or second masculine plural, iina as second feminine singular, na as third or second feminine plural; and una as second feminine singular. But these meanings overlap with—rather than neatly adding to—the categorical contrasts of the prefix set.

2.3. We need, therefore, separate and conflated matrices, as for Fore and Potawatomi, to show the total field.

Note in (16a) that the recurrent formative reflect ambiguities—neutralization of matrix contrasts—of an extensive degree. The t as a prefix formative appears somewhere in every column (s, d, p) of (16a) and in three rows (3f, 2m, 2f). The y appears somewhere in columns s, d, p; and in rows 3m, 3f. Similarly, in (16b) suffix formative u appears in columns s, d, p, and in rows 3m, 3f, 2m, 1; and so on.

The prefix ambiguities of (16a), however, are in part resolved by suffix matrix (16b) and vice versa. To show most clearly the

It would appear, furthermore, that a theory in which formative joins morpheme to present total field structure might eventually help in the description of the integration of Arabic consonantal root formative with vowel formative. We shall not attempt to explore this possibility here.

technique of patterning by which this is accomplished, we abstract from prefix matrix (16a) a smaller feminine matrix (17a) of persons 3 and 2; and from suffix matrix (16b) a matrix (17b) of feminine 3, 2.

(17a) Feminine prefix   (17b) Feminine suffix

	s	d	p		s	d	p
3f	t	t	y	3f	u	aani	na
2f	t	t	t	2f	iina	aani	na

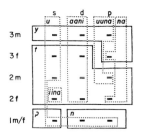

(18=conflated 16a, 16b) Field Structure of Arabic Imperfect Strong-Verb Affixes

In (17a) the third person contrasts with second person in the plural whereas in (17b) it contrasts in the singular. (A conflated prefix-suffix masculine set is not necessary to set up contrast of third with second masculine since they already contrast for all columns of s, d, p in the prefix matrix (16a).)

If, now, in (18) we conflate (16a) and (16b) we see the total field structure. Solid lines group contrastive formatives of (16a). Dotted lines group contrastive formatives of (16b). All cells are differentiated except for the ambiguity remaining between 3fs and 2ms; 3fd and 2md and 2fd; 1d and 1p.

3. Most of the following principles have been illustrated in some detail here. Others are implied, only: for their illustration see the theoretical article referred to in footnote 1.

Interchange of arrangements of rows and columns in a morphological matrix helps one to discover regularities, ranking, and segmentation of pattern—whether submorphemic or intermorphemic.

Pattern is most likely to emerge when the permutations bring occurrences of a particular formative into blocks which form an adjacent set. An L shape implies a ranking of category involvement.

A conflated structure (of a set of affixal sets containing the same category dimensions) arises from the union and intersection of the matrix formatives.

The form-meaning co-occurrence requirement for the existence of a natural language system can be satisfied by formatives as form, plus categories as meaning, even when the form-meaning requirement is achieved only by the interplay of various one-to-many and many-to-one relationships of formative to category within a single matrix or within a conflated field of contiguous or noncontiguous matrices.

A simple morpheme is a vector formative. A simple matrix is composed only of vector formatives. An ideal matrix has only ideal (single-cell) formatives. (Therefore maximum morphemic irregularity—exclusively single-cell formatives—leads to maximum matrix simplicity, i.e., ideal matrix.) Morphophonemic symbolization allows one to present certain regular or irregular changes in the useful guise of pseudo-simple morphemes and matrices.

A matrix as an emic unit can be well-defined via contrast, variation, and distribution in class, sequence, and higher-level matrix. A morphological meaning is definable as a category of an emic morphological matrix.

Emic matrices may prove to be subject to historical reconstruction and to occur in diachronic oscillation from approximations of simple toward ideal matrix, and from ideal toward simple matrix structures.

A CLASSIFICATION
OF DIBABAWON ACTIVE VERBS

JANNETTE FORSTER and MYRA L. BARNARD

Verbs in Dibabawon[1]) constitute a distribution class, typically manifesting the predicate of verbal clauses or the head slot of a verb phrase filling such a predicate slot. A major division within the distribution class is between stative and active verbs. Stative verbs describe a state or effect produced on an affectant by a process or event and fill the head slot of the predicate of stative verbal clauses. Active verbs describe an action or activity performed by an actor and fill the head slot of the predicate of active verbal clauses. The purpose of the present paper is to suggest a method for the classification of Dibabawon active verb stems in terms of co-occurrence restrictions in the situational string and in the clause level grammatical string. Basic to the method is the assumption that there is a situational hierarchy which is relevant to the description of a given language and which is distinct from the grammatical hierarchy.[2])

---

[1]) Dibabawon is a Manobo language spoken in northern Davao province, Mindanao, Philippines. In the analysis of verb classes presented in this paper, extensive use was made of a concordance of 60,000 words of Dibabawon text processed through the IBM 1410 computer of the University of Oklahoma by the Linguistic Information Retrieval Project of the Summer Institute of Linguistics and the University of Oklahoma Research Institute. The project was sponsored by Grant GS-270 of the National Science Foundation. The texts were gathered by the authors during 1961–1963 from eleven different informants, and cover a wide range of subjects.

[2]) Pike has regarded the situational role as one of the contrastive features of a tagmeme, so that an actor-as-subject, for example, is a different tagmeme from a recipient-of-action-as-subject. See his *Language in relation to a unified theory of the structure of human behavior*, Glendale (now Santa Ana), California, 1954, § 7.6, for a discussion of this. In 'Discourse Analysis and Tagmeme Matrices', *Oceanic Linguistics* 3.21 (1964), Pike notes that 'David Thomas

The situational string of an active verb includes the action described by the verb, the participants directly and indirectly involved in the performance of the action, the setting of the action in time and space, and optionally such things as the reason for the action, the means of performing the action, and the distance covered when the action involves motion. Not all slots of the situational string are relevant in distinguishing verb classes. Some, such as those giving the setting in time and space, can occur with any verb. Others, such as causer (one requesting or permitting the actor to perform the action), beneficiary (one for whose benefit the action is performed), objective (that which the actor goes to get), and concomitant (that which is included in the action, often in a subordinate or incidental way) are only indirectly involved in the performance of the action, and can be said to be optional in their occurrence with the verb. There are four participants directly involved in the action of active verbs, and the obligatory presence of one or more of these in the situational string is the basis for certain divisions of these verbs.[3] The four direct participant slots are actor (one performing the action), goal (that acted upon), instrument (that with which the action is performed), and site (that toward or from which the action is directed).

---

has suggested ... the setting up of situational hierarchies as different from grammatical ones', and Thomas in 'Transformational Paradigms from Clause Roots', *Anthropological Linguistics* (January 1964) takes the situational roles (dramatis personae of the action) into account in describing the clause roots which underlie different batteries of grammatical structures.

[3] Elements that are obligatory in the situation may be explicit in the discourse or they may be left unspecified if they are present in the extralinguistic environment or if they are part of the shared experience of all members of the speech community. Hockett speaks of the 'valence' of a particular verb for an appropriate object, whether in the linguistic context or in the nonspeech environment (*A course in modern linguistics*, 248–49 [1958]). Thus in his illustration of two people approaching a car and one saying 'I'll drive', the car is the situational object even though it is not mentioned in the sentence. In the situation reported through the sentence 'I'll slice the bread', native speakers of English understand that the action of slicing requires an instrument and that the usual instrument is a knife and does not need to be specified. Whether these obligatory elements are in the deep grammar, as Hockett suggests (249), or whether they are part of a separate hierarchy, they are relevant to the understanding and analysis of the language at more than one point.

Since the situational slots are correlated with grammatical slots in ways which vary depending upon the verb class, a classification made solely on the basis of the situational string is not adequate. The correlations between situational slots and grammatical slots are most conveniently described in terms of the verbal clause string. Since our concern in this paper is verb classes, not clause structure as such, the correlations will be discussed only for kernel clauses.[4]

There are four clause level grammatical slots (hereafter referred to simply as grammatical slots) which are relevant to our classification of Dibabawon active verbs – subject, object, associate, and referent. Each of these when it occurs in the grammatical string of a verbal clause can potentially function simultaneously as the topic of the clause; the focus inflection of the verb identifies its function as subject, etc. For example, with the tense indicated by *og-* or *-g-* prefixed to the stem, the absence of an overt focus marker signals subject focus, *-on* signals object focus, *-i* signals associate focus, and *-an* signals referent focus. A classification of Dibabawon verbs based on the grammatical slots occurring in the clause or on the potential focus of the verb is not adequate without some reference to the underlying situational string because verbs which can occur in the same grammatical construction do not necessarily occur in the same situational string, and vice versa.

DIAGRAM 1

Correlations between situational slots
and grammatical slots with Dibabawon active verb classes.

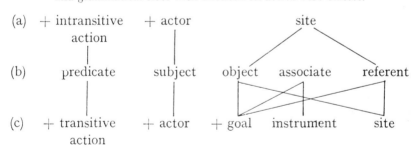

4) The situational string of a causative voice verb includes an obligatory causer slot. For the correlations between situational and clause level grammatical slots with a causative voice verb see Forster, 'Dual structure of Dibabawon verbal clauses' in *Oceanic Linguistics* 3.26–48 (1964).

Diagram 1 shows (a) the situational slots possible with an intransitive verb manifesting the action, (b) the grammatical slots of a verbal clause through which the action is reported, and (c) the situational slots possible with a transitive verb. The lines connecting the situational slots of (a) and (c) with the grammatical slots of (b) indicate the correlations that have been observed. This is a composite diagram and as such it does not show all of the restrictions of occurrence. All active verbs in Dibabawon have an obligatory actor in the situational string, and in addition all transitive verbs have an obligatory goal. Other restrictions of occurrence are described in connection with the verb class to which they are relevant.[5] The classification of verbs presented in this paper is not necessarily exhaustive. As more verbs are examined it may be that additional classes will be distinguished on the basis of differences in the obligatory situational slots and their correlations with grammatical slots.

1.   Intransitive verbs are classified as simple intransitive (i), object intransitive (io), and referent intransitive (ir), according to the situational slots obligatory to each class and the correlated grammatical slots of the verbal clause through which the action is reported. The situational slot of goal is obligatorily absent with all intransitive verbs.

1.1.   The situational string of a simple intransitive verb has an obligatory actor and an obligatory absence of all other direct participants. In a verbal clause through which the situation is reported, the actor is correlated with the grammatical slot of subject.

The examples are given in tagmemic notation with Dibabawon citation and English gloss followed by slot : filler for each situational and grammatical tagmeme. Fillers not present in the cited verbal clause but found elsewhere in the linguistic context are included in parentheses in the situational tagmeme. Fillers understood from extralinguistic context are included in parentheses and given in English only. The symbol –c→ between situational tagmeme and

---

[5] Note that these correlations hold only when the situational slots obligatory to the verb are reported through a verbal clause in which that verb manifests the head of the predicate. If any of the participants are known from extralinguistic context, or if they are reported through some other grammatical construction, these correlations do not hold.

grammatical tagmeme is read 'correlated with'. Abbreviations used include iP = intransitive verbal predicate, (sf) = subject focus, S/T = subject with simultaneous function of topic. Other abbreviations will be identified in the sections in which they are introduced.
(1) *oglangkob ki* ⁶) 'we lie face down' = simple intransitive action: *langkob* 'lie face down' –c➤ iP(sf): *oglangkob*, actor: singular speaker and hearer 'we' –c➤ S/T: *ki*.
(2) *madaas ogtulin kan ibabaoy* 'the domestic pig will grow rapidly' = simple intransitive action: *tulin* 'grow' –c➤ iP(sf): *madaas ogtulin*, actor: (*babuy* 'pig') –c➤ S/T: *kan ibabaoy*.
    Other verbs in this class include *baguus* 'roar' (of wind, airplane), *gimata* 'wake up', *sakindog* 'stand up', *sinogow* 'weep', *lipodong* 'sleep'.

1.2.   The situational string of an object intransitive verb has an obligatory actor and an obligatory site. In a verbal clause through which the situation is reported, the actor is correlated with the grammatical slot of subject, and the site is correlated with the grammatical slot of object. When the object tagmeme of an intransitive clause is not simultaneously functioning as topic of the clause its filler can include a location orientation particle, whereas the filler of the object tagmeme of a transitive clause cannot. This formal difference in the clause reflects the situational distinction between site and goal. Abbreviations introduced in the examples are ioP = object intransitive verbal predicate, (of) = object focus, S = subject, O = object, O/T = object with simultaneous function of topic.
(3) *wadaq logwaq si Pedro duqon ki Maria* 'Pedro did not appear to Maria' = object intransitive action: *logwaq* 'emerge' –c➤ ioP(sf): *wadaq logwaq*, actor: *Pedro* –c➤ S/T: *si Pedro*, site: *Maria* –c➤ O: *duqon ki Maria*.
(4) *puli kud oglogwaqon sikan uma ku* 'I'll just emerge at my farm' = object intransitive action: *logwaq* 'emerge' –c➤ ioP(of): *puli...d oglogwaqon*, actor: singular speaker 'I' –c➤ S: *ku*, site: *uma* 'farm' –c➤ O/T: *sikan uma ku*.

---

⁶) In the Dibabawon citations, *q* represents glottal stop, *ng* represents velar nasal, and except in proper names *o* represents an unrounded central vowel. All of the examples occur in text materials with the exception of (18) which was volunteered as an illustration of the verb form.

Only two other verbs have been observed in this class, *duguk* 'approach' and *abut* 'reach'.

1.3.   The situational string of a referent intransitive verb has an obligatory actor and an obligatory site. In a verbal clause through which the situation is reported, the actor is correlated with the grammatical slot of subject, and the site is correlated with the grammatical slot of referent. Abbreviations introduced in the examples are irP = referent intransitive verbal predicate, (rf) = referent focus, R = referent, R/T = referent with simultaneous function of topic.

(5) *duqon ka bayaq soqi danow* 'you pass this lake' = referent intransitive action:*bayaq* 'pass' –c→ irP(sf):*bayaq*, actor:singular hearer 'you' –c→ S/T:*ka*, site:*danow* 'lake' –c→ R:*duqon...soqi danow*.

(6) *bayaqan tad si Rasagadang* 'let's pass Rasagadang' = referent intransitive action:*bayaq* 'pass' –c→ irP(rf):*bayaqan...d*, actor:singular speaker and hearer 'we' –c→ S:*ta*, site:*Rasagadang* –c→ R/T: *si Rasagadang*.

(7) *oglaguyan ka* 'it might run from you' = referent intransitive action:*laguy* 'run' –c→ irP(rf):*oglaguyan*, actor:(*gibang* 'lizard'), site:singular hearer 'you' –c→ R/T:*ka*.

Other verbs in this class include *agpot* 'reside', *andiyaq* 'go there', *laboy* 'pass by', *layang* 'fly', *uliq* 'return'.

2.   There are three hyperclasses of transitive verbs, defined according to the grammatical slot with which the situational slot of goal is correlated. The hyperclasses are object-goal, associate-goal, and referent-goal.[7] In the class labels, the letter immediately following t (transitive) indicates the grammatical slot with which the goal is correlated.

2.1.   Object-goal transitive verbs are classified as object transitive (to), object associate transitive (toa), object associate referent

[7] These three divisions have also been observed for Maranao transitive verbs where they are attested by differences in the causative inflection of the verbs. This has been described in 'Verb stem classes in Maranao transitive clauses', by R. G. Ward and J. Forster, *Anthropological Linguistics*, 9 (6):30–42 (June 1967).

transitive (toar), and object referent transitive (tor), according to the situational slots obligatory to each class and the correlated grammatical slots of the verbal clause through which the action is reported.

2.1.1.   The situational string of an object transitive verb has an obligatory actor and an obligatory goal. In a verbal clause through which the situation is reported, the actor is correlated with the grammatical slot of subject, and the goal is correlated with the grammatical slot of object. In the examples the abbreviation toP = object transitive verbal predicate.

(8) *ogdaa ki to baqaw ta* 'we will take our provisions' = object transitive action:*daa* 'take' –c⟶ toP(sf):*ogdaa*, actor:singular speaker and hearer 'we' –c⟶ S/T:*ki*, goal:*baqaw* 'provisions' –c⟶ O:*to baqaw ta*.

(9) *ogdaaqon kud soqi bataq* 'I will take this child' = object transitive action:*daa* 'take' –c⟶ toP(of):*ogdaaqon...d*, actor:singular speaker 'I' –c⟶ S:*ku*, goal:*bataq* 'child' –c⟶ O/T:*soqi bataq*.

(10) *nigdawat to kandidu sikan bataq* 'the child picked up the kettle' = object transitive action:*dawat* 'pick up' –c⟶ toP(sf):*nigdawat*, actor:*bataq* 'child' –c⟶ S/T:*sikan bataq*, goal:*kandidu* 'kettle' –c⟶ O:*to kandidu*.

(11) *pigdawat sikan babuy sikan bataq* 'the child picked up the pig' = object transitive action:*dawat* 'pick up' –c⟶ toP(of):*pigdawat*, actor:*bataq* 'child' –c⟶ S:*sikan bataq*, goal:*babuy* 'pig' –c⟶ O/T:*sikan babuy*.

Other verbs in this class include *agow* 'snatch', *ahaq* 'watch', *ani* 'harvest', *baba* 'carry', *bidbid* 'twist', *bugow* 'drive', *bunuq* 'murder', *dinog* 'hear', *dodoo* 'drive', *koqon* 'eat', *minyoq* 'marry', *pood* 'fell', *pudut* 'get'. Two verbs have been observed to have membership in this class and in the referent transitive (tr) class with no apparent difference in meaning: *dakop* 'capture' and *saqab* 'overtake'.

2.1.2.   The situational string of an object associate transitive verb has an obligatory actor, an obligatory goal, and an obligatory instrument. In a verbal clause through which the situation is reported, the actor is correlated with the grammatical slot of subject, the goal is correlated with the grammatical slot of object, and the instrument is correlated with the grammatical slot of associate. An instrument is obligatory in the situational string of a verb if something other than a part of the actor (such as his hand) is necessary to the performance of the action. Frequently the instrument is specific to the verb, as *ahu* 'pestle' to *bayu* 'pound grain', and is not realized in the linguistic context unless an unusual instrument or a special variety of the instrument is used. The grammatical slot of associate when correlated with the situational slot of instrument does not occur with the simultaneous function of topic of a kernel verbal clause in over 60,000 words of text.[8] In unelicited material, when a verb that requires a situational instrument occurs with associate focus in the predicate of a kernel verbal clause, the instrument will be correlated with a grammatical slot in some other construction and the associate-as-topic of the clause will be manifested by a (zero) third person pronoun. An associate-as-topic correlated with a situational instrument and manifested by a noun phrase can be readily elicited, so that the restriction observed in text materials is at least partly stylistic. It does, nevertheless, serve as a formal contrast with the associate-as-topic correlated with a situational goal, which regularly occurs manifested by a noun phrase in unelicited text material. Abbreviations introduced in the examples are toaP = object associate transitive verbal predicate, (af) = associate focus, A = associate, A/T = associate with simultaneous function of topic.

(12) *nigpanaq a to aliwas* 'I shot a buck monkey' = object associate transitive action:*panaq* 'shoot with arrow' –c→ toaP(sf):*nigpanaq*, actor:singular speaker 'I' –c→ S/T:*a*, goal:*aliwas* 'buck monkey' –c→ O:*to aliwas*, instrument:(*tunud* 'arrow').

(13) *ogpanaqon ku suyaq aliwas* 'I will shoot that buck monkey' = object associate transitive action:*panaq* 'shoot with arrow' –c→ toaP(of):*ogpanaqon*, actor:singular speaker 'I' –c→ S:*ku*, goal: *aliwas* 'buck monkey' –c→ O/T:*suyaq aliwas*, instrument: (*tunud* 'arrow').

(14) *ogpilakon dan on kan babuy* 'they speared the pig' = object associate transitive action:*pilak* 'spear' –c→ toaP(of):*ogpilakon*... *on*, actor:plural third person 'they' –c→ S:*dan*, goal:*babuy* 'pig' –c→ O/T:*kan babuy*, instrument:(spear).

---

[8] We are indebted to Carl Dubois of the Summer Institute of Linguistics for pointing out this limitation of distribution in text materials he had examined from the Sarangani Manobo dialect of southern Davao province.

(15) *daaqa now on ton tabaaq su iyan igpilak ta soqi babuy* 'you take the war spear because we will use it to spear this pig' = object transitive action:*daa* 'take' –c→ toP(of):*daaqa...on*, actor:plural hearers 'you' –c→ S:*now*, goal:*tabaaq* 'war spear' –c→ O/T:*ton tabaaq, su iyan* 'because', object associate transitive action:*pilak* 'spear' –c→ toaP(af):*igpilak*, actor:singular speaker and hearer 'we' –c→ S:*ta*, goal:*babuy* 'pig' –c→ O:*soqi babuy*, instrument:(*tabaaq* 'war spear') –c→ A/T:Ø.

Other verbs in this class include *bakus* 'fetter', *baodbod* 'grind', *dupuk* 'pulverize', *gotgot* 'cut with sawing motion', *gupaa* 'segment', *latus* 'whip', *ligis* 'crush', *tigbas* 'slash', *tadtad* 'slice', *tiuk* 'string as beads', *tongos* 'wrap'. There is a group of verbs that has membership in this class and in the referent associate transitive (tra) class with no apparent difference of meaning. This group includes *lopon* 'obstruct', *sampong* 'blindfold', *songsong* 'plug', *tuus* 'cover'.

2.1.3. The situational string of an object associate referent transitive verb has an obligatory actor, an obligatory goal, an obligatory instrument, and an obligatory site.[9] In a verbal clause through which the situation is reported, the actor is correlated with the grammatical slot of subject, the goal is correlated with the grammatical slot of object, the instrument is correlated with the grammatical slot of associate, and the site is correlated with the grammatical slot of referent. No example has been found in text of more than three of the direct participant slots correlated with grammatical slots in a single verbal clause. In the examples the abbreviation toarP = object associate referent transitive verbal predicate.
(16) *pinanampodan to liqog kan hariq kan mongo bawbataq* 'the king beheaded the young men' = object associate referent transitive action: *tampod* 'sever' –c→ toarP(rf):*pinanampodan*, actor:*hariq* 'king' –c→ S:*kan hariq*, goal:*liqog* 'neck' –c→ O:*to liqog*, site:*bawbataq* 'young man' –c→ R/T:*kan mongo bawbataq*, instrument:(*kampilan* 'sword').
(17) *ogtampodon ku to liqog soqidi kampilan ku* 'I'll sever the necks

---

[9] A ditransitive class will have to be described if it can be established that in the situational string of some verbs two goals are obligatory rather than a goal and a site as we have described them here. In favor of a ditransitive class is the absence in our data of any example of a location orientation particle occurring in the referent slot with *tampod* 'sever' or *kuyab* 'cleanse'.

with my sword' = object associate referent transitive action:*tampod*
'sever' –c→ toarP(of):*ogtampodon*, actor:singular speaker 'I' –c→
S:*ku*, goal:*liqog* 'neck' –c→ O/T:*to liqog*, instrument:*kampilan*
'sword' –c→ A:*soqidi kampilan ku*, site:(*bawbataq* 'young man').

(18) *pahid ka sikan buling duqon to pisngi nu* 'wipe the soot from
your cheek' = object associate referent transitive action:*pahid*
'wipe' –c→ toarP(sf):*pahid*, actor:singular hearer 'you' –c→ S/T:*ka*,
goal:*buling* 'soot' –c→ O:*sikan buling*, site:*pisngi* 'cheek' –c→ R:
duqon to pisngi nu, instrument:(cloth).

(19) *dayun impahid duqon kan pigkagat din* 'then he wiped off the
one he had bitten with it' = object associate referent transitive
action:*pahid* 'wipe' –c→ toarP(af):*dayun impahid*, actor:(*bakosan*
'constrictor'), goal:(blood), instrument:(*daanut to kayu* 'inner bark
of tree') –c→ A/T:Ø, site:(*pamaquwan* 'snake') –c→ R:*kan pigkagat
din*.

Other verbs in this class include *kagis* 'shave', *kuyab* 'cleanse',
palis 'peel', *sauk* 'dip'.

2.1.4.   The situational string of an object referent transitive
verb has an obligatory actor, an obligatory goal, and an obligatory
site. In a verbal clause through which the situation is reported, the
actor is correlated with the grammatical slot of subject, the goal is
correlated with the grammatical slot of object, and the site is
correlated with the grammatical slot of referent. In the examples
the abbreviation torP = object referent transitive verbal predicate.

(20) *dayun piglingat ni Sumimbahag kan amuq duqon kan puut*
'then Sumimbahag removed the monkey from the sticky sap' =
object referent transitive action:*lingat* 'remove' –c→ torP(of):*dayun
piglingat*, actor:*Sumimbahag* –c→ S:*ni Sumimbahag*, goal:*amuq*
'monkey' –c→ O/T:*kan amuq*, site:*puut* 'sticky sap' –c→ R:*duqon
kan puut*.

(21) *ogtuntun on man sikan patiukan* 'they lowered the beehive' =
object referent transitive action:*tuntun* 'lower' –c→ torP(sf):*ogtuntun on man*, actor:(*monggqotow* 'people') –c→ S/T:Ø, goal:*patiukan*
'beehive' –c→ O:*sikan patiukan*, site:(ground).

(22) *ogtuntunan kad ki Madagunay* 'I'll lower Madagunay to you' =
object referent transitive action:*tuntun* 'lower' –c→ torP(rf):*ogtuntunan...d*, actor:(*Mabasag*, singular speaker), goal:*Madagunay*
–c→ O:*ki Madagunay*, site:singular hearer 'you' –c→ R/T:*ka*.

(23) *tuntuna a now diyaq soqi lugiq* 'you must lower me into this hole' = object referent transitive action: *tuntun* 'lower' –c➤ torP(of): *tuntuna*, actor: plural hearers 'you' –c➤ S: *now*, goal: singular speaker 'I' –c➤ O/T: *a*, site: *lugiq* 'hole' –c➤ R: *diyaq soqi lugiq*.

Other verbs in this class include *bagnus* 'extract', *batun* 'raise', *buyuq* 'request', *halin* 'transfer', *padpad* 'drop', *pispis* 'pluck'. There is a group of verbs that has membership in this and the associate referent transitive (tar) class with no apparent difference of meaning. This group includes *bilin* 'leave', *ligwat* 'wedge', *tanom* 'plant', *uug* 'drop'.

2.2. Associate-goal transitive verbs are classified as associate transitive (ta) and associate referent transitive (tar) according to the situational slots obligatory to each class and the correlated grammatical slots of the verbal clause through which the action is reported. In each class the obligatory situational goal is correlated with the grammatical slot of associate.

2.2.1. The situational string of an associate transitive verb has an obligatory actor and an obligatory goal. In a verbal clause through which the situation is reported, the actor is correlated with the grammatical slot of subject and the goal is correlated with the grammatical slot of associate. In the examples the abbreviation taP = associate transitive verbal predicate.

(24) *dagow man ogqanak kad on* 'perhaps you are about to give birth' = associate transitive action: *qanak* 'offspring' –c➤ taP(sf): *dagow man ogqanak...d on*, actor: singular hearer 'you' –c➤ S/T: *ka*, goal: (*qanak* 'offspring').

(25) *wadaq a iqanak dini to Macgum* 'I wasn't born here in Macgum' = associate transitive action: *qanak* 'offspring' –c➤ taP(af): *wadaq ...iqanak*, actor: (mother), goal: singular speaker 'I' –c➤ A/T: *a. dini to Macgum* = location.

Other verbs in this class include *timbag* 'discard', *gukat* 'fling'.

2.2.2. The situational string of an associate referent transitive verb has an obligatory actor, an obligatory goal, and an obligatory site. In a verbal clause through which the situation is reported, the actor is correlated with the grammatical slot of subject, the goal is correlated with the grammatical slot of associate, and the site is correlated with the grammatical slot of referent. In the examples the

158

abbreviation tarP = associate referent transitive verbal predicate.
(26) *ogbogoy ad iyu to sobuquk no allang* 'I will give you one of my
slaves' = associate referent transitive action:*bogoy* 'give' –c→
tarP(sf):*ogbogoy...d*, actor:singular speaker 'I' –c→ S/T:*a*, goal:
allang 'slave' –c→ A:*to sobuquk no allang*, site:plural hearers 'you'
–c→ R:*iyu*.

(27) *imbogoy dan on sikan mongo tagudaa diyaq ki Abla* 'they gave
their baggage to Abla' = associate referent transitive action:*bogoy*
'give' –c→ tarP(af):*imbogoy...on*, actor:plural third person 'they'
–c→ S:*dan*, goal:*tagudaa* 'baggage' –c→ A/T:*sikan mongo tagudaa*,
site:*Abla* –c→ R:*diyaq ki Abla*.

(28) *pigbogayan a dayun to mayur noy to pusii* 'our mayor promptly
gave me a gun' = associate referent transitive action:*bogoy* 'give'
–c→ tarP(rf):*pigbogayan... dayun*, actor:*mayur* 'mayor' –c→ S:*to
mayur noy*, goal:*pusii* 'gun' –c→ A:*to pusii*, site:singular speaker
'I' –c→ R/T:*a*.

Other verbs in this class include *baqot* 'add', *botang* 'place',
hobong 'hide', *sood* 'insert', *tagwoy* 'proffer', *taguq* 'insert', *toqon*
'insert in ground'. There is a group of verbs which forms a subclass
of associate referent transitive in which the site can occur correlated
with either a referent slot or an object slot without any apparent
difference of meaning. No transitive class has been identified in
which the site is correlated only with an object and for this reason
we have not defined an associate object transitive class. The verbs
in the subclass include *dogpak* 'pitch', *hawoo* 'toss', *timbag* 'throw'.

2.3.   Referent-goal transitive verbs are classified as referent
transitive (tr), referent associate transitive (tra), and referent
associate referent transitive (trar). In each class the obligatory
situational goal is correlated with the grammatical slot of referent.

2.3.1.   The situational string of a referent transitive verb has an
obligatory actor and an obligatory goal. In a verbal clause through
which the situation is reported, the actor is correlated with the
grammatical slot of subject and the goal is correlated with the
grammatical slot of referent. In the examples the abbreviation
trP = referent transitive verbal predicate.

(29) *himatoy kow to manuk no dadua* 'you kill two chickens' =
referent transitive action:*himatoy* 'kill' –c→ trP(sf):*himatoy*, actor:

plural hearers 'you' –c⇾ S/T:*kow*, goal:*manuk* 'chicken' –c⇾ R:*to manuk no dadua.*

(30) *pighimatayan din kan kuntara din* 'he killed his enemy' = referent transitive action:*himatoy* 'kill' –c⇾ trP(rf):*pighimatayan*, actor:singular third person 'he' –c⇾ S:*din*, goal:*kuntara* 'enemy' –c⇾ R/T:*kan kuntara din.*

Other verbs in this class include *bandog* 'illuminate', *bantoy* 'guard', *boag* 'separate', *duma* 'accompany', *lonaq* 'indwell', *sabuk* 'release', *salig* 'trust', *tabang* 'pick up', *tagad* 'wait'.

2.3.2.   The situational string of a referent associate transitive verb has an obligatory actor, an obligatory goal, and an obligatory instrument. In a verbal clause through which the situation is reported, the actor is correlated with the grammatical slot of subject, the goal is correlated with the grammatical slot of referent, and the instrument is correlated with the grammatical slot of associate. In the examples the abbreviation traP = referent associate transitive verbal predicate.

(31) *ogluluqub a* 'I will cover myself with it' = referent associate transitive action:*luqub* 'cover' –c⇾ traP(sf):*ogluluqub*, actor:singular speaker 'I' –c⇾ S/T:*a*, goal:(I), instrument:(*hikam* 'mat').

(32) *batuna din kan babuy aw luqubi din to hikam* 'he hoisted the pig and covered it with a mat' = object referent transitive action: *batun* 'hoist' –c⇾ torP(of):*batuna*, actor:singular third person 'he' –c⇾ S:*din*, goal:*babuy* 'pig' O/T:*kan babuy*, site:(*pinayag* 'hut'), *aw* 'and', referent associate transitive action: *luqub* 'cover' –c⇾ traP (rf):*luqubi*, actor:singular third person 'he' –c⇾ S:*din*, goal:(*babuy* 'pig') –c⇾ R/T:Ø, instrument:*hikam* 'mat' –c⇾ A:*to hikam.*

(33)   *kan linas to lawaqan, iglopon din to lugiq no pighimu din* 'with bark of a tree he blocked the hole he had made' = referent associate transitive action:*lopon* 'obstruct' –c⇾ traP(af):*iglopon*, actor:singular third person 'he' –c⇾ S:*din*, goal:*lugiq* 'hole' –c⇾ R:*to lugiq no pighimu din*, instrument:*linas* 'bark' –c⇾ eA/T:*kan linas to lawaqan.* Note that this is a derived clause with the emphasized associate as topic (eA/T) tagmeme in prepredicate position.

Other verbs in this class include *soqob* 'cover with a lid', *sampong* 'blindfold', *songsong* 'plug', *tuus* 'cover with leaves'.

2.3.3.   The situational string of a referent associate referent transitive verb has an obligatory actor, an obligatory goal, an obligatory instrument, and an obligatory site. In a verbal clause through which the situation is reported, the actor is correlated with the grammatical slot of subject, the goal is correlated with the grammatical slot of referent, the instrument is correlated with the grammatical slot of associate, and the site is correlated with a second grammatical slot of referent. In the examples the abbreviation trarP = referent associate referent transitive verbal predicate.

(34) *bayad kow to dadua no kapisus* 'you must pay two pesos' = referent associate referent transitive action:*bayad* 'pay' –c→ trarP (sf):*bayad*, actor:plural hearers 'you' –c→ S/T:*kow*, goal:(wages), instrument:*pisus* 'peso' –c→ A:*to dadua no kapisus*, site:(singular speaker 'I').

(35) *pigbayadan tiboq diyaq ki Margarito Guminang* 'he paid Margarito Guminang for it all' = referent associate referent transitive action:*bayad* 'pay' –c→ trarP(rf): *pigbayadan*, actor:(*Kener*), goal: *tiboq* 'all' –c→ R/T:*tiboq*, instrument:(*sapiq* 'money'), site:*Margartio Guminang* –c→ R:*diyaq ki Margarito Guminang*.

(36) *ogbayadan ku ikow to lima no kapisus* 'I will pay you five pesos' = referent associate referent transitive action:*bayad* 'pay' –c→ trarP(rf):*ogbayadan*, actor:singular speaker 'I' –c→ S:*ku*, goal: (wages), instrument:*pisus* 'peso' –c→ A:*to lima no kapisus*, site: singular hearer 'you' –c→ R/T:*ikow*.

(37) *iyan igbayad ku iyu to babuy no kadlaganon* 'in fact I will pay you a wild pig' = referent associate referent transitive action: *bayad* 'pay' –c→ trarP(af):*igbayad*, actor:singular speaker 'I' –c→ S:*ku*, goal:(wages), instrument:*babuy* 'pig' –c→ A/T:*to babuy no kadlaganon*, site:plural hearers 'you' –c→ R:*iyu*. The particle *iyan* marks this as a derived construction.

Bayad is the only verb we have observed in this class.

Summer Institute of Linguistics, Nasuli,
Malaybalay, Bukidhon, Philippines

A hierarchical study of neutralization in Kasem

JOHN C. CALLOW

Institute of Linguistics, Box 47, Achimota, Ghana

(Received 11 January 1967)

The grammar of Kasem[1] is being analysed in terms of a hierarchical model (cf. Halliday, 1961; Bendor-Samuel, 1963), the (ascending) levels of relevance to this paper being word, phrase, clause, string, and sentence. (The 'string' is the unit which functions in the sentence and consists of a tightly bound sequence of clauses, the non-initial clauses operating under extensive restrictions with respect to their structure. This type of syntactic unit appears to be characteristic of many Gur languages and is often referred to as a 'series' or 'serial construction'. For a recent discussion in some detail of this unit, under the term 'clause clusters', see Pike, 1966: 55–78.) At the word level in this hierarchy, a system of categories can be set up to account for the form of every verb word, i.e. so that every verb word can be completely 'parsed' or described in terms of these categories. But one of the characteristic features of this system of categories is that there is extensive neutralization between the categories. The question, then, that this paper seeks to discuss is this: are the ambiguities inherent in the verb word resolved within the language as a whole? An answer is here presented which seeks to relate the resolution of the ambiguities to the different levels of the grammatical hierarchy, as set up.

In presenting the patterns of neutralization in the verb system, I will make considerable use of Pike's theory of matrices, as developed over the past few years.[2] Interest in this theory was stimulated by discussion with Pike at the Institute of Linguistics workshop held in Accra, Ghana, during November and December 1965, as it has the considerable advantage of providing a means both

---

[1] Kasem is the language of the Kasena, an ethnic group which is found on both sides of the northern border between Ghana and Upper Volta, and which numbers approximately 60,000. It is assigned to the Grusi subdivision of the Gur (Voltaic) language group within the Niger-Congo language family (after Greenberg). The data for this paper was collected in Paga, in the Upper Region of Ghana, between November 1962 and June 1965.

[2] For a general statement of Pike's matrix theory, see Pike (1962), and for an extended application to West African languages, see Pike (1966). For the use of matrices specifically to study categories across levels, see Ham (1965). It should be noted, however, that there are certain theoretical differences between this approach and that of Pat Ham. In this paper, categories are established for each level independently, and no categories are introduced which are irrelevant to it. This does not appear to be so in Ham (1965) where the categories established for the clause are considered as relevant at every lower level. Thus, for Kasem, the distinction between Affirmative and Negative is established at the phrase level (see Matrix 6 below) but not at the word level (see Matrix 1), where there is no such distinction. It should be noted, therefore, that it is

to display and manipulate a particular 'field' (to use Pike's term, 1959) of
data, as a field. The variety of forms of the verb word constitute such a 'field',
and matrices are therefore used to present and manipulate this data so as to
bring the patterns of neutralization sharply into focus.

The paper will be presented in three major sections. The first will describe the
system of categories set up for the verb word and the neutralizations within that
system; the second will discuss how these neutralizations may be progressively
resolved by aspects of the syntax of the levels above the word; and the third will
illustrate the paper by resolving the ambiguities in a section of narrative text.

1. CATEGORIES OF THE VERB WORD AND THEIR NEUTRALIZATION

The maximum number of forms that a verb word can exhibit is six, and the
minimum, for the purposes of this study, two. (The purpose of this paper can be
achieved without studying every detail of the verb system. In particular, three
limitations are imposed on the data to be discussed. The first is that 'mono-
aspectual' verbs are excluded, i.e. verbs that can occur in only one aspect. The
second is that consonant final stems only will be considered in detail since the
vowel final stems can be treated as a limited type of the consonant final stems.
The third is that the larger body of material will be restricted to formal narration
as this has been the most closely studied so far.) Three categories are established
to account for these forms, and these are shown in Matrix 1, illustrated by the
forms of the verb meaning 'to hoe, farm'. (The consonant phonemes of Kasem

Matrix 1. Categories of the verb word

		Absolute	Non-Absolute
Imperfect		/vàda/	/vàdi/
Perfect	Past	/vàga/	/vàgi/
	Future	/và/	
	Imperative	/vǎdi/	

are /p t c k, b d j g, m n ny ŋ, f s v z, l w y/. The vowel phonemes are /i ɪ e ɛ,
ə a, u ʊ o ɔ/, but a prosodic type of notation is used to write them taking into

not said that this distinction is neutralized at the word level; rather, it has no existence,
having no relevance, at that level.

The research for this paper was in part financed by a grant from the U.S. Office of
Education, under contract 5-14-065, through the Center for Research in Language
and Language Behavior of the University of Michigan. A preliminary version of the
paper was read at a meeting of the Linguistic Association of Great Britain in November
1966.

account the system of vowel harmony that operates for the word (i.e. for the stem and suffix). The five vowels /ɪ ɛ a ɔ ʊ/ belong to one harmonic set and will be written with 'i e a o u' respectively; the other five vowels /i e ə o u/ belong to a second harmonic set and words in this harmony will be written with an 'h' in the determining syllable. By using this orthographic system, constant mention of harmonic alternatives for the verb suffixes is avoided, considerably simplifying the description. There are also four tones, high, mid, low, and rising, indicated respectively by /ˊ ˉ ˇ ˋ/ on the first syllable of the tone unit. Suffixes are always atonal.)

The three categories established for the verb word may be conveniently referred to as Aspect, Tense, and Case. The category of Aspect consists of a two-term system, Imperfect and Perfect. The meaning of the Imperfect Aspect is 'any type of repeated action (frequentative, process, habitual, etc.) or state, without reference to time' and of the Perfect Aspect is 'any type of non-repeated action or single event, without reference to time'. The category of Tense consists of a three-term system, Past, Future and Imperative. The category of Case consists of a two-term system, Absolute and Non-Absolute. The Absolute context is one in which the verb is not closely linked, grammatically or phonologically, with what follows it. The Absolute does not seem, however, to be a purely pausal form, as (i) in the Perfect Past Negative verbal phrase the Non-Absolute form occurs regularly before pause, and (ii) the Absolute form can occur when it precedes locative and adverb phrases, often fluctuating with the Non-Absolute in these cases. Thus, /o twih de mama/ or /o tuh de mama/ 'he comes every day' where /twih/ is the Absolute form, and /tuh/ is the Non-Absolute form. Within this system, then, the form /vàdi/ would be described as the Imperfect Non-Absolute, the form /vàga/ as the Perfect Past Absolute, etc.

The form of Matrix 1 highlights certain peculiarities of the system of categories set up for the verb word. The distinction between the Absolute and the Non-Absolute is relevant to the Imperfect and the Perfect Past only; and whereas the Perfect Aspect has a threefold tense distinction, the Imperfect Aspect has none.

A system of four verb sets is established for Kasem on the basis of the suffixes exhibited by the verb in the two Absolute contexts. There are three such suffixes, /-a/, /-i/, and zero, symbolized in this paper as /-ø/. The suffix /-a/ is affixed to both consonant and vowel final stems; the suffix /-i/ is found affixed to vowel stems only; and the suffix /-ø/ is found affixed to both consonants and vowel final stems, having the form /-i/ following consonants and zero following vowels. This analysis may seem rather unusual, but the following are the three main reasons for adopting it. (i) The suffix /-i/, affixed to vowel stems, is found in contexts where consonant final stems are never found; (ii) consonant final and vowel final stems, in the same context, occur with the forms /-i/ and zero respectively; (iii) the form /-i/, found with consonant final stems, is readily lost in speech, and may well be regarded as the equivalent of a zero suffix, as absolute final consonants do not occur in Kasem (although they are found in many of the related languages). The four verb sets are labelled A to D, and their mutual relationships are shown in Matrix 2.

Matrix 2. The verb sets

		Perf. /-a/	Past Abs. /-ø/
Imperf. Abs.	/-a/	A	D
	/-i/	B	C

In order to study the details of the system of verb sets, and the patterns of neutralization, they are presented in a matrix with the six verb forms defining the columns and the verb sets and subsets the rows. The numeral following a set letter refers to morphologically defined subsets, the lower case letter to phonological types within the sets and subsets. The interstices of the matrix are filled by typical verbs from each set and type.

Matrix 3. Details of the verb sets and word level categories

	Imperfect		Past		Perfect Fut.	Imper.	
	Abs.	Non-Abs.	Abs.	Non-Abs.			
A1	/vàda/	/vàdi/	/vàga/	/vàgi/	/và/	/vădi/	'to hoe'
A2	/ŋòna/	/ŋòni/	/ŋòga/	/ŋògi/	/ŋò/	/ŋŏni/	'to steal'
A3a	/tùa/	/tù/	/tìga/	/tìgi/	/tì/	/tŭ/	'to die'
A3b	/lùa/	/lò/	/lòga/	/lògi/	/lò/	/lŏ/	'to build'
A3c	/tìa/	/tè/	/tàga/	/tàgi/	/tà/	/tă/	'to tell'
A4a	/dùna/	/dùni/	/dùna/	/dùni/	/dù/	/dŭni/	'to chew'
A4b	/jāana/	/jāani/	/jāana/	/jāani/	/jā/	/jā/	'to seize'
B	/té/	/tá/	/tága/	/tági/	/tá/	/tá/	'to shoot'
C	/bwèh/	/bòh/	/bòhŋi/	/bòhŋi/	/bòhŋi/	/bŏhŋi/	'to call'
D1a	/màga/	/màgi/	/màgi/	/màgi/	/màgi/	/măgi/	'to beat'
D1b	/tóga/	/tógi/	/tógi/	/tógi/	/tógi/	/tógi/	'to follow'

To facilitate the discussion of the patterns of neutralization, the following devices will be used. Each distinct segmental stem shape exhibited by a given verb will be numbered from left to right. Thus, the verb 'to hoe' in the first row has three such verb stems, /vad-/, /vag-/, and /va-/, whereas the verb 'to follow' in the last row has only one stem, /tog-/. Then, /vad-/, /vag-/, and /va-/ are given the numbers 1, 2 and 3 respectively, but /tog-/ the number 1 only. Further, if a stem has an overt suffix, i.e. /-a/ or /-i/, it will be followed by a +. Thus, /vada/ would be rewritten 1+, /vadi/ simply as 1. Finally, a stem shape with a distinctive tone will be followed by an asterisk, so that, for instance, /vădi/ would be symbolized as 1*. Replacing the entries, then, in Matrix 3 with this symbolic notation, we obtain Matrix 4.

Matrix 4. Symbolic representation of Matrix 3

| | Imperfect | | Perfect | | | |
| | | | Past | | Fut. | Imper. |
	Abs.	Non-Abs.	Abs.	Non-Abs.		
A1	1+	1	2+	2	3	1*
A2	1+	1	2+	2	3	1*
A3a	1+	1	2+	2	3	1*
A3b	1+	1	2+	2	1	1*
A3c	1+	1	2+	2	3	3*
A4a	1+	1	1+	1	2	1*
A4b	1+	1	1+	1	2	2
B	1+	1	2+	2	1	1
C	1+	1	2	2	2	2*
D1a	1+	1	1	1	1	1*
D1b	1+	1	1	1	1	1

This matrix will now be rearranged, first by collapsing the first three rows, which are identical in pattern; second, by permuting the rows so that there is an approximately increasing degree of neutralization in successive rows; and third, by putting the two Absolute columns together. Further, for convenience of reference, the columns will now be labelled from a to f, and the rows from 1 to 9.

Three distinct patterns of neutralization can be seen in Matrix 5. First, there is no neutralization at all for the first two rows, so that no higher level considerations are needed for these verbs, which represent about 4 per cent (20/500) of the current verb stock. Second, each row has its own distinctive patterns of neutralization, so that the set to which a verb belongs is a determining factor in the patterns of neutralization. Third, apart from forms symbolized by column a, all other possible form-pairs are neutralized somewhere in the system, as follows: b = c in rows 8 and 9, b = d = e in rows 5, 8 and 9, b = f in row

9; c = d in rows 6 to 9, c = e in rows 3, 4, 8 and 9, c = f in rows 4 and 9; d = e in rows 5, 8 and 9, d = f in row 9; e = f in rows, 4, 7 and 9. Also, a = b in rows 6 and 7.

Matrix 5. Patterns of neutralization in the verb word

		Impf. Abs.	Pf. Past Abs.	Pf. Impf. Non-Abs.	Pf. Past Non-Abs.	Pf. Fut.	Pf. Imper.	Neut[ns].
		a	b	c	d	e	f	
A1, 2, 3a	1	1+	2+	1	2	3	1*	none
A3c	2	1+	2+	1	2	3	3*	none
A3b	3	1+	2+	1	2	1	1*	c = e
B	4	1+	2+	1	2	1	1	c = e = f
C	5	1+	2	1	2	2	2*	b = d = e
A4a	6	1+	1+	1	1	2	1*	a = b c = d
A4b	7	1+	1+	1	1	2	2	a = b c = d e = f
D1a	8	1+	1	1	1	1	1*	b = c = d = e
D1b	9	1+	1	1	1	1	1	b = c = d = e = f

In discussing these extensive neutralizations, it should be noted that where columns a to d are concerned, neutralization can occur only in the appropriate Absolute or Non-Absolute context. This implies that the ambiguities b = c and b = d are always resolvable from the context, and so will not be further considered.

2. RESOLUTION OF THE AMBIGUITIES AT THE HIGHER LEVELS
2.1. *The phrase level.* Matrix 6 shows the system of categories set up for the verb phrase. To establish these categories it is necessary to take into consideration the first two orders of preverbal particles, and these are shown in the interstices of Matrix 6, followed by a 'V' indicating 'verb'. The constituents of the verb phrase shown here are obligatory.

Matrix 6. The system of categories for the verb phrase

		Past	Future	Consec.	Imperat.
Imperfect	Affirm.	V	wú tà V	màà V	tà V
	Negative	bā V	bá tà V	màà bā V	yí tà V
Perfect	Affirm.	V	wú V	mā V	V
	Negative	wù V	bá V	—	yí V

It will be observed that at the phrase level, there are no ambiguities in the Negative at all – every form of the verb phrase involving the category of Negative is clearly and unambiguously distinguished from every other. In the Affirmative, however, this is not so, but there is neutralization between the Imperfect Past, the Perfect Past and the Perfect Imperative. Put in other terms, this means that the forms of the verb phrase involving either of the categories Future or Consecutive are all distinct. This means that the Perfect Future form of the verb is always distinguished at the phrase level as this is the form used in both Future and Consecutive phrases.

If we now rewrite Matrix 5, allowing for the phrase level resolution of the Perfect Future, and also eliminating rows 1 and 2 as having no neutralizations, we obtain Matrix 7. To make the remaining patterns of neutralization more perspicuous, column f, the Perfect Imperative, is placed between columns a and b (the Absolute columns), on the one hand, and columns c and d (the Non-Absolute columns), on the other. Circles are used to link together neutralized forms in any given row.

Matrix 7. Patterns of neutralization after resolution at the phrase level

		Absolute		Pf.	Non-Absolute		
		Impf.	Pf. Past	Imper.	Impf.	Pf. Past	
		a	b	f	ċ	d	
B	4	1+	2+	(1	1)	2	c = f
A4a	6	(1+	1+)	1*	(1	1)	a = b c = d
A4b	7	(1+	1+)	2	(1	1)	a = b c = d
D1a	8	1+	1	1*	(1	1)	c = d
D1b	9	1+	(1	(1)	1	1)	b = f c = d = f

The remaining neutralizations can now be conveniently divided into two groups – those that involve the Perfect Imperative, and those that do not. The Perfect Imperative is neutralized in rows 4 and 9 with the Imperfect Non-Absolute; and in row 9 with the Perfect Past in both the Absolute and the Non-Absolute contexts. All the other neutralizations are between the Imperfect and the Perfect Past, in all (Absolute or Non-Absolute) contexts.

For examples of resolution of ambiguities at the phrase level see examples 1, 2, 9, 15 and 17 in the commentary on the text given below.

2.2. *The clause level.* Clauses containing a verbal phrase are divided into two major classes according to their function in the string, termed primary and secondary clauses. Since secondary clauses admit of a distinction of Aspect only, and since the aspect is determined by the string in which they occur, discussion of the secondary clause will be taken up in connexion with the string level in the next section.

The primary clause is divided into two main types – the statement and the imperative, these two being distinguished by intonation superimposed on the lexical and syntactic pitch. (It can be stated in general that the imperative clause has raised overall pitch, narrower intervals, and absence of downdrift.) The imperative is thus clearly marked at the clause level, so that neutralizations involving column f, the Perfect Imperative (c = f in row 4, b = f in row 9, and c = f, d = f in row 9) are now resolved. The neutralizations remaining are all between the Imperfect and the Perfect Past, in all contexts (cf. Matrix 7).

Since there is no example of the Perfect Imperative in the portion of text material that is analysed in section 3, an example is given here. In each case, the clause followed by an exclamation mark is noticeably raised in pitch and the intervals narrowed.

/mú ò làadi ò wí bà yági! bà yági! bà yí dūli!/
emph. he shouted he saying they leave they leave they not throw

'He shouted that they should leave them and stop throwing (stones)'

/yági/ is a Group Dɪb verb, so that b = c = d = e = f is its pattern of neutralization, as is also the case with /dūli/. In the case of /yági/ the ambiguity is resolved at the clause level, in the case of /dūli/ at both the phrase (/yí/ marks the Perfect Negative Imperative verb phrase; cf. Matrix 6, p. 38) and the clause levels. Therefore the forms /yági/ and /dūli/ are analysed as the Perfect Imperative forms (f).

2.3. *The string level.* The string consists of a primary clause optionally followed by a number of secondary clauses, and one of the characteristic features of the string is that it is uniform with respect to Aspect, i.e. all the verbs in the string are either Perfect or Imperfect,[3] the Aspect being indicated by the tones of the pronoun subjects of the secondary clauses, mid tone in Perfect strings and low tone in Imperfect strings. At the string level, therefore, the final ambiguity between the Imperfect and the Perfect Past is resolved, for if the string is one with Perfect Aspect, then the verb in its primary clause must be the Perfect Past form (in a secondary clause it is the Perfect Future) as the other possible forms would have already been resolved at lower levels. (For examples of resolution of ambiguities at the string level, see examples 3, 4, 6 and 16 in the commentary on the text.)

One final problem remains, however. If the primary clause is not followed by a series of secondary clauses indicating the Aspect of the string, and if it itself is not marked as Perfect Future or Perfect Imperative, how can it be determined whether the verb form is that of the Imperfect or the Perfect Past?

---

[3] Certain forms of the Perfect string may contain a verb in the Imperfect Aspect, but such forms are rare and well defined.

There are two principal solutions to this problem, one at the string level, the other at the sentence level. If the primary clause of the string is complex in structure, i.e. if it consists of what may broadly be described as a clause 'couplet', then the Aspect is marked within the primary clause in the same way as it is within the string. Since there are no examples of this construction in the appended text, a couple are given here.

/ò yà máŋi ò yàhdi wú. . . ./
he past already he not-know that . . .
'He hadn't known before that . . .'

In this case, the first five words form a complex clause, and it is marked as an Imperfect one by the low tone pronoun between the two verbs. /máŋi/ would therefore be analysed as the Imperfect Non-Absolute form of the verb.

/ò máŋi ō vùh Nàvŏdo/
he already he go Navrongo
'He has already gone to Navrongo'

In this complex clause, the mid tone pronoun indicates that it is a Perfect string, so that /máŋi/ would here be analysed as the Perfect Past Non-Absolute.

If, on the other hand, the primary clause is not complex, then it is necessary to take into account the position of the primary clause in the sentence; this will be discussed in the next section.

2.4. *The sentence level.* The simple sentence consists of an independent string, optionally followed and/or preceded by a dependent string. In all three of these places the Imperfect Aspect is the marked one, either by the form of the verb itself, or by preverbal particles. If the primary clause is in an initial dependent string, then the preverbal particle /mǎà/ indicates that it is in the Imperfect Aspect, and absence of it shows a Perfect string. This is also true for the independent string, but it should be noted that the phrase level implications of /mǎà/ in this place are different. If the primary clause is in a final dependent string, then the Imperfect Aspect is marked by the preverbal particle /tà/. Again, since there are no examples in the appended text of initial and final dependent strings in the Imperfect Aspect, these are given below.

/ò lán nà mǎà vèh tú, .../
she now as — going as
'As she was on her way, . . . '

Because of the presence of the /mǎà/, the verb form /vèh/ is analysed as being in the Imperfect Aspect, the context also being Non-Absolute.

/. . . sī bā jwà tà yɛ̌h Pàga kùhdi nà būbū tèh tú/
purpose they fut. — knowing Paga bottom sub. began how sub.
'so that they will know how Paga was founded'

In this case, the /sī/ introduces a final dependent string, and the /tà/ marks it as in the Imperfect Aspect. Hence, /yĕh/ is analysed as the Imperfect Non-Absolute form.

For examples of Perfect forms of the verb being resolved at the sentence level, see examples 5, 11, 12 and 13 in the commentary on the text.

2.5. *Some general comments.* Before taking up the detailed study of the resolution of ambiguities as exemplified in some narrative text, a few comments on the above sections will be made. It has been shown that successive levels in the grammatical hierarchy can be used to resolve the ambiguities arising from neutralizations of categories found in the verb word, but what has not yet been emphasized is that there is a recognizable pattern to these successive resolutions. Each level above the word does not simply resolve some random ambiguities but, rather, resolves a specific major ambiguity. At the phrase level, ambiguities involving the Perfect Future are resolved; at the clause level, ambiguities involving the Perfect Imperative are resolved; and at the string and sentence levels, ambiguities involving the Perfect Past and the Imperfect are resolved. It is clear, therefore, that a characteristic feature of each level here discussed is that it distinguishes one of the categories relevant to the verb word.

There are two other interesting features of this system of neutralizations. The verb set D comprises about 80 per cent of the present verb stock (400/500) and it is also the verb set that has the most extensive neutralizations (see Matrix 5), and consequently requires all the levels for the resolution of its ambiguities. Further, the fundamental distinction in the verb system is that of Aspect; (this is the only distinction made for verb set D1b); and this is the distinction that is resolved at the highest levels of the hierarchy.

3. EXEMPLIFICATION FROM NARRATIVE TEXT

The above statements concerning the resolution of the ambiguities in the verb system will now be demonstrated on some narrative text material. The text will be given with an interlinear literal translation, and will be followed by a free translation. Each verb in the text will be underlined and will be followed by an index number which refers to the subsequent comments. The text, of course, includes verbs of every type, in particular vowel final and mono-aspectual verbs which have not been discussed in this paper. No detailed comments will be made on the mono-aspectual verbs, but the vowel final verbs will be discussed within the general framework already established.

/nōonu   mú   wū   dá.   ō   mā   zàɲi[1]   dē   dìdì   sŏŋo   nī.   ò   māà
man   emph. is   there he   —   got-up   day one   house in   he   —

vèh[2]   ò   kátogo   sŏŋŏ.   ò   nà   nūhɲi[3]   ō   yíh[4]   máncōhŋo   nī
going   his girl-friend house he   when   went-out   he   reached   front yard   in

tú,	mú	ò	nē[5]	ò	sŏŋo	máncōhŋo	nī	dǎla	yám;	yà	bíbíhli[6]
when	emph.	he	saw	his	house	front yard	in	logs	the	they	rolling

yà	twī[7]	yà	tógi[6]	ò	yíhga	yà	māà	kĭa.[8]	ō	mā	bwèh[1]
they	falling	they	following	his	face	they	—	passing	he	—	asked

wí	yà	māà	vèh[2]	yǎhm	mú.	yā	mā	láhdi[9]	wí	yà
saying	they	—	going	where?	emph.	they	—	replied	saying	their

wū	mú	wè[10]	pī	yà	māà	vèh[2]	sī	yā	gwàadi[11]
stomach	emph.	aching	result	they	—	going	purpose	they	dig-up

!ihdi.	nōonu	wúm	mā	mòni;[1]	ò	yáhli	dàadi[12]	fí	sī	dī
medicine	man	the	—	laughed	his	tooth	left	little	purpose	it

gōhdi.[13]	dǎla	yám	dáa	mā	jóohdi[9]	yā	tà-ú[14]	wí	ò	tā
fall-out	logs	the	again	—	returned	they	told-him	saying	he	yet

wù	nē[15]	ŋòh.	ò	nā	làga,	sī	ō	jóohdi[13]	ō	zù[16]	nàbōoh
not	saw	thing	he	if	wants	purpose	he	return	he	enter	cowyard

kúm;	mú	ò	wú	nā[17]	ŋòh./
the	emph.	he	will	see	thing

Free translation

Once upon a time there was a man. One day, he got up in his house and was setting off for his girl-friend's house. When he had got into the cleared area in front of the house ('front yard') he saw there the logs (that are used for sitting on) rolling away past him. He asked them where they were going and they replied that, as their stomachs were aching, they were going to dig up some medicine. The man laughed so much that his tooth almost fell out. The logs then told him that he hadn't seen anything as yet – if he wanted to, he should go back into the area where the animals were kept ('cowyard') and then he would see something.

Commentary

(N.B. The verbs that are underlined, but not numbered, are all verbs that occur in the Imperfect Aspect only.)

1. /zàŋi/. Set D1a: b = c = d = e. Resolved at the PHRASE level by the particle /mā/ as the Perfect Consecutive Affirmative verbal phrase; hence, the verb is the Perfect Future (e).
2. /vèh/. Set A3 (vowel final): c = d. Resolved at the PHRASE level by the particle /māà/ as the Imperfect Consecutive Affirmative verbal phrase; the context is Non-Absolute; hence, the Imperfect Non-Absolute form (c).
3. /nūhŋi/. Set D1b: b = c = d = e = f. Resolved at the STRING level as

Perfect as a member of a Perfect string; further resolved at the SENTENCE level as the Perfect Past since it is the primary clause in a string in the initial dependent place in the sentence; context Non-Absolute. Hence, analysed as the Perfect Past Non-Absolute form (d).

4. /yíh/. Set Dɪb (vowel final): b = c = d = e = f. Resolved at the STRING level as Perfect as a member of a Perfect string; also a secondary clause in that string. Hence, the Perfect Future form (e).

5. /nē/. Set B (vowel final): a = c = d. Resolved at the SENTENCE level as it is a primary clause in the independent place in the sentence without the markers of the Imperfect; also, the context is Non-Absolute. Hence, the Perfect Past Non-Absolute (d).

6. /bíbíhli/. Set Dɪb; b = c = d = e = f. Resolved at the STRING level as Imperfect since it is a member of an Imperfect string; context Non-Absolute. Hence, the Imperfect Non-Absolute form (c).

7. /twī/. Set B (vowel final): unambiguous at the word level as the Imperfect Absolute (a).

8. /kia̯/. Set Dɪb (vowel final): b = c = d = e = f. Unambiguous at the word level as the Imperfect Absolute (a). (Note that in this case it is also marked at the phrase level as Imperfect by the particle /màà/, and at the string level by being a member of an Imperfect string.)

9. /láhdi/. Set Dɪb: b = c = d = e = f. Resolved at the PHRASE level by the particle /mā/ as the Perfect Consecutive Affirmative verbal phrase; hence, the Perfect Future form (e).

10. /wè/. Set B. Unambiguous at the word level as the Imperfect Absolute form (a). (This is a case of the Imperfect being indicated by the form of the verb itself in a primary clause in the independent place in a sentence.)

11. /gwàadi/. Set Dɪa: b = c = d = e. /gwàadi/ is in a primary clause in a final dependent place in the sentence. Therefore, resolved at the SENTENCE level as Perfect, since there is no marker of the Imperfect. Hence, the Perfect Future form of the verb (e).

12. /dàadi/. Set Dɪa: b = c = d = e. /ò yáhli dàadi fí/ is a primary clause in the independent place in the sentence, and it is not marked as Imperfect. Hence, resolved at the SENTENCE level as the Perfect Past. In this case, the context (i.e. a following /fí/) is indeterminate as to whether it is Absolute or Non-Absolute. The form is therefore either the Perfect Past Absolute (b) or the Perfect Past Non-Absolute (d).

13. /gōhdi/. Set Dɪb: b = c = d = e = f. Resolved at the SENTENCE level in the same way as 11 (q.v.) as the Perfect Future form (e).

14. /tà/. Set A3c. Unambiguous at the word level as the Perfect Future form (e). (Note that this is confirmed by its being a secondary clause in a Perfect string.)

15. /nē/. Set B (vowel final): a = c = d. Resolved at the PHRASE level by the

particle /wù/ as the Perfect Past Negative verb phrase. Hence the Perfect Past Non-Absolute form (d). (Cf. with 5 above. This is the same form of the same verb, but the ambiguity is resolved at different levels in the two cases.)

16. /zù/. Set A1 (vowel final): d = e. Resolved at the STRING level as a secondary clause in a Perfect string. Hence, the Perfect Future form (e).

17. /nā/. Set B (vowel final): e = f. Resolved at the PHRASE level by the particle /wú/ as the Perfect Future Affirmative verb phrase. Hence, the Perfect Future form (e).

REFERENCES

Bendor-Samuel, J. T. (1963). A structure-function description of Terena phrases. *Canadian Journal of Linguistics* **8**. 59–70.

Halliday, M. A. K. (1961). Categories of the theory of grammar. *Word* **17**. 241–292.

Ham, P. (1965). Multilevel influence on Apinayé multi-dimensional clause structure. *Linguistics* **15**. 5–32.

Pike, K. L. (1959). Language as particle, wave and field. *Texas Quarterly* **2**. 2.

Pike, K. L. (1962). Dimensions of grammatical constructions. *Language* **38**. 221–244.

Pike, K. L. (1966). *Tagmemic and Matrix Linguistics Applied to Selected African Languages.* U.S. Department of Health, Education, and Welfare, Office of Education, Bureau of Research.

Syntax
below the sentence

RULES AS COMPONENTS OF TAGMEMES
IN THE ENGLISH VERB PHRASE

Kenneth L. PIKE and Evelyn G. PIKE

1. Indices[1] for tone and for tagmeme

This paper attempts to incorporate into the structure of a tagmeme certain rules as contrastive features of that tagmeme[2]. The crucial point here is that the rules thus mentioned are not elements which are to be applied to a prior phrase structure made up of units but which are out-

---

[1] List of abbreviations and symbols

Act	active	Monemph	nonemphatic
BR	bireceptive	Nuc	nucleus
BS	bistative	o, p, n_3, n_4	rule indices, see sect. 9
BT	bitransitive	P	phrase
CV	current relevance	Part	participle
D	descriptive	Pass	passive
-D	suffix morpheme	Rt	root
	meaning 'past time'	SA	semiattributive
I	intransitive	SS	semistative
i, j, k, m, n_1, n_2	rule indices, see sect. 4	ST	semitransitive
Indic	indicative	S	stative
Inf	infinitive	T	transitive
Mar	margin	V	verb
Mn	main verb	-Z	suffix morpheme
Mo	modal		meaning '3s present time'
-N	suffix morpheme	3s	third person singular
	meaning 'past state'		

⟨ ⟩ is a class symbol enclosing the only member of that class. e.q. ⟨*not*⟩.
+ obligatory to the construction
± optional to the construction
+/− obligatorily present or absent under specified conditions.
∼ indicates phonologically-conditioned allomorphs.
∞ indicates lexically or tagmemically conditioned allomorphs.
y⟨z y replaces z
verb root₁ the subscript number indicates root index classes.
      For further explanation see section 6.
  -x indicates a suffix.

[2] We have profited substantially by discussing these principles with Peter H. Fries

side those units; rather the rules are essential features characterizing
tagmemes. The rules are emic features of tagmemes, rather than themselves being emic units in their own right.

Analogues of this viewpoint are present in the prior literature, both
for the treatment of the phoneme and for the treatment of the morpheme. As for the phoneme, it has long been argued in tagmemics that
there is a distinction in theoretical terms between an emic contrastive
feature of a phoneme, as over against the phonemic unit itself[3].

For some years before that, we had given to morphemes — not to
phonemes or constructions — explicit tags or 'indices' to show that they
were responsible for (or controlled) certain phonological changes in
words accompanying them. These changes could not be attributed to the
phonemic shape of the controlling morphemes, which in certain instances were completely homophonous with noncontrolling ones. Rather,
the accompanying controlling lexical entry, as such, had to be tagged as
an arbitrary source for the introduction of the changes. For example, in
tone studies where this was especially prominent, one could have in
Mixtec of Mexico two homophonous morphemes, such as *kee* 'to go' and
kee 'to eat' which differentially affected the tone of a following word
such as *isò* 'rabbit':

  kee isò 'The rabbit will go away'
  kee isó 'The rabbit will eat'

where the change from basic mid-plus-low tone (of 'rabbit') to derived
mid-plus-high tone is caused by the preceding word 'eat'. With the indices added, as information which does not reflect phonemic content,
note the same items again, as

  kee[a] *isò* 'The rabbit will go away'
  kee[b] *isó* 'The rabbit will eat'

where index (a) refers to a form which causes no change, whereas (b)
refers to a set of forms which induces this— or other— changes, under
appropriate circumstances. The changes are complex, with very highly
intricate pattern. It is not merely a question of an occasional change,
nor of one simple rule, but of a large interlocking set of rules, which we
cannot give here[4]. The motivation for this kind of approach was very

---

[3] See the first document on tagmemics as such, in Kenneth L. Pike, *Language in Relation to a Unified Theory of the Structure of Human Behavior,* Part I (1954), Part II (1955), Part III (1960); for
explicit discussion see section 8.35, or see the revised edition, (The Hague, Mouton, 1967).

[4] See Kenneth L. Pike, *Tone Languages,* pp. 81–82, 91–92. (Ann Arbor, University of Michigan
Press, 1948.)

great. On the one hand, it allowed for the retention of an enormous amount of experience in the relevance of a phonemic script for tone, both in the ability to present materials which could be used for foreign language learning, and in the presenting of an alphabet which could be read by native speakers directly. It preserved all and only the surface contrasts which were needed for these two purposes. On the other hand, the morphophonemic tags in the lexicon, and the lists of words which operate alike under such rule conditions, plus associated matrices of the more complex pronomial sets of interlocking relations, allow one to see the over all structure of the system as it operates.

In the present article, in this tradition we add *indices to tagmemes* (rather than to morphemes) and show their effect on neighboring forms in the English verb phrase. The use of "rules" in tagmemics is not new—they have been used from the beginning, but in different ways, and without the term rule being applied to them. Specifically, for example, that which we will call here a *placement* rule has been a part of the standard equipment of tagmemics since 1954, but presented in the formulas by way of arrows which showed optional placement[5]. Similarly, that which we might call a *rule for optional occurrence* has been standard in tagmemics from the beginning[6], but written in the form of a ± sign before a tagmeme, without this sign specifically being called a rule. In the present article we continue these matters, but if we call them rules − in order for some current readers to follow the argument more easily − we do so under specific names of differential rule types, so that their differential roles in the theory are not erased.

More recently, Robert E. Longacre[7] has taken the lead in developing a variety of tagmemic apparatus which combines a somewhat classical tagmemic formula (including signs for optionality) and lists of types of fillers, with an appended set of footnotes which are explicitly a *part of the formal apparatus*; neither part is intended to operate by itself. Longacre has also brought this notation to bear on the presentation of the English verb phrase[8].

---

[5] See *Language*, section 7.744.

[6] See *Language*, section 7.745.

[7] See, for an initial instance, Longacre's article with Kenneth Jacobs, Patterns and Rules in Tzotzil Grammar, *Foundations*, 3.325−89 (1967).

[8] In "A Hierarchical Look at the English Verb Phrase", a paper presented, for the Center for Applied Linguistics, to a conference on the English verb, at Harper's Ferry, 1968. To appear in *Journal of Philippine Linguistics*. We are drawing heavily on Longacre's treatment, both in selection of data and in his preliminary tagmemic analysis. He, in turn, is indebted to the work by F.R. Palmer, *A Linguistic Study of the English Verb* (London, 1965), for his background data.

Our intent here is not to add further insights into the basic data of
the English verb phrase, but is rather to explore the implications of at-
tributing a rule to a specific tagmeme of a construction directly in the
formal notation.

2. Constraints on a tagmemic solution

We share some of Longacre's reasons for wanting a tagmemic presentation of the data on English verb phrase. We share a hierarchical view
of language, within which there is explicit desire to retain, wherever possible, words as constituents, and words as constituents in a hierarchical
order as distributed in phrases, with phrases distributed in clauses. Similarly, we wish the auxiliary to be treated as directly part of the verb
phrase — much more closely bound to the verb than is an infinitive
complement following the main verb. In Longacre's terms: 'This approach finds it uncongenial (1) to sever the auxiliary complex from
within the verb phrase and treat it as a separate part of the clause; or
(2) to combine the verb and its complement into one phrase; or (3) consider that stems of one word and inflectional elements on another word
combine into one structural unit.' We may, in fact, specify several constraints which we would put on the acceptability of any tagmemic solution to these — or any other — data.

We wish, further, for the solution of the English verb phrase to be coherent with the theory as a whole. *Motivation*, therefore, is that of *coherence* with the total theory, rather than, first of all, immediate simplicity of a particular rule, or similarity with a rule needed in some one
other bit of grammar selected in an *ad hoc* fashion to motivate the first
one. (From this point of view, that is to say, two situations which rein-
force one another by demanding the same rule, can still be *ad hoc* relative to a theory as a whole. A Cadillac differential may be better en-
gineered than a Ford differential — but it should not be lightly used to replace a broken Ford part.) Similarly, a part of the description should be
coherent with the description, as a whole, of that *particular* language —
not just with the theory as a whole. (Here, again, we emphasize *systemic
coherence* rather than item coherence.) But the theory wants units preserved, where possible, since it claims that if constituents are cavalierly
ignored, eventually no theory could survive — not even one of transformational grammar, since it must eventually be based on some 'phrase

structure' constituents[9]. The theory wishes hierarchical structure to be preserved, in relation to unit preservation.

3. Allo constructions for the active indicative verb phrase

We now give in table 1 summary data for one kind of verb phrase which we wish to describe. We have sorted out the illustrations in the table so that the first half gives illustrations without modals. The second half repeats the same kinds of constructions as the first half, but with modals added.

We then display, in table 2, some construction symbols for data to be represented in the tagmemic formula for each of the eight subsets (*allo constructions*) of the positive materials from table 1 (allowing also for other main verbs in addition to 'eat'). The name of a phrase level tagmeme slot appears at the top of each column. Then in the appropriate cell in the column appears the name of the word construction which fills that slot; and within the parentheses are indicated the constituents of that word, with + and ± signs used to show obligatory and optional occurrence of the constituents. On the other hand the use of separate formulas for each of these allo-constructions would be awkward in two respects: (1) It would take eight allo-formulas to show the data; and (2) it would miss certain generalizations. As for the first, allo-constructions 1a and 1b cannot be combined readily, since the marginal verb of 1b puts a constraint on the ending of the main verb (i.e. the main verb must come with *-ing*). In 1c a similar but different constraint (i.e. main verb must be accompanied by the -N 'past state') requires that 1c be differentiated from 1a and 1b. The combination of the two constraints appears in 1d. The modals, 2a–d, lose none of the constraints of 1a–d, but add further ones. In addition, however, those allo-constructions formulas would not in one simple symbol or rule show that tense comes in every instance in every formula on the first verb of that formula; in the allo-construction formulas this fact would be shown separately each time. Similarly,

---

[9] Note, therefore, that this comprises a starting point in our search for a description of the English verb phrase, differing from that of the early transformationalists. See Noam Chomsky, *Syntactic Structures* (The Hague, Mouton, 1957). We have rejected that kind of splitting of words which was suggested by Zellig Harris to obtain discontinuous morphemes such as . . . *us.* . *us* of *filius bonus* meaning 'male' (see Pike's *Language*, sections 6.54, 7.322 and 7.56).

Table 1
Active indicative non-emphatic verb phrase data.

		Mo(dal)	Neg	C(urrent) R(elevance) [have]		State [be]		Em(pty)		Nuc(leus)
1a	(I)	–	–	–	–	–	–	–	–	eat
	(I)	–	–	–	–	–	–	do	n't	eat
	(He)	–	–	–	–	–	–	–	–	eats
	(He)	–	–	–	–	–	–	does	n't	eat
	(He)	–	–	–	–	–	–	–	–	ate
	(He)	–	–	–	–	–	–	did	n't	eat
1b	(I)	–	–	–	–	'm	–	–	–	eating
	(I)	–	–	–	–	'm	not	–	–	eating
	(I)	–	–	–	–	was	n't	–	–	eating
	(He)	–	–	–	–	is	–	–	–	eating
	(He)	–	–	–	–	is	n't	–	–	eating
	(You)	–	–	–	–	're	–	–	–	eating
	(You)	–	–	–	–	were	–	–	–	eating
1c	(I)	–	–	've	–	–	–	–	–	eaten
	(I)	–	–	have	n't	–	–	–	–	eaten
	(He)	–	–	's	–	–	–	–	–	eaten
	(He)	–	–	has	n't	–	–	–	–	eaten
	(I)	–	–	'd	–	–	–	–	–	eaten
	(I)	–	–	'd	not	–	–	–	–	eaten
1d	(I)	–	–	've	–	been	–	–	–	eating
	(I)	–	–	have	n't	been	–	–	–	eating
	(He)	–	–	has	–	been	–	–	–	eating
	(I)	–	–	had	–	been	–	–	–	eating
	(I)	–	–	had	n't	been	–	–	–	eating
2a	(I)	will	–	–	–	–	–	–	–	eat
	(I)	wo	n't	–	–	–	–	–	–	eat
	(I)	would	–	–	–	–	–	–	–	eat
	(I)	would	n't	–	–	–	–	–	–	eat
	(I)	'll	–	–	–	–	–	–	–	eat
	(I)	'd	–	–	–	–	–	–	–	eat
2b	(I)	will	–	–	–	be	–	–	–	eating
	(I)	wo	n't	–	–	be	–	–	–	eating
	(I)	would	–	–	–	be	–	–	–	eating
2c	(I)	would	–	have	–	–	–	–	–	eaten
2d	(I)	will	–	have	–	been	–	–	–	eating
	(I)	wo	n't	have	–	been	–	–	–	eating
	(I)	would	n't	have	–	been	–	–	–	eating

Table 2

A tabulation of eight Allo-constructions of the active indicative positive verb phrase.

	Modal Margin	Current Relevance Margin	State Margin	Nucleus
Allo				
1a	—	—	—	MnV(VRt ± -Z/-D)*
1b	—	—	StateV(+*be* ± -Z/-D)	MnV(VRt + -*ing*)
1c	—	CRV(+*have* ± -Z/-D)	—	MnV(+VRt + -N)
1d	—	CRV(+*have* ± -Z/-D)	StateV(*be* + -N)	MnV(+VRt + -*ing*)
2a	MoV(+MoRt ± -Z/-D)	—	—	MnV(+VRt)
2b	MoV(MoRt ± -Z/-D)	—	StateV(+*be*)	MnV(+VRt + -*ing*)
2c	MoV(+MoRt ± -Z/-D)	CRV(+*have*)	—	MnV(+VRt + -N)
2d	MoV(+MoRt ± -Z/-D)	CRV(+*have*)	StateV(+*be* + -N)	MnV(+VRt + -*ing*)

*Abbreviations: MoV Modal Verb; MoRt: Modal Root; CRV: Current Relevance Verb; StateV: State Verb; MnV: Main Verb.
Two levels of construction are shown: word level (in parentheses) and phrase level.

nothing in the allo-construction formulas would provide a specific symbol to tell the reader that whatever verb (marginal or nuclear) follows
CRV, that that second verb would carry -N 'past state'; and no symbol
within the formulas would tell him that *-ing* will always follow, on the
main verb, StateV. From these points of view, therefore, a set of allo-
construction formulas would be cumbersome. In the next section we
intend to represent all of these construction variants with a single phrase
formula.

4. Verb phrase formula with indices for various monolevel or multilevel effects

Longacre's rules (by giving a single basic formula including all the auxiliaries, accompanied by a set of rules specifying these co-occurrence
facts) avoid the redundacy. We now wish to get equivalent results, but
by a different mechanism. On the *phrase level* of the hierarchical structure we add *indices* to the respective tagmemes to predict their action
affecting other tagmemes.

In the phrase formula we give only[10] a classical tagmemic slot followed, after a colon, by a classical grammatical filler class, plus the added
index preceding the slot label.

Phrase Level Formulas

Act(ive) Indic(ative Nonemph(atic) V(erb) P(hrase) =
   $\pm i$ Mar:MoV $\pm n_1$ Mar: ⟨*not*⟩ $\pm j$ Mar:CRV $\pm k$ Mar:StateV $+/-n_2$
   Mar:EmptyV $+m$ Nuc:ActIndicMnV

Accompanying the phrase-level formulas are word-level formulas. In
classical tagmemic fashion there must be one of these to represent the
internal breakdown of any label for a word construction which occurs
as a filler in the phrase-level formula. We need, therefore, a breakdown
formula for Mo(dal) V(erb), C(urrent) R(elevance)V, StateV, EmptyV,
and Act(ive) Indic(ative) M(ai)nV. On the other hand, no breakdown
formula is needed for ⟨*not*⟩ since it is grammatically simple. (Angle

[10] Current tagmemic theory is developing much more complex formulas than this. See, for example, Thomas P. Klammer, *The Structure of Dialogue Paragraphs in Written English Dramatic and
Narrative Discourse* (University of Michigan dissertation, 1971). Formulas of four cells, six, or
nine, are being developed for various purposes. Most extensively, see volumes edited by Austin
Hale and Ronald Trail, in *Clause, Sentence, and Discourse in Selected Languages of Nepal and
India,* Summer Institute of Linguistics Publications in Linguistics and Related Fields, Volumes
40, 41, 1973. To appear.

brackets are used to indicate that the enclosed form is the only member
of its class, and hence is also the name of that class.)
Word Level Formulas

MoV = + Nuc:MoRt + Mar: [m] +/− Tense
CRV = + Nuc: ⟨*have*⟩ [i] −/+ Mar: [m] +/− Tense
StateV = + Nuc: ⟨*be*⟩ [i] −/+ Mar: [m] +/− Tense
$\qquad$ [j] +/− ⟨-N⟩
EmptyV = + Nuc: ⟨*do*⟩ [i] −/+ Mar: [m] +/− Tense
$\qquad$ [j] +/− ⟨-N⟩
$\qquad$ [k] +/− ⟨-*ing*⟩
ActIndiMnV = + Nuc: MnVRt [i] −/+ Mar: [m] +/− Tense
$\qquad$ [j] +/− ⟨-N⟩
$\qquad$ [k] +/− ⟨-*ing*⟩

Similarly, to accompany these formulas, there must be a set of *morpheme classes* which represent every filler of a slot if the filler is not itself complex. Thus there need to be morpheme-class lists for MoRt, for tense, for ⟨*have*⟩, for ⟨*be*⟩, for ⟨-N⟩, ⟨*do*⟩, ⟨-*ing*⟩, ⟨*not*⟩ and for MnVRt. We will give these later, after first commenting on certain components of these formulas.

We next define and discuss the rule indices i, j, m, n_1, n_2 :
Rule Indices For Rule Types:

  i Requires the choice of the minus option for the margin in the next verb tagmeme in the verb phrase.
    Comment: This applies whether that verb as a whole is itself marginal or nuclear to the phrase. It is a *surpressing rule* for word-phrase variants, and works *progressively*, operating on the *surface output* of the phrase. It is *multi-level* in its action (see below).
  j Requires the choice of ⟨-N⟩ for the margin of the next verb of the surface structure.
    Comment: this is a *selection* rule for phrase-word variants; it is progressive in impact, and is multi-level in action.
  k Requires the choice of ⟨-*ing*⟩ for the margin of the next verb tagmeme of the verb phrase.
    Comment: A selection rule, operating on the surface output; progressive; multi-level.
  m Requires the choice of tense in the margin of the first verb tagmeme of the verb phrase.
    Comment: A selection rule operating on the surface output; it is multi-level. But this rule is *regressive* in its action.

n_1 Occurs following the first verb tagmeme of the verb phrase.
Comment: A *placement* rule, operating on the surface structure.
(We previously discussed, above, rules for optional placement, as
having been used in early tagmemic formulations. We find these re-
occurring here via n_1. The rule could have been given in terms of
classical tagmemic lines and arrows for the optional placement; the
clumsiness of the arrows is avoided by this index.)

n_2 The EmptyV occurs only with the negative, and only if no other
verb tagmeme occurs in a margin slot in the verb phrase.
Comment: This is an *insertion* rule, adding a semantically *empty*
element regressively on the surface structure. Note: Whenever the
negative immediately precedes the nucleus of the verb phrase, there
is then ambiguity. In one alternative, the negative plus the verb together fill the nuclear slot. This is a source of double negative, and i
used infrequently. We do not discuss that ploblem in its ramificatio

We now elaborate on the rule statements and comments just given.

All rules which operate by adding tagmemes to the level under consideration, or deleting total tagmemes from that level, or marking them
optional (as with ± tagmemes on that level), or moving them will be called *'mono level'* rules, since they affect elements of the string as *wholes.*

With i, j and m, however, a radically different kind of rule is added:
These rules are *multi-level,* since they do not merely move, add, or delete a tagmeme from the string of tagmemes on the hierarchical level
under consideration, but *operate down inside* a tagmeme of that string.
In addition, this operation inside a tagmeme of the string is applied to
a tagmeme of the string *other than the controlling one which carries
the index.*

Thus, for example, the index j controls some characteristic of the next
succeeding surface in the phrase; whatever that next verb is — whether it
be the state verb or the main verb — one must move down inside the verb,
to a lower level of structure, and put constraints on the choice of its suffixes. Specifically, it will require that the succeeding verb in the string
carry the suffix -N 'past state'. Thus the "influence" of the C(urrent)
R(elevance) tagmeme "moves forward" across-to-and-down-inside the
next tagmeme. It is this combination of progressive influence plus lower
level application which forces us to consider this a different kind of rule
from those of same-level placement, deletion, insertion or optionality.

The same considerations hold when the influence (as by index i) is a
lower-level deleting factor — when the influence moves forward and down

inside the vext verb of the phrase, to delete any suffix there. Similarly, we are still dealing with a multi-level rule when the influence works backwards and down inside, as for index m. Here, the rule says to go back to the front of the phrase, after all surface deletions or additions have been taken care of, and then – and only then – apply to that first verb (whether marginal or nuclear) the selection of some tense form. That is, this rule is also multi-level, since it works simultaneously across tagmemes and down into a lower level of the string; but it is regressive rather than progressive.

As an alternative to a regressive rule, it is possible to state this one progressively. The price one pays for this is to set up a symbol before the phrase, neither attaching it to a tagmeme, nor treating it as a component of any one tagmeme. This, as we see it, is the Chomsky solution – but we do not care to follow it, in spite of its formal elegance, since it loses for us the desired advantage of dealing with tagmemes as constituents.

A second alternative would appear to be to apply the symbol m to the first verb tagmeme of the phrase. When this is done, however, another awkward result occurs – so awkward that we reject it. With the m applied to the first verb tagmeme (the modal verb) the result is satisfactory when the plus option of the ± symbol of that tagmeme is activated; but the m is lost from the formula, in this situation, if one activates the minus option of that verb tagmeme. In that case, after the m has been lost, one comes to the next verb tagmeme which should now get the person-tense suffix, but there is no index to tell us how that should be done. In fact, the loss of tense from the phrase as a whole would not show up until one went clear down into the word-level generation, and found somewhere – it is not quite clear where – that tense was lacking, but was needed. There would have to be some tag or some index on each lower level to warn the generating machine that if the modal were not there, the person-tense should be added at least someplace.

A further alternative: Add the m index to each verb tagmeme, both marginal and nuclear, but with the stipulation that only the first occurrence in the surface string should be activated. This tends to be less insightful than our preferred solution, if we assume that surface position in the phrase is in fact the controlling factor.

In our view, however, it is simpler to assume[11] that a language such as

[11] For footnote, see next page.

English does in fact occasionally have a regressive rule, and that the controlling-controlled domain of such a rule can cross levels.

We have one further comment on the phrase-level formula: The Empty Verb margin is shown as $+/-$. By this we mean that the tagmeme is obligatorily absent under certain stated conditions, whereas a simple $\pm$ has no conditions given. In the instance of the tagmeme for the empty verb, the conditions for occurrence are given by the rule n_2, the insertion rule.

We now turn briefly to a consideration of the word-level formulas. No new rules are added, and it is not necessary to have in the word-level formulas any special reference back to the rule indices from the phrase level. The generativeness of the formulas, from phrase level through word level to morpheme classes, operates correctly if the appropriate $+$, $\pm$ and $+/-$ elements are given, along with the potential fillers. But this puts some burden on the reader to make certain that the indices from tagmemes on the phrase level have had their appropriate effect on adjacent tagmemes on that level, and down inside them to the word level. We have felt, therefore, that it was simpler for the reader if we put in *reminders* of the rules on the word level at the appropriate place.

Since these are reminders, and not new rules, we have enclosed the indices in square brackets. Thus, when [m] occurs, it says to the reader: 'If m is supposed to apply here, then choose (the plus option for) person-tense; but if [m] does not apply, choose (the minus option) to eliminate person-tense from this word structure. Similar readings are given to [j] and [k]. The reading for [i] is slightly different. It comes, not where it would affect the choice of a particular filler, but preceding the tagmeme as a whole[12]. In that position, it is directly followed by $-/+$ (rather than $+/-$) to indicate that if [i] is supposed to apply at this point, then the margin as a whole should be deleted; but that if [i] is not to apply, then (1) the margin must be present and (2) [k], [j], or [m] may apply.

Note, furthermore, that there is a *convenience* to the *ordering* of these rules, but not a necessity. That is, if one first applies the [i] rule for the tagmeme as a whole, and the margin is eliminated, then one does not need

---

[11] Regressive rules, though probably less frequent than progressive rules, are well known and useful in description. See Eugene A. Nida, *Morphology: the Descriptive Analysis of Words,* second edition, pp. 283–293, 21–41 (Ann Arbor, University of Michigan Press, 1949). In phonetics, anticipation of articulation leads to regressive etic effects on phonemes, just as slow decay of an articulatory position leads to progressive effect.

[12] Christopher Smeall suggested this alternative to us.

to bother (for the empty verb, say) to determine whether or not [j], [k], [m], apply. But if one wishes to first apply [j], or [k], or [m], and make a choice on that ground, this does not damage us – since if [i] then applies, it will eliminate them at a later stage.

Similarly, we have built in a bit of redundancy into these bracketed indices, to let the reader more easily follow the results, even though this is not necessary for results. Specifically, for example, in the margin for the modal verb we have included [m]+/– tense. But the formula for the tagmeme itself already includes a plus for that margin, and the only filler given as a possibility is person-tense, so that no choice is involved other than [m]. Since, in addition, the modal verb comes first, and since [m] requires that the first verb of the phrase carry tense, there is a redundancy. We could have eliminated the [m]+/–, and merely have given the tense here. For anyone, therefore, who prefers maximum simplicity in the formula (with a slight penalty to the reader, however) these word formulas could be reworked with the redundant bracket eliminated.

We wish now to show the reader that these formulas are formal, and generative, for the materials seen in table 1. We give, therefore, step-by-step instructions for proceeding from our phrase-level formula to the output of table 1.

5. Steps for generating[13] the verb phrase

We now wish to present a mechanical procedure for the utilization of the formula of the Active Indicative Non-emphatic Verb Phrase. In order to produce a sample of that phrase, the following steps can be taken:

Step 1. Flip a coin for each ± tagmeme. (Heads for plus, tails for minus.) Hold any tagmemes with +/–, –/+, or +. (This order of application saves a lot of work in applying rules to tagmemes that later get washed out – i.e., it saves going down to the morpheme level, only to have the morphemes washed out by later rules.)

---

[13] The first attempt to make explicit the generative power of a tagmemic formula is found in Robert E. Longacre, *Grammar Discovery Procedures* (The Hague, Mouton, 1964), further attention to generativeness in tagmemics has been given by Walter A. Cook, in "The Generative Power of a Tagmemic Grammar," *Monograph Series on Languages and Linguistics,* 20.27–41 (Georgetown University, School of Languages and Linguistics, 1967). After we had presented this paper to a Linguistic forum at the University of Oklahoma in the summer of 1972, Joseph Grimes suggested that we might find related kinds of approaches in the work of W.A. Woods, "Transital Network Grammar for Natural Language Analysis," in *Communications of the ACM,* 13.10.591–606 (1970).

Step 2. Check any +/− or −/+ rule and handle, if possible, here.

Step 3. Check for any rule indices in the held tagmeme string.

(a) Make any changes of order, as indicated, and then delete the index.

(b) Where a given index 'x' of one tagmeme affects another tagmeme, mark 'x' on the filler of the affected tagmeme, and delete that index from the controlling tagmeme.

Step 4. Apply Step 4 to each of the held tagmemes of step 3, beginning with the first one and repeating the cycle successively with the others.

(a) If only one label occurs in the filler set, use it, unless choice is conditioned by +/− rules. If several occur, at least one of which has an index, use the one whose index matches a carried-down index. Otherwise, flip a coin to choose one of them. Hold.

(b) If the label represents a morpheme class, write it down, while letting any index carried down from higher levels exercise its impact here. (If there is no error, one should find the complementary reminder already present at the lower level, waiting for decision of its +/−.) Hold.

(c) If the label represents a syntagmeme with included tagmemes (e.g. a word-level formula), write the new formula, and carry down before it any index from step 3.

(d) If the 'x' of the formula from step (a) correlates with an '[x]+/−' of a filler in the new formula of step (c), apply the rule (or carry down to the next level, if necessary) and eliminate the index.

(e) Carry down elements of each filler. Hold.

Step 5. Repeat step 4 for each included syntagmeme formula growing out of step 4(e). (Note exit, at morpheme class, via step 4(b).) Carry down morpheme classes.

Step 6. Take each morpheme class in the held string, and flip a coin to choose a member of the class (heads for top half of list, tails for bottom half; repeat flips until one morpheme is obtained). (See attached list of morpheme classes.) If the class has only one member (shown by list or by angular brackets), choose it. Hold.

Step 7. If there is only one allomorph listed for the first morpheme, record it. If more than one allo is present in the listing, compare with adjacent morphemes in the string, and choose according to conditioning rules as given in section 6 below. Record result. Repeat for all morphemes. (Note: A residue will remain, if the result is conditioned by a level of structure higher than that contained in the highest level treated.

Here, clause-level choices of *I* versus *you* and *he*, affect *am, are*; flip for these choices, beyond the generative mechanisms presented.)

Step 8. Delete spaces between morphemes within a string represented by a word-level formula. Delete, also, space before enclitic abbreviations such as *-n't, -'ve*.

Step 9. Check to see if output is acceptable. (Note: In this special instance, we have given prior definition of acceptability as being comparable to the entries in table 1.)

We show just one sample of the application of these steps. See table 3 for the derivation of (*they*) *weren't pointing*. Note that, in step 1, flips of the coin came up tails for modal and current-relevance tagmemes, so they were deleted; heads retained negative, and state verb; neither +/− nor + (for empty verb and for main verb) is eligible for deletion by coin flip. In step 2, the empty verb possibility is deleted in view of retention of state verb in step 1. Step 3 places the negative after the first verb retained in step 1; in addition, the m is moved from the main verb tagmeme to the state verb filler; and the k is moved from the state tagmeme to the main verb filler.

Step 4 applies separately to the tagmemes of state, negative, and main verb. For the first of these, step 4(a) carries down the single filler construction (with the index which was attached at step 3). Since it is more than a morpheme class, step 4(b) does not apply. Instead, step 4(c) carries down the index but replaces the filler label (state verb) with the full formula from the list of word-level formulas. Step 4(d) then notes the identities of the index m before-and-within the formula, applies it, by retaining tense (and eliminating the index and all other options). Step 4(e) carries down the filler of the nuclear slot, deleting the nuclear label. Then step 5 repeats, as necessary, step 4 for the remaining tagmemes.

Step 6 chooses specific morphemes: for ⟨*be*⟩, *be* (no alternatives, for this one-member class); for main verb root, *point*. Step 7 carries down *point* and *-ing* (no alternatives), but chooses *were* for *be* plus 'past', and *n't* for *not*. (For rules controlling this step, see section 6.) Step 8 deletes spaces within words or before enclitic abbreviations, to give *weren't* and *pointing*.

Table 3

Derivation of *They weren't positive*.

Formula	±i Mar:MoV	±n₁ Mar:⟨not⟩	±j Mar:CRV	±k Mar:StateV	+/− n₂ Mar:EmptyV	+m Nuc:ActIndMnV
Step 1	−*	+n₁ Mar:⟨not⟩	−	+k Mar:StateV	−	→
Step 2		→	↗	→		
Step 3			↗	Mar:m+StateV	Mar:⟨not⟩	Nuc:k+ActIndMnV
Step 4(a)				Mar:m+StateV	Step 5 repeat 4: ⟨not⟩	Step 5 repeat 4: k+ActIndMnV
Step 4(b)					⟨not⟩	
Step 4(c)				m+[+Nuc:⟨be⟩ [i] −/+ Mar:[m]+/− Tense [j]+/− ⟨N⟩]	→	k+[+Nuc:MnVRt [i] −/+ M:[m]+/− Tense [j]+/− ⟨N⟩ [k]+/− ⟨-ing⟩]
Step 4(d)				Nuc:⟨be⟩ +Mar: Tense	→	Nuc:MnVRt +Mar:⟨ing⟩
Step 4(e)				⟨be⟩ Tense	→	MnVRt -ing
Step 5 [See step 4, repeating]				be were (−D 'past time')	→	
Step 6				be	→	point ing
Step 7				were	n't	point ing
Step 8					weren't	pointing

* The minus and plus in the row for step 1 refer to 'tails and heads' of the flip of the coin.

6. Rule indices for allomorphs grammatically, lexically, and phonologically conditioned

Next we give a list of morphemes sufficiently detailed to allow the reader to see how the generative steps work – and specifically to give data necessary for the implementation of steps 6 and 7.

Morpheme Classes

Nuclear verb root class:

MnVRt

Bitransitive (BT)

give$_6$ 'to bestow without a return': *I gave a ball to the child.*

hang$_{11}$ 'to suspend': *I hung the clothes on the line.* See SS for peripheral meaning.

place$_1$ 'to put in a location': *I place the book on the table.*

slip$_1$ 'to pass something to another without arousing attention': *I slipped him a book.* See ST for central meaning.

take$_7$ 'to transport something to or from a location': *I took the cup from her.*

tow$_1$ 'to drag something to or from a location or direction': *I towed the boat toward the beach.*

will$_1$ 'to bequeath': *I will my house to my son.* See T.

write$_8$ (rait ∞ rɪt) 'to form symbols on a surface as a missive': *I wrote a letter to her.* See T for central meaning. rɪt precedes -N 'past state'.

Transitive (T)

beat$_5$ 'to strike repeatedly' or 'to gain victory over': *I beat the flax. I beat their contestant.*

bend$_6$ 'to change the shape of': *I bent the wire.* See R for peripheral meaning.

bleed$_4$ 'to remove blood from': *I bled the chickens.* See R for central meaning.

braid$_1$ 'to interwind': *I braided her hair.*

cut$_2$ 'to sever sharply': *I cut the fabric.*

do$_{10}$ (du ∞ də ∞ dɪ) 'to perform': *I did the work.* See ⟨do⟩ for tagmemically-conditioned meaning.

də precedes -Z '3s present time' or -N 'past state' ∞ dɪ precedes -D 'past time'.

feel$_3$ (fil ∞ fɛl) 'to touch': *I felt the soft blanket.* See D for peripheral meaning. fɛl precedes -D 'past time' or -N 'past state'.

fill$_1$ 'to cause the occupancy of the whole of': *I filled her cup.*

hit$_2$ 'to strike': *I hit the tree.*

hum$_1$ 'to make a vocal melody with closed lips': *I hummed a tune.*

kick$_1$ 'to strike with the foot': *I kicked the stone.*

open$_1$ 'to move from a shut position': *I opened the box.*

plead$_{1/4}$ 'to speak in support of': *I pled his case.*

point$_1$ 'to indicate a direction either physically or figuratively': *I pointed to the sign.*

read$_4$ 'to understand the symbols of writing...': *I read the book.*

see$_{12}$ 'to perceive by the eye': *I saw the child.*

sing$_{13}$ 'to make a vocal melody': *I sang a song.*

will$_1$ 'to determine by act of choice': *I willed his capitulation.* See also BT.

write$_8$ (rait ∞ rɪt) 'to form symbols on a surface for communication': *I wrote the book.* See DT for peripheral meaning. rɪt precedes -N 'past state'.

Semitransitive (ST)

come$_{14}$ 'to approach': *I came here.*

flee$_1$ (fli ∞ flɛ) 'to go away rapidly': *I fled from the turmoil.* flɛ precedes -D 'past time' or -N 'past state'.

go$_{15}$ (go ∞ wɛn ∞ gɔ) 'to move away, depart': *I went downtown.* wɛn precedes -D 'past time' ∞ gɔ precedes -N 'past state'.

slip$_1$ 'to make a sliding movement': *I slipped in the mud.* See BT for peripheral meaning.

Intransitive (I)

shudder$_{1/3}$ 'to shiver as with fear': *I shuddered visibly.*

Bireceptive (BR)

receive$_1$ 'to take in or accept': *I received the prize.*

Receptive (R)

bend$_6$ 'to change shape': *The wire bent.* See T for central meaning.

bleed$_4$ 'to emit blood': *The chicken bled profusely.* See T for peripheral meaning.

Bistative (BS)

cost$_2$ 'to elicit a price': *The book cost me five dollars.*

Stative (S)

have$_1$ ((hæv ~ v) ∞ (hæ ∞ ∅)) 'to possess': *I have three apples.* See ⟨*have*⟩ for tagmemically conditioned meaning. hæ precedes -Z '3s present time' or -D 'past time' or -N 'past state'; ∞ ∅ in faster speech before -Z '3s present time' or -D 'past time': *I'd gone. He's gone.* (hæ v ~ v) occurs other than environments mentioned above and in these other environments v occurs in faster speech: *I've three apples.*

Semistative (SS)

be$_5$ 'to be located': *I am in my study.* See SA for a second central meaning. See also ⟨*be*⟩ for tagmemically conditioned meaning. bi ∞ æm ~ m '1s, present time';∞ ɪ ~ ∅ preceding '3s present time';∞ ar ~ r 'all other persons, present time';∞ wəz '1, 3s' preceding -D 'past time';∞ wr 'all other persons' preceding -D 'past time';∞ bɪ preceding -N 'past state'. The phonologically-varying allomorphs tend to occur in faster speech in the Non-Emphatic VP.

hang$_{11}$ 'to dangle': *I hung on the ropes (where I had been knocked).* See BT for central meaning.

Descriptive (D)

feel$_3$ 'to sense a state': *I feel tired.* See T for allomorph statement and central meaning.

rest$_1$ 'to remain at ease': *I rested quietly.*

Semiattributive (SA)

be$_5$ 'equated to or to have characteristics of': *John is president.* See SS for allomorph statements and a second central meaning; see also ⟨*be*⟩ for tagmemically-conditioned meaning.

Etc. (Other verb types are not illustrated here.)

Marginal verb root classes

MoRt

can$_{16}$ (kæn ∞ kʊ) 'to be able'. k precedes -D 'past time': *could.*

may$_{17}$ (me ∞ mai) 'possibility'. mai precedes -D 'past time': *might.*

shall$_{16}$ (sæl ∞ sʊ) 'future to a given time', occasionally fluctuates with *will.* s precedes -D 'past time': *should.*

will$_{17}$ (wɪl ∞ wʊ) 'future to a given time'. wɪ precedes -D 'past time': *would.*

⟨*have*⟩$_1$ 'current relevance' cf. S MnVbRt for allomorph statement and central meaning.

⟨*be*⟩$_5$ 'state' cf. SS MnVbRt for allomorph statement and central meaning.

Suffix classes

Tense

-D ((-əd ~ -d ~ -t) all other allomorphs listed below ∞ etc.) 'past time'
-əd ~ -d ~ -t following VbRt index classes 1, 10, 16: -əd with those ending in alveolar stops: *bend, point*; -d with those ending in voiced sounds except the alveolar stops: *burn, fill, hang, hum, see*; -t with those ending voiceless sounds except the alveolar stop: *place, slip*
∞ -t following VbRt index classes 3, 15, 17: *feel, go*

∞ -t < d with 9: *bend*

∞ -∅ with 2, 5: *be, beat, cost*

∞ ɛ < i with 4: *plead, bleed*

∞ e < ɪ with 6: *give*

∞ e < ə with 14: *come*

∞ æ <ə with 13: *sing*

∞ ʊ < e with 7: *take*

∞ ə < æ with 11: *hang* (This has been listed above also because of the fluctuation of *hung* with *hanged*.)

∞ o < ai with 8: *write, arise*

∞ ɔ < i with 12: *see*

∞ any other classes not listed here.

-Z ((-əz ~ -z ~ -s) ∞ -∅)) '3s present time'

-əz ~ -z ~ -s following all VbRt index classes except 16, 17. -əz with those ending in sibilants: *place, please*, etc.; -z with those ending in non-sibilant voiced sounds: *give, read, open, fill*; -s with those ending in non-sibilant voiceless sounds: *point, hit, write*

∞ -∅ following VbRt index class 16, 17

⟨-N⟩ 'past state'.

Same allomorphs occurring with the same VbRt index classes as those of the -D 'past time' morpheme, except for those listed below:

-ən ~ -n following VbRt index classes 5, 6, 7, 8, 12, 15: -ən with those members ending in a consonant: *beat, give, take*; -n occurring with members ending in a vowel: *go, see*

∞ ə < i with VbRt index class 13: *sing*

∞ -∅ with VbRt index class 14: *come*, etc.

⟨-ing⟩ 'present state'.

Other morpheme classes

⟨not⟩ (nat ∞ -nt) 'negation'

-nt occurs in Nonemphatic VP unless the preceding form is contracted: *I haven't eaten. I've not eaten.*

⟨to⟩ '(empty of meaning)'

⟨do⟩$_{10}$ '(empty of meaning)'. See T MnVbRt for allomorph statement and central meaning.

   This material is intended to be neither complete nor accurate with regard to number of allomorphs or meaning of morphemes, but is rather designed to allow the reader to get a sampling of the outworking of rules needed to get down to the allomorph level. First, certain main verb roots are partially sorted into sets according to their occurrence in transitivity type (or 'case frame') in a way which we do not attempt to justify here[14]. This sorting is treated as grammatical since it is basic to the structure of syntagmemes, including subject-predicate arrangements and focus.

Further sorting by grammatical slots separates the modals from main verbs. For this class, we treat *can* versus *could* as showing tense – but if we wish to keep the generalization that the m index transfers tense to the first verb of the phrase, then the modals must be shown as having a third person suffix when the subject is third person. To accomplish this, we treat -Z '3s present time' as having a *grammatically-conditioned allomorph which is zero*[15].

The subscript number with each verb root indicates the index class to which that root belongs. The index class is determined by the specific and unique set of allomorphs of the suffixal morphemes with which each verb root occurs. The allomorphs, and in some instances allomorph subsets, of a given morpheme are *lexically-conditioned variants* marked by [∞]; those subsets within such lexically-conditioned variants are *phonologically-conditioned* and marked by [~][16]. For example: $give_6$ occurs with e $<$ ɩ of the -D 'past state' morpheme: *I gave*; with (-ən ~ -n) of the -N 'past state' morpheme: *I have given*; with (-əz ~ -z ~ -s) of the -Z '3s present time' morpheme: *He gives*. We will make this kind of listing below for each of the 17 index classes in our data. The allomorphs of each suffixal morpheme will occur in the same order as in the example above, i.e. -D, -N, -Z.

1: (-əd ~ -d ~ -t), (-əd ~ -d ~ -t), (-əz ~ -z ~ -s)
2: ∅, ∅, (-əz ~ -z ~ -s)
3: -t, -t, (-əz ~ -z ~ -s)
4: ɛ $<$ i, ɛ $<$ i, (-əz ~ -z ~ -s)
5: ∅, (-ən ~ -n), (-əz ~ -z ~ -s)
6: e $<$ ɩ, (-ən ~ -n), (-əz ~ -z ~ -s)
7: ʊ $<$ e, (-ən ~ -n), (-əz ~ -z ~ -s)
8: o $<$ ai, (-ən ~ -n), (-əz ~ -z ~ -s)
9: t $<$ d, t $<$ d, (-əz ~ -z ~ -s)

---

[14] Cf. reference to Hale in footnote 9.
[15] There are alternative analyses which would be quite acceptable within our view.
[16] We are able to utilize, in this framework, the insights of Nida from his *Morphology*. (Reference in footnote 11.)

10: (-əd ~ -d ~ -t), (-ən ~ -n), (-əz ~ -z ~ -s)
11: ə < æ , (ə < æ), (-əz ~ -z ~ -s)
12: ɔ < i, (-ən ~ -n), (-əz ~ -z ~ -s)
13: æ < ɪ , ə < ɪ , (-əz ~ -z ~ -s)
14: e < ə, ∅ (-əz ~ -z ~ -s)
15: -t, (-ən ~ -n), (əz ~ -z ~ -s)
16: (əd ~ -d ~ -t), #, ∅
17: -t, #, ∅

The conditioning *source* of the phonologically-conditioned variants of the suffix is the phonemic shape of the verb root to which the suffix is attached. These *phonological rules* are a feature of the suffixal morpheme and are stated above in the morpheme-class listing of that morpheme. *The final phoneme* of the phonemic transcription (or sometimes other appropriate orthography) constitutes an *implicit phonemic index* dividing these verb roots.

Note, further, that these rules are *ordered from grammar to lexicon to phonology*. The phonological /-əz ~ -z ~ -s/ or the /əd ~ -d ~ -t/ apply as *regular* but only *after* the lexically-conditioning verb roots have been determined. The lexical conditioning is based on the grammatical classes. (Note the grammatical-lexical difference between the tense suffix of modals and main verbs mentioned above.)

Thus far, the controlling influence has been *progressive* – from stem to suffix; but indices may also be appropriate for sets of suffixes which work *regressively* to control the phonology of the stem. This we have, in our data, for /ɪ-/ from *be* before /-z/ '3s present time'; or for /wɛn-/ and /gɔ-/ from *go* before lexically-conditioning 'past time' and 'past state'. Such elements are infrequent[17] in our data. When both progressive and regressive rules are at work simultaneously, we have *fusion* of two items; in such instances segmentation is sometimes impossible. If the phonological sources are not in evidence (as *assimilation*), the fusion must be treated as lexically-conditioned. Note *were*, and *am* from *be* (cf. listing under SS).

In this section we have thus far been concerned with morphemes in which two or more allomorphs differ phonologically, whether the conditioning source is grammatical, lexical, or phonological. But we also have *allomorphs differing semantically*, which are *tagmemically condi-*

---

[17] Alternatively (and often more practically) an index symbol can be omitted, and the items listed as exceptions – defined as non-indexed deviations from a regular pattern.

tioned. It is precisely here that we treat *do* as the main verb 'to act' but having a *semantically-zero variant* (glossed as '(empty verb)') occurring in a marginal slot of the verb phrase. So, also, *be* — which as main verb appears to us currently to have the central meanings of 'to be located', (SS) and 'equated to' or 'have characteristics of' (SA) — has in the margin of the verb phrase a grammatically-conditioned semantic allomorphs which is here glossed as 'state'. Similarly, *have* has semantic conditioning to 'current relevance'[18], in the phrase margin. In spite of the conditioning of meaning by the tagmeme we have here nevertheless attributed the meaning to the morpheme. It is possible, instead, to attribute these special meanings to the tagmemic slots themselves. Under different descriptive circumstances, therefore, we would say that *neutralization of semantic contrast* occurs here between morphemic meaning and tagmemic meaning, with the meaning attributed to both.

We have not given numerical or letter indices to these semantically-conditioned allomorphs, but have rather named them by some semantic feature — e.g. 'state'. (The theoretical importance of these materials to a *wave* perspective on language — and part of the motivation for our approach to conditioned semantic change — will be discussed in section 8 — suggesting a *semantic "rule"* type far more general than those we have been discussing thus far.)

Other allomorphs differing semantically — not phonologically — also occur in our data. Specifically, for example, the English verb roots require indices in the lexicon to specify their transitivity type — whether bitransitive, transitive, intransitive, and so on. Rather than attaching to each root a formal symbol, however, we have sorted the verb roots into lists, labelling these lists as wholes.

Some of the verb roots occur in two or more classes, with slightly different meanings. In such instances, it is usually possible to intuit one of the meanings (and usages) as *basic* (or *normal*, or *unmarked*) and the others as *derived*. The rule for transitivity conditioning of a set of semantic components of a main verb is that the predicate slot of the construction type in which the verb happens to occur has a structural meaning — and that this meaning affects the basic lexical meaning of the verb root. For *feel* (as in *I felt* [= *touched*] *the soft blanket*), for

---

[18] We have not ourselves attempted to deal in detail, however, with the meanings of these marginal verbs. We have, rather, given only crude definitions; the gloss 'current relevance' is taken from W. Freeman Twaddell in *The English Verb Auxiliaries* (Providence, Brown University Press, 1960).

example, the basic meaning is 'transitive'; this verb also occurs in our
listing, here, with the semantic component 'descriptive' (as in *I felt
tired*). In these instances, semantic change is noticeable: In the first, an
action by someone or something is signaled, whereas in the second it is
a state of someone that is signaled. We have double listed and cross ref-
erenced such items.

7. Hyperclass and hierarchy

We now turn to certain general considerations growing out of these
results. The rules indicated by the indices on the tagmemes are applicable to the verb phrase, whether that verb phrase has as its main verb
any of the set bitransitive, transitive, intransitive, etc. Yet each of these
verb sets is a different *distribution class*, since they come in slots of different clause types, respectively. What, then, comprises the class '*verb*'?
It is not a distribution class, for the reason just given, but is rather *a
class of distribution classes* – that is, a *hyperclass*.

Similarly, the verb phrases represented here make up a hyperclass set.
Thus in these materials *the rules apply to a hyperclass*. This fact, in
turn, is precisely one of the elements which led to the setting up of hyperclasses in the first place[19]. Whenever a generalization cuts across distribution classes, applying to a class of such classes, a hyperclass unit is
set up to represent the domain of that generalization. Thus hyperclasses
are involved whenever one mentions terms such as 'noun', 'noun phrase',
'clause', or 'sentence'.

From a tagmemic point of view, there is added motivation given to
the concept of *hierarchy*, by the fact that these rules have a hyper-class
feature, affecting verb and verb phrase, which in part identifies those
levels. Similarly, the need for re-ordering tagmemes in the 'surface' sequence, the ordering of deletions of tagmemes, and the application of
the indexed rules to a 'surface' which is defined in terms of one or more
of these levels, all point to the desirability of retaining hierarchical level
as a theoretical construct.

Note further, that this is specifically related to the desire to keep the
word undivided. By doing so, various kinds of rule relationships can be
shown (in terms, for example, of the generating steps) which may be

[19] See *Language*, sections 11.43, 11.73.

obscured if the level-structure is not retained explicitly both in the underlying theory and in the generating steps. It is not sufficient, for clarity of this rule output, merely to see what material can be generated in some mechanical fashion. We are after more than a machine to generate some output; we are after a device which shows how forms are generated *in relation to levels* which are detectable by various kinds of rule generalizations (and presumably — though not discussed here — to be supported by psycholinguistic evidence).

In this connection, we have treated "auxiliary" not as a constituent separate from the verb on the clause level, but rather as a modifying marginal element within the verb phrase. This, we feel along with Longacre, is intuitively and formally much more desirable than splitting off the auxiliary as if it were on a par with, say, subject and greater-predicate-minus-auxiliary.

8. Grammar as wave

Another important principle can be observed in operation here. It has been shown elsewhere[20] that it is inadequate to analyze a grammar merely as a set of particles — whether given by formula or by list or by other mechanism. Synchronically one can detect *wave-like changes of freedom of occurrence combined with changes of meaning and changes of modificational structure* which show that grammatical fusion occurs which is analogous to phonological fusion within stress groups. In such a setting the nucleus as a grammatical unit is seen as least subject to such change. Here, then, we find a setting for *the development of modals* precisely because there are marginal and nuclear elements within the verb phrase. It is assumed, in this view, that as a main verb moves away from (its usage as a filler of) a nuclear slot to (being a filler of) a marginal slot, that its freedoms will be cut — it will have less freedom to carry suffixes; less freedom to be accompanied by tagmemes of time, place, condition; and is more likely to undergo some conditional change of meaning.

It is precisely this, we affirm, which has happened to a word like *do* meaning 'to perform'. When it becomes a marginal element in the

[20] See Kenneth L. Pike, "Grammar as Wave", in *Monograph Series on Languages and Linguistics* 20.1–14 (Georgetown University, School of Languages and Linguistics, 1967).

phrase, as in *he doesn't eat,* loss of meaning or change of meaning is
there (see section 6). This kind of change is unmotivated in any theory
which does not have the ability to discuss within its basic assumptions
the wave-like character of grammar. In tagmemics, however, it is a standard device available to motivate the relating of *do* as nucleus of a verb
phrase to the *emically same* but *etically different* (conditioned) *do* as
marginal.

In some instances, furthermore, the deterioration of a marginal element when removed from the nucleus can go so far that it cannot easily
be related to the nuclear form any longer. In such instances, one has the
descriptive dynamics available (in tagmemic grammar-as-wave) for the
development of particles. The moment at which a conditioned verb
would become a newly-detached particle would – not suprisingly, in
wave theory – be *indeterminate.*

We give in table 4 a summary of an earlier stage of the development
of the English modals, for which we draw on the discussion by Yoko
Saito[21]. There the ' "auxiliarization" in progress during the Middle
English period' is seen, such that '*shal* and *moot* seem to have developed
into pure auxiliaries earlier than *wil, may,* and *can*'. Note, in the table,
that *shal* has lost, in Middle English, forms for infinitive and past participle, but has gained the right to appear as the first of two auxiliaries.

9. The infinitive verb phrase

Thus far we have dealt with only one of the verb phrase types treated
by Longacre. He gives formulas for active and passive types for each of
the cross-classificatory types of indicative, infinitive, participle, imperative, and emphatic, with a gap at passive-emphatic. We shall not attempt to duplicate that material here, but refer the reader to it. We
shall, however, add just two more phrase formulas at points where
further rule types are needed:

[21] "Semantic System of ME Modal Auxiliaries", in *Studies in English Linguistics* 1.30–34
(Tokyo, Asahi Press, 1972).
    For discussion of elements like *want to, have got, are the ones to, keep on...ing, had
better, used to,* treated as 'true auxiliaries' but 'not themselves one homologous group' –
and in our view seen as representing the wave-like development of modals or auxiliaries –
see William J. Stevens, "The Catenative Auxiliaries in English", in *Language Sciences* 23.21–24
(1972).

Table 4
Development of modals in the ME period (after Saito).

	Have forms for infinitive, past participles, and *-ing*	Can occur, in general, as first component of a combination of two auxiliaries (no main verb occurs here)	Can express either the basic meaning, or a special meaning (an 'overtone') when followed by to-infinitive of a main verb
shal	–	+	+
moot	–	–	–
wil	+	–	–
may	+	–	–
can	+	–	–

Rule Indices for Rule Types (continued):

  o Requires *-ing* in the margin of the first verb tagmeme of the phrase.

      Comment: This is a multi-level regressive selection rule (cf. m).

  p The plus option may be chosen only if the ⟨*having*⟩ margin (as well as the StateV margin) occurs in the phrase.

      Comment: This is an occurrence rule for phrase variants.

n_3 May occur preceding *to* or any one of the verb tagmemes.

      Comment: A placement rule for phrase variants.

n_4 Occurs here or following the ⟨*having*⟩ margin.

In order to illustrate rule n_3, we give the formula for the non-emphatic infinitive verb phrase:

Phrase Level Formulas (continued):

ActInf(initive)VP = $\pm n_3$ Mar:⟨*not*⟩ +i Relater:⟨*to*⟩

$\pm$j Mar:CRV(=⟨*have*⟩) ±k Mar:StateV +Nuc:ActInfMnV.

Word-Level Formulas (continued):

ActInfMnV = +Nuc:MnVRt [i]−/+ Mar:[j]+/− ⟨-N⟩

                             [k]+/−⟨-*ing*⟩

This infinitive phrase formula differs from the indicative one in several respects: (1) The *not* can precede the whole formula; this requires the rule index n_3. (2) The sign ⟨*to*⟩ is an obligatory relator, (3) that carries the i index which in the active form was carried by the modal-verb tagmeme. (4) No tense suffix appear in the phrase, so that (5) the current-relevance verb appears only in its root form — and thus can be optionally represented either (a) as CRV subject to the stated rules, or (b) directly as a morpheme class containing the one member ⟨*have*⟩ (our formula,

Table 5
Active non-emphatic infinitive verb phrase

–	to	–	–	–	–	–	eat
not	to	–	–	–	–	–	eat
–	to	–	–	–	be	–	eating
not	to	–	–	–	be	–	eating
–	to	–	have	–	–	–	eaten
not	to	–	have	–	–	–	eaten
–	to	–	have	–	been	–	eating
–	to	not	have	–	been	–	eating
–	to	–	have	not	been	–	eating
–	to	–	have	–	been	not	eating

above, supplies the reader with the option in parentheses). (6) The lack
of tense also deletes the need for an m rule.

10. The passive-participle verb phrase

We also give one formula which involves both participle and passive,
in order to illustrate the o, p, and n_4 rules added above:
Phrase Level Formulas (continued)
Pass(ive)Part(iciple)VP = $\pm n_4$ Mar:⟨*not*⟩ ±j Mar:⟨*having*⟩ + o Mar:Part
StateV +/– p Mar-as-progressive: ⟨*being*⟩ + Nuc:PassMnV.
Word Level Formulas (continued)
⟨*having*⟩ = Frozen: +*have* + *-ing*
    Optionally: replace ⟨*having*⟩, in the phrase formula, with PartCRV,
    then:
    PartCRV = +Nuc: ⟨*have*⟩ + Mar:[o]+/– ⟨*-ing*⟩
PartStateV = +Nuc:⟨*be*⟩ + Mar:[o]+/– ⟨*-ing*⟩
                                    [j]+/– ⟨*-N*⟩
⟨*being*⟩ = Frozen: +*be* + *-ing*
    Optionally: replace ⟨*being*⟩, in the phrase formula, with
    ProgressiveStateV, then:
ProgressiveStateV = +Nuc:⟨*be*⟩ +Mar:⟨*-ing*⟩
PassMnV = +Nuc-as-passive-action:MnVRt +Mar-as-passive-aspect:⟨*-N*⟩.
    In the passive-participle verb phrase, notice (1) that the negative, via
n_4, may precede the entire phrase or any of its verbal tagmemes. (2)
Greater simplicity of formula and rule structure is achieved by dealing
with *having* and *being* as frozen forms (cf. section 9) than by giving
them word-level formulas of a slot-filler type. (The frozen forms allow

for no substitutions – or deletions – either of root or of suffix, whether freely or due to index rule.) (3) The index k does not occur; if it were – incorrectly – retained, it would wrongly change *eaten* to *eating* after *being* or *been*. (4) The index o is a regressive rule, like m, but determines the occurrence of *-ing* rather than tense. (5) There is sometimes homonymy, according to this analysis, between the tagmeme Mar-as-progressive, with its filler exclusively *being*, and the tagmeme immediately preceding it (see *been* in *having been eaten*) with its filler class made up of *been* and *being*. For the first illustration in table 6, *being eaten*, we treat *being* as filling the state slot rather than the progressive slot, (a) because of the meaning difference and (b) since, if the *being* of *being eaten* were to be treated as filling the progressive slot, this (along with its corresponding negative) would be the only example in which the tagmeme Mar:StateV would not be present in a passive verb phrase.

An important principle may be deduced from the emperical usefulness of treating the frozen forms as units. Whereas for most rule development we seek broader and broader applicability of a generalization, in order to capture "reality", we suddenly find natural data working the other way: There is a need for *a reversing of generalization* – for *narrowing rules* – rules which are needed (a) both to capture *naturalness* of representation (or for efficiency), and (b) to reflect that aspect of *language change which leads to exceptions, idioms, and fusion*. It is high time that our *theoretical* interest take account of that *increasing particularity* in language which is a concomitant of its continuing development of rules and generalizations. Language theory with either of the two without the other is not rich enough to account for language as it is observed.

The conclusion that such a view of fusion is not *ad hoc* to these syntax rules can be supported by the need for a similar view of fusion on a morphological level. It has elsewhere been demonstrated – with data totally independent of the structures treated here – that language theory must include provision for rules and counter rules, for fusion due to phonological merger of morphemes within rhythm units counteracted by analogical extension of matrix formatives which re-establish a system of simple morphemes[22].

---

[22] See discussion of this historical principle, and of re-establishment of equilibrium which has been upset by fusion, in Kenneth L. Pike, "Theoretical Implications of Matrix Permutation in Fore (New Guinea)". *Anthropological Linguistics* 5.8.1–23 (1963), and "Non-Linear Order and Anti-Redundancy in German Morphological Matrices", *Zeitschrift für Mundartforschung* 32.206 (1965).

Table 6
Passive participle verb phrase.

—	—	—	being	—	eaten
not	—	—	being	—	eaten
—	having	—	been	—	eaten
not	having	—	been	—	eaten
—	having	not	been	—	eaten
—	having	—	been	being	eaten

For the remaining kinds of verb phrases (active and passive, whether indicative, infinitive, participial, imperative, emphatic) one should see Longacre for general fillers, contents, and footnoted rules.

11. The tagmeme viewed as a multi-level rule

Once we view a set of tagmemic formulas as containing a variety of rule types, it is intriguing to ask: Can the tagmeme itself be seen, in this perspective, as a rule operating on a set of contrasting features? The answer — yes. In this sense a *tagmeme can be seen as the representation of a multi-level rule which correlates a position in a higher-level construction with a constructional unit which is (at least) one level lower in the hierarchy of constructional units.* This is the "slot-and 'filler' " aspect of tagmemics. Since, however, such a rule has constructions as elements, and such constructions are defined — in our theory — as sequences of tagmemes, the specifying of the tagmeme in terms of rules leads in one step to the re-establishment of the tagmeme as a constructional unit, with sequences of the tagmemes comprising syntagmemes — i.e. emic constructions. But the tagmeme fillers at the *lowest* level of the grammatical hierarchy are morpheme classes, not constructions; and morpheme classes rather than constructions may also fill slots in some higher-level construction: cf. not only *boy, -s, two,* but also *if,* and *but.*

Summer Institute of Linguistics

KENNETH JACOBS AND ROBERT E. LONGACRE

PATTERNS AND RULES IN TZOTZIL GRAMMAR

In keeping with a conviction that patterns are primary in human activity, linguistic taxonomy takes pattern and pattern-point as primitives. Tagmemics assigns a position of privilege to the syntagmeme and tagmeme. The former is a pattern which consists of a structurally contrastive string on a given level of hierarchical structure (whether phonological, grammatical, or lexical). The latter is a functional point within that pattern along with the set of items manifesting the function. In tagmemic grammars syntagmemes are presented as formulas, i.e. concatenated strings of tagmemes related as n-tuples. Ideally the syntagmeme may be regarded as the Cartesian product of the sets which manifest all its tagmemes. It must be kept in mind, however, that (a) certain tagmemes are obligatory; others are optional; (b) special combinatorial constraints may limit the number of tagmemes whose exponents may enter into the Cartesian product in any given manifestation of a syntagmeme; (c) when a subset of one tagmeme enters into the product then it may require a subset – including the null set – of another tagmeme. Besides these combinatorial and exponential constraints there may need to be permutation rules whenever the tagmemes may, under given conditions, occur in an order other than that given in the formula.

This article is intended to exemplify a description of a language which begins with pattern (syntagmeme) and pattern-point (tagmeme) but which elaborates via (partially ordered) rules. The formulas present contrasting wholes relevant to the structure of the language, in this case the Tzotzil of Southern Mexico.[1] Such a starting point entails a certain inevitable redundancy in that patterns are only partially different. Each set of patterns is preceded by general rules relevant to that set as a whole. Many of the patterns are also accompanied by special rules relevant only to that pattern. Whenever possible rules are not repeated. The general rules, formulas, and

---

[1] Tzotzil is a Mayan language spoken by about 65000 speakers in the state of Chiapas, Mexico. The dialect here studied is Chamula, spoken around San Cristobal de Las Casas. The data were gathered from 1962–5. The principal informant was Domingo Hernandez from San Juan, Chamula. The analysis and writing of this paper was largely done at the Centro Linguistico Manuel Gamio, Ixmiquilpan, Hidalgo, Mexico. – For some previous articles on Tzotzil grammar see Colin Delgaty, 'Tzotzil Verb Phrase Structure', in *Mayan Studies*, I, Norman 1960, pp. 82–120, and Alfa Delgaty, 'Notes on Dependent versus Independent Nouns in Tsotsil', *William Cameron Townsend en el Vigisimoquinto aniversario del Instituto Linguistico de Verano*, Mexico, D.F., 1961, pp. 413–20.

special rules are presented in boxes. They are considered to constitute the grammar in the narrowest sense of the word. This apparatus is accompanied by commentary and illustrative material. In the Appendix relevant sets are given and in some cases charted.

This paper deals with Tzotzil phrases and clauses. In Tzotzil, as in many (if not all) Mayan languages, it does not seem profitable to distinguish word from phrase as grammatical levels.[2] While there is a stem (or derivative level) there is but one further grammatical level between stem and clause. This intermediate level, which we here term the phrase is characterized by varying degrees of phonological cohesion correlating roughly with the distance of elements from the stem.

I. VERB PHRASES

Phrases 100–300 are verb phrases. Within the verb phrases 100 are active; 200 are passive; and 300 are stative, gerundive, and existential. Decade numbers indicate: 10 intransitive; 20 transitive; 30 ditransitive; 40 agentive (only in 200); 50 stative; 60 gerundive; and 70 existential (the latter three only in 300). Unit numbers indicate: 1 indicative; 2 subjunctive; 3 negative; 4 imperative; and 5 cohortative.

General Rules for Verb Phrases

ASP X AUX
  V1.   When ASP: asp 1/4/5/8/9, then -AUX.

Position of ASP
  V2.   ASP: asp 8/9 follows STEM.

Permutations of MOD
  V3.   MODAL: o *permanent*, occurs only post-STEM (PLUR).
  V4.   When +AUX, then MOD/LIM MOD may permute to post-AUX (SUBJN).
  V5.   When ASP: asp 1/4, then MOD/LIM MOD may permute to post-ASP (SUBJN).

Re. ASP: asp 1
  V6.   When ASP: asp 1 X 1/3 pers A in 120, 131, then asp 1: ta; otherwise asp 1: ta . . . x-.

---

[2] Cf. Colin Delgaty, 'Tzotzil Verb Phrase Structure', p. 83; Clarence and Katherine Church, 'The Jacaltec Noun Phrase', in *Mayan Studies*, I, pp. 158–170, esp. p. 160, fn. 4. Also note concerning K'ekchi in Longacre, *Grammar Discovery Procedures*, pp. 42–3.

> V7. Whenever asp 1:ta ... x- occurs contiguous to SUBJN and/or MOD/LIM MOD, then ta ... x- brackets these elements.
>
> Re. any tagmeme Z: pers A/B
> V8. Z: pers B precedes (ACT) STEM.
> V9. Z: pers A X PLUR: pers A'; Z: pers B X PLUR: pers B'.
> V10. ACT: per A a- *you* ~X DO/IO: per B i- *me*; rather ACT: per A a-*you* X DO/IO: per C -un *me*.
>
> Re. any tagmeme Z:3 per pl C
> V11. SUBJN: -uc follows Z:3 per pl C.
>
> Re. PLUR: pers A'/B' X DO/IO: pers pl C.
> V12. PLUR: B' ~X DO/IO: pers pl C.
> V13. PLUR: 1 per excl A' X DO/IO: 2 per pl C.
> V14. PLUR: 2/3 pers A' X DO/IO: 1 per excl C.
>
> Re. permutation of PLUR: A'
> V15. PLUR: A' follows DO/IO: 2 pers C.
>
> NEG X MOD X REST
> V16. When NEG: mu and +REST, then +MOD.
>
> Special exponents of DO/IO
> V17. DO/IO: *jba*[3] *self 1 per*; aba *self 2 per*; sba *self 3 per;* in 120–30.

V1. Auxiliary does not occur with the aspects listed in this rule. With aspects 2, 3, 6, and 7, however, Auxiliary is optional.

V2. Aside from aspect 8 or 9 which follows the Stem, aspects 1–7 occur somewhere preceding the Stem as indicated in the various formulas. While aspect 7 has null manifestation it is assumed to occur where the majority of the prefixes occur.

V3. This rule tells us that when Modal tagmeme is manifested by o *permanent* it occurs only post-Stem plus or minus the Pluralizer.

[3] The orthographic symbols of this paper correspond to the following Tzotzil phonemes (cf. Nadine Weathers, 'Tsotsil Phonemes with Special Reference to Allophones of b', *International Journal of American Linguistics*, April 1947, 108–11):

b = b	ch = č	ch' = chʔ	j = h	i = i
p = p	' = ʔ	m = m	v = v	e = e
t = t	t' = tʔ	n = n	y = y	a = a
c/qu = k	c'/q'u = kʔ	s = s	l = l	o = o
ts = c	ts' = tsʔ	x = š	r = r	u = u

V4. In the formulas for non-negative phrases in the active and passive systems the Modal tagmemes are assigned a position out beyond the Stem plus or minus the Pluralizer. This rule tells us that in the presence of an Auxiliary the Modal tagmemes may permute to a position following the Auxiliary or the Auxiliary plus the Subjunctive marker.

V5. The presence of aspects 1 or 4 permits a similar permutation of the Modal tagmemes to a position following Aspect or Aspect plus the Subjunctive marker.

V6. This rule states the distribution of the two allomorphs of the morpheme which manifest aspect 1.

V7. Whenever for any reason (cf. rules V3–V5), the subjunctive particle -uc, a Modal, the Limited Modal manifested by ono'ox, or a sequence of -uc plus Modal or Limited Modal would occur contiguous to the allomorph ta ... x- of aspect 1, the former are bracketed by the latter.

V8. In this rule, Z symbolizes any tagmeme marking participant, i.e. Subject tagmeme of an intransitive verb, Direct Object of a transitive verb, Indirect Object of a ditransitive verb (whether active or passive), or Subject as goal of a passive transitive verb. Whenever any of these tagmemes is manifested by persons of set B that tagmeme precedes the Stem in intransitive and passive and precedes the Actor in transitive and ditransitive. This is true whether or not so indicated in a particular formula. Thus in the formula for phrase 111 SUBJ:pers B/C/D occurs following the Stem. Nevertheless, pursuant to this rule Subject manifested by persons of set B must precede the Stem. Persons of set C and D occur as indicated in all formulas.

V9. The Pluralizer tagmeme pluralizes one and only one of the tagmemes representing participants. If such a tagmeme is manifested by persons of set A then that tagmeme may be pluralized only by the Pluralizer tagmeme manifested by the persons of set A'. Similarily a tagmeme manifested by persons of set B may be pluralized only by persons of set B'. Thus, in a transitive verb when persons of set B manifest Object and persons of set A manifest Actor either Object or Actor may be pluralized, but not both.

V10. Whenever anywhere in the formulas for transitive and ditransitive verb phrases the Actor is manifested by persons of set A and the Direct Object or Indirect Object is manifested by persons of set B, the restriction represented in this rule is relevant. The specific morpheme a- *you* of persons set A may not co-occur with i- *me* of persons set B. In this case the morpheme i- *me* is replaced by -un *me* of persons set C.

chamajun *you will hit me* (ch- aspect 3 *incomplete*, a- actor per A *2 per*, maj transitive stem *to hit*, -un direct object per C *1 per*)

V11. This rule tells us that the subjunctive particle -uc will follow the tagmeme that is manifested by third person plural of set C.

V12. Anywhere in the formulas for transitive and ditransitive verb phrases the Pluralizer tagmeme manifested by persons of set B′ will not co-occur with Direct Object or Indirect Object manifested by persons plural of set C.

V13. Anywhere in the formulas for transitive and ditransitive verb phrases the Pluralizer tagmeme manifested by first person exclusive of set A′ may co-occur with Direct Object or Indirect Object manifested by second person plural of set C.

V14. Anywhere in the formulas for transitive and ditransitive verb phrases the Pluralizer tagmeme manifested by second or third persons of set A′ may co-occur with Direct Object or Indirect Object manifested by first person exclusive of set C.

V15. This rule states the permutation that occurs when Pluralizer manifested by set A′ (cf. rule V13) occurs with Direct Object or Indirect Object manifested by second persons of set C.

V16. Negative verb phrases are characterized by many special co-occurrence restrictions, only some of which can be summarized in general rules. This rule states that whenever the Negative tagmeme is manifested by mu and whenever the Restrictive tagmeme occurs also; then the Modal tagmeme must occur.

V17. This rule states a special set of exponents of Direct Object and Indirect Object. Occurrence of these exponents determines reflexive subtypes of the transitive and ditransitive verb phrases.

ta smil sba *he will kill himself* (ta aspect 1 *incomplete*, s- actor per A *3 per*, mil transitive stem *to kill*, sba direct object *self 3 per*)

laj yalbe sbaic *they said among themselves* (laj aspect 4 *complete*, y- actor per A *3 per*, al transitive stem *to say*, -be referent, sba indirect object *self 3 per*, -ic plural per A′ *3 per*)

Phrase 111 (act. intr. indic. verb phrase) = +ASP:asp 1–3/5–7/9 ±AUX:aux +STEM:is ±PLUR:pers B′ +SUBJ:pers B/C/D ±MOD:mod⁴ ±DIR:dir.
1. When ASP:asp 9, then SUBJ:pers C.
2. Otherwise, When -AUX, then SUBJ:pers B; when +AUX, then SUBJ:pers D.

---

⁴ Occasionally a cluster of two modal particles may occur in a verb phrase.

In the active intransitive indicative verb phrase the Subject is the actor without a goal. The obligatory tagmemes of this phrase are: Aspect, Stem, and Subject. The optional tagmemes are: Auxiliary, Plural, Modal, and Directional.

Rule 1 indicates all variants in which the Aspect tagmeme is manifested by aspect 9. As stated in general rule V1 the optional Auxiliary tagmeme does not occur with this aspect. As stated in general rule V2 aspect 9 follows the Stem tagmeme. The Subject tagmeme is manifested by persons of set C.

> c'otemoxuc xa *you have arrived* (c'ot intransitive stem *to arrive*, -em aspect 9 *perfect*, -oxuc subject per C*2 per plural*, xa modal *attained*)

Rule 2 indicates the manner in which choice between Subject manifested by persons of set B and Subject manifested by persons of set D is determined by absence or presence of Auxiliary. With aspects 2, 3, 6, and 7 (cf. V1) presence of Auxiliary is optional with consequent difference in choice of person sets. As stated in V8 persons of set B precede the Stem.

> xamuyubajic xa *you are happy* (x- aspect 2 *incomplete*, a- subject per B *2 per*, muyubaj intransitive stem *to be happy*, -ic pluralizer per B′ *2 per*, xa modal *attained*)

> chibatcutic *we will go* (ch- aspect 3 *incomplete*, i- subject per B *1 per*, bat intransitive stem *to go*, -cutic pluralizer per B′ *1 per exclusive*)

> ijelav bal *he passed going* (i- aspect 6 *complete*, # subject per B *3 per*, jelav intransitive stem *to pass*, bal directional *going*)

> vayic ox *they were sleeping* (# aspect 7 *complete*, # subject per B *3 per*, vay intransitive stem *to sleep*, -ic pluralizer per B′ *3 per*, ox modal *unattained*)

> xba ve'an *you are going to eat* (x- aspect 2 *incomplete*, ba auxiliary *to go*, ve' intransitive stem *to eat*, -an subject per D *2 per*)

> chba abtejcun *I am going to eat* (ch- aspect 3 *incomplete*, ba auxiliary *to go*, abtej intransitive stem *to work*, -cun subject per D *1 per*)

> ic'ot vaycutic *arriving we slept* (i- aspect 6 *complete*, c'ot auxiliary *to arrive*, vay intransitive verb *to sleep*, -cutic subject per D *1 per plural inclusive*)

tal vayicuc xa *coming they slept* (# aspect 7 *complete*, tal auxiliary *to come*, vay intransitive stem *to sleep*, -icuc subject per D *3 per plural*, xa modal *attained*)

Rule V1 states that of the aspects which occur with this phrase type, aspect 1 and 5 do not co-occur with an Auxiliary. Accordingly (rule 2), Subject is manifested by persons of set B. When aspect 1 occurs and the Modal permutes to pre-Stem (V5), then allomorph ta ... x- of the former brackets the latter as stated in general rule V7.

ta me ximuyotic ech'el *we will go up passing* (ta ... x- aspect 1 *incomplete*, me modal *polite emphatic*, i- subject per B *1 per*, muy intransitive stem *to go up*, -otic pluralizer per B' *1 per plural inclusive*)

lacolic to ox *you were free* (l- aspect 5 *complete*[5], a- subject per B *2 per*, col intransitive stem *to be free*, -ic pluralizer per B' *2 per plural*, to modal *yet*, ox modal *unattained*)

Phrase 112 (act. intr. subjn. verb phrase) = +ASP:asp 1–3/7/9 ±AUX:aux +/-SUBJN:-uc +STEM:is ±PLUR:pers B' +SUBJ :pers B/C/D ±LIM MOD:ono'ox ±DIR:dir.
1. When ASP:asp 1, then SUBJ:pers B.
2. When ASP:asp 9, then SUBJ:pers C.
3. Otherwise, SUBJ:pers D.
4. When ASP:asp 1/9, then +SUBJN; when ASP:asp 9, then SUBJN follows (post-STEM) ASP.
5. When ASP:asp 2/3, then +AUX and +SUBJN.
6. When ASP:asp 7, then +AUX iff +SUBJN.

In the active intransitive subjunctive verb phrase the same relation exists between Subject and Stem as in the indicative. The subjunctive phrase, however, denotes: (1) the act or state not as fact but merely entertained in thought; (2) a conditional element in a proposition; or (3) something desired but not yet realized. Only in this active subjunctive phrase type and in the passive phrase type may the sign of the subjunctive be omitted.

Rules 1 and 4 together summarize variants in which aspect 1 occurs. According to general rule V1 this aspect does not co-occur with Auxiliary tagmeme. The Subjunctive marker is obligatory, Subject is manifested by

---

[5] In phrases 111–3 aspect 5 co-occurs only with 1/2 pers.

persons B (which precedes Stem according to V8), and Limited Modal may precede Subject (V5).

> tauc ono'ox xicomcutic *if we would only stay* (ta ... x- aspect
> 1 *incomplete*, -uc subjunctive, ono'ox limited modal *only*, i-
> subject per B *1 per*, com intransitive stem *to stay*, -cutic pluralizer
> B' *1 per plural exclusive*)

Rules 2 and 4 summarize variants in which aspect 9 occurs. According to general rule V2, this aspect is post-Stem; while according to V1 it does not co-occur with the Auxiliary tagmeme. Here, as in 122 and 132, the occurrence of a post-Stem Aspect particle determines the permutation of the Subjunctive -uc to a position immediately following the Aspect particle. Subject is manifested by persons of set C.

> ve'emucoxuc ono'ox tal *had you only eaten coming* (ve' intran-
> sitive stem *to eat*, -em aspect 9 *perfect*, -uc subjunctive, -oxuc
> subject per C *2 per plural*, ono'ox limited modal *only*, tal direc-
> tional *coming*)

Rule 3 states that all other variants of 112 have Subject manifested by persons of set D. Rule 5 states that with aspects 2 and 3, both Auxiliary and Subjunctive are obligatory. Rule 6 states that with aspect 7 either both Auxiliary and Subjunctive occur or neither. General rule V4 states that Limited Modal may permute to pre-Stem in the presence of an Auxiliary. Forms without the Subjunctive marker -uc are still recognizable as subjunctive phrases. In the absence of an Auxiliary, persons of set D unambiguously indicate 112, 222, or 232 (cf. 111, special rule 2).

> xlicuc abtejan ono'ox *if you would only begin to work* (x- aspect
> 2 *incomplete*, lic auxiliary *to begin*, -uc subjunctive, abtej
> intransitive stem *to work*, -an subject per D *2 per*, ono'ox
> limited modal *only*)
>
> chbatuc ochicuc *if they would go and enter* (ch- aspect 3 *incom-
> plete*, bat auxiliary *to go*, -uc subjunctive, och intransitive stem
> *to enter*, -icuc subject per D *3 per plural*)
>
> sutcun ono'ox tal *had I only returned coming* (# aspect 7 *com-
> plete*, sut intransitive stem *to return*, -cun subject per D *1 per*,
> ono'ox limited modal *only*, tal directional *coming*)
>
> batuc muyutic *had we gone and gone up* (# aspect 7 *complete*,
> bat auxiliary *to go*, -uc subjunctive, muy intransitive stem *to go
> up*, -cutic subject per D *1 per plural inclusive*)

V. CLAUSES

Clauses are classified as: 10 intransitive; 20 transitive; 30 ditransitive; 40 transitive passive; 50 ditransitive passive; 60 nominal; and 70 relator-axis. Verb types are not in one-to-one correspondence with clause types. Thus, although active transitive verbs are distinguished as to indicative, subjunctive, negative, imperative, and cohortative, (active) transitive clauses distinguish only non-injunctive (simply labelled transitive) clauses which may have indicative, subjunctive, and negative verbs; and injunctive clauses which may have imperative or cohortative verbs.

General Rules for Clauses 11–62

Cl. 1. Any clause not containing a final embedded clause may terminate with a post-Peripheral Ter: X (terminal tagmeme manifested by particles of set X).

Cl 2. (Post-nuclear) periphery = $\pm$ Ref: 502B $\pm$ Acc: 502A $\pm$ Adv: (403, 404) -I, 501, 601, 71.

Cl 3. Ref occurs in 11, 41, 51, 61; in 21, 31 iff 21, 31:: Axis of 71.

Cl 4. Acc and Adv: (403, 404) - I occur in 11–32.

Cl 5. Adv: 601 does not occur in 12, 22, 32.

Cl 6. Adv: 71 does not occur in 62.

Cl 7. Otherwise, Adv: 501, 601, 71 occurs in 11–62.

Cl 8.   Adv may permute to pre-predicate.
Cl 9.   Adv: 601 must permute to pre-predicate.
Cl 10. Any peripheral tagmeme may occur more than once in a clause.

The peripheral Referential tagmeme is manifested only by phrase 502 B (referential phrase). This tagmeme occurs in clauses 11, 41, 51, and 61. In the other clause types Referential never occurs. Referential tagmeme never permutes to pre-predicate.

Referential tagmeme has a broad semantic range. In clause 11 the Referential usually signifies causative.

> tey icham oxvo' cu'un (clause 11) *there three people died because of me* (tey adverbial phrase 601 *there*, icham predicate verb phrase 111 *they died*, oxvo' subject noun phrase 404 *three people*, cu'un referential phrase 502 B causative *because of me*)

> chi'abtej yu'un ti vinique (clause 11) *I work because of the man* (chi'abtej predicate verb phrase 111 *I work*, yu'un ti vinique referential phrase 502 B causative *because of the man*)

In clause 11 the Referential tagmeme sometimes signifies the person to whom the action of the Predicate refers.

> isacub yu'un (clause 11) *the day dawned on him* (isacub predicate verb phrase 111 *the day dawned*, yu'un referential phrase 502 B referential *on him*)

In clauses 41, 51, and 61 the Referential tagmeme signifies agent; that is, the one who performs the action signified by the Predicate.

> icomtsanat ta sna yu'un ti vinique (clause 41) *he was left in his house by the man* (icomtsanat predicate verb phrase 221 *he was left*, ta sna adverbail phrase 501 B *in his house*, yu'un ti vinique referential phrase 502 B agent *by the man*)

> i'ac'bat yu'un ti antse (clause 41) *it was given to him by the woman* (i'ac'bat predicate verb phrase 231 *it was given to him*, yu'un ti antse referential phrase 502 B agent *by the woman*)

> naca stenel bal yu'unic (clause 61) *simply the throwing of it away by them* (naca adverbial phrase 601 *simply*, stenel bal predicate verb phrase 361 *the throwing of it away*, yu'unic referential phrase 502 B agent *by them*)

Referential tagmeme may occur in clause 21 or 31 only on the condition that that clause manifest Axis in a clause 71. As in some instances of occurrence of referential with clause 11, referential in clause 21 and 31 refers to the person who stands in some sort of oblique reference to the action of the predicate.

> c'usi laj jpastic yu'un ti jchi'iltac (clause 71) *what have we done wrong to our friends?* (c'usi relator stative relator phrase 602 *what*, laj jpastic yu'un ti jchi'iltac axis clause 21 contains yu'un ti jchi'iltac referential phrase 502 B *to our friends*)

Peripheral Accompaniment tagmeme is manifested only by phrase 502 A (accompaniment phrase). This tagmeme occurs most frequently in clauses 11, 21, and 31. It rarely occurs in 12, 22, or 32; and never occurs in other clause types. Accompaniment tagmeme never permutes to pre-predicate.

> ilo'ilaj schi'uc ti yajnil reye (clause 11) *she chatted with the wife of the king* (ilo'ilaj predicate verb phrase 111 *she chatted*, schi'uc ti yajnil reye accompaniment phrase 502 A *with the wife of the king*)

> chba jsa'cutic abtel schi'uc ti quits'ine (clause 21) *I'm going to look for work with my younger brother* (chba jsa'cutic predicate verb phrase 121 *I'm going to look for*, abtel direct object noun phrase 401 *work*, schi'uc ti quits'ine accompaniment phrase 502 A *with my younger brother*)

> laj yalbe sbaic schi'uc ti yits'ine (clause 31) *he talked it over with his younger brother* (laj yalbe sbaic predicate verb phrase 131 *they talked it over among themselves*, schi'uc ti yits'ine accompaniment phrase 502 A *with his younger brother*)

The peripheral Adverbial tagmeme varies somewhat widely both in manifestation and meaning. Occurrence of particular variants in the various clause types is here given.

Adverbial may be manifested by noun phrase 403 and 404. Whenever the Adverbial tagmeme is manifested by a noun phrase it signifies measurement of time or amount. The phrase-level Identifier is obligatorily absent from the noun phrase which tends to be brief. This variant rarely permutes to a prepredicate position. It occurs only in clauses 11–32. Its occurrence in clauses 12, 22, and 32 is rare.

> ja' no'ox yes ta spas jujun ac'obal (clause 21) *only like that he does it each night* (ja' no'ox yes adverbial *only like that* [ja' no'ox phrase 601 *only*, yes phrase 601 *like that*], ta spas predicate

verb phrase 121 *he does*, jujun ac'obal adverbial noun phrase 403 *each night*)

chcac'betic sc'a'al jujuti jujun javil (clause 31) *we put in a little bit of fertilizer each year* (chcac'betic predicate verb phrase 131 *we put in*, sc'a'al direct object noun phrase 402 *fertilizer*, jujuti jujun javil adverbial *a little bit each year* [jujuti noun phrase 404 *a little bit*, jujun javil noun phrase 403 *each year*])

Adverbial tagmeme manifested by prepositional phrase 501 may signify manner in clauses 11–41. It occurs most frequently with this meaning in clause 11, but only rarely with this meaning in clauses 12, 22, and 32. This semantic variant may permute (although rarely) to pre-predicate.

ta ox xlaj ta milel (clause 11) *she was to die by killing* (ta ox xlaj predicate verb phrase 111 *she was to die*, ta milel adverbial phrase 501 *by killing*)

tey iyac' ta loq'uesel ti sbec' sate (clause 21) *there he permitted the removal of his eye* (tey adverbial phrase 601 *there*, iyac' predicate verb phrase 121 *he permitted*, ta loq'uesel adverbial phrase 501 *the removal*, ti sbec' sate direct object noun phrase 402 *his eye*)

mu ta jta ta sa'el (clause 21) *I won't find it by looking* (mu ta jta predicate verb phrase 123 *I won't find it*, ta sa'el adverbial phrase 501 *by looking*)

Adverbial manifested by prepositional phrase 501 may also signify measure of time, amount, place, and person or thing. This semantic variant occurs in all the clause types. It occurs most frequently in clause 11. It rarely permutes to a prepredicate position.

tey x'oc'olet icom ta yoc te' (clause 11) *there weeping he stayed at the foot of the tree* (tey x'oc'olet adverbial *there weeping* (tey phrase 601 *there*, x'oc'olet phrase 601 *weeping*), icom predicate verb phrase 111 *he stayed*, ta yoc te' adverbial phrase 501 *at the foot of the tree*)

jelav ta ora (clause 11) *he passed quickly* (jelav predicate verb phrase 111 *he passed*, ta ora adverbial phrase 501 *quickly*)

chacac'be avabtel ta mal c'ac'al (clause 31) *I'll give you your work in the afternoon* (chacac'be predicate verb phrase 131 *I'll give to you*, avabtel direct object noun phrase 401 *your work*, ta mal c'ac'al adverbial phrase 501 *in the afternoon*) laj smil ta machita (clause 21) *she killed him with a machete* (laj smil predicate verb phrase 121 *she killed him*, ta machita adverbial phrase 501 *with a machete*)

Adverbial may be manifested by Adverbial phrase 601. Adverbial phrase 601 may signify manner and measure (places in 61–62). Adverbial tagmeme manifested by adverbial phrase 601 occurs only in pre-predicate position. It may occur several times in the same clause (up to three in our present corpus). This variant occurs in all the clauses except 12, 22, and 32.

tey nan ta scol (clause 11) *in all probility he will get well* (tey nan adverbial phrase 601 *in all probability*, ta scol predicate verb phrase 111 *he will get well*)

ja' no'ox laj jman (clause 21) *I only bought it* (ja' no'ox adverbial phrase 601 *only*, laj jman predicate verb phrase 121 *I bought it*)

jun yo'nton tey javal chvay (clause 11) *content there mouth up he sleeps* (jun yo'nton tey javal adverbial *content there mouth up* [jun yo'nton phrase 601 *content*, tey phrase 601 *there*, javal phrase 601 *mouth up*], chvay predicate verb phrase 111 *he sleeps*)

li' xa me oy ti ts'i'e (clause 61) *here is the dog* (li' xa me adverbial phrase 601 *here*, oy predicate existential phrase 371 *there* is, ti ts'i'e subject noun phrase 401 *the dog*)

Adverbial may be manifested by axis relator clause (71). Whenever the Adverbial tagmeme is manifested by an axis relator clause it signifies place. This variant occurs in all the clause types except 62. It rarely permutes to pre-predicate.

isutic bal ti bu oy ono'oxe (clause 11) *they returned to where they had always been* (isutic bal predicate verb phrase 111 *they returned*, ti bu oy ono'oxe adverbial clause 71 *where they had always been*)

laj st'ujanic ti osil bu lec (clause 21) *they chose the land where it was good* (laj st'ujanic predicate verb phrase 121 *they chose*, ti osil direct object noun phrase 401 *the land*, bu lec adverbial clause 71 *where it was good*)

chotol ti vinique bu ch-ech' ti te'tical chije (clause 61) *the man sat where the deer passed* (chotol predicate phrase 351 *sitting*, ti vinique subject noun phrase 401 *the man*, bu ch-ech' ti te'tical chije adverbial clause 71 *where the deer passed*)

Clause 11 (intr.) = (+Pi: 111–3 ±S: 401–6, 61, 71) ±REF ±ACC ±ADV.
1. Read no more than three tagmemes.
2. S may permute to precede Predicate or to follow periphery.

The Intransitive Predicate is the only obligatory tagmeme. Subject is an optional nuclear. The remaining tagmemes are peripheral. The Intransitive Predicate is manifested by intransitive indicative, subjunctive, and negative verb phrases (111–3). Presumably, Subject is manifested by any noun phrase (401–6), and by certain clause structures. The most common manifestation of Subject in the texts of our corpus are 401–2. Of the clause manifestations of Subject two are documented: (1) nominal clause (61) with Predicate manifested by existential phrase (371); (2) relator-axis clause (71).

No more than three tagmemes occur per clause. Clauses of two tagmemes are the most common. The most frequent linear ordering of tagmemes is that found in the formula, but either Subject or Adverbial (see general rules Cl 8, Cl 9) may permute to pre-predicate, while Subject may occur post-peripheral.

meltsaj xa li avotique (clause 11) *your tortillas are prepared* (meltsaj xa predicate verb phrase 111 *are prepared*, li avotique subject noun phrase 401 *your tortillas*)

mu sbat ta ora ti sc'a'al ti banamile (clause 11) *the fertilizer of the land doesn't leave immediately* (mu sbat predicate verb phrase 113 *it doesn't leave*, ta ora adverb phrase 501 *immediately*, ti sc'a'al ti banamile subject noun phrase 402 *the fertilizer of the land*)

oy jlom cristiano muc bu ch-abtej (clause 11) *there are some people who don't work* (oy jlom cristiano subject variant of clause 61 whose predicate takes the existential indicative phrase 371 *there are some people*, muc bu ch-abtej predicate verb phrase 113 *they don't work*)

xul ta joltic ti c'u s'elan ti banamile (clause 11) *we remember what the land is like* (xul predicate verb phrase 111 *it returns*, ta joltic adverb phrase 501 *to our heads*, ti c'u s'elan ti banamile subject relator axis clause 71 *what the land is like*)

tey xa jmoj batic schi'uc ti sbanquile (clause 11) *there together he went with his older brother* (tey xa jmoj adverbial *there to-*

gether [tey xa phrase 601 *there,* jmoj phrase 601 *together*], batic predicate verb phrase 111 *they went,* schi'uc ti sbanquile accompaniment phrase 502 A *with his older brother*)

mu lecuc ch-abtej ti vinique (clause 11) *the man doesn't work well* (mu lecuc adverb phrase 601 *not well,* ch-abtej predicate verb phrase 111 *he works,* ti vinique subject noun phrase 401 *the man*)

mu c'u xut xloc' ti mute (clause 11) *there is nothing the bird can do to get out* (mu c'u xut adverbial phrase 601 *there is nothing to do,* xloc' predicate verb phrase 111 *he gets out,* ti mute subject noun phrase 401 *the bird*)

Clause 12 (intr. inj.) = (+ Pi: 114–5) $\pm$ ACC $\pm$ ADV.

The most frequent reading is Intransitive Injunctive Predicate manifested by either intransitive imperative verb phrase (114) or intransitive cohortative (115). Characteristically these clauses are brief. Accompaniment is rare in this type. As stated in general rules (Cl 8, Cl 9), Adverbial may permute to prepredicate.

abtejan ta ora clause 12 *you work now*! (abtejan predicate verb phrase 114 *you work,* ta ora adverbial phrase 501 *now*)

ba ve'cutic ta jna (clause 12) *let's go eat at my house* (ba ve'cutic predicate verb phrase 114 *let's go eat,* ta jna adverbial *at my house*)

batanic schi'uc ti vinique (clause 12) *you go with the man* (batanic predicate verb phrase 114 *you go,* schi'uc ti vinique accompaniment phrase 502 A *with the man*)

ac'otajan oxib velta (clause 12) *you dance three times* (ac'otajan predicate verb phrase 114 *you dance,* oxib velta adverbial noun phrase 403 *three times*)

ac'o chamuc (clause 12) *let him die* (ac'o chamuc predicate verb phrase 115 *let him die*)

APPENDIX: MANIFESTING SETS

A. Reference table of person marker sets

	PERSON A				PERSON B		PERSON C	PERSON D
	w/cons. init. stems		w/vow. init. stems		B	B′		
	A	A′	A	A′				
1s	j-		c-		i-		-un	-cun
2s	a-		av-		a-		-ot	-an
3s	s-		y-/#-		#-		-#	-uc
1pl excl	j ... cutic		c ... cutic		i ... cutic		-uncutic	-cuncutic
1pl incl	j ... tic		c ... tic		i ... otic		-otic	-cutic
2pl	a ... ic		av ... ic		a ... ic		-oxuc	-anic
3pl	s ... ic		y ... ic		# ... ic		-ic	-icuc

B. Sets of relevance to verb phrase structure

Aspect-mode

asp. 1	ta/ta ... x-	incomplete
asp. 2	x-	incomplete
asp. 3	ch-	incomplete
asp. 4	laj	complete
asp. 5	l-	complete
asp. 6	i-	complete
asp. 7	#-	complete
asp. 8	-oj	perfect
asp. 9	-em	perfect

Auxiliary

ay	to have been there
bat/ba	to go
c′ot	to arrive (away)
ech′	to pass
laj	to finish
lic	to begin
och	to enter
sut	to return
tal	to come
vul	to arrive (here)

Modal

ca	reason
me	polite
nan	little uncertainty
no′ox/no′	limited
o	permanent
ono′ox/ono′	always
ox	unattained
quic	proving
to	still
van	uncertainty
xa	attained

Directional

balel/bal	going
comel	staying
ech′el	passing
jelavel	going ahead
loq′uel	going/coming out
muyel	going up
talel/tal	coming
yalel	going down

C. Sets of relevance to noun phrase structure

Article

ti	the
ati	the (anaphoric)
li	the
ali	the (anaphoric)
taj	the one there
ataj	the one there (anaphoric)

Classifier

bej	small round things
bus	things piled up
cot	animals
lic	flat thin things
mec	trips
ten	events
vo'	people
—	
—	

Modifier 1

antsiquil	female
bats'i	right
biq'uit	small
,nu	bad
querem	male
ts'et	left
uni	small
—	
—	

Modifier 2

ach'	new
c'ox	small
ic'al	black
mas	more
me'anal	poor
me'lal	widow
me'on	orphan
tsajal	red
ts'eil	raw
—	
—	

Numeral 1

jayib	many
jun	one
chib	two
oxib	three
chanib	four
vo'ob	five
vaquib	six
vucub	seven
vaxaquib	eight
baluneb	nine
lajuneb	ten
buluchib	eleven
lajcheb	twelve
oxlajuneb	thirteen
—	
—	

Numeral 2

ju-	each
j-	one
cha'-	two
ox-	three
chan-	four
vo'-	five
vac-	six
vuc-	seven
vaxac-	eight
balun-	nine
lajun-	ten
buluch-	eleven
lajcheb-	twelve
oxlajun-	thirteen
—	
—	

Specifier

yan	other
otro	other
jaylaj	every

D. Other sets

Peripheral particles X		*Stative-relator Y*	
ec	included	baq'uin	when
noxtoc	again	bu	where
tajmec	superlative	buch'u/buch'utic	who
umbi	in view of that	c'u/c'usi/c'usitic	what
un	emphatic	c'u cha'al	what for
xtoc	also	c'u s'elan	what like
		c'uxi	how
		jayib	how many

Summer Institute of Linguistics

CONJOINING IN A TAGMEMIC GRAMMAR OF ENGLISH*

Alton L. BECKER

1. Introduction

In *Syntactic Structures* Noam Chomsky wrote:
... the possibility of conjunction offers one of the best criteria for
the initial determination of phrase structure. We can simplify the description of conjunction if we try to set up constituents in such a way
that the following rule will hold:
   If S_1 and S_2 are grammatical sentences, and S_1 differs from S_2 only
in that X appears in S_1 where Y appears in S_2 ... and X and Y are
constituents of the same type in S_1 and S_2, respectively, then S_3 is a
sentence, where S_3 is the result of replacing X by X + and + Y in S_1...[1].
Chomsky goes on to argue, in substance, that a phrase structure grammar (as he defines it) has no way of incorporating such a rule — that is,
a rule which describes a binary transform. And because this rule leads
to considerable simplification in writing a grammar, 'it provides', he
writes, 'one of the best criteria for determining how to set up constituents'[2].
   I wish to argue that Chomsky was right in giving great importance to
the description of conjoining, that it does indeed put a number of important constraints on the way we describe the constituents of a grammatical string, and that, therefore, the specification of tagmemic conjoining rules will be both interesting in allowing us to compare and
evaluate grammatical theories and necessary in establishing criteria

* This article was supported in part by the Center for Research on Language and Language Behavior, University of Michigan, under contract OEC-3-6-061784-0508. The author is also indebted to Kenneth L. Pike for extended discussions about parts of the paper.
[1] *Syntactic Structures* (The Hague: Mouton & Co., 1957)p. 36
[2] *Syntactic Structures* (The Hague: Mouton & Co., 1957)p. 38

which a grammatical description must meet. In this paper I would like
to report on my attempts to describe conjoining in English, focusing
particularly on two important changes which I think are necessary in
Longacre's generative model of tagmemics[3]. Because of limited time
and becausing conjoining is extremely complex, I will further confine
my remarks to conjoining with *and* at the clause level, realizing that
many problems in the description of conjoining remain.

Why is the description of conjoining of such importance in writing a
grammar? There are two basic reasons:

(1) Conjoining, like embedding, is theoretically an open-ended (recursive) operation. Though there are undoubtedly psychological and
rhetorical constraints on all recursive rules, there seems no reason why,
given a particular string like

John, Bill, and Frank are here,

we cannot always add one more item to the list:

John, Bill, Frank, and Larry are here.

Furthermore, this recursiveness is not the same operation as recursive
embedding; or, in plain language, coordination is different from sub-
ordination. Conjoining is an operation repeating constituents of a construction (syntagmeme) at a particular level (e.g., sentence, clause,
phrase, word), while subjoining, on the other hand, is an operation not
of repeating but of restricting a particular constituent in a construction.
Conjoining adds to the number of constituents at a level; subjoining does
not. I think it important not to confuse these two kinds of recursiveness, if we wish a grammar to reveal not just the form but also the relationships of elements in a string. Conjoining, then, requires that a grammar be able to describe what I will call linear recursiveness.

(2) The second reason why conjoining is an important constraint on
the form of a grammar is that it is an especially context sensitive operation. As Chomsky observed, conjoined constituents must be 'constituents of the same type'. The difficulty lies in saying what 'of the same
type' means[4]. Clearly, the form of the conjoined elements does not determine whether or not they may be conjoined. That is, class labels like
Noun Phrase, Prepositional Phrase, Adverb, etc., do not provide sufficient information about the constituents of a string to allow us to write
conjoining rules. Conjoined constituents can have different forms:

---

[3] Sketched in the introduction of Robert Longacre, *Grammar Discovery Procedures* (The Hague:
Mouton & Co., 1964).
[4] For footnote, see next page.

John stepped into the water carefully and without a word.

And constituents of the same form cannot always be conjoined:

*John danced with Mary and with a limp.

Furthermore, if we define 'of the same type' as 'dominated by the same node in a phrase structure tree', we cannot easily explain such conjoinings as,

I floated and he swam across the lake[5].

Also, conjoining or coordination is a label for at least three different linearly recursive operations: conjoining proper, disjoining, and alternating[6]. That is, conjoining with *and* is different from conjoining with *but* and *or*, as the following three sentences demonstrate:

John danced with Mary and with Sue, too.

John danced with Mary or with Sue (*too).

*John danced with Mary but with Sue.

Conjoining clearly requires more information about constituents of a construction than can be derived from a tree diagram. Conjoinable constituents are not necessarily those of the same form or those dominated by the same node in a phrase structure tree.

2. Linear recursiveness in a tagmemic grammar

In the introduction to *Grammar Discovery Procedures*, Longacre sketches a grammatical model which might be called Generative Tagmemics. That is, he attempts to make explicit operations or rules which

---

[4] Chomsky's rule has been qualified by Lila R. Gleitman in 'Coordinating Conjunctions in English', *Language* 41 (1965): 260–293. A way of describing conjoining which bears, I think, some resemblance to that discussed below is suggested in Charles J. Fillmore, 'Toward a Modern Theory of Case' (prepublication copy), a longer version of Fillmore, 'A proposal concerning English prepositions' in *Monograph Series on Languages and Linguistics Number 19*, Georgetown University Institute of Languages and Linguistics, Washington, D.C. I was given his paper too late for it to have any effect on this paper, unfortunately.

[5] Example taken from Andreas Koutsoudas, *Writing Transformational Grammars*. (New York: McGraw-Hill, 1966) p. 249.

[6] Several uses of *and* are not here considered as conjoining; e.g. *It went faster and faster.* (Intensification), *Go and get it!* (Sequence), *He danced with Mary, and very well, too.* (Emphasis). Also, there is a set of clause patterns in which the subject and accompaniment tagmemes conjoin; e.g. *John danced with Mary* versus *John and Mary danced* (also *fought, talked, argued*, etc.). For a listing of various uses of *and* and other conjunctions, see *Prepositions, Conjunctions, Relative Pronouns and Adverbs*. (New York: Funk and Wagnalls Co., 1953).

were often implicit in tagmemic grammars. Though I think he left out at least one important feature of tagmemics in his reformulation — as I shall point out later — he does isolate the three general kinds of generative operations which are motivated by the traditional tagmemic assumptions about language[7]. These operations or rules, if you wish, are:

(1) 'Adjoining rules', or 'reading rules', which specify the ways that tagmemes or string constituents may be adjoined in syntagmemes or constructions at the different grammatical levels. Reading rules use three kinds of symbols: 'cover symbols' for tagmemes representing formal relational categories in syntagmemes (e.g. Subject, Predicate, Object, Complement, etc.), 'signs' preceding each tagmeme symbol representing various collocational options (e.g. +, ±, +(...), etc.), and 'superscripts' representing the option of repeating a tagmeme in a particular reading (e.g. S^n) (I shall have more to say about these superscripts when I discuss tagmemic conjoining rules.).

(2) 'Permutation rules' which specify the ways that tagmemes in a particular reading can be reordered. These rules are important in conjoining, for conjoined constituents cannot be permuted separately:

John bathes in the morning and at night.

In the morning and at night John bathes.

*In the morning John bathes at night[8].

(3) 'Replacement rules', or 'exponence rules', which specify the constructions at various levels that can manifest the formal relational categories (tagmeme symbols). For instance, these rules specify that the relational category *Subject* can be manifested by different kinds of noun phrases, pronoun phrases, relative clauses, etc. It is these rules which allow recursive embedding in tagmemic grammars.

Which of these rules, or what combination of them, can describe linear recursiveness, particularly conjoining? It seems to me that conjoining is a particular kind of reading or adjoining operation which must be carried out before the permutation rules can apply. Longacre's superscripts are motivated by the need for linear recursiveness. In fact, I shall argue that repeating a tagmeme is equivalent to conjoining; for if a tag-

---

[7] These assumptions are neatly summarized in Kenneth L. Pike, 'Beyond the Sentence', *College Composition and Communication* 15 (1964): 129–135.

[8] We might have *In the morning John bathes, and at night.* Poetic language is characterized by greater freedom of permutation.

meme is actually repeated, then a conjunction marker (*and, but, or,* and others, including special intonation) is obligatory:

John fishes with a fly-rod.
(Subject, Predicate, Instrumental)

John fishes with a fly-rod and with a casting-rod.
(... Instrumental^2)

*John fishes with a fly-rod with a casting-rod.
Notice that if the rule that repeating a tagmeme requires a conjunction (including special intonation), then the analysis of a sentence like,

I live at 2165 Newport in Ann Arbor,
requires recognizing at least two Location tagmemes, perhaps Area Location and Point Location. If there are two Location tagmemes here, then they can be permuted independently, as indeed they can, for we might say – with special contrastive emphasis,

In Ann Arbor I live at 2165 Newport.
though not,

*At 2165 Newport I live in Ann Arbor.
Here I am foreshadowing my next point – that tagmemes must be differentiated much more than they frequently are in order to describe linear recursiveness, among other things. This is a clear instance of what I think Chomsky meant when he said that the description of conjoining 'provides one of the best criteria for determining how to set up constituents'.

Though Longacre's superscripts can describe some conjoinings, there are others which they cannot at present describe. First of all, sequences of tagmemes as well as single tagmemes can be conjoined:

John runs slowly and walks quickly.

I float and John swims across the lake.

John walks quickly in the morning and slowly in the afternoon.
Because conjoining or repeating involves both single tagmemes and sequences of tagmemes, superscripts on single tagmemes are inadequate. Hence I propose, as the first of two changes in Longacre's model, that a rather different kind of tagmeme be introduced into the reading rules. The rules presently account for only two of three basic kinds of grammatical relations: 'subordinate relations' (satellite tagmemes) and what I shall call for want of a better term 'interordinate relations' (relations of nuclear tagmemes to each other). The new tagmeme will describe 'coordinate relations', a third general kind of grammatical relation. It

differs somewhat from other tagmemes in that it defines an operation, similar to the phoneme defining an operation that Pike has recently suggested[9]. I will symbolize this new tagmeme as $\pm K^n$, indicating that it is optional and recursive. It will replace all the superscripts in Longacre's reading rules. Tentatively we can say that K (or the coordinate relation) adjoins X_2 to X_1 in which X = any tagmeme or sequence of tagmemes in the reading[10].

If we have the clause level reading,

Subject Predicate Object Frequency K

then any tagmeme or linear sequence of tagmemes (short of the whole syntagmeme which may be conjoined at the sentence level) may be repeated, giving us the readings,

Subject and Subject ...
'John and Mary hold the child every morning'.

Subject Predicate and Subject Predicate ...
'John holds and Mary washes the child every morning'.

Subject Predicate Object and Subject Predicate Object ...
'John holds the child and Mary washes the dishes every morning'.

... Predicate and Predicate ...
'John holds and washes the child every morning.'

... Predicate Object and Predicate Object ...
'John holds the child and washes its face every morning'.

... Predicate Object Frequency and Predicate Object Frequency ...
'John holds the child every morning and washes the dishes every night'.

... Object and Object ...
'John holds the child and his wife every morning'.

... Object Frequency and Object Frequency ...
'John holds the child every morning and his wife every night'.

... Frequency and Frequency ...
'John holds the child every morning and every night'.

---

[9] See Kenneth L. Pike, *Tagmemic and Matrix Linguistics Applied to Selected African Languages* (Final Report of Research carried out under Office of Education Contract No. OE-5-14-065; November, 1966), section 6.2.8 'Theory of Phoneme Types as Item, Process, and Relation', where Pike recognizes 'lowering influence' as a phoneme /!/ in several African tone languages.

[10] This rule is suggested, in part, by the conjunction rule in Zellig S. Harris, *String Analysis of Sentence Structure* (The Hague: Mouton & Co., 1962) pp. 39-40.

However, the operation also permits such an anomalous string as,
   *'John and the book hold the child every morning'.
   *'John holds and the book contains the child every morning'.
   *'John and where I was are here every morning'.
Obviously the operation must be qualified further. Not all tagmemes are
K-equivalent or conjoinable. We must add to the rule as follows:
   $\pm K^n$ in which K adjoins X_2 to X_1, and X_1 and X_2 are K-equivalent.
The question now is, how can we describe K-equivalence; or in Chom-
sky's terms, when are X_1 and X_2 constituents of the same type? This
brings me to the second proposed change in Longacre's generative model
of tagmemics.

3. Deep structure in a tagmemic grammar

As we have seen, K-equivalence cannot be determined either from the
grammatical function (relational category) or the manifesting forms of
a tagmeme. That is, different forms may be conjoined:
   John stepped into the water carefully and without a word.
And tagmemes of the same grammatical function (e.g. Subject) often
may not be conjoined:
   *John and where I was are here.
Hence, a tagmeme notation which marks only these two features of tagmemes (function and form) does not supply enough information to determine K-equivalence. I would argue that this limited notation (e.g.
Subject: noun phrase) reveals only the surface structure of syntag-
memes.

In order to go beyond surface structure it is essential, I believe, to realize the importance of traditional tagmemic designations like Subject-
as-Actor, Subject-as-Goal, or even Subject-as-Location and Subject-as-
Time[11], etc. Often we try to do without these complex designations, or
we mix grammatical categories (Subject, Predicate, Object, etc.) with

---

[11] In Kenneth L. Pike, *Language in Relation to a Unified Theory of the Structure of Human Behavior,* Chapter 7 (The Hague: Mouton & Co., 1967) tagmemes are repeatedly referred to as 'actor-as-subject' or 'recipient-of-action-as-subject'. The importance of this distinction is discussed in detail in Pike, 'Discourse Analysis and Tagmeme Matrices', *Oceanic Linguistics* III (Summer, 1964): 5–25.

these semantic categories (Actor, Location, Time, Purpose, etc.)[12]. To exclude them is to limit our grammars to a description of surface structure, making it impossible, I think, for us to explain such a phenomenon as conjoining. To mix these grammatical and semantic categories is to obliterate the important difference between surface and deep structure. Perhaps I can clarify my point with some examples.

In all the following sentences, grammatical meaning is invariant while grammatical form changes:

Subject-as-actor: John feeds the cat in the morning.
Subject-as-goal: The cat is fed by John in the morning.
Subject-as-time: In the morning is when John feeds the cat.
Subject-as-action: Feeding is done in the morning. (Stylistic deletions)

In a tagmemic grammar, the relations between these sentences is not a transformational derivation from an underlying base sentence but rather a change of focus on semantic categories, conditioned chiefly by discourse constraints[13]. In the first sentence there is subject focus on actor, in the second, subject focus on goal, etc.

The concept of the tagmeme as I am presenting it here — and it is really not very new — can be represented in a diagram (suggested to me by Kenneth Pike). In fig. 1, A (Grammatical form) represents relational categories in a construction (or syntagmeme), such as Subject, Object, Predicate, Complement, Modifier, etc. B (Grammatical meaning) represents what I have been calling the semantic categories in a construction, such as Actor, Goal, Location, etc. C (Lexical form) represents morpheme classes, such as Noun, Verb, Pronoun, Adjective, etc. D (Lexical meaning), which I will not discuss in detail here, represents semantic equivalence, as in the possible anaphoric relationship between *John, the boy, he, his* in a given text. (This element D is of great importance in formal discourse analysis.)

Reading rules can now be seen as ordered within a matrix (fig. 2) in which the various semantic categories (B in fig. 1) intersect with con-

---

[12] For an example of a grammar in which grammatical and semantic categories are mixed, see Nguyen Dang Liem, *English Grammar* (a combined tagmemic and transformational approach) Linguistic Circle of Canberra Publications, Series C, No. 3 (Canberra, 1966).

[13] Some of these constraints are discussed in A.L. Becker, 'Item and Field: A Way into Complexity' in *On Teaching English to Speakers of Other Languages* (Carol J. Kreidler, ed. Series II Champaign: National Council of Teachers of English, 1966). See also S.N. Jacobson, 'A Modifiable Routine for Connecting Related Sentences of English Text', in Garvin and Spolsky, *Computation in Linguistics* (Bloomington: Indiana University Press, 1966).

	Grammar	Lexicon
Form (Surface structure)	A	C
Meaning (Deep structure)	B	(D)

Example: Subject$_{\text{Actor}}$: Noun$_{\text{(young male human)}}$

Fig. 1. Elements of Complex Tagmeme Symbol A_B: C_D

struction (syntagmeme) types; the cells at these intersections are filled
·by relational categories (A in fig. 1). Neither the rows nor the columns
in this matrix are anywhere near complete; nor am I sure I can complete
them quickly for numerous problems remain, among them the handling
of negation and disjunction, which seem closely interrelated. However,
we can tentatively say that readings proceed left to right across rows,
including the reading of the new tagmeme $\pm K^n$; permutation rules then
reorder tagmemes in a reading, and exponence rules eventually give
values for the symbols C and D.

We can now describe K-equivalence, which is determined by the deep
structure of syntagmemes, in terms of the semantic categories. The rule
for conjoining with *and* or a conditioned variant of *and* (e.g. special intonation pre-terminally when conjoining is repeated) at the clause level
is simply that clause-level tagmemes are K-equivalent if their grammatical
form and meaning (A and B in fig. 1) are identical. This rule allows sentences like,

John stepped into the water carefully and without a word.

I floated and he swam across the lake.

John danced with Mary and with Sue.

John bathes in the morning and at night.

John runs slowly and walks quickly.

The rule does not allow the following sentences:

*John danced with Mary and with a limp.

*John and where I was are here.

*The man is and hit me.

*He took John home and Mary seriously.

*I want to know why John and when Mary are coming.

Certainly the rule I have given will have to be qualified. For instance,
first person pronouns cannot be conjoined except as parts of sequences:

Semantic categories: (grammatical meaning)

Syntagmeme types: (form)	actor	item	...	assert	motion	equation	transaction	...	direct goal	indirect goal	quality	accomp.	inst.	location (1)
1.	+S			±A	+P							±M		±M
2.		+S		±A		+P					+C			±M
3.	+S			±A			+P		±O			±M		±M
4.		+C			+S	+P					+S			±M
5.				±A	+S	+P					+C			±M
Etc.														

	location (2)	direction	time	manner	cause	purpose	...	conjunction	disjunction	alternation	... etc.
1.	±M	±M	±M	±M	±M	±M		±K^n	±K^n	±K^n	
2.	±M		±M	±M	±M	±M		±K^n	±K^n	±K^n	
3.	±M	±M	±M	±M	±M	±M		±K^n	±K^n	±K^n	
4.	±M	±M	±M		±M	±M		±K^n	±K^n	±K^n	
5.	±M	±M	±M		±M	±M		±K^n	±K^n	±K^n	
Etc.											

Examples:

1. John will run with Mary to school.
2. The book may be wet.
3. John can dance the polka with Mary.
4. Black is the color of my true love's hair.
5. Skiing can be pleasant on a sunny day.

*I and I are going.

But: I must and I will succeed.

However we explain exceptions[14] or qualify the rule, and in spite of the numerous complexities of linear recursiveness which have perforce gone unmentioned here, I hope I have demonstrated some of the constraints which the description of conjoining puts on tagmemic reading rules, especially the need to distinguish between surface structure and deep structure in tagmemic grammars.

University of Michigan

---

[14] K-equivalence, interestingly, is never identity. If a tagmeme is repeated, it does not mean the same thing in both instances, e.g. *There are books and books* and *Take that and that!* Repeating linguistic units very often signals that a new referent is intended and hence is a very important feature of discourse, e.g. *John saw the movie and John did his homework.* This sentence suggests to me that two people named John are involved. In the following sentence there is some ambiguity whether one or two people are involved: *John saw the movie and he did his homework.* In the next sentence, though, only one person is involved: *John saw the movie and did his homework.* I have considered deletion, therefore, a feature of sentence-level, discourse constrained conjoining, very similar to other anaphoric markers. See Rolf Karlsen, *Studies in the Connection of Clauses in Current English: Zero, Ellipsis, and Explicit Form* (Bergen: J.W. Eides, 1959) for a thorough discussion of the anaphoric function of deletion.

A SYNTACTIC PARADIGM

KENNETH L. PIKE

University of Michigan

I. CONTROLLED REDUNDANCY IN A CITATION PARADIGM

In a previous article I showed how matrix theory[1] could be used to present some features of the relations between well-defined constructions. I claimed there that a traditional paradigm illustrates one kind of matrix on a word level but that matrix theory provides the basis for paradigms on syntactic levels as well.

Here I wish to give one small syntactic paradigm to illustrate this point. For structural data, I chose an article by James C. Dean.[2] It has the advantage of brevity, so that re-statement of its essential components can be fairly complete without being tedious. In addition, it represents a Philippine structure so different from Indo-European—or, for that matter, from American Indian languages —and so little understood by those who are not specialists in Malayo-Polynesian, that any light thrown on its structure is likely to be welcome.

Our procedure will be, first, to set up and discuss the relationships between Bilaan clause types through a display of a crucial kernel matrix. We show derivatives of the matrix by multiplication of that kernel in various ways.

We then come to the transitive paradigm itself. This is displayed in three forms: (a) as a citation paradigm, (b) as a tagmemic-notation paradigm, and (c) as a tagmatic-notation paradigm.

The CITATION PARADIGM consists of sample clauses chosen so as to illustrate contrasts between members of the paradigm. The same morphemes are retained wherever possible. Every change in illustrative lexemes is intended to force on the reader's attention some element of structural significance. The continued use of the same lexemes allows the reader to keep a few in view—all that are needed, in principle, to illustrate the entire contrastive structure.

Forced memory of a large number of items and the elaborate search for substitution relations of comparable forms are deliberately avoided by this built-in redundancy of the paradigm. Simplicity of description here is assumed to include presentation designed for ease of understanding. Paradigmatic redundancy, is welcomed when it serves to stimulate the reader's perception and to aid his understanding—rather than rejected by some esthetic criterion of rhetoric which proves irrelevant or harmful to the perception of linguistic pattern.

In order to help the reader to obtain insight into the structure, we wish to control all but one variable at a time, so that contrastive elements of that variable

[1] 'Dimensions of grammatical constructions', *Lg.* 38.221–44 (1962).

[2] 'Some principal grammatical relations of Bilaan', *Oceania linguistic monographs* 3.59–64 (1958). For convenience I have changed a few of Dean's orthographic symbols. For description of the sound system, see his article 'The phonemes of Bilaan', *Philippine journal of science* 84.311-22 (1955). The Bilaan dialect represented is spoken in Kablan, Tupi, Cotabato, Mindanao.

will be clearly in evidence. Lexicon, therefore, is held constant unless the structure demands lexical replacement or addition. A syntax paradigm exploits this CONTROLLED REDUNDANCY. This explains why paradigms have been used for centuries in pedagogical treatments.

Note that by these examples we are trying to illuminate and illustrate the structure. Validity of the forms,[3] as a related goal, is best assured by excerpting the illustrative material from running text. But this is equally true for all kinds of linguistic analysis. It negates neither here nor elsewhere the value of speed in reaching the tentative conclusions and directness of understanding gained from elicited paradigms.

The TAGMEMIC-NOTATION PARADIGM shows in a formal manner the internal structure of the contrastive clauses and the relations between their components. It does so in the simplest, most direct manner by an emic notation of one symbol-complex per included tagmeme—and one tagmeme per symbol. If alternative forms of a construction are possible, only one is represented here, chosen as the most frequent or as in some sense normal or basic.

The TAGMATIC-NOTATION PARADIGM, the third form used here, then supplies the details of alternative or expanded forms of the emic constructions. It gives each tagmeme of each construction variant an etic notation by symbolizing not only the functional slot involved but also the class of lexemes filling it.

Discussion of various problems in the transitive analysis will be followed by a brief presentation of a possible intransitive structure, and a few hints as to the nature of further Bilaan constructions. Finally, English will be contrasted with Bilaan at certain relevant points.

II. THE TRANSITIVE MATRIX

The crucial core—or kernel, or nucleus—of Bilaan structure includes a class of transitive clauses which are formally distinct and which have their formal contrasts paralleled by construction meaning.[4] By the construction differences the hearer is informed that the observer's (or speaker's) attention is oriented toward the relation between the action of the predicate and its actor, or between an action and its goal, or between an action and some other person, thing, or locality relevant to it. In each of these types the physical event—the etic situation, the denotation—is constant, and signalled by the transitivity of the clause. But the emic focus—the directed attention of the observer (or speaker) to one of the relations of the activity as reported—becomes contrastive. Some one of the substantive components of the clause serves as the FOCUS-COMPLEMENT[5] of this

---

[3] Additional illustrations have been supplied to me by Dean when those in his article lack the redundancy of lexical items required for the paradigm. Some of these he was unable to check in the field. To be sure, therefore, the reader must use Dean's published forms, which include illustrations of the types and morpheme classes (but not always with the identical morphemes) shown here.

[4] Sometimes called voice. See Howard McKaughan, *The inflection and syntax of Maranao verbs* (*Publications of the Institute of National Language*; Manila, 1958).

[5] The term FOCUS applied directly to the actor or to the goal is found in A. Healey's 'Notes on Yogad', *Oceania linguistic monographs* 3.77-82, and in Phyllis M. Healey's *An*

FOCUSSED ACTIVITY-RELATION of the predicate and often is formally marked as such.

In an English translation of a Bilaan clause one may add to the predicate a subscript $_{at}$ for an actor-focussed activity relation, but $_{gt}$ for a goal-focussed activity relation and $_{rt}$ for a referent-focussed relation, and an arrow pointing toward the actor or goal or referent which is the complement of that activity relationship. The contrastive translations then may appear as: (*It is the*) *cat*← (*that*) *catches*$_{at}$ (*the*) *rat*. (*It is the*) *rat*← (*that the*) *cat catches*$_{gt}$. (*It is for the*) *man*← (*that the*) *cat catches*$_{rt}$ (*the*) *rat*.

The first two clauses might also be translated as English active and passive: (*The*) *cat*← *catches*$_{at}$ (*the*) *rat*. (*The*) *rat*← *is caught*$_{gt}$ (*by the*) *cat*. But deep-seated differences in structure between an English passive clause and a Bilaan goal-focussed-activity clause make the former translation for the moment preferable. (In §7 I shall outline some of these important structural differences. First, however, I wish to present the formal structure of the Bilaan clause.)

We are now ready to set up a simple column matrix listing these three formal clause types, named for the contrastive forms of their activity relationships. In (1) I use M_k to represent the kernel (the nucleus) of the activity-clause system. TC represents transitive clause (with actor-focussed, goal-focussed, or referent-focussed activity). Our later formulas justify the treatment of the first two of these constructions as well-defined[6] units.

$$(1) \quad M_k = TC_{at}$$
$$TC_{gt}$$
$$*TC_{rt}$$

The third construction is marked with an asterisk because Dean's material does not provide the data necessary to treat it here. In Abrams' data,[7] however, a small residue in the system contrasts TC_{gt} with TC_{rt}. The referent type is not needed for our presentation of a model for a syntax paradigm, and will not be mentioned again until later in the paper; but it must be kept in mind by those interested in comparing Philippine systems with English.

Agta grammar (Manila, 1960). The latter is based on a master's thesis written at the University of Sydney, 1958.

Some students of Philippine language—among them McKaughan and Wolfenden—tell me that this use of focus makes the actor or goal too prominent. This in turn leads to difficulty in distinguishing between focus and emphasis, and fails to give central attention to the activity itself and its relationships. For this reason I have developed the phrases 'focussed activity-relation' and 'focus complement' in order to place priority on the verb.

[6] Any well-defined unit must be seen in reference (a) to the contrastive components which set it apart from other units and which simultaneously allow its identification; (b) to the variant forms in which it physically occurs; and (c) to its distribution in a class of units, in a hierarchical sequence (or string or spacial display) of units, and in a matrix (or contrastive pattern) of units. Thus the units in (1) comprise a matrix and are in part defined, in turn, by their place in this matrix pattern. See also the reference in fn. 1.

[7] Norman D. Abrams, *The verb complex in Bilaan* (unpublished master's thesis, University of Washington, 1960). This contains many details of the general verb morphology and of the morphological and syntactic aspects of focus. It amplifies Dean's shorter paper, and implies types of verb bases not treated there. The dialect described is that of the Sanangani district of southeast Cotobato, and of the Koronadal area.

In addition to structural attention focussed on activity relations, Bilaan gives formal attention to emphasis. Focus is not emphasis. Focus reports the observer's attention to one of several relations—without essential emotional overtones—between a predicate and some other part of a clause; the focus-complement substantive is viewed only in reference to that relationship, not as in focus of itself. In emphasis, on the contrary, some one substantive is singled out for a direct isolated overlay of emotional connotation without formal (emic) reference to or dependence upon its relation to the activity to which it is in (etic) fact related. The formal independence of emphasis allows it to function as a variable which is formally separate from the focus complement.

In English, emphasis is usually achieved by suprasegmental intensity, length, and pitch (although it can also be handled in part by special segmental lexemes such as *indeed*). In Bilaan the emphasis—like a focussed activity-relation—is signalled segmentally. We translate the Bilaan emphasis into English orthography, therefore, by small capital letters representing any unspecified variety of English suprasegmental intensity: (*It is the*) cat← (*that*) catches$_{at}$ (*the*) RAT. (*It is the*) CAT← (*that*) catches$_{at}$ (*the*) rat. (*It is the*) rat← (*that the*) CAT catches$_{gt}$. (*It is the*) RAT← (*that the*) cat catches$_{gt}$.

In the first two illustrations, *cat* as focus-complement actor is first nonemphatic, then emphatic. Similarly *rat*, as focus-complement goal in the second pair of illustrations, varies in emphasis. We see, therefore, that the marked activity-focus relation is essential to the basic contrasts of the kernel matrix, whereas emphasis is an optional component which may be added to any of the substantive tagmemes of the clause without affecting its kernel structure.

For this reason it proves useful to treat emphasis as adding a class of further but less basic clause types to the system. This is shown in (2) as matrix multiplication, with $_e$ representing emphasis: $_{ea}$ emphatic actor, $_{eg}$ emphatic goal.

$$(2) \quad _e M_k = {}_{ea}TC_{af}, \; {}_{ea}TC_{gf}, \; {}_{eg}TC_{af}, \; {}_{eg}TC_{gf}$$

If, now, we arrange (2) in matrix form $_e M$, we obtain (3); we arbitrarily retain nonemphasis in the matrix by adding a zero-emphasis column. Here A_{fc} is actor-focus complement, G_{fc} goal-focus complement.

(3) Transitive Clause $_e M$:

	$_e$Zero	$_e$A	$_e$G
A_{fc}	TC_{af}	$_{ea}TC_{af}$	$_{eg}TC_{af}$
G_{fc}	TC_{gf}	$_{ea}TC_{gf}$	$_{eg}TC_{gf}$

But (3) does not include some apparently intransitive forms of Dean's data. These have actor-focussed activity forms without the complexity of a substantive goal elsewhere in the clause. Why not start with the simpler intransitive clauses as the kernel matrix rather than the transitive? The answer seems to be that grasping the pattern of Bilaan or many other Philippine languages requires an appreciation of focus contrasts as basic. This cannot be demonstrated unless one begins with the transitive, where both actor-focussed activity and goal-focussed activity come into view.

This judgment then forces the question: can the intransitive matrix be derived from the transitive? It can indeed. But to do so it is necessary to multiply the transitive matrix by a component which applies a minus feature for goal. If $-TC_{gf}$ is used to mean the obligatory absence of the goal-focus cell of M_k, and Int to mean intransitive, then the nonemphatic and the emphatic intransitive clauses are seen in (4) and (5).

$$(4)\ IntC\ =\ Int \cdot (M_k\ -TC_{gf})$$
$$(5)\ {}_eIntC\ =\ {}_e \cdot (Int \cdot [M_k -TC_{gf}])$$

That is, the intransitive clause matrix is derived from (3) by changing T to Int and by striking out the bottom row and the righthand column.

III. THE TRANSITIVE CITATION PARADIGM

We are now ready to present in (6) the transitive syntactic paradigm in citation form. The citation forms are kept as uniform as possible, for reasons given in §I. Words illustrating the same tagmeme or tagmeme class or tagmeme variant (allotagma) are wherever possible kept in a vertical column. Gaps in the permitted occurrence of the tagmeme or allotagma are shown by dots.

The rows in (6) come in pairs, representing the basic contrast of actor-focussed versus goal-focussed activity. Symbols at the left in (6) come from matrix (3). The presentation of pairs is chosen successively from each column of (3).

The M (or am) in the verb *kamfeʔ* 'catch' is part of a variant morpheme which helps to signal the actor-focussed activity construction; the comparable goal-focussed activity in the same verb is seen signalled by N. As in the English sentences of §II, an arrow pointed toward a Bilaan pronoun shows it to be a focus complement; $_{af}$ and $_{gf}$ label activity-focus types; capital letters show emphasis.

Sentences (6e, 6e'), with asterisk, show how the analogous pattern might possibly be filled—but without documentation in available data.

(6) Transitive Clause in Citation Paradigm

(6a)	TC_{af}	...	*kaMfeʔ*	→*ale*	*dun*	'...	Catch$_{af}$	→they him'
(6a')		(...	*kaMfeʔ*	→*ɨ*	*dale*	'...	Catch$_{af}$	→he them'.)
(6b)	TC_{gf}	...	*kaNfeʔ*	-*la*	→*ɨ*	'...	Catch$_{gf}$	they →him'
(6b')		(...	*kaNfeʔ*	-*an*	→*ale*	'...	Catch$_{gf}$	he →them')
(6c)	$_{ea}TC_{af}$	*DALE*←	*kaMfeʔ*	...	*dun*	'THEY←	catch$_{af}$	... him'
(6c')		(*KANEN*←	*kaMfeʔ*	...	*dale*	'HE←	catch$_{af}$	... them')
(6d)	$_{ea}TC_{gf}$	*DALE*	*kaNfeʔ*	-*la*	→*ɨ*	'THEY	catch$_{gf}$	they →him'
(6d')		(*KANEN*	*kaNfeʔ*	-*an*	→*ale*	'HE	catch$_{gf}$	he →them')
(6e)	$_{eg}TC_{af}$	**KANEN*	*kaMfeʔ*	→*ale*	...	'HIM	catch$_{af}$	→they ...'
(6e')		**(DALE*	*kaMfeʔ*	→*ɨ*	...	'THEM	catch$_{af}$	→he ...')
(6f)	~	...	*kaMfeʔ*	→*ale*	*KANEN*	'...	catch$_{af}$	→they HIM'
(6f')		(...	*kaMfeʔ*	→*ɨ*	*DALE*	'...	catch$_{af}$	→he THEM')
(6g)	$_{eg}TC_{gf}$	*KANEN*←	*kaNfeʔ*	-*la*	...	'HIM←	catch$_{gf}$	they ...'
(6g')		(*DALE*←	*kaNfeʔ*	-*an*	...	'THEM←	catch$_{gf}$	he ...')
(6h)	~	...	*kaNfeʔ*	-*la*	→*KANEN*	'...	catch$_{gf}$	they →HIM'
(6h')		(...	*kaNfeʔ*	-*an*	→*DALE*	'...	catch$_{gf}$	he →THEM')

Various observations can be made by scanning the paradigm and its translation. Note that in the first permitted structural position only emphatic forms occur—but that an emphatic goal optionally comes last (6f, 6g, 6h). The emphatics either are out of focus or serve as the focus complement. The third singular emphatic pronominal form, actor or goal, is *kanen* 'he, him', whether or not it serves as focus complement; third plural emphatic is *dale* 'they, them'. Predicates, in the second position, contrast by their markers for actor-focussed versus goal-focussed activity.

More difficult to see, but present in the data, is the crucial membership in four pronoun classes, and the priority ranking of their functions.[8] Some such characteristic seems to be typical of many Philippine languages. Highest structural priority in descriptive order of selection goes to the emphatics (*kanen*, *dale*). Regardless of focus or of actor-versus-goal function, the emphatic set is used when two or three of the functions are simultaneously present. Second priority goes to the focus-complement set represented here by # 'he, him' and *ale* 'they, them'. Whether the pronoun is in actor or goal function this set is used if it carries simultaneous focus-complement function. Zero priority goes to two contrastive sets of pronouns when they are neither emphatic nor serving as focus complement. In zero-priority the actor function (a suffix class) is expressed by -*an* 'he', -*la* 'they'; the goal function by *dun* 'him', *dale* 'them'.

Note, then, that only *kanen* and *dale* stand in first position, with or without an arrow; only -*an* and -*la* in third, never with an arrow; # and *ale* both in third and in fourth, always with an arrow. This specialization of pronouns for tagmemic function characterizes Bilaan.

Such an arrangement of pronominal sets, however, raises theoretical questions. What is the morphemic status of these forms? What is their tagmemic status? And how must # be analyzed?

The ranking of pronouns into functional sets affects all the persons. Yet no one person shows overt contrasting forms for all four sets. Third person singular has four forms in contrast, but one of these (the focus-complement third person) is zero. Nevertheless, by using both third singular and third plural in the citation paradigm, the four sets can be filled out overtly and contrastively for at least one of the persons for each function.

In this presentation we are assuming that the third-person-singular morphs of each functional set are contrastive morphemes, not allomorphs of a single morpheme. This solution may appear surprising, in view of the fact that elsewhere[9] I have treated English *he* and *him* as allomorphs of {*he*} tagmemically conditioned. The Bilaan analysis is forced on us (a) because of the formal correlation of pronoun focus-complement with marked verb structure; (b) because of the form-meaning contrast of focus-complement versus nonfocus-complement pronouns in identical tagmemic slots, as in (6a) versus (6b); and (c) because structural ambiguities would result if all the forms of one person were rewritten with a single morphophonemic spelling. In such a rewrite the contrastive pronominal forms (6a, 6b, 6h) would be the same, concealing overt formal differences which in fact parallel the semantic ones.

[8] The emphatic set, however, is ambiguous with the nonfocus object set except for third person singular *kanen* versus *dun*. Otherwise the contrast is neutralized. (For complete lists, see Dean 60.) Dean feels, however, that the contrast is vital to an understanding of the system.

[9] *Language in relation to a unified theory of the structure of human behavior* 1.84b (Glendale [now Santa Ana], 1954), 3.14(z) (1960).

This conclusion, in turn, leads to # 'he←, him←' as having some formal status. We do not treat it as a zero morpheme, for no overt allomorph would then be part of it. (Tagmemic theory rejects all totally zero units.) Our solution, therefore, is to assume that the tagmeme of actor here has *ale* as an overt manifesting variant, and # as a covert variant. Then # becomes a symbol, directly, of the presence of the actor tagmeme in zero-variant form. Thus # in (6) is not a zero morpheme, but a zero allotagma. The dots, on the other hand, represent neither a zero allomorph nor a zero allotagma but merely the absence of any manifestation of a tagmeme at a given point, and the absence of any compelling reason to expect a tagmeme there.

All of this, however, leads to a still deeper structural issue. If # and *ale* in (6a, 6e, 6f) manifest an actor tagmeme, what tagmeme do *-la* and *-an* manifest in (6b, 6d, 6g, 6h)? Do both pronoun sets represent precisely the same tagmeme of actor? Are they not rather functionally—tagmemically—somehow in contrast? And is not the actor manifested in (6d) by *kanen* and *dale* in contrast with goal tagmeme manifested in (6e) by *kanen* and *dale* in the same apparent position? And are not all of these, in turn, in some kind of functional contrast with *KANEN* and *DALE* as emphatic actor and emphatic goal, as in (6c, 6g)? Finally, what should be done to formalize the fact that # and *ale* sometimes manifest actor (6a, *6e, 6f) and sometimes goal (6b, 6d)?

My solution to these problems is to set up two special tagmemes, neither of which ever has a manifestation apart from another tagmeme. Emphatic tagmeme is characterized (a) by prepredicate position (6c, 6d, *6e, 6g) with free distribution-variant under goal forms to post-actor position (6f, 6h); (b) by the special set of emphatic pronouns *kanen, dale* as filler of its slot; (c) by a semantic component of emphasis; (d) by simultaneous (portmanteau) manifestation with actor (6c, 6d), or simultaneous goal (*6e, 6f, 6g, 6h). Tagmemes in Bilaan, then, can be simultaneously present[10] in tagmeme composites, as in other languages we may find simultaneous phonemes or simultaneous morphemes.

A similar analysis must then be adopted so as to set up a tagmeme of focus-complement. This one can be simultaneous with actor or with goal tagmeme, or with the tagmeme composite actor-plus-emphasis or goal-plus-emphasis. The focus-complement tagmeme is characterized (a) by the manifesting pronoun class #, *ale* (or by overranking emphatic *KANEN* or *DALE*); (b) by postpredicate actor or goal positions (or by overranking prepredicate emphatic position); (c) by correlation with a focus indicator for actor or goal in the predicate; and (d) by a semantic component of focus complement.[11]

The actor tagmeme outside a tagmeme composite is seen in (6b, 6d, 6g, 6h). Characterizing the simple actor is (a) the nonemphatic, nonfocus-complement

[10] See Velma B. Pickett, *The grammatical hierarchy of Isthmus Zapotec* (Language dissertation No. 56; Baltimore, 1960). She sets up for various purposes simultaneous tagmemes in Double Function. See 69–71, 78–79, for relative or interrogative tagmeme simultaneous with subject, object, time, location, and manner tagmeme. See 56 and 35 for her clause and phrase formulas in tagmemic notation. Presumably English *who* etc. could well be handled by related techniques. See also my *Language* 3.71b, 74a (1960).

[11] Or of 'topic'—the term used by McKaughan (18) for the meaning and name of the focus complement. See fn. 5.

pronoun class -*an*, -*la*; (b) position immediately after the predicate; (c) a semantic
component as actor; and (d) negative concord (i.e. no concord) with goal-focussed
predicate tagmeme. (But as part of an emphatic tagmeme composite, or of a
focussed-emphatic tagmeme composite, it takes on the priority characteristics
referred to under emphasis and focus.)

Comparably, the simple noncomposite goal tagmeme of (6a) and (6c) has
(a) a manifesting class of nonemphatic nonfocus-complement pronouns *dun*,
dale; (b) position after nonemphatic actor; (c) a semantic component as goal;
and (d) negative concord with an actor-focussed predicate.

How can all this extra information be symbolized? The citation paradigm
appears deceptively simple. Some kind of notation is needed to show the simultaneity of tagmeme structurings with its intricate priority interplay of
pronominal sets. For this we turn to a tagmemic notation.

IV. The Structure Paradigm

If one modification is made, the simultaneity of tagmemes in the clause string
can be shown in (7) by symbols introduced in earlier sections. We add a vertical
bar between letter symbols of a tagmeme composite, thus: $A|_{fc}$, as representing
simultaneous actor and focus-complement tagmemes.

(7) Transitive Clause in Tagmemic-Notation Paradigm

(7-6a)	TC_{af}	$\{\ldots$	TP_{af} $A|_{fc}$	$G\}$
(7-6c)	$_{ea}TC_{af}$	$\{_e|A|_{fc}$	TP_{af} $\ldots$	$G\}$
(7-6e)	$_{eg}TC_{af}$	$\{_e|G$	TP_{af} $A|_{fc}$	$\ldots\}$
(7-6b)	TC_{gf}	$\{\ldots$	TP_{gf} A	$G|_{fc}\}$
(7-6d)	$_{ea}TC_{gf}$	$\{_a|A$	TP_{gf} A_{cr}	$G|_{fc}\}$
(7-6g)	$_{eg}TC_{gf}$	$\{_e|G|_{fc}$	TP_{gf} A	$\ldots\}$

I have rearranged the paradigm, dropping the grouping into pairs of contrasting focussed activity gained from the columns of matrix (3). I have regrouped
the clause types into two triples by way of the two rows of (3), so as to bring out
further relationships between the actor-focussed set as a whole and the goal-
focussed set as a whole. Cross reference of the formulas of (7) to those of (6) is
provided by using a composite number; (7-6d) labels the new treatment of (6d).

This notation points up a further fact: that the emphasis tagmeme has a
specific position before predicate but the focus-complement tagmeme has none.
Moreover, the lack of a vertical bar within the complex symbol for predicate
shows that we consider the actor-focussed predicate to be a single tagmeme (on
the clause level of structure) in contrast with the goal-focussed tagmeme. Within
the predicate, on the other hand, there is a word-level string of tagmemes. In a
full-scale grammar we would here have to discuss (a) the tagmeme slots within
each kind of verb structure, plotting each kind of verb construction for this
purpose separately; (b) the morpheme classes entering the slots; (c) the contrasts
between various kinds of verb constructions; (d) relations between the verb
constructions (or their included constituents) and noun (or other) structures;
and (e) any allomorphic variations within morpheme classes or constructions.

All of this is morphological discussion and lies outside the scope of the present paper (and of Dean's) except for a general reference to the essential -M- and -N- signals of focus. Here we have ignored all morphological variants of these signals. Our concern with internal components of the verb has been exclusively with samples of those units which signal the interlocking of the morphological with the syntactic level—i.e. of word with clause. (If we were analyzing the verb in detail, we would expect to set up a tagmeme of focus, on the morphological level. The morphemes represented by -M- and -N- would fill this tagmemic slot.) For a description of the elaborate morphophonemics of a Philippine language cf. rather McKaughan's treatment;[12] for our purpose the morphological detail would at this point only obscure the syntactic relations.

The overall simplicity of the formulas of (7) is due to their emic representation. Variants in the position of tagmemes, variants in the internal structure of the tagmemes (the etic components of the tagmemes in terms of filler classes or their variants), clause variants which result from clause expansions through optional tagmemes of time, location, and so on (not discussed by Dean)—all of these complicating characteristics have been omitted. The fact that we are listing stripped-down emic summaries of constructions through formulas without tagmeme variants and without construction variants is symbolized in (7) by the braces enclosing each emic clause formula.

One symbol of (7-6d), so far unexplained, is also important to the structure. The notation A_{cr} represents a special cross-referent tagmeme filling the regular actor slot when tagmeme A occurs in $_e|A$ of $_{ea}TC_{gf}$. Here two actor tagmemes are required. The second actor tagmeme occurs in cross reference to the first. The permitted classes in the two actor slots are not completely interchangeable. The postpredicate actor tagmeme is the more restricted of the two. Only the non-focus-complement actor pronoun may come there. But either a noun (or noun phrase) or a pronoun will be found manifesting A (with or without $_e$ or $_{fc}$). We are forced to give attention to the particular classes which are allowed to enter the various slots.

The emic listing of clause constituents in (7), furthermore, does not provide symbols for the variants of structure which arise from freedom in the placement of the tagmeme composites $_e|G$ and $_e|G|_{fc}$ from (6e $\sim$ 6f, 6g $\sim$ 6h). These composites occur either in the prepredicate slot normal to the emphasis tagmeme or in the postactor slot normal to nonemphatic goal. (An alternate analysis might deny the presence of $|_{fc}$ in $_e|A|_{fc}$ and in $_e|G|_{fc}$ since the only signal for its presence comes from the verb. Dean, however, marks such items as still in focus; I follow his analysis.)

Matrix (8) now supplies this lack of symbols for etic detail in (7) with a tagmatic slot-and-class paradigm. The fact that it is an etic display of the constructions, rather than an emic one like (7), is symbolized by enclosing each etic clause formula in square brackets. Parentheses enclose the fillers of the slots. In predicate slots one finds a transitive verb with the actor-focus or goal-focus markers -*m*- or -*n*-. In all other slots except A_{cr} one finds both noun and pronoun.

---

[12] See reference in fn. 4.

The labels Pr_e, Pr_{fc}, $Pr_{uf}A$, $Pr_{uf}G$ denote emphatic pronoun, focus-complement pronoun, nonfocus-complement actor, and nonfocus-complement goal pronoun. Pointed brackets enclose one typical member of the class to remind the reader of the make-up of the class, and as a key to Dean's description, which labels the classes by these particular examples.

(8) Transitive Clause in Tagmatic-Notation Paradigm

(8-6a)	TC_{af}	[...	TP_{af} (TV_m)	$A\vert_{fc}$ $(N/Pr_{fc} \langle ale\rangle)$	G $(N/Pr_{uf}G \langle dun\rangle)]$
(8-6c)	$_{ea}TC_{af}$	$\lbrack_e\vert A\vert_{fc}$ $(N/Pr_e \langle kanen\rangle)$	TP_{af} (TV_m)	...	G $(N/Pr_{uf}G \langle dun\rangle)]$
(8-6e)	$_{eg}TC_{af}$	$[^\bullet_e\vert G$ $(N/Pr_e \langle kanen\rangle)$	TP_{af} (TV_m)	$A\vert_{fc}$ $(N/Pr_{fc} \langle ale\rangle)$	...]
(8-6f)	~	[...	TP_{af} (TV_m)	$A\vert_{fc}$ $(N/Pr \langle ale\rangle)$	$_e\vert G$ $(N/Pr_e \langle kanen\rangle)]$
(8-6b)	TC_{gf}	[...	TP_{gf} (TV_n)	A $(N/Pr_{uf}A \langle -an\rangle)$	$G\vert_{fc}$ $(N/Pr_{fc} \langle ale\rangle)]$
(8-6d)	$_{ea}TC_{gf}$	$\lbrack_e\vert A$ $(N/Pr_e \langle kanen\rangle)$	TP_{gf} (TV_n)	A_{cr} $(Pr_{uf}A \langle -an\rangle)$	$G\vert_{fc}$ $(N/Pr_{fc} \langle ale\rangle)]$
(8-6g)	$_{eg}TC_{gf}$	$\lbrack_e\vert G$ $(N/Pr_e \langle kanen\rangle)$	TP_{gf} (TV_n)	A $(N/Pr_{uf}A \langle -an\rangle)$	...]
(8-6h)	~	[...	TP_{gf} (TV_n)	A $(N/Pr_{uf}A \langle -an\rangle)$	$G\vert_{fc}$ $(N/Pr_e \langle kanen\rangle)]$

Paradigm (8) may also be called an etic TESTING MATRIX, since with this kind of data (supplemented with comparable matrices for word constructions, phrase constructions, and construction of sentence, paragraph, and discourse at their respective levels) the accuracy of a syntactic description[13] and the productive applicability of the system in speech can be matched for fit against the material available for analysis.

Yet (8) calls for further particulars to demonstrate its full validity. It predicts the occurrence of nouns in all A (except A_{cr}) or G positions—whether or not in simultaneous occurrence with $_e\vert$ and $\vert_{fc}$. It predicts also some ambiguity when nouns are used. Inasmuch as the symbol N remains unchanged in tagmeme slots A, G, $A\vert_{fc}$, $G\vert_{fc}$, $_e\vert A$, $_e\vert G$, $_e\vert A\vert_{fc}$, and $_e\vert G\vert_{fc}$, it implies that the nouns (or noun phrases) in those slots are identical. If this is true, then when the nouns *kuku?* 'cat' and *ungeh* 'rat' are used, the forms (9-6c) and (9-6e) become identical. One cannot tell here whether it is actor or goal which begins the clause or follows the verb.

(9-6c) $_{ea}TC_{af}$: *kuku? kamfe? ungeh* '(The) CAT ← catches$_{af}$ (the) rat.'
(9-6e) $_{eg}TC_{af}$: *kuku? kamfe? ungeh* '(It is the) CAT (that the) rat ← catches$_{af}$.'

This ambiguity does not occur in goal-focussed clauses, however, since $_{ea}TC_{gf}$ (8-6d) is distinguished from $_{eg}TC_{gf}$ (8-6g) by the obligatory presence of a cross-referent actor pronoun in the former.

Further ambiguity develops at another place in the paradigm, but does not appear directly through (8). Its source lies below the emic level of the clause construction and even below the level of tagmemic representation of etic construction variants of the clause. It arises in an etic variant (an allotagma) of the tagmeme $\vert_{fc}$ simultaneous with A or G (but never with $_e\vert$).

[13] The same data must be known, I believe, tacitly or explicitly, for an adequate test, regardless of the theory under which the analysis is made or the style in which it is presented.

Note that this claims no more than when we affirm that a phonemic description cannot be checked for accuracy against the data, nor used for producing accurate pronunciation, unless the (emic) phonological symbols are accompanied by an (etic) commentary or by an (etic) symbolism relating the systemic generalizations to physical articulation. No variety of phonemic theory can avoid this requirement.

To solve this problem we have available, above, the relevant data and the requisite theory. We combine forms (6a', 6b, 6e', 6f') from the citation matrix with a discussion of third-person allotagmatic # of A|_{fc} and of G|_{fc} of (7) and with a discussion of the nominal ambiguity of noun function in (9-6c, 9-6e).

The emic symbol for the fillers of a tagmemic slot does not differentiate between the overt and covert allotagmatic fillers of that slot. Similarly, the label Pr_{fc}, standing for the emic class of focus-complement pronouns, does not symbolize the overt and covert etic variants of the class. And finally, the selected illustrative member of that emic class ⟨ale⟩ does not display the zero. Where, then, would the zero allotagma (zero manifestation) of Pr_{fc} appear in the formulaic description? Where, that is, except in the citation paradigm (6)?

Tagmemic theory is explicit on this point. Tagmemes, as well-defined units, include in their complete description any needed reference to their variants (as well as to their contrastive-identificational features and to their distribution in class, in sequence, and in matrix).[14] Just as we have used braces and brackets to distinguish the emic from the etic nature of construction formulas, so now we use the same symbols for the tagmemes themselves. Braces enclose an emic notation of tagmemes; brackets enclose symbols for allotagmas. This notation becomes important whenever the analyst is discussing the tagmemes as such, rather than the tagmemically-represented construction variants. The tagmeme composite {A|_{fc}}, for example, has among its variants both [A|_{fc} ⟨ale⟩] and [A|_{fc} ⟨#⟩]. (We could have further differentiated matrix (7) from (8) by italicizing the tagmeme symbols of (7) but not the same symbols when representing only the tagmemic slots of (8). We have assumed, however, that braces and brackets make this difference explicit enough, just as we use only one set of symbols for phonemes between diagonals and for phones between brackets.)

V. Intransitive paradigm

Now that our basic approach has been illustrated and paradigmatic symbols have been set up for handling the transitive clause, the intransitive clause can be presented without much comment. The intransitive citation paradigm appears as (10).

(10) Intransitive Clause in Citation Paradigm

(10a)		IntC_{af}	...	Mngel	→ale	...	'...	Cry_{af}	→they	...'
(10a')			(...	Mngel	→#	...	'...	Cry_{af}	→he	...')
(10a")			(...	Mngel	→kuku?	...	'...	Cry_{af}	→cat	...')
(10b)		_{ea}IntC_{af}	DALE	Mngel	→(...)	...	'THEY	cry_{af}	→(...)	...'
(10c)			DALE	Mngel	→ale	...	'THEY	cry_{af}	→they	...'
(10b'-c')			(KANEN	Mngel	→#	...	'HE	cry_{af}	→#	...')
(10b"-c")			(KUKU?	Mngel	→#	...	'CAT	cry_{af}	→#	...')
(10d)		~	...	Mngel	→ale	DALE	'...	Cry_{af}	→they	THEY'
(10d')			(...	Mngel	→#	KANEN	'...	Cry_{af}	→he	HE')
(10d")			(...	Mngel	→#	KUKU?	'...	Cry_{af}	→it	CAT')

A new set of stems appears in (10), illustrated by mngel 'to cry'. It is the correlation of this stem type with the absence of goal forms which forces the sym-

---

[14] See fn. 6.

bolizing of intransitive actor-focussed activity as distinct from transitive. The focus signal M appears here initial in the word.[15]

By comparing (10b) with (10c) we note that the cross-referent pronoun after the verb (that is, $A_{cr|fc}$) may be included or be left out of the intransitive clause. (This makes it somewhat different in functional load from the obligatory A_{cr} in transitive 7-6d.) In each instance, however, the arrow indicates that the slot is in focus whether filled or not; when filled, it shows the focus-complement set of pronouns.

I have used the sign # exclusively for the focus-complement third person, which occurs only as zero. The absence of third person plural cross referent is shown by parentheses around the dots in (10b). This is not zero in the same sense, since the optional focus-complement *ale* is present there in (10c). Since we do not wish to change direction of focus during the optional absence of *ale*, the arrow points to the empty slots.

Note the ambiguity between (10a″) and (10d″): '(The) cat ← cries $_{af}$' versus '(It) ←, (the) CAT, cries $_{af}$'. The third singular in (10d″) $A_{cr|fc}$—but not the same tagmeme in third plural form in (10d)—is zero, opening the door to this ambiguity.

The emic paradigm for intransitive is seen in (11).

(11) Intransitive Clause in Tagmemic-Notation Paradigm

(11-10a)	$IntC_{af}$	{...	$+IntP_{af}$	$+A|_{fc}$}
(11-10b–d)	$_{ea}IntC_{af}$	{$+_e$|A	$+IntP_{af}$	$\pm A_{cr|fc}$}

The optional nature of $A_{cr|fc}$ is symbolized by $\pm$ in the emic representation of (11-10b–d). (Obligatory occurrence of other tagmemes is shown by $+$.) This freedom is limited to the construction variant which carries the emphatic tagmeme in normal initial position. The restriction will enter the notation only when the etic variants of (11) are shown in (12).

(12) Intransitive Clause in Tagmatic-Notation Paradigm

(12-10a)	$IntC_{af}$	[...	$+IntP_{af}$ (IntV$_m$)	$+A|_{fc}$ (N/Pr$_{fc}$ ⟨ale⟩)	...]
(12-10b–c)	$_{ea}IntC_{af}$	[$+_e$|A (N/Pr$_e$ ⟨kanen⟩)	$+IntP_{af}$ (IntV$_m$)	$\pm A_{cr|fc}$ (Pr$_{fc}$ ⟨ale⟩)	...]
(12-10d)	~	[...	$+IntP_{af}$ (IntV$_m$)	$+A_{cr|fc}$ (Pr$_{fc}$ ⟨ale⟩)	$+_e$|A (N/Pr$_e$ ⟨kanen⟩)]

In (12), two different kinds of variants require symbols. Whereas the EXPANSION VARIANT of (10b–c), seen with its optional addition, is simply shown by the $\pm$ in (12-10b–c), a TRANSFORM VARIANT requires an alternant formula as in (12-10d). Variants of constructions,[16] whether of the expansion or the transform type, can be handled as alternants of which neither has priority over the other. Or one variant of a pair may be treated as a base or norm from which the other is derived by a rule. Derivation of the transform variant (12-10d) from a clause base

---

[15] Either because of morphophonemic changes due to the particular phoneme sequence beginning the stem, or because of some complexity of relation between intransitive and stative relationships not discussed in Dean's article but perhaps implied by Abrams. (See fn. 7).

[16] Compare similar alternative treatments of allomorphs and allophones.

(12-10b–c) requires the rule that the initial emphatic tagmeme complex be trans-posed to clause-final position and that the sign $\pm$ be changed to $+$ before $A_{cr|fc}$. The base-plus-rule approach, however, makes it difficult to display paradigms and matrices of well-defined units and their variants.

VI. NOUN PHRASES

In Dean's article there is little treatment of Bilaan phrases. He has supplied me with a few further forms, which reveal an interesting interlocking between some components of the clause paradigms and certain noun phrases which have one noun as head and another noun (or pronoun) as possessor. In (13) and (14) these are shown in citation and in tagmemic-notation paradigms (Po possessor, NPh noun phrase, H head).

(13) Possessor Noun Phrase in Citation Paradigm

(13a)	PoNPh	...	ungeh	-la	'...	rat	their'
(13a')		...	ungeh	kuku?	'...	rat	cat's'
(13b)	ₑPoNPh	DALE	ungeh	...	'THEIR	rat	...'

(14) Possessor Noun Phrase in Tagmemic-Notation Paradigm

(14-13a)	PoNPh	[···		HNPh (N)	Po (N/Pr$_{uf}$A $\langle$-an$\rangle$)]
(14-13b)	ₑPoNPh	[ₑ|Po (N/Pr$_e$ $\langle$kanen$\rangle$)		HNPh (N)	···]

In (14-13a) the set of regular pronominal possessors of an item is the same set as the nonfocus-complement actor of (8-6b). The emphatic pronominal set of (14-13b) is the same as the actor in (8-6d) or the goal in (8-6g). The order rela-tion of pronoun Pr$_e$ and of pronoun Pr$_{uf}$A to the head of the noun phrase is the same—before and after respectively—as it is to the predicate of the clause.[17]

An emphatic tagmeme occurs in the possessor noun phrase (14-13b). Our notation ₑ| is the same as for the substantives in the actor and goal tagmeme com-plexes of the clause, and shows that our analysis treats this tagmeme as identical with the one that occurs simultaneously with such an actor or goal (in 8-6d and 8-6g, for example). The emphatic tagmeme, then, occurs on a par both with a clause-tagmeme string and with a noun-phrase string; it functions on two differ-ent structural levels.

Sharply different in character are noun phrases with a marker *di*. These have some relationship to referent function translatable as 'to me', 'for me', and the like. From Abram's material I gather that the particle *di* occurs when the noun phrase is not functioning as a focus complement. Similarly, Dean's material has a few sentences in which a particle *i* occurs with a noun functioning as actor or goal. Abrams shows this particle as occurring optionally.

Many Philippine languages, however, use a particle to mark any noun phrase

---

[17] This fact adds weight to our treatment of focussed actor (or goal) as a focus comple-ment to the predicate rather than as a central topic or as a center of focus itself. It suggests, further, that we have here a structural argument from noun-phrase analogy for treating the predicate as the nucleus of the clause with both actor and goal as in some sense marginal or lateral to it.

as a focus complement. In Maranao,[18] *so* marks a phrase as focus-complement subject, focus-complement object, or focus-complement instrument. When functioning as a nonfocus-complement, a Maranao subject noun phrase takes *o*, an object takes *sa*, a referent takes *ko* (with cooccurrent subjective or objective voice—i.e. actor- or goal-focussed activity in the verb) or *sa* ~ *ko* (with cooccurrent instrumental voice), an instrument takes *ko* (with cooccurrent objective or referential voice) or *so* (with cooccurrent instrumental voice). In Tagalog,[19] each of the voices takes as an obligatory focus-complement marker the particle *ang*. Markers of this type in Maranao and Tagalog prevent much of the Bilaan ambiguity of (9-6c) and (9-6e). In languages where focus markers occur regularly with noun phrases, the order of tagmemes in the clause does not need to be as rigid as it appears to be in Bilaan.

VII. BILAAN AND ENGLISH

In view of the widespread activity-focus system, with three or four voices in many Philippine languages, it is not surprising that Bilaan, as Abrams suggests, has a restricted contrast between referent-focussed and goal-focussed activity. For certain verbs, he says, the *n*- marker in the verb takes over a function of signalling reference-focussed activity, with a zero marker for goal-focussed activity. This is shown in (15–16).[20] I mark the constructions with an asterisk because the difference in dialect source between Dean and Abrams may make the illustration inapplicable to the Bilaan dialect which Dean describes.

(15) *bat-an ale* 'He throws them'

(16) *n-bat-an ale* 'He throws (to) them'

The importance of this material to us is that it helps to point up one difference between English and many languages of the Philippines. Whereas English has only an active and a passive voice, some Philippine languages have several voices. For this reason we tentatively added the referent clause type to the matrix of (1), even though there was not enough material to add it to our syntax paradigm. Certain of the formal differences between English active and passive clauses and the Bilaan clauses with activity focussed toward actor, goal, and referent are symbolized in (17) and (18).

(17) English Voices
    (17a) $S_a \leftarrow \ \rightarrow P_{af}$ G
    (17b) $S_g \leftarrow \ \rightarrow P_{gf}$ Agent

(18) Bilaan Voices
    (18a) P_{af} $\rightarrow A_{fc}$ G
    (18b) P_{gf} A $\rightarrow G_{fc}$
    (18c) *P_{rf} A   G $\rightarrow R_{fc}$
    (18d) ~*P_{rf} A $\rightarrow R_{fc}$ G

---

[18] See the table in McKaughan 19. See also McKaughan, 'Overt relation markers in Maranao', *Lg.* 38.47–51 (1962).

[19] See Table 5 in Elmer Wolfenden, *A re-statement of Tagalog grammar* 16 (Manila, 1961).

[20] From Abrams 10.

Comparing (17a) with (17b) we affirm that English S_a is a subject-as-actor tagmeme differing from homophonous S_g, a subject-as-goal tagmeme. The two are members of a distribution class of homophonous subject tagmemes,[21] contrasting in transformations (S_g tagmeme of passive clause transforms to G tagmeme of active; S_a of active clause transforms to agent of passive) and in semantic relations. What holds them together in an emic class of tagmemes is their position before the predicate and their tie to the predicate in person and number (*The boys run : The boy runs*). This tie is symbolized by the arrow pointing right, to the predicate; the arrow pointing left, to the subject, implies the component of observer focus on actor-oriented or goal-oriented activity.

In (18a–d) the Bilaan differences show up clearly. No single distribution class of subject containing actor, goal, and referent tagmemes can be fruitfully postulated; different distributional positions are retained for actor and for goal. No concord of person and number links the predicate with the focus complement. The tentative listing (*) of the referent clause type in (18c) implies a more complex voice system for Bilaan than for English. The referent alternant in (18d) allows the focus complement to be drawn back closer to the predicate—provided, however, that this alternant is not used if the two substantives are members of the same subclass, so that their use might result in ambiguity.[22]

[21] See my *Language* 1.131 (1954), 3.13a(c), 16a(jj) (1960).

[22] Thus, Abrams indicates (11) that there is in variation the order of *kayu* 'tree' and *balo* 'bolo knife' in *k-an-lang-gu kayu balo : k-an-lang-gu balo kayu*. The degree to which variation occurs in that dialect, however, is not clear from his material. Possibly a special order sometimes occurs when one of two (or more) substantives is a noun and the other a pronoun.

Syntax
sentence level

SENTENCE STRUCTURE AS A STATEMENT CALCULUS

ROBERT E. LONGACRE

Summer Institute of Linguistics

Sentence (as opposed to clause) structure involves a combination of predications into larger units much as in the statement calculus of formal logic, but requires a richer apparatus. An over-all taxonomic scheme—relevant to sentence structures in many parts of the world—is presented. After showing how structurally distinct parts of the sentence are relevant to the structure of paragraphs and discourses, a detailed classification of English sentence types is presented. The parameters of the resulting over-all system are suggestive of universal parameters of relation and contrast among sentences.

Sentence structure in the sense of combination of clauses into larger units has been little studied. What is usually termed sentence structure in linguistic literature is rather clause structure. The clause is the proper domain of such grammatical relations as predicates of various sorts, objects, complements, benefactives, and adjuncts. It is also the domain of the lexical, situational, or semiological relations which Fillmore (1968a, b) has called CASE. These have had parallel development within the framework of tagmemic theory by members of the Philippine Branch of the Summer Institute of Linguistics.[1] Whether grammatical or lexical-situational, all these relations are the linguistic counterpart of the predicate calculus. Sentence structure, however, is the linguistic counterpart of the statement calculus, although it involves a richer and more varied scheme of relations than those found in formal logic. Thus, while we find conjunction, alternation, and implication relevant to both formal logic and natural languages, the latter require finer distinctions, plus recognition of further relations.

In this article,[2] I suggest an over-all taxonomic scheme for the sentence, show that this scheme has implications for the structure of paragraphs and discourses, classify English sentence types, and suggest some universal parameters for systems of sentence types.

10. Clauses combine to form sentences in two ways: (1) as PERIPHERAL (or subordinate) elements plus NUCLEUS; and (2) as intra-nuclear combinations. The latter are more reminiscent of the statement calculus of formal logic; but the former embrace features of considerable importance, and are here described first.

Clauses which are found in the Periphery of the sentence can best be seen in their full structural context by considering the sentence as a whole, the place of the Periphery within the sentence, and the distribution of subordinate clauses within the Periphery. Careful study will further reveal that the subordinate

*Language, 46. 783-815, 1970, reprinted by permission.

[1] Articles by members of the Philippine Branch of the Summer Institute of Linguistics include Pike 1964, Forster 1964, Miller 1964. More recent work in Philippine languages includes Reid 1966, Forster & Barnard 1968, Hall 1969.
[2] Cf. Longacre 1967:15–25; 1968, vol. 2. The latter volume is a summary of joint research with some 20 colleagues of the Philippine Branch of the Summer Institute of Linguistics.

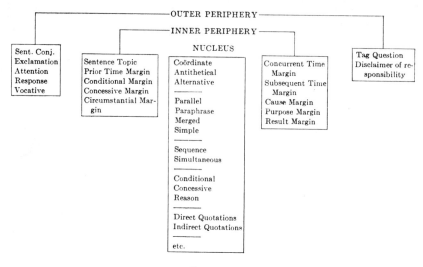

FIGURE 1

(1) Linear order on the chart is intended to reflect a statistically common ordering among the world's languages.

(2) Outer Periphery items permute to grammatical junctures within Inner Periphery and Nucleus in many languages.

(3) Nuclear sentence strings may occur recursively within the Inner Periphery and the Nucleus.

(4) A particle such as English *then* intervenes in many languages between certain preposed Sentence Margins and the Nucleus.

(5) In the Outer Periphery, the symbol 'Sent. Conj.' stands for a set of positions, such as SENTENCE CONJUNCTION, SENTENCE ADVERB, and SENTENCE MODIFIER, e.g. *and, nevertheless, obviously*...

'clauses' might better be regarded as subordinated sentences occurring recursively within the Periphery of the sentence—but more of this in its proper place.

Figure 1 presents an over-all view of the sentence. It is non-language-specific in that it is empirically based on studies in English, some ten Meso-American languages, some twenty-four Philippine languages, and a few scattered languages from other areas. First of all, the scheme recognizes the sentence Nucleus as the domain of such relations as coördination, antithesis, alternation, certain types of parallelism and paraphrase, certain time relations such as sequence and simultaneity, certain types of implication, and quotation. These relations will be illustrated with English examples in later sections of this paper. The Periphery (which may, on occasion, interrupt the linear order of the Nucleus) is divided into outer and inner parts, which differ considerably in function.

11. Tagmemes of the OUTER PERIPHERY include various sorts of SENTENCE CONJUNCTIONS, SENTENCE ADVERBS, and SENTENCE MODIFIERS as well as elements here labeled EXCLAMATION, ATTENTION, RESPONSE, and VOCATIVE. The first three elements may occur individually, or in a sentence-initial cluster such as *And, on the other hand, obviously* ... EXCLAMATION is a function expounded by various bywords, epithets, and four-letter words; more than one may occur in sequence. ATTENTION is expounded by such words as *hey!* RESPONSE is expounded by affirmative, negative, or noncommittal particles. VOCATIVE is expounded by personal names, terms of kinship and other relations, or further substitutes. Linear ordering of these elements is language-specific. A common position for them is near the opening of the sentence where their relative linear ordering can be observed in a given language. Nevertheless, in many languages some of these outer-peripheral elements permute to a grammatical juncture almost anywhere within the interior of the sentence. This is, in fact, one feature which frequently distinguishes them from tagmemes of the Inner Periphery. Thus, a Sentence Conjunction like *however* often is found in the interior of the sentence (some strict stylists prescribe that it must not be used as a Sentence Conjunction in sentence-initial position): *However, John went downtown. John, however, went downtown. John went downtown, however. John went, however, downtown.* In other than simple sentences: *John, however, went downtown, and Mary stayed home. John went downtown, however, and Mary stayed home.* Similarly, exponents of the Vocative can also be distributed within the sentence: *Mary, he's just trying to string you along and deceive you. He's just trying, Mary, to string you along and deceive you. He's just trying to string you along, Mary, and deceive you. He's just trying to string you along and deceive you, Mary.* Obviously, careful work is needed here to determine, within a particular language, which permutations are possible.

Two other outer-peripheral tagmemes are given a sentence-final position in Figure 1. English has a very specialized device for forming tag questions—use of modal or auxiliary, deletion of main verb, use of anaphoric pronoun, and presence of negative to elicit a positive answer, while absence of negative elicits a negative answer: *You'll go downtown for me, won't you? You won't go downtown alone at this hour of the night, will you?* It seems best to consider that this structure determines a further nuclear sentence pattern in English, and it is so treated in a later section of this paper. In many languages, however, a simpler device, i.e. a sentence-final particle, is used to indicate a tag question. This particle may, furthermore, permute to sentence-interior position, where it occurs contiguous to the particular word that is being questioned. Similarly, many languages contain a particle which, by indicating that what one says comes from another source, allows the speaker to disclaim responsibility for the utterance. This particle may also permute to the interior, where, in some languages, it may occur several times within the boundaries of a single sentence.

Occurrence of outer-peripheral tagmemes is somewhat conditioned by broader constraints of paragraph and discourse structure. Obviously, the purpose of the Sentence Conjunction and similar elements is to bind a sentence into surrounding context: is a given sentence simply an addition to the preceding context, is it antithetical, does it explain or exemplify what preceded, is it a result of or reason for what preceded? The choice of a given conjunction frequently answers such questions. The Sentence Conjunction may, however, introduce not just the sentence of which it is phonologically and grammatically a part, but a whole section of discourse.

Tagmemes such as Attention and Vocative most typically occur in sections of dialogue. Furthermore, embedded sentences do not normally contain these, or for that matter other tagmemes of the Outer Periphery—except for sentences which are embedded as direct quotations.

12. The INNER PERIPHERY is more intimately associated with the Nucleus than is the Outer Periphery. Furthermore, embedded sentences may contain tagmemes of the Inner Periphery.

The SENTENCE TOPIC is an element which occurs early in the sentence string. It often directly follows the Sentence Conjunction of the Outer Periphery, without other outer tagmemes being present. The Sentence Topic is expounded by a substantive phrase (or embedded clause or sentence) and is usually cross-referenced by something within the Nucleus of the sentence. In particular languages, particles such as *as for* or *even* may introduce the exponent of Sentence Topic; or it may have no introducer. Thus: *As for John, his horse died. Even my father, he was disturbed by what they were doing in the name of law and order. Risk, that is what adds spice to life and makes it worth while.*

The other tagmemes of the Inner Periphery are SENTENCE MARGINS. They are expounded by elements that occur with any of the various Nuclei—although, as in any and all grammatical constructions, particular collocational restrictions may make impossible a complete paradigm.

Three distinct TIME MARGINS occur in many languages, appearing most naturally in sentences which refer to events rather than to descriptions or states. When a Time Margin refers to an action which is antecedent to that found in the Nucleus, it is a PRIOR Time Margin; it regularly precedes the Nucleus, and in some languages is limited to that position: *After/when Ed came downstairs, Mary slipped out the front door, went around the house, and came in the back door.* Here the example is a coördinate sentence with a Prior Time Margin. CONCURRENT Time Margins refer to actions which at least partially overlap with that reported in the sentence Nucleus. Such margins are not limited to pre-nuclear position and are, indeed, in some languages limited to post-nuclear: *While Ed was coming downstairs, Mary slipped out the front door, went around the house, and came in the back door.* A SUBSEQUENT Time Margin is illustrated by: *Mary stayed there until Ed came downstairs.*

Implicational Margins, i.e. CONDITIONAL or CONCESSIVE Margins, are found in many languages. To be classified as Margins rather than as features of the Nucleus, such elements must be non-specific to particular following constructions. In English, a general condition (not contrafactual) goes with a following sentence base with a modicum of cross-reference and restriction. By contrast (see §31.4), contrafactual conditions involve mutual restriction and double-talk within both the *if* and *then* parts of the sentence. With the same sentence Nucleus, both Conditional and Concessive Margins may occur: *If Ed slept five minutes overtime, his father got cross with him and made things generally unpleasant. Although Ed never slept more than five minutes overtime, his father got cross with him and made things generally unpleasant.*

Teleological Margins (CAUSE, PURPOSE, and CIRCUMSTANTIAL) are also of common occurrence. The Cause and Purpose Margins are often postposed to the Nucleus, while the Circumstantial Margin is more commonly preposed. Cause and Purpose Margins involve embedded sentence structures in many languages. This length and complexity makes it less awkward to have them occur sentence-finally. In English the Margins may occur either preposed or postposed. The following example of Cause Margin precedes the same Nucleus employed above: *Because Ed occasionally slept five minutes overtime, his father got cross with him and made things generally unpleasant.* With the following Paraphrase Sentence, a postposed and more complex Cause Margin occurs: *She got very angry, she threw a temper tantrum worthy of a three-year-old child, because she knew that it would be tolerated and might even result in her getting her way again, as in past years.* The following examples of Purpose Margin are preposed and postposed respectively: *In order to keep Ed from sleeping five minutes overtime, his father got cross with him and made things generally unpleasant. She got very angry, she threw a temper tantrum worthy of a three-year-old child, so that she might get her way again, as she had done in past years to the detriment of the whole family.* The Circumstantial Margin is a sort of watered-down or weakened Cause Margin: *Since (or In that) she knew that it would be tolerated, she got very angry, she threw a temper tantrum worthy of a three-year-old child.*

In the general scheme of the sentence, a Result Margin is indicated; but English has no such Sentence Margin. The English *so* does not introduce a Result Margin in a sentence such as the following, but is rather a link within the Nucleus of a Result Sentence (§31.5): *She called me, so I went.* Similarly, the English word *for* does not introduce a Cause Margin, but is rather a link in a Reason Sentence (§31.5): *I went along with them, for there was nothing else to do.*

In some languages, certain conjunctions may occur as links between preposed Margins and the following Nucleus. Such margin-nucleus linking conjunctions are not specific to any given Margin. Were they specific to a given Margin, then the whole margin-conjunction-nucleus complex would better be re-interpreted as a new derived Nucleus (cf. §31.4). English *then*, which expresses chronological or logical sequence, may occur after a preposed Prior Time Margin, a Conditional Margin, or a Circumstantial Margin, before the sentence Nucleus: *After he came, then I left. If he's a philanthropist, then I'm one too. Since he's there, then I'm not really needed. Then* also occurs within COÖRDINATE and CONTRA-FACTUAL Sentences whenever its lexical meaning is appropriate: *He came and then I left. Had he come at the moment, then all would have been well.*

13. It is convenient to consider that Sentence Margins of the various sorts, when their exponents are something other than a phrase, are expounded not by clauses but by sentences. Often the string which follows a subordinating conjunction or relator is a single clause. Nevertheless, a single clause is a simple (or minimal) sentence. Furthermore, Sentence Margins are slots where nuclear sentence patterns may recursively be embedded within other sentences. Thus, an Antithetical Sentence may be embedded with a Cause Margin: *I don't want to marry her, because she's rich but I'm poor.* Or a Coördinate Sentence may be so embedded: *I don't want to marry her, because she's rich and her folks don't respect me.* Or a Paraphrase Sentence: *I don't want to marry her, because she's rich, she's never known a day of hard work in her life.* Or an Alternative Sentence: *I don't want to marry her, because either she's rich or she's pretending to come from a* *wealthy family.* Or an Indirect Quotation Sentence: *I don't want to marry her, because she told me that her father was a millionaire.*

20. The division of the sentence into Outer Periphery, Inner Periphery, and Nucleus not only provides a convenient internal taxonomy of the sentence, but also yields divisions of considerable relevance to the structure of discourses and paragraphs. I have already noted that the distribution of initial elements of the Outer Periphery correlates with certain features of discourse structure. It remains to document here the relevance of the Inner Periphery to such higher-level structures.

Five commonly occurring discourse genres are:[3] NARRATIVE, PROCEDURAL, EXPOSITORY, HORTATORY, and DRAMATIC. NARRATIVE discourse is characterized by time sequence in accomplished (past) time. PROCEDURAL discourse is characterized by time sequence in projected (present or future) time.[4] The former tells a story; the latter prescribes a course of action, or tells how to make something.[5] EXPOSITORY discourse is subject-matter oriented; chronological considerations, if present, are not focal. HORTATORY discourse does not depend on time sequence but refers to projected time (present or future); it has an obligatory second person component. While Expository discourse is essentially an essay, Hortatory discourse is essentially a sermon, in the sense of a discourse aimed at influencing conduct. DRAMATIC discourse is distinct from all these in that it is a narrative without an overt narrator; rather, every participant speaks out in multiple first-second person interplay.

In cementing together the parts of a discourse, tagmemes of the Inner Periphery are often crucial. For example, in Narrative and Procedural discourse, Prior Time Margins are pivotal. Thus a new episode of a story may begin: *When John woke up the next morning* ... or *After the ball was over* ... In a Procedural discourse such links may take the form: *When you have thoroughly mixed the dry ingredients* ... or *When the paint has dried for two hours* ... Alternatively, such links may not be by way of 'when' clauses (Prior Time Margins), but by way of consecutive time horizons that encode as Concurrent Time Margins. Thus, successive paragraphs of a story may begin with: *That morning* ... , *At six o'clock in the evening* ... , *The next day* ... , *Two solid weeks passed* ... , etc. In

---

[3] Cf. Longacre 1968:1.1–50. This volume also reflects the joint research with 11 colleagues of the Philippine Branch of the Summer Institute of Linguistics.

[4] To understand the function of tense in discourses, it is necessary to distinguish time as a lexical category from tense as a grammatical category. Accomplished versus projected time is a lexical distinction. A given lexical category of time must be encoded into grammatical tenses. Thus, accomplished time in Latin historiography is frequently encoded by the present tense. All that is required is that the over-all discourse—especially its opening—make it clear that the events have already taken place, i.e. that lexically we are dealing with accomplished time. In Bontoc Narrative discourse, L. Reid reports that it is customary to begin with past tense forms, shift to non-past for the body of the narrative, then shift again to past tense forms near its close.

[5] Narrative discourses which tell how a particular object was made, or a particular activity carried out at a given time in the past, are distinct from Procedural discourses, even though both may serve to instruct one in the making of an object or carrying out of an activity. Here the intent of a discourse seems to belong to the lexicon while the form seems better assigned to the grammar.

a Procedural discourse, similar links may occur but do not refer to past events: *Whenever you want to begin* ... , *Twenty-four hours later* ... , *At noon of the same day* ... , *At sundown* ...

Paragraphs may be classified (Longacre 1968:1.53–190) into narrative, procedural, expository, hortatory, and dialogue types. Although there is a matching of discourse genre to paragraph type, it is nevertheless important to note that a discourse of a given genre is not necessarily composed exclusively (or even preponderantly) of the corresponding paragraph type. Thus, a Narrative discourse may include any sort of paragraph; all that matters is that they be linked in a chronological framework.

Internal linkage within paragraphs is much like that found between paragraphs. Note the two examples from Tolkien 1969 in Figure 2.[6] Both examples are of narrative paragraphs. In the first example the function expounded by the first sentence is that of paragraph setting; it introduces the cake and says a few things about it. The Nucleus of the paragraph consists of three analogous functional elements which I term BUILD-UPS (BU); they report successive events (or event complexes) of the paragraph as encoded in grammatical sentences.[7] In the sentence which expounds the first BU, we are told that the cake was cut up and proved just sufficient for each child to have one large slice. BU_2 is expounded not by a sentence but by an embedded expository paragraph, which consists of two sentences—a topic sentence (which I call a TEXT) and a further sentence which explains and expands the Text (and is therefore called the EXPOSITION). The material which expounds BU_2 advances the action of the paragraph by telling us that the slices disappeared and the children—with varying luck—found trinkets and trifles baked in them. The final BU (BU_n) climaxes the paragraph by telling us that the magic star was not found (although it had been baked into the cake). BU_2 is linked to BU_n by virtue of the Prior Time Margin that begins the sentence which expounds the latter. Thus, *when the cake was all eaten* refers back to *The slices soon disappeared* at the onset of the embedded paragraph which expounds BU_2. Also, the parallelism of *when the cake was all eaten* to *When it was all cut up* in BU_1 serves to carry the story through two consecutive time horizons within that paragraph: between the two lies the eating of the cake. The point to note, however, is that skillful use of Time Margins is partly responsible for the effectiveness of the paragraph.

The second example has no paragraph setting, but plunges immediately into the action of the paragraph. It has but two BU tagmemes, the first of which is expounded by a long Coördinate Sentence. The second and climactic BU is expounded by an expository paragraph which has a Preliminary tagmeme (like Setting in a narrative paragraph), a Text, and two Exposition tagmemes. In

[6] By permission from Houghton Mifflin Company, Boston.

[7] Here again a distinction of grammar and lexicon is needed. The grammar of the paragraph fits grammatical sentences into grammatical slots within the paragraph. In a narrative paragraph, the speaker has the option of grouping more than one event into the same sentence. The lexical structure of the paragraph needs, however, to be traced out in its own right, regardless of the boundaries of grammatical sentences—although there may prove to be lexical strings to which the name lexical sentence would not be inappropriate. Thus, lexically a narrative paragraph is a string of events (see Longacre 1968:1.64–7).

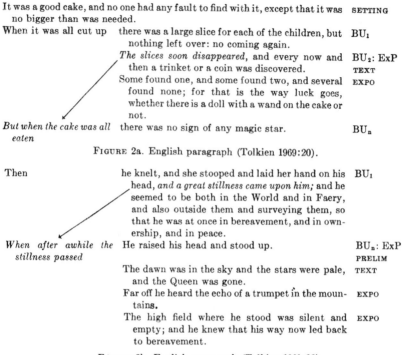

It was a good cake, and no one had any fault to find with it, except that it was   SETTING
no bigger than was needed.

When it was all cut up   there was a large slice for each of the children, but   BU₁
nothing left over: no coming again.

The slices soon disappeared, and every now and   BU₂: ExP
then a trinket or a coin was discovered.   TEXT

Some found one, and some found two, and several   EXPO
found none; for that is the way luck goes,
whether there is a doll with a wand on the cake or
not.

But when the cake was all   there was no sign of any magic star.   BUₙ
eaten

FIGURE 2a. English paragraph (Tolkien 1969:20).

Then   he knelt, and she stooped and laid her hand on his   BU₁
head, *and a great stillness came upon him;* and he
seemed to be both in the World and in Faery,
and also outside them and surveying them, so
that he was at once in bereavement, and in own-
ership, and in peace.

When after awhile the   He raised his head and stood up.   BUₙ: ExP
stillness passed   PRELIM

The dawn was in the sky and the stars were pale,   TEXT
and the Queen was gone.

Far off he heard the echo of a trumpet in the moun-   EXPO
tains.

The high field where he stood was silent and   EXPO
empty; and he knew that his way now led back
to bereavement.

FIGURE 2b. English paragraph (Tolkien 1969:38).

the sentence which expounds Preliminary, an action is reported (*he raised his head and stood up*) which precedes the explanatory material constituting the rest of the paragraph. The Text states that the stars were pale and the Queen was gone. This is developed in two further sentences, one of which reports that far-off echoes of trumpets could be heard from the Queen's party as they withdrew, and the other of which states the emptiness of the field and the feeling of loss. The thing to notice, however, is the role of the Prior Time Margin in connecting the material which expounds BU₁ to that which expounds BUₙ. Thus, *when after a while the stillness passed* refers back to *and a great stillness came upon him* (which is indeed further developed in the balance of that same sentence). The transition between the two main events of the paragraph is clearly marked by exploitation of this sentence-level feature.

In some linguistic areas of the world (e.g. South America, the Philippines), use of Time Margins to mark progress from one BU to another within a narrative paragraph is much more regular and frequent than in English. I document this with a translation of a narrative paragraph from Sarangani Bilaan (Philippines) (Figure 3).[8] In this paragraph there is a Setting expounded by the Simple Sen-

---

[8] This diagram is reproduced from Longacre 1968:1.69. Sarangani Bilaan data are from McLachlin & Blackburn (unpublished MS, 1968). We regret to report the untimely death of Betty McLachlin in an automobile accident, August, 1969.

	And then it was afternoon now	SETTING
	and we were playing volleyball	BU₁
And I wasn't (playing) very long	and I saw Nini come up to me.	BU₂
( )	She said, 'Father, they said for you to come home.'	BU₃
And when I heard that	I went home.	BU₄
And arriving at the house	Uyen said to me, 'They said for you to go upstairs.'	BU₅
And when I heard that	then I went upstairs.	BU₆
And when I arrived upstairs	then Barb said to me, 'Have Uyen come up also.'	BU₇
And when I heard that	then I said to Uyen, 'She said for you to come up.'	BU₈
( )	Then Uyen came up also. .	BU₉
And when Uyen arrived beside us	Barb said to us, 'Sit down.'	BU₁₀
And when we were sitting	Barb said to me, she said, 'A letter has just arrived ... big mother is very sick ... you are to go home, it says.'	BU₁₁
And when I heard that	first I was just silent; for a long time I didn't speak.	BU₁₂
And when I was able to talk	then I said, 'They wouldn't send that letter here quickly if mother hadn't died, but she is already dead.'	BU₁₃
And when we had finished talking about the letter	then we cried.	BUₙ
	And I said, 'Oh, it is really so that mother has already died.'	TERMINUS

FIGURE 3. Sarangani Bilaan paragraph (from McLachlin & Blackburn).

tence: 'And then it was afternoon now.' A string of fourteen Build-ups follows. Except at the onset of the sentences which expound BU₃ and BU₉, each sentence of the paragraph Nucleus begins with a Prior Time Margin which refers to the previous sentence. Lexically, some of these subordinated constructions simply repeat a verb from the previous sentence. Thus, in BU₁₁ the verb *sit* is repeated from the previous sentence. In BU₂ the verb *play* is implied but does not actually occur. Other subordinated constructions employ a lexical reciprocal of a verb which occurs in the previous sentence. Thus BU₄, BU₆, BU₈, and BU₁₂ employ the verb *hear*, which answers to the verb *say* in the sentence which in each case

| It is unpleasant to be submerged by an avalanche, but we must allow the person to undergo this experience | *in order that he realise that his system has no answer to the crucial questions of life.* | EXHOR |

↙

| *He must come to know that his roof is a false protection from the storm of what is,* and then we can talk to him of the storm of the Judgment of God. | | REASON |

FIGURE 4a. English hortatory paragraph with Reason tagmeme (Schaeffer 1968:129).

| Hell or any such concept is unthinkable to *modern man* | *because he has been brain-washed into accepting the monolithic belief of naturalism which surrounds him.* | TEXT |

↙

| We of the West are not brain-washed by our State but we are brain-washed by our culture | | REASON |

↘

| even the *modern radicals* are radicals in a very limited circle. | (because ...) | EXPO |

FIGURE 4b. English expository paragraph with Reason tagmeme (Schaeffer 1968:129).

| They are *my* kind; they are my people; they are not something else; they're that which I am. | | TEXT |

↘

| I can really understand them | because I am who they are | RESULT |

FIGURE 5. English expository paragraph with Result tagmeme (Schaeffer 1969:120).

precedes. Other subordinated constructions employ a lexical item which indicates a carrying forward or completion of an action indicated in the previous sentence. Thus, in BU$_5$, BU$_7$, and BU$_{10}$, the verb *arrive* complements *go* and *come* in the previous sentences while *able to talk* complements *just silent* and *didn't speak* in the previous sentence. Similarly, in BU$_n$, *finished talking* complements the verb *say* in the previous sentence. So frequent is this use of a Prior Time Margin, linking nuclear sentences of narrative paragraphs, that the possibility of supplying it when absent is a good test for whether or not a succeeding sentence within a narrative paragraph qualifies as a further BU tagmeme. Thus, in BU$_3$ we could supply in sentence-initial the Sarangani Bilaan equivalent of 'And when she arrived'. Similarly, in BU$_9$ we could supply the equivalent of 'And when she heard this'.

Time Margins are by no means the only margins used in linking sentences within the nuclei of paragraphs. In expository paragraphs, a topic sentence (or Text) is paraphrased in further sentences (Expositions), as in the embedded expository paragraphs found in the two English examples above. But in hortatory paragraphs (and less frequently in expository paragraphs) paraphrases occur in which Purpose, Cause, and Conditional Margins figure. Use of these margins figures prominently in hortatory discourse which is aimed at influencing conduct, and which therefore contains appeals to possible results of actions, reasons for taking a given course of action, and warnings as to consequences of not heeding the counsel given. Notice the accompanying passages (Figure 4) from a contemporary Christian apologete (Francis Schaeffer).[9] In the first example an Antithetical sentence expounds the Exhortation tagmeme. This sentence ends with a Purpose Margin, which is taken up and paraphrased in the following sentence, which I therefore consider to expound a Reason tagmeme.[10] In the paraphrase which occurs in the second sentence, *he must come to know* corresponds to *that he may realize* in the first sentence; *his roof is a false protection* corresponds to *his system has no answers;* and *from the storm of what is* corresponds to *to the crucial questions of life.* The second sentence proceeds to tack on a further member that is parallel to its first member: *and then we can talk to him of the storm of the Judgment of God.* This is, indeed, one frequent use of Coördinate Sentences in discourse—to attach, to some systematic paraphrase which occurs in the regular development of a paragraph, an additional but parallel element.

The second example from the same author (Schaeffer 1968:129) is similar, but comes from an expository paragraph and involves a Cause Margin. Actually it is taken from the center of a paragraph—so that what is here labeled Text is actually an Exposition of an earlier Text; this does not, however, affect the value of the illustration. The first sentence ends with a Cause Margin, referring to modern man's being brain-washed into acceptance of the monolithic belief in naturalism. The reference to brain-washing is taken up and explained in the following sentence, which is therefore considered to expound a Reason tagmeme. But what of the third and last sentence? Here we can easily suppose that a final Cause Margin could be added, such as *because they are brain-washed by their culture.* Furthermore, *modern radical* is a species of *modern man,* and considering that sentence 3 implies a similar Cause Margin to that stated in sentence 1 and developed in sentence 2, we conclude that sentence 3 is simply an Exposition of the Text. So, the reference in sentence 3 to modern radicals being *radical in a limited circle* is not dissimilar to the assertion that certain concepts are *unthinkable to modern man.*

A further example from the same author (Figure 5) illustrates the inverse of a Reason tagmeme, viz. a Cause Margin in sentence 2 which paraphrases sentence 1.[11] This I call a RESULT tagmeme. Thus, in this example, *because I am what they are* in sentence 2 summarizes the whole of the long Paraphrase sentence which expounds the Text.

Conditional Margins figure in WARNING tagmemes in hortatory paragraphs, and in ALTERNATE-STEP tagmemes in procedural paragraphs. Thus, in a hortatory paragraph there may be an Exhortation expounded by *Don't go out of your way to get a police record.* The next sentence may be *If you do, you may find it difficult someday to get employment.* This second sentence has a preposed Condi-

[9] From Schaeffer 1968:129, used by permission of Inter-Varsity Press, Downers Grove, Illinois.

[10] For the formal definition of such paragraph-level tagmemes as Reason, Result etc., in terms of relevant parts of the grammatical sentence, see Longacre 1968:1.111-23.

[11] The quotation is from Schaeffer 1969:120, used by permission of Inter-Varsity Press, Downers Grove, Illinois.

tional Margin that reverses the negative-affirmative value of the preceding sentence. Furthermore, it adds novel material not found previously in the paragraph. I have considered this to be the formal structure of a Warning tagmeme. In a procedural paragraph, a pair of Alternative Steps may be expounded by sentences each of which contains a preposed Conditional Margin. Thus a sentence *Inspect the motor to see how badly worn it is* may be followed by a sentence: *If the cylinders are not scored nor the pistons loose, then just put in new valves and rings.* The next sentence may be: *If the cylinders are worn (it is best to measure with a micrometer), then pull the block and do a complete motor job.* Considering the first sentence to expound a Step tagmeme, then those following expound two Alternative Steps. Such Alternative Steps are often expounded by sentences which begin with Conditional Margins—although the second of two Alternative Steps may begin with a word such as *otherwise*.

Sentence margins are not necessarily exploited for purposes of intra-paragraph linkage. In paragraphs where they are so exploited, the flow of the paragraph is directed through them. In paragraphs where they are not so exploited, the main flow of the paragraph bypasses them. They may be compared, then, to eddies or backwash areas. Nevertheless, material out of the flow in its own paragraph may serve to cross-reference to material in a previous paragraph, or to foreshadow material in succeeding paragraphs. Material out of flow in a given paragraph may, therefore, serve to link paragraphs, and be quite relevant to the flow of the discourse.

To conclude this section, I note that the setting up of sentence margins is well motivated. Not only are such tagmemes useful to the description of the sentence itself, but their use in linking sentence to sentence leads us into the heart of paragraph and discourse structure.

30. In the previous sections I have illustrated various elements of the sentence Periphery, and have shown that the Inner Periphery is of considerable relevance to the structure of paragraphs and discourses. It remains to describe the combinations of clauses and other elements within the nucleus of the sentence. Here, as already said, we require a richer apparatus than that of the statement calculus—yet not an apparatus dissimilar in kind.

I present here the Sentence Nuclei of English as a representative system of sentences. Over twenty such systems have been posited for as many Philippine languages, while further such systems have been suggested for several Mexican Indian languages.[12]

To begin with, English may be described in terms of two sub-systems: (1) a system of sentences whose Nuclei are characterized by conjoining and quotation; and (b) a system of Merged Sentences (the latter term will be explained and exemplified in §32).

31. Sentence Nuclei which are characterized by conjoining or quotation constitute a system with three series and five orders (Figure 6). The three series

---

[12] Besides the numerous data papers summarized in the Philippine Project report referred to above, also note the following papers dealing with the sentence structure of Mexican Indian languages: Engel & Longacre 1963, Lind 1964, and Reid et al. 1968 (especially pp. 49–73, a contribution by Ruth Bishop).

	1. Juxtaposition	2. Concatenation	3. Explanation	4. Implication	5. Quotation
LOOSE	PARAPHRASE ø synonyms [rejects *and*]	COÖRDINATE ... *and* (δ) ... [a subtype: sequence]	REASON ... *for* ...	CONCESSIVE { *even if* ... / *even though* ... / *although* ... } → { *still* ... / *yet* ... / *nevertheless* }	DIRECT QUOTATION [without adaptation of Quoted to speaker's viewpoint]
TIGHT	RECAPITULATION ø repeats verb [rejects *and*]	ANTITHETICAL ... *but/yet/only* (δ) ... [subtypes with negative, antonyms, and gradients]	RESULT ... *so* ... / *so* ... *that* ... and *too* (Adj) ... *to* (Vb) / *because* ... *therefore* ...	CONTRAFACTUAL { *if* (+ past) / Aux S Vb in past } ... *(then)* +past	INDIRECT QUOTATION [with adaptation of Quoted to speaker's viewpoint]
BALANCED	ECHO QUESTION [subtypes: Aff. answer, Neg. answer]	ALTERNATIVE ... *(either)* or (δ) ... / ... *(neither)* nor (δ) ...	EQUATIONAL *it* + *be* (and others)	CORRELATIVE *as* ... *so* ... *as many as* ... *so many*	INDIRECT QUESTION *ask* { *whether* ... / *if* ... }

δ = deletion possibilities in non-initial sentence base

FIGURE 6. English sentence Nuclei (Conjoining and Quotation).

are LOOSE, TIGHT, and BALANCED. TIGHT sentences show relatively more internal restriction, cohesion, and cross-reference than do the corresponding LOOSE sentences.[13] BALANCED sentences are characterized by a setting of one part against another by alternation, correlation, or equation. The orders of sentence types show a certain progress in the manner of relating component bases—just as the series show progress in degree of cohesion. Thus, JUXTAPOSITION characterizes the first column; here there is no sentence-medial conjunction. CONCATENATION characterizes the second column; here occur conjunctions that are indisputably coördinate, viz. *and*, *but*, and *or*. Logical relations characterize the next two orders: EXPLANATION involves *for* and *so* which, while coördinators in English, somewhat resemble *because* and *in order to*. A third sentence type, the EQUATIONAL, seems to belong here as well. In the IMPLICATION order occur *if ... then*, *although ... still*, *as many as ... so many*, and other sequences of conjunctions which cross-reference each other within the sentence. Finally, the last order, QUOTATION, involves a relating of one clause to another in a manner not unlike that of embedding one as the goal of the other—although there are good and sufficient reasons for not considering this to be the structure. Juxtaposition, Concatenation, Explanation, Implication, Quotation—all display movement along a parameter from weak association without conjunction, all the way to an association so intimate as to be reminiscent of clause structure. To this system the Simple Sentence is extra-systemic. It is, however, a sentence type in that it may have the full Periphery found in a sentence whose Nucleus is highly complex and involves a whole series of clauses.

31.1. Some of the basic contrasts of the system may be best understood by inspection of the Concatenation order of sentence types. The COÖRDINATE Sentence is basically different from the ANTITHETICAL Sentence. The former is a loose sequence of sentence bases connected with *and* between successive bases, or with juxtaposition between each pair of bases except the last pair which are linked with *and*. This type of conjoining is non-committal as to chronology, in that events may be reported regardless of whether the chronology is sequential, simultaneous, or irrelevant. If the component clauses are short and parallel in structure, the link *and* may be entirely omitted. Thus, the Coördinate Sentence which follows seems to require *and* between the last pair of sentence bases: *I went over to Gaul, saw the situation there, and conquered it for Rome.* The following Coördinate Sentence is, however, acceptable without the conjunction: *I came, I saw, I conquered.* Deletion of the subject of the clause which expounds the second base is common when the subjects have the same referents: *I went downtown and (I) bought a hamburger.* Other patterns of deletion are possible, e.g. gapping as defined and described by Ross 1968.

By contrast, the Antithetical Sentence has not an indefinite number of bases, but two: a THESIS and an ANTITHESIS, with an intervening ADVERSATIVE expounded most typically by *but* but sometimes by *yet* or *only*. Lexically, the Anti-

[13] No claim is made that precisely the same degree of loose-tight contrast characterizes all such pairs of sentences across the chart from left to right. All that is required is that, internally within a given column, the sentence type which is represented in the top row be characterized by less restriction and cross-reference than that in the middle row.

thetical Sentence is characterized by more restriction than characterizes the Coördinate Sentence. The two bases of the Antithetical Sentence contrast in four ways:

(a) One of the two bases is a DENIED ALTERNATIVE. This is true of all the following examples:

He's not a sinner, he's a saint.
He's not a paragon of virtue, but he's a good man.
He's not dead, but alive.
It's not good, it's bad.
It's not hot, but it's warm.

Given the alternatives *Is he a sinner or a saint?*, an Antithetical Sentence may be formed: *He's not a sinner, he's a saint*. With deletion of the second Subject and Predicate, we get *He's not a sinner but a saint*. With gradients of a variable presented as alternatives in such a sentence as *Is it hot or just warm?*, we derive the Antithetical Sentence *It's not hot, it's just warm; or It's not hot, but it's warm*.

(b) Both bases are CONTRASTING PARALLEL STRUCTURES (contrast of whole situation). Thus: *My horse is black but yours is white*. Note that such sentences do not imply such an alternative base as **Is my horse black or is yours white?* The situation here is not that of ascribing one predicate to a participant in preference to another predicate (as in Denied Alternative); rather, both participants and predicates are contrasted.

(c) The second base presents a CONSIDERATION WHICH COUNTER-BALANCES that presented in the first base. While this is similar to that found in the previous group, the contrast may be more diffuse: *You have a body with eyes and ears and hands and feet, but your body is temporary. It is hard for me to remember to drink water, but the sight of someone drinking reminds me to drink and I try to remind myself as often as possible.*

(d) An EXPECTED CONSEQUENT is denied. Thus: *He came but didn't stay. He spoke to her but she didn't reply. They started out for Paris but never arrived.*

Various patterns of deletion (including systematic omission of *but* in certain environments) and transformation (including the *although* paraphrase) occur; their domain must be described seriatim for each subtype here mentioned. Thus, an *although* paraphrase is not possible in a Denied Alternative when antonyms are involved: **Although he's not dead he's alive*; but it is possible in a Denied Alternative with gradients of a variable: *Although it's not hot, it's warm.*

The ALTERNATIVE Sentence turns on the word *or*, or on repeated conjunctions such as *either ... or* and *neither ... nor*. Its lexical restrictions are similar to but distinct from those of the Antithetical Sentence. Aside from the antonyms and gradients which may characterize both a denied alternative in the Antithetical Sentence and the Alternative Sentence itself, there are some further possibilities in the latter. Thus, an Alternative Sentence may present a predicate and an identical denied predicate in a fashion which has no corresponding Antithetical Sentence: *Is he coming or not?* and *He's either coming or he isn't*; but not **He's not not coming, he's coming*. Furthermore, Alternative Sentences do not necessarily turn on an excluded middle, and may therefore have more than two bases: *If the roof continues to leak, then either find a way to repair it cheaply, or sell the* *house, or turn it into a slum tenement.* Occasionally an Alternative Sentence is simply a choice of synonyms or closely related lexical items.[14] Thus a sentence such as *We must try to better our lot in life, raise our standard of living, or do something to improve ourselves* does not really present alternatives, but rather alternative ways of phrasing the same thing. Such sentences are a frequent device of orators and preachers. Again, for the various varieties of Alternative Sentence, rules of deletion and paraphrase must be stated.

The choice of *and* vs. *but* vs. *or* in sentence-medial position is not, therefore, a trivial one.[15] The number and lexical nature of the sentence bases within a sentence are affected by choice of conjunction. Furthermore, patterns of deletion and paraphrase differ according to choice of medial conjunction. In brief, distribution of these three English conjunctions is best understood in reference to whole patterns of which they are part.

31.2. In that the system here described is characterized by either conjoining or quotation, I turn now to the order of Quotation sentences (the last column in Fig. 6). These sentences resemble clause structures in that the quotation itself could be considered as the object of the verb. Consider, however, the sentences: *He said, 'I'm going downtown.' 'I'm going downtown', he said, 'but you stay right here and don't follow me.' 'Let me alone,' said her husband quickly. Abraham Lincoln said, 'Fourscore and seven years ago our Fathers brought forth upon this continent a new nation, conceived in liberty and dedicated to the proposition that all men are created equal. Now we are engaged in a great civil war, testing whether that nation or any nation so conceived and so dedicated can long endure ...'* We may divide such Direct Quotation Sentences into two tagmemes: a Quotation Formula, and a Quoted. The exponents of both tagmemes are sufficiently distinctive that considerable complication is encountered in trying to rationalize them as clause structures. The Quotation Formula is expounded by a transitive (or bitransitive) clause of somewhat specialized lexical and grammatical structure. Thus in Direct Quotation Sentences such clauses must employ a verb of speech or its equivalent. Verb and subject permute more freely than is ordinary (witness *said her husband* above). Furthermore, the verb plus subject may be interposed between parts of the so-called object. The so-called object—which we here term the Quoted—is of much greater length and complexity than we are accustomed to note in clause structures. In Direct Quotation Sentences, the Quoted may be expounded by an embedded paragraph or discourse. Essentially, therefore, Quotation Sentences take clause-level stuff and restructure it on the sentence level.

[14] This was first pointed out by Ballard 1968.

[15] Again, however, a distinction between lexical and grammatical structure is needed here. The Coördinate Sentence *I went downtown and Mary stayed home* and the Antithetical Sentence *I went downtown but Mary stayed home* do not reflect any fundamental difference in the situation being described, but they do reflect a difference in the intent of the speaker. In the former sentence, the speaker desires only to couple the two events in one conceptual framework, as in some way connected or parallel. In the second sentence, the speaker wants to present the two events as contrastive, to set one against the other. Non-contrastive coupling is expressed by choice of the Coördinate Sentence; contrastive coupling is expressed by choice of the Antithetical Sentence. The same lexical material is found in both sentences—either as some non-committal lexical coupling, or as two lexical sentences, which are conjoined in grammatically different ways.

Direct Quotation Sentences are intended to give the words of a speaker without adaptation to the viewpoint of the one who reports them. Features already mentioned are: (1) This sentence necessarily contains a verb of speech or its equivalent (e.g. *he thought, he said to himself*). (2) The Quotation Formula may precede, follow, or be interposed within the Quoted. Note the above examples as well as the following: *He said, 'I'll go over there tomorrow.' 'Tomorrow,' he said, 'I'll go see about it.'*

INDIRECT QUOTATION Sentences are of two varieties: (a) with verbs of speech or their equivalent in the Quotation Formula, and with adaptation of the words of the Quoted to the viewpoint of the reporter; and (b) with verbs of thinking, knowledge, sensation, and the like in the Quotation Formula, followed by an exponent of Quoted parallel to that found in (a). In both varieties an optional sign of Quoted, expounded by *that*, may appear. The adaptation of the words of the Quoted to the viewpoint of the reporter affects pronouns and expressions of time and place. Thus the Direct Quotation Sentence *He said, 'I'll go over there tomorrow'* can be reported as an Indirect Quotation Sentence one day later: *He said that he would come here today.* In the Indirect Quotation the lexical items *go, over there,* and *tomorrow* are replaced by *come, here,* and *today.* In addition the modal *will* is changed to *would* to agree with the tense of the verb in the Quotation Formula. Furthermore, it is possible to place a contrastive intonation peak on the verb in the Quotation Formula; this plus a non-final intonation on the end of the sentence enables the reporter to cast doubt on the intentions, veracity, or ability of the original speaker to keep his word: *He* SAID *he would come here today* ... It is impossible to do this in the Direct Quotation; to attempt to do it is to confuse the hearer and cause him to believe that you are actually using an Indirect Quotation. Finally, the Quotation Formula of the Indirect Quotation may not permute as does that of the Direct Quotation.

It is evident that the Indirect Quotation is a tighter structure than the Direct Quotation. The Quotation Formula and the Quoted cohere more closely in the former sentence type, which may also be characterized by the overt link *that* between its two parts, which cannot permute with each other.

A third type of Quotation Sentence, the INDIRECT QUESTION, differs from the Indirect Quotation in that it employs the verb *ask* (or some lexical equivalent, including *didn't know* and *wondered*) in its Quotation Formula, and embeds a yes-no question or content question in its Quoted. The Sign of the Quote is *whether* or *if* when the former embeds; the second alternative is always implied but need not be stated: *He asked if you were interested (or not).* If the embedded question is a content question, no sign of quote appears; rather, the interrogative word serves this function: *He asked when you were coming.* All such questions are indirect. Direct Questions may be considered to be simply further examples of Direct Quotation Sentences. The Indirect Question, especially in its alternative subtype, resembles the Alternative Sentence, and both are in the Balanced series of sentences.

31.3. Column one of Figure 6 contains an order of JUXTAPOSITION Sentences —all of which reject any internal conjunction or link. PARAPHRASE Sentences are the loosest. They employ synonyms or paraphrases to express the same idea twice: *She was angry; she was utterly furious at the perfidy of the man. It's the* *most beautiful place on the island; it's a veritable paradise.* RECAPITULATION Sentences are tighter in that they require the repetition of the verb of the first base within the second base. By so doing, the sentence achieves a certain poignancy and emphasis. Thus, *I went home, I went home to see what was really going on* gives an impression of drama and suspense that is not given by simply saying *I went home to see what was really going on.* The impression of suspense is heightened by rallentando and pause in sentence medial. Finally, the ECHO QUESTION gives us a Balanced sentence with a weighted alternative loaded in favor of the desired answer. Thus, *You won't go down town alone, will you?* elicits such an answer as *Of course not, you couldn't think I was that stupid!* On the contrary *You'll go down town right now, won't you?* is designed to elicit such an answer as *I certainly will, don't you worry!* In both cases the Echo Question is in principle a repetition of the verb and subject of the first base with deletion of the main verb. As such, Echo Questions take their place in the order of Juxtaposed sentences.

31.4. Column four of Figure 6 contains an order of IMPLICATION Sentences. While Implication is usually expressed as a Conditional or Concessive Margin followed by a Nucleus, Implication Sentences are more specialized structures. In CONCESSIVE Sentences, the Concessive Margin is incorporated into the Nucleus by means of a counter-balancing and cross-referencing particle such as *still, yet,* and *nevertheless.* The addition of such a medial conjunction is non-trivial. Semantically and functionally, such an added link is similar to the *but* of an Antithetical Sentence—which is admittedly a coördinator. The effect of adding the medial conjunction is to create patterns of cross-referencing particles such as *even though ... still, though ... nevertheless,* and *although ... yet,* which become fundamental parts of the framework of this particular Nucleus. Perhaps these patterns of cross-reference are created at the cost of partially weakening the original bond between the relator (such as *even if, though,* or *although*) and the axis which follows. Thus, a Conditional Margin such as *Even though things are bad* is considered to be expounded by a Relator-Axis sentence in which Relator is expounded by *even though* and the Axis by what follows. The whole may be preposed to a Nucleus such as *they could get worse.* When one adds, however, a medial link such as *nevertheless,* a pattern of cross-referencing conjunctions *even though ... nevertheless* is set up, which in turn weakens the original Relator-Axis bond in the exponent of the incorporated margin. The Concessive Sentence has then four parts: CONCESSIVE MARKER expounded by *even if, though, although;* CONCESSION expounded by clause or sentence (such as *things are bad*); CONCESSIVE LINK expounded by *still, yet,* and *nevertheless;* and COUNTER-CONSIDERATION expounded by a clause or sentence (such as *they could get worse*). Once thus constituted, such a sentence may suffer radical deletion in which the Concessive Marker is omitted and the Concession stripped to the lexically relevant word, as in: *Tired, nevertheless he was ready.*

The CONTRAFACTUAL Sentence is an even tighter structure than the Concessive Sentence. This is seen in the fact that, while the Concessive Sentence creates a Nucleus by the fairly superficial device of bringing in a medial coördinating link, the Contrafactual Sentence achieves its unity by tense sequence (past in both bases) and (in one optional structure) by eliminating the *if* in the protasis in favor of an interrogative structure with split verb phrase. At all events a species of double-talk results in which each base is to be understood as the opposite of its apparent positive-negative value. Thus *Had he arrived, all would have been well* implies *He didn't arrive* and *all isn't well.* A Contrafactual Sentence can always be incorporated into an Antithetical Sentence by adding a *but* and an Antithesis. Thus *Had he arrived, all would have been well* may be expanded to *Had he arrived, all would have been well—but he didn't.*

The CORRELATIVE Sentence encodes a biconditional implication. *As Maine goes so goes the nation* means *Maine goes Republican if-and-only-if the nation goes Republican.* Similarly biconditional is: *As many as were on the outside, that/so many were also on the inside.* The mutual implication encoded in this sentence type indicates that it is the Balanced member of its order.

31.5. Finally, order three of Figure 6 embraces a trio of sentence types which express logical relations of a weaker order than implication; we give the label EXPLANATION to this order. I posit here a REASON Sentence which contains a medial *for*, a RESULT Sentence which contains a medial *so*, and an EQUATIONAL Sentence which includes sentences with initial expletives and other elements.

The case for considering *for* and *so* to be coördinators and not subordinators is well summarized by Williams (1966:67–70). He points out that clauses introduced by *for* and *so* do not permute to sentence initial position as do clauses introduced by subordinating conjunctions, that *for* and *so* clauses do not embed after other subordinators (cf. *Bill stayed, because though I left Tom came* and *Things went better when after I left Bill arrived*), and passes on from Gleitman a pronoun antecedent test that seems to put *for* and *so* into the set of the coördinators. Williams also gives evidence that sentences with medial *for* permit greater freedom of surrounding base structure than do sentences with medial *so*. For this reason I have considered Reason Sentences to belong to the Loose series and Result Sentences to belong to the Tight series. I also include under the latter some further related structures.

Reason Sentences are illustrated by the following: *Ponder this well, for there may be grave consequences. I gave in to her demands, for there was nothing else to do. I gave in, for what else could I do? What could I do, for there was simply no place to go? Why should I be concerned, for who cares what happens to me?* With considerable freedom various sorts of indicative, interrogative, and imperative structures occur on both sides of *for*.

Result Sentences show a variety of related structures besides those which contain a medial *so*. Thus we can say *The soup was very hot, so we couldn't eat it.* But we can also say *The soup was so hot that we couldn't eat it* and, even more simply, *The soup was too hot to eat.* The latter structure is more similar to those of the Merged Sentences which are described in the next section. A related but less likely construction is *Because the soup was very hot therefore we couldn't eat it.* The latter simply brings the exponent of a Cause Margin into the Nucleus by addition of the counter-balancing particle *therefore* (cf. the Concessive Sentence).

Reason and Result Sentences are related as inverses: *We couldn't eat the soup, for it was very hot. The soup was very hot, so we couldn't eat it.* A relation of this sort between two sentences does not argue that they are not separate sentence types. Sentence types may be derivationally related without constituting the same type (cf. Direct and Indirect Quotations, some Antithetical and Concessive Sentences, some Indirect Questions and Alternative Sentences).

Constructions with initial expletive *it* are not conveniently analysed into clause structures. The fact that they obligatorily embed another clause gives them a combinatorial property more like that which we encounter on the sentence level. I propose therefore to call such constructions and other similar ones Equational Sentences. A sentence such as *It's a fact that all such optimism is misplaced* is a sentence-level equation, as is also the equivalent *That all such optimism is misplaced is a fact*. Medial conjunction may be a further clue that a sentence-level rather than a clause-level equation is intended: *What is not good is therefore necessarily bad*. A further variant of this sentence type incorporates the exponent of a Cause or Purpose Margin into the Nucleus of the sentence: *The reason he can't go is because he's getting married. His main purpose in coming is so that he can confuse the issues.*

32. In contrast to the English sentences which are characterized by conjoining or quotation, there is a further system of sentences which consist of clauses that are more intimately associated. To these we give the name MERGED Sentences (Longacre 1968:2.154–64, and 1969).

In the system of English sentences which has already been described, Order One consists of Juxtaposed Sentences. Such sentences have no medial conjunction but employ rather a semi-final phonological juncture. Various lexical constraints characterize the three Juxtaposed Sentence types. The Merged Sentences reflect a further structural specialization which results in a more intimate nexus than that found in Juxtaposed Sentences. Thus, phonologically the Merged Sentences drop the medial semi-final juncture and give the whole sentence a phonological unity like that found in a single clause. Grammatically, the Merged Sentences require that the second sentence base not contain a finite verb phrase, but rather infinitive or participial phrases, or just verb word structures. Furthermore, some of these Merged Sentences contain a substantive phrase that is syntactically in double function, e.g. object of the verb in the first sentence base but subject of the verb in the second sentence base. Lexically, the Merged Sentences are specialized in that the set of verbs which may expound the predicate of the clause which expounds the first sentence base is a distinct and separate set in every type of Merged Sentence. Thus, phonologically, grammatically, and lexically, Merged Sentences contrast with the sentence types which constitute the system already described.

The data for the study of English Merged Sentences have been carefully assembled and classified by Palmer (1965:150–79). Although Palmer describes these structures as 'Complex Verb Phrases', he presents cogent arguments that such structures are a combination of clauses and that one clause is not embedded within the other (155–7). On the contrary, he argues, the component clauses combine to form a new structure. In commenting on a sentence such as *I got him to persuade her to ask him to change his mind*, he argues that *him to persuade her to ask him to change his mind* is not the object of *got*, nor is *her to ask him to change his mind* the object of *persuade*, nor is *to change his mind* the object of *ask*. Rather

'All that is required is a hierarchical analysis in which the downgraded clause is quite deliberately not assigned status as a clause element, object or complement.' He then goes on to argue that, transformationally, *He got her to do it* is derived from *he got* plus *She does it*—with proper adaptations and qualifications.

Much of what I suggest here is essentially a restatement of Palmer. I have copied out his sets and subsets of verbs which are possible in the first clause of what I term a Merged Sentence. I consider these sets and subsets to determine etic varieties of the Merged Sentence. Then I have shuffled and reshuffled these etic varieties in an effort to group them according to a discrete number of contrasting Merged Sentences. In the process I sometimes combine varieties of constructions that Palmer handles separately.

English Merged Sentences constitute a system with two series and five orders (Figure 7). The two series are distinguished in that one series consists of sentences which have the same subject in both clauses and never contain a noun in double function, while the other series consists of sentences which either have different subjects in the two clauses or have an option of same or different subjects. When the subjects are different in the two clauses and the verbs in the first clause are active, then a noun in double function may occur. The five orders are distinguished as five values ranging from loose to tight. At one end of this parameter occurs an order of sentences (MANNER and TELIC) which permit full infinitive phrases, active and passive, in the predicate of the second clause. At the other end of this parameter occurs an order of sentences (PASSIVE and SENSATION) which permit only verb words, not verb phrases, in the predicate of the second clause. The former order of sentences is considered to represent the loosest Merged Sentence structures, while the latter represents the tightest. In the three intervening orders occur sentence structures with intermediate degrees of restriction in the predicate of the second clause.

In describing the system of English Merged Sentences I first describe the extremities of the system, i.e. the Manner, Telic, Passive, and Sensation Sentences, then the intervening orders of Merged Sentence.

32.1. In the MANNER Merged Sentence, the verb of the first clause is lexically a manner modifier of the verb in the second clause. As already stated, the subject is the same in this order of Merged Sentences, no noun phrase occurs in double function, and the second verb may be an active or passive infinitive verb phrase. According to Palmer (161), verbs that occur in clause one are the following: *appear, chance, come, happen, hasten, manage, proceed, seem, tend,* (negatively) *fail, neglect, omit.* The verbs *risk* and *try* (handled elsewhere by Palmer) are very similar in their adverbial modification of the following verb, but these two verbs take only the *-ing* form of the second verb. The verb *chance* takes either the infinitive phrase or the *-ing* form. Developing Palmer's statement that these verbs 'could be replaced by an adverbial phrase and the second verb used in a finite form', I note such paraphrases as the following where Merged Sentences are parallel to simple one-clause sentences with a corresponding adverb:

He chanced to make some money (He made some money by chance.)
He appeared to succeed (He apparently succeeded.)
He won't fail to do it (He'll do it without fail.)

MINIMAL INFINITIVE PHRASES

	1 Full Inf Ph	2 V₁ directed toward V₂	3 Only A Inf Ph	4 Min Inf + word structures	5 Only word structures
Same Subject — (←NPh→)	MANNER V₁ modifies V₂ $V_2 = \begin{cases} \text{A/P Inf Ph} \\ \text{(V-ing)} \end{cases}$ come, hasten, seem, happen, chance, risk, try	CONATIVE V₁ expresses effort relative to V₂ $V_2 = \begin{cases} \text{min A/P Inf Ph} \\ \text{(V-ing?)} \end{cases}$ attempt, strive, learn	PREDISPOSITION intent of V₁ (not) carried out in V₂ $V_2 = \text{min A Inf Ph}$ remember, forget	OBLIGATION V₁ modal of V₂ (should) $V_2 = \begin{cases} \text{min A/P Inf Ph} \\ \text{V-ing} \end{cases}$ need, want (implies a further actor)	PASSIVE V₁ passive V₂ $V_2 = \text{V-N}$ get
Diff. Subject Same/Diff. Subject +/±(←NPh→)	TELIC +/− NPh V₁ = verbal/mental activity relative to V₂ $V_2 = \begin{cases} \text{A/P Inf Ph} \\ \text{V-ing} \end{cases}$ agree, ask, expect, intend, advise, warn	ASPECTUAL +/− NPh V₁ qualifies V₂ in respect to inception, continuance, or terminus $V_2 = \begin{cases} \text{min A/P Inf Ph} \\ \text{min A/P Part Ph} \end{cases}$ begin, start, continue, cease, keep, stop	RECIPROCAL (always implies a NPh) $V_2 = \begin{cases} \text{min A Inf Ph} \\ \text{V*} \end{cases}$ help, let, know(?)	CAUSATIVE + NPh V₁ is effective cause of V₂ $V_2 = \begin{cases} \text{min A Inf Ph} \\ \text{V*} \\ \text{V-ing} \\ \text{V-N} \end{cases}$ have, get, make, cause(?)	SENSATION + NPh V₁ reports V₂ (cf. Ind Q) $V_2 = \begin{cases} \text{V*} \\ \text{V-ing} \\ \text{V-N} \end{cases}$ see, hear, feel, catch, observe, remember, recollect

FIGURE 7. English Merged Sentences.

and less closely:

He proceeded to say ... (He said next ...)

The infinitive phrase is not restricted to its minimal form:

He happened to have been seen there two days before.

He happened to have seen him two days before.

He happens to be going there.

With the verbs *risk* and *try:*

He risked doing it again.

He tried rigging up a connection.

For both the above there are paraphrases that reveal the adverbial thrust of V_1: *He did it again at risk. He tentatively rigged up a connection.* Palmer (163) points out that *try* has other meanings, but that as used here it means 'experimentation.' Thus, *He tried to rig up a connection* contains the verb *try* used in the sense of effort and belongs to what I term the Conative Merged Sentence.

In the TELIC Merged Sentence, the verb of the first clause expresses verbal or mental activity relative to the action expressed by the verb of the second clause. In that this Merged Sentence type belongs to the second series, same or different actors are possible; and, given the latter, a noun may occur in double function. In common with the Manner Merged Sentence, the predicate of the second clause may be an infinitive phrase of any structure, except that the *-ing* form may occur in V_2 when a small subset of three verbs occurs as V_1. These various considerations are best met by recognizing three variants of this sentence type. Each variant is determined by the subset of verbs that occurs in the first clause. I take these subsets directly from Palmer.

In subtype (a) the actors of the two clauses are identical. The set of verbs found in the first clause (Palmer, 160–1) comprises: *agree, aim, arrange, ask, aspire, beg, choose, condescend, consent, decide, decline, elect, expect, hesitate, hope, long, mean, offer, prepare, promise, refuse, scorn, stand, swear, threaten, undertake, want, wish,* and *(don't) care.*

The following paradigmatic example illustrates the possible range of structure:

I expect to tell about it.

I expect to be telling about it soon.

Symbols for Figure 7:

V = Verb

Inf Ph = Infinitive Phrase

A = Active

P = Passive

Min = Minimal

-N = Past participle inflection of the English verb

V ⚹ = Uninflected verb stem

←NPh→ = Noun Phrase in double function with preceding and following verb

Part Ph = Participle (or gerund) Phrase

+ = Obligatory occurrence

− = Obligatory absence

± = Optional occurrence

+/− = Present or absent under specific conditions

+/± = Obligatory or optional under specific conditions

> I expect to have told about it by then.
> I expect to have been telling about it for some time before that date.
> I expect to be told about it.
> I expect to have been told about it by then.
> I expect to be being told about it more or less constantly.

Subtype (b) has different actors, and a noun phrase in double function occurs between the two clauses. The subset of verbs that occurs in the first clause (Palmer, 170) overlaps some (in six verbs) with the subsets in subtype (a): *advise, allow, ask, beg, challenge, choose, command, compel, dare, direct, drive, expect, force, intend, invite, lead, mean, motion, oblige, order, press, remind, teach, tell, tempt, trouble, trust, urge, warn, give* (+ Noun Phrase + *to understand*). When the first clause is passive, no noun in double function occurs:

> They advised me to go.
> I challenge you to have finished this job by noon.
> I expect him to be defeated.
> He warned me to be expecting trouble.
> I was advised to go.
> I was challenged to have finished this job by noon.
> He was expected to be defeated.
> He was warned to be expecting trouble.

A small subset of three verbs, *intend, plan, propose* (Palmer, 166), determines subtype (c) of this phrase type. This subtype has the peculiarity that not only may infinitive phrases occur in the second clause, but also the form of the verb inflected with -*ing:*

> I intend to finish by then.
> I intend to have finished by then.
> I intend finishing by then.
> I plan to go (going) there tomorrow.
> I propose to ignore (ignoring) him.
> I intended to be overpowered by him.
> I plan to be ignored; what's the use?

32.2. The PASSIVE Merged Sentence is a periphrastic way of expressing passivity by means of the verb *get*. V_2 is restricted to the participial form. The verb *get* is a versatile verb, and its use in the Passive Merged Sentence is distinct from its use in the Causative Merged Sentence. Note the following examples: *He got nominated* vs. *He got himself nominated;* and *He got killed* (through no fault of his own) vs. *He got himself killed* (with a possible suggestion of blame). Thus we might also say *In spite of strenuous efforts to avoid nomination, he got nominated*; and *He pulled all possible strings and got himself nominated.* The sentences *He got himself killed* and *He got himself nominated* are therefore considered here to be Causative Merged Sentences, parallel in structure to *He got John killed* and *He got John nominated.*

Some more varied examples of the Passive Merged Sentence follow:

> He gets punished all the time.
> He was getting punished almost daily.
> He hasn't been getting punished now quite so regularly as before.

Of all the Merged Sentences, this type is the most similar to a single clause which contains a single verb phrase. However, because of its parallelism to other Merged Sentences here posited, it seems best to include it also in this system of English sentences.

The SENSATION Merged Sentence requires different actors in its two component clauses. It has a medial noun phrase in double function, except when the first clause is passive (this restriction is general in the whole system of Merged Sentences). V_2 is simply a word (W) structure, i.e. the uninflected form of the verb, or the -*ing* form, or the -N (participial) form. The set of verbs found in the predicate of the first clause includes three subsets: (a) *hear, feel, smell, see, watch, notice* (but not *taste*) (Palmer, 170); (b) *catch, find, observe;*[16] and (c) *remember, forget, regret, recollect, recall.*[17]

The first subset determines a variant of this Merged Sentence in which V_2 has all the structural possibilities found in this type, i.e. W #, W + -*ing*, and W + -N. The choice between the first two gives contrasting non-progressive and progressive meanings. As Palmer (170) observes, *I saw them crossing the river* does not imply that we know they reached the other side, while *I saw them cross the river* implies that we saw them reach the other side. Other examples:

I heard the bullet go past my ear.

I heard the artillery shells zooming overhead.

I felt it crawl/crawling up my back.

I smelled it cooking (but apparently not *I smelled it cook*).

I watched them depart/departing.

I noticed him mowing the front lawn (but apparently not *I noticed him mow the front lawn*).

I saw our team beaten badly.

I heard it played by the Philharmonic Symphony Orchestra.

If the first clause is passive (only *see* and *hear*), only the -*ing* form of the verb occurs in the second clause:

They were last seen crossing the river.

They were heard radioing for help.

With the second subset of verbs in the first clause, only the -*ing* form of the verb occurs in the second clause. The passive in the first clause is generally possible here for all the verbs of this subset:

Grandma caught them stealing cookies.

They were caught stealing cookies.

He found them sleeping.

They were found sleeping.

They observed him transmitting signals by semaphore.

He was observed transmitting signals by semaphore.

With the verbs of the third subset in the first clause, only the -*ing* form occurs in the second clause, and the first clause may not be passive:

He remembers me saying something like that.

---

[16] Palmer, 171 (minus the verb *perceive*).

[17] Palmer, 173 (I add the verbs *recollect, recall*).

I'd forgotten him doing that.
I don't recollect him coming at all.

The latter subset also occurs with a construction involving possessive pronouns and participle phrases (active and passive) instead of word structures. Possibly this is no longer a Merged Sentence, but a participle phrase as a nominal construction in the object slot of a clause:

I'd forgotten his saying that.
I'd forgotten his having said that.
I'll always remember his having been answered so adequately by one of his own students.

It is of interest that almost all these verbs in all three subsets are **verbs** used in the indirect Quotation formulas of non-speech Indirect Quotation Sentences:

I saw that they were crossing the river.
I heard that he was coming.
I smelled right away that dinner was cooking.
I noticed that there was something wrong (but not with *watched*).
I felt that it was wrong.
I found that they were sleeping (but not with *caught*).
I observed that he was transmitting.
I remembered that he had helped me.

Nevertheless, the Sensation Merged Sentence is not a transformation of such non-speech Indirect Quotations. The Merged Sentence *I saw them crossing the river* simply reports that I saw them as they were crossing the river; the emphasis is on seeing them as they performed a given act. But in the non-speech Indirect Quotation *I saw that they were crossing the river*, the emphasis is on the FACT that I saw them.

32.3. Conative and Aspectual types form the second order of Merged Sentences in Figure 7. In respect to the predicate of the second clause, this order neither permits the full gamut of infinitive verb phrase structure (as in order 1) nor restricts structure to verb words (as in order 5). Rather, minimal active or passive infinitive verb phrases occur, as well as minimal active or passive participle phrases in the Aspectual Sentence.

In Conative Merged Sentences, V_1 includes *attempt, try, strive* (Palmer, 161). As with any sentence in series one, the actors of the two clauses are the same:

She is attempting to outperform her brother.
She's trying to accomplish something.
He tried to help.
Try to come.
Strive to be regarded well.
Attempt to be recognized.
He's trying to be noticed.

Conative Merged Sentences with *try*, expressing commands, may be transformed to Coördinate Sentences in colloquial speech: *Try and come. Try and help.*

In the Aspectual Merged Sentence, V_1 qualifies V_2 in regard to inception, continuance, or termination. In that the structure of V_2 may be active/passive minimal infinitive phrase or active/passive minimal participle phrase, the possible forms of V_2 may be illustrated as follows: *to take, to be taken, taking, being taken.* There are three variants of this Merged Sentence.

In subtype (a) the actors of the two clauses are the same: the full range of permitted structure (minimal active/passive infinitive phrase; minimal active/ passive participle phrase) occurs; and the set of verbs occurring as V_1 comprises *begin, start, continue, cease* (Palmer, 165):

He began to talk/talking.
He started to talk/talking.
He continued to talk/talking.
He ceased to talk/talking.
He began to be considered persona non grata.
He continued being talked about.
He ceased being considered for the job.
He continued to be considered undesirable.

(Some of the passive forms are comparatively rare and strained).

In subtype (b), the actors of the two clauses are also the same; but only the active or passive participle phrase occurs as V_2. The set of verbs occurring as V_1 (Palmer, 162) comprises *keep, finish, stop,* and possibly *get*:

He keeps talking.
He kept being criticized.
She stopped doing it.
When the factory finishes being retooled ... (Again, the passive forms are more rare).
They got talking.[18]

Subtype (c) has different actors in its two clauses, and has only *-ing* verbs in its second clause. These forms could be considered to be only word structures, but comparison with the two other subtypes leads us to consider them to be minimal active participle phrases. The set of verbs in the first clause comprises *start, set, keep, stop.*[19] These verbs may be made passive, in which case no syntactically ambivalent noun occurs:

He started them talking.
He started the motor running.
He kept them going.
He stopped them stealing.

---

[18] The occurrence of both *got to talk* and *got talking* would appear to throw these constructions into the first subtype. *Got to talk,* however, means something different, equivalent to *was permitted to talk.*

[19] Palmer, 171. He includes *leave*—which is somewhat aberrant, however, in that it may also occur with an -N form of V_2:

He left them standing there.
They were left standing there.
He left them stranded there.
They were left stranded there.

They were started talking.
They were kept going.
They were stopped stealing.

32.4. The PREDISPOSITION and RECIPROCAL types constitute the third order of Merged Sentences. Only minimal active infinitive verb phrases occur as V_2; in the second type, however, an uninflected verb may also occur as V_2.

In that the Predisposition Merged Sentence belongs to series one, it has the same actor in both clauses. This sentence type reports in V_1 an intention (V_2) that is either remembered and carried out, or is forgotten and not carried out. The two verbs that occur as V_1 are, therefore, *remember* and *forget*. Thus, *I remembered to go* implies *I went*, while *I forgot to go* implies *I didn't go*. Palmer (166) points out that sentences such as *I remembered going there* and *I forgot going there* imply something quite different, viz. that one went there, but either does or does not recollect doing so.

The Reciprocal Merged Sentence implies, but does not necessarily state, a noun phrase in dual function. The verbs *help* and *let* figure as V_1.

With *help* as V_1, a minimal active infinitive verb phrase or an uninflected verb may occur as V_2:

I helped (them) do it.
Please help (me/him/her) put the books away.
You can help (me/us/them) push the car.
I helped them to find the house.
They were helped to find the house.

With *let* as V_1, only the uninflected form of the verb occurs as V_2. When V_1 is active, the presence of a noun phrase in double function is required, except for certain special idioms:

They let him go.
He was let go.
They let him hurt her badly.
He was let stay there too long.

Palmer (160) discusses special idiomatic combinations of *let* plus a second verb. He presents interesting pairs such as *He let fall that he would be coming* vs. *We must not let such an opportunity slip*, and *He let go the rope* vs. *He let the rope go*. These examples seem to establish that a noun phrase in dual function is present even in such idioms as *let fall*, *let slip*, and *let go*, but that the noun phrase which is object of V_1 and subject of V_2 is shifted to the object position after V_2. In a pair of verbs such as *let live*, an object such as *others* is possibly implied although unstated. More difficult to rationalize are Palmer's examples such as *He let fly with his foot*. Here apparently a base such as *He let his foot fly* is indicated, but the noun in dual function emerges as an instrumental phrase.[20]

[20] Some further examples of Palmer's on the same page involve idioms such as *make do*, *hear tell*, and *hear say*, similar in some ways to the structures here described as Reciprocal Merged Sentences. Thus *We have to make do with soup this evening* is not dissimilar from *We will have to make the soup do this evening*. Nevertheless, the former sentence refers to getting along with only soup, while the latter refers to having to get along with that quantity of soup because there is no more.

Palmer also points out (169) that the verb *know* has certain uses as V_1 that are not dissimilar to the structures here grouped under the Reciprocal Merged Sentence, but that this occurrence 'is confined to questions with *ever* or to statements with *never* or other semi-negatives', such as *Have you ever known them (to) come on time?*

It is plain that this Merged Sentence type is subject to considerable idiomatic development and specialization. This, however, far from being an analytical drawback, reinforces the uniqueness of this Merged Sentence type.

32.5. The OBLIGATION and CAUSATIVE types constitute the fourth order of Merged Sentences.

With the Obligation Merged Sentence, V_2 may be a minimal active infinitive verb phrase, an *-ing* form of the verb, or a minimal passive infinitive verb phrase. With the active infinitive as exponent of the predicate of the second clause, no further actor is implied than the one stated in clause one. With the latter two exponents, a further actor is implied while the actor of clause one becomes goal. As V_1, *need* occurs freely. Palmer (167) also lists *want, deserve*, and *require;* some of these uses may be more British than American. The function of the first clause resembles that of the English modal *should:*

He needs to clean the car.
The car needs cleaning.
The car needs to be cleaned.

Beside *He needs to watch*, Palmer cites *The man wants to watch;* and beside *He needs watching* he cites *The man wants watching.*

In the Causative Merged Sentence,[21] V_1 expresses the effective cause of the action encoded in V_2. The actors of the two clauses are different, and there is an obligatory noun phrase in dual function. When V_1 is *have*, V_2 may be only a word structure, with either no inflectional suffix, or with *-ing* or -N. When V_1 is *get*, a word structure with *-ing* or with -N may occur as V_2, but a minimal active infinitive phrase may also occur there. *Get* as first verb may be made passive:

I had him tell me all about it.
I've had him writing all afternoon.
I have him writing another essay.
I can't have you do that.
I can't have you doing that.
I can't have that done.
I won't have you hurt.
I'll have you know that you are wrong.
I got him to go.
I got him going.
I finally got him nominated.
He was got moving.
He was got to go.

A few other verbs possibly pattern as first verbs in a Causative Merged Sentence, but do not co-occur with the full gamut of possibilities in V_2. Thus *make*

---

[21] Cf. Palmer, 169, for *have*, and 173 for this use of *get*.

as V_1 is followed by an uninflected verb when *make* is active, and is followed by a minimal active infinitive verb phrase when *make* is passive:

> He made me do it.
> He was made to do it.

Cause as V_1 co-occurs with minimal active or passive infinitive verb phrase as V_2. Sentences which contain *cause* as V_1 are, therefore, quite divergent structurally from other examples of Causative Merged Sentence, and may possibly belong elsewhere taxonomically:

> I caused him to pay attention.
> I caused him to be elected.
> I'll cause you to feel differently about it.

32.6. Other putative Merged Sentences exist which might better be analysed as verbs having verbals as clause-level objects. To this class, in my opinion, belong constructions involving a miscellaneous assortment of verbs also listed by Palmer (163–4): *avoid, consider, deny, enjoy, miss, postpone, practice, (don't) fancy,* and *(don't) mind*. All these occur with *-ing* verbals as clause-level objects:

> I avoided talking to her.
> I denied knowing him.
> I don't mind eating roast dog.
> I practice playing the harpsichord.

Note that possessive pronouns or adjectives can be used with at least some of the above—thus demonstrating that they are really substantive phrases:

> I avoided any and all talking to her.
> I don't mind your eating roast dog.

Also similar are 'preferment' verbs such as *detest, dislike, fancy, hate,* etc. (Palmer, 164–5, 171–2). These take active or passive infinitive or participial phrases:

> I like to do that.
> I hate to be preached at all the time.
> I resent being told what I already know.
> I like swimming.

Again, at least some of the above demonstrably act like substantives: *I like slow, languid swimming* (see also the end of §32.2, above).

Palmer (174–5) specifically excludes from his 'complex phrase' infinitives which express purpose and result. I concur with him in that I exclude these from my Merged Sentences.

32.7. It is interesting that not only may indefinitely long chains of Merged Sentences with ever deeper embedding occur (as in *She got him to ask her to persuade John to petition the Emperor*), but also members of the first system described in §31 may embed within the Merged Sentences. In the following battery of examples, various sorts of Conjoining and Quotation Sentences embed within the Telic Merged Sentence:

> I want him to be enthusiastic, to go overboard on the matter (embedded Paraphrase Sentence).

I want him to do it, to do it with all his heart (embedded Recapitulation Sentence).

I want him to come and see about it (embedded Coördinate Sentence).

I wanted John to come and Mary to go (embedded Coördinate Sentence).

I wanted John to come but Mary to remain where she was (embedded Antithetical Sentence).

I want John to leave or Mary to order him out (embedded Alternative Sentence).

I wanted John to leave or Mary to (embedded Alternative Sentence).

I wanted John to go unless he had reason for staying (embedded Simple Sentence with Conditional Margin).

I wanted John to say 'Get out!' (embedded Direct Quotation Sentence).

I wanted John to say that she should get out (embedded Indirect Quotation Sentence).

I wanted John to ask her whether she liked him or not (embedded Indirect Question Sentence).

40. It is worth pondering whether the two systems of sentences described for English may not be related in some still larger system. A beginning clue is that the Merged Sentences represent a manner of associating two bases that is more intimate than the sort of conjoining found in Juxtaposed Sentences. Therefore, in reference to Figure 6 (Conjoining and Quotation Sentences), the Merged Sentences represent a topological region to the left of Column 1, Juxtaposition. A further consideration is that Merged Sentence types which have only the same actor in both bases and may not have a noun phrase in dual function are therefore even more intimately coupled than those that may have different actors and such a noun phrase in dual function. This means that the former belongs topologically to a region to the left of the latter. A third consideration is that the five orders of Merged Sentences show a gradation from loose to tight that is similar to that posited in the system of Conjoining and Quotation, where there are loose and tight series of sentences. In brief, the system of Merged Sentences belongs topologically to a region to the left of the Juxtaposed Sentences and above that of the Balanced Sentences. The only irregularity is that the Merged Sentences have five values of Loose-to-Tight grading, while the main system has but two values at this point plus a third value (Balanced) not found in the Merged Sentences. The result of these observations is given in Figure 8.

If these observations are valid, they suggest the following statements regard-

Merged (same)	Merged (same/diff)	Juxtaposition	Concatenation	Explanation	Implication	Quotation	
Manner	Telic	Paraphrase	Coördinate	Reason	Concessive	Direct Quotation	Loose
Conative	Aspectual						
Predisposition	Reciprocal						
Obligation	Causative	Recapitulation	Antithetical	Result	Contrafactual	Indirect Quotation	Tight
Passive	Sensation						
		Echo Question	Alternative	Equational	Correlative	Alternative Question	Balanced

FIGURE 8. Interrelations of English sentence types.

ing sentences in languages in general: (1) Sentence types form a system—never simply an inventory list. (2) A system is not necessarily free from local irregularities, lacunae, etc.

A possible parallel is the periodic chart of the chemical elements. While there is considerable system, beauty of arrangement, and even parallelism of many elements within the same column, local areas of irregularity (e.g. the rare earths) occur as well.

Sentence systems are specific to given languages. What is universal is the type of parameter found. Thus two or three series will occur in a sentence system, i.e. loose vs. tight, or loose vs. tight vs. balanced. The orders of sentences which occur may be arranged as values of a parameter from left to right, according to progressive intimacy of association. Areas of possible irregularity the world over are the Merged Sentences (when several distinct types are found) and Quotation Sentences. These types of sentences often form sub-systems within the larger system.

REFERENCES

BALLARD, LEE. 1968. Inibaloi sentence structure. Unpublished MS.
ENGEL, RALPH, and ROBERT LONGACRE. 1963. Syntactic matrices in Ostuacan Zoque. IJAL 29.331–44.
FILLMORE, CHARLES J. 1968a. The case for case. Universals in linguistic theory, ed. by Emmon Bach and Robert Harms, 1–90. New York: Holt, Rinehart & Winston.
——. 1968b. The grammar of hitting and breaking. To appear in Studies in English transformational grammar, ed. by R. Jacobs and Peter Rosenbaum. Waltham, Mass.: Ginn-Blaisdell.
FORSTER, JANNETTE. 1964. Dual structure of Dibabawon verbal clauses. Oceanic Linguistics 3.26–48.
——, and MYRA L. BARNARD. 1968. A classification of Dibabawon verbs. Lingua 20.265–8.
HALL, WILLIAM C. 1969. A classification of Siocon Subanon verbs. Anthropological Linguistics 2:7.209–15.
LIND, JOHN. 1964. Clause and sentence level syntagmemes in Sierra Populuca. IJAL 30.341–54.
LONGACRE, ROBERT E. 1967. The notion of sentence. Georgetown University monograph series on languages and linguistics, 20 (ed. by E. L. Blansitt, Jr.), 15–25.
——. 1968. Discourse, paragraph and sentence structure in selected Philippine languages. 3 vols. U.S. Department of Health, Education, and Welfare, Final Report, Contract No.0-8-062838-0391. (Vols. 1–2 now published as SIL publications in linguistics and related fields, 21; Santa Ana, Calif., [1970].)
——. 1969. A hierarchical look at the English verb phrase (what it is—what it isn't). Paper read at the Conference on the English Verb, Martin's Ferry, April, 1969.
McLACHLIN, BETTY, and BARBARA BLACKBURN. 1968. An outline of Sarangani Bilaan discourse and paragraph structure. Unpublished MS.
MILLER, JEANNE. 1964. The role of verb stems in the Mamanwa kernel verbal clauses. Oceanic Linguistics 3.87–100.
PALMER, F. R. 1965. A linguistic study of the English verb. London: Longmans.
PIKE, KENNETH L. 1964. Discourse analysis and tagmeme matrices. Oceanic Linguistics 3.5–25.
REID, AILEEN; RUTH BISHOP; ELLA BUTTON; and ROBERT LONGACRE. 1968. Totonac: from clause to discourse. (Summer Institute of Linguistics publications in linguistics and related fields, 17.) Norman, Oklahoma.

REID, LAWRENCE A. 1966. An Ivatan syntax. (Oceanic Linguistics, special publications, 2.) Honolulu: University of Hawaii Press.

ROSS, JOHN. 1968. Gapping and the order of constituents. Unpublished MS.

SCHAEFFER, FRANCIS A. 1968. The God who is there. Downers Grove, Ill.: Inter-Varsity Press.

——. 1969. Death in the city. Downers Grove, Ill.: Inter-Varsity Press.

TOLKIEN, J. R. R. 1969. Smith of Wooten Major. New York: Ballantine Books.

WILLIAMS, JOSEPH M. 1966. Some grammatical characteristics of continuous discourse. Doctoral dissertation, University of Wisconsin.

[Received 17 April 1970]

Syntax
above the sentence

DISCOURSE ANALYSIS AND TAGMEME MATRICES

Kenneth L. Pike, University of Michigan

This paper[1] suggests the directions in which we are moving to develop matrices and tagmeme concepts in reference to constant situational roles (of a plot) within changing grammatical roles. Earlier work has shown how constructions can be placed in a matrix,[2] how syntax paradigms can utilize matrices with the vertical dimensions representing constructions and horizontal dimensions representing sequences of tagmemes in order to get a quick view of a language structure,[3] and how replacement of morphological formatives in cells of the matrix, with rows and columns permuted or conflated, can reveal pattern.[4] Each of these types of presentations has been useful in developing a theory of language as field, and in the methodology of language analysis.

It seemed probable, however, that one ought to be able to construct a matrix in which single tagmemes fill the cells, and in which neither of the dimensions intersecting with these cells is of the type of sequence arrangement such as occurred in the tagmemic representation of the syntax paradigm. This gap in theory disturbed us for some two years. Recently, however, in connection with certain studies in the Philippines, material came to our attention which pointed out several possible ways by which tagmeme matrices could be constructed which would be useful both in the study of language universals and in the handling of problems of particular language systems.

The solution requires the symbolization of certain situational invariants--called situational roles--without which a plot cannot be understood, nor a consistent discourse generated.

I. Problems in Discourse Sequence

In the Spring of 1963, members of the Summer Institute of Linguistics, studying thirty languages, met with their informants at a workshop in Mindanao to discuss problems, some of which continue to recur in these related languages.

(a) A transitive clause may be present--let us say--with predicate, subject, object, as in Killed John the tiger (i. e. , John killed the tiger) in contrast to a causative transitive clause such

as <u>Killed</u> <u>Bill</u> <u>John</u> <u>the</u> <u>tiger</u> (i.e., <u>Bill</u> <u>caused</u> <u>John</u> <u>to</u> <u>kill</u> <u>the</u>
<u>tiger</u>) with predicate, subject, object, referent (as second object).
<u>John</u> as subject in the first, noncausative clause, parallels in
form <u>Bill</u> as subject of the causative clause. Subject in these
two sentence types is signalled by a marked personal noun phrase,
or by a pronoun phrase, or by a marked nonpersonal noun phrase,
or by a pronoun selection. <u>John</u> is thus marked as subject in the
first clause but not in the second where its relation to the real-
world situation is the same but its grammatical structure is
different. (For a related English problem note <u>He</u> <u>killed</u> <u>the</u>
<u>tiger</u> versus <u>Bill</u> <u>caused</u> <u>him</u> <u>to</u> <u>kill</u> <u>the</u> <u>tiger</u>, in which the change
of <u>he</u> to <u>him</u> marks change of grammatical but not situational
role.) Several questions were forced to attention by this: (1) How
could <u>John</u> and <u>Bill</u> be treated as subject--as filling the same
structural slot in the grammar--in the two respective clause types,
and yet be so different in reference to the real-world situation
involved? (2) How should this be symbolized in tagmemic formulas?

The answer could not be given as simply one of active versus
passive versus causative clauses, or the like, since further
relationships also occurred in which items such as time or location,
which could be added to either of the clause types cited, could also
fill various grammatical roles.

(b) Related to the first problem is a second one where,
again, change of grammatical role does not signal a change in
real-world situation. If, in <u>John</u> <u>killed</u> <u>the</u> <u>tiger</u>, the subject <u>John</u>
(and the predicate) are so marked that <u>John</u> is given special
attention as the topic of the statement (see the problem of focus,
three paragraphs below) then it may be moved into the predicate
role of an equational (identificational) clause; at the same time
the remainder of the clause is nominalized by a particle marking
it for focus (topic) and is moved into the topic slot of the two-part
equational clause, following the predicate. This yields something
like [<u>There</u> <u>is</u> <u>the</u> <u>one</u> <u>who</u>] <u>killed</u> <u>the</u> <u>tiger</u>, <u>namely</u> <u>John.</u> (When
some tagmeme other than subject--say object or referent-- is in
focus, it likewise may be moved to the equational-predicate slot,
with the clause remainder again marked for topic.) It is not the
purpose of this article to discuss such structures. Rather, we
merely note that there is an extraordinary capacity for the
particular item from the real-world situation to be placed into a
variety of grammatical relations from one sentence type to another.
If, therefore, one wishes to be able to see in the formulas of a
sentence or sequence of sentences anything whatever about the

relationship of its parts to the real world, it is necessary to do more than list the grammatical function of the slot and the class of items in that slot. Somehow one must be told the relationship of each tagmeme to the real world, in addition to its grammatical function.

(c) A third problem, in turn, grew out of the second. In following a story one needs to be able to know what has happened to a particular person in the plot from one sentence to the next. Discourse structure demands more than a symbolization of the grammatical structure of separate sentences, and more than the listing of the classes of words of particular sentences. Granted the specification both of class and of grammatical function, one could still end up with no idea whatever of the relationship of these items to each other, as reflected in the real world, and with no idea whatever of the relation of these in reference to the development of the story as a whole.

(d) Even more disconcerting were slight hints that choice of sentence structure is determined not by random selection, but that one sentence type in a story demands that a limited selection of sentence types follow it such that the actors involved must flow-- within certain limits--from one point in the story to another via one grammatical structure to another. These hints could neither be checked for accuracy nor rejected, without further kinds of data and formulaic representation.

(e) A fifth problem crisscrossed with these others. Even within a sequence of subject, object, predicate in a single sentence, deep structural changes reflect particular ties either between subject and predicate, or between object and predicate, or between predicate and--say--a referent of some other element in the sentence. This tie reflects something about the attitude of the speaker (who is uttering the sentence) towards the components of the sentence. That is, he can especially direct his attention (in a manner called focus--indicating the topic of the statement) towards the subject, or toward the relationship of the subject to the predicate (something like active sentences do in English), or toward the relation between object and predicate (such as the subject-predicate relation of the passive in English). In some Philippine languages there are four such focus possibilities in clause types.[5]

(f) Crisscrossing this change of attention is some kind of related but structurally contrastive emphasis. Emphatic attention

directed toward the particular tagmeme in the construction does
not involve its grammatical concord or tie with any other tagmeme.
This differentiates it from the directed attention--which we have
called focus--where a tie between two tagmemes is involved.
Emphasis, furthermore, is independently applicable to tagmemes
without restriction as to their prior involvement in focus.
Therefore a tagmeme could be simultaneously focussed and
emphatic, or unfocussed unemphatic, or focussed unemphatic,
or unfocussed emphatic. [6]

Here, also, it is desirable to try to follow the attention
of the speaker and his attitude as he discusses the course of
events in a single episode.

II. Symbols for Situational Roles Added to Symbols for Grammatical
     Roles

In order to be able to understand the descriptions being
brought to the attention of the workshop, and in order to be able
to follow the internal relationships of a sentence in their structural
meanings, we adopted the following rule - of - thumb for a tentative
presentation of data: To the symbol for each tagmemic slot--to each
symbol for grammatical role--would be added a subscript which
indicated its real-world function--a symbol of its situational role.
Thus when the subject John was serving as actor in John killed the
tiger, the subject tagmeme would be shown as $Subj_{ac}$ (subject-as-
actor); the tiger as object in the same sentence would be represented
as Obj_g (object-as-goal). When the tagmeme Bill (which is
grammatically marked as subject in Bill caused John to kill the
tiger) is the causer of the action, however, it would be symbolized
as $Subj_c$ (subject-as-causer); in that same sentence the tagmeme
symbol for John as grammatical object would carry a subscript
to show that its real-world function was actor: O_{ac}; and the tiger
would be Ref_g (referent-as-goal), grammatically marked as
carrying a further referent role while continuing its situational
role as goal of the event.

It should be noted that we had already utilized such materials
for contrast in tagmemes in English, when we had two subject
tagmemes as actor and as goal respectively as John saw Bill
versus John was seen by Bill. [7]

Sometimes, furthermore, two tagmemes serve simultaneously
in the one portmanteau grammar slot. Thus, in English, the

sentence <u>John came</u> is paralleled by the sentence Who came?, but with the subject-as-actor in <u>Who came</u>? simultaneously containing an interrogative tagmeme. Such problems have previously been discussed for Zapotec, [8] an American Indian language, and for Bilaan of the Philippines. [9] In the Philippine situation, however, we now need to go much further, since a topic slot can be filled by location[10] or by time. [11] Thus to follow an episode or discourse it is necessary to be able to trace, throughout, not only the actor and goal of a particular action but all kinds of elements in the stories such as time, location, and the like.

For our purpose here I shall refer to these as <u>situational roles</u>, [12] with the actors involved as <u>dramatis personae</u> serving in participant roles which are a subvariety of situational role.

III.   Flow of Situational Roles through Discourse

Our aims in studying discourse are both analytical and generative. In analysis, we wish to understand how a discourse is constructed. Generatively, we wish to be able to talk, tell stories, and produce literature.

These problems are both practical and theoretical. Practically, we have found that the production of separate, well-formed, correct sentences in sequence by no means guarantees either intelligibility of a discourse or correctness of its structure. Any one sentence may be produced correctly, but with the total discourse unintelligible since the understanding of a sentence may require a particular set of mind ready to receive it--an expectancy developed in preceding sentences; or the second sentence may be required to contain within it particular cues which interlock it with preceding and following sentences for intelligibility. [13]

The particular direction in which our discourse research moved in the Philippine studies was determined by the idea that discourse ambiguity would be eliminated for these languages by two procedures: (1) the search in a corpus of unelicited text for conditioned sequences of sentence types--e. g. , equational types following non-equational types under conditioning or quasi-conditioning circumstances; (2) the eliciting of <u>directed-plot</u> text.

Technology of the first type seems routine--but has not yet given extensive results. The eliciting technology of the second

suggests (a) that the analyst choose a strictly limited set of
situational roles, appropriate to the culture--e. g. , the mother
(as causer) of a boy (as actor) killing (as action) a monkey (as
goal) with an arrow (as instrument) in the forest (as scene) for
his sister (as beneficiary); (b) that the story be elicited bit by
bit, with the informant kept aware of total context. [14]

To this data we then wished to apply tagmemic formulas
in which the slot symbol included the grammatical-role representation,
with the situational-role representation as a subscript to the
grammatical representation. As subscripts, causer, actor, goal,
location, beneficiary, and instrument, would be retained unchanged
through the story.

It was hoped that the flow of situational roles through the
changing construction types would illuminate the composition of
the tagmemic types occurring in the various constructions and
the sentence sequence required by this story.

Then the story was to be re-elicited in several ways.
Whereas the story first was to be told by an outside observer--the
informant--about the incident, the repeat was to be elicited as if
the mother were telling the story; (I asked him to go. . . and he. . .);
then re-elicited as told by the boy (My mother told me to go. ..so
I. .); again, from the viewpoint of the sister (Mother told my
brother. . . and he reported to me that. . .); and (if folktales allow
animals to talk--which is by no means certain in some Philippine
areas) from the point of view of the monkey (or he may be replaced
with an eligible talker, in a fighting scene); with the story re-elicited,
if possible, from--say--the mother's viewpoint, but with her
emotional attitude changed by having focus of attention removed
from the hunger of the sister to pride in the achievement of the
son.

Here the intent is to find out how observer viewpoint affects
the flow of situational roles through the constructions, and the flow
of constructions through the discourse.

Tagmemic theory insists that no sentence is well described
unless its external distribution is given. Any unit of human behavior
(whether grammatical, lexical, physical, conceptual) includes as
one of its components its external distribution in a more inclusive
class, in a sequence of hierarchically-ordered events (or spacially
ordered events), and in a network of contrastive vectors of a
matrix. [15]

Before full definitions or descriptions of sentences, clauses, and phrases can be given, their discourse potential must be known. Tagmemic theory does not allow theory of grammar to start with sentence--or with any other one unit. The total system, including discourse, must be part of the setting within which any one unit is discovered, or adequately presented.[16]

Note that in the analysis of the discourse any one situational role such as "actor" does not represent a generalized <u>class</u> of actors, such as would normally be represented in a generalized tagmemic formula, but must rather represent some <u>one particular actor</u> from the real-world episode. If one were to use miscellaneous sentences--which would result from having a variety of real-world actors, miscellaneously interchanged without reference to plot--then one could never be sure what the conditions of sequence were involved. <u>Plot</u>, then, becomes part of the meaning of a total episode--a <u>contrastive feature</u> of that episode, and relevant to determining its <u>formal</u> structure.

On the other hand this plot restriction definitely did not require that a particular situational role be represented by the same lexical item at each occurrence of the role. It could be given by noun, by pronoun, by direct reference, by indirect reference, at any grammatical level--by separate sentence, by filler of some clause slot, or in whatever way was convenient and permissible. Note, for example, that in the following list of English sentences the role of <u>possession</u> can be represented in various ways. Verb in context: <u>John owns the book</u>; <u>The book is owned by</u> John; <u>John owns it</u>; <u>He owns it</u>; <u>It is the book that John owns</u>; <u>It is John that owns the book</u>; <u>The book belongs to John</u>. Noun in context: <u>John's possession of the book</u>; <u>his possession of the</u> book; <u>John is possessor of the book</u>; <u>The possessor of the book is John</u>; <u>The possession of the book is in John's hands</u>; <u>The book's possession is in John's hands</u>. Affix in context: <u>John's book</u>; <u>It is John's book</u>; <u>The book of John's</u>; <u>The book is John's</u>. Pronoun: <u>The book is your's</u>, John; <u>his book</u>; <u>a book of his</u>. The <u>-ing</u> form of the Verb: <u>the book belonging to John</u>.

IV. Tagmeme Matrix with Situational Role Times Grammatical Role

It was at this point that it became clear that a matrix could be constructed with tagmemes in the cells. By putting to the left

the various kinds of situational relations--roles in the real world--
and by putting across the top of the matrix the various grammatical
roles, cells would be provided for the tagmeme symbol showing the
complex of the two roles. [17]

A brief sample is given, with some of the cells filled, in
Figure 1. In this figure we have not attempted to fill all of the
cells, but have given only a few samples such as subject-as-actor,
subject-as-goal, subject-as-action, subject-as-causer, subject-
as-place; object-as-actor, object-as-goal, object-as-action,
object-as-causer.

	Subject	Object	Predicate	Time ...
Actor	S_{ac}	O_{ac}		
Goal	S_g	O_g		
Action	S_{act}	O_{act}		
Causer	S_{cau}	O_{cau}		
Place	S_p			
Instrument				
Enabler				
Time				
Beneficiary				
...				

Fig. 1   Tagmeme Matrix of Situational Times Grammatical
Roles

The reason for this incompleteness is an empirical one:
the kind of matrix suggested here is etic. It implies, therefore,
etic universals--a list of all known tagmeme types reported in the
world. Such a classification will be a very great advantage to
field workers in the future--and we are working toward the

preparation of such an etics of tagma types. Yet any such etic scheme is the conflation[18] of known but diverse emic systems of various languages. Such an etics implies the conflation into a single etic matrix of an adequate sampling of the emic systems of various languages of the world. Since, however, not even one such matrix has been finished for any area of the world, an adequate generalized etic scheme must be delayed. Even now, however, this preliminary bit has proved fruitful in the Philippines in stimulating our workers to have a checklist of the kinds of situational relationships to watch for in the role flow through discourse.

How many such cells might there ultimately be in a universal etics of situational roles? Or when should one stop constructing cells, if an unlimited number of semantic components can be recognized in the world? The reply can in part be treated structurally. No new row or column should be added to the charts until it has been demonstrated as structurally necessary in some language. Symbols for situational and grammatical vectors should not be created ad hoc for the sake of developing a larger diagram, but should represent the reported constructions.[19]

Will not some of the tagmas in the cells be homophonous? Definitely yes. We have already indicated that in English the tagmemes of subject-as-actor and subject-as-goal in John saw Bill and John was seen by Bill may be homophonous (that is, may have the same filler class in the contrastive tagmemic slots). Tagmemic theory allows homophonous tagmemes as it also allows homophonous morphemes. How, then, can they be contrasted? The answer seems to be clear in principle though sometimes difficult to apply--with presumably some indeterminacies which will remain. Two tagmemes are contrastive (even if homophonous at some of their manifestations) if the constructions in which they occur expand differently (contain different optional tagmemes) or if the constructions lead to or allow different transformations.[20]

The contrast between situational role and grammar role needs to be carefully handled, but techniques for doing so are only in part developed. We have mentioned one specific instance: subject-as-actor versus subject-as-causer in some of the Philippine languages; both tagmemes carry the same particle or pronominal marker, identifying the grammatical role of each as subject (as "source" of the event). The contrastive situational roles of actor versus causer would be recognizable by the different transform potential from one clause type to another (actor <u>boy</u> as grammatical object in <u>The mother caused the boy to shoot the monkey</u>, becomes subject in <u>The boy shot the monkey</u>), and by their relation to the real world as well.   In English, similarly, subject-as-actor (in an active sentence) and subject-as-goal (in a passive sentence) are both marked as subject grammatically (each precedes the predicate, and each is tied to the predicate by concord of singularity or plurality); and subject-as-actor transforms to agent from the clause <u>John saw the boy</u> to <u>The boy was seen by John.</u>

V.   Grammatical Levels as a Dimension in the Tagmeme Matrix

        In Figure 1 we assume that the grammatical role was specifiable without subdivision.   Underlying it was the further assumption that we were dealing with clause-level grammatical roles.   If one checks on the English illustration for <u>possession</u> given in III, however, it becomes obvious that this assumption is too simple and that the situation roles migrate not only to different clause slots, but to slots on other grammatical levels as well.   Ultimately, therefore, an etics of roles must be flexible enough to leave room for this kind of role flow across boundaries of levels.   In Fig. 2 we now suggest a framework within which this might be developed.   Grammatical levels are given at the left--discourse, utterance-response units, monologue, sentence, clause, phrase, word, morpheme--and other layers could be introduced as needed.   Across the top come the situational roles.   Tagmemes symbolized for both grammatical and situational roles come in the cells.

```
                    Actor    Goal    Possession    ...

Discourse

Utterance-Response

Monologue

Sentence

Clause

Phrase

Word

Morpheme

...
```

Fig. 2   Matrix of Construction Times Situational Role,
with Tagmemes in the Cells

A difficulty arises as soon as one attempts this: The
figure is too simple.   Each level of the grammatical hierarchy
must itself be broken into a spectrum of contrastive discourse
types, sentence types, phrase types, etc.   Each of these, in
turn, would then have to be broken into their respective
grammatical slots.   Only then would one be able to have the cells
cut fine enough to begin to accommodate all of the specific tagmas
combining grammatical role with situational role.   In addition,
the boundary between situational role and lexical component is
not yet clear enough to prevent excessive representation of
lexical differences.   Judgment as to the useful cut-off point for
the etics here--as for any other etic scheme--would have to be an
empirical one, but one for which experience is still not available
as a good guide.

VI.   Tagmeme Matrices with Observer Role as a Dimension

In I (e, f) we pointed out that one of the problems in handling
the Philippine languages was that specially-contrastive clause types

reflect observer attention and observer emphasis. We now must
try to find a way in which these can be worked into a tagmeme
matrix. If they are left out, much of the relevant material in
the Philippine languages will be unrepresented in our format.

In the handling of the syntax paradigm article[21] the problems
of observer attention--focus--and the problem of observer emphasis
were reflected in English translations such as It is indeed the boy
that catches the rat; It is indeed the rat that the boy catches; It
is indeed the BOY that catches the rat; It is indeed the RAT that
the boy catches. The fact that these can, with some awkwardness,
be translated into English (with special lexicon--indeed--and clause
structure for attention, and with stress--here written with caps--
for emphasis) is evidence that in an English discourse the migration
of situational roles through varying grammatical roles can also be
handled through special clause structures which reflect not only
these observer attitudes but others.

To illustrate this fact we return to the citation of variants
of John's book, with expansions of various grammatical types which
show change of observer attitude--attitudes ranging from certainty
to uncertainty, to negation, to query, to hypothesis, etc.: It is
indeed John's book; Of course it's his book; John's book?; Is it
John's book?; You say it is John's book!;[22] Suppose it's John's;
No, it couldn't be his; Definitely it is not John's book; If it is John's
book; Although it is John's book; Would that it were John's book;
They say it is John's book; John, your book!; Oh, that is the book
that John owns; etc.[23]

We wish, then, to be able to represent in the cells certain
tagmemes which signal observer components as simultaneous with
other situational roles and grammatical roles. First, in Fig. 3,
we leave room for the tagmemes directly in the cells. On the left
we place the tagmemes taken from the cells of Fig. 1. We let that
dimension itself be a complex of grammatical role with situational
role. It is obvious that such a list cannot be complete, since Fig. 1
is itself not remotely complete. Hence the dots at the left indicate
that as of the moment these can be expanded to indefinite number.
Along the top, on the other hand, we now add observer roles.[24]
Here, likewise, empirical studies are only at the beginning, and
a universal etics will have to wait for a sampling of an adequate
number of languages before the most helpful etics can be developed.
From the Philippine languages, as already mentioned, we can
abstract focus (directed attention) and emphasis. Surprise,

disappointment, negation, query, doubt, quotation, hesitation, and the like, can be added to this dimension. Tagmeme complexes-- simultaneous, (portmanteau) tagmemes--may need to be placed in the cells.

In the cells we put only a few tagmeme complexes as illustrative. Note subject-as-actor with simultaneous focus, subject-as-actor with simultaneous emphasis, subject-as-actor with simultaneous surprise. The tagmemic theory by which these are related needs further study. In these cells, the added observer role is treated as an added tagmeme simultaneous with the one listed to the left of the verticle bar[25] in the cell. There appears to be no reason, however, why a tagmeme could not contain an observer component alone.

	Focus	Emphasis	Surprise . . .
S_{ac}	S_{ac} | f	S_{ac} | e	S_{ac} | sur
S_g			
O_{ac}			
O_g			
. . .			

Fig. 3 Matrix with Tagmemes (marked for grammatical
and situational roles) Times Observer's Role

Since this type of matrix would get totally out of hand if the basic tagmeme list at the left were made as large as the previous figures implied it might be, it will prove necessary to use some type of matrix multiplication[26] to cut down the complexity of the table. It is not clear yet how this can best be done. Perhaps it could be handled, as in Fig. 4. Observer roles are placed along the top as in Fig. 3. Then, to the left, would be various matrices from different grammatical levels of Fig. 2. If, for example, the first row in Fig. 4 were to represent a matrix of all clause types, each with its tagmeme sequence, and each tagmeme with its

grammatical and situational roles, then the column multiplications
would state that an observer role could be added to each relevant
part of the respective clause matrices. Fig. 4 suggests this by
having a matrix of clause types in the first row, observer focus
in the first column, and the cell filled by a matrix times observer
focus. The next row has a matrix of phrase types; its first column
is filled by the phrase matrix times focus. We do not attempt to
fill in the other cells since this is intended to be suggestive only.

                     Focus   Emphasis   Surprise   . . .

Matrix of Clause Types M_{cl}. Foc.

Matrix of Phrase Types M_{ph} . Foc.

    . . .

        Fig. 4 Matrix with Matrices Times Observer Role

VII. Conclusion

        We have attempted to show the practical and theoretical
advantages of relating two components of language structure: On
the one hand, discourse structure requires for its study techniques
by which one can recognize continuity of individual situational
invariants--situational roles--as they migrate through the structure.
On the other hand, these elements representing situations in the
real world find themselves garbed in different dress; they appear
in various grammatical roles and are represented by differing
lexical items. Therefore the study of discourse structure must be
supplemented by a study of tagmeme structure represented in a
way which allows one to see both the grammatical role and the
invariant situational role.

        Ideally one might expect to construct some kind of flow
chart for optional or obligatory sequence of situational roles
through grammatical roles within a discourse plot. Ideally, also,
one should be able to develop an etics of tagmeme display such
that dimensions of situation and grammatical role can be presented
so that one has easily available a summary of tagma types which
have been discovered around the world and which are available for

recognition and treatment. These latter role displays, however,
must be overlaid with observer components brought to bear upon
the presentation of these roles, and the selection of the grammatical
kinds of structure which allow these observer roles to be represented.

NOTES

1. Presented at the summer meeting of the Linguistic
Society of America, July 27, 1963, Seattle.

2. Dimensions of grammatical constructions, Language,
38. 221-44, (1962). See, in this volume, papers by Weaver
(Ranking of personal pronouns in Agusan Manobo), Lusted-Whittle-
Reid (The use of matrix technique in an analysis of Atta personal
pronouns), Reid (A matrix analysis of Bontoc case-marking
particles), Shand (Tense, focus, and mode in Ilianen Manobo),
and Morey (The interrelationship of aspect and focus on four
grammatical levels of Ata).

3. A syntactic paradigm, Language, 39. 216-30, (1963).
See, in this volume, papers by Forster (Dual structure of Dibabawon
verbal clauses), and Newell (Independent clause types of Batad
Ifugao).

4. Matrix permutation and conflation, a paper presented
at the winter meeting of the Linguistic Society of America,
December, 1962, New York; to appear (in two parts) in the
International Journal of American Linguistics and Anthropological
Linguistics. See, also, papers in this volume by Reid (A matrix
analysis of Bontoc case-marking particles), and Lusted-Whittle-
Reid (The use of matrix technique in the analysis of Atta personal
pronouns).

5. See Howard McKaughan, The Inflection and Syntax of
Maranao Verbs, Manila, (1958); and see, in this volume, articles
by Forster (Dibabawon verbal clauses), and Newell (Clause types
of Batad Ifugao), Morey (Interrelationship of aspect and focus),
Shand (Tense, focus, and mode in Ilianen Manobo), Reid (Bontoc
case-marking particles), and Lee (Non-focus verbs in Maguindanao).

6. For my earlier tagmemic treatment of this problem,
see reference to A Syntactic Paradigm in fn. 3.

7. See my Language in Relation to a Unified Theory of the Structure of Human Behavior, Glendale (now Santa Ana), California, 1954, § 7. 6. Note that the distribution class of tagmemes called subject, in English, includes both the tagmeme actor-as-subject and the tagmeme recipient-of-action-as-subject (and presumably various other types in John is tired, etc.).

Note that this approach leaves room for discussion of the subject of a passive verb as "logical object"--i. e. , with situational role as goal.

8. See Velma B. Pickett, The Grammatical Hierarchy of Isthmus Zapotec, Language, Dissertation No. 56, 1960, p. 78.

For the opposite situation, in which a single situational role fills two grammatical roles, note English reflexive in I hit myself. Compare It rained with a pseudo-situational role filling the obligatory subject slot, and contrast it with Rain rained drawn from Dibabawon (data from Jan Forster) in which the nonpersonal situational element fills both the subject and the predicate slots.

9. For simultaneous function of actor with focus, and for object with focus, or for actor with emphasis, goal with emphasis, or action with focus with emphasis, and goal with focus and emphasis, note my Syntactic Paradigm.

10. Compare here in English Here is the place.

11. Compare now in English Now is the strategic hour.

12. Compare the comments of Robert Longacre who in another connection (in Grammar Discovery Procedure: A Field Manual, The Hague, to appear in 1964) refers to the plot (predicate), dramatis personae (for actor, etc.), props, scenery, and so on.

Recent development of space-time role matrices of Philip Bock (The Social Structure of a Canadian Indian Reserve, Ph. D. thesis, Harvard University, 1962) describing anthropologically many of these kinds of components in a sample specific social situation may eventually help define situational roles for tagmemic discourse analysis.

David Thomas has suggested--independently of Bock's material--the setting up of situational hierarchies as different from grammatical ones.

We note that ambiguities in grammatical roles are often disambiguated by situational role when these are known from earlier parts of a discourse. Linguistic analysis, dependencies, and generative power must not be assumed to start or end with sentences. Sentence structures are but one construction in a hierarchy of interlocking levels of grammar and situation, such that the total system of form and meaning must be treated as a composite whole.

13. This was most forcefully called to our attention by James Lauriot, of the Summer Institute of Linguistics, a decade ago when some New Testament translation in Shipibo failed to produce adequate intelligibility. He developed analytical devices to test for cues to sequence of situational roles in discourse. By taking a story, and asking in succession for each sentence who did what, what was done to whom, where did it occur, etc., the multiple ambiguities--from his point of view as an outsider--were gradually resolved. A most elaborate and unexpected set of cues was found to reside in different parts of the sentence structures. Preliminary descriptions of this material were prepared, with hierarchical ordering of some of these elements, but have not appeared in print.

For brief description of paragraph elements of a related language, see Eugene A. Loos, Capanahua Narration Structure, Texas Studies in Literature and Language, 4, Supplement, 697-742 (1963).

14. The first phase of such an eliciting technique, with similar roles, is seen in Eugene A. Nida, Morphology[2], Ann Arbor, (1949), p. 185.

Testing of the more extensive tagmemic discourse analysis suggested here is being carried on by Elmer Wolfenden.

15. See, for example, abbreviated statement in the Syntactic Paradigm, fn. 6, and see feature mode, manifestation mode, and distribution mode as the organizing principle of units described in my Language. . . Behavior, §§ 6.4-6, 7.3-5, 8.3-5.

16. Such elicited material has been begun by Elmer Wolfenden. Results were not available at the time this paper was written.

17. The particular classes of fillers of the slots are not under attention at this moment--whether noun, adjective, etc. These would be added in a tagmatic symbolization. For the difference between the two matrix types, note illustrations given in A Syntactic Paradigm, pp. 223, 225, 227.

18. See Matrix Permutation and Conflation (reference in fn. 4), for the way such conflations are handled, within a single language.

19. For explicit discussion of limits on the adding of structural units--limits imposed by a suggested dual criterion-- note extensive empirical treatment of the subject in Robert E. Longacre, Grammar Discovery...(reference in fn. 13).

20. Note, as we indicated above, that in my Language... Behavior§7, expansion and transform were mentioned. The extensive development of transformational theory currently under way by Zellig Harris, Noam Chomsky, and others should contribute greatly to the finesse with which such technology can be developed. Here, in the long run, may well develop one of their greatest contributions--though the authors currently would probably prefer to think that their contribution lies elsewhere. For documents on transformational grammar, note listings and discussion in Volume III (1960) of my Language... Behavior; for a current bibliography of transform materials, see Julian C. Boyd and Harold V. King, Annotated Bibliography of Generative Grammar, Language Learning, 12. 307-12, (1962).

21. See reference in fn. 3.

22. Various intonational devices can be added here to increase the range. I assume that the reader can add these for surprise, doubt, and the like, without further help at this point.

23. Recent transformational approaches should prove very helpful in showing us how to move from one of these types to another by way of grammatical rules.

David Thomas has called to my attention, for example, the concept of 'a battery of transformations' in the work of Henry Hiz̆ (Congrammaticality, Batteries of Transformations and Grammatical Categories, Structure of Language and its Mathematical Aspects, Proceedings of Symposia in Applied Mathematics, Providence,

Rhode Island, 12. 43-55, 1961). Here Hiž deals with sets of
related sentences defined by substitution classes marked by
retained numerals but differing by the order and the 'constants'
comprising members of closed classes. See, also, Zellig Harris
who states: 'The consideration of meaning mentioned above is
relevant because some major element of meaning seems to be
held constant under transformation'; and 'But aside from such
differences, transforms seem to hold invariant what might be
interpreted as the information content'; and 'The man was bitten
by the dog (N_2 v be V en by N_1) describes more or less the same
situation as The dog bit the man, and is a transform of N_1 v V N_2,...'
in his article Co-Occurence and Transformation in Linguistic
Structure, Language, 33. 290 (1957).

In this paper we are more directly interested, however, in
the fact that these tagmemes flow through the discourse in ways
which have controls outside the sentence. No sentence generating
process by itself (i.e., not going beyond the sentence) is sufficient
to meet the requirements of a theoretical construct needed to cover
these structural discourse restrictions and sequence relations, or
to provide the practical methodology needed to find and to describe
them.

24. Since this paper was presented to the Linguistic Society,
I have noticed the relevance to this problem of a paper by Roman
Jakobson: Shifters, Verbal Categories, and the Russian Verb
(Russian Language Project, Harvard University, 1957).

Two kinds of matrices are implied or presented. The first
contrasts message with code and leads to four cells (1) a message
about a message (M/M)--after Vološinov--as a quotation or quotation
indicator; (2) a code about a code (C/C)--after Gardiner--as a
personal name meaning the one 'to whom the name is assigned';
(3) a message referring to the code, any elucidating interpretation
or translation of an utterance (M/C); (4) a code referring to the
message (C/M)-- called a 'shifter', after Jespersen--such that the
shifter cannot be defined without reference to the given message--as
I. (This last category is highly relevant to tagmemic discourse
structure since it helps follow the continuing reference to a particular
person or other situational role throughout the plot.)

The second of Jakobson's implied matrices has one dimension
contrasting the speech ([S]) itself with the narrated topic ([n]) and a
second dimension contrasting the event itself (E) with one of the

participants (P), giving E^s, E^n, P^s, P^n. (The distinction of participant versus nonparticipant seems to be related to our handling of observer.)

The partial interrelation of these two sets of contrasts provides Jakobson a background system for the discussion of Russian verbal categories.

25. Note A Syntactic Paradigm, pp. 218-19, for detailed discussion.

26. See my Dimensions... (reference in fn. 2), pp. 226-29, for this concept, in which each cell of a matrix is modified by some superimposed component.

D. LEE BALLARD, ROBERT J. CONRAD, and ROBERT E. LONGACRE

THE DEEP AND SURFACE GRAMMAR OF
INTERCLAUSAL RELATIONS

1

This paper is both an accident and an example of making a virtue out of necessity. The first author of the paper, while participating in a field workshop directed by the third author, produced a description of the sentence types of a Philippine language, Inibaloi.[1] The paper diverged in several ways from descriptions of sentence structures in other Philippine languages under study at the same workshop.[2] The divergence seemed occasioned by Ballard's persistent interest in matters of structural meaning, substitutability of sentence-medial conjunctions, and accompanying informant reactions. Ballard set up certain sentence types, e.g. Coordination versus Simultaneity versus Sequence, with temporal considerations involved in the latter two types but not in the first. He attempted to match the situation which was encoded in each sentence type with the inventory of medial conjunctions which distinguish the various types. In doing this, he had to posit a set of conjunctions in some of the sentence types with a ranking conjunction – diagnostic of its sentence type – at the head of each set. Thus, the medial conjunction *jey*[3], 'while', 'at the same time', was considered to be diagnostic of the Simultaneous Sentence and was posited as the sole and sufficient marker

---

[1] Inibaloi is the language of approximately 40000 people in the southern two-thirds of Benguet Province, Central Luzon, Philippines. The examples in this paper are from text material gathered in various parts of Benguet Province but primarily in the municipality of Kabayan, where the first author was resident for five years, 1961–1966.

This workshop program and the research on Inibaloi were carried out under Office of Education (U. S. Department of Health, Education, and Welfare) contract No. 0-8-062838-0391.

[2] Monographs or articles on sentence structure in the following languages and by the following authors have been submitted for publication in various outlets: 'Central Bontoc', by Lawrence Reid; 'Agta', by Roy Mayfield; 'Siocon Subanon', by William Hall; 'Tausug', by Lois and Seymour Ashley; 'Western Bukidnon Manobo', by Richard Elkins. For some indication of the contents of these and other subject data papers which are as yet unsubmitted for publication, see Longacre, *Philippine Languages: Discourse, Paragraph, and Sentence Structure*, Vol. II.

[3] The orthography, with but a few simplifications, is that used in printed Inibaloi. The phonemes of Inibaloi, pronounced as their English counterpart unless otherwise indicated, are as follows: consonants b, d, g, j, k, k (backed), l, m, n, ng, p, r, s, sh, t, w, and y; vowels a (low central), i (high-to-mid front), e (high-to-mid central), o (high-to-mid back). Glottal stop is not written between vowels nor word-initially; it is written as a hyphen in clusters with another consonant.

of that construction which expresses various sorts of chronological overlap. The medial conjunction *tan* 'and' was considered to be diagnostic of the Coordinate Sentence. Conjunction *asan* 'and then' was considered to be diagnostic of the Sequence Sentence. But *jey* was also considered to be a further marker of both Coordination and of Sequence, while *tan* was considered to occur in Sequence Sentences as well as in Coordinate. A further conjunction *jet* 'and' was also considered to occur in Coordinate and Sequence Sentences. A substitution test was proposed in which the informant was asked in a given sentence that if he were to change the medial conjunction to some other conjunction, what would be his choice? The informant was quite willing to cooperate in this. It turned out that there were sentences with a medial *jey* or *jet* wherein, on reflection, the informant was of a mind to substitute *tan* 'and'; such sentences regardless of the original conjunction were termed Coordinate Sentences. There were other sentences with medial *jey, jet,* or *tan* wherein the informant, on reflection, was minded to substitute *asan* 'and then'; such sentences were termed Sequence Sentences. And so, what initially appeared to be a quite viable system of sentence types was assembled.

The present paper[4] is a complete reworking of the original Ballard paper in terms of structural tension between deep grammar and surface grammar relations. That it is based on Inibaloi rather than on English[5] is initially accidental. We were far advanced into an analysis of this sort before the potential importance for language in general was realized. On the other hand – and here we make a virtue of necessity – an analysis based on English would not necessarily compel interest in anything outside of English, while an analysis of some language other than English inevitably invites comparison with English or other European languages. At any rate, as is readily evident in this paper, the deep grammar relations here described are for the most part quite relevant to English sentence structure.

Ballard's original paper involved the following difficulties: (1) It seemed to reduce to synonyms or quasi-synonyms conjunctions that were intuitively felt to be different. (2) It seemed to rob the speaker of a set of options that are properly his. (3) It seemed to fail to take account of the fact that the same

---

[4] Under OE contract 0-9-097756-4409(014): 'Hierarchy and Universality of Discourse Constituents' (New Guinea Languages). The deep structure apparatus worked out in the analysis of Inibaloi is also being applied to languages of New Guinea which are the more immediate focus of the project. In this paper Ballard continues to be responsible for the Inibaloi data, its selection, and its interpretation, while Longacre has written most of the expository sections. Robert Conrad, also of the Summer Institute of Linguistics, has monitored application and adaptation of the predicate and statement calculi used to symbolize deep structures. Section 3 is largely his compilation.

[5] For an analysis of surface structures in English sentences (with some unformalized treatment of deep structures), see Longacre (1970).

situational relation (or some linguistic structuring based on the situation) might be encoded different ways for differing purposes in varied parts of a discourse.[6] The matter of coupling versus temporal overlap versus temporal succession is a case in point. Inibaloi seems to be more interested in temporal relations on the sentence level than English as seen in the fact that distinct conjunctions of simple one-morpheme structure occur in sentence medial to distinguish three differing relations: thus *tan* marks coupling; *jey*, temporal overlap, and *asan*, temporal succession. On the other hand, in both English and Inibaloi – though with more paraphrasis in English – it is possible to encode the identical situation so as to express any of the three relations. Suppose, for example, a situation in which John leaves the apartment and goes downtown exactly seven minutes by the clock before Mary, his wife, comes home. John may report this event the next day in the words, 'I went downtown and Mary came home'. If he chooses this wording, he disavows interest in temporal considerations. On the other hand, John may find himself in a situation where it is of crucial importance to establish the succession of events. He may therefore say, 'I went downtown and then Mary came home'. In still other circumstances John may want to emphasize that the two events were not far apart and that succession between them is of no importance. In this case he may say 'About the time that I went downtown Mary came home'. In Inibaloi the three varying conceptualizations of the situation are deftly shown by simple choice of sentence-medial *tan* 'and' versus *asan* 'and then', 'subsequently' versus *jey* 'at the same time'. This analysis of John's three ways of reporting the same situation does not reduce the distinctive conjunctions to synonyms, but preserves their essentially different thrust, while at the same time it recognizes the option of the speaker to conceptualize the same situation differently, and ties in well with the purpose of the discourse (or part of the discourse) in which John's sentence is found.

At this point the general parallelism of all this to certain matters having to do with the internal structure of clauses becomes apparent. In clause structure, several theoretical frameworks converge in establishing that not one set of relations but two such sets are needed to describe the internal structure of predications. Fillmore's case grammar works with deep grammar categories such as Agentive, Instrumental, Dative, Factitive, Locative, and Objective, versus the more well-known surface categories such as Subject, Object, indirect Object (or Benefactive) and Adjuncts.[7] Within the framework of tagmemics, the tradition is now old in respect to the analysis of Philippine languages that two sets of relations – often called 'situational'

[6] For some criticisms of Ballard's original paper, see Longacre 1968, Vol. II, 64–65; 88–92; 124–25.
[7] Fillmore, 1966, 1968a, b.

versus 'grammatical' categories – are needed. Thus, while the overt grammar
of a typical Philippine language clearly marks Subject, Object, Referent, and
Associative, other covert categories such as Actor, Causer, Goal, Instrument,
and Site move in and out of these overtly marked slots.[8] The covert categories are posited by noting contrasting collocational behaviour of close
synonyms as well as by noting transformations involving identical lexical
items. Stratificational grammar relegates what corresponds to Fillmore's
cases and Philippine 'situational categories' to a sememic stratum.[9] Whatever
the theoretical persuasion, transformational-generative, tagmemic, or stratificational, it is recognized that two sets of categories are needed. The categories, while slot-like, really mark relations of various noun phrases to the
verb which encodes the action of the predication.[10]

The parallelism of these considerations to sentence level relations is not
difficult to see. The situational string of a man opening a door with a key can
be variously encoded. The choice of alternative encodings is a part of the
speaker's conceptualizing activity correlating with the purpose of the
discourse or part of a discourse being formed. Presumably when the speaker
chooses to say 'The man opened the door with the key', he is either uninterested in any special focus within the clause or he is focusing on the man as
the agent. If he chooses, however, to say 'The key opened the door' or perhaps
'This key opened the door' he is focusing on the key itself to the temporary
exclusion of interest in the man who turned the key. Similarly, if he chooses
to say 'The door opened' – especially with some such addition as 'The door
opened slowly and silently' – he is focusing on the door itself or the manner of
its opening. This focus is not quite so exclusive of the possible agent if a
passive is chosen: 'The door was opened (it didn't open by itself, stupid!)'.
These alternative encodings of the same situation are not dissimilar in
principle from John's different encodings of his going downtown and Mary's
coming home.

This present paper is committed, therefore, to the thesis that a set of deep
grammar relations needs to be posited to account for the moving of same
or very similar lexical material through changing patterns of interclausal
relations. The sentence, as the immediately ascending hierarchical level
above clause, needs such a set of relations if we are to understand the
dynamics of that level. Most, however, of the relations here catalogued
will also prove relevant to the understanding of paragraph structures –
although the latter are beyond the scope of this paper.

[8] Forster, 1964; Miller, 1964; Pike, 1964; Reid, 1966; Forster and Barnard, 1968; Hall, 1969.
[9] Gleason, 1966; Tabor, 1966; Cromack, 1968; Stennes, 1969.
[10] Longacre, 1965, 1967.

It is proposed to label these relations 'deep grammar' relations as opposed to 'surface grammar' relations – and to stay within the framework of tagmemic theory.[11] The terms are not too fortunate in that 'surface' has a way of sounding simular to superficial, while 'deep' can be taken to mean 'more relevant'. At the onset it is necessary to rid ourselves of this notion – unless we are uninterested in language as communication and profess

---

[11] Attempts have been made by various practitioners of tagmemics in recent years (M. R. Wise, Al Wheeler, and Longacre, to name three) to handle all relations we are here calling deep grammar as *lexicon*. The feeling has been that since tagmemics professes belief in trimodalism, why not let the lexicon be the domain of what TG grammar calls 'deep grammar'? This paper marks the end of this endeavour on the part of the third author of this article. I do not believe that trimodalism need be equated with a belief in three hierarchies as such; all modes are not equally hierarchical in structure. This was my original position in Longacre, 1964, p. 23. I believe that the search for a lexical hierarchy has been frustratingly illusive. The lexicon is properly the domain of the dictionary-maker where we encounter meaning which is primarily of the non-slot-class, non-linear variety, but rather meaning involving real-world (or 'as if' real world) reference, and meaning established ultimately by the interplay of item and context (Longacre, 1958). It is to be conceded, of course, that collocational strings of lexical items can scarcely be discussed without reference to a rudimentary grammar (more of the deep than of the surface variety) and perhaps to a rudimentary phonology as well, but this does not mean that the minimal frame of reference has to belong to the lexicon itself. Nor does the fact that deep grammar is a minimal grammatical frame for discussing lexical items in and of itself make the categories of deep grammar part of the lexicon. In so far as linear strings are relevant within the lexicon proper they are collocational strings (cf. EXPECTANCY CHAINS) which comprise either (a) statistical probabilities of co-occurrence; or (b) observed co-occurrences within a given text or group of texts and peculiar to those texts. The latter are the sort of arrays obtained by Zellig Harris' Discourse Analysis.

Good reasons can be argued for keeping deep grammar categories in the grammar rather than in the lexicon: (1) Once put into the lexicon the debate threatens to be endless and inconclusive as to how to divide grammar from lexicon; every practitioner of tagmemics has a different answer. But if deep grammar categories are in the grammar and if no hard and fast division is to be posited between them and surface features (such as *must* be posited if they are different modes of structure), then we can settle for a polarization in which certain features of structure are relatively surface and the others relatively deep. (2) The type of category or relation posited in the deep grammar is not different in kind from that found in surface structures. Thus deep structure actor, goal, benefactive, instrument are not different in kind from subject, object, indirect, etc.; they are a rather more regular version of the latter freed from surface inconsistencies of encoding. So also coupling, contrast, overlap, succession are not very different in kind from coordination, antithesis, simultaneity, and sequence in surface structures. Again, however, they are more precise and defineable than the surface categories which must be defined in a given language partly in terms of varying and partially overlapping mappings of deep structures. (3) Last but not least we are less embarrassed to have these covert and obliquely marked categories as grammar – albeit deep grammar – when we come to a language where without warning on one or more structural levels there seems to be a dearth of surface structure features and where grammatical distinctions must lean heavily on deep structure categories.

Meanwhile Becker (1967) and Platt (1970) have within the framework of tagmemics been handling as 'grammatical meaning' what I here term 'deep grammar'. They have, therefore, kept these categories within grammar proper and not attempted to shift them to the lexicon.

interest only in language as design. Without the surface patterns speech is impossible. Furthermore, without contrasting surface patterns which afford the speaker a certain variety of options language would be wooden and comparatively expressionless. Surface patterns themselves involve meaning components which are added to those of the encoded deep structures. But surface structures are empty without deep structures to encode within them. Language must be understood as an interplay between the two sets of structures without one-to-one mapping between them. This means that enough structure must be put into each to make such interplay possible. We must not put all meaning components into the deep structure, because choice of the surface structure pattern is meaningful. If surface structure cannot be dispensed with – witness the recent spate of interest in surface constraints among advocates of transformational-generative grammar [12] – then we are out to make the most of it.

It is proposed here that within a taxonomic framework such as tagmemics – and one with an incurable interest in language particulars (not to the exclusion of interest in universals) – a taxonomy of the depths as well as of the surface is possible. The dissolution of 'deep grammar' within some trans-formational-generative circle into general semantic structures of an ever more abstract variety has been an interesting phenomenon of our times.[13] It is our contention, however, that a surface taxonomy of form within a language determines a similar taxonomy of deep relations, and that the two taxonomies stand and fall together. The deep grammar here advocated is not the deepest possible level – it stops short of dissolution into general semantic or logical categories. It stops in fact where the structure of a given language indicates a cut-off point in that it sets up no more deep structure categories than are required to account for surface encodings.

The matter of a cut-off point in the elaboration of deep grammar structures is an important one. Consider the Inibaloi data in Section 2.2 of this paper. The deep structures are all found in English and even the surface encodings which are indicated are not dissimilar in the two languages. A (juxtaposed) Paraphrase Sentence is posited in the surface structure of the Inibaloi (and in English). A category of PARAPHRASE is also set up in the deep grammar with the following subcategories: IDENTITY-EQUIVALENCE; GENERIC-SPECIFIC and SPECIFIC-GENERIC; STATEMENT-SPECIFICATION; with NEGATED ANTONYM in second position. (Sentences with NEGATED ANTONYM in first position encode only as Antithetical Sentence, cf. English 'It's not white but black' or 'He's not courageous; on the contrary, he's rather cowardly'.) The first five sub-

---

[12] Ross, 1967; Lakoff, 1969; Perlmutter, 1970.
[13] McCawley, 1967.

categories all encode as the surface structure Paraphrase Sentence. Of these subcategories, statement-specification encodes regularly as a Paraphrase Sentence, and rarely (once in our present corpus) as a Nucleus plus Cause Margin$_2$. The first subcategory, Identity-Equivalence, encodes somewhat rarely as an Addition Sentence or a Nucleus plus Cause Margin$_2$, and somewhat more frequently as an Alternative Sentence ('We should try to raise our standard of living, or endeavour to better our life, or do something to improve our condition.'). Apparently encoding as an Alternative Sentence is obligatory when more than two predications are involved. Generic-specific occasionally encodes in some surface structure which expresses cause and result (Cause Margin$_1$ plus Nucleus) – here the putative cause is a tautology and logically fallacious (cf. English 'They don't taste good because they're bitter.'). Generic-specific also encodes as a Simultaneous Sentence. Specific-generic does not happen to have any similar encoding in the data of Ballard's paper but this may be fortuitous. Finally, negated antonym in second position may encode as a Simultaneous Sentence, a Coordinate Sentence or an Alternative Sentence. It is evident that no two subcategories of PARAPHRASE in the deep structure encode in the same fashion throughout in respect to possible surface structures. Therefore, it is valid to posit these subcategories of Paraphrase in that they are needed if we are to discuss coherently alternative encodings in surface grammar.

The informant reactions noted by Ballard in the course of his 'change-the-conjunction' game with his Inibaloi informant are also of considerable importance. They directly witness to the native speaker's recognition of deep structure categories which are not in one-to-one correspondence with surface structure encodings. This witness can be taken in conjunction with that afforded by observing alternative encodings of similar lexical stuff in varying surface patterns. This twofold witness is of special relevance to the Coordinate Sentence in several respects: (1) An environment in which the informant regularly shifted *jey* 'while' to *tan* 'and' was that in which both sentence bases were expounded by clauses containing descriptives as their predicates, e.g. 'It is big while (*jey*) it is long'. This willingness of the informant to substitute *tan* 'and' in place of *jey* 'while' correlates with the fact that many examples of Coordinate Sentences contain bases expounded by clause with this sort of predicate. (2) The deep grammar relation which we may call COUPLING is typically a joining of two bases with differing predicates and the same terms, or of two bases with differing predicates and with different terms. The former sort of coupling may be encoded either as Coordinate (with *tan*) or as Simultaneous Sentence (with *jey*). By contrast, the surface structure Parallel Sentence with no medial conjunction encodes a coupling of bases with the same predicates but a differing set of terms, e.g.

'They speak English; their wives speak English; their children speak English'. Occasional examples occur of this variety of deep structure coupling encoded as Coordinate Sentence with medial *tan*. It is significant to note that in these cases there is resort to chiastic arrangement – as if to break up the neat parallelism of the Parallel Sentence when the same lexical stuff encodes as a Coordinate Sentence: 'And the plates were gold, and gold was the table'. (3) Certain Coordinate Sentences which occur in text by competent speakers can nevertheless be shifted by a same or different speaker to Sequence Sentences by substitution of medial *asan* 'and then', for *tan* 'and'. Here the informant seems to be responding to deep structure SUCCESSION in making this substitution. (4) An occasional sentence which clearly involves deep structure CONTRAST ('they would work when the moon was out and they would sleep when the sun was out' – with contrast between 'work' and 'sleep' as well as between 'moon' and 'sun') occurs in text encoded as a Coordinate Sentence. (5) Finally, there are occasional examples of precisely the same lexical stuff that regularly encodes as Paraphrase Sentence encoded as Coordinate Sentence. What emerges then? For one thing: the Coordinate Sentence is a preferred encoding of a certain type of coupling, but that it may also encode a variety of deep grammar relations (and de-emphasize) parallelism, succession, contrast, and paraphrase whenever these relations are not really germane to a discourse or some part of it.

It is also true that certain varieties of Antithetical Sentence – a surface structure which may have medial *nem* 'but', *jey* 'while' or no link at all – permit substitution of *nem* for *jey* or null. Even without this substitution it seems obvious that there are certain sentences with medial *jey* which are not simultaneous. English and Inibaloi are structurally similar at this point. Thus, although the English word 'while' clearly is used as a subordinator (not a coordinator as in Inibaloi) to express temporal overlap ('I browsed through the bookstore while my wife shopped') there are as clearly other uses that can by no amount of special pleading be construed as simultaneous: 'We groan under a heavy load of taxation while our ancestors paid scarcely any taxes'. It appears also that in such a sentence as the following, where chronology is not in focus at all but rather description, the English word 'while' also simply expounds antithetical link: 'Oxygen is a colorless, odorless, tasteless gas, while chlorine is green and has a pungent odor'.

Informant reaction as to transformational possibilities (between surface structures) is also of interest in identifying the deep structure or structures encoded into the Inibaloi Result Sentence – a surface structure of but two bases with intervening (*jet*) *isonga* or (*jet*) *nakol ni* 'therefore, as a result, so'. Certain of these sentences appear to be giving explanation of a situation, so we at one time posited within the deep structure of implication a special relation 'EXPLANATION'. Then we recalled that the informant permitted all such examples to be transformed to the structure Cause Margin$_1$ plus Nucleus. There seemed therefore to be no justification for setting up Explanation versus EFFICIENT CAUSE since the two putative deep structures encode the same way in surface structures.

Deep structures make a better framework for discussing specific collocational chains (lexically) than do surface structures -- since the sheer variety of the latter can confuse the basic collocations. A case in point is what we might call EXPECTANCY CHAINS. Certain groups of verbs often occur linked together in chains of chronological or logical expectancy, so that when one member of the chain occurs, we expect to see a closely consecutive member appear next. Thus, 'set out' and 'arrive' are found in such expectancy chains the world over. We are not surprised therefore to find Sequence Sentences of the sort 'He set out for London and arrived there yesterday'. The same chain figures in frustration as encoded both in Antithetical Sentences and in Concessive Margin plus Nucleus: 'He set out but didn't arrive' or 'Although he set out, he didn't arrive'. Here there is an expected consequent 'arrive' but instead the expected consequent is negated. The same expectancy chain figures in links between successive sentences in a discourse: 'He set out for London at 6:00 in the morning. On arrival in the late afternoon, he...'.

It seems apparent that the deep structure relations -- which are on the situational or real-world side of language rather than on its more formal side -- are more universal than the surface structures which encode them. It proves convenient then to compare languages as structures first via the deep structures and secondarily via surface structures. Nevertheless, although most of the relations posited in this paper for Inibaloi would seem to make a fair bid for universality, it remains that they are posited specifically for Inibaloi in order to facilitate discussion of encoding of deep structures into surface structures in that language. It may be conjectured that deep structure relations found on the clause level as well as those found on the sentence and paragraph levels are to a high percentage the same around the world. Nevertheless local variations of the general scheme are found in particular linguistic areas while individual languages within an area have further idiosyncrasies in their deep structure. Care needs to be taken in the study of a particular language neither to thoughtlessly posit structures that are not known elsewhere nor to confine that language to a procrustean bed by forbidding it any novelty. Meanwhile, universals within a linguistic area are especially significant to the study of languages within that area. At all events, the student of language who is aware of the deep grammar as well as the surface grammar within even one language has no small advantage over one simply familiar with surface structures of several languages.

It is possible that a frequent cause of sentences of marginal grammaticality is unusual or bizarre encodings of deep structures into surface structures which do not regularly encode them. In the Inibaloi materials some of our most aberrant examples of unusual encodings were corrected in text materials subsequently edited by native speakers for publication in literacy materials.

In the subsequent sections of this paper we present in Section 2 a brief summary of Inibaloi Sentence Types (surface patterns) followed by a description of certain selected sentence types along with the deep structures that they may encode. In any case where such a distinction seems feasible, we divide these encodings into regular encodings and less frequent encodings. A few carefully chosen Inibaloi examples accompany each surface structure along with the various encodings. As it seems relevant, parallels and contrasts with English structure are pointed out. Section 3 contains a summary of all deep structures whether or not they are referred to in Section 2. This amounts to a reverse indexing of the deep structures according to the surface structures into which they encode.

2

The Inibaloi sentence is a linear string which consists of an Outer Periphery, an Inner Periphery, and a Nucleus. Only the Nuclei contrast from sentence type to sentence type. The contrastive nuclei (nine of which are here described) determine twenty sentence types in the surface structure of the language. These twenty sentence types constitute a system which is represented in Table I. These types naturally group into pairs which share certain taxonomic features. We have refrained, however, from giving taxonomic labels to each distinctive pair. Each member of each pair may be classified as tight or loose according to the relative amount of structural restriction and versatility of encoding of deep structures. Thus Indirect Quote is a tighter structure than the Direct Quote in that the former requires adjustment of the substance of the quotation to the viewpoint of the reporter while the latter does not. The Eventuation Sentence, a general type of sequence structure with *asan* 'and then', is loose while the Contingency Sentence employs the same conjunction in a tighter construction involving implication and balanced conjunctions in sentence initial and sentence medial. Again, the Antithetical Sentence – with three possible medial conjunctions and seven possible encoded deep structures is looser than the Surprise Sentence with choice of two medial conjunctions and but one encoded deep structure. In general, in progress from left to right across the chart we notice a progress from clause-like structures (Simple and Direction Sentences) to columns 2 and 3 that are linked by juxtaposition (with an optional overt conjunction in

TABLE I

Inibaloi sentence systems

2.1 Simple	2.3 Parallel	2.5 Introduction	2.7 Simultaneous	2.9 Surprise	2.11 Contingency	2.13 Sequence	2.15 Reason	2.17 Indirect question	2.19 Indirect quote
ø	ø	ø	*jey*	*ngaran ni*	*ampot…asan*	ø	ø	QF₅ *nem*	QF₂ QF₃ QF₄ *ey/nem*

2.2 Direction	2.4 Paraphrase	2.6 Identification	2.8 Coordinate	2.10 Antithetical	2.12 Eventuation	2.14 Addition	2.16 Result	2.18 Alternative	2.20 Direct quote
ø	ø	*ø/jet*	*tan*	*nem/jey/ø*	*asan*	*jet*	*isonga/ nakol ni*	*ono*	QF₁ QF₂ *ey*

Identification in column 3) to columns 4 and 5 which contain conjoined structures, to columns 6 and 7 which encode some element of temporal succession, to column 8 which encodes implication, to the last two columns which encode quotation and alternation – which is in some ways similar to Indirect Question with which it pairs. This progression involves increasing intimacy of association from column 2 on in what we might conceptualize as juxtaposition, conjoining, chaining, implication, and quotation. The sentence types not described in detail in this paper are here exemplified with one example each:

Simple Sentence (with various preposed and postposed margins)

> *Jet* **TM**: *idi   inshel sha ira   sotan,* **CausM**$_2$: *tep   inon-an*
> and   when caught they them those   because saw
> *ko ira ni inbalod sha   so shiya iskowidaan,* **N**: *tedo   ira*
> I   them tied/up they   at   school   three they
> *sotan* **CausM**$_2$: *tep   kinebsil   sha'y eshom...*
> those   because let/get/away they some
> 'And when they captured those men, because I saw them when they had bound them here at the school, there were three of them, because they let some get away...'

Direction Sentence

> *Eti,   akad   ka ka panbayo ni balon   mo.*
> come go/home you you thresh   trail/food your
> 'OK, go home (and) thresh (the rice) for your meals on the trail.'

Introduction Sentence

> *Wara'y naktel la baka; insedad mi sotan.*
> was   chilled cow   boiled we that
> 'There was a cow that died from the cold; we cooked that one.'

Identification Sentence

> *Mengibesheng ira   ni wakal; si-kato'y iba-jatan   sha so ni*
> string/up   they vines   that   place/to/hang they
> *ketap   sha.*
> blanket their
> 'They would string up vines; that was what they would hang their blankets on (to air them).'

Surprise Sentence

> *Kowan to ey an   menayshay ali   nodta shaka panshayshaya;*
> say   he   go/to dig   here at/the they   digging
> **ngaran ni**   *sipkaren ni sangkap kono'y posel.*
> what/do/you/know graze   tool   hearsay knotty/wood.
> 'His intent was to dig where (the workers) were digging; what
> do you know his digging tool scraped a pine knot.'

Contingency Sentence

> **Asan** *ali   kaedaw wara'y inbetkag ko.*
> then   here came is   sent   I
> 'Then he came I sent someone for him.' Free: 'He didn't come
> until I sent someone for him.'

Reason Sentence

> *Say ninemneman   sha so niyay jey wara'y talon,   no*
> reason/to/think they   this   be   second/crop
> *sina-shom, emebitil   i too.*
> sometimes have/famine people
> 'The reason why they thought (to plant) a second crop of rice,
> sometimes the people are caught in famine.'

Result Sentence

> *...Piyan to ngarod   ja onshokey i biyag sha'n sampamilja;*
> want he emphatic   long   life   their one/family/unit
> **isonga**   *piyan to'n mankepi.*
> therefore want he   feast
> '...He certainly wants that the life of that family be long; therefore
> he wants to celebrate *kapi*.'

Indirect Question

> *Ekak amta* **lk**: *nem* **Base**: *ngaran to'n taw-en nontan.*
> not-I know   what   year   then
> 'I don't know what year that was.'

Indirect Quote

> *Inkowan sha* **lk**: *ey* **Base**: *eg sha piyan i pilak.*
> said   they   not they want   money
> 'They said that they didn't want money.'

Direct Quote

> *Kowan to kono*   lk: *ey* Base: *Jo di   olop jet idaw jo*
> say   he hearsay   you here fetch and bring you
> *la'd ma Peshis.*
> to
> 'He said, "Go fetch him and bring him to Peshis".'

The Sentence Margins are a special group of peripheral tagmemes which because of their special surface structures and their tendency to occur indifferently with various nuclei, are considered to be distinct from the latter. Margin tagmemes are only occasionally expounded by noun phrase (cf. Temporal Margin); more frequently exponents of these tagmemes are at least of clausal structure and not infrequently involve a combination of clauses. Since a single-clause unit can be interpreted as a Simple Sentence it proves convenient to consider all non-phrasal exponents of Sentence Margins to be RELATOR-AXIS SENTENCES, i.e. sentences which are formally subordinated by means of a preposed Relator such as 'because', 'if', 'when', and 'in order to'. Seven margin tagmemes (Cause$_1$, Cause$_2$, Conditional$_1$, Conditional$_2$, Concessive, Purpose, and Temporal) are posited; and seven corresponding subtypes of the Relator-Axis Sentence. In that the Sentence Margin tagmemes cluster around the Nucleus they constitute along with the two Sentence Topic tagmemes an inner periphery as opposed to Exclamation, Sentence Conjunction, and Vocative which constitute the outer periphery of the sentence.

Two Cause Margin tagmemes (which prepose the Inibaloi equivalent of 'because') and two Conditional Margins have been posited. While the Cause Margins do not contrast with each other semantically they involve differing Relators and contrast positionally with almost no overlap: Cause Margin$_1$ occurs only pre-nucleus; and Cause Margin$_2$ occurs pre-nucleus only when preceded by another peripheral tagmeme and otherwise occurs only post-nucleus.

The two Conditional Margin tagmemes also involve differing Relators: *no, into no,* and *kamo ni* in Conditional Margin$_1$ and *nem* in Conditional Margin$_2$. Positionally Conditional Margin$_1$ tends to occur pre-nucleus (95% of occurrences), and Conditional Margin$_2$ tends to occur post-nucleus (75% of occurrences). On initial inspection the two Conditional Margins do not seem to be functionally very distinct. On closer inspection, however, it turns out that (1) while either (in conjunction with a following nucleus) may encode deep structure Hypothetical, Conditional Margin$_1$ but not Conditional Margin$_2$ encodes Contrafactual and (rarely) Succession, and (2)

Conditional Margin$_2$ but not Conditional Margin$_1$ encodes the temporal relation of Overlap. Conditional Margin$_2$ refers often, then, to temporal relations while Conditional Margin$_1$ is more strictly implicational. This is reinforced by the observation that words such as *bilangey* 'supposing' frequently occur in our data with Conditional Margin$_1$ as well as negatives while the latter do not occur in exponents of Conditional Margin$_2$.

A few examples are enlightening. Thus in the dialogue (from text material) that follows, the second speaker changes from Conditional Margin$_2$ to Conditional Margin$_1$:

Speaker 1: *Si Handro i binidin ko ey Pangamag ka ni ikdogan to* nem *man-ikdog.*
'Handro was the one I ordered: "Make a nest (for the hen) when she begins to lay eggs".'

Speaker 2: *Talaka'n iamagkan to* no *aman-ikdog.*
'Probably he will make one for her if she is laying.'

As an experiment, the following minimal pair was given to an informant to distinguish:

Asan nak bayshi nem *wara'y pidaken ko.*
'I will pay for it when I get some money.'
Asan nak bayshi no *wara'y pidaken ko.*
'I will pay for it when I get some money.'

The informant reacted that in the latter case the store owner would not extend credit! In the former case, he might, depending on the man.

Concessive Margin is expounded by a Relator-Axis Sentence introduced by the Inibaloi equivalent of 'although'. Purpose Margin involves the Inibaloi equivalent of 'in order to'. Temporal Margin involves the Inibaloi equivalents of 'when' or 'while'.

Periods in examples cited indicate sentence-final juncture; commas and semi-colons indicate non-final juncture; and no punctuation indicates no break in intonation. It may be noted that the phonological sentence and the grammatical sentence usually coincide. Sometimes, however, two phonological sentences constitute one grammatical sentence. The criterion for combining two phonological sentences as one grammatical sentence is structural. A sentence type is defined by its structure, whether or not the bases are optionally divided phonologically by sentence-final juncture. Thus, the sentence *At ondawak. Nem akak dimaw.* 'I was to go. But I didn't go.' is grammatically an Antithetical Sentence, even though phonologically it is two sentences. The converse is not true. The unity of a phonological sentence is never violated by dividing it into two grammatical sentences.

Lists of exponents of base tagmemes in bi-dimensional arrays are those exponents that have been observed in text material. Such lists are, therefore, not exhaustive. When an exponent is cited as "any sentence", this is based on actual observation of a majority of sentence types and on there being no obvious restriction on occurrence of the rest. It is to be understood that the bi-dimensional arrays given for each sentence type represent only the nucleus of the sentence. A periphery – not specified in the arrays – accompanies each Sentence type. Each array contains a surface structure and deep structure component. The symbols for the latter are taken – with adaptation and elaboration – from the predicate and statement calculi of formal logic.

In the Inibaloi examples square brackets enclose the relevant part of an example as opposed to extraneous material.

2.1. *Parallel Sentence*

The Parallel Sentence (see Table II) is a juxtaposed structure without medial link, but with characteristic intonation joining the two bases. The majority of examples – in fact all that certainly belong to this type – have identical predications but contain a set of terms with members differing from base to base. In many of these examples the predicates are existential.

TABLE II

Parallel sentence

+ Base$_1$ (Proposition$_1$)	+ Base$_2$ (Proposition$_2$)...	+ Base$_n$ (Proposition$_n$)
Ind Cl	Ind Cl	Ind Cl
Coupling P(a) ∧ P(b)		... ∧ P(n)

Rules: 1. Bases may permute
2. Between each of the bases intonation rises to a peak which is similar to utterance-final intonation, but usually higher.

2.1.1. Coupling, P(a) ∧ P(b) ∧ ... ∧ P(n)

1   *Wara'd tan   i apag, wara'd tan   i dokto, wara'd tan   i inepoy,*
     is   there meat is   there camote is   there rice
     wara'd tan   i kankanen.
     is   there   dessert
     'There is meat, there is camote, there is rice, there is dessert.'

2   *Iman i Idoko,   iman i Pangasinan, iman ali'y too   di'd*
     there   Ilocano there   there here people here-from
     ma Bontoc.

'There are Ilocanos, there are Pangasinans, there are people here from Bontoc.'

3   *Aliwa et ngo'n tayo mosmos-an i mangardin bengat, aliwa*
not   instead   we   all/together   gardening   only   not
et ngo'n tayo mos-an   i man-oma bengat, aliwa'n tayo et ngo
instead   we   all/together   farming   only   not   ,we   instead
mosmos-an i ob-obda bengat ta say wara'd ja baley.
all/together   work   only   is-in   house.
'We shouldn't only do gardening, we shouldn't only do rice farming, we shouldn't only do that work which is in the village.'

2.2. *Paraphrase Sentence*

The Paraphrase Sentence (see Table III) is also a juxtaposed structure without medial link. There is apparently more variety of exponents – in terms of embedded surface structure sentence type – in the second base than in the first.

Five distinguishable deep structures are encoded as this sentence type: (1) A predication followed by a predication employing the same exponent of predicate or synonym, i.e. Identity-Equivalence paraphrase. (2) A predication involving a predicator of relatively generic meaning followed by a predication involving a predicator of relatively specific meaning. (3) The converse of (2), i.e. a predication involving a predicator of relatively specific meaning followed by a predication involving a predicator of relatively generic meaning. (4) A predication stating an effect followed by a predication stating the above plus specification of a participant, Statement-Specification paraphrase. (5) A predication involving a predicator followed by a predication whose predicator is a denied antonym (or situational opposite) of the first. It is apparent that all the above are distinct deep structures because they have varying surface structure encodings. Thus, (1), (2) and (5) are the most versatile in regard to surface structure encoding while (3) is the most restricted in that it encodes only as Paraphrase Sentence. Deep structure (4) is also relatively restricted in that besides Paraphrase Sentence itself, it encodes only as Nucleus plus Cause Margin$_2$. Besides Paraphrase Sentence, (1) may encode with some frequency as Addition Sentence, and Nucleus plus Cause Margin$_2$. Possible further encodings of (2) are Simultaneous Sentence and Cause Margin$_1$ plus Nucleus. Additional encodings of (5) are Simultaneous Sentence, Coordinate Sentence, and Alternative Sentence. For examples of each of the above see the appropriate sentence types.

Apparently all these deep structures also encode in the English Paraphrase Sentence which is, as in Inibaloi, a juxtaposed structure. Exact repetition of the predicate probably constitutes in English a special sentence type, the

Recapitulation Sentence which conveys special effect or dramatic addition: 'I went home; I went home to see what was really going on.'

TABLE III

Paraphrase sentence

+ Base₁ (Remark)		+ Base₂ (Paraphrase)	
Ind Cl		Ind Cl	
Simple S		Simple S	
Ind Quote S		Ind Quote S	
		Simult S	
		Parallel S	
Identity-Equivalence	Pa ∧	[Pa ≢ P′a]	
	Pa ∧	Pa′	
Generic-Specific	gPa ∧	sPa	
Specific-Generic	sPa ∧	gPa	
Statement-Specification	Pa ∧	$\left\{\begin{array}{l} \text{Pba} \\ \text{Pab} \\ \text{Pax} \end{array}\right.$	
Negated Antonym	Pa ∧	$\overline{\text{Pa}}$′	

2.2.1. *Identity-Equivalence.* The first two examples are Pa ∧ Pa′; the last two are Pa ∧ Pa and Pa ∧ P′a respectively.

1   *Dimaw i solsharo; shakel i Japan na dimaw.*
      went   soldiers many   went
      'The soldiers went; many Japanese went.' (In this example the 'soldiers' are Japanese.)

2   .   *...Todokan ni too'n   emin ey mapteng gayam i religion, mapteng*
      consent   people all   good   after/all   good
      gayam i mesoshot i Biblia.
      after/all follow
      '...All the people will consent that after all religion is good, (that) it is good to follow the Bible.'
      (In this example, 'religion' and 'following the Bible' are equivalent expressions.)

3   *Tayo ira   di   pidiwen; tayo pidiwen ima   ketap   sha'n shakel.*
      we   them here steal   we   steal   those blankets their many
      'We will go steal them; we will steal all those blankets of theirs.'

4   *Enshi nontan; aneng ali'd   Bagiw.*
      not   then   not/yet here-from

'There was no (dynamite) at that time; it had not yet come from Baguio.'

2.2.2. *Genetic-Specific*, gPa ∧ sPa:

1   *Indaw sha'y nowang shima sakey   da'n barrio; ininat sha'y*
    took they carabao to-the another   led   they
    nowang.
    carabao
    'They took the carabao to another barrio; they led the carabao.'
    (The Predicator of Base₁ is the generic word *daw* 'go, bring, take';
    inat in Base₂ is specific: 'lead by a rope'.)

2   *Jet an   ma ira inbaliw   ni mabediw; sha ira*
    and go/to   them cross/with crosser   they them
    innangonangoy.
    swim/with
    'And those who were good at crossing the river took them across;
    they swam across with them.' (The predicator of Base₁ is *baliw*
    'cross'; *nangoy* in Base₂ is specifically 'swim'.)

2.2.3. *Specific-Generic*, sPa ∧ gPa:

1   *Isonga   emekkit sota too'n shaka ikoday; emankemag-i'n*
    therefore dried   the person they drying be/dry
    pasia tep   maka bolan.
    very because one   month
    'So the person they are mummifying dries up; he gets very dry
    because (they do it) for one month.' (The Predicator in Base₁
    is the relatively specific term *kekit*, which collocates only with
    living things; *maga* in Base₂ is very generic.)

2   *Sotan i shaka ikowan, ta   [enshi'y maysediw ni tapey,*
    that   they say   because none buy/with   rice/wine
    enshi'y maytomkal.]
    none   buy/with
    'That is what they say because [there is no money to pay for the
    rice wine; there is no money to buy it with.]' (In this example
    saliw in Base₁ is a specific term for buying alcoholic beverages;
    tomkal in Base₂ is very generic.)

2.2.4. *Statement-Specification*, Pa ∧ { Pba / Pab / Pax

1   *Nan-oli   sotan na nan-ispay; dimaw da'd Sayangan.*
    returned that   spy   went   to
    'That spy returned; he went to Sayangan.' (Base$_2$ gives a speci-
    fication of the location tagmeme, which is only implicit in Base$_1$.)

2   *Tep   inalpeng   ma; dimpeng   nen Dabonay ja*
    because unconscious   knock/unconscious
    bii.
    woman
    'Because he was unconscious; Dabonay, a woman, had knocked
    him unconscious.' (Base$_1$ gives a specification of the agent
    tagmeme, which is only implicit in Base$_2$.)

2.2.5. With a negated antonym in Base$_2$, Pa $\wedge$ $\bar{P}''$a:

1   *Mapteng noman   i nemnem ni dalakay; eg   sha ikowan ey*
    good   certainly thoughts of old/men not they say
    iraka mesiwasiwat.
    they   being/distracted.
    'The old men have good thoughts; they do not say that they are
    being distracted from their work.' (To say that one is being dis-
    tracted from one's work to do a service to the community is a
    negation of 'having good thoughts', but this is negated.)

2   *Jet idi   inshel sha ira   sotan... tedo ira   sotan tep*
    and when caught they them those   three they those because
    [kinebsil sha i eshom; eg   sha sina-kop].
    let/slip they others not they overtake
    'And when they captured them... there were three of them,
    because [they had let the others get away; they didn't catch them].'

2.3. *Simultaneous Sentence*

The Simultaneous Sentence (see Table IV) consists of two or three bases
chained together with intervening Simultaneous Link expounded by *jey*
'while', 'at the same time', 'and'. Examples of three-base sentences are rare.
The bases may permute. Primarily this sentence type encodes deep structure
Overlap of which two varieties can be distinguished on the basis of surface
grammar encoding (stated in terms of two-base sentences): (1) With the
second base encoding a continuum (a continuous activity or state) and the
first encoding either a coterminous continuum or an event which takes place
during the continuum encoded in the second base. (2) With the first base
encoding a continuum during which the event encoded in the second base
takes place. This sentence type may also include, however, Succession. By

choice of this surface structure, successive events so encoded are conceptualized as being in close sequence, or taking place at roughly the same time (much like the English 'about the time that...', or 'as soon as'). The Simultaneous Sentence may also encode differing predicates (in this case descriptives) with the same subject. Coupling of this sort is regularly encoded as a Coordinate Sentence. Two varieties of Paraphrase – one with a generic predication followed by a specific and another with a predication followed by the negated antonym have also been observed as encoded in this sentence type. In these latter non-chronological uses *jey* is apparently used to emphasize logical rather than chronological connections.

English encodes Overlap in varied ways, e.g. via the subordinating conjunction 'while' or by means of structures embedded in noun phrases 'at the time that' or 'about the time that' or by means of 'during' plus a nominalized clause.

TABLE IV

Simultaneous sentence

+ Base₁ (Action₁)	+ Sim Lk	+ Base₂ (Action₂)	±[+ Sim Lk	+ Base₃ (Action₃)]
Ind Cl Simple S	*jey*	Ind Cl Simple S Dir Quote S	*jey*	(probably the same as Base₂,
Overlap P̲	∧	Q̲		but only examples
P̣	∧	Q̲		here are:
P̲	∧	Q̣		P ∧ Q ∧ R)
Succession P̣	∧	Q̣(Cf. Eventuation S)		
Coupling Pa	∧	Qa (Cf. Coord. S)		
Paraphrase gP̥	∧	sP̥ (Cf. Paraph. S)		
Pa	∧	P̥̄′ (Cf. Paraph..S)		

Rule: Bases may permute.

2.3.1. With Base₂ encoding a continuous action or state and Base₁ encoding either an event which takes place during that continuum (Overlap), P ∧ Q̲ or a coterminous continuum (Overlap), P̲ ∧ Q̲. Examples 1–2 are P̣ ∧ Q̲, and 3–4 are P̲ ∧ Q̣.

1   *Idi emengenop, [naogip i asawa to jey emenoso'y nga-nga].*
       when hunting   sleep   wife   his   nursing   baby

'While he was hunting, [his wife went to sleep while the baby was nursing].'

2   *Eg metakwaban* **jey** *nandabos kita.*
         not be/opened   naked   we
         'No one opens (the door) when they're naked.'

3   *...Kaonnanginangis* **jey** *kaontiyetiyed ja ondaw da nodta baley*
             kept/crying   climbing   go   to   house
         shi Bayojok.
         of
         '...He kept on crying as he was climbing up to the house of Bayojok's family.'

4   *Jet kaonshalashalang sota disdis   ni dagidab,* **jey** *kaondisdisdis*
         and blazing/on   the shavings of reeds   cleaning
         ngo ni dagidab.
         also   reeds
         'And the shavings of the reeds blazed on, while he kept on cleaning the reeds.'

2.3.2. With Base$_1$ encoding a continuous activity or state and Base$_2$ encoding an event which takes place within the continuum encoded in Base$_1$, $\underline{P} \wedge \underset{.}{Q}$.

1   *Marama nontan nin*   *i shaka pengenap ni kabosol sha,*
         current then   for/a/while they looking   enemies their
         jey *on-akarak ali'd jay.*
             go/home-I here here
         'At that time they were looking for their enemies, and I came home.'

2   *Kamika mesa-pat ma* **jey** *ibonget ko's Itengan da...*
         we   up/above   angry/at I
         'We had gone uphill a little when I got very angry at Itengan...'

3   *Wara ni pinsak, wara'y asawa to'd   naydaem* **jey** *onmotok ali'y*
         was   once was wife his-at inside   arrived here
         apo to'n toray – sota kowan sha la ey commission – ja manbisita
         boss his rulers   the say   they   visit
         ni iskowida.
             school/children
         'Once his wife was inside (his house) when his superiors arrived – what they call a commission – to visit the school children.'

2.3.3. With the bases encoding events in immediate chronological succession, P ∧ Q:

1 *Shaka iba-jat* **jey** *inbes-ig*   *sha; shaka iba-jat*
   they   hang/up   drop/violently they they   hang/up
   jey *inbes-ig*   *sha.*
       drop/violently they
   'They would lift (them) up by a rope and drop (them) violently to
   the ground; they did this repeatedly.' (The two events, the
   lifting and the dropping, obviously occur in chronological
   sequence, but the two actions are probably conceptualized by the
   speaker as taking place in roughly the same time span.)

2 *Nem   inewat   nonta kowan sha ey mengan,* [*toka ewata*
   when received the   say   they   eat   he   received
   jey *ikespig tola'd ma bo-day*].
       throw he-to   ground
   'When the person they intended to eat received (the food they
   sent), [he received it and then threw it on the ground].'

3 *Inanbakoit ta emin i too   nontan,* **jey** *onmotok ma ali'y Kastil.*
   evacuated all   people there   arrived   here Spanish
   '(When the warning was received), all the people evacuated (to the
   mountains), and the Spanish arrived.' (In this example, the
   people had no sooner reached safety in the mountains when the
   Spanish soldiers came into view down the valley.)

2.3.4. The following examples of Simultaneous Sentences encode a deep
structure, Pa ∧ Qa, which is usually encoded as a Coordinate Sentence:

1 *Kamo ni inaypi-ket shima debeng et, eg   kita makasapol:* [*debeng*
   if   wedged   in-the deep   not we able/find   deep
   jey *shakel i shanom*].
       much   water
   'If the (drowned man's body) is wedged in the deep water, we
   won't be able to find it: [it is deep and the river is high.]'

2 *Si Dabonay da, ekayang* **jey** *ebadeg...*
                 tall   big
   'Dabonay, she was tall, and she was big...'

2.3.5. The following examples of Simultaneous Sentence encode a deep
structure which is usually encoded as Paraphrase Sentence. Examples 1–2 have
negated antonyms in Base$_2$; example 3 is Generic-Specific. Examples 2 and 3
are Simultaneous Sentences embedded in Conditional Margins:

1   *Inpanejaw sha, nem* [*kini-toan to* **jey** *eg to intoloy   i tayaw*].
     had/dance they but cut/short he   not he continue   dance
     'They had him dance the *tayaw*, but [he cut short the dance and
     did not continue it].'

2   *Sama kantong, no* [*maykagsha'y batang   to niman* **jey** *eg pay*
     the   if prematurely cut/down its now   not yet
     epospos i ogso   to], *kenshat   ta mapteng i dowem   to.*
     used/up blossom its necessarily   good   ripeness its
     'The *kantong* banana, if [it is cut down prematurely, that is
     before its blossom is fully absorbed], it is certain to be nice and
     ripe.'

3   *No* [*shakel* l*c pasia*, **jey** *wara'y epat ta polo'n kaban*], *mi*
     if   much   very   is   four   tens cavans we
     odopen i truck jet ikalka mi'd ma anian.
     fetch   and load we-in the place/to/harvest.
     'If [there is a great amount, that is there are forty cavans], we
     fetch a truck and load it on in the field.'

2.4. *Coordinate Sentence*

The Coordinate Sentence (see Table V) couples two or three sentence bases
by means of *tan* 'and' which links the bases. Coupling thus encoded in the
Coordinate Sentence semantically is noncommittal in contrast to more
specific modes of relating bases such as parallelism, paraphrase, contrast,
temporal succession, and temporal overlap. The Coordinate link *tan*
typically couples predications that are distinct but from the same lexical
domain, e.g. 'old' and 'tough'; 'scorched' and 'thirsty'; 'be sickly' and
'won't get rich'; and 'don't know' and 'be afraid'. Terms of the predications
may be identical (Pa ∧ Qa) or different (Pa ∧ Qb). Sometimes the latter are
resultant on partitioning the universal set by means of *eshom* 'some' ...
eshom 'others'. Examples with more than two bases are rare; it is assumed
that there is no structural distinction in exponents of the bases of three-base
Coordinate Sentences as opposed to those with but two bases.

A few scattered examples of Coordinate Sentence encode deep structures
more typically encoded as other sentence types. Thus example 1 in 2.4.3
has a medial *tan* but does not couple distinct predications but rather identical
ones. In that the set of terms which marks subject has distinct members in the
two predications, P(a) ∧ P(b), it is evident that the deep structure encoded
here is that found regularly in the Parallel Sentence. A chiastic arrangement
breaks up, however, the parallelism which is at any rate de-emphasized by
encoding as a Coordinate Sentence. The example in 2.4.5 encodes situational

antonyms ('forest' versus ' living there') with negation of the second antonym – exactly as in the Paraphrase Sentence which regularly encodes such structures. By resorting to coordination in this sentence, the paraphrase is de-emphasized. A further example in 2.4.4 encodes contrastive material, i.e. antonyms, of the sort usually encoded in the Antithetical Sentence; here contrast is de-emphasized. Other examples of Coordinate Sentence clearly reflect situations in which chronological succession is involved; by choice of the Coordinate Sentence for surface structure encoding, the chronological succession is not treated as focal.

The English Coordinate Sentence with 'and' is also quite receptive of varied deep structure encodings. On reinforcing 'and' to 'and then' the English Coordinate Sentence regularly expresses Succession. In general, however, English Sentence types do not make time as focal a consideration as does Inibaloi.

TABLE V

Coordinate sentence

$+ \text{Base}_1(\text{Head}_1)$	$+ \text{Coor Lk}$	$+ \text{Base}_2(\text{Head}_2)$	$\pm [+ \text{Coor Lk} + \text{Base}_3(\text{Head}_3)]$	
Ind Cl Simple S Simult S	*tan*	Ind Cl Simple S	*tan*	Probably as for Base₁
Coupling	Pa ∧	Qa		
	Pa ∧	Qb		
	P(a) ∧	P(b) (Cf. Parallel S)		
Paraphrase	Pa ∧	P̄"a (Cf. Paraph. S)		
Contrast	P(a) ∧	P"(b) (Cf. Anti S)		
Succession	Pa ∧	Qa (Cf. Sequence S)		

Bases may permute

2.4.1. Coupling of different predicates with same terms, Pa ∧ Qa:

1   *Nasnaskitan shi shontog*   **tan** *nassho'n pasia.*
     scorched   on mountain and thirsty   very
     'He was scorched by the sun on the mountain, and he was very thirsty.'

2   *Naka mannengis tep*   [*enshi'y kenen ko* **tan** *ayshi'y*
     I   crying   because none   eat   I   none
     panbaljan   *ko.*]
     place/to/live my
     'I am crying because [I have nothing to eat and no place to live].'

2.4.2. Coupling of different predicates with different terms, Pa ∧ Qb:

1   *Ipadtian   to ira   ni nowang ono baka,* **tan** *menginat ira   ni*
        butcher/for he them   carabao or cow and lead   they
        baka tan nowang   ja iakad   sha.
        cow and carabao   take/home they
        'He was to butcher for them a carabao or cow, and they were to
        lead a cow and carabao with them home.'

2   *Wara ma'y anak   sha, jet [etoling i eshom* **tan** *ediyag*
        was   children their and dark   some and cross-eyed
        i eshom].
        some
        'They had children, and [some were dark-skinned and some were
        cross-eyed]'.

2.4.3. The following two examples of Coordinate Sentence encode a deep
structure, P(a) ∧ P(b), which is usually encoded as Parallel Sentence. The
parallelism is broken by a transposition of elements in Base₂:

1   *Jet sota pingkan ja panganan sha, balitok* **tan** *balitok i damisaan.*
        and the plate   eat/on   they gold   and gold   table
        'And the plates they ate on were gold, and the table was gold.'

2   *Enshi kono'y an esharasharal,* **tan** *sota naytowen na salaw,*
        none hearsay   destroyed   the standing   rice/wine/jar
        enshi'y an etowang.
        none   overturned
        'They say there was nothing (in the house) that was damaged,
        and the rice wine jars that were standing, none were overturned.'
        (This example is not well-formed in that while the predicates
        are close synonyms, they are not identical.)

2.4.4. The following example of Coordinate Sentence encodes a deep structure (Contrast), P(a) ∧ P″(b), which is usually encoded as Antithetical
Sentence:

1   *Jet emin na too,   iraka man-obda nem   onbolan* **tan** *iraka*
        and all   people they working when moon   and they
        maokip nem   onsekit.
        sleep   when sun/shines
        'And all the people, they would work when the moon was out,
        and they would sleep when the sun was out.'

2.4.5. The following example of Coordinate Sentence encodes a deep structure (Negated Antonym), Pa ∧ P̄"a, which is usually encoded as Paraphrase Sentence:

1   *Nonta bayag   da, ja [kakadasan iyay ja dogad* **tan** *ayshi'y*
       long/ago   forest   this   place and none
      nanbaley], shakel i baay.
       living   many   vines
      'Long ago when [this place was a forest and no one lived here],
      there were many vines.' (Although we do not get the expected
      identity of terms.)

2.4.6. The following example of Coordinate Sentence encodes deep structure (Temporal Succession), Pa ∧ Qa, which is usually encoded as Sequence, Addition, or Temporal Margin plus Nucleus:

1   *Say mapteng, on-akad kayo nin,* **tan** *no kabasan,   daw*
       good   go/home you first and   tomorrow come
      kayo di.
       you here
      'What is good, you all go home for now, and tomorrow, come
      back here.' (That this is an unusual encoding of Temporal
      Succession is evidenced by the fact that when the text from which
      this sentence was taken was edited for use in literacy, the surface
      encoding was changed from a Coordinate Sentence to an Addition
      Sentence.)

2.5. *Eventuation Sentence*

The Eventuation Sentence (see Table VI) encodes temporal Succession between two or more bases which are linked by *asan* 'and then'. No more than four such bases have been found linked into an eventuation sentence. In many examples of two base structures, it is evident that the first predication indicates some sort of time span or series of activities or events on completion of which the event encoded in the second predication takes place. Even in examples that do not indicate such span or activity complex in the first base it seems implied that the action encoded in the second base is contingent on completion of what is encoded in the first base. This sentence then seems to imply 'Activity A completed, then B'. In the deep structure component of the tagmemic apparatus we assume either a span-event with same subject, or event-event with the same subject. The only extant example of a four-base structure seems to encode span-span-span-event.

The special rules at the bottom of the apparatus state tactical constraints essential to a well-formed Eventuation Sentence.

TABLE VI

Eventuation sentence

+Base$_1$(Anterior)	+Ev Lk	+Base$_2$(Subsequent$_1$)...	±[+Ev Lk	+Base$_n$(Subsequent$_n$)]
Ind Cl Simple S Dir Quote S	*asan*	Ind Cl Simple S	*asan*	Ind Cl Simple S Ind Quote S
Succession $\underline{\text{Pa}}$ $\underset{\bullet}{\text{Pa}}$	$\wedge$ $\wedge$	$\underset{\bullet}{\text{Qa}}$ $\underset{\bullet}{\text{Qa}}$		The only example of a multi-based Event S is: $\underline{\text{P}} \wedge \underline{\text{Q}} \wedge \underline{\text{R}} \wedge \underline{\text{S}} \wedge \underset{\bullet}{\text{T}}$

Rules: 1. Exponent *asan* of Ev Lk attracts the subjects pronoun in the clause in the following base.
2. Tense is usually progressive in the clause in the base that follows *asan*, and there is a special set of morphophonemic rules.

2.5.1. With bases encoding a span followed by an event, $\underline{\text{Pa}} \wedge \underset{\bullet}{\text{Qa}}$:

1 *Esolokan i tedo'n polo'n akew asan shaka ibka.*
more three tens days they bury
'(The mummifying) would go more than thirty days, and then they would bury him.'

2 *Nandigat ira ni ekal nonta pagey nin asan shaka*
had/difficulty they taking/away the rice first they
ekala mowan i kiyew jet asdeg to'n ebadeg.
take/away again wood and fairly big
'They had difficulty taking off the rice first, and then they took off also the wood (beams), and they were fairly large.'

2.5.2. With bases encoding two punctiliar events, $\underset{\bullet}{\text{Pa}} \wedge \underset{\bullet}{\text{Qa}}$:

1 *Inkowan nonta imok ey,* [*Menongpitak nin asan naka*
said the mosquito whistle-I first and/then I
kaleta'y kemkemti].
bite firefly
'The mosquito said, ["I will whistle first, and then I will sting the firefly"].'

2.5.3. The following five-base sentence encodes span-span-span-span-event, $\underline{\text{P}} \wedge \underline{\text{Q}} \wedge \underline{\text{R}} \wedge \underline{\text{S}} \wedge \underset{\bullet}{\text{T}}$: [13a]

[13a] This footnote is to be found on p. 118.

1   *No   akaotan i kaybebkaan   ni tokod, mengisepat ira   ni*
              when dug/out place/to/bury of post   raise   they
              inam-am   jet   menginom ira ni tapey,   asan   shaka
              floor/beam and drink   they   rice/wine and/then they
              isepat i baniwal,   jet   no   alasshosi, menginom mowan ira
              raise   ceiling/beam and when noon   drink   again   they
              ni tapey,   asan   iraka mangan, ja sid-an sha ma sota aso
              rice/wine and/then they eat   eat   they   the dog
              ono kanshing, asan   shaka itodoy   mowan i kayang ni
              or goat   and/then they continue again   raising of
              baniwal   nem meksheng ira'n mengan ni alasshosi, tan
              ceiling/beam when finish   they eat   at noon   and
              ikayang sha'y kalosod tan dekatan   sha, asan   shaka atpi.
              raise   they rafters and cross-piece they and/then they   roof
              'When the postholes are dug, they raise the floor beams, and they
              drink rice wine; then they raise the ceiling beams, and when it is
              noon, they drink rice wine again; then they eat, feeding on the
              dog or goat (provided by the owner of the house); then they
              continue raising the ceiling beams after the noon meal, and they
              raise the rafters, and they put on the cross-pieces to which the
              roofing is attached; and then they roof (the house).' (Base$_1$ and
              Base$_2$ are expounded by an embedded Addition Sentence, Base$_3$
              by a Paraphrase Sentence, Base$_4$ by a Coordinate Sentence of
              three bases, and Base$_5$ by an independent clause.)

2.6. *Sequence Sentence*

The Sequence Sentence (see Table VII) encodes two or more events in chronological Succession. With some frequency more than two bases occur. The subject is the same in all bases. This distinguishes the Sequence Sentence from, e.g., the Parallel Sentence where subjects are frequently different in that it is required in the successive bases that one set of terms must differ from base to base.

The English sentence 'I came, I saw, I conquered' corresponds rather closely to the Sequence Sentence of Inibaloi. This particular example is, however, a translation from Latin. Whether such constructions are frequent and native to English enough to warrant our setting up a similar sentence type in English is another question. I have considered that, granting sufficient parallelism of structure in an English Coordinate Sentence, the conjunction *and* could be omitted and that resultant structures are but variations of the Coordinate Sentence.

TABLE VII

Sequence sentence

+ Base$_1$ (Event$_1$)	+ Base$_2$ (Event$_2$) ...		+ Base$_n$ (Event$_n$)
Ind Cl	Ind Cl		Ind Cl
		Ind Quote S	
Simple S	Simple S		Simple S
Succession Pa ∧	Qa	... ∧	Na

2.6.1. Several bases encoding a sequence of punctiliar events:
Pa ∧ Qa ∧ ... ∧ Na.

1   *Sikmaten nen Governor Gaelan itan na solat; binasa to;*
     catch   that   letter read   he
     in-oli   to di   sotan na solat.
     brought/back he here that   letter
     'Gov. Gaelan received the letter; he read it; he returned it personally here.'

2   *Dayta, tinopik   sota ketap   ko; sina-shad   ko; kowan ko ey*
     that   folded-I the blanket my over/shoulder I   say   I
     si-kak i ondaw.
        I   go
     'At that, I folded up my blanket; I threw it over my shoulder; I said I would be the one to go.'

3   *Kina-jat   sha sota toktok; inbonong   sha.*
     took/from/water they the   head   prayed/over they
     'They took the head out (of the caldron); they prayed over it.'

2.7. *Addition Sentence*

The Addition Sentence (see Table VIII) consists of two or more bases chained together with intervening Additional Link expounded by *jet* 'and', 'in addition'. Primarily this Sentence type encodes two deep structures: (1) Succession of events (or rarely, event-span) with either the same term as subject or with the second term of the first predication as subject of the second predication. Multi-based structures are exclusively of this variety. Three- and four-base structures may be explained as combinations of Pa ∧ Qa and of Pab ∧ Qb in some recognizable pattern, e.g. Pa ∧ Qab ∧ Rab ∧ Sb in four-base sentences. (2) Efficient Cause in which two-base structures encode the logical antecedent as Base$_1$ and the logical consequent as Base$_2$. The extant examples of the latter Base$_1$ refer to a state, often emotional.

Material that regularly goes into other sentence types occasionally encodes as surface structure with medial *jet*. Extant examples of such encodings include Paraphrase of the Identity-Equivalence variety, Coupling, and Existence-Predication. Use of *jet* in these varied encodings plus its more regular uses (here in this sentence type, and in the Identification Sentence) establish this conjunction as a very versatile semantic element. An alternative analysis to that here suggested would be to set up as subtypes of the following sentences the corresponding strings with medial *jet*: Paraphrase, Coordinate, and Introduction. The conjunction *jet* is not, however, of frequent use with the deep structures regularly encoded in these sentence types.

This Inibaloi sentence type encodes deep structures most frequently encoded as the Coordinate Sentence in English.

TABLE VIII

Addition sentence

+ Base$_1$ (Statement)	+ Add Lk	+ Base$_2$ (Addition$_1$)...	± [+Add Lk	+ Base$_n$(Addition$_n$)]
Ind Cl	*jet*	Ind Cl	*jet*	Ind Cl
Simple S		Simple S		
Coordinate S		Dir Quote S		
		Paraph. S		
Succession	Pa ∧	Qa		Multi-based
	Pab ∧	Qb		sentences up to three
				and four bases, e.g.
				Pa ∧ Qab ∧ Rab ∧ Sb
Efficient Cause	P ∧	[P ⊃ Q]		
Paraphrase	Pa ∧	P′a (Cf. Paraph. S)		
Coupling	Pa ∧	Qa (Cf. Coord. S)		
Existence-predication	∃Pa ∧	[Pa ≡ Pba] (Cf. Intro. S)		

2.7.1. With bases encoding successive events, Pa ∧ Qa:

1   *Kinidkiran sha'y kambang sha,* **jet** *indoto sha sota biyog.*
     scraped they pots their cooked they the soot
     'They scraped their pots and cooked the soot (from them).'

2   *Binoshasan sha sota kapi* **jet** *indaw sha'd San Fernando.*
     harvested they the coffee took they-to San Fernando
     'They harvested the coffee and took it to San Fernando.'

2.7.2. With bases encoding reciprocal events in which the goal of the first base is the actor in the second base, Pab ∧ Qb:

1   *In-oran   sha* **jet** *idi   nalbeng, timolok   sota bii.*
put/in/rain they and when wet   consented the girl
'They put her out in the rain, and when she was wet, the girl consented.'

2   *Sota aasawa sha   ngo, itakin   sha* **jet** *iraka menedos.*
the wives   their also take/along they   they cleaning
'Their wives as well, they took (them) along, and they would clean (the rice terrace walls).'

2.7.3. With multiple bases involving both succession and reciprocity (as in 2.7.1 and 2.7.2).

1   *Kasoreng kono   ondetep kono   ngo* **jet** *simbi   to'd ma*
finally   hearsay dived   hearsay also and reached he-in the
shanom, ja nanpi-ket   shima diyang shi shanom **jet**
water   wedged/himself in   cave in water and
inteded   (to) kono **jet** *dimekeng shima shanom.*
held/down he hearsay and bloated in-the water
'Finally he dived in too and reached him in the water, wedged in a cave under the water, and he held him under the water, and he became bloated in the water.'

2   *…Kowan sha, ka di   pangotkot ni dokto   shima despag*
say   they you here dig   camote at-that below
shima inon-an tayo **jet** *mengan kito* **jet** *on-oli kito'n emin.*
at-that saw   we   eat   we   return we   all
'…They said, "Go dig camote down below at that (place) we saw, and we will eat, and we will all return (home)".'

2.7.4. The following examples of Addition Sentence encode that deep structure (Efficient Cause) which is usually encoded as Cause Margin, $P \wedge [P \supset Q]$:

1   *Timakot kono   ira* **jet** *inay-olop   ali   sha.*
afraid   hearsay they   taken/along here they
'They were afraid, they said, and they (consented to) come along here.'

2   *Teg-in na pasia* **jet** *nanngaran ima shontog   ni empoti; esa-keban*
cold   very   turned/to   mountain white covered
ni empoti'n emin, ja sota kowan tayo ey angshap.
white   all   the say   we   frost
'It was very cold, and that mountain turned white; it was covered by white completely - what we call "frost".' (Base$_2$ is expounded by an embedded Paraphrase Sentence.)

3   *Diningketan sha* jet *siged.*
     sweetened   they   good
     'They sweetened it, and it was good.'

2.7.5. The following Addition Sentences encode deep structure that is usually encoded as other sentence types: Paraphrase Sentence (example 1), Introduction Sentence (example 2), Coordinate Sentence, i.e. Coupling (example 3):

1   *Inandabos kono*   jet *ingkal   to'n emin i baro   to.*
     naked   hearsay   removed she all   clothes her
     'She was naked, and she had removed all her clothes.'

2   *Wara'y epakdal   la sais,* jet *intomkal   to ni binangday.*
     was   left/over   10¢   used/to/buy he   rice/cake
     'There were ten centavos left over, and he used it to buy rice cakes.'

3   *Makelting kono   tan ekayang,* jet *enshokey kono'y   bowek to.*
     pretty   hearsay and tall   long   hearsay hair   her
     'She was pretty and she was tall, and her hair was long.' (Base$_1$ is expounded by an embedded Coordinate Sentence.)

2.8. *Antithetical Sentence*

The Antithetical Sentence (see Table IX) consists of two opposed bases optionally joined by *nem* or *nem ag* 'but' or by *jey* 'while, but'. It is convenient to add exponent $\emptyset$ in cases when neither link is present. There are several distinct subtypes, not all of which take the full set of exponents, *nem* (*ag*), *jey*, and $\emptyset$ – symbolized as ⟨*nem*⟩ in the apparatus.

Antithetical Sentences which encode deep structure Contrast are of three varieties: (1) Those with same or different predicates in the two bases and a contrasting pair of terms but with an overt negative in the first base; and with medial *nem* or *jey*; (2) those with a pair of antonyms or situational opposites in both bases and a contrasting pair of terms with any exponent of link; and (3) those with identical predicates in the two bases, with a negative and a reference to the universal set as a term in the first base, and with a deleted predicate with a corresponding term which is a member of the universal set ('No one spoke up but Fianza') in the second base. The latter take exponents *jey* and $\emptyset$ of link. A further variety (4) of Antithetical Sentence encodes a deep structure Paraphrase of the negated antonym – antonym variety, $\bar{P}''a \wedge Pa$. That this is truly an Antithetical Sentence is seen in the fact that it shares with subvarieties (1) and (3) above a negative in its first base. Three other varieties of Antithetical Sentence encode deep structure Frustration (Implication). In subvariety (5) a chain of logical or temporal expectancy is presupposed ($P \supset Q$) but in place of the expected logical or temporal consequence we get a predication with the contrary positive-negative value, as in 'I looked for it but couldn't find it' where 'looking' normally anticipates 'finding'. This variety occurs with all exponents of antithetical link. With the permutation of the Thesis and Antithesis in the surface structure we get (6) another subvariety of this sentence type in which only *jey* expounds link. A further subvariety (7) of which there are only a few examples involves a bringing-together of premises which mutually conflict in that they imply contradictory consequents. Thus, while $P \supset Q$ and $R \supset \bar{Q}$, both P and R may be encoded as an Antithetical Sentence. This subvariety has antithetical link expounded only by *jey*.

The deep structures here described encode also as the English Antithetical Sentence. Structure (3) also encodes regularly in English by means of the preposition word 'except'. English is parallel to Inibaloi in its use of 'while' in Antithetical Sentences.

TABLE IX

Antithetical sentence

+ Base₁ (Thesis)		± Anti Lk	+ Base₂ (Antithesis)
Ind Cl		*nem (ag)*	Ind Cl
Any S type		*jey*	Simple S
		(ø)	Add. S
			Simult. S
Contrast	$\bar{P}(a)$	∧ *nem/jey*	$[P(b) \not\equiv Q(b)]$
	$P(a)$	∧ ⟨*nem*⟩	$P''(b)$
	$P(\overline{U-a})$	∧ *jey*/ø	$P(a) \wedge (a \in U)$
Paraphrase	$\bar{P}''a$	∧ ⟨*nem*⟩	P_a
Frustration	$(P \supset Q) \wedge P$	∧ ⟨*nem*⟩	Q_β
	$(P \supset Q) \wedge (R \supset \bar{Q}) \wedge P$	∧ *jey*	R

Rule: When Anti. Lk: *jey* and when $(P \supset Q) \wedge P \wedge Q_\beta$, then P and Q_β may permute.

2.8.1. With an overt negative in Base₁ (Contrast), $\bar{P}(a) \wedge [P(b) \not\equiv Q(b)]$

1   *Eg onpatok shi kagaban   ja maykemot shi eshom*
    not roost in chicken/house mix   into other
    ma manok, **nem** *si-kato, kaonpatok shi kadasan ja nay-askang*
        chicken but he   roosts   in tree   adjacent
    shi kagaban.
    to chicken/house.
    'He would not roost in the chicken house with the other chickens,

but him, he roosted in a tree that was near the chicken house.'
(In this example the chicken house is contrasted with the tree
near the chicken house as a roosting place. The first predication
is negated.)

2   *Ekak met   ninemanemat i baliw   niyay ja shanom,* **nem**
    not-I emphatic try   crossing of-the   river   but
    si-kato'y kaonbaliw ni olay ja kaonsabi son si-kak.
    she   crossed   always   reach   me
    'I never once tried to cross this river, but she was the one who
    always crossed to come to me.'

3   *Eg to kono   ininat sotan na animal,* **jey** *songpit kono'y*
    not he hearsay lead   those   whistle hearsay
    timawal   son si-kara.
    summoned   them
    'He did not lead those animals with ropes, but (his) whistle was
    what called them.' (The two predicates in this example are quasi-
    synonyms. The contrast is between 'led the animals with ropes'
    and 'use of a whistle'.)

2.8.2. With pair of antonyms or situational opposites in both bases (Contrast), $P(a) \wedge P''(b)$:

1   *Nem idi   edakay ira, eg ira   onposi,* **nem** *sota talaw,*
    but when old/men they not they able   but the stars
    imonong   ira'n marikit tan makedsang.
    remained they young and strong
    'But when they were old, they were feeble, but the stars, they
    remained young and strong.' (Here, 'old' and 'feeble' are con-
    trasted with their antonyms 'young' and 'strong', as well as
    'human beings' with 'stars'.)

2   *Kasta   met i si-kami'n iBenguet,   abos mi'n nankebay-an;*
    likewise   we   Benguet/people only   left
    enshi la ira   sota kait   mi.
    not   they the companions our
    'Likewise those of us from Benguet, we are the only ones left; our
    companions are all gone (i.e. dead).'

2.8.3. With identical predicates in the two bases, with a negative and a
reference to the universal set in $Base_1$ and with the exception to the universal
negation given in $Base_2$, $P(\overline{U-a}) \wedge P(a) \wedge (a \in U)$:

1   *Enshi et   kono'y sha ibayad **jey** anak to'n kaoshirianan ja*
             none instead hearsay they pay/with   child his youngest
             naoges.
             ugly
             'There was nothing they had to pay for it with but his youngest
             child who was ugly.'

2   *Enshi et   kono i an   onbaliw **jey** sota dabas.*
             none instead hearsay go/to cross/river   the sow
             'None crossed the river except the sow.'

3   *Wara'y sakey ja too shi Tinek ja edapo ali'd   Tokokan, ja*
             is   one   man in   from here-from
             nanngaran ni Itip; an   enganop, jet [ayshi an   bintik nonta
             named   go/to hunt   and none go/to run/to
             *kabajan na olsa ja inenopan to **jey** shiyay ali...]*
             female   deer   hunting he   here this/direction
             'There was a man in Tinek who was from Tokokan, whose name
             was Itip. He went hunting, and [the deer he was chasing came no
             place but here...]'

2.8.4. With Base₁ encoding a negated antonym of the Predicator of Base₂ (Paraphrase), $\bar{P}''a \wedge Pa$:

1   *Jet eg kono   inanpiging ni inkaysepa to shima bajisbisan,*
             and not hearsay   tilted   landing   its at-the under/eaves
             nem *inandeteg kono...*
             but straight   hearsay
             'It was not tilted when it landed under the eaves, but it was
             straight...' (In this example, 'tilted' is an antonym of 'straight'
             but is itself negated.)

2   *No mankosdey ira, shaka ibonong so nen Matong ja [eg to*
             if feast   they they pray   to   not she
             *ipalobos i pagey, dokto, tan eshom ja ondeshek, **nem***
             allow   rice camote and other   go/deep but
             pan-itapew   to et   ira].
             keep/on/surface she instead them
             'When they celebrate *kosdey*, they pray to Matong that [she not
             allow the rice, camotes, and other (plants) to go deep (where the
             underworld people will get them), but rather that she cause them
             to stay on the surface instead].' (Here, 'go deep' is the negation of
             'stay on the surface', but 'go deep' is itself negated.)

3   *Kowan to ey Ayshi, eg tayo bonoen ira;   may-idaw ira'd*
say   he   no   not we kill   them taken   they-to
Trinidad.
'He said, "No, we won't kill them; they will be taken to Trinidad".'

2.8.5. With a frustration of the logical or temporal sequence, $(P \supset Q) \wedge$
$\wedge P \wedge Q_\beta$:

1   *Kinedked ko'y bokdew ko,* **nem** *ekak etey.*
cut   I   throat my but not-I die
'I cut my throat, but I didn't die.' (In this example, 'cutting one's
throat' presupposes dying, but this is negated in Base$_2$.)

2   *Idi   naksheng ira'y talaw ja nan-emes, inenap sha'y baro*
when finished they stars   bathing sought they clothes
sha, **nem** *eg sha simpol.*
their but   not they found
'When the stars had finished bathing, they looked for their
clothes, but they didn't find them.' ('Looked for' presupposes
finding, but this is negated.)

3   *Toka ikoyokoyod   kono* **jey** *eg ma-ma-kal.*
            continually/pulled hearsay   not come/loose
'He pulled and pulled, but it wouldn't come loose.'

4   *Jet emin-ano'n   kaondaw shi emanshidos; eg sha iaknan.*
and how/many/times went   to feast   not they give/to
'And many times he would go to feasts, (but) they wouldn't give
him (anything to eat).' (In Inibaloi culture it is assumed that
everybody attending a feast is fed, but this logical sequence is
negated in Base$_2$.)

2.8.6. With the same deep structure as 2.8.5 but with a permutation of
Thesis and Antithesis.

1   *Idi   on-an to [sotan na singa inay-apil i kapangani   nonta*
when see   he that   like different place/to/eat of/the
shaka bagbag-a, **jey** *pamiljara   metlaeng],   kowan nonta*
they send   family-their just/the/same say   the
pastol ey Sajay i naykontra shi bilin   nen Apo Shiyos.
pastor this   contrary to command of God
'When the pastor saw [that their servants ate in a different place,
in spite of the fact that they were relatives of theirs], he said, **"This**

is contrary to the commands of God".' (Here, the presupposition is that since they were relatives they should be accorded equal eating privileges, but this is not the case.)

2   *Shaka nenginengisi,* **jey** *powek   shi Nawal.*
        they   cried/for   typhoon at
        'They cried and cried for (the dead frog – which is taboo) in spite of the fact that it was during a typhoon at Nawal.' (Here, the danger from the typhoon implies care not to violate taboo, but instead the violation of the taboo is indicated in Base$_1$.)

2.8.7. With premises implying contradictory consequents, $(P \supset Q) \land \land (R \supset \bar{Q}) \land P \land R$:

1   *Nonta agsapa,   anet   onbaliwak shi shanom* **jey** *debeng i shanom.*
        morning almost cross-I   in water   deep   water
        'This morning, I was about to cross the river, but the river was deep (i.e. I didn't cross).'

2.9. *Alternative Sentence*

The Alternative Sentence (see Table X) consists of two or more bases joined by the Alternative Link expounded by *ono* 'or'. There is frequent ellipsis within the second base of interrogative Alternative Sentences.

When alternation is encoded in this sentence type, more than two bases may not occur when the second base contains a predicate that is the negation of the first base. With an alternation that turns on choice of corresponding terms, or choice of predicates, or choice of temporal or spatial modifiers, a further base or bases is possible, provided that the lexical items involved do not imply an excluded middle, i.e. provided that they are not antonyms or situational opposites.

This sentence type also encodes paraphrase of the Identity-Equivalence type, i.e. paraphrase which involves synonyms. Here, as in English, an Inibaloi speaker (especially common in oratory) may pile up synonyms connected with 'or' – much as if an unstated 'or in other words...' or 'we might say...' were involved.

Again, English Alternative Sentence is quite parallel to the Inibaloi structure here described and illustrated. One use of the English Alternative Sentence, that of encoding Warning, is unlike Inibaloi: 'Better not let our torches go out or we will have a hard time finding our way home'. This encodes not as an Inibaloi Alternative Sentence but as a Result Sentence (not illustrated in this paper) in which the connective exposing 'result' here comes to mean 'otherwise'.

TABLE X

Alternative sentence

+ Base$_1$ (Alternative$_1$)	+ Alt Lk	+ Base$_2$ (Alternative$_2$)...	±[+ Alt Lk	+ Base$_n$ (Alternative$_n$)]
Ind Cl Simple S Ampl S Dir Quote S	*ono*	Ind Cl Simple S Sequence S Dir Quote S	*ono*	Ind Cl Simple S
Alternation with excluded middle { Pa Pa Pa Pax	# # # #	P̄a P″a Pa″ Pax″	...> ...> ...>	
Alternation without excluded middle { Pa Pa Pax	> > >	Qa Pb Pay	...> ...> ...>	Na Pn Pan
Paraphrase Pa Pa	< <	P'₁a P̄a	...<	P'$_n$a (Cf. Paraph. S) (Cf. Paraph. S)

2.9.1. Alternation examples 1–2 involve a negation in $Base_2$, $Pa \neq \bar{P}a$; example 3 has the same predicate in both bases (but deleted in second base), $Pa \vee Pb$; example 4 situationally involves only two alternatives, $Pa \neq Pa''$; examples 5–7 have differing predicates which belong to the same domain, $Pa \vee Qa$; examples 8 and 9 have the alternation turning on spatial or temporal relations, $Pax \vee Pay$. Further examples of excluded middle are not illustrated below.

1   *...Ikowan ma   ni dalakay ey Maytodoy, **ono** enshi?*
        say   now   old/men   continue   or not
        '...The old men would then say, "Shall we continue with it or not?"'

2   *Jet mengidik   ka di   **ono** ayshi?*
        and half-thresh you here or   not
        'And will you thresh the rice and bring it here or not?'

3   *Si-kato'y on-elbat, **ono** si Malakas metlaeng?*
        he   transfer or   just/the/same
        'Will he be the one to take (the chickens) to his place, or will it be Malakas just the same?'

4   *Jet kaon-an   to nem [binediw ni daki, **ono** binediw ni bii].*
        and way/to/see if   crossed boy or   crossed girl
        'And (we) will see if [the boy crossed (the river), or the girl crossed (the river)].' (In the context, there were only two alternatives being considered, so this example implies an excluded middle.)

5   *Inkowan to nen Castro ey mesopol   ja [paelbat mo ma manok,*
        said   he to   necessary   transfer you chickens
        ono *al-en mo di].*
        or   bring you here
        'Castro said that it is necessary [for you to move (your) chickens or for you to bring them here].'

6   *No ngaaw i apko   masinakit ira tan eg ira onbaknang,*
        if bad   gall/bladder sickly   they and not they get/rich
        ono *sepnakan sha ni   sakey mowan na keshel.*
        or   feast/for they with one   again   pig
        'If the gall bladder gives a bad omen, they will be sickly and they will not get rich, or as an alternative, they celebrate *sepnak* for (the house) with another pig.'

7   *No memintedo ja sepnakan sha,* [*bebtikan   sha sota baley*
     if   three-times   feast/for they run/away/from they the house
     ono *a-tanen sha,* **ono** *idako sha   sotan na baley jet   mandeka*
     or   move   they or   sell   they that   house and make
     ira   mowan ni sakey ja bado].
     they again   one   new
     'If they celebrate *sepnak* three times for (the house and the omens
     are always bad), [they abandon the house, or they move it, or
     they sell the house and build another new one].' (In this example,
     the three bases show that there is no implication of an excluded
     middle.)

8   *No kasta,   Bagiw ali   shalnen mo   metlaeng   nem on-ali*
     if   like/that   here route   you just/the/same when return
     ka,   ono seventy-three?
     you or
     'If it's like that, will you come via Bagiw when you return, or
     (kilometer) 73?'

9   *Ima   pay* (*i*) *sawal   ni epat ta akew,* **ono** *esheshokey pay nem*
     there still   over/ten by four   days or   longer   still if
     wara'y kabaalan ni anak   to, no wara'y mebedin na mansilbi.
     is   ability   of children his if is   can   serve
     'There are (some funerals) that go fourteen days, or it is longer
     still if his children have the means, (and) if there are (animals) to
     serve.'

2.9.2. The following examples of Alternative Sentences encode deep structures which are usually encoded as Paraphrase Sentence. Examples 1 and 2
are of Identity-Equivalence Paraphrase, Pa $\wedge$ P$_1'$a $\wedge$ ... $\wedge$ P$_n'$a, and example 3
is of Paraphrase with a negated antonym in Base$_2$, Pa $\wedge$ P̄"a:

1   *Isonga   emin na partido   ni metey, iraka mengiopo,   **ono** iraka*
     therefore all   relatives of dead   they contributing   they
     mengioffer, **ono** *iraka mengi-kan shiya kadnan ni emetey...*
     offering   they giving   at   place of dead
     'Therefore all the relatives of the dead one, they are making
     funeral contributions, (*ono*) they are offering, (*ono*) they are
     giving at the house of the dead one...'

2   ...*Jet shi Benguet ali'y tosoka idakoi ni ketap   pa* [*toka*
        and in   here he   sell   blanket   he
     pedeka   ono toka pa-ebel].
     have/made   he   have/woven

'...And in Benguet here was where he would sell the blankets [that he had had made (*ono*) he had had woven].'

3   *Saman i kaon-anan no* [*mapteng nga too,*   **ono** *aliwa'n*
       that   way/to/see if good   person   not
       mangishas].
       lazy
       'That is the way to see if [he is a good person (*ono*) not lazy].'

3. DEEP STRUCTURE REVERSE INDEX AND DEFINITION OF SYMBOLS

3.1. In this section we summarize the deep structures which are mentioned in the previous two sections of this paper and indicate how they encode into surface structures. In that this is a reverse indexing of material given in the previous sections, it is given in outline form so as to make it as concise and useful as possible. The first surface structure listed indicates the most frequent encoding of each type of deep structure.

I.   Conjoining
     1. Coupling
        (1) $Pa \wedge Qa$ Coordinate, Simultaneous, Addition
        (2) $Pa \wedge Qb$ Coordinate
        (3) $P(a) \wedge P(b) \wedge ... \wedge P(n)$ Parallel, Coordinate
     2. Contrast
        (1) $\bar{P}(a) \wedge [P(b) \not\equiv Q(b)]$ Antithetical, Nucleus + Cause Margin$_2$
        (2) $P(a) \wedge P''(b)$ Antithetical, Coordinate
        (3) $P(\overline{U-a}) \wedge P(a) \wedge (a \in U)$ Antithetical
II. Paraphrase
     1. Affirmation
        (1) Identity-Equivalence
            $Pa \wedge [Pa \not\equiv P'a]$ Paraphrase, Addition
            $Pa \wedge Pa'$ Paraphrase, Nucleus + Cause Margin$_2$
            $Pa \wedge P'_1a \wedge P'_2a \wedge ... \wedge P'_na$ Alternative
        (2) Generic-Specific
            $gPa \wedge sPa$ Paraphrase, Simultaneous, Cause Margin$_1$ + Nucleus, Nucleus + Cause Margin$_2$
        (3) Specific-Generic
            $sPa \wedge gPa$ Paraphrase

(4) Statement-Specification

$$Pa \wedge \begin{cases} Pba \\ Pab \\ Pax \end{cases}$$ Paraphrase, Nucleus + Cause Margin$_2$

2. Negated Antonym

(1) Pa $\wedge$ P''a   Paraphrase, Simultaneous, Coordinate, Alternative

(2) P''a $\wedge$ Pa   Antithetical

III. Temporal

  1. Overlap

    (1) Coterminous

      P̲ $\wedge$ Q̲   Simultaneous, Temporal Margin + Nucleus, Nucleus + Conditional Margin$_2$

    (2) Punctiliar-continuous

      Ṗ $\wedge$ Q̲   Simultaneous, Temporal Margin + Nucleus

    (3) Continuous-punctiliar

      P̲ $\wedge$ Q̇   Simultaneous, Temporal Margin + Nucleus, Nucleus + Conditional Margin$_2$

  2. Succession

    (1) Span-event[14]

      P̄ $\wedge$ Q̇   Eventuation, Temporal Margin + Nucleus, Conditional Margin$_1$ + Nucleus

    (2) Event-event

      Pa $\wedge$ Qa $\wedge$ ... $\wedge$ Na   Sequence, Addition

      Ṗab $\wedge$ Qb   Addition

      Ṗ $\wedge$ Q̇   Eventuation, Simultaneous, Temporal Margin + Nucleus, Coordinate

    (3) Event-span

      Ṗ $\wedge$ Q̲   Temporal Margin + Nucleus

IV. Implication

  1. Realization

    (1) Hypothetical

[14] This same structure can be expanded to P̲ $\wedge$ Q̲ $\wedge$ R̲ $\wedge$ Ṡ.

$$P \supset Q$$

Conditional Margin$_1$ + Nucleus, Nucleus + Conditional Margin$_2$

(2) Contrafactual

$$P_\beta \wedge [P_\beta \supset Q_\beta] \wedge [P \supset Q]$$ Conditional Margin$_1$ + Nucleus

(3) Warning

$$(P \supset Q) \wedge \bar{P} \wedge Q$$ Result

(4) With universal quantifier of temporal or participant [15]

$$P_{\forall t} \supset Q$$ Conditional Margin$_1$ + Nucleus

$$P_{\forall(a)} \supset [Qa \not\equiv Q_{ba}]$$ Concessive Margin + Nucleus

(5) Contingency

$$[P \not\equiv \underline{P} \quad] \supset Q ; P \supset \underline{Q}$$ Contingency

2. Frustration

(1) Surprise

$$(P \supset Q) \wedge P \wedge R$$ Surprise

(2) Expectancy Reversal

$$(P \supset Q) \wedge P \wedge Q_\beta$$ Antithetical, Concessive Margin + Nucleus, Direction

(3) Conflicting Premises

$$(P \supset Q) \wedge (R \supset \bar{Q}) \wedge$$
$$\wedge P \wedge R$$
Antithetical, Concessive Margin + Nucleus

(4) Mistaken Idea

$$(Q_\beta) \wedge tP \wedge Q$$ Indirect Quote

3. Causation

(1) Efficient Cause

$$P \wedge [P \supset Q]$$ Cause Margin$_1$ + Nucleus, Nucleus + Cause Margin$_2$, Addition, Reason, Result, Contingency

(2) Final Cause

$$P \wedge [P \supset pQ]$$ Reason, Nucleus + Purpose Margin

$$Pa \wedge [Pa \supset pQa]$$ Direction

(3) Intent

$$iP \wedge Q$$ Indirect Quote

V.   Alternation (all subvarieties of this deep structure are encoded as Alternative Sentence) [16]

---

[15] The following two formulas could be used to distinguish accomplished implication from hypothetical implication: $P_{\forall t} \wedge [P_{\forall t} \supset Q]$, $P_{\forall a} \wedge [P_{\forall a} \supset Q]$. This distinction is not made here because there is no corresponding difference in the surface structure.

[16] Although not distinguished in Inibaloi, these three subvarieties have different surface structures in the Nii language of the Western Highlands District of New Guinea, as reported by Alfred Stucky of the Summer Institute of Linguistics.

1. With excluded middle (exclusive disjunction)
   (1) By negation
   $$Pa \not\equiv \bar{P}a$$
   (2) By antonym
   $$Pa \not\equiv P''a$$
   $$Pa \not\equiv Pa''$$
   $$Pax \not\equiv Pax''$$
2. Without excluded middle (inclusive disjunction)
   $$Pa \lor Pb \lor ... \lor Pn$$
   $$Pa \lor Qa \lor ... \lor Na$$
   $$Pax \lor Pay \lor ... \lor Pan$$

VI. Amplification
   1. Existence-predication
      $$\exists Pa \land [Qa \not\equiv Qba] \qquad \text{Introduction, Addition}$$
   2. Predication-equation
      $$Pab \land Ebc \qquad \text{Identification}$$

VII. Reporting
   1. Speech
      $$wP \land Q \qquad \text{Direct Quote, Indirect Quote, Indirect Question}$$
   2. Awareness
      $$aP \land Q \qquad \text{Indirect Quote, Indirect Question}$$
   3. Metalanguage
      $$cP \land Q \qquad \text{Indirect Quote}$$

3.2. *Definition of Symbols:*

$a \in U$	Term a is an element of set U.
a, b, ..., n	Terms of predicates, always written immediately to the right of the predication containing them.
x, y	Further predicate terms with a spacial or temporal function.
a'	Synonym or situational equivalent of term a.
a"	Antonym or situational opposite of term a.
Eab	Equational predication, "term a is b".
P, Q, R (but not U)	Predicates.[17] If terms have been assigned to some or all of the variables to form an acceptable statement, the result is called a predication. With no

---

[17] This is an attempt to follow the general use of 'predicate' in the predicate calculus as an expression containing variables such that an assignment of values results in a statement. The term predication is reserved for predicates to which some or all of the values have been assigned.

terms specified, predicate symbols without temporal quantifiers refer to the entire predication. With terms specified, they refer to the predicator only.

$\bar{P}$ Negation of predicate P.

P′   Predication involving a synonym or situational equivalent of a lexical item with the same function in P.

P″   Predication involving an antonym or situational opposite of a lexical item with the same function in P.

The following three symbols are used as temporal quantifiers of predicates:

$\underline{P}$ P denoting a non-punctiliar activity or state.

$\bar{P}$ P denoting a punctiliar event.

$\underline{\dot{P}} \wedge Q$ P denoting a non-punctiliar activity or state which overlaps in time with a punctiliar event in Q.

$P \supset Q$ If P, then Q.

Pa   P with first term (actor) a.

Pab   P with first term (actor) a, and a subsequent term b which may or may not function as goal.

$Pa \wedge Qb$ P with first term (actor) a, and Q with first term (actor) b, distinct from a. If no terms are specified in a predicate, it is understood that the actors may be either the same or different.

$Pa \wedge Qa$ P with first term (actor) a, and Q with the same first term (actor) a.

$P(a) \wedge P(b) \wedge \ldots \wedge P(n)$ Conjunction of n identical predications with non-identical terms having the same function in each predication.

P_β Operator$_\beta$ changes the positive-negative value of P so that every predicate in the expression takes one of the two values. For example, $[P_\beta \supset Q_\beta] \wedge$ $\wedge P \wedge Q$ means any one of the four possibilities: $[\bar{P} \supset \bar{Q}] \wedge P \wedge Q$, $[\bar{P} \supset Q] \wedge P \wedge \bar{Q}$, $[P \supset \bar{Q}] \wedge \bar{P} \wedge Q$, or $[P \supset Q] \wedge \bar{P} \wedge \bar{Q}$.

$P(a)$ P involving term a which has the same function as any other term or terms enclosed in parentheses in the same expression.

$P \vee Q$ P or Q or both (inclusive disjunction).

$P \not\equiv Q$	Either P or Q, but not both (exclusive disjunction).
$P_{\forall a}$	P with universally quantified participant term a which may or may not have the same function in other predications in the expression.
$P_{\forall t}$	P with universally quantified temporal term t which may or may not have the same function in other predications in the expression.
$P(U)$	P with universal set U as a term which has the same function as other terms in the expression which are enclosed in parentheses. For example, in $\bar{P}(U) \wedge P(a)$, U has the same function in $\bar{P}$ as term a has in P.

The following seven symbols occur with subscripts preposed to predicate symbols, distinct from the terms of the respective predicates, which occur postposed. These preposed subscripts relate P to a following predicate in the same expression.

aP	P with a reporting function denoting awareness of a statement in the following predicate.
cP	Metalanguage predicate with a calling or naming relationship to the following predicate.
gP	P involving a more generic term which contrasts with a corresponding and more specific term in predicate sP.
iP	P denoting an intent relationship with the following predicate.
sP	P involving a more specific term which contrasts with a corresponding and more generic term in gP.
tP	P which denotes a mistaken idea in the following predicate.
wP	P which denotes reported speech in the following predicate, with no implication about whether or not the statement results in a corresponding action.

The following symbol is similar to the seven above, but relates to the preceding predicate instead.

pQ	Q has a purposive relationship (final cause) to the preceding predicate. That is, the preceding predicate was for the purpose of Q.

∃P	Existential[18] predication. "There is _____."
t	Predicate term with a temporal function.
U	Universal set, such as the set of all people or all places.
U−a	Complement of set U − a.
∀a	Universal quantifier, "for every term a."
∃	Existential quantifier.
(□)	Expression enclosed in parentheses, which must be more than just a predicate term, is an unstated presupposition with respect to the remainder of the expression not so enclosed.
[□]	Expression so enclosed must be grouped as one unit.

$$P \land \begin{cases} P \\ Q \\ R \end{cases}$$ The three expressions $P \land P$, $P \land Q$, and $P \land R$.

Summer Institute of Linguistics

BIBLIOGRAPHY

Becker, A. L.: 1967, *A Generative Description of the English Subject Tagmeme*, Doctoral dissertation, University of Michigan, Ann Arbor.

Church, A.: 1956, *Introduction to Mathematical Logic*, Vol. I, Princeton University Press, Princeton, N. J.

Cromack, R. E.: 1968, *Language Systems and Discourse Structure in Cashinawa*, Doctoral dissertation, Hartford Seminary Foundation.

Fillmore, C. J.: 1966, 'A Proposal Concerning English Prepositions', *Monograph Series on Languages and Linguistics*, Number 19 (ed. by F. P. Dinneen, S.J.), Georgetown University, Washington D.C., pp. 19–34.

Fillmore, C. J.: 1968a, 'The Case for Case', *Universals in Linguistic Theory* (ed. by E. Bach and R. Harms), New York, pp. 1–90.

Fillmore, C. J.: 1968b, 'The Grammar of Hitting and Breaking', *Studies in English Transformational Grammar* (ed. by R. Jacobs and Peter Rosenbaum).

Forster, J.: 1964, 'Dual Structure of Dibabawon Verbal Clauses', *Oceanic Linguistics* **3.1**, 26–48.

Forster, J. and Barnard, M. L.: 1968, 'A Classification of Dibabawon Verbs', *Lingua* **20**, 265–68.

Gleason, H. A., Jr.: 1964, 'The Organization of Language: a Stratificational View', *Monograph Series on Languages and Linguistics*, Number 17 (ed. by C. I. J. M. Stuart), Georgetown University, Washington, D.C., pp. 75–96.

Hall, W. C.: 1969, 'A Classification of Siocon Subanon Verbs', *Anthropological Linguistics* **11.7**, 209–15.

Lakoff, G.: 1969, 'Global Rules', 44th Annual Meeting, L.S.A., Dec. 29–31, San Francisco.

[18] The notation (∃x) P(x) is not used here because of conflict with the definition of P(x) in this presentation.

Longacre, R. E.: 1958, 'Items in Context: their Bearing on Translation Theory', *Language* 34, 482–91.

Longacre, R. E.: 1964, 'Prologemena to Lexical Structure', *Linguistics* 5, 5–24.

Longacre, R. E.: 1965, 'Some Fundamental Insights of Tagmemics', *Language* 41, 65–75.

Longacre, R. E.: 1967, 'Reply to Postal's Review of Grammar Discovery Procedures', *IJAL* 33, 323–48.

Longacre, R. E.: 1968, *Philippine Languages: Discourse, Paragraph, and Sentence Structure*, Summer Institute of Linguistics and Related Fields, No. 21.

Longacre, R. E.: 1970, 'Sentence Structure as a Statement Calculus', *Language* 46, No. 4 (December).

McCawley, J. D.: 1967, 'The Respective Downfalls of Deep Structure and Autonomous Syntax', 42nd Annual Meeting, L.S.A., Dec. 28–30, Chicago, Ill.

Miller, J.: 1964, 'The Role of Verb Stems in the Mamanwa Kernal Verbal Clauses', *Oceanic Linguistics* 3.1, 87–100.

Perlmutter, D. M.: 1970, 'Surface Structure Constraints in Syntax', *Linguistic Inquiry* 1.2, 187–255.

Pike, K. L.: 1964, 'Discourse Analysis and Tagmeme Matrices', *Oceanic Linguistics* 3.1, 5–25.

Platt, J. T.: 1970, *Grammatical Form and Grammatical Meaning*, Doctoral dissertation, Monash University, Melbourne.

Reid, L. A.: 1966, 'An Ivatan Syntax', *Oceanic Linguistics*, Special Publication No. 2, University of Hawaii.

Ross, J. R.: 1967, 'Constraints on Variables in Syntax', unpublished doctoral dissertation, MIT.

Stennes, L. H.: 1969, *The Identification of Participants in Adam Fulani*, Doctoral dissertation, Hartford Seminary Foundation.

Stoll, R. R.: 1963, *Set Theory and Logic*, Freeman, San Francisco, Calif.

Tabor, C. R.: 1966, *The Structure of Sango Narrative*, Hartford Studies in Linguistics, No. 17, 2 vols.

[13a] [Footnote to p. 97.] This same example also includes further exponents of non-final bases of the Eventuation Sentence: Coordinate Sentence, Paraphrase Sentence, Addition Sentence. It seems probable that a variety of sentence types over and beyond those indicated in the bidimensional array expound bases of the Eventuation. Apparently, however, it is not self-embedding, i.e. Eventuation Sentence does not expound a base of the Eventuation Sentence.

NARRATIVE VERSUS OTHER DISCOURSE GENRE

Robert E. LONGACRE

Narrative can be systematically distinguished in various ways from other discourse genre. Above all, narrative contains *plot*. The plot structure of the rhetorician is related to but not isomorphic with the surface structure grammar on the discourse level. Nevertheless, many narratives have recognizable surface structure *Peaks* — marked in a variety of ways — which correspond to such units of plot structure as Climax and Denouement. This paper attempts to document these assertions by reference to the structure of folk tales from Mexico, Philippines, and New Guinea and to modern novels and short stories[1].

1. Discourse genre

Chart 1 summarizes some of the broad characteristics of discourse genre. Notice that this is not fine-grained enough to isolate specific types of discourse, but merely indicates genre. I have attempted to show some parameters of contrast which distinguish the five genre here subsumed. The scheme is not exhaustive. Certainly other genre of discourse exist as well, e.g., Epistolary discourse or letters, where we have surface requirements (partially dictated by the very format of the page) in certain areas of the world. And of course this scheme includes only prose discourse; it doesn't include verse or song.

[1] The Philippine studies were carried out 1967–1968 under OE Contract No. 0-8-062838-0391. The final report of this project is Longacre 1968. The New Guinea studies were carried out in 1970 under a similar Contract OE No. 0-9-097756-4409(014). The final report on the latter has been submitted to Georgetown University Press under the title 'Hierarchy and Universality of Discourse Constituents (New Guinea Languages)'. Work on discourse structure in Mexican Indian languages was carried out before the Philippine contract as well as between Philippine and New Guinea contracts. This paper also owes something to discussions with students while giving a course in discourse structure at the Linguistic Institute of LSA during the summer of 1971.

Chart 1
Some discourse genre.

	– Prescriptive	+ Prescriptive
+ Succession (chronological)	Narrative (many types) 1. 1/3 persons 2. Actor oriented 3. Accomplished time encodes as past or present 4. Chronological linkage	Procedural (many types; includes instructional) 1. Pseudo (non-specific person) 2. Goal oriented 3. Projected time encodes as past, present, or future 4. Chronological linkage
	Drama 1. Multiple 1/2 person 3. Accomplished time as concurrent 5. Dialogue paragraphs without quotation formulas	
– Succession (chronological)	Expository (several types, includes descriptive) 1. Any person (usually 3rd) 2. Subject matter oriented 3. Time not focal 4. Logical linkage	Hortatory (sermons, pep talks, etc.) 1. 2nd person 2. Addressee oriented 3. Commands, suggestions encode as imperatives or 'softened' commands 4. Logical linkage

1.1. The genre included here are: narrative, procedural, drama, expository, and hortatory. Narrative is, of course, story and is our main focus in this paper. Procedural is 'how-to-do-it' or 'how-it-is-done' text. Drama is text which consists entirely of dialogue. Expository genre includes essays, scientific articles, and descriptive material. Hortatory includes sermons, pep talks, etc. I think that these discourse genre could be arranged in order of vividness. Certainly the most vivid discourse is drama; the second most vivid is narrative; possibly the third most vivid is procedural. I would reckon that expository is still more vivid than than hortatory, the sermon (in the narrow sense of pure exhortation) being possibly the dullest of all discourses. I think that this is documentable by watching a congregation on Sunday morning. As long as the preacher limits himself to 'You should do this, you shouldn't do that' and cites motivations, warnings and so forth, people sleep. When he gets to a part of this sermon where he tells a story as a brief illustration of some point, even the children wake up and want to know how the story is going to come out.

1.2. I suggest two parameters to describe the discourse genre embraced in this system: (chronological) succession which may be plus or minus; and prescriptive, which has the same two values.

Chronological succession is important both to narrative, i.e., telling a story, and to giving procedure. One has to have ordered steps in most procedures if they are to proceed. One has to say, 'Do this, then do that', or 'Having done this, then do that', and so forth. Procedural and hortatory discourse are plus Prescriptive in that they prescribe, i.e., tell us either how to dor or how to make something (procedural discourse) or what we ought to do or ought not to do (hortatory discourse). This Prescriptive element does not normally characterize Narrative, Drama, and Expository discourse.

1.3. Again, however, we must distinguish here intent as related to the deep structure, and form as related to the surface structure. Thus the primary aims of the various genre are somewhat as follows: Narrative and Drama: to entertain (fiction) or to inform (history, whether past or current); Procedural: to tell how-to-do, or how-it-is-done; Expository: to explain or describe; Hortatory: to influence conduct. It seems that each of these surface structure genre primarily exists to encode its matching deep structure. Nevertheless, there may be non-isomorphic mapping so that a surface structure encodes something other than its primary encoding. Thus Narrative and Drama – clearly distinct from each other in surface structure but with similar primary deep structure encoding – may be used to give procedure ('This is how a master builder built *his* house'), to explain a subject or to give moral lessons (fable and parable). In such cases, the deep structures of Procedure, Exposition, and Exhortation are expressed in surface structure Narrative or Drama rather than in the genre where they primiarly encode.

1.4. In the interior of the various boxes, certain further numbered parameters are indicated. Number 1 refers to person. Narrative discourse is usually first or third person – although occasionally we have the phenomenon in current Western literature of a story in second person (This is the story of your life, you were born, you did so and so). Most Narratives are, however, first or third person. First person accounts tend to be more formal. Even within third person accounts there are some very interesting differences having to do with the viewpoint of the narrator himself vis-a-vis the viewpoint of characters of the story. The narrator may be neutral as to viewpoint or he may walk in and stand by one particular character so that the reader sees the story unfold through the eyes of this third person and views the activities of the other third persons through his eyes. More of this later.

Procedural discourse essentially employs a nonspecific person, indicated by an impersonal form of the verb or some stylized use of a pronoun. Some languages use *you*: 'First you do this, then you do that'. Others prefer first person inclusive of second person; 'this is how we all do it', or first person exclusive, and even third person: 'The hunter does this, then does that', or 'they do this, then do that'. There may be options within the same language implying again different and specific Procedural text types. For instance, if we say, 'This is how we (not including you) do it', there may be an implicit admission that you (as a foreigner) wouldn't want to try this out but this is how we do it. If, on the other hand, we say 'This is how we (including you) do it' this amounts to a tacit invitation for you to try it out yourself or join in the activity.

Continuing with Expository and Hortatory discourse, Expository discourse can be in any person, but in that it is subject matter oriented it is usually third person. Hortatory discourse involves a second person component in its deep structure but may not have such a person in its surface structure. That is, in Trique (Mexico) Hortatory discourse it is rather impolite to say *you*, and is much better form to say *we* (including you). This puts oneself in the same category as the person to whom you are talking. Hortatory discourse may be given in third person: 'A good _____ does so and so, he is always on the job, he supports his family, he tills his cornfield', meaning of course,'you should be on the job, take care of your family, and till your cornfield'. The second person component is in the deep structure even though it is not found as such in the surface structure. So much for parameter one within the boxes.

1.5. Let us make short shrift of parameter two. Narrative discourse is mainly actor oriented, i.e., the deep structure agent is subject. Procedural discourse is goal oriented — the object of the activity, the thing done or the thing made is what one focuses on. In some languages as in Oksapmin (New Guinea), one may go through a whole Procedural text and never specify an actor or use a personal pronoun at all, because it is simply not necessary and the morphology of the language permits us to have verbs without specifying their agent. Expository discourse is subject matter oriented. Hortatory discourse is addressee oriented which correlates with the second person orientation.

1.6. Parameter 3 has to do with time. Deep structure accomplished time is encoded in Narrative discourse. Accomplished time may encode as the past tense or as an historical present tense in the surface structure. Procedural discourse is usually in deep structure projected time – unless one is recounting a procedure no longer followed but only of historical interest. Some sort of habitual or customary deep structure component is, at all events, found as well. Most frequently these deep structure components (projected time, habitual or customary) encode as some sort of non-past tense, i.e., as a present or a future. A surface structure past tense is not impossible, however, and is documented for a few languages (e.g., Eastern Otomi of Mexico, Voigtlander, n.d.; and Keley-i Kallahan of the Philippines, Reid, n.d.). Special conventions and constraints govern such use of past tense to encode projected time with habitual import. In Expository discourse, time is not focused on (unless it be an essay about time!). In Hortatory discourse deep structure commands, suggestions, etc. encode as imperatives of various sorts, jussives and hortatives in the surface structure. Sometimes these are softened down in various conventionalized ways. Thus, in some New Guinea cultures one tones down imperatives in the presence of older people, whom one does not baldly order around.

1.7. Parameter 4 has to do with linkage of parts of a discourse to each other. Correlating with the fact that both Narrative and Procedural are characterized by chronological succession, the linkage within Narrative and Procedural discourse is chronological linkage. This is more important than the particular stuff of the given paragraphs that make up the narrative discourse. A narrative discourse actually may have very few narrative paragraphs, but if the paragraphs are arranged in chronological order, we still have a story rather than an essay. Expository and Hortatory discourse are characterized not by chronological but by logical linkage. Of the two, Hortatory is probably looser in its connections than Expository which requires that we progress in an orderly and logical way from topic to topic.

1.8. In all this I have not taken into account Drama. Drama is, as we said, a more vivid form of discourse than Narrative. It is characterized by multiple first and second person, i.e., multiple 'I-thou' situations in which person speaks directly to person without the intervention of a narrator. Drama presents accomplished time as concurrent. This usually requires surface structure present tenses except when speaking of the past or anticipating the future. Drama has dialogue paragraphs without quotation formulas. Rather than saying 'John said to Mary', 'Mary answered him', John simply speaks out, then Mary speaks out. In oral dramatic texts from certain groups in the Philippines, we can not employ the convention of Western drama of identifying the speakers on the margin of the page. Imagine, therefore, a page of Western drama with names of dramatic personae out in the margin, then imagine a dialogue with such names deleted but one so well framed that one knows who is talking to whom and when scenes and acts shift simply by what people say to each other. This is Philippine dramatic text.

2. Some special characteristics of narrative

Narrative we said is a vivid form of discourse, exceeded in vividness only by drama.

2.1. One special characteristic of Narrative is its necessary preoccupation with the problem of participant identification. You must keep track of who does what to whom or the story falls flat on its face. Some important work has been done here by practitioners of stratificational grammar (Taber, Stenner, Cromack) and by Mary Ruth Wise.

There's also the matter of narrator viewpoint versus participant viewpoint. In some stories, the narrator is very self-consciously narrating. In the rather well known novel circulating at present, *The French Lieutenant's Woman*, the narrator is so self-conscious that at one point he pauses to say in effect: 'Well, shall I finish the story this way or shall I finish the story that way, what shall we do? I'm just like God, I'm sitting up here making these people do what I want them to do'. In *The House of the Seven Gables* which I will be referring to quite frequently, Hawthorne's point of view as narrator crops us again and again throughout the story. Chapter 2 is a case in point. As Hawthorne describes to us an important day in the life of Hepzibah Pyncheon he remarks 'Far from us the indecorum of assisting, even in imagination, at a maiden lady's toilet. Our story must therefore await Miss Hepzibah at the threshold of her chamber...' Further on, he refers to the house as being empty except for Hepzibah and 'a disembodied listener like ourself'. Further on, Hawthorne remarks 'Let us pardon her one other pause...' Still a few pages further he remarks 'All this time, however, we are loitering faint-heartedly on the threshold of our story. In very truth, we have an invincible reluctance to disclose what Miss Hepzibah Pyncheon was about to do'.

2.2. Above all, Narrative is distinct from other genre in that Narrative has plot. To be true, some plots may be in very low relief. Thus, a first person account may be episodic, if not rambling. On the other hand a well-written novel in third person may be episodic as well. Willa Cather's *Shadow on the Rock* is such a novel. It procedes in chronological order, year by year as a young girl grows up in early French Quebec. There is little struggle – certainly no perceptible build-up or climax. Yet it is a charming story, well told. The deep structure of such a narrative is a string of deep structure Episodes; these group in inconsistent fashion into surface structure Episodes expounded by paragraphs and by embedded discourses.

By contrast, other narrative texts have a perceptible Climax or Peak. What rhetoricians have since classical times identified as plot structure (originally for drama) necessarily involves such a Climax. As suggested above, I would like to see plot used for Narrative in general – even those of episodic nature where the plot is in low relief due to absence of any perceptible Climax or Peak.

In integrating the rhetoricians' anatomy of plot into linguistic structure, we begin with noting that the rhetoricians' scheme is the *deep structure* of climactic narrative. The deep structure here, as everywhere, is in no necessary one-to-one correspondence with surface structure features. Nevertheless, we would expect the surface structure to have features similar to those of the deep structure but to mark them less consistently. This is what we find.

2.3. Chart 2 suggests a correlation of the deep and surface features of discourse. The deep structure, given at the bottom of the chart, are the rhetoricians' scheme[2]. The surface structures are given at the top of the

---

[2] I am indebted to Thrall, Hibbard, and Holman for the particular form of that scheme as given here but the antecedent tradition goes back to classic times.

Chart 2
Narrative discourse with surface peak.

	Title	Aperture	Stage	(Pre-peak) episodes	Peak	Peak'	(Post-peak) episodes	Closure	Finis
Surface structure	Formulaic phrase/ sentence		Expository paragraph/ discourse	Paragraph/ discourse (usually narrative or dialogue)	1. Crowded stage 2. Rhetorical underlining 3. Shifts in:	See peak	See pre-peak episodes	Of varied structure especially expository paragraph, but can be expository discourse, narrative discourse, hortatory discourse (= moral?)	Formulaic phrase/ sentence
				Narrative paragraph/ discourse	Articulated by means of 1. Time horizons in succession 2. Back-reference in paragraph/ discourse to the preceding 3. Conjunctions 4. Juxtaposition, i.e. clear structural transition to another paragraph or embedded discourse	(a) Tense (b) Person (c) Vantage point (d) Orientation (e) Relative amount of conjunctions and transition (f) Length of units (sentence, paragraph, embedded discourse) (g) From narrative to rhetorical question, apostrophe, dialogue, or drama			
Deep structure (plot)	Surface features only	1. Exposition 'Lay it out'		2. Inciting moment 'Get something going' 3. Developing conflict 'Keep the heat on'	4. Climax 'Knot it all up proper'	5. Denouement 'Loosen it'	6. Final suspense (surface structure episodes) 'Keep untangling'	7. Conclusion 'Wrap it up'	Surface feature only

A. Climax may encode as peak and denouement as peak'

Or: B. Climax may encode as pre-peak episode and denouement as peak

Or: C. Climax may encode as peak and denouement as post-peak episode

As stage

As episodes

chart. Arrows mark encoding of deep structures into surface structures. Notice that the Title and the (formulaic) Aperture ('Once upon a time') are considered to be features of the surface only. The story, as regards its deep structure, gets under way with (1) Exposition, 'Lay it out'. Here crucial information of time, place, local color, and participants is given. With (2) Inciting Moment 'Get something going', the planned and predictable is broken up in some manner. Thus, a man who has plodded to work faithfully for 25 years passing certain points at certain hours runs into something quite unexpected on the way to work – and thereby hangs a tale. With (3) Developing Conflict 'Keep the heat on', the situation intensifies – or deteriorates – depending on one's viewpoint. (4) Climax 'Knot it all up proper' is where everything comes to a head, if not head-on collision. Here is where the author really messes it up, brings in contradictions, and adds all sorts of tangles until confrontation is inevitable. (5) Denouement, 'Loosen it', a crucial event happens which makes resolution possible. Things begin to loosen up. We can see a way out, even if not to a happy ending. (6) Final Suspense 'Keep untangling', work out details of the resolution. (7) Conclusion 'Wrap it up' brings the story to some sort of decent – or indecent – end.

2.4. The correlation of the features of plot with surface structure is our next question. Exposition often corresponds to a slot which we can call Stage in the surface structure. Many times Stage is expounded by an expository paragraph or even a short embedded expository discourse. It may however, be a subsidiary narrative which is necessary to get the main narrative going. For Tolkien's three volume trilogy a complete narrative discourse of book length, *The Hobbit,* serves as Stage for the following work *The Lord of the Rings.* Stage sometimes has very special characteristics, as in Carl Sandburg's *Abraham Lincoln, Volume 2, The War Years.* Sandburg has here as the third paragraph of this volume a long run-on sentence which goes on for about two and a half pages: 'Only tall stacks of documents recording the steel of fact and the fog of dream could tell the intricate tale of the shaping of a national fate; of _____; of _____; of _____; etc.' This sentence includes many scattered anecdotal observations about life in the United States at the beginning of 1861, about social issues, economic problems and storms and stresses in the body politic. A sentence of this length occurs nowhere else in the volume. It is appropriately reserved for Stage.

Inciting Moment and Developing Conflict in the deep structure, i.e., the plot, usually encode as surface structure Episodes. I have been unable to find any particular surface structure features which distinguish an Episode which encodes the Inciting Moment from any other Episode.

I use the term *Peak* to refer to any episode-like unit set apart by special surface structure features and corresponding to the Climax or the Denouement in the deep structure. Where the surface structure distinguishes these two deep structure units, I posit *Peak* (Climax) versus *Peak'* (denouement). Climax and/or Denouement may, however, be marked in no special way in the surface structure but may on the contrary simply encode as further surface structure Episodes. In the latter case the surface structure of the Narrative is episodic even though there are Climax and Denouement in the deep or plot structure.

The Final Suspense encodes as one or more post-Peak Episodes, while Conclusion is more likely to have special marking in the surface structure – often some non-narrative paragraph or discourse. When the surface structure Closure is a Hortatory paragraph or discourse, it is possibly a special *Moral* slot. The (formulaic) Finis, is considered to be a feature only of the surface. This latter may be a formulaic sentence like 'That's all; we're through' or even a printed word 'Finis'.

3. Marking of surface structure peak

What I am especially interested in in the balance of this paper is the devices available for marking surface structure Peaks. I think this is crucial because if we can identify surface structure Peaks, then we can have pre-peak Episodes and post-peak Episodes and can consequently articulate a considerable amount of the surface structure of the Narrative.

While chart 2 indicates *Peak* and *Peak'* in the surface structure, I will describe these jointly except when it seems that there is evidence for separating them in referring to a given short story, novel, or folk tale.

3.1. One hallmark of Peak (often encoding deep structure Climax) is the crowded stage. Think of a Shakespearian play where at the dramatic height of the play everybody except very subsidiary characters are on stage; the stage is crowded, there's a lot going on. This we can see in a novel such as *A Tale of Two Cities* by Dickens where the Peak (deep structure Climax) is the second trial of Charles Darnay (including the reading of a long letter as evidence). Every important character is there and some lesser characters: Charles Darnay, his father-in-law, his wife, Madame Defarge, her husband, 'Vengeance', Mr. Lorry, Barsad, and Sydney Carton who becomes the hero of the story. Only a few lesser characters (e.g., Miss Pross) are not at the trial scene.

3.2. Another characteristic is what I call rhetorical underlining. The author, or narrator (in the case of oral literature) does not want you to miss that this is the important point of the story so he takes a few extra words to tell it. He may employ parallelism, paraphrase, and tautologies of various sorts to be sure that you don't miss the point. A colleague of mine was taking a course in creative writing at the University of Michigan. Her professor once said, "At this point in the story, I want more words. It goes by too fast". And so the surface structure Peak often has some such rhetorical underlining. It's as if you took a pencil and underlined certain lines of what you are writing.

I'm thinking of two Mixe texts (recorded by Willard Van Haitsma) which we studied at a Mexican linguistic workshop. One text looked as if it should have some sort of Climax or Denouement in the plot structure. It had to do with a certain man who went through a series of vicissitudes and eventually emerged as king. That looked like a rather important thing, didn't it? But Van Haitsma as consultee and myself as consultant argued repeatedly about where the Peak was in the story. Then there was another Mixe story which is a fairly mundane story from our point of view as aliens but which the Mixes like quite well. Now this story has a point in it where a man composes a song. He is out in the woods and he composes a song. We're told this several times in the same paragraph and then in the next paragraph we're told the whole thing over again once more. It appears that there is a surface structure Peak which is marked here very clearly. What to us is unexciting, to the Mixe is exciting. Apparently this second story has a surface structure Peak while the first story is episodic in its surface structure – whatever you make of its plot structure.

3.3. Now aside from rhetorical underlining, let's look at this matter which I call shifts of various sorts. If the story has a surface structure Peak of some kind, there are various ways in which the author can indicate a change of pace or viewpoint and thus tells us that something important is happening at this juncture of the story.

A shift in surface structure tense can be the clue. There is a Fore (New Guinea) folk tale "Small People can be Useful", in which a monster which was eating the sugar cane is destroyed by two small dwarves who shoot him full of arrows. There are far past, recent past, past, present, and future tenses in this language. The story starts off in the far past tense, 'A long time ago'. As it proceeds and as the plot thickens, there's a shift to recent past. Right at the deep structure Climax of the story it shifts into present tense and then at the Closure of the story we're told 'that's how it happened a long time ago' and the far past tense is again employed.

In Kosena (New Guinea) this happens too. Here, as in Fore, the tense shift happens only in formal legend as opposed to informal first person narrative which has no such shift. In informal first person narrative, there is usually recent past or remote past according to whether a person is telling a story of recent events or of something that happened in his earlier years.

The novel *A Tale of Two Cities* – already referred to – has a tense shift at a great moment of the story. After the trial and after Sydney Carton has taken the place of Charles Darnay in jail, the drugged Darnay and his family are fleeing in the coach from Paris. Suddenly we find here that the story is in present tense. This adds vividness and excitement and here marks a Peak' which encodes part of the deep structure Denouement of the story. We can thus distinguish Peak (Climax) from Peak' (Denouement) in the surface structure of *A Tale of Two Cities*. *The House of the Seven Gables* uses a very similar device. As Judge Pyncheon sits dead in the parlor of the house, suddenly the story shifts into present tense: 'Judge Pyncheon ... still sits in the old parlor... The Judge has not shifted his position for a long while now. He has not stirred hand or foot... He holds his watch in his left hand...' Present tenses and perfectives here mark a Peak which encodes deep structure Denouement – since Climax, unmarked in the surface structure, encodes simply as an Episode.

3.4. There may also be person shifts. This is noticeable not only in Narrative, but in certain Procedural texts which likewise mark a Peak. Such Procedural discourses are similar to Narrative discourse in that they have some sort of a Target Procedure to which the whole text is directed. All procedures are going somewhere, in the sense that they proceed towards some goal. The goal, however, may not be marked in the surface structure. Where it is marked we have a phenomenon not dissimilar from that which is found in Narrative discourse. Thus, in Dibabawon (Southern Philippines) Game Procurement texts we find that person shifts correlate in some texts with onset of Peak. One such text runs: 'We (inclusive), when we go to shoot fish... We do this, we do that... and then when you see it you spear it'. Here there is a shift to second person right at the Target Procedure where you actually spear the fish. Another such text runs: 'The bird hunters among the Dibabawons, they do so and so, they make certain preparations... They build a bird blind... And then he shoots the bird'. Again, at the point of actually obtaining the game, there is a shift to third person. Such shifts are not always this exact. They are somewhat approximate. They tend to occur, however, somewhere around the Peak of the procedures.

Now to go back to *A Tale of Two Cities* by Charles Dickens. Right at that crucial scene where they are fleeing from Paris, about half way through that section suddenly we find that we are there in the stage-coach too: 'Houses in twos and threes pass by us... The hard, uneven pavement is under us... Sometimes, we strike into the skirting mud...' Here we have not only present tense (as previously noted) but first person plural as well. The whole section ends up: 'The wind is rushing after us and the clouds are flying after us, and the moon is plunging after us, and the whole wild night is in pursuit of us, but so far we are pursued by nothing else'. This is the only spot in the whole novel where 'we' is used to take the reader to the scene of the action itself. Here, the person shift reinforces the tense shift in marking the Peak′ (Denouement).

Likewise, to refer again to *The House of the Seven Gables*, at the point where we have the shift to present tense there is also a person shift. That is, Hawthorne begins to address the dead Judge Pyncheon as he sits in his chair: 'Why Judge, it is already two hours... Pray, pray, Judge Pyncheon, look at your watch now... Up, therefore, Judge Pyncheon, up! Canst thou not brush the fly away? Art thou too sluggish?...' Thus, for about twelve pages, he heckles the dead Judge[3].

---

[3] Some Philippine languages use a person shift of this sort not to mark climax, but through a story. There are sentences like 'When Ukap went upstairs to give the food to his mother, then you said to your mother'. Here 'you' equals 'Ukap'. This characteristically takes place within a sentence, which starts out in third person and shifts to second person. Data from Hazel Wrigglesworth.

3.5. There may be a change in what I call vantage point. I do not mean by this, viewpoint in the sense of sympathy with a character of a story. I mean rather, by whom do we stand, through whose eyes do we view the story? Let us suppose a story about Peter, Paul, and Mary. In this story we find such sentences as: 'Peter and Mary come to Paul ... Peter and Mary go from Paul ... Peter and Mary bring things to Paul ... Peter and Mary take things away from Paul ... Peter and Mary become visible to Paul ... Peter and Mary pass out of the sight of Paul ...' Furthermore, we are told the inner thoughts of Paul but not the inner thoughts of Peter and Mary. In such a story you can almost draw vector lines to Paul as being the focal person.

While a story may consistently hold to one vantage point throughout, it is not unusual to find shifts in vantage point. Such a shift most naturally occurs near Peak of the story and consequently marks such a Peak in the surface structure.

The Open Boat by Stephen Crane, has four men adrift in a boat. A ship has sunk. At first we are not certain if any one of the four is singled out for vantage point. As the story progresses, however, we get hints that the correspondent may be more focal than the other three because we're occasionally told briefly something of what the correspondent is thinking. By contrast, we have to infer from the actions and facial expressions of the other three what they are thinking. Finally, when you get to the point of the story where they beach the ship and make for land, where one person drowns and three get through including the correspondent, at that point we're very sure that the correspondent is focal in the story. The captain passed by him floating on a piece of wood. The shore became visible to him. The carpenter passed out of sight and drowned. Furthermore, now we're told extensively and in detail the thoughts which flashed through the mind of the correspondent. This overt shift to the vantage point of the correspondent partially marks the Peak of the story. Furthermore, this can be documented (not simply impressionistically asserted) by attention to motion verbs and similar phenomena[4]. We are looking at things that we can put our thumb on as overt features of the surface structure of the narrative.

A short story, "Indian Justice" by Freyre (translated from Spanish by Colford) illustrates change of vantage point. The story has to do with

---

[4] It was Fillmore (in a personal conversation) who first alerted me to the importance of motion verbs in establishing what I here call vantage point.

two travelers on the Antiplano of Bolivia who are *personae non gratae* with the Indians of that region because they have pulled some shady land deals. The story starts out with the Indians coming to the two travelers or going from them. Likewise things appear to them and things disappear from them. Clearly the two travelers are the vantage point of the early part of the story. Finally at the end of the story, the Indians are the vantage point and the travelers are passive as they are brought in to the waiting Indians and slowly butchered by them. Here, shift in vantage point marks the Peak' (Denouement); the Peak is otherwise marked.

Vantage point is morphologically marked in the structure of Oksapmin (New Guinea). In one sort of Oksapmin narrative, one can single out one person or one set of persons as the vantage point of a story in the third person. All verbs which refer to these people as agents must have one type of verb morphology while all verbs which refer to other people must have a different type of verb morphology. Thus, some verbs are marked as 'participant viewer', while other verbs are marked as 'participant viewed'. You are made certain by the very verb morphology at whose side you are standing in the course of the story. This device also serves for keeping participants straight in the course of the story.

3.6. Now let's look at what I here call Orientation for want of a better name. By Orientation I largely mean what is encoded as surface structure subject. Most languages can encode more than one case as surface structure subject. In Narrative, very commonly the agent is encoded as subject, and goal (or patient) is encoded as object. One sort of shift that can occur here simply involves switching the particular dramatis personae which occur as subject (agent) and object (goal). Thus, a story that starts out with a certain character A as subject (agent) and another character B as object (goal) can end up with B as subject (agent) and A as object (goal). This happens where the phenomenon of role reversal occurs in a story; so that the victim becomes the aggressor and the persecutor becomes the victim at the Peak of the story. This is very common. There may also be other shifts, however, e.g., A as subject (agent) and B as object (goal) may be shifted so that B becomes subject (goal) and A drops into the background.

Instrument as surface structure subject can be used effectively to picture impersonal forces closing in on the main characters of the story. Thus, in the story "Indian Justice" by Freyre we are told that the horn continues to blow although of course someone is blowing it; we're told that boulders come crashing down although presumably someone is pushing the boulders down off the hilltop; and we're even told that the two men felt as if they were being carried along by forces beyond their control. There is no doubt that the encoding of instrument as subject has a lot to do with the feeling created in this part of the story (Peak, deep structure Climax) that impersonal forces are closing in on the two main characters. In "A Field of Rice" by Pearl Buck at the Peak (Climax) of the story there is a shift to goal and location as subject, i.e., the 'rice', the 'seed', the 'ricefield', the 'ground', 'the clay bottom', are subjects. This is at the point of tension in the story where the rice crop is failing because it has been planted wrongly under the influence of the Commissar in rural Red China.

In summary, Orientation has largely to do then with the matter of what case is encoded as subject and hence the matter of what a particular portion of a discourse is oriented to. Is it oriented to agent, to goal, or to instrument or to location? A shift in orientation can indicate a 'great moment of the story', i.e., either a Peak (Climax) or Peak' (Denouement).

3.7. A shift in the relative amount of conjunctions and transition may also be relevant. Thus, in Ilianen Manobo oral literature, a typical story such as "The Story of Ukap" starts out in a very deliberate way with a lot of conjunctions and long conjunctive complexes which carefully mark transitions within the story and balance the action of one character against the action of another character. About two-thirds of the way through the story, this feature fades out and very few conjunctions are used for the balance of the story. Rather, simple juxtaposition of sentence with sentence and paragraph with paragraph is found. There's a perceptible change in the pace of the whole story in that where we once had deliberate and overt transition, we now have implicit and covert transition between the main parts of the story which picks up its pace at this point and rolls on toward its end. Here the shift of pace signals transition to Peak.

3.8. The sheer length of units (clauses, sentences, paragraphs, embedded discourse) may be important as well. Thus, we may find at the Peak of a story a shift to short, fragmentary, crisp sentences, which emphasize the change of pace. The shocker is that in certain New Guinea highland languages, quite the opposite takes place, viz. a long sentence at Peak. Thus, in Wojokeso (New Guinea) there is a folk legend "Woodchip" which has at its Peak' (the Peak is otherwise marked) a paragraph whose second sentence is twice as long as any found previously in the story. This has a parallel in a Procedural text, "House Building" whose Target Procedure consists of a single sentence which is likewise far longer than any previous sentence in the discourse. The effect is much as if we had an English text with sentences of moderate length and then suddenly hit a long two-page run-on sentence with medial 'and-a's.

While any part of a discourse may presumably be expounded by an embedded discourse (a string of paragraphs which belong together), the surface structure Peak of a narrative may be marked by an embedded discourse which is explicitly quoted – such as a letter, speech, or sermon. Thus, the surface structure Peak (deep structure climax) of *A Tale of Two Cities* is the second trial of Charles Darnay. The story of this trial is recounted in what is implicitly an embedded discourse. But the Peak of this embedded discourse is the reading of a long letter written by a former prisoner in the Bastille. This long letter occupies about sixteen pages of the novel and sheds much light on obscure corners of the story as previously given. As Peak of the embedded discourse (trial scene) it also marks Peak of the novel itself (just as Akron is the highest point in Summit County which is in turn the highest county in Ohio).

Likewise, a favorite device of Ayn Rand's (cf. *Fountainhead, Atlas Shrugged*) is to mark Peak (Climax) of a novel by a rather lengthy speech by the main character.

Labov's observation that we may have background material either at the beginning of the story or near the climax of the story, has relevance here. Background material medial or towards the end of a discourse may result from the fact that there is an embedded discourse at Peak, and that this embedded discourse has its own deep structure Exposition (surface structure Stage).

3.9. A further feature available for marking Peak is shift to drama, dialogue, rhetorical question, or apostrophe (direct address of the author to one of his characters). Keep in mind what I said about drama being a very vivid style of discourse in which you drop out quotation formulas, and people speak out in multiple 'I-thou' relations. *The Open Boat* by Stephen Crane close to its Climax has a stretch of drama. Here we are not told that B said so-and-so to A or that A said so-and-so to B, but the various characters simply speak out one to the other. Only what they say gives clues to who speaks. This gives a heightened vividness to the story that is part of the structural marking of its Peak.

A short story "Michael Egerton" by Reynolds Price has no dialogue, in fact, no direct speech until the Peak of the story where there is a stretch of dialogue. So in one case it's a shift from dialogue as such to drama, and in the other case it's a shift from narration to dialogue.

I referred to Ilianen Manobo folk tales where conjunctions are used very deliberately at the start of a story, but drop out about two-thirds of the way through the story, as the story proceeds rapidly towards its end. At about the point where the conjunctions drop out you begin to note also a preponderance of dialogue in the story as well. This also makes for a change of pace.

Rhetorical question may be used with effect at the Peak of the story. For instance in referring to the Wojokeso story, "Woodchip" with the extra long sentence at the end, I said that this sentence marked Peak' (Denouement) and that there was also marking of a Peak (deep structure Climax) earlier in the story. The earlier Peak (Climax) is expounded by a rather long paragraph which contains a rhetorical question "Now why did he do that?" and the answer, "He did it because so and so." There is also considerable parallelism and paraphrase within the same paragraph. Since these features are not found elsewhere in the story, presumably the rhetorical question and the accompanying rhetorical underlining mark the surface structure Peak (Climax) while the extra long sentence in the following paragraph of the story marks Peak' (Denouement). To refer again to the chapter "Governor Pyncheon" of *The House of the Seven Gables*, (part of the Peak' of the novel), I have counted 53 rhetorical questions in that chapter. The next to the last paragraph of the chapter is a series of 8 such questions; only the terminal sentence of the paragraph is not a rhetorical question. So here sits Judge Pyncheon dead in the chair and Hawthorne is bombarding him with a barrage of rhetorical questions which the fellow isn't in any condition to answer. The intensity of this barrage of rhetorical questions is exceeded only by the book of Job — whose Peak in chapters 38–41 consists largely of such questions.

3.10. What is the moral of all this? The moral is: almost any surface structure grammatical feature may be used to mark Peak if it brings about a shift of pace in the story. These features are identifiable and countable. We can therefore confidently assert that a Peak is there in the formal structure of the text. Furthermore, we are sometimes justified in talking about surface structure Peak (Climax) versus surface structure Peak' (Denouement) as well. When both Peak and Peak' occur they are marked in different ways. Finally, as stated earlier, if we can note how a story begins, peaks, and ends, much of the remaining surface grammar of the narrative can be plotted in reference to these three points.

Summer Institute of Linguistics

Bibliography

Barnard, Myra Lou. Dibabawon Text in *Discourse, Paragraph, and Sentence Structure in Selected Philippine Languages. Volume III. Text Material* by Robert E. Longacre, 1969. pp. 269–299.

Buck, Pearl S. "A Field of Rice". *Ten Modern American Short Stories* edited by David A. Sohn. New York: Bantam Pathfinders Editions, 1965. pp. 111–123.

Cather, Willa. *Shadows on the Rock.* New York: Knopf; New York: Random.

Crane, Stephen. "The Open Boat". *Great American Short Stories* edited by Wallace and Mary Stegner. New York: Dell Publishing Co., Inc., 1957. pp. 257–286.

Cromack, Robert Earl. *Language Systems and Discourse Structure in Cashinawa.* Connecticut: The Hartford Seminary Foundation, 1968.

Dickens, Charles. *A Tale of Two Cities.* New York: Washington Square Press, Inc., 1965.

Freyre, Ricardo Jaimes. "Indian Justice". *Classic Tales from Spanish America* edited and translated by William E. Colford. New York: Barron's Educational Series, Inc., 1962.

Fowles, John. *The French Lieutenant's Woman.* Boston: Little, Brown and Company, 1969.

Hawthorne, Nathaniel. *The House of the Seven Gables.* New York: Holt, Rinehart and Winston, 1965.

Labov, William, Paul Cohen, Clarence Robins and John Lewis. *A Study of the non-standard English of Negro and Puerto Rican Speakers in New York City,* Cooperative Research Report No. 3288. New York: Columbia University, 1968.

Lawrence, Marshall. *Oksapmin Discourse and Paragraph Structure.* Unpublished manuscript, 1970.

Price, Reynolds. "Michael Egerton". *Ten Modern American Short Stories* edited by David A. Sohn. New York: Bantam Pathfinders Editions, 1965. pp. 81–87.

Rand, Ayn. *Atlas Shrugged.* New York: The New American Library, 1943.

Rand, Ayn. *Fountainhead.* New York: The New American Library, 1957.

Reid, Lawrence A. *Tense Sequence in Procedural Discourse.* Unpublished manuscript, nd.

Sandburg, Carl. *Abraham Lincoln, Volume II, The War Years, 1861–1864.* New York: Dell Publishing Co., Inc., 1954.

Scott, Graham. *Higher Levels of Fore Grammar.* Unpublished manuscript, 1970.

Stennes, Leslie Herman. *The Identification of Participants in Adamawa Fulani.* Connecticut: The Hartford Seminary Foundation, 1969.

Taber, Charles Russell. *The Structure of Sango Narrative,* Volumes I and II. Connecticut: The Hartford Seminary Foundation, 1966.
Thrall, William F., Addison Hibbard, C. Hugh Holman. *A Handbook to Literature.* New York: The Odyssey Press, 1961. pp. 156–158.
Tolkien, J.R.R. *The Hobbit.* New York: Ballantine Books, Inc., 1966.
Tolkien, J.R.R. *The Lord of the Rings.* New York: Ballantine Books, Inc., 1965.
Van Haitsma, Willard. *Discourse and Paragraph Structure of Coatlan Mixe.* Unpublished manuscript, nd.
Voigtlander, Katherine. *Use of Lexical Margins in Flow of Discourse, Eastern Otomi, Mexico.* Unpublished manuscript, nd.
West, Dorothy. *Wojokeso Texts Appended to Wojokeso Sentence, Paragraph, and Discourse Analysis.* Unpublished manuscript, nd.
Wise, Mary Ruth. *Identification of Participants in Discourse: A Study of Aspects of Form and Meaning in Nomatsiguenga.* Michigan: University of Michigan, 1968.
Wrigglesworth, Hazel. *Discourse and Paragraph Structure of Ilianen Manobo* to appear in *Philippine Discourse and Paragraph Structure in Memory of Betty McLachlin.* Canberra: Australian National University.
Wrigglesworth, Hazel. "Story of Ukap" in *Discourse, Paragraph, and Sentence Structure in Selected Philippine Languages. Volume III Text.Material* by Robert E. Longacre, 1969. pp. 192–268.

THOMAS P. KLAMMER, University of Michigan
CAROL J. COMPTON, University of Michigan

SOME RECENT CONTRIBUTIONS TO TAGMEMIC ANALYSIS OF DISCOURSE*

With a few exceptions, American linguists have traditionally concerned themselves chiefly with language units at the sentence level or below. This artificial limitation upon linguistic inquiry is reflected in, and perhaps partially due to, Bloomfield's idea that "each sentence is an independent linguistic form, not included by virtue of any grammatical construction in any larger linguistic form" (Bloomfield, 1933.170). However, in recent years linguists working within a tagmemic framework have been interested in a more comprehensive view of language and have thus turned their attention to a focus upon language units at a level higher than the sentence, in particular, the paragraph and the discourse. This article deals, in part, with two such tagmemic studies, at the same time showing how these new analytic tools might be applied to language materials quite different in nature from those under examination in the original studies, as well as pointing to the promise that tagmemic analysis of discourse holds for the future.

The three-volume work *Discourse, Paragraph, and Sentence Structure in Selected Philippine Languages*, edited by Robert E. Longacre (1968), reports on work done with 25 languages and dialects of the Philippines. The intent of this broadly-based study was to do research on hierarchical levels above those regularly investigated by other linguists. In addition to the volumes edited by Longacre, the 1968 University of Michigan Ph.D. dissertation by Mary Ruth Wise entitled *Identification of Participants in Discourse: A Study of Aspects of Form and Meaning in Nomatsiguenga* makes a major contribution to tagmemic theory of discourse analysis. Concerned primarily with uncovering the means by which the referents of pronouns belonging to the elaborate pronominal system of the South American Nomatsiguenga language are identified, Wise shows that, in relation to both encoding and decoding, participant identification depends partly upon cues occurring in structural systems beyond the level of the individual sentence.

These works by Longacre and Wise provide a foundation for

*We are grateful to Kenneth L. Pike for turning our attention to this exciting field of endeavor.

discourse analysis in other languages, including English. In
some of our own exploratory investigations we have used the
familiar children's tale *Little Red Riding Hood,* a simple, relatively short discourse unit. It will provide useful illustrations here
for some of the chief concepts used in the tagmemic analysis of
discourse.

Longacre begins his discussion by suggesting, on the basis
of the Philippine data, a typology of discourse genres. His typology is founded on the notion that, within a given language, there
is a finite number of discourse types, where these types or
genres are defined by certain characteristics held in common by
the members of the particular genres. Limiting themselves to
prose (and thereby excluding songs and poems), Longacre and his
colleagues found four main discourse types and several minor
ones in the Philippine languages investigated. The four main
genres may be most simply characterized as follows: *Narrative
Discourse* recounts some sort of story; *Procedural Discourse* tells
how to do something; *Expository Discourse* expounds a subject or
explains something; and *Hortatory Discourse* attempts to influence
or change conduct, beliefs, and attitudes.

The major formal characteristics which distinguish each of
these genres from the others are presented in Figure 1. The rows

FIGURE 1	Time: Accomplished or Not Focal	+Projected Time
+Sequence in Time	Narrative Discourse	Procedural Discourse
	1 or 3 Person oriented	1/2/3 Person oriented
-Sequence in Time	Expository Discourse	Hortatory Discourse
	Subject-matter Oriented	2 Person Oriented

Main Genres of Discourse Distinguished (after Longacre, 1968.1.2)

of the matrix represent the presence or absence of a sequence in time, and the columns represent the setting in time, whether in projected time, that is, in the future, or not in projected time, which includes both accomplished (past) time and a lack of partic- ular focus on setting in time.

LRRH is obviously a *Narrative Discourse*. It is characterized by its presentation of a sequence in time, its setting in past or accomplished time (*"Once upon a time* there *was . . ."*), and its orientation to a third person point of view. *LRRH* is not a *Procedural Discourse*, for although Procedural Discourse shares the characteristic of sequence in time with Narrative Discourse, it is nevertheless set in projected time (since, in the languages investigated, the procedures it specifies are still to be carried out) and it may occur in the second person, as well as the first or third (*"You do this, and then you do that."*). *Expository Discourse* does not exhibit a necessary sequence in time, nor does it focus on a particular setting in time. It is oriented toward the subject matter it explains rather than being characteristically limited to a first, second, or third person point of view. *Hortatory Discourse* also lacks an obligatory sequence in time; it is set in projected time (since it tries to bring about *new* behavior and attitudes), and it is oriented toward the second person (*"You ought to do this."*)

For each discourse genre, Longacre has specified a *tagmeme formula* on the basis of the Philippine data. In the case of Narra- tive Discourse, for example, Longacre (1968.I.5) gives the follow- ing formula:

±Aperture±Episode+Denouement+Anti-denouement±Closure±Finis

The symbol + indicates obligatory presence; the ± indicates optional presence; *Episode* may occur more than once. Each of the terms preceded by + or ± represents a function-slot which may be filled or expounded by one of a number of possible grammatical units. Thus an Episode in a Narrative might be e*xpounded* by an embedded discourse, a paragraph or group of paragraphs, or a single sentence. A function-slot together with the set of units that can expound it are together called a *tagmeme*. Various other subtypes of Narrative, e.g., Monoclimactic and Episodic, have formulas differing slightly from this one, which happens to repre- sent a Diclimactic Narrative.

LRRH might be analyzed according to Longacre's formula for Narratives in a way similar to the following:

Aperture. In a typical Narrative, Aperture provides temporal and spatial setting and introduces at least some of the principal dramatis personae. In the version of *LRRH* used for this analysis, the Aperture consists of two sentences: "Once upon a time there was a little girl whose mother had made her a red hood and cape to match. Everyone called her Little Red Riding Hood."

Episode. We have divided *LRRH* into three Episodes. In the first, LRRH is given the task of carrying goodies to Grandmother's house, and preparations are made for the journey. In the second Episode, LRRH encounters the apparently friendly wolf in the midst of her trip through the woods to Grandmother's. In the third, the wolf races ahead to Grandmother's house, frightens the poor old lady out of her house, disguises himself in her nightclothes, and gets into her bed.

Denouement. The Denouement in Longacre's terminology contains the climax of the story. In *LRRH*, we have included in the Denouement LRRH's arrival at Grandmother's, her realization of the wolf's identity, and the arrival at the last moment of the woodchopper.

Closure. The Closure tagmeme typically offers some final comment on the participants. In *LRRH*, the Closure consists of the final two sentences: "Then they all sat down and had tea and bread and butter, and honey. It was a happy occasion, for they knew that the wicked wolf could never bother anyone again."

An analysis such as this can be done quite easily on an intuitive basis without detailed linguistic analysis. But when we desire greater precision and wish, for example, to mark the boundaries of the units expounding discourse-level slots such as Episode and Denouement and to identify the formal criteria that establish such units and thus confirm our intuitions, the task of discourse analysis becomes more difficult. It quickly becomes necessary to leave the conception of a single structure mode that we have discussed so far, and to reassert one of the fundamental tagmemic postulates, namely , the trimodal nature of language structure.

Both Longacre and Wise view language units as hierarchically structured. But, in keeping with their tagmemic frame of reference, they insist on the inadequacy of a single hierarchy. Instead of a monohierarchical structure, Longacre and Wise propose trimodal structural hierarchies. Longacre calls these the phonological, grammatical, and lexical hierarchies, while Wise labels them phonological, grammatical, and lexemic.

Although there are differences between Longacre's and Wise's conceptions of these three hierarchies in that Wise develops more fully what she calls the lexemic hierarchy, whereas the emphasis of Longacre's work is with the grammatical hierarchy, we can discuss what is essential to the idea of trimodal structuring without emphasizing their disagreements. The phonological hierarchy, which is to some extent replaced by a ''graphical'' hierarchy in written materials, ranges from phonemes at the lowest level, to syllables, to stress groups, to higher level phonological units. Although elaborated by neither Longacre nor Wise, the phonological hierarchy would be crucial in accounting for patterns of rhythm, meter, and rhyme in poetry. The grammatical hierarchy ranges from morpheme at the lowest level, through stem, word, phrase, clause, sentence, and paragraph, to discourse at the highest level. The third hierarchy, which, for convenience, we shall refer to as ''lexical'' in this discussion, though not identical for Longacre and Wise, is similar to the grammatical hierarchy in its structure, with units more or less analogous in size and position on the hierarchy to units on the grammatical hierarchy.

Although the lexical hierarchy is superficially similar to the grammatical, it is in reality very different. The lexical structure of language units is based on logical-chronological relationships and situational roles. These criteria determine units by no means in a constant one-to-one correspondence with units on the grammatical hierarchy. At the clause level, for example, lexical functions such as agent and goal do not always correspond to grammatical subject and object respectively, as in passive clauses. At the discourse level, the grammatical ordering of episodes in the linear narration is not always the same as the strictly chronological ordering of events on the lexical hierarchy. In *LRRH*, an illustration of this difference is found when LRRH's mother tells her, ''I'm making fresh bread for Grandmother . . . The woodchopper stopped by this morning to tell me that she is ill.'' The order of these two sentences, here given as they appear in the story, is the grammatical order, the narration order. Chronologically, however, the event of the woodchopper's stopping by precedes, and is in fact, a partial cause of, the event of Mother's making bread for Grandmother. The grammatical order of these two sentences thus contrasts with their lexical order.

In other, non-Narrative genres of discourse, the lexical order corresponds to ''logical'' order. An *Expository Discourse*, for example, might have practically any surface order, depending on the rhetorical inclinations of the speaker or writer. Its lexical order, on the other hand, might correspond to the structure of a formal syllogism, with major premise, minor premise, and conclusion.

The indeterminacy which makes difficult the precise identification of the boundaries of units expounding discourse slots is, in part, a product of this frequent lack of congruence between lexical and grammatical units. This is illustrated at the boundary between the second and third Episodes of *LRRH*. Quoted here are the last two sentences of the second Episode and the first sentence of the third.

And she began to pick the blossoms that grew near the path. She was so busy that she did not see the wolf put down the basket and slip quietly away.
                        — Episode boundary —
Little Red Riding Hood did not know that while she picked flowers the wolf was running through the woods to her grandmother's cottage.

The Episode boundary we have marked is a grammatical boundary. That is, it marks a break between sections of the linear "telling" of the tale, a division between subunits in the narration. Lexically there is also a unit boundary indicated here, but it is not so clearly reflected in the surface order of the story. The lexical division we are referring to is that between the events of LRRH's picking blossoms and the wolf's running to Grandmother's. But marking that boundary precisely in the text is difficult because there is here an "inter-leaving" of lexically separate events in the grammatical progression of the narration — LRRH's picking and the wolf's running are referred to on both sides of the grammatical Episode boundary. Lexical and grammatical structures at the discourse level are thus out of phase and not precisely co-terminous at this point in the narrative.

Another fundamental tagmemic postulate, developed in relation to discourse analysis more extensively by Wise than by Longacre, is that of language units as form-meaning composites. She expands this idea with a matrix similar to that given in Figure 2. "The three aspects of meaning," she says, ", — the plot of the events

FIGURE 2

Aspects of Meaning / Aspects of Form

	Leximic	Grammatical	Phonological
Observer Viewpoint	"LRRH", not "Daughter"	"Once upon a time there was . . ."	
Plot of the Events Narrated			
Social Setting	"Mother" "Grandmother"		wolf's imitation of Grandmother's voice

Composites of Form and Meaning
in a Narrative
(Cf. Wise, 1968.10)

narrated, the observer's viewpoint, and the social setting – are
phenomena in the 'real world,' independent of linguistic form,
i.e., they are non-language specific and remain invariable under
paraphrase or translation. They intersect with the aspects of form
– lexemic, grammatical, and phonological – which are often language specific. At the intersections there are linguistic units
each of which is a composite of an aspect of form and an aspect
of meaning" (Wise, 1968.9).

For example, in *LRRH* we find that the intersection of Social
Setting with Lexemic form partially accounts for the particular
lexical items which are the names of the participants – i.e., the
names "Mother" and "Grandmother" reflect directly the social
situation in which these participants function in the narrative.
The fact that   LRRH   is called   "LRRH"   and not
"Daughter" is explained by the intersection of Observer Viewpoint and Lexemic form, since the observer (the narrator) through
most of the story is focusing on and viewing events in relation to
LRRH. "Mother" and "Grandmother" not only reflect the actual
social situation, but also are the names by which LRRH identifies these participants. By using these lexical items, the narrator
directs the reader's attention and interest to the focal character
of the story.

At the intersection of Phonological form with Plot meaning, we
find the high weak voice quality with which the wolf attempts to
impersonate Grandmother. Furthermore, the particular grammatical
formula "Once upon a time there was . . . " which occurs at the
beginning of this version of *LRRH* and is characteristic of so
many children's fairy tales might be explained by the intersection
of Grammatical form with Observer Viewpoint. The formula indicates not only the usual fairy tale setting in the indefinite past
("Once upon a time"), but also the backgrounding of the persona
of the narrator with a resultant freedom for the narration to focus
upon and see things in relation to the main character("there was "
rather than, e.g., "I personally was present when . . .").

Longacre and Wise have presented what seems to us to be
groundbreaking studies for the tagmemic analysis of discourse.
But they are not alone in their interest in the tagmemic analysis
of language units beyond the sentence. Tagmemic theory, developed most extensively in Pike (1967), has from its inception emphasized a broad conception of language and refused to narrow its
attention solely to sentences or smaller linguistic units. Initial,
and in light of later developments, very fruitful insights for discourse analysis were offered by Pike (1964 a, b, c,; 1965; 1967;

and elsewhere). Becker (1965) outlined a tagmemic theory of paragraph structure and in so doing aimed in part at making linguistic research of ''more than peripheral interest to rhetoricians and literary scholars '' (237). Young and Becker (1965) showed the relevance of tagmemics for a modern theory of rhetoric and sketched in the initial outlines of such a theory. Seeking empirical confirmation for Becker's tagmemic theory of paragraph structure, Young and Becker (1966) and Koen, Becker, and Young (1967) conducted experiments in which college undergraduates were asked to place paragraph markers at appropriate sentence junctures in both English and nonsense passages. In the results the authors found support for the notion that the paragraph is a multisystemic unit which is identified on the basis of ''three interlocking, simultaneously-operating 'systems' in written material,'' which, following Becker, they label lexical, grammatical,- and rhetorical. In spoken language, a fourth (phonological) system is expected to operate (Koen, Becker, and Young, 1967.526). These ''systems'' are clearly related to the three hierarchies of Longacre and Wise, with initial investigation indicating that the grammatical hierarchy of Longacre and Wise includes both the grammatical and rhetorical systems of Becker. The most recent contribution growing out of these studies is Young, Becker, and Pike (1970), *Rhetoric: Discovery and Change.* Constructing a coherent and comprehensive rhetoric on a foundation of tagmemic theory, the authors offer an approach to the teaching of writing that emphasizes the process of discovering knowledge in combination with the process of communicating it.

New directions for the tagmemic analysis of discourse are indicated by a number of questions with which we are presently concerned. How can tagmemics contribute to a closer intergration between linguistics and certain kinds of literary research? What is the role of intonation and high-level phonological units in the structure of discourse? What new light can the insights achieved in discourse analysis shed on more general problems of human communication, problems which involve not only grammatical, phonological, and lexical hierarchies, but graphic, pictorial, and kinesic as well? Finally, what new frontiers might the techniques of the tagmemic analysis of discourse open up for teachers, both in second language instruction and in the teaching of native language skills? We are convinced that seeking answers to these and related questions charts an exciting course for future study, in a portion of which we are already engaged.

REFERENCES

Becker, Alton L. 1965. A tagmemic approach to paragraph analysis *College composition and communication* 16:5. 237-42.
Bloomfield, Leonard. 1933. *Language.* New York. Holt.
Koen, Frank, Alton L. Becker, and Richard E. Young. 1967. The psychological reality of the paragraph. *Studies in language and language behavior,* vol. 4, ed. H.L. Lane and E.M. Zale, 526-38. Ann Arbor. Center for Research on Language and Language Behavior, The University of Michigan.
Little Red Riding Hood. 1961. Racine, Wisc. Whitman Publishing Co.
Longacre, Robert E., ed. 1968. *Discourse, paragraph, and sentence structure in selected Philippine languages.* 3 vols. Santa Ana, Cal. The Summer Institute of Linguistics.
Pike, Kenneth L. 1964. a. Beyond the sentence. *College composition and communication* 15. 129-35.
—————— . .1964. b. Discourse analysis and tagmeme matrices. *Oceanic linguistics* 3 (Summer). 5-25.
—————— . 1964. c. A linguistic contribution to the teaching of composition. *College composition and communication* 15. 82-88.
—————— . 1965. Language — where science and poetry meet. *College English* 26. 283-92.
—————— . 1967. *Language in relation to a unified theory of the structure of human behavior.* 2nd ed. The Hague. Mouton
Wise, Mary Ruth. 1968. *Identification of participants in discourse: a study of aspects of form and meaning in Nomatsiguenga.* Ph.D. dissertation, The University of Michigan.

Young, Richard E. and Alton L. Becker. 1965. Toward a modern theory of rhetoric: a tagmemic contribution. *Harvard educational review* 35:4. 450-68.

—————————. 1966. The role of lexical and grammatical cues in paragraph recognition. *Studies in language and language behavior*, vol. 2, ed. H.L. Lane, pages not numbered. Ann Arbor. Center for Research on Language and Language Behavior, The University of Michigan.

Young, Richard E., Alton L. Becker, and Kenneth L. Pike. 1970. *Rhetoric: discovery and change*. New York. Harcourt.

SOCIAL ROLES, PLOT ROLES, AND FOCAL ROLES IN A NOMATSIGUENGA CAMPA MYTH*

Mary Ruth WISE

1. Introduction

The characters in a Nomatsiguenga Campa myth simultaneously play three different types of roles: The roles related to SOCIAL STRUCTURE are primarily the kinship relations between the characters. The roles in the PLOT are villain (and co-villain), victim(s), and mediator(s). The roles related to the OBSERVER VIEWPOINT in telling the story are focal and non-focal roles, i.e., whether the character is the focus of attention or not. The systems in which these different types of roles operate are sketched briefly in sections 2–4, and certain aspects of the *Tosorintsi* 'deity' myth are described in order to show how the systems are intimately inter-related and, therefore, only partially autonomous (sect. 5). One version of that myth is given in full in sect. 6.

2. The system of kinship terms

In Nomatsiguenga Campa myths[1], as well as other types of discourse, the characters are often referred to by kinship terms rather than by name. Such terms specify, in part, the social roles of characters in any given discourse and are drawn from the system of Nomatsiguenga kinship terms[2].

The dimensions of contrast in the system are generation, sex, and bifurcation[3].

The generations distinguished are Ego's own generation (G^0), second

---

* This paper was read at the XXXIX International Congress of Americanists, Lima, Perú, 1970.
[1] For footnote, see next page.
[2] For footnote, see page 391.
[3] For footnote, see page 391.

[1] The Nomatsiguenga dialect of Campa is spoken by approximately 1 000 persons living along the Sanamoro or Pangoa river sysem which flows into the Perené and along the headwaters of the Anapati which flows into the Ené. This area is surrounded by speakers of the Ashéninca dialect of Campa. Nomatsiguenga is mutually unintelligible with that dialect as well as with Pajonal Campa and Machiguenga. Although most Nomatsiguenga men are bilingual in Ashéninca Campa and their own language, the converse is not true because of sociological factors.

This paper is drawn from Wise, 1968. The field work during which data for that study were gathered was supported in part by National Science Foundation grant GS-1137. My data were supplemented by that gathered by Mr. and Mrs. Harold Shaver working under the auspices of the Summer Institute of Linguistics. I am deeply indebted to them for their hospitality during my own field work among the Nomatsiguenga and for the free access which they granted to their field notes. In fact, the version of the Tosorintsi myth presented here was narrated by Mr. Andres Chompati and transcribed by Mr. Shaver with the aid of Mr. Pablo Chimanca :a prior to my field work on the language. A version narrated by Mr. Julio Mishicuri in September, 1966, is essentially the same in structure, but is much longer since it includes more episodes.

The transcription of the text, as well as other Nomatsiguenga words, follows in most respects Mr. Shaver's phonemic analysis in 'Phonemics and Morphophonemics of Nomatsiguenga', unpublished manuscript. It differs in that /i/ and /y/ are both transcribed /i/ in this paper and in that the contrast between high and low tone is not indicated. The phonemes posited are enclosed in slant lines in charts A and B, the principal allophones of the phonemes are enclosed in brackets, and the orthographic symbols used in the transcription are enclosed in quotation marks.

Chart A

Consonant phonemes, allophones, and ortographic symbols for Nomatsiguenga.

		Labial	Alveolar	Velar
Stop		/p/[p] "p" [p^W]	/t/[t] "t"	/k/[k] "k" [k^W] [k^y]
Nasal		/m/[m] "m" [m^W]	/n/[n] "n"	/ŋ/[ŋ] "ng"* [ŋ^W] [ŋ^y]
Fricative	Vd.	/β/[β] "b" [β^W] [b]	/r/[r] "r" [1]	/γ/[γ] "g" [γ^W] [γ^y]
Fricative	Vl.		/s/[s] "s"	/h/[h] "h"
Affricate			/ts/[ts] "ts"	

* /ŋ/ is transcribed as "n" preceding a velar stop and as "ng" elsewhere.

generation (G²), first ascending generation (G⁺¹), and first descending generation (G⁻¹). In the second generation removed from Ego no distinction is made between ascending and descending relation, i.e., grandparents and grandchildren are referred to by the same set of terms. Also in that generation the bifurcation distinction, i.e., the contrast between parallel and cross relation is neutralized.

The sex distinction takes two different forms: in Ego's own generation and the second generation, the essential sex distinction made is whether the relative is the same or different sex than Ego, whereas in the first ascending and first descending generations the sex distinction made is whether the relative is male or female[4].

For example, in chart 1 *ren* in *irenti* 'his brother or parallel cousin' or in *orento* 'her sister or parallel cousin', refers to a parallel relative of the same sex and generation as Ego. In contrast, *tom* in *itomi* 'his son or

---

[1] (continued)

Chart B

Vowel phonemes, allophones, and orthographic symbols for Nomatsiguenga.

	Front	Central	Back
High	/i/[i] "i"		/o/[u] "o"
	[ɩ]		[o]
Mid		/ė/[ė] "ë"	
Low	/e/[ɛ] "e"	/a/[a] "a"	
	[æ]	[ə]	

[2] My necessarily superficial observation of Nomatsiguenga social organization leads me to believe that it is similar to that of the linguistically related Amuesha where matrilocal residence and bride service are expected during the early years of a girl's first marriage. The use of a single set of terms to refer to cross relatives or affines is compatible with cross cousin marriage which is the preferred pattern among the Amuesha and appears to be also among the Nomatsiguenga.

[3] This kind of analysis of a system of kinship terms is similar to componential analysis as developed independently by Goodenough (1956) and Lounsbury (1956). It is also similar to the kind of analysis of various levels of grammatical and lexical structure presented in Wise (1968). In that study contrastive sets of categories of meaning comprise the dimensions of contrast for each system described. For a theoretical discussion of dimensions of contrast in language systems, see Pike (1962).

[4] These different forms of the sex distinction can be considered variants of a single dimension of contrast. For a similar treatment of variants in the sex of the linking relative and a theoretical discussion of the problem see Lounsbury (1964).

Chart 1

System of kinship terms in Nomatsiguenga giving third person forms. The term for a male's relative is given in the top line of each cell and that for a female's relative is given in the lower line.

Same sex as Ego			Different Sex than Ego	
	Parallel	Gross (and affinal)	Parallel	Cross (and affinal)
G^2		*i-tsia-ri-ne* *o-tsia-ro-ne*		*i-sio-ro* *o-sa-ri*
G^0	i-ren-ti o-ren-to	ir-ani-ri o-nato-to	iri-tsi-ro o-hari-ri	
	Male Relative		Female Relative	
G^{+1}	*ir-i-ri* *i-ri*	*iri-kongi-ri* *o-kongi-ri*	*i-ni-ro* *o-ni-ro*	*ir-agi-ro* *agi-ro*
G^{-1}	*i-tom-i* *o-tom-i*	*i-ti-ne-ri* *o-ti-ne-ri*	*iri-sin-to* *o-sin-to*	*ir-ani-ro* *eba*

parallel nephew', or in *otomi* 'her son or parallel nephew' refers to a parallel male relative of the first descending generation.

In chart 1 the system of kinship terms is presented utilizing the dimensions of contrast described above. The forms given are those used to refer to the relatives of someone other than speaker or addressee, i.e., third person. The prefix *i-* ∞ (*ir-* ~ *iri-*) indicates third person masculine possessor while the prefix *o-* ∞ ∅ indicates third person feminine possessor (or non-masculine in the total structure of the language). The suffix *-ri* ∞ *-ti* ∞ *-i* indicates male relative while the suffix *-ro* ∞ *-to* ∞ ∅ indicates female relative. The suffix *-ne* indicates possessed noun; it obligatory occurs with certain roots.

As can be seen from the preceding discussion the sex distinction in the root does not indicate sex of relative in some cases and in other cases does not indicate whether or not the relative is the same sex as Ego. Nevertheless, in the total word — possessive prefix, root, and gender suffix — both the sex of the relative and the sex of Ego are distinguished in every case. Compare for example, *i-tsia-ri-ne* 'his-relative of same sex, second generation-masculine-possessed, i.e., his grandfather or his grandson' with *o-tsia-ro-ne* 'her-relative of same sex, second generation-feminine possessed, i.e., her grandmother or her granddaughter'. In some cases, the

Chart 2

Vocative forms of kinship terms. The term for a male's relative is given in the top line of each cell and that for a female's relative in the lower.

	Same sex as Ego		Different sex than Ego	
G²	Parallel	Cross (and affinal)	Parallel	Cross (and affinal)
	tsia-ri-ne *tsia-ro-ne*		*no-sio-ro* *na-sa-ri/tsia-ne*	
G⁰	*ige* *ni-ren-to*	*(n-)ani* *na-nato-to*	*tsi-o* *hai*	
	Male Relative		Female Relative	
G¹	*paba(-ti)/apa(-ti)* *paba(-ti)/apa(-ti)*	*koki* *no-kongi-ri*	*ina(-to)* *ina(-to)*	*agiro-ntsi* *n-agiro*
G⁻¹	*no-tom-i* *no-tom-i*	*na-ti* *na-ti-ne-ri*	*na-sin-to* *na-sin-to*	*ni-ani-o* *n-eba*

root of a term also indicates the sex of Ego. Thus, *ani* in *ir-ani-ri* refers to a man's cross cousin of the same sex whereas *nato* in *o-nato-to* refers to a woman's cross cousin of the same sex.

In chart 2 the vocative forms of the kinship terms are presented. These forms are also used by Ego in referring to his relatives, thus, *ige*, for example, is either 'brother (vocative) or my brother'. Some of these forms do not include possessive prefixes, e.g., *ige* 'brother (of a man)'; others optionally include them, e.g., *ani* or *(n-)ani* 'brother-in-law or my brother-in-law'; and still others optionally include gender suffixes, e.g., *paba(-ti)* or *paba* 'papa'[5].

The system as presented in charts 1 and 2 is somewhat asymmetrical: A single term — *isioro* for relative of a male Ego and *osari* for female Ego refers to a relative in the second generation removed or a cross relative of different sex than in Ego's own generation. In contrast, two terms refer to these relatives when they are the same sex as Ego, e.g., *itsiarine* and *irenti* for male Ego in chart 1. There is, however, an obsolete usage of *sa*, as in *i-sa-ri*, which yields a more symmetrical system. Formerly, *sa* was the term for a relative of the second generation removed of the same

[5] Parentheses enclose optional elements in chart 2 as well as in other sections of the paper.

Chart 3
Alternate system for male Ego.

Same sex as Ego		Different sex than Ego	
Parallel	Cross	Parallel	Cross
G^2 *i-sa-ri* (obsolete) or *i-tsia-ri-ne* (occasional current usage)		*i-sio-ro*	
G^0	*ir-ani-ri*	*iri-tsi-ro*	

sex as Ego or for a parallel relative of Ego's generation and sex. This alternate system is shown in chart 3.

In the *Tosorintsi* myth given in section 6, the reader will note the obsolete usage of *isari*. One informant explained that *isari* was formerly used for *itsiarine* but that Mabireri and his relative were of the same generation, 'like brothers', rather than grandfather and grandson. In one biographical narrative in the data *itsiarine* is also used in the sense of 'brother', i.e., a parallel relative of a male Ego's own generation. It also occurs in this sense in one instance in the Tosorintsi myth. Both *isari* and *itsiarine* are translated as 'his relative' when they are used in the sense of a parallel relative of a male Ego's own generation.

3. Plot roles in relation to the structure of a myth

The plot roles of the characters in a myth are villain(s), victim(s), and mediator(s)[6]. The characters who play these roles are, in general, different in each chapter of a myth. However, in each new chapter at least one participant is included who was referred to in some preceding chapter, e.g., Mabireri's relative appears in the first and third chapters of the Tosorintsi myth, while Mabireri appears in the first and second. This carry-over helps to link the chapters into a single coherent story. In order

---

[6] The plot roles posited are adapted from Propp's work originally published in 1928, but more widely known after an English edition appeared in 1958. The analytical concepts which he applied to Russian fairy tales were further developed and modified by Dundes (1964) while studying North American Indian folklore. No attempt is made in the present paper to follow either Propp or Dundes in detail.

to relate these plot roles to the structure of a myth as a whole, a brief sketch of myths and chapters is given first and then the order in which the characters appear is described.

A myth as a whole includes the following units: an obligatory introduction, at least one chapter, an optional elucidation, and an obligatory closure.

The introduction unit may be manifested by a noun phrase stating the title as in illustration (1), by a sentence or paragraph summarizing the narrative as in (2), or by a sentence stating the situation as in (3).

(1) *ira sanguiro* 'that snail'

(2) *i-o-sebatanaka tsiapaini hirai kibatsi*
HE-CAUSATIVE-TO_QUAKE CHAPAI LONG_AGO EARTH
'Chapai caused an earthquake long ago'.

(3) *matsiguenga pihiri hiraira*
PERSON BAT LONG_AGO
'The bat used to be a person'.

The elucidation unit is manifested by one or more explanatory paragraphs. A paragraph taken from the Mosquito myth is given in (4) as an example.

(4) *irooti ora inanta monio-niro yamĕka,*
THAT'S_WHY THAT THERE_ARE MOSQUITOES-BAD NOW
inanta yamĕ monio arokenta i-tonganĕ aroke
THERE_ARE NOW MOSQUITOES BECAUSE HE-EXPLODE ALREADY
i-tonganĕ kanta aroke i-porokane atiroko
HE-EXPLODE THERE ALREADY HE-GO EVERY-PLACE
i-ngantahi-ri. irooti ora inanta
HE-WOULD_SAY-HIM THAT'S_WHY THAT THERE_ARE
monio-niro yamai. matsiguenga i-ngantingani hiraira
MOSQUITOES-BAD NOW PERSON HE-IS_SAID_OF BEFORE
i-aagantini monio-niro
HE-EAT MOSQUITO-BAD
'There are pesky mosquitoes now because Mosquito exploded and went in all directions. That's what they used to say. That's why there are mosquitoes now. He used to be a person and ate people'.

The closure unit is usually manifested by a terminative sentence such as *aro o-karati* NOW IT-CUTS-OFF 'that's all'. One informant's question "didn't he say 'that's all'?" after listening to a narrative where it was omitted is evidence of its obligatory nature.

The main body of a myth comprises one or more chapters. The following units are included within a chapter: an optional summary, an optional statement of a situation, an obligatory conflict, an obligatory mediation, and an obligatory resolution. In the actual narration of the story, these units may occur in the order named or in the following order: summary, situation, resolution, conflict, mediation.

Within the conflict unit, a conflict or problem caused by the villain is narrated. Then, in the mediation unit a way to resolve the problem is decided upon and carried into action. In the resolution unit, which is usually brief, the problem is finally resolved.

The following schema of the myth (illustration 5) given in section 6 will serve to illustrate the structure of chapters within a myth. (The numbers in parentheses refer to the numbers of successive clauses in section 6.)[7]

(5) Introduction (1—5)

Chapter 1	Conflict (6—23)
Chapter 2	Summary (24—25)
	Conflict (26—74)
	Mediation (75—100 or 75—115)
	Resolution (101—117 or 116—117)[8]
Chapter 3	Situation (118—136)
	Conflict (137—177)
	Mediation (178—220)
	Resolution (221—256)
Closure	(257)

The villain of each chapter in a myth is usually introduced first: he is named in the summary or the statement of the situation if one of those units occur, or in the conflict unit if those units are omitted. The victim is usually introduced after the villain when the narration of the conflict is begun. The mediator is introduced later — often not until the mediation unit. The villain's fate is stated in the resolution unit. For example, in the story about *monio-niro* 'Mosquito,' who used to eat people, Mosquito is introduced in the topic sentence. The way he tempted people — the victims — to visit him by always having plenty of fish on hand for

---

[7] Informant reaction would seem to indicate that the mediation unit of Chapter 2 includes ¦ clauses 75—115, and the resolution unit includes clauses 116—117. It seems possible, however, that the first alternative given in the schema could also fit this particular story.

[8] A more detailed account of ways in which focus of attention is indicated in Nomatsiguenga clauses is given in Wise (1968) pp. 156—162.

them to eat and then killed them while they were in a deep sleep from overeating is narrated first. Later a mediator, one of the people who realized what was happening to his relatives, is introduced and manages to confront Mosquito with his guilt. The problem is resolved when Mosquito turns into mosquitoes which still feed on blood but do not kill their prey.

On the other hand, the mediator may be introduced first, if his role as mediator is overtly stated. For example, in one version of the *mantsiakori* 'Moon' myth, Moon is introduced first. His role as mediator is made clear in the summary where it is stated that he is the one who made manioc for people to eat. Nevertheless, the details of how Moon made manioc are not given until the mediation unit later in the chapter.

4. Focal and non-focal roles in a narrative

The observer viewpoint in telling a story divides the characters into those playing focal and non-focal roles. In telling a biographical narrative the narrator may choose a character to be the focus of attention. Different narrators of the same event may focus attention on different characters. In contrast, a particular fixed character in each chapter of a myth is the focus of attention, i.e., the character in focus does not vary with different narrators. The narrator of a myth indicates his uninvolved viewpoint, in which choice of focus of attention is ruled out, by phrases such as those in (6) and (7).

(6) *ingantingani kara hiraira* 'he was said of a long time ago, i.e., it's said thus he did a long time ago'.

(7) *yamai hirai i-kengitsatomoeti-na-ro naro ora*
NOW BEFORE HE-NARRATIVE-IN_PRESENCE_OF-ME-IT ME
na-kemantabita naro arosatapage
THAT I-LISTEN I A-LITTLE
'Now (the story-teller) told in my presence that which I listened to a little (and will now tell you)'.

Whether the focus of attention is fixed by the structure of the story itself, as in myth, or is chosen by the narrator, as in biographical narrative, it is indicated by similar means. One of the means by which the character who is in focus is indicated is by naming a participant as the beneficiary of an action. Thus, in a story of a fishing trip the fact that 'father' is in focus of attention is indicated by *-ne-ri* in (8).

(8) *na-karata-si-ki-ne-ri ora i-obasiat-an-ka-ro*
'I-CUT-PURPOSIVE...BENEFACTIVE-HIM THAT HE-STOP_
CRACKS-INSTRUMENTAL...IT
'I cut (the leaves) for him in order that he stop up the cracks (in the dam).'

Another means by which focus is indicated is by unusual use of the gender distinction. Affixal forms of pronominal morphemes are obligatory as constituent units of finite active verbs; the prefix *i-* indicates third person masculine or feminine subject. A mixed group is ordinarily referred to by *i-* with the plural suffix *-ig*. Occasionally, however, the non-masculine pronominal prefix *o-* occurs with the plural suffix *-ig* referring to a mixed group; this form indicates that the observer's focus of attention is upon a woman who is part of the group. Yet another way of indicating focus of attention will be illustrated in the next section.

5. Interrelations of roles in the Tosorintsi myth

Within each chapter of the Tosorintsi myth, the victims are changed into another form by the villain in the conflict unit. In the mediation unit someone intervenes on behalf of the others, and in the resolution unit the villain is changed into another form. The plot roles of the characters and their fates are summarized in chart 4. (Note that the first chapter lacks the mediation and resolution units in the version presented in this paper.)

Chart 4

Plot roles in chapters in the Mabireri myth. Fates of villains and victims are shown by the symbol > followed by a noun phrase.

	Chapter 1	Chapter 2	Chapter 3
Conflict Unit	Villain: Mabireri Co-villain: Mabireri's relative (the boy) Victim: children > termites	Villain: Mabireri Victim: People > rocks	Villain: Mabireri's relative Victim baby > rock
Mediation Unit		Mediator: some of the people	Mediator: baby's mother, sister and father
Resolution Unit		Villain > ashes	Villain > pifayo palm with edible fruit

Chart 5
Correlations between plot roles and social kinship roles of characters in the Mabireri myth.

Pairs of Participants	Plot roles in chapters	Kinship roles
		Parallel relatives
Mabireri and his relative	Villain and co-villain	Brothers or parallel cousins
People and some of them	Victim and mediator	Brothers or parallel cousins
Baby and mother	Victim and mediator	Son and mother
Baby and sister	Victim and mediator	Brother and sister
Baby and father	Victim and mediator	Son and father
		Cross relatives
Mabireri and people	Villain and victim	Brothers-in-law or cross cousins
Mabireri's relative and baby	Villain and victim	Mother's brother and sister's son (uncle and nephew)
Mabireri's relative and baby's sister	Villain and mediator	Mother's brother and sister's daughter (uncle and niece)
Mabireri's relative and baby's father	Villain and mediator	Brothers-in-law

Simultaneously, the characters play kinship roles indicating their social relations to one another. The roles played by each were deduced from the various kinship terms by which they are referred to or by which they address one another in the story. These roles are interrelated with the plot roles in that those who side together are parallel relatives while those who are against each other are cross relatives[9]. The plot roles and kinship roles of each pair of participants are shown in chart 5.

As seen in chart 5, Mabireri and his relative *isari* (cf. chart 3 and relevant discussion in section 2 on the use of this term) side together as villain and co-villain and are parallel relatives of the same generation. Similarly, the father and the baby side together as mediator and victim and are parallel relatives.

On the other hand, Mabireri and the people he turned into rocks are cross relatives, i.e., cross cousins or brothers-in-law. Similarly, the relative as villain and the baby as victim are also cross relatives, i.e., mother's brother and sister's son.

[9] Further field work might reveal that the cross relative relationship of villain and victim in myth reflects something of current relations between cross relatives. It may be, for example, that there is a certain amount of tension in the relationship between cross relatives but not in that between parallel relatives. Etnographic data are not sufficient at present, however, to make such correlations. The joking relation between cross cousins of the same sex among the neighboring Amuesha can perhaps be considered a manifestation of underlying tensions.

The role of the baby's mother is ambivalent. As the relative's sister, i.e., a parallel relative, she saved him from being burned along with Mariberi. (Note that this particular pair is not shown on the chart because of the ambivalence.) As the conflict in the third chapter develops, however, her role as the mother of the baby becomes more important. In that role she is on the opposite side from her brother who turned his cross nephew, the baby, into a rock.

The observer's focus of attention is yet another role which is intimately interrelated with the plot roles and social roles. The interrelation is shown in that kinship roles are expressed in terms of a character's relation to the participant who is focus of attention. In the third chapter, for example, the relative is the focus of attention. Therefore, the mother and the father are quoted as saying at different points 'he, i.e., the relative, turned his nephew into a rock on me' rather than 'he turned my son into a rock'. By expressing the kinship roles of villain and victim in terms of the character who is focus of attention the social roles, plot roles, and focal roles in a Nomatsiguenga myth are all closely intertwined and only partially autonomous. All three must be considered for a complete understanding of the part each character plays in a myth.

6. One version of the Tosorintsi myth

The Tosorintsi myth, as narrated by Mr. Andres Chompati, is given in full below as partial documentation of the different kinds of roles discussed in the previous sections.

A free translation of the myth is given first. In that section numbers preceding paragraphs indicate the clause numbers of the vernacular text included in each paragraph. A literal translation is given beneath each clause of the vernacular text. Pronominal affixes and affixes particularly relevant to participant roles, e.g., causative and benefactive, are given a literal translation. Affixes which are not translated, e.g., aspect, are indicated by the symbol |. . .| in the literal translation but their meanings are reflected in the free translation.

Free translation:

(Chapter 1, 1—5) 'Thus Mariberi did long ago when he changed [people into rocks, etc.]. He was said of long ago.

(6—23) 'While he was changing [people into rocks, etc.] there was his relative whom he carried. It's said and I listened a little when [the old story-tell told it in my presence. Mabireri would carry him and carry him; he would go far. His relative would advise him when he saw any children climbing. [Relative impatiently:] 'Who is that climbing, relative?' Since Mabireri knew [he would answer]: 'It's just termites' [and the children turned into termites]. [Again relative:] 'Whoever is that climbing?' 'It's just termites,' Mabireri said [and they, too, turned into termites].

(Chapter 2, 24–35) 'After a while the people were disgusted (with Mariberi). He would say to them: 'Brother-in-law, go dam the stream so that I can roast fish in leaves after a while.' 'Let's go dam the stream,' they said to one another. They all went; they were gone.

(36–40) 'Rapidly they piled up the rocks. They piled and piled, then they brought [leaves] and dried up the stream.

(41–50) 'After they finished, [Mabireri said], 'I'll go see my brother-in-law and roast fish in leaves and eat it right there.' He left and arrived where they had dammed the stream.

(51–67) 'He said, 'Have you dried up the stream, brother-in-law?' 'Yes, I've dried it. Take some [fish], brother-in-law.' '[Oh] you gave me just a bunch of leaves,' he said. He thought it was leaves but it was really fish. Then he blew: 'may he turn into a rock.' Right then Mabireri turned [the one who had handed it to him] into a rock. If the man hadn't given him leaves, he wouldn't have changed him.

(68–74) 'Another time he would send them to dam the stream and right then he would change another person into a rock. Again and again he sent them to dam the stream and changed others into rocks.

(75–88) 'Then they were really disgusted with him. 'Now truly, what can we do to him? How many times will he go on changing our people [into rocks]? Come let's kill him,' one of them said. They were really disgusted. Then Mabireri, the deity, said to them, 'brother-in-law, go dam the stream.' 'Okay, let's go, all of us, and dam the stream as brother-in-law ordered us.'

(89–91) 'They all went to dam the stream. The rocks sounded *toro, toro, toro* [as they piled them up]. Rapidly they caused the stream to dry up.

(92–99) 'Mabireri arrived there and looked around. 'Have you dried it?' 'Yes, we've dried it, have some [fish].' They took [a bunch to give him] but just gave him leaves. 'Have some fish.'

(100–109) 'They had already piled lots of wood in the fire. Mabireri was there by the fire shading his eyes [from it]. 'Now!' they grabbed him and lifted him up and threw him into the fire. 'Good enough for

him! Thus, no one will change us [into rocks] any longer.' They hurried
to finish gathering the fish.

(110–117) "Tear down the dam [so his ashes will wash down].' They
tore down the dam; the water rushed in *siararara*. His ashes rose to the
top and floated. They were gone; he ascended to the sky.

(Chapter 3, 118–136) 'Now the relative [a boy] whom Mabireri had
carried was left alone. One of the people went down the river and said to
him, 'Your relative has been burned.' 'Come let's kill him, too, lest he
follow in Mabireri's steps and change us into rocks,' they said. But the
boy's sister said, 'Don't burn him; I'll take him for my servant, he can
help me.' So she took him home with her. 'Stay here with someone [us],'
[she said to him].

(137–146) 'Then she said to the boy, 'Swing your nephew in his hammock for me so that I can make something for you to wear without in-
terruption.' 'Okay.' He swung the baby, and as he swung he said: 'Swing
swing *tsionia*. Swinging may [he] appear termite. Swing, swing may [he]
appear a rock. Swing may [he] appear a termite.'

(147–166) 'Then his sister scolded him, 'Don't play that way; don't
talk that way lest you change your little nephew. You'll do just like the
one who used to carry you, you'll change us.' 'Sis, I'm going now to go
tear down the canal my dead relative dug with me some time ago.'
'Don't go,' she said, 'lest you burn it. You say you're thinking of the
canal your dead relative dug with you. [Forget it.] You [just] stay here
and swing your nephew for me so that I can hurry and make [your robe].'
Then he went on swinging him.

(167–177) 'Suddenly the boy disappeared; he was gone there where he
had been thinking of to his relative's canal. Then his sister said, 'What's
happened that my son hasn't cried; he's been sleeping a long time?' She
got up [and looked], and there was only a rock lying there in the baby's
hammock.

(178–196) 'Then she said, 'That worthless brother of mine has
changed his little nephew into a rock on me. Where's he gone now?' 'Run
go tell your father.' So the daughter ran and advised him, 'My uncle has
changed my little brother.' The baby's father ran. 'His uncle has changed
his little nephew into a rock on me,' [the mother said]. 'Go follow him
and beat him to death. He was going to tear down his relative's canal, he
said a little while ago.' 'Now why on earth has my worthless brother-in-
law changed his little nephew on me? I'll go beat him to death,' [the
father said].

(197–210) 'The father left and came out [of the jungle] there where already his [brother-in-law's] corn was. [It had just been planted as the boy went along and had grown up miraculously.] He came out [farther] and already there was corn maturing. He came out [farther] and already the ears were ripening. He came out again, and again, and again; then, as he arrived, he heard the boy pounding rocks there where he was feeling for crabs.

(211–220) 'Upon arriving he called to him, 'You worthless brother-in-law, why did you change your nephew on me? Come I'll kill you.' He answered, 'No don't kill me, instead nail me down with a pifayo tree stake. Then I'll turn into a pifayo tree and you can eat my fruit.'

(221–233) 'The father took him to nail him. 'Where shall I nail you, brother-in-law?' 'Here on my head.' Then he hammered, *tok* (hammering sound). 'Harder, brother-in-law.' *Tok*. 'Harder, brother-in-law.' *Tok*. 'Harder, brother-in-law.' *Tok*. 'Harder, brother-in-law.' *Tok*. 'Harder, brother-in-law,' he said.

(234–247) ''Now when you strike inside me, brother-in-law, run just a little ways, stop, turn around and look at me. That way the pifayo fruit will ripen quickly and not one will fall to the ground immaturely. [Go on hitting] harder, brother-in-law.' He continued to strike, *tok*. 'Harder, brother-in-law.' *Tok*; he struck inside!

(248–256) 'Go, run.' He ran. 'Look around, brother-in-law, look around.' But he didn't stop. He was gone for the boy's hot springs [which his blood turned into] were really frightful.

(257) 'That's all.'

(1) *aro   i-kanta hirai*
   NOW   HE-DO BEFORE
(2) *ira   mabireri-ta-tsi*
   THAT   MABIRERI....UNSPECIFIED_PERSON
(3) *i-nganti-ngani*
   HE–IS_SAID_OF–PASSIVE
(4) *kara   i-pegainatanti*
   WHEN   HE-CHANGE_INTO
(5) *i-nganti-ngani kara hiraira*
   HE–IS_SAID_OF–PASSIVE WHEN BEFORE
(6) *i-pegainatanti*
   HE–CHANGE_INTO
(7) *ainta   i-sari*
   THERE_IS   HIS-RELATIVE

(8) *i-kë-ri*
   HE-CARRY-HIM
(9) *ira   komantageti-ri*
   THAT   ADVISE-HIM
(10) *o-kanta-gani*
   IT-IS_SAID-PASSIVE
(11) *na-kamëmati   arosatapagi   naro*
   I-LISTEN   A_LITTLE   I
(12) *i-kengitsata-mo-eti-na-ro*   *naro*
   HE-NARRATE-IN_PRESENCE_OF. . .ME-IT   ME
(13) *i-ngianë-ri*
   HE-CARRY-HIM
(14) *i-ngianë-ri*
   HE-CARRY-HIM
(15) *i-riata   hanta*
   HE-GO   FAR
(16) *i-raniopë*
   HE-SEE
(17) *pairiraka   i-rata-ig-e hanekihegi*
   WHOEVER   HE-CLIMB-PLURAL. . . CHILDREN
(18) *pairi ata-tsi-ri*   *ira-ri-na-sari*
   WHO CLIMB-UNSPECIFIED_PERSON. . . THAT-BUT MY-RELATIV
(19) *atirama   i-rate*
   SINCE   HE-KNOW
(20) *iri-anti   kahiro*
   HE-ONLY   TERMITE
(21) *pairiroko   atobintëngi-tsi-ne*
   WHO_MAYBE   CLIMB-UNSPECIFIED_PERSON. . .
(22) *iri-anti   kahiro*
   HE-ONLY   TERMITE
(23) *i-kanë-ri*
   HE-SAY_TO-HIM
(24) *aro   i-kanka*
   NOW   HE-DO
(25) *i-tsirisiobagitaka*
   HE-DISGUSTED
(26) *i-kanti-ri   ir-aniri*
   HE-SAY_TO-HIM   HIS-BROTHER_IN_LAW

(27) *n-ani*   *n-ani*
MY-BROTHER_IN_LAW   MY-BROTHER_IN_LAW
pi-ngomointegiteni
YOU-DAM_STREAM

(28) *pi-ngomointegite*
YOU-DAM_STREAM

(29) *ora*   *n-atasiibageginteta*   *mitiri*   *karaka*
THAT   I-ROAST_IN_LEAVES   FISH   LATER

(30) *intsome*
LET'S_GO

(31) *o-ngomo-ig-ete*
WE-DAM_STREAM-PLURAL. . .

(32) *intsome*
LET'S_GO

(33) *intsome*
LET'S_GO

(34) *i-tsongaitanak-a*
HE-FINISH_AWAY-REFLEXIVE

(35) *hatake*   *(∅)-inane*
GONE   HE-EXIST

(36) *omanapage*   *i-komopë-ro*
RAPIDLY   HE-DAM_STREAM-IT

(37) *i-komopë-ro*
HE-DAM_STREAM-IT

(38) *i-komopë-ro*
HE-DAM_STREAM-IT

(39) *i-agë-ro*
HE-TAKE-IT

(40) *i-ogakë-ro*
HE-DRY-IT

(41) *i-ogakë-ro*
HE-DRY-IT

(42) *kanta*   *i-atahe*   *iriro*
THERE   HE-GO   HE

(43) *aro*   *na-niahateni*   *n-anirirangi*
NOW   I-GO_SEE   MY-BROTHER_IN_LAW. . .

(44) *n-atasibaigitëteta*   *mitiri*
I-ROAST_IN_LEAVES   FISH

(45) *aito*   *na-hagabagëgiteta*
RIGHT_THEN   I-EAT
(46) *i-ake*
HE-GO
(47) *i-ake*
HE-GO
(48) *i-agaitinai*
HE-ARRIVE_AT_RIVER
(49) *i-agaitinai*
HE-ARRIVE_AT_RIVER
(50) *kanta*   *i-komo-ig-e*
THERE   HE-DAM_STREAM-PLURAL
(51) *i-kane*
HE-SAY
(52) *p-ogakë-ro-ma*   *n-ani*
YOU-DRY-IT. . .   MY-BROTHER_IN_LAW
(53) *hee*   *n-ogake-ro*
YES   I-DRY-IT
(54) *n-ogake-ro*
I-DRY-IT
(55) *ne-ri-ka*   *n-ani*
TAKE-HIM   MY-BROTHER_IN_LAW
(56) *iro-ntiri*   *somantosira*   *po-pai-na*
IT-ONLY   LEAVES   YOU-GIVE-ME
(57) *i-kanke-ri*
HE-SAY_TO-HIM
(58) *i-hiti-ro*   *somantosi*
HE-THINK-IT   LEAVES
(59) *i-hiti-ri*   *ira mitiri*
HE-THINK-HIM   THAT FISH
(60) *aka*   *iriro*   *mitiri*   *inabita*
BUT   HE   FISH   EXIST
(61) *irorota-me*   *i-me-ri ora somantosi*
IT-CONDITIONAL   HE-GIVE-HIM THAT LEAVES
(62) *kero-me*   *i-pegi-ri*
NOT-CONDITIONAL   HE-CHANGE_INTO (ROCK)-HIM
(63) *aro*   *i-kanti*
NOW   HE-SAY

(64) *iro-ntiri   po-pai-na   somantosi*
IT-ONLY   YOU-GIVE-ME   LEAVES
(65) *i-piakani   piho*
HE-CHANGE_INTO (BLEW) PIHO
(66) *mopë   i-megi-ma*
ROCK   HE-CHANGE_INTO-MAY
(67) *aito i-pegobike-ri   mopë*
RIGHT_THEN HE-CHANGE_INTO-HIM ROCK
(68) *aro   i-kanka*
NOW   HE-DO
(69) *i-gati-ri*
HE-SEND-HIM
(70) *komota-tsi*
DAM_STREAM-UNSPECIFIED_PERSON
(71) *aito   i-megobitahi-ri*
RIGHT_THEN   HE-CHANGE_INTO-HIM
(72) *i-gati-ri*
HE-SEND-HIM
(73) *komota-tsi*
DAM_STREAM-UNSPECIFIED_PERSON
(74) *aito   i-megobitahi-ri*
RIGHT_THEN   HE-CHANGE_INTO-HIM
(75) *aro   i-tsirisiaka-ri*
NOW   HE-DISGUSTED_WITH-HIM
(76) *kanta   atirosonoriko   a-nganti-ri-ra*
THERE   HOW_TRULY_MAYBE   WE-DO-HIM. . .
(77) *te   e-raita   i-megainatënte yaka*
NO   US-HOW_MANY_TIMES   HE-CHANGE_INTO HERE
(78) *intsome*
LET'S_GO
(79) *a-tagi-ri*
WE-BURN-HIM
(80) *i-kanke*
HE-SAY
(81) *iri-raiko   i-tsirisiobagita*
HE-HOW_MANY_TIMES   HE-DISGUSTED_WITH
(82) *i-kanti ira   mabireri   tosorintsi-ta-tsi*
HE-SAY THAT   MABIRERI DEITY. . .UNSPECIFIED-PERSON

(83) *i-kanti-ri ora*
    HE-SAY_TO-HIM ((HESITATION)[5]
(84) *n-ani pi-ngomointegite*
    BROTHER_IN_LAW YOU-DAM_STREAM
(85) *aro   intsoma-ig-e*
    NOW   LET'S_GO-PLURAL. . .
(86) *intsoma-ig-e   omagaro*
    LET'S_GO-PLURAL. . .   ALL
(87) *kara   o-ngomoitegite*
    THERE   WE-DAM_STREAM
(88) *ka   i-gaki-na n-aniri*
    THERE HE-SEND-ME MY-BROTHER_IN_LAW
(89) *i-ata-si-ke-ro*
    HE-GO-PURPOSIVE. . .IT
(90) *i-komo-ig-apë*   *toro toro toro*
    HE-DAM_STREAM-PLURAL. . .   SOUND OF PILING UP ROCKS
(91) *omanapage   omanapage   i-o-biriatë-ro*
    RAPIDLY   RAPIDLY   HE-CAUSATIVE-DRY-IT
(92) *areepa   i-areepa   kanta*
    (HESITATION) HE-ARRIVE   THERE
(93) *i-netsapë-ro*
    HE-LOOK_ARRIVING-IT
(94) *p-ogake-ro*
    YOU-DRY-IT
(95) *hee   n-ogake-ro*
    YES   I-DRY-IT
(96) *ne-ri-ka*
    TAKE-HIM. . .
(97) *i-agë*
    HE-TAKE
(98) *ora   somántosi   i-pë-ri*
    THAT   LEAVES HE-GIVE-HIM
(99) *ne-ri-ka mitiri*
    TAKE-HIM. . .   FISH
(100) *aroka aro i-tsimabota-ig-ë*
    NOW_IF NOW HE-PILE_FIREWOOD-PLURAL. . .
(101) *i-tsimaboke*   *kanta*
    HE-PILE_FIREWOOD   THERE

(102) *kanta irironi kanta kanta-tsi*   *nega*
THERE HE THERE DO-UNSPECIFIED_PERSON   WHERE
(103) *i-otapitapiogitaka*   *kara*   *tsitsi-kë*
HE-SHADE_EYES_WITH_HAND   THERE   FIRE_AT
(104) *ha*   *i-agë-ri*
NOW!   HE-TAKE-HIM
(105) *i-tsomake-ri*
HE-LIFT-HIM
(106) *i-hokobogitë-ri*   *kanta*
HE-THROW_INTO_FIRE-HIM   THERE
(107) *asate*   *pi-nganti-ri*
GOOD_ENOUGH   YOU-DO-HIM
(108) *negara*   *te iri-raita*   *pegainate-i-ne*
WHERE NO   HE-HOW_MANY_TIMES   CHANGE_INTO-US. . .
(109) *omanapage   i-obitë-ri*   *mitirira*
RAPIDLY   HE-GATHER-HIM FISH
(110) *i-tsonganake-ri*
HE-FINISH-HIM
(111) *kanta*   *pi-ntisongë-go-të-ri*
THERE YOU-TEAR_DOWN_DAM-INCLUDED. . .HIM
(112) *i-tisongë-go-të-ri*   *siaararararara*
HE-TEAR_DOWN_DAM-INCLUDED. . .HIM SOUND_OF_WATER
RUSHING DOWN
(113) *i-gomantareganaka*
HE-RISE_ASHES
(114) *kanta*   *i-amatë*
THERE   HE-FLOAT
(115) *i-amatane*
HE-FLOAT
(116) *hatake*
GONE
(117) *i-sorokire-ngani*
HE-ASCEND_TO_SKY-PASSIVE
(118) *irinibani ira*   *irinibani*   *ira*   *i-giani*
(HESITATION) HE_ALONE HE   HE-CARRY
(119) *i-abatetane*   *komatenta*
HE-GO_DOWNRIVER   DOWNRIVER
(120) *i-kanti-ri*
HE-SAY_TO-HIM

(121) *i-take-ngani*   *pi-tsiarineni*
HE-BURN-PASSIVE YOUR-DEAD_RELATIVE

(122) *aro intsome*
NOW LET'S_GO

(123) *a-ntsibatë-go-tantima-ri*
WE-KILL-INCLUDED. . .HIM

(124) *iriro-ke*   *agaganai-ro-ni*
HE-AND PASS_ON-IT. . .

(125) *i-ripegana-i-ri*   *i-tsiarine*
HE-CHANGE_INTO-US. . . HIS-RELATIVE

(126) *i-megaibagentina-i*
HE-CHANGE_INTO-US

(127) *i-kanke*
HE-SAY

(128) *o-kanti*   *ora*   *iri-tsiro*
SHE-SAY THAT HIS-SISTER

(129) *kero pi-tagi-ri*
NOT YOU-BURN-HIM

(130) *n-agai-ri-ni*
I-TAKE-HIM. . .

(131) *no-meraro*   *irirota*
MY-SERVANT HE

(132) *no-merataima-na-ro*
I-COMMAND-ME-IT

(133) *oka*   *iagairi iagairi*   *p-agai-ri*   *kanta*
THAT (HESITATION) SHE-TOOK-HIM THERE

(134) *o-tentaha-ri*   *pongotsi-kë*
SHE-TOOK-HIM HOUSE-AT

(135) *p-inaga*   *pairini*
YOU-REMAIN WHO

(136) *p-inaga*   *pairini kanta*
YOU-REMAIN WHO THERE

(137) *aro*   *o-kanti-ri okantiri ora*
NOW SHE-SAY_TO-HIM (HESITATION)

(138) *pi-sionkati-na-ri*   *pi-tinerira*
YOU-HAMMOCK_SWING-(BENEFACTIVE)- ME-HIM YOUR-NEPHEW

(139) *pi-sionkati-na-ri*
YOU-HAMMOCK_SWING-(BENEFACTIVE)-ME-HIM
pi-tinerira
YOUR-NEPHEW

(140) *omanata n-agat-anon-tahë-mi*
RAPIDLY I-TAKE-BENEFACTIVE. . . YOU
(141) *pi-ngaera*
YOU-WEAR
(142) *aro*
NOW
(143) *i-sionka*
HE-HAMMOCK_SWING
(144) *i-sionkatë-ri*
HE-HAMMOCK_SWING-HIM
(145) *i-kanti   i-kanti ora*
HE-SAY   (HESITATION)
(146) (song follows): *sionka sionka tsionia isionka*
SWING SWING TSIONIA HE_SWING
tsiomontë   kahiro   tsiomontë
APPEAR   TERMITE   APPEAR
sionka sionka tsiomontë mapi tsiomontë isionka tsiomontë
SWING SWING APPEAR ROCK APPEAR HE_SWING APPEAR
kahiro   tsiomontë
TERMITE   APPEAR
(147) *aro   o-kanti*
NOW   SHE-SAY
(148) *pi-gesantëbagiti*
YOU-PLAY_BADLY
(149) *pi-kantabagiti*
YOU-SAY_AIMLESSLY
(150) *kara po-megatë-na-ri*
THERE YOU-CHANGE_INTO-(BENEFACTIVE)-ME-HIM
ika pi-tineri-ani
THAT YOUR-NEPHEW-LITTLE
(151) *po-sigana-ri*
YOU-FOLLOW-HIM
(152) *hanaari   kihi-mi hirai   ora*
LIKE_HIM   CARRY-YOU BEFORE   (HESITATION)
(153) *po-megaibagentana-i*
YOU-CHANGE_INTO-US
(154) *hoe aro na-hake*
SISTER NOW I-GO

(155) *na-ntisongëte*   *i-ginareni*
      I-TEAR_DOWN_DAM   HIS-CANAL
(156) *i-kinat-agi-i-na-ni*
      HE-DIG-ACCOMPANIMENT. . .ME. . .
      na-sarini hirai
      MY-DEAD_RELATIVE BEFORE
(157) *o-ngantimata*
      SHE-SAY
(158) *kero pi-ati*
      NOT YOU-GO
(159) *pi-sagantë-ro-ka*
      YOU-BURN-IT-IF
(160) *pi-sagantë-ro-ri*
      YOU-BURN-IT. . .
(161) *pi-kengetinai-ri*   *i-ginareni*
      YOU-THINK-HIM   HIS-CANAL
(162) *i-kinat-ag-i-mi*
      HE-DIG-ACCOMPANIMENT. . .YOU
      pisarini   *hirai*
      YOUR_DEAD_RELATIVE   BEFORE
(163) *pi-ngane*
      YOU-SAY
(164) *pi-sionkati-na-ri*
      YOU-HAMMOCK_SWING_(BENEFACTIVE)-
      pi-tineri
      ME-HIM YOUR-NEPHEW
(165) *omanata*   *na-ngant-anon-ti-mi*
      RAPIDLY   I-DO-BENEFACTIVE. . .YOU
(166) *aike*   *i-sionka*   *sionkatë-ri*
      THEN   HE-SWING   SWING-HIM
(167) *aro*   *i-peganaka*
      NOW   HE-CHANGE_INTO
(168) *aro*   *i-peganaka*
      NOW   HE-CHANGE_INTO
(169) *hatake*
      GONE
(170) *hatake inane*
      GONE HE_EXIST

(171) *kanta   i-kenganake-ri-kënta*
THERE   HE-THINK-HIM-AT_THERE
i-ginarekë i-sari
HIS-CANAL HIS-RELATIVE

(172) *aro   o-kanti*
NOW   SHE-SAY

(173) *ati   i-piaka*
WHERE   HE-CHANGE_INTO

(174) *te   i-raragahema   no-tomirangi*
NO   HE-CRY   MY-SON

(175) *iri-raiko   naarai   i-samë*
HE-RECENTLY   RECENTLY   HE-SLEEP

(176) *o-kabitanaka*
SHE-GET_UP

(177) *iro-nti mopë kisagesëga-tsi-a*
IT-ONLY ROCK LIE-UNSPECIFIED_PERSON. . .
kara i-sionkarokë
THERE HIS-HAMMOCK_IN

(178) *aro   o-kanti*
NOW   SHE-SAY

(179) *i-pegatanai-na-ri-niri*
HE-CHANGE_INTO-(BENEFACTIVE)-ME-HIM. . .
i-tineri-ani   hai-kimingarani
HIS-NEPHEW-LITTLE   BROTHER-WORTHLESS

(180) *atike i-ake   yamai*
WHERE HE-GO   NOW

(181) *pi-ha*
YOU-GO

(182) *pi-ngomantëti-ri p-iri*
YOU-ADVISE-HIM YOUR-FATHER

(183) *pi-siganaka iri-sinto*
SHE-RUN HIS-DAUGHTER

(184) *o-komantëti-ri*
SHE-ADVISE-HIM

(185) *i-peganai-ri-metsi   hai-ani no-kongiri-rangi*
HE-CHANGE_INTO-HIM. . .   BROTHER-LITTLE MY-UNCLE. . .

(186) *i-sigopë ir-iri*
HE-RUN HIS-FATHER

(187) *i-pegatanai-na-ri*
HE-CHANGE_INTO-(BENEFACTIVE)-ME-HIM
i-tineri-ani   *iri-kongiri*   *ora*
HIS-NEPHEW-LITTLE HIS-UNCLE (HESITATION)
(188) *pi-hate*
YOU-GO
(189) *pi-giatë-ri*
YOU-FOLLOW-HIM
(190) *pi-takiti-ri*   *ora*
YOU-KILL_WITH_STICK-HIM (HESITATION)
(191) *pi-takiti-ri*   *ora*
YOU-KILL_WITH_STICK-HIM (HESITATION)
(192) *i-ginare*   *i-sari*   *i-ntisongëte*
HIS-CANAL HIS-RELATIVE HE-TEAR_DOWN_DAM
(193) *i-kanëni naarai*
HE-SAY RECENTLY
(194) *atirasonori i-kanta*
HOW_TRULY HE-DO
(195) *i-pegatanai-na-ri i-tineri-ani n-aniri-kiminga*
HE-CHANGE_INTO-(BENEFACTIVE)-ME-HIM HIS-NEPHEW-
LITTLE MY-BROTHER_IN_LAW-WORTHLESS
(196) *na-takiti-ri-ta*
I-KILL_WITH_STICK-HIM. . .
(197) *i-ake*
HE-GO
(198) *aroke aroke p-ine*
(HESITATION) NOW_AND IT-EXIST
(199) *i-ake*
HE-GO
(200) *i-kontetane*
HE-COME_OUT
(201) *aroke p-inane singi*   *i-singine*
NOW_AND IT-EXIST CORN   HIS-CORN
(202) *i-kontetane*
HE-COME_OUT
(203) *aroke p-agabagaka*
NOW_AND IT-MATURING-EARS
(204) *i-kontëtane*
HE-COME_OUT

(204a) *aroke*   *o-këterigisigi*
NOW_AND   IT-RIPENING_EARS

(205) *i-kontetane*   *basini*
HE-COME_OUT   ANOTHER

(206) *i-konetane basini*
HE-COME_OUT ANOTHER

(207) *i-kontetane basini aro*
HE-COME_OUT ANOTHER NOW

(208) *i-kemopë-ri pëng pëng pëng*
HE-HEAR_ARRIVING-HIM SOUND OF ROCK POUNDING

(209) *i-kanti-ro mopë*
HE-DO-IT ROCK

(210) *kanta*   *i-pasati-ri*   *ir-osirote*
THERE   HE-FEEL_FOR-HIM   HIS-CRAB

(211) *i-kaimë-go-tapë-ri*   *n-ani*
HE-CALL-INCLUDED-ARRIVING-HIM MY-BROTHER_IN_LAW

(212) *po-pegatanai-na-ri-niko*
YOU-CHANGE_INTO-(BENEFACTIVE)-ME-HIM. . .
pi-tineri-kimingarani
YOUR-NEPHEW-WORTHLESS_ONE

(213) *hoke*
COME

(214) *no-pasati-mi*
I-KILL-YOU

(215) *ma*   *kero*   *pi-pasati-na*   *n-ani*
NO   NOT   YOU-KILL-ME   MY-BROTHER_IN_LAW

(216) *kero*   *pi-pasati-na*
NOT   YOU-KILL-ME

(217) *po-pëakitigi-na ora*   *iroro këri-tsobiteki*
YOU-NAIL-ME (HESITATION) IT PIFAYO_TREE-STĄKE
ora
(HESITATION)

(218) *aro*   *këri no-meganëma*
NOW   PIFAYO I-CHANGE_INTO_REFLEXIVE

(219) *aro*   *po-pë-na-niri*
NOW   YOU-EAT-ME

(220) *i-kanë-ri*   *i-kanke-ri*
(HESITATION)   HE-SAY_TO-HIM

(221) *i-agë-ri*
    HE-TAKE-HIM
(222) *i-pëake-ri*
    HE-NAIL-HIM
(223) *ati   no-pëake-mi   n-ani*
    WHERE I-NAIL-YOU MY-BROTHER_IN_LAW
(224) *yaka   na-gitokëka*
    HERE MY-HEAD_ON
(225) *aro   i-pëake-ri   tok*
    NOW HE-NAIL-HIM HITTING_SOUND
(226) *kabeni   n-ani*
    HARDER MY-BROTHER_IN_LAW
(227) *tok*
    HITTING_SOUND
(228) *kabeni   n-ani*
    HARDER MY-BROTHER_IN_LAW
(229) *tok*
    HITTING_SOUND
(230) *kabeni   n-ani*
    HARDER MY-BROTHER_IN_LAW
(231) *tok*
    HITTING_SOUND
(232) *kabeni   n-ani*
    HARDER MY-BROTHER_IN_LAW
(233) *i-kanka*
    HE-SAY
(234) *aike   i-osananke-ri*
    THEN HE-STRUCK_INSIDE-HIM
(235) *aroka   p-osananki-na   n-ani*
    NOW_IF YOU-STRIKE_INSIDE-ME MY BROTHER_IN_LAW
(236) *pi-sigëmaigitigima*
    YOU-RUN_A_LITTLE_WAY
(237) *p-aratianke*
    YOU-HALT_THERE
(238) *pi-pisitakima*
    YOU-TURN_AROUND
(239) *pi-niabintëma   tëika*
    YOU-LOOK_BEHIND (HESITATION)

(240) *aroke tsonabatëkeragitake*   *këri*
NOW_AND RIPENING_NOT_WASTE   PIFAYO_FRUIT
∅-inane
IT-EXIST

(241) *i-siganaka*
HE-RUN

(242) *kabeni*   *n-ani*
HARDER   MY-BROTHER_IN_LAW

(243) *tok*
HITTING_SOUND

(244) *i-ogagane-ri*
HE-CONTINUE-HIM

(245) *kabeni*   *n-ani*
HARDER   MY-BROTHER_IN_LAW

(246) *tok*
HITTING_SOUND

(247) *sanare*
STRIKE_INSIDE

(248) *pi-ha*
YOU-GO

(249) *pi-siganëma*
YOU-RUN

(250) *i-siganaka*
HE-RUN

(251) *pi-nebintima*   *n-ani*
YOU-LOOK_BEHIND   MY-BROTHER_IN_LAW

(252) *ni-nebintima*   *n-ani*
YOU-LOOK_BEHIND   MY-BROTHER_IN_LAW

(253) *te*
NO

(254) *hatake*
GONE

(255) *o-ngantima*
IT-DO

(256) *o-gobengaka*   *ora i-maganite*
IT-FEARFUL   THAT HIS-HOT_SPRINGS

(257) *aro*   *o-karati*
NOW   IT-CUT_OFF

Summer Institute of Linguistics

418   *M.R. Wise*

Bibliography

Dundes, A. (1964) *The Morphology of North American Indian Folktales.* Folklore Fellows Communications. No. 195. Helsinki: Suomalainen Tiedeakatemia.

Goodenough, W.H. (1956) Componential Analysis and the Study of Meaning. *Language* 32. 195–216.

Lounsbury, F.G. (1956) A Semantic Analysis of the Pawnee Kinship Usage. *Language* 32. 158–194.

Pike, K.L. (1962) Dimensions of Grammatical Constructions. *Language* 38.221–244.

Propp, V. (1958) *Morphology of the Folktale.* Translated by Laurence Scott from 1928 original. Indiana University Publications in Anthropology Folklore and Linguistics, No. 10.

Wise, M.R. (1968) *Identification of Participants in Discourse: A Study of Aspects of Form and Meaning in Nomatsiguenga.* University of Michigan Ph. D. Dissertation.

SOME GRAMMATICAL FEATURES OF
LEGENDARY NARRATIVE IN ANCASH QUECHUA

Helen LARSEN

In the early stages of the grammatical analysis of the Huaraz dialect of Ancash Quechua, the data were divided into three classes of discourse to be studied separately[1]. These tentative classes were legendary narrative, personal account narrative, and conversation. Although the initial division was made intuitively, some distinctive grammatical features based on differences in time and location orientations and on differences in focus of attention have since become apparent which support the validity of this division.

The legendary narrative is a complete unit, creating its own background context at the onset. This is followed by a series of events leading to a conclusion. The focus of attention is, in general, on the lead character. Time is oriented toward sequence of action without reference to the time of the speech event, and location toward the movement of the dramatis personae. Neither the speaker nor the addressee(s) are involved in the events of the narrative.

The personal account differs from the legendary narrative in that the

---

[1] An earlier version of this paper, 'Algunos rasgos distintivos de la narración tradicional en el Quechua de Ancash' was read at the XXXIX International Congress of Americanists, Lima, Perú, 1970.

The analysis presented is based on field work carried out from 1966–1969 in Marcará, a town of some 3,000 Quechua speakers in the province of Carhuaz, department of Ancash, Perú. The principal informants were Mr. Elías Huayané and Miss Leocadia Granados. An IBM Concordance of Ancash Quechua texts, produced under the sponsorship of National Science Foundation grant GS–1605, was useful in the analysis of the data.

Discussions with James Loriot have had considerable influence on my views of Quechua grammar. I am indebted to Mary Ruth Wise for help in this presentation of the analysis. Her dissertation (Wise, 1968) was influential in shaping my viewpoint on the nature of discourse structure.

speaker is involved in the events of the narrative as either lead character
or observer so that the story is told from his viewpoint. The action sequence is the focus of attention. As the speaker is relating what has
happened, the place and time of the speech act function as location and
time orientations to his story. In this class of narrative, also, the addressee
is uninvolved in the events being related.

Conversation, unlike the narratives, is not oriented to past events. The
location and time orientations are 'here' and 'now'. Addressee is involved in that a response is required of him.

In this paper the grammatical features which characterize the legendary narrative will be described. These features are: (1) the structure of
the narrative sentence, (2) the narrative verb ending, (3) the form of the
noun phrase, and (4) the topic markers. A cursory study of narrative
material from the Province of Pomabamba, also in the Department of
Ancash, revealed that many of the same forms described below occur in
the Pomabamba material, but their distribution and function vary considerably from that of the Huaraz dialect. Although one would expect
to find even more variation in less closely related Quechua dialects,
many of the grammatical features described probably occur in most of
them.

Only a beginning has been made in the analysis of structures beyond
the sentence, but three major divisions of the legendary narrative have
been posited: background, body, and conclusion. These divisions will
serve as the basis for our discussion. In the background unit the identity
of the lead character is established. He is referred to by one of his roles
in society, such as: an orphan or a young boy. This reference suggests
something of the conflict which he as lead character will have to resolve.
The background is short, consisting of only one or two sentences. The
body of the narrative is a sequence of actions grouped into event units,
or as the folklorists refer to them, functions (Propp, 1958). The narrative
terminates with a conclusion, which, like the background, is short. These
divisions differ not only in content but also in the variations of the narrative sentence which occur in each.

1. Narrative sentence

The narrative sentence, the basic grammatical unit of the narrative, consists of one or more clauses and a sentence marking construction. In its fullest variation the sentence marking construction has three parts, two of which are connective. Its parts are as follows[2]:

1. Antecedent connective
   (a) demonstrative   (b) dependent clause =
       tsay   preceding verb root
                            and dependent
                            endings (*-pti-n*)/(*-r*)
2. Sequence connective
   -na
3. Reportive
   -sh

The third and final unit of the construction, *-sh*, reportive marker, indicates that the speaker heard the information and is passing it on. In the personal account narrative the verifier *-m* occurs rather than *-sh*. (Allomorphs *-shi* and *-mi* occur following closed syllables.) Parker, describing these morphemes for the Ayacucho dialect, states:

> /-mI/ generalmente se agrega a la frase de la cláusula que indica la información mas importante de la cláusula, frecuentemente relativa al tópico hecho explícito en la misma. ... En contraste con los otros encliticos de comentario (/-shI/ y /-chA/) indica que se habla por experiencia o convicción personal, *pero ne se puede traducir* [italics mine] (1965, p. 94).

In my opinion, Parker was unable to adequately translate, describe

---

[2] The transcription of examples and the text in this paper is based on the phonemic analysis with the following exceptions:
(a) Long vowels are transcribed by vowel and the morphophoneme {H} in first person markers and certain affixes such as /čo:/ 'in', which is transcribed "choh". In these environments, therefore, the following morphophonemic transcriptions are used:
/i:/ (/e:/ in Marcará) < {ih}
/a:/   < {ah}
/u:/ (/o:/ in Marcará) < {uh}
(b) Vowels followed by the morphophoneme {Y} are transcribed morphophonemically as follows:
/e:/ < {ay}
/i:/ < {uy}
/i/ < {iy}
Other orthographic symbols used in native Quechua words are: /p/ "p", /t/ "t", /k/ "k", /q/ "q", /m/ "m", /n/ "n", /ñ/ "ñ", /s/ "s", /š/ "sh", /n/ "n", /¢/ "ts", /č/ "ch", /l/ "l", /λ/ "ll", /r/ "r", /w/ "w", /y/ "y", /i/ "i", /a/ "a", /u/ "u", /a:/ "aa", /o:/ "oo". In Spanish loan words the following additional symbols are used: /b/ "b", /d/ "d", /g/ "g", /f/ "f", /s/ "c", /e/ "e", /o/ "o".

the function, or state the distribution of these morphemes because his
syntactic description was limited to the clause. It is suggested here that
they do not pertain to the clause, the level at which he analyzed them,
but rather to a higher level unit in the discourse. In the Huaraz dialect
they characterize the sentence in narratives. Although its function differs somewhat, -*mi* is the sentence marker in conversation also.

The first and second units of the sentence marking construction function as connectives. The second unit, -*na*, is a time connective indicating
sequence. It could be translated 'then when'. The first unit refers to an
antecedent in the discourse by means of *tsay* 'that'. A dependent clause
also occurs in this antecedent connective unit; it includes obligatorily a
verb root plus affixes with a dependent verb ending, and optionally
other clause level units appropriate to that particular verb. Most frequently the verb root is a repetition of the one which immediately preceded. Occasionally, however, it is a verb expressing the natural result of
the previous one. For example, 'having arrived' occurs when the preceding verb was 'he went'. The forms -*pti-n* or -*r* 'having done that' are the
dependent endings of the verb. -*pti-n* indicates that the following clause
will have a different subject from that of the dependent clause while -*r*
indicates that the subject will be the same in both clauses.

As mentioned previously, the narrative sentence varies according to
its place in the narrative. For example, in the background unit the connectives of the sentence marking construction are not required and,
therefore, the obligatory reportive marker occurs phonologically attached
to the first grammatical unit of the clause. When sufficient background
information has been given, the action sequence or the body of the narrative is initiated; and the fullest variant of the construction, with its two
connectives, occurs as the first unit of each sentence. Its function is to
connect grammatically that which has already been related to the clause
which follows.

Note the variations of this construction in the folktale which is included in section 6. In sentence (1) the identity of the character is established as background to the sequence of events which are to follow.
Because there is no connective relationship, only the reportive marker
occurs, phonologically attached to the first grammatical unit of the main
clause.

(1) *huk nuna-sh*   *kanaq*   *kima tsuriyuk*
    a man-reportive marker   he was   three sons having
    There was a man who had three sons.

In (3), the form of the sentence marking construction indicates that the connective relationship is not temporal since -*na* does not occur. There is, nevertheless, a connective relationship to the previous action indicated by *tsay* 'that (being)'.

(3) *tsay-shi*   *ayukuyaanaq   tsay ishkaq*
    that(being)-reportive marker   they went   those two
    mayor kaqkuna
    older ones
    So the two older ones went away.

The variations, illustrated in sentences (5), (10) and (39), are apparently stylistically determined rather than formally. The demonstrative *tsay* can replace the entire dependent clause as in sentence (5) or it can be deleted leaving only the dependent clause, as in sentence (10).

(5) *tsay-na-sh*   *mayor kaq*
    that(being)-sequence-reportive marker   older one
    wawqinkunaqa niyan "..."
    his brothers   they say "..."
    Then the older brothers said, "..."

(10) *niptin-na-sh*   *huknin   wawqinna   nin*
     saying-sequence-reportive marker   one of   his brother   he says
     When he said that one of his brothers answered him.

(39) *tsay lluqaykaptin-na-sh*   *palumaqa*
     that climbing up-sequence-reportive marker   dove
     lapapapap   ayukun
     sound of flying   he goes
     When he was climbing up then a dove flew away (sound of flying).

At times the clause is connected to something other than an antecedent action, e.g., a locative — as in (16) and (17), a purpose or other dependent clause — as in (35) — or a temporal. In such a case, that unit occurs first in order in the sentence and the sequence connective and the reportive marker are phonologically attached to it.

(35) *tsaynoh kaykaayaptin-na-sh*   *hukna   chaarin*
     like that being-sequence-reportive marker   another one   he arrives
     That being the case another one arrived.

(16) *tsay kuchunchoh-na-sh*   *kanaq   monti*
     that shore-on-sequence-reportive marker   there was   a tree
     And there, on that shore, was a tree.

(17) *tsay montiman-na-sh*   *lluqakurkun*
    that tree into-sequence-reportive marker   he (was) climbed up
    And he had climbed up into that tree.

I conclude then that the sentence marking construction, rather than
being analyzed as a unit of the clause, should be considered a unit of the
narrative sentence and, hence, a distinguishing feature of narrative discourse structure.

2. Narrative verb ending

Another grammatical feature which characterizes legendary narrative
is the distinctive independent verb ending -*naq*. In other classes of discourse the verb endings indicate person and an orientation which is usually referred to as tense. This legendary narrative form, -*naq*, however,
specifies only by implication that the action is past and the actor third
person.

In the body of the narrative, when connectives of antecedent action
and sequence have been initiated as part of the sentence marking construction, the full form of the verb ending -*naq* is replaced by a short form -*n*,
as in sentence (5). This short form continues throughout the narrative
as long as there is connected sequence of action. If the sequence is interrupted to give some background information the full form is again used,
as in sentence (16).

3. Noun phrase formation and components

In legendary narrative the components of the noun phrases which
refer to the various characters are determined, in general, by the following criteria:

First, by place in the discourse. The first reference to a character gives
the pertinent information for establishing his identity. Every subsequent
reference has anaphoric features. For example, the lead character may be
referred to as 'a man', then as 'that man' and thereafter as 'man' plus a
marker which indicates antecedent reference without having to repeat
'that' with each occurrence. This marker is termed 'topic marker' and
will be more fully discussed below.

A second criterion is the relationship of the character to the lead character of the narrative. The lead character has his own identity and is referred to with a noun phrase which indicates something of his role in society. Other characters are usually referred to with a noun phrase which indicates their kinship relation to him. The grammatical manifestation is a possessive noun phrase such as 'his brother'.

Thirdly, the reference to a character may change to be in accord with the circumstances and characters of a new function unit. For example, the first references to a character may be 'child', while in new circumstances he is referred to as 'young man'. A character other than the lead may be in focus in one of the function units; in that case the phrase which normally refers to a third character is replaced by one which indicates his kinship relation to the new focus character. For example, if the lead character of the narrative is a man but the focus character of a given function unit is that man's father-in-law, the woman who was referred to as 'his wife' is now referred to as 'his daughter'. A character with a very minor role, however, frequently retains the original kinship reference although that reference may not properly relate him to the new focus character.

A fourth criterion is the distribution of the noun phrase. For example, the demonstrative *tsay* generally does not occur as a component of the noun phrase if it is functioning as direct object rather than subject of a clause. A further example is seen when a character is referred to in a direct quotation; in this instance the phrase is formed from the point of view of the one who is quoted but is derived from the form of the reference in narrative portions.

This section has been concerned with the factors which determine the components and form of the noun phrase as it occurs in a connected discourse. Although further investigation is necessary, it is apparent that there are other factors which determine whether or not the noun phrase will be deleted altogether from a clause. At the present stage of investigation, it appears likely (but has not yet been confirmed) that a noun phrase is required even though its occurrence results in redundancy of information at the boundary of a high level discourse unit tentatively termed paragraph.

4. Topic markers

The topic markers are a group of three morphemes which function in

the narrative, not as the topic marker of the clause as Solá (1958) and
Parker (1965) have indicated, but as part of discourse structure. They
are *-qa, -na,* and *-pis.* Although their function and meaning are difficult
to understand or describe, in legendary narrative these morphemes have
a more restricted function which facilitates analysis somewhat. The connective relationships of the action of the narrative are maintained by
the sentence marking construction. In a similar manner, the connected-
ness of the noun phrases referring to the characters is maintained by the
occurrence of the topic markers. Perhaps 'antecedent referent marker in
connected discourse' would be a better term than 'topic marker'.

In the body of the narrative, the connectives of action and sequence
having been initiated, *tsay* 'that' is replaced with *-qa,* in the noun
phrases referring to characters which have previously been introduced.
The occurrence of *-qa* indicates that the clause in which the noun phrase
occurs is part of the connected action sequence and that the character is
identical with one referred to previously. *-qa* is more or less equivalent
to 'the' in English[3].

Although *-qa* occurs most frequently, *-na* replaces it in certain instances and indicates that the subject of that particular clause is part of
a group which was previously referred to. The distribution of *-pis* which
can also replace *-qa* cannot be adequately described as yet.

Usually these topic markers occur phonologically attached to the
noun phrase which functions as subject of the clause. Occasionally they
are attached to a phrase functioning as direct object, indirect object or
location noun phrase. In such a case, they indicate emphasis.

5. Anaphoric reference in illustrative text

In the narrative text given in section 6, the references to the lead
character will illustrate various anaphoric noun phrase forms, and the
occurrence of the topic markers.

In sentence (1), the lead is introduced as his father's son, one of a
group of three brothers. His father is the focus character of this background unit. In the next reference, sentence (3), the lead is singled out
as the youngest of the brothers. The form *kaq* indicates an oppositional

---

[3] I am indebted to Peter Landerman for the suggestion that *-qa* is more or less equivalent to the
definite article in English.

relationship to a previous referent, in this case the two brothers. In sentence (4) *tsay* 'that' indicates an antecedent reference but now clearly puts him in the role of lead character with the use of the term 'little one' which indicates something of his social role. The occurrence of *-qa* along with *tsay* indicates that the sequence of action of the narrative is being initiated. In sentences (6), (8) and (11), he is referred to by the simple form 'boy', a term which implies that he is the lead character. In sentence (15) there is a new set of circumstances: he is blind and, therefore, the reference is 'the blind (one)'. In sentences (14) and (18) the pronoun 'he' occurs. This pronomial form is infrequently used in Quechua narrative. Its occurrence indicates that the referent is either the lead character or the focus of attention of the function unit in which it occurs. Again in sentences (33) and (38) the reference is the simple form 'boy'. The final reference, in sentence (43b), again groups him with his two brothers. The noun phrase is marked by *-n* to indicate that these are the same three which were referred to previously. There are two references to him in direct quotations (sentences (32) and (10)). The reference identifies him as the same character as that of the narrative but is made from the viewpoint of the person who is being quoted.

Other characters of this story include the two older brothers of the lead character. In sentence (1) they are introduced, as was the younger brother, as the sons of their father. When they are singled out in sentence (3) the phrase has the antecedent referent *tsay* which indicates that they were spoken about before but the ending *-q* which occurs on the word 'two' indicates that this is the first time they have been mentioned as that particular group. The form *kaq* also indicates an opposition, a group being split up. In sentences (5) and (7) the anaphoric reference is in relationship to the lead character, their younger brother, and *-qa* occurs indicating that the sentences are part of the body of the narrative. In sentence (10) the reference is to only one of the brothers. The noun phrase has an anaphoric form *huknin* meaning 'one of them' which indicates his relationship to the group of two and *wawqin* 'brother' his relationship to the lead character. *-na* replaces *-qa* indicating that the character is part of a group which has been previously referred to. The final references are in sentence (43b). Because the sentence is a part of the conclusion, the narrative action sequence has been terminated, and the topic marker does not occur.

In summary, the following are some of the distinctive grammatical features of the legendary narrative: the sentence marking construction with an antecedent connective, the sequence connective, and the reportive

marker; the narrative independent verb ending with its full and short forms:
criteria arising from structure which determine the form, components, and
occurrence of the noun phrase; and finally the topic markers. Although
many questions remain unanswered, my studies to date confirm the hypothesis that it is necessary to posit units beyond the simple sentence, i.e.,
beyond the clause, in order to adequately account for these features.

6. Illustrative text

A literal translation is given interlinearly, while a free translation follows
the complete text. Sentence numbers in the text correspond with those
referred to in sections 1–5. Morphemes separated by hyphens but not
translated are indicated . . . in the interlinear English.

(1) *huk nuna-sh   ka-naq   kima tsuri-yuk*
    a man-reportive   be-narrative ending   three sons-having

(2) *tsay nuna-sh   wanukiyku-naq   kima-n   tsuri-n-ta*
    that man-reportive   die-narrative ending   three-the son   his-object
           haqiri-naq
    marker   leave-narrative-ending

(3) *tsay-shi   ayuku-yaa-naq   tsay ishka-q mayor*
    that-reportive   go-plural-narrative ending   that two   older
    ka-q-kuna   menor ka-q-ta   haqiriyku-r
    one-plural   younger one-. . .-object marker   leaving behind-. . .

(4) *y   tsay-shi   tsay nuspi-qa   ni-naq   "nuqa-pis*
    and   that-reportive   that kid-topic   say-narrative ending I-topic
    qam-kuna-wan   aywayta-m   muna-h"   ni-r
    you-plural-with   to go-verifier   want-I   saying
    qati-naq
    following-narrative ending

(5) *tsay-na-sh   mayor ka-q   wawqi-n-kuna-qa*
    that-sequence-reportive   older one-. . .   brother-his-plural-topic
    ni-ya-n   "mana-m.   qam-ta-qa   apay-niyki-ta
    say-plural-he   no-verifier   you-object marker-topic   to take-you
    muna-ya-h-tsu   ima-q   taq   shamu-nki   qam-qa
    want-plural-I-negative   what-for   question   come-you   you-topic
    quedakiy   nuqa-kuna-qa   allapa   karu-ta-m   ayuku-ya-h"
    stay here   I-plural-topic   very   far-to-verifier   go-plural-I

ni-shpa   waapu muna-ya-n-tsu   apayta
say-ing   angry want-plural-he-negative   to take along

(6) *tsay-na-sh   wamra-qa karullapa karullapa qati-n*
that-sequence-reportive   boy-topic afar off afar off follow-he
por fin huk   chusyaq   hirka-man feyu-man
finally   a   uninhabited hill-at   bad place-at
chaari-ya-n
arrive-plural-he

(7) *tsay-choh-na-sh   hamakuri-ya-n tsay mayor ka-q*
that-in-sequence-reportive rest-plural-he   that older one
wawqi-n-kuna-qa
brother-his-plural-topic

(8) *tsay-man-na-sh   charku-n   qipa-n-ta   wamra-qa*
that-to-sequence-reportive arrive-he behind-him-. . . boy-topic

(9) *tsay-na-sh   mirkapa-ta   miku-ya-pti-n*
that-sequence-reportive   lunch-object marker eat-plural-when-he
ni-n   "pacha-h-mi   waqa-n nuqa-ta-pis
say-he stomach-my-verifier cry-it   I-object marker-topic
qu-yaa-ma-y"
give-plural-. . .-me

(10) *ni-pti-n-na-sh   huknin wawqi-n-na   ni-n*
say-when-he-sequence-reportive one of brother-his-topic say-he
"qam-ta   qu-yaa-na-q   ka-pti-n-qa
you-object marker   give-plural-. . .-. . . being-if. . .-. . .
nawi-yki-ta   mah hurqariyki-y huknin-ta."
eye-your-object marker remove-. . .   one of them-object marker

(11) *tsay-na-sh   hurqari-n   wamra-qa*
that-sequence-reportive   take out-he boy-topic
pacha-n-paqraykur   huknin nawi-n-ta
stomach-his-because of   one of eye-his-object marker
ichiklla-ta   quri-ya-n   ni pacha-n-pis
little bit-object marker give-plural-he   not stomach-his-topic
junta-n-tsu
full-he-negative

(12) *tsay-na-sh   peru mana   taq*
that-sequence-reportive but   not   exclamatory
pacha-h-pis   junta-n-tsu   mas-ta
stomach-my-topic full-ending-negative more-object marker

muna-h   "ni-n   "mah   mas-ta
want   say-he well   more-object marker
qu-yaa-na-q-paq-qa   *huknin*
give-plural-. . .-. . .-in order to-topic   the other
nawi-yki-ta   raq hurquriyki-y."   *ni-ya-n*
eye-your-object marker   also take it out-ending   say-plural-he
hurqurilla-n   huknin   nawi-n-ta
took it out-he   the other   eye-his-object marker
pacha-n-paqraykur
stomach-his-because of

(13) *tsay-na-sh   tsay-choh   ichik-lla-ta*
that-sequence-reportive   that-in   only-a little-object marker
quyku-r   haqiriyku-r   ayuku-yaa-naq
giving him-. . .   leaving-. . .   go away-plural-narrative ending
wisku-ta   dejaliyku-r
blind-object marker   leaving-. . .

(14) *tsay ayuku-yaa-shqa-n-yaq-na-sh*   *pay-qa*
that go-plural-meanwhile-. . .-. . .-sequence reportive   he-topic
mana   rika-shpa   ka-naq
not   see-ing   be-narrative ending

(15) *imanoh-lla-chi   tsay   naani-ta-qa*   *llutan-pa*
how-I don't know   that   road-object marker-topic   any old way-. . .
llutan-pa   aywa-naq   wisku   por fin
any old way-. . .   go-narrative ending   blind man   finally
huk qucha   kuchu-n-man   chaa-naq
a lake   shore-its-to   arrive-narrative ending

(16) *tsay   kuchu-n-choh-na-sh*   *ka-naq*   *monti*
that   shore-its-in-sequence-reportive   be-narrative ending   tree

(17) *tsay monti-man-na-sh*   *lluqa-ku-rku-n*
that tree-up into-sequence-reportive   climb-up into-. . .-he

(18) *tsay-choh-na-sh*   *media   nochi-na   casi*
that-in-sequence-reportive   mid   night-topic   almost
riyarayka-n   pay-qa   ni   punu-n-tsu   monti-lla-choh
being awake-he   he-topic   not   sleep-he-negative   tree-only-in
lluqa-shqa-lla
climb-was-poor thing

(19) *pullan paqas-na-sh*   *punku-na   waqa-n*
middle night-sequence-reportive   door-topic   cry-he

(*tallran bun blan*) *ni-shpa libru-pis kichaka-n punku-pis*
ideophonic saying book-topic is open-it door-topic
kichaka-n mesa-pis tanrara-n
is open-it table-topic resound-it

(20) *tsay-na-sh* "*ima taq. may-choh taq.*
then-sequence-reportive what question where-in question
wayi-ku ka-n may-choh taq kay-choh."
house-question be-it where-in question here
wiyarayka-n upaallalla
listen-he silently

(21) *tsay mas ratitu-ta-na-sh chaari-ya-n*
that later minute-. . .-sequence-reportive arrive-plural-he
(*tun tun tun tun tun*) *punku-ta takakuri-n*
ideophonic door-object marker knock on-he

(22) *tsay-na-sh huknin-qa* "*pasa*" *ni-shpa*
that-sequence-reportive one of them-topic come in say-ing
ni-n kukun "*ima taq.*" *ni-shpa wiyarayka-n*
say-ending chief what question say-ing listening-he

(23) *mas ratu-na-sh atska-q-na hukllay-lla-pa*
more minutes-sequence-reportive lots-. . .-topic one-only-by
hukllay-lla-pa chaa-ya-n por fin llenakaari-ya-n
one-only-by arrive-plural-he finally fill-up-plural-he

(24) *despues-na-sh qallayku-ya-n ni-shpa* "*buenu*
after-sequence-reportive begin-plural-he saying okay
kanan-qa mah musya-shun ima-ta-sh
now-topic know-we will what-object marker-reportive
rura-yaa-mu-shqa." *ni-shpa-na tapunaku-r primeru tapuri-n*
do-plural-. . . saying then ask-ing first ask-he
"*qam-qa ima-ta taq ruramu-rqu-nki.*"
you-topic what-object marker question do-past-you
ni-shpa
say-ing

(25) *tsay-na-sh* "*nuqa-qa mishi*
that-sequence-reportive I-topic cat
tuku-shqa-lla-m tayka-rqu-h cocina-n-choh
pretend-was-only-verifier sit-past-I kitchen-its-in
despues-mi wallpa ishpay-ta
later-verifier chicken urine-object marker

haka   mullka-ta   *y   qitu-ta*
guinea pig dirt-object marker   and   dirt-object marker
hitarpu-rqu-h   warmi-n-pa   kashki-n-man   tsay-na-m
dump in-past-I   woman-her-. . . soup-her-into that sequence-verifier
quwa-n-qa   *maqa-shqa   peliya-shqa   warmi-n-wan*
husband-her-topic   beat-past   fight-past   woman-his-with
ishka-n-ta-m   *peliya-tsi-mu-rqu-h*
two-the-object marker-verifier   fight-made-. . .-past-I

(26) *tsay-na-sh*   "*alli-m   ka-nqa   tsay-qa*
that-sequence-reportive   good-verifier be-will that-topic
nuqa-ntsik-paq-mi."   (paq paq paq)   paqchiyku-ya-n
I-plural-for-verifier   ideophonic   clap-plural-he

(27) *tsay-na-sh*   *kushi-shqa   paqchi-r   usha-ri-r-na*
that sequence-reportive   happy-was   clap-ping   finish-. . .-ing-then
huknin-ta-na   *tapuri-n   "qam-qa*
another-object marker-topic   ask-he   you-topic
ima-ta   *taq*   *rura-rqu-nki."*
what-object marker   question   do-past-you

(28) *ni-pti-n-na-sh*   "*nuqa-qa   ruramu-rqu-h   huk*
say-when-he-sequence-verifier   I-topic   do-past-I   a
casadu-ta-wan
married man-object marker-with
casada-ta-m   *juntaramu-rqu-h."*
married woman-object marker-verifier   put together-past-I
"*muy bien   alli-m   tsay-qa   nuqa-ntsik-paq-mi   ka-nqa."*
very well   good-verifier   that-topic   I-plural-for-verifier   be-will
ni-shpa   llutaypa   paqchiyku-ya-n
say-ing   terrible   clapped-plural-he

(29) *huk-ta-na-sh*   *tapu-n   "qam-qa*
another-object marker-sequence-reportive   ask-he   you-topic
ima-ta   *taq*   *ruramu-rqu-nki."   ni-shpa "nuqa-qa*
what-object marker   question   do-past-you   say-ing   I-topic
juntamu-rqu-h   soltera-ta-wan
join-past-I   young lady-object marker-with
solteru-ta-m."   "*ah   tsay-qa   bruju-pa-m."*
young man-object marker-verifier   oh   that-topic   witch-of-verifier
ni-shpa   ni   paqchi-ya-n-pis-tsu
say-ing   not even   clap-plural-he-. . .-negative

(30) *huk-ta-na-sh*   *tapu-n*   "*y*   *qam-qa*
another-object marker-sequence-reportive   ask-he   and   you-topic
ima-ta   *taq*   *ruramu-rqu-nki.*"   *ni-shpa*
what-object marker   question   do-past-you   say-ing
"*nuqa-qa   llapan   pueblu   upunan*
I-topic   all   town   that which is to drink
pukyu-ta-m   *tsapaykamu-rqu-h.*"   *ni-shpa*
pool-object marker-verifier   cover it up-past-I   say-ing

(31) *ni-pti-n-na-sh*   "*ah   y   tsay-mi*
say-when-he-sequence-reportive   oh   and   that-verifier
peliyakiykaa-ya-n   tsay-qa   *nuqa-ntsik-paq-mi   ka-nqa   y*
fighting-plural-he   that-topic   I-plural-for-verifier   be-will   and
remediu   ka-n-ku   *ni-n*   "*aw-mi*   *ka-n-mi*   *huk*
remedy   be-it-question   say-he   yes-verifier   be-it-verifier   a
kankar   rumi-lla-m   *tsaparayka-n.*"   "*ah yah*"
flat   rock-only-verifier   is covering-he   oh OK

(32) *huk-ta-na-sh*   *tapuri-n*   "*y*   *qam-qa*
another-object marker-sequence-reportive   ask-he   and   you-topic
ima-ta   *taq*   *ruramu-rqu-nki.*"   "*nuqa-qa*
what-object marker   question   do-past-you   I-topic
ishka-n   wawqi-n-kuna-wan-mi   *huknin   ichik   wamra-pa*
two-the   brother-he-plural-with-verifier   another   little   boy-of
nawi-n-ta   *hurqaratsi-rqu-h.*"   *ni-shpa   ni-n*
eye-his-object marker   make take out-past-I   say-ing   say-he
"*alli-m*   *tsay-qa*   *nuqa-ntsik-paq-mi.*"
good-verifier   that-topic   I-plural-for-verifier

(33) *paqchiri-ya-pti-n-na-sh*   *wamra-qa*
clap-. . .-when-he-sequence-reportive   boy-topic
wiyarayka-shqa-n-ta-na   *ni-n*   "*peru   nuqa   taq*   *ka-h*
listening-while-he-then   say-he   but   I   exclamatory   be-I
nuqa-ta   *taq*   *nawi-h-ta*
I-object marker   exclamatory   eye-my-object marker
hurqaratsi-yaa-ma-shqa   *ni-shpa   mantsaka-shqa*
make to take out-plural-me-he   say-ing   afraid being-was
wiyarayka-n
listening-he

(34) *wiyarayka-pti-n-na-sh*   "*ka-n-ku*   *remediu*
listening-when-he-sequence-reportive   be-he-question   remedy

tsay-paq-qa." ni-n "aw-mi   ka-n-mi   paluma-pa
that-for-topic say-he yes-verifier be-he-verifier   dove-of
ruru-n-lla-m."   "ah yah" ni-shpa apuntari-r-na
egg-its-only-verifier oh OK   say-ing writing down-. . .-then

(35) *tsay-noh kaykaa-ya-pti-n-na-sh   huk-na*
that-like   being-plural-when-he-sequence-reportive another-topic
chaari-n   (ay ay ay ay ay)   ni-shpa "ima   taq
arrive-he   sound of suffering   say-ing what question
pasaykushu-rqu-nki."   ni-n
happen you-past-he   say-he

(36) *tsay-na-sh   ni-n   "nuqa-ta-qa*
that-sequence-reportive   say-he I-object marker-topic
maqayka-yaa-ma-shqa   allapa-m
beat-plural-me-he   very much-verifier
wanunahchoh-mi   escapamu-rqu-h.   rumi
when I was just about to die-verifier   escape-past-I   stone
tuku-shqa-lla-m   hitarayka-rqu-h huk restauranti-choh
pretend-was-. . .-verifier   laying-past-I   a   restaurant-in
y   tsay-mi   mosa-ta   platu-n
and   that-verifier   girl-object marker   plates-her
allapaaku-shqa-n-ta   ishkiyka-tsi-rqu-h y   tsay-mi
carry-was-it-object marker   fall-make-past-I   and   that-verifier
tsariyka-yaa-ma-r herieru-man apayka-yaa-ma-r maachu-wan
grab-plural-me   iron-to   take-plural-me   hammer-with
golpi-yaa-ma-shqa paki-na-h-paq   peru mana
hit-plural-me-he   break-. . .-me-order to   but   not
paki-pti-h-na-m   "kay rumi-qa   ima-noh
break-when-I-sequence-reportive this   stone-topic   what-like
rumi-chi."   ni-r   "hitara-yaa-ma-shqa."   (ay ay ay ay)
stone-verifier   say-ing   throw out-plural-me-he   ideophonic
ni-shpa kayka-n   "alli-m   tsay-qa   nuqa-ntsik-paq-mi
say-ing   being-he   good-verifier   that-topic   I-plural-for-verifier
buenu   cholu."   ni-shpa   paqchirkaari-ya-n
OK   well done   say-ing   clap-plural-he

(37) *por-fin tsay-noh   kaykaa-ya-pti-n-na-sh*
finally   that-like   being-plural-when-he-sequence-verifier
gallu-qa   cantayku-n
rooster-topic   crow-he

(38) *cantayku-pti-n-na-sh*   *ah hora-na*
sing-when-he-sequence-reportive oh time-now
witsiku-shun-na."   ni-shpa (tanran blan bun) ni-shpa
separate-we will-now say-ing ideophonic   say-ing
yarqurkaari-ya-n   wayi-pita-qa   wamra-qa
went out-plural-he house-from-topic boy-topic
wiyarayka-shqa-n-ta   tsay hora-na   qallakurkulla-n
listening-meanwhile. . .-. . . that very hour-then began-he
monti-man lluqa-r   mas   lluqa-n   lluqa-n
tree-into   climb-ing more climb-he climb-he
(39) *tsay lluqayka-pti-n-na-sh   paluma-qa*
that climb up-when-he-sequence-reportive dove-topic
(lapapapap) ayuku-n "may-choh taq   kayka-n."
ideophonic go-it   where-in   question be-he
ni-shpa-na mas   lluqa-n ashi-r   ashi-r   lamka-r
say-ing-then more climb-he look-ing look-ing feel-ing
lamka-r por fin tariri-n   ruru-ta
feel-ing finally find it-he egg-object marker
(40) *tariri-r-na-sh   tunarkaari-n   nawi-n-man*
finding it-. . .-sequence-reportive push into place-he eye-his-into
(41) *tsay-na-sh   rikachakaramu-n relombra-y-pa*
that-sequence-reportive look around-he really-shining. . .-. . .
relombra-r nawi-n-qa   lindu por fin tsay-pita
shining   eye-his-topic nice finally there-from
bajariyku-r ayuku-n wawqi-n-kuna   qipa-n-ta
coming down go-he brother-his-plural right behind them. . .-. . .
wawqi-n-kuna-ta   ashi-r   y
brother-his-plural-object marker looking for-. . . and
wawqi-n-kuna   qipa-n-choh   yurirku-n
brother-his-plural behind-his-in appear-he
(42) *tsay-na-sh   wawqi-n-kuna-qa*
that-sequence-reportive brother-his-plural-topic
mantsa-kaa-ya-n   "peru kay cholu-ta-qa
fear-become-plural-he but   this kid-object marker-topic
wisku-ta   taq   haqimu-rqa-ntsik taq
blind-object marker question leave-past-we   question
kay nawi-n sanu   qipa-ntsik-choh yurirka-mu-n." ni-shpa
this eye-his healed behind-our-in arrive-he say-ing

mantsakaari-ya-n
become afraid-plural-he

(43) *tsay-na-sh   ni-n*
that-sequence-verifier   say-he

[1] *"nuqa-qa   kay   qipa-yki-kuna-ta-m   ayukamu-rqu-h*
I-topic   this   behind-you-. . .-verifier   come-past-I

[2] *qipa-yki-kuna-choh   rikakaamu-h*
behind-your-plural-in   see-I

[3] *nuqa-ta   haqi-yaa-ma-rqa-yki*
I-object marker   leave-plural-me-past-you
wisku-ta-m
blind-object marker-verifier

[4] *peru kanan   cuentari-ya-shqa-yki   allapa   feyu-m*
but   now   tell-plural-you-I   very   awful-verifier
wiyayku-rqu-h   kanan
hear-past-I   now

[5] *nuqa   tsay   wisku   kayka-r-mi   aywa-rqa-h   mana   naani-pa*
I   that   blind   be-ing-verifier   go-past-I   not   road-by
y   tari-rqa-h   huk   qucha-ta   y   tsay   qucha
and   find-past-I   a   lake-object marker   and   that   lake
kuchu-n-choh   monti   ka-naq   tsay-man
shore-its-on   tree   be-narrative ending   that-into
lluqakurku-rqa-h
climb up-past-I

[6] *y   media   nochi-na-m   tsay   qucha-choh*
and   mid   night-sequence-verifier   that   lake-in
bulla-ta   rura-r   yurirku-ya-n   atska-q   nuna
noise-object marker   do-ing   arrive-plural-he   lots of-. . .   people

[7] *y   despues-mi   parla-ya-n   "ima-ta   taq*
and   after-verifier   talk-plural-he   what-object marker   question
rura-rqu-nki."   ni-shpa   tapunaku-r   libru-man
do-past-you   say-ing   asking each other-. . .   book-into
apunta-ya-n
write-plural-he

[8] *tsay-mi   tsay-choh   wiya-rqu-h   "soltera-ta-wan*
that-verifier   there-in   listen-past-. . .   miss-object marker-with
solteru-ta-m   juntamu-rqu-h."   ni-shpa   ni-n
youth-object marker-verifier   join-past-I   say-ing   say-he

[9] *tsay-paq-mi*   *paqchi-ya-n-tsu*
that-for-verifier   clap-plural-he-negative
"casadu-ta-wan
married man-object marker-with
casada-ta-m   *juntamu-rqu-h."*
married woman-object marker-verifier join-past-I
ni-ya-pti-n-mi   *sellama*   *kushiku-ya-n*
say-plural-when-he-verifier very-much happy-plural-he

[10] *despues-mi* *"ishka-n* *wawqi-n-kuna-wan-mi*   *huknin*
after-verifier two-the   brother-his-plural-with-verifier another
wawqi-n-pa-ta   *nawi-n-ta*
brother-his-of-object marker eye-his-object marker
hurqaratsi-rqu-h."   *wiya-rqu-h*
make to take out-past-I hear-past-I

[11] *y*   *tsay-mi*   *ni-ya-rqu-n*   *"remediu ka-n-ku*
and that-verifier say-plural-past-he remedy be-it-question
tsay-paq." *ni-ya-rqu-n*   *"aw-mi"*
that-for say-plural-past-he yes-verifier

[12] *ni-ya-pti-n-na-m*   *"ima taq"*   *ni-rqa-n*
say-plural-when-he-sequence-verifier what question say-past-he

[13] *tsay-mi*   *"paluma-pa ruru-n-mi."*   *ni-rqa-n*
that-verifier dove-of   egg-his-verifier say-past-he

[14] *y*   *tsay-na-m*   *nuqa-qa ashi-rqu-h y*
and that-sequence-verifier I-topic   look-past-I and
tariri-rqu-h y   tsay churakurku-rqu-h   y   rikachakari-rqu-h
find-past-I and that put into place-past-I and see-past-I

[15] *razunpa-m*   *mana alli-ta*   *rurayaka-ntsik*
right-verifier not   good-object marker do-we
diablu-pa ruray-nin-ta   *kay nuqa-ntsik qam-kuna*
devil-of doing-his-object marker this I-plural   you-plural
nawi-h-ta   *hurqa-tsi-yaa-ma-rqu-nki*   *y*
eye-my-object marker take out-make-plural-me-past-you and
asi wakin-kuna-pis   *mana-m*   *alli-tsu*
so others-plural-topic not-verifier good-negative

[16] *y*   *razunpa-m*   *mana alli-man aywa-na-paq*
and its true-verifier not   good-to go-. . .-in order to
huti-ntsik apuntarayka-n."   *ni-shpa*
name-our is writing down-he say-ing

(43b) *willa-naq*   *ishka-n*   *wawqi-n-kuna-ta*
      advise-narrative ending   two-the   brother-his-plural-object marker
      y   *wawqi-n-kuna*   *mantsaka-shqa*
      and   brother-his-plural   afraid-was
      quedaku-yaa-naq   *kaku-yaa-naq*   *kima-n*
      stay-plural-narrative ending   be-plural-narrative ending   three-the
      tsaychoh-na   *yachaku-yaa-naq*
      there-then   live-plural-narrative ending
Free translation:

(1) Once there was a man who had three sons. (2) The man died and the three sons were left alone.

(3) Then the two older sons decided to go away and leave the youngest behind. (4) The youngest said, "I want to go with you." And he tried to follow them. (5) The older brothers said, "No, we don't want to take you. Why do you want to come? You stay here. We're going on a very long trip." Angered, they didn't want to take him along. (6) But the boy did follow his brothers from a distance until they arrived at an uninhabited fearful hill. (7) His brothers rested there; (8) the boy got there a little later.

(9) After they had eaten their lunch, he said, "I'm hungry. Give me something to eat, too." (10) One of his brothers answered, "If you want us to give you something, pluck out one of your eyes." (11) Then the boy plucked out one of his eyes and they gave him a little to eat. But he was still hungry. (12) "But I'm still hungry. Give me more!" he told them "If you want more," they said, "pluck out your other eye." So he plucked out his other eye because he was so hungry. (13) Then they gave him a little more to eat and went away leaving their brother blind.

(14) Meanwhile, he wasn't able to see and they had already gone. (15) I can't imagine how he could find his way but finally the blind youth came to the shore of a lake. (16) By the shore there was a tree, (17) which he climbed into.

(18) Later the poor boy was still awake at nearly midnight because he couldn't sleep in the tree. (19) Then at midnight he heard a door bang. The book was opened, the door was opened, the table resounded. (20) Then he thought, "Is there a house near here?" Silently he listened. (21) A few minutes later some men arrived. They knocked on the door: tun, tun, tun, tun, tun. (22) The chief said, "Come in." The boy listened, thinking, "What is this?" (23) A little later many men began to arrive one by one. They kept coming until the house was jammed.

(24) Then they began to say, "Now we will see what we have done." The chief asked of one, "What have you done?" (25) He answered, "I sat in the kitchen pretending to be a cat. Later I put chicken urine and guinea pig excreta and other filth in the woman's soup. Her husband came out and beat her up. I made them fight." "That's a good way for us to be." They all clapped for him: paq paq paq.

(27) When they finished their happy applause, he asked another, "What did you do?" (28) He answered, "Here's what I did. I brought together a married man and another man's wife." They said, "That is very good." They applauded loudly.

(29) He asked another, "What did you do?" He answered, "I joined a young man and a young woman." But he was told, "That's a witchdoctor practice." And they did not clap for him at all.

(30) Another was asked, "And what did you do?" He answered, "I cut off the supply of drinking water for a whole town, and they are all fighting." He was told, "That's good, Is there a way this can be undone?" "Yes," he said, "there is only a flat rock covering the water." "Okay, that's good."

(32) He asked another, "And you – what did you do?" He answered, "I caused two brothers to make their little brother pluck his eyes out." "Excellent," said the chief, "that's exactly how we do!" When they finished clapping, the youth – listening to all this – thought to himself, "Hey, that's me. It was my eyes they made me pluck out!" Now he was really afraid as he went on eavesdropping. (34) Still listening he heard someone ask, "Is there any remedy for that?" "Yes," was the answer, "there is – the egg of a dove." Oh, I see," he said, writing it down in the book.

(35) While they were still doing that, another arrived groaning in pain. "What happened to you?" he was asked. (36) He said, "They really beat me up. At death's door I escaped. I was pretending to be a stone on the floor in a restaurant. I made the waitress trip over me while she was carrying a stack of plates. Someone picked me up and took me to the workroom to break me in pieces with a hammer. When I didn't break, they asked, "What kind of stone is this?" So they threw me out. Ow, ohhh," he groaned. "Well done," he was told. "That's how we do it." They gave him a rousing ovation.

(37) Thus it went until the cock crew. (38) When they heard the rooster, they said, "It is now time for us to go." The door slammed; the book closed; the table resounded and they all left.

The boy having heard all, climbed higher and higher in the tree. (39)
While he was climbing, he heard the sound of a bird flying. "Where can
it be?" he wondered. He climbed higher and higher searching by feeling
all over. Finally he found the egg. (40) Eagerly he forced it into place in
his eye socket. (41) He was able to look all around and see clearly.

Leaving the tree, he started down the road his brothers had taken to
search for them. And he came up right behind them. (42) They were
seized with fear. "But," they exclaimed, "we left this boy behind, blind!
How can he be here now with his eyes restored?" They were really afraid.
(43) So he related the whole story for them: I followed you. You left me
blind. But I heard this horrible thing. Because I was blind I couldn't
make my way well but I came to a lake with a tree near the shore. I
climbed the tree. About midnight lots of people came making a great
deal of noise. Each one was asked how he had done. And they wrote it
all down in a book. One said he'd brought a young man and young
woman together. For him they did not clap. Another said he'd brought
together a married man and a married woman. For him they cheered.
Then one told how he had caused two brothers to make their younger
brother pluck his eyes out. Someone asked if there was a remedy for
that. The fellow answered that there was – a dove's egg. So I searched
and found one. I could see when I put it in.

"It is true that when we do bad things we are doing the devil's work
You made me take out my eyes and other things. That was bad. It is
true that our names are written down in that book when we do bad
things." (43b) He finished his narrative. His two brothers were still very
much afraid.

The three of them settled there together and lived happily ever after.

Summer Institute of Linguistics

Bibliography

Levengood, Margaret and Helen Larsen. "Descriptive Sketch of Huaylas Quechua," forthcoming
in *Les Langues du Monde*.
Parker, Gary. (1965) *Gramática del Quechua Ayacuchano,* Universidad Nacional Mayor de San
Marcos. Lima, Perú.
Wise, Mary Ruth. (1968) *Identification of Participants in Discourse: A study of Aspects of Form
and Meaning in Nomatsiguenga,* University of Michigan Ph.D. Dissertation. Published in
Summer Institute of Linguistics Publications in Linguistics and Related Fields, No.28 (1971).

Analysis of society

SOCIAL STRUCTURE AND LANGUAGE STRUCTURE[1]

Philip K. BOCK

The search for valid analogies between the structure of language and the structure of other aspects of culture is an important part of modern anthropological thought. Recent students of this problem seem to fall into two general groups: (1) those fellows of Whorf who, in a variety of ways, are seeking *congruencies* between the language and the cultural values, perceptions, or practices of some particular society, and (2) those who, like Pike, are attempting to formulate unified theories of the structure of human behavior within which language appears as a special, though central, case (Pike 1954–1960).

The present paper is in the latter tradition. I shall suggest several analogies between language structure and social structure. These analogies have elsewhere led to the formulation of descriptive statements of the structural units of a community and the relationships among these units[2].

Fundamental to this undertaking is the proposition that all linguistic forms (morphemes, morphological and syntactic structures, etc.) constitute a sub-class of the more general category *cultural forms*. Following Redfield's definition of culture as "conventional understandings, manifest in act and artifact" (1941: 132), I propose to define a cultural form as:

a set of inter-related, partially arbitrary expectations, understandings beliefs or agreements, shared by the members of some social group, which can be shown to influence (or to have influenced) the behavior of some members of that group (Bock 1962:156).

Linguistic forms are cultural forms *par excellence* for, in general, there

---

[1] The first portion of this paper was read at the annual meeting of the American Anthropological Association in San Francisco, November, 1963. I am indebted to Kenneth L. Pike, Dell H. Hymes, and the late Clyde Kluckhohn for assistance and encouragement.

[2] Bock (1962: 154–249). The ethnographic and ethnohistorical sections of my dissertation will soon be published as a Bulletin of the National Museum of Canada.

is an extremely high consensus among the members of a speech community as to the defining characteristics and potential distribution of the phonemes, morphemes, tagmemes, etc., known to the group. These partially arbitrary understandings and expectations, most of them unconscious or pre-conscious, influence the verbal behavior of group members in predictable and dependable ways. Indeed, this "influence" is so regular that the linguistic is able to formulate a description of the structure of a language on the basis of a relatively limited number of observations (a corpus).

The contrastive definition of a finite number of linguistic forms and the rigorous statement of their potentials for co-occurrence constitute an adequate description of the structure of a language.[3] I suggest, similarly, that the cultural forms influencing other than verbal behavior may be contrastively defined and their relationship stated systematically and economically. Furthermore, I would maintain that at least three types of units are necessary to such a description: (1) social roles (and classes of roles), (2) periods (and dimensions) of social time, and (3) areas (and dimensions) of social space.

Like linguistic forms, social roles also constitute a sub-class of cultural forms. Each role consists of expectations regarding the behavior of classes of individuals or "actors" The partially arbitrary and inter-related behavioral expectations making up any given social role will be referred to as the *attributes* of that role (cf. Bruner et al., 1956. 25—49). One or more of these attributes will be "criterial" (Bruner et al., 1956.30) or "pivotal" (Nadel, 1957.32) in the categorization of actors as legitimate performers of the role. Other associated or "entailed" attributes may be viewed as either free or conditioned behavioral variants. Finally, social roles may be grouped into *role-classes* on the basis of their shared attributes and/or their substitutability in some environment.

From this point of view, the linguistic analog of the social role is the morpheme with its free and conditioned allomorphs and its membership in distributional classes of morphemes. Let us now explore two aspects of these analogous units: their internal structure and their external distribution.

Brown (Bruner et al., 1956. 263—264) has argued that morphemes are cognitive categories and that phonemes are their attributes: it is the

[3] This is a minimum requirement for an adequate description of a corpus. I accept, in principle the further requirement that a description be generative; however, there is no need to burden the present paper with what would necessarily be a highly programmatic discussion.

unique *selection* and *arrangement* of these attributes (which are themselves categories on another level of analysis) which defines each morpheme. Every language system prescribes certain arrangements and pro-
scribes others. According to most linguists, the phoneme-attributes are
themselves meaningless, and it is only in certain traditional combinations that they carry meaning.

The similarity of these features to the internal structure of social roles
may not be immediately evident, but I shall try to demonstrate the uti-
lity of the analogy. First of all, behavioral attributes – be they abstract
(mild joking, exercise of jural authority) or concrete (speaks to audience,
prepares food) – may pertain to many roles in a given culture, while
some attributes have cross-cultural relevance. Thus it is the distinctive
selection and arrangement of such attributes which makes possible the
contrastive identification of any one role in a particular culture. Just as
meaningless phonemes function to keep utterances apart, for purposes
of structural description the manifestation (performance) of any behavioral attribute may be viewed as inherently meaningless *except* as it combines with other attributes to contrastively define a particular social
role.

Specification of the attributes making up the *internal structure* of a
role or morpheme is, of course, only one part of the analysis. Equally
important is the statement of the potential *external distribution* of these
units.

The external distribution of a social role consists, in the first instance,
of its relationships with other social roles, i.e., its privileges of co-occurrence. Merton has dealt with this problem from a rather different perspective in his writings on the "role-set". Merton uses this concept to
refer to "that complement of role-relationships in which persons are
involved by virtue of occupying a particular social status" (1957.110).
He emphasizes that each social status involves "not a single associated
role, but an array of roles", so that, for example, "the status of school
teacher in the United States has its distinctive role-set, in which are
found pupils, colleagues, the school principal and superintendent, the
Board of Education, professional associations, and, on occasion, local
patriotic organizations" (1957. 110–111).

Merton's theoretical interest in this concept focuses on the "functional problem of articulating the components of numerous role-sets. . .
so that an appreciable degree of social regularity obtains" and status oc-
cupants are not subjected to "extreme conflict in their role-sets"

(1957. 111). He discusses several social mechanisms which serve to articulate role-sets and thus mitigate the impact of diverse expectations upon a status occupant. But the fact remains that radically different behavioral expectations *are* attached to the role of "teacher" in connection with various members of the corresponding role-set. Phrased differently the attributes of a role vary with — are conditioned by — the other roles with which it occurs, just as the phonemic shape of a morpheme may be conditioned by its occurrence with different distribution classes of morphemes.

The general principle may be stated as follows: the behavioral manifestation (or performance) of a particular allomorph or role variant is conditioned by its external distribution. Thus a structural statement describing which variants of the role "teacher" occur with which members of its associated role-set would be of the same *general form* as a statement describing which allomorphs of, say, the English plural morpheme [-S] occur with different phonological and morphological classes of noun stems (see table 1).

In table 1 we see that a social role may be composed of several different sub-sets of behavioral expectations (variants $a_1, a_2. \ldots a_n$), and which of these is manifested depends (in part) upon which of the roles in its role-set (B, C. ... J) it occurs with. Borrowing again from linguistic theory, we may say that these variants are in *complementary distribution* if they never occur in the same environments (i.e., in relation to the same member of the role set), and thus we may speak of them as conditioned variants of the same structural unit: alloroles of the same roleme.

If no such environmental factors can be found which appear to condition the occurrence of different role variants, the latter may be said to be in free variation; but we must also consider the possibility that there are environmental factors other than the presence of other roles which

Table 1
Isomorphism of two structural statements.

Role A, 'teacher'	Morpheme [-S], 'plural':
variant a_1 with B, 'pupil'	/-s/ with Class 1 noun stems
variant a_2 with C, 'colleague'	/-z/ with Class 2 noun stems
variant a_3 with D, 'principal'	/-əz/ with Class 3 noun stems
etc.	etc.

may affect the manifestation of these units. It is in this regard that we now turn briefly to the notions of social space and social time.

Social space and social time

The performance of a social role projects a definition of the situation, and this situation involves an ordered series of behavioral expectations — what Goffman has called a "plan for the co-operative activity that follows" (1959. 12–13). I would argue that recurrent social situations are themselves cultural forms having determinate distributions in social space and social time. I have defined a *situation* as "a *cultural form* consisting primarily of understandings concerning the scheduling of, and allocation of space for, the occurrence of *other* cultural forms" (Bock 1962. 158). In other words, a situation (as a unit of social structure) is here viewed as a kind of four-dimensional cognitive map within which social roles are located. For example, to say that a certain part of a building is a classroom is to imply that during certain socially defined periods of time ("classtime") the social roles of "teacher" and "pupil" are *expected* to occur within it. Such socially defined units of space and time may also condition the manifestation of social roles (and other cultural forms).

On closer investigation, it will appear that the "class" (or any other social situation) is *internally structured* in terms of social space and social time with varying expectations attaching to sub-areas of the classroom and sub-periods of class time. On the other hand, the "class" as a total situation is *externally distributed* into larger dimensions of social time (the school week or term) and areas of social space (the school building or campus) just as the component social roles are distributed into classes of roles.

Now if a role performance projects a situation, and if a situation implies a set of roles, it would appear that we are dealing with the kind of correlation between a functional "slot" and class of "fillers" analogous to the unit of grammatical structure which Pike calls the *tagmeme* (Pike 1960. 121–122). Grammatical descriptions employing the tagmeme concept tend — like most descriptive statements in phonology and morphology — to be *linear* in form: they represent the obligatory or optional occurrence of tagmemes within a phrase, clause, or sentence as formulae which are isomorphic with the temporal sequence of these

Table 2
The descriptive model.

Situation "Class"	Time: Class meeting

Space:
    Classroom
	Roles:
	    + teacher
	    + pupil
	    ± student-teacher

+ indicates obligatory occurrence
± indicates optional occurrence

units in speech (cf. Elson and Pickett 1962). Descriptions of social structure must, however, deal with the non-sequential or, broadly speaking, spatial relationships among social roles, as well as the linear and cyclical temporal sequences.

Thus the basic descriptive model (table 2) which emerges from this approach is one which states the optional or obligatory occurrence of social roles (and their variants) within a situation-matrix bounded by a period of social time and an area of social space.

Given such a situation-matrix as a fundamental unit, it is possible to focus either upon its internal structure, spelling this out in considerable detail, or upon its external distribution, relating the component social roles, time periods, and spatial areas to more inclusive classes and dimensions. In these ways the structural relationship of the situation as a whole to other recurrent situations in the system may be economically described.

An example of structural description

A recurrent situation on the Micmac Indian Reserve studied by the author in 1961 will be used to illustrate how the method of structural description outlined above may be applied[4]. The structural description of any one situation occurring in a human community must necessarily refer to other situations; therefore, a notational system was devised to facilitate cross-referencing. The elements of this are given in table 3.

---

[4] A narrative description of the wake, based upon participant-observation in four separate occurrences and several informant interviews, will be found in Bock (1962. 148–149).

Table 3

Notational system for structural description.

Upper case letters (S, T, R, M) refer to cultural forms: areas of social space (S), periods of time (T), social roles (R), or matrices (M).

Integers following upper case letters label specific cultural forms.

Lower case letters (s, t, r) designate *variants* of cultural forms.

Decimals following lower case letters label variants of cultural forms.

Upper case clusters (SC, TC, RC) designate *classes* of cultural forms.

Letters following hyphens (e.g., RC-A) are used to label specific *classes* of cultural forms.

An integer preceding a letter, separated from it by a period, refers to a *matrix* other than the one under consideration.

Examples: 3.SC-A: Space class "A" of matrix # 3.

4.R-B.1: Role # 1 from role class "B" of matrix # 4.

t-5.2: Variant # 2 of time period # 5 (of the matrix under consideration).

The matrix to be presented (table 4) describes the Indian-style wake, a situation which occurs nightly during the period between the death and the burial of an adult member of this Micmac Band. The external distribution of this period (14.TC-A: Time of Wake) is thus into the *life cycle* of individual Band members and into the night period of the daily cycle. The participating roles are contrastively defined in this and other situations. The reader should bear in mind that the matrix and its component cultural forms represent sets of expectations which influence the behavior of participating individuals; they do not represent the individuals themselves.

The external distribution and internal structure (segmentation) of SC-A: "Place of Wake" are self-explanatory, though it should be noted that the precise physical arrangements may vary from one manifestation to the next. Thus, the structural description must be general enough to allow for non-structural variations (due, for example, to the different floor plans of Indian homes) while indicating the kinds of areas in terms of which the participants orient their behavior.

The internal structure of TC-A: "Time of Wake" is given in a linear notation with single or double slashes separating the component periods and colons including those periods which are repeated alternately; thus, //:T-3/T-4:// indicates the expected alternation of 'Singing Time' with "Intermission" when the exact number of alternations is not structurally determined. The occurrence of periods of time or social roles is assumed to be obligatory unless marked as optional by the presence of the symbol, ±. Separate treatment of the internal structure of the time dimension,

Table 4
Situation-matrix #14: Indian wake.

M-14		T-1	T-2	T-3	T-4	T-5
S-1: Bier	s-1.1: nucleus	R-1	R-1	R-1	R-1	R-1
Area	s-1.2: margin	±R-2			±R-2	
S-2: Front area			R-3	R-4		r-2.1
S-3: Audience Area			R-2	R-2	±R-2 ±R-4	r-2.2 R-4
S-4: Marginal	s-4.1: kitchen				r-2.1	
Area	s-4.2: outside	r-2.2			±r-2.2 ±R-4	

14.SC-A: Place of wake – external distribution into 9.S-A.1: House site (usually that occupied by deceased)
S-1:   Bier area
s-1.1: nucleus – contains coffin
s-1.2: margin – area immediately surrounding coffin
S-2:   Front area – focal region of performances during T-2, -3, and -5.
S-3:   Audience area – seating area for R-2: Mourner
S-4:   Marginal area – residual space, including
s-4.1: kitchen area
s-4.2: outside of house
14.TC-A: Time of wake – external distribution (see discussion above).
      TC-A = //T-1/T-2//:T-3/T-4://±T-5//://:T-3/T-4://
T-1:   Gathering time – participants arrive at SC-A: Place of wake
T-2:   Prayer time – saying of the Rosary by R-3: Prayer leader
T-3:   Singing time – several hymns sung with brief pauses in between
T-4:   Intermission – longer pause in singing
T-5:   Meal time – optional serving of meal (about midnight)
14.RC-A: Participant roles – external distribution noted for each:
R-1:   Corpse – from 3:RC-A: Band Member
R-2:   Mourner
r-2.1: Host – member of 9.RC-A: Household group (of deceased)
r-2.2: Other – residual category
R-3: Prayer leader
r-3.1: Priest – from 3.R-B.1.1: Priest
r-3.2: Other – from 14.R-4
R-4:   Singer – usually from 11.R-A.4: Choir member

though confusing at first, vastly simplifies the form of the matrix (which otherwise require several identical columns) and makes possible independent consideration of the structure of social time.

For some of the more complex matrices, it is useful to set up several role classes; but in M-14, all the participants may be viewed as manifesting a single role class. The contrastive segmentation of RC-A into its component units may be accomplished in a number of ways. There is, at present, no motivation within the theory for the use of binary features; however, by pressing the linguistic analogy in this direction it is possible to differentiate the four members of this role class by means of three attributes, each of which has a positive and a negative pole: (a) Living/Dead; (b) Leads Prayers/Responds; and (c) Sings/Listens. Our social roles may then be contrastively defined as bundles or non-equivalent sets of these attributes; the structural statement may be made in tabular form or, as below, in linear form:

R-1: 'Corpse' = [-a] (Dead; other attributes irrelevant)
R-2: 'Mourner' = [a, -b, -c] (Living, Responds; Listens)
R-3: 'Prayer Leader' = [a, b] (Living, Leads Prayers)
R-4: 'Singer' = [a, c] (Living; Sings)

Given such a statement, natural classes or sub-classes of roles may be rigorously defined through the use of elementary logical notions. For example, RC-A may be defined as the intersection of sets containing *a* with those containing -*a*.

The role of "Mourner" (R-2) occurs in two variant forms (r-2.1; r-2.2) but as can be seen from the matrix these variants have different distribution potentials during only certain periods of the wake, while during T-2 and T-3 their distributions are identical. This may be viewed as a case of conditioned variation with neutralization occurring in some environments. The variants of R-3: "Prayer Leader" may be distinguished on the basis of their respective external distributions, but within M-14 they appear to be in free variation (i.e., either r-3.1 or r-3.2 occurs in the environment S-2 at T-2).

Discussion

The goal of structural description in ethnography, as in linguistics, is the contrastive identification of cultural forms and the rigorous statement of their distribution. A situation-matrix such as that presented above does exactly this. It cannot do more, nor does it pretend to. Thus, M-14 does not explain or give the meaning of the Indian wake any more than a grammar of English explains a particular sentence-type. The "item and arrangement" (Hockett 1954) approach adopted in this example may be supplemented by more process-oriented (even transformational) statements (cf. Bock, 1962. 225-226), but the aim remains strictly *formal*. Content enters the analysis only for the purpose of contrast.

Yet it is clear that a formal analysis which lacks all content is as meaningless as a grammar without an accompanying lexicon. How then are we to introduce cultural content into a structural description? One solution is to add to the contrastive role definitions what Nadel (1957) called the "entailed" attributes — the host of behavioral expectations that seem to follow from the assumption of a role. Here Merton's notion of the "role set" again becomes useful since we may further specify (in our role lexicon) the variable attributes which are manifested only in certain relationships. Similarly, the recognition of classes of roles simplifies the specification of content since many normally non-contrastive attributes may be defined for some abstract role class (such as "citizen" or "adult male") and then allowed to carry over to all of its component roles.

One further example will indicate the way in which cultural content may be related to structural description. A central part of the Indian wake involves the singing (during 14.T-3) of certain traditional hymns for the dead. Though I personally lack the musicological and linguistic skills necessary to perform a structural analysis of these hymns, I feel quite certain that they constitute a class of cultural forms with distinctive formal features. And even if I am unable to analyze their internal structure, I am in a position to say something about their external distribution: they are manifested (i.e., expected to be performed) in the environment S-2 at T-3 of M-14. Furthermore, knowledge of these hymns and the ability to perform them are attributes of a particular social role (14.R-4: Singer), while the hymns themselves are members of a larger class of musical forms and might best be described as variants of the hymns used at other religious services. Finally, if material objects (such as the coffin) are treated as manifestations of still other cultural forms[5], their internal structure, class membership, external distribution,

---

[5] For footnote, see next page.

and role correlates can be stated within the same type of structural framework, making possible the formal descriptive integration of most aspects of a culture.

The extensions of structural description suggested in the last two paragraphs are largely programmatic. The first attempt by the author to apply this approach to a body of field data (Bock, 1962. 184–221) had more restricted aims and, even so, met with variable success in analyzing different situations. Ritual situations (such as the wake) yielded most readily to analysis, for in ritual, spatial and temporal boundaries are usually clear-cut, role-performances are carefully rehearsed, and the attributes which serve to contrast different roles are consciously emphasized and reinforced by highly visible and redundant cues. Indeed, it might be possible to define the process of *ritualization* in terms of the degree to which temporal, spatial, and role cues are made explicit and redundant for the purpose of insuring smooth and error-free interaction. A possible linguistic analog may be found in C.F. Voegelin's concept of "noncasual speech" (1960. 57–68).

Other types of situations are more difficult to describe in structural terms: units of social space or social time may overlap, resulting in indeterminate boundaries; the complex conditioning of roles by distributional factors may obscure the nature of the underlying units; and an insufficient or biased corpus of observations may lead to faulty analysis. But these difficulties are all similar to problems faced by the linguist in morphological analysis; and insofar as language is a part of culture, we may expect that equally complex patterning will be found in social structure.

In spite of the difficulties encountered, the attempt to formulate a structural description of some social group can be revealing; for by formalizing our conceptions of social structure we are led into a systematic search for the cultural forms in terms of which men orient their behavior in space, in time, and in relation to other actors.

University of New Mexico

---

[5] How one views the relationship of artifacts to culture depends of course, on one's view of the nature of culture (cf. Osgood, 1951). From the point of view expressed in this paper, the relationship is seen as analogous to that between speech and language: i.e., the material objects are expressions (manifestations) of cognitive units (expectations, etc.) which the ethnographer formulates as cultural forms. (Cf. Pike, 1960. 115–118).

Bibliography

Bock, Philip K. 1962. *The Social Structure of a Canadian Indian Reserve.* Unpublished Ph. D. dissertation, Harvard University, Cambridge, Mass.

Bruner, J.S., J.J. Goodnow and G.A. Austin. 1956. *A Study of Thinking.* New York: John Wiley and Sons, Inc.

Elson, B. and V. Pickett. 1962. *An Introduction to Morphology and Syntax.* Santa Ana: Summer Institute of Linguistics.

Goffman, Erving. 1959. *The Presentation of Self in Everyday Life.* Garden City: Doubleday Anchor Books.

Hockett, Charles F. 1954. Two Models of Grammatical Description. *Word* 10:210–231.

Merton, Robert K. 1957. The Role Set: Problems in Sociological Theory. *British Journal of Sociology* 8:106–120.

Nadel, S.F. 1957. *The Theory of Social Structure.* Glencoe: Free Press.

Osgood, Cornelius. 1951. Culture: its Empirical and Non-Empirical Character. *Southwestern Journal of Anthropology* 7:202–214.

Pike, Kenneth L. 1954–1960. *Language in Relation to a Unified Theory of the Structure of Human Behavior,* Parts I, II and III, Preliminary Edition. Glendale: Summer Institute of Linguistics.

Redfield, Robert. 1941. *The Folk Culture of Yucatan.* Chicago: University of Chicago Press.

Voegelin, C.F. 1960. "Casual and Noncasual Utterances Within Unified Structure" in *Style in Language* (ed. by Thomas A. Sebeok), pp. 57–68. New York: Technology Press and John Wiley and Sons, Inc.

INDEX

Abrams, N.D., 237, 246, 248, 249
Actor, 5, 41, 61
Adequacy, 56
Adjoining, 226
Africa, 44, 46, 81, 106
Aguaruna, 38
Algonquian, 135
Allomorph, 82, 85–90, 194–198
Allotone, 110, 111
Ambiguity, 62, 166, 170–173, 233, 302
Amuesha, 391, 399
Analysis, 55
Anaphora, 426–428
Arabic, 144–146
Ashley, L., 307
Ashley, S., 307
Aspect, 163–168
Ata, 300
Auca, 27
Austin, G.A., 452
Auxiliary, 199, 200
Aymara, 75, 78

Bach, E., 11, 18
Backlooping, 19, 20, 22
Ballard, D.L., 43, 52, 282, 313
Bandhu, C.M., 57
Barnard, M.L., 42, 251, 282, 310, 354, 375
Becker, A.L., 35, 42, 44, 52–54, 230, 311,
    354, 385–387
Behavior, 2–4
Bendor-Samuel, J.T., 125, 133, 161, 173
Bieri, D., 57
Bilaan, 234–249, 258, 259
Bishop, R.G., 26, 34, 262, 282
Blackburn, B., 258, 259, 282
Bloomfield, L., 5, 11, 20, 139, 144, 377, 386

Bock, P., 39, 53, 301, 441, 445, 446, 450, 452
Bolinger, D.L., 24, 34
Bolivia, 75, 371
Bontoc, 300
Boyd, J.C., 303
Brazil, 125
Brend, R.M., 37, 39, 53
Brown, J., 442
Bruner, J.S., 442, 452
Buck, P.S., 375
Button, E.M., 26, 34, 282

Campa, 389–418
Campos, D.A., 105
Carson, M., 81
Case, 13, 42, 60–65, 163–168, 238, 242–249,
    309–311
Castillo, J.M., 105
Categories, 230
Cather, W., 375
Caughley, R., 57, 70, 74
Cayley diagram, 47
Chepang, 57, 68, 70, 72, 73
Chimanca, P., 390
Chipaya, 75–79
Choice, 32
Chompati, A., 390, 400
Chomsky, N., 6, 7, 18, 56, 73, 179, 223, 225,
    227, 302
Church, A., 354
Church, C., 18, 206
Church, K., 18, 206
Citation, 239–242
Clause, 5, 12, 16, 19, 21, 24, 26, 27, 29,
    31–33, 38, 42, 60, 65, 66, 69–73,
    167, 168, 213–219, 225–229,
    236–249, 251, 262

Cohen, P., 375
Coherence, 178
Colford, 370
Composition, 44
Concord, 41
Conflation, 144–146
Conjoining, 223–233, 263–265
Conrad, R., 43, 52
Constituent, 63
Constraints, 43, 178, 179, 223–225
Construction, *see also* Syntagmeme, 16, 17, 30, 38, 56, 179–181, 225, 237, 285–305
Context, 224
Contrast, 3–5, 25, 26, 29, 33, 36, 77, 78, 83, 84, 88–100, 109, 126–128, 205, 237, 262–282, 316
Contreras, H., 11
Conversation, 47, 48
Cook, W.A., 17, 35, 42, 43, 53, 187
Couplet, 111–124
Cox, D., 17
Crane, S., 370, 373, 375
Crawford, J.C., 78
Cree, 135
Cromack, R.B., 310, 354, 362, 375
Cultural forms, 441, 442
Cycling, 71, 72

Daly, J., 106
Data collection, 8
Davis, I., 75
Dean, J.C., 235, 237, 246, 248
Deep structure, 56, 229–233, 308–354, 361
Delgaty, A., 205
Delgaty, C., 205, 206
Derivation, 58, 65–66, 70–73, 190
Description, 224, 449–453
Dhangar, 57
Dibabawon, 147–160, 300, 368
Dickens, C., 367, 369, 373, 375
Discourse, 32, 35, 41–44, 46, 256–262, 285–305, 356, 357, 377–387, 419–440
Discourse genre, 357, 362, 378
Display, 73
Distribution, 4, 5, 37, 101–103, 130–132
Distribution mode, *see* Distribution
Double function, 23
Downstep, 81, 106–108
Dramatis personae, 12

Dubois, C., 154
Dundes, A., 394, 418

Einstein, A., 2
Eliot, T.S., 5
Elkins, R., 307
Elson, B., 29, 34, 446, 452
Embedding, 17, 19, 20, 22
Emic, 2, 3, 6, 146, 236, 242–245
Emphasis, 238, 240–249
Enclitic, 119–122
Engel, R., 21, 262, 282
English, 12, 13, 26, 27, 42, 46, 58, 64, 65, 175–204, 223–233, 241, 248, 249, 251–283, 288–291, 296, 301, 308, 309, 312, 313, 327, 331, 335, 337, 340, 344, 426, 444
Erickson, B., 75, 140, 143, 144
Etic, 2, 3, 6, 243–245
Evaluation, 223
Expansion, 20, 246
Exponents, 205–219

Feature, 31, 39, 40, 56, 62–65, 69, 176, 204
Feature mode, *see* Contrast
Field, *see also* Matrix, 5, 6, 22, 23, 25, 26, 28, 45, 46, 77–79, 162
Filler, 5, 24, 60, 445
Fillmore, C.J., 23, 35, 42, 53, 60, 61, 74, 225, 309, 354, 370
Focus, 42, 67, 236, 238, 240–249, 287, 296, 397–400
Fodor, J., 11
Fore, 145, 368
Form, 13, 24, 40, 42, 43, 382–384
Formalism, 51, 52, 55
Formative, 40, 135–146
Formula, 43, 56, 78, 179, 182, 183, 205–222, 234
Formula exponation, 17
Formula permutation, 17, 18
Formula reading, 17
Forster, J., 149, 152, 251, 282, 300, 310, 354
Fowles, J., 375
Freyre, R.J., 371, 375
Fries, P.H., 45, 175, 370
Function, *see also* Slot, 11–13, 15, 24, 25, 28, 30–33, 58–60, 135–146
Function-set, 12
Fusion, 44, 45, 203

Gardiner, 304
Garvin, P., 230
Generalization, 36
Generativeness, 35, 43, 78, 187, 191–198, 225
German, 41
Gesture, 52
Ghana, 161
Gleason, H.A., 44, 53, 82, 135, 138, 310, 354
Gleitman, L.R., 225
Glock, N., 44, 53
God's truth, 6, 7
Goffman, E., 445, 452
Goodenough, W., 391, 418
Goodnow, J.J., 452
Gordon, K., 57
Grammar, 4, 8, 11, 25, 41, 42, 44, 45, 57–73, 148–160, 205–222, 285–305
Grammatical form, 230
Grammatical hierarchy, 381, 382, 384
Grammatical meaning, 230, 311
Granados, L., 419
Greek, 13
Grimes, J.E., 35, 37, 44, 47, 53, 187
Gur, 161
Gustafsson, U., 57

Hale, A., 35, 47, 57, 74, 182, 195
Hall, W.C., 251, 282, 307, 310, 354
Halliday, M.A.K., 8, 17, 61, 173
Ham, P., 161
Harris, Z.S., 14, 19, 179, 228, 303, 311
Hawthorne, N., 362, 375
Healey, A., 236
Healey, P.M., 237
Hearer, 32
Hernandez, D., 205
Heuristics, 12, 28
Hibbard, A., 365, 375
Hierarchy, *see also* Level, 4, 8, 19–22, 29–32, 35, 37, 56, 103, 104, 161, 179, 198, 199
Hiẓ, H., 303, 304
Hjelmslev, L.J., 2
Hockett, C.F., 135, 139, 140, 143, 144, 148, 450, 452
Hocus pocus, 6
Hollenbach, B.E., *see* Erickson
Holman, C.H., 365, 375
Huayaní, E., 419
Huddleston, R., 56, 74
Human behavior, 39
Hyperclass, 152, 198, 199

Identification, 36
Identity, 233
Ifugao, 300
India, 57
Indices, 176, 177, 182–187, 191–198, 201
Infinitive, 196, 200–202
Influence, 184
Information, 31
Inibaloi, 307–355

Jacobs, G., 40, 54, 177
Jacobson, S.N., 230
Jakobson, R., 304
Japanese, 14, 15
Jespersen, O., 304
Jirel, 57, 68, 70
Job, 374
Jordan, E.H., 13, 15

Kallahan, K., 361
Kanite, 39
Karlsen, R., 233
Kasem, 161–173
Kasena, 161
Katz, J., 11
Kernel, 38, 237
Kham, 57, 68, 71, 73
King, H.V., 303
Kinship, 389–394
Klammer, T.P., 57, 74, 182
Koen, F.M., 53, 385, 386
Kosena, 368
Kotia, 57
Koutsoudas, A., 225
Kreidler, C.J., 230

Labov, W., 373, 375
Lakoff, G., 23, 312, 354
Landerman, P., 426
Larsen, H., 440
Larson, M., 38
Latin, 13
Lauriot, J., 302
Lawrence, M., 375
Leach, G.N., 31
Lees, R., 11
Level, *see also* Hierarchy, 18, 29, 30, 204
Level skipping, 22
Levengood, M., 440
Lewis, J., 375
Lexeme, 43
Lexemic structure, 44

Lexical form, 230
Lexical hierarchy, 381, 382, 384
Lexical meaning, 230
Lexicon, 4, 8, 11, 42, 61, 62
Lexis, 8
Liem, N.D., 26, 230
Lind, J., 262, 282
Listener, *see* Hearer
Loans, 133
Longacre, R.E., 1, 6, 8, 11, 18, 19, 21, 23, 24, 26, 28–30, 32, 34, 35, 43–48, 52, 53, 177, 178, 187, 199, 200, 204, 206, 224–227, 251, 256–258, 262, 270, 282, 301, 303, 309–311, 355, 377–380, 384, 386
Loos, E.A., 307
Loriot, J., 419
Lounsbury, F.G., 391, 418
Lowe, I., 35, 53, 54
Lusted, R., 300

Magar, 57, 68
Maguindanao, 300
Maithili, 57
Malayo-Polynesian, 13
Manandhar, T., 57
Manifestation mode, *see* Variation
Manobo, 154, 300, 372, 374
Maranao, 147, 152, 300
Margin, 199, 200, 252–256, 320
Martinez, T., 81
Mathematics, 35, 46–52
Matrix, *see also* Field, 35, 38–41, 63, 64, 70–73, 77, 78, 135–146, 161–168, 230, 231, 235–249, 281, 285–305, 382, 383, 446–449
Mayan, 75–79, 205
Mayfield, R., 307
McCawley, J.D., 312, 355
McKaughan, H., 236, 237, 241, 248, 300
McLachlin, B., 258, 259, 282
Meaning, 40–43, 382–384
Meeusen, A.E., 135
Merton, R.K., 443, 444, 450, 452
Mexico, 81, 105, 205, 357
Micmac, 446–449
Miller, G.A., 18
Miller, J., 12, 13, 251, 282, 310, 355
Mishicuri, J., 390
Mixe, 78, 367
Mixteco, 81–134, 176

Modal, 195, 201
Mode, 3
Model choice, 47, 48
Models, 47
Morey, V., 300
Morpheme, 4, 40, 41, 82, 85–90, 183, 191–198
Morphemic patterning, 135–146
Morphophonemics, 40, 176, 177
Morphotonemics, 85–90
Music, 48
Myth, 389–418

Nadel, S.F., 442, 450, 452
Narrative, 170–173, 362–375, 379–384, 419–440
Narrator, 397, 398
Nasality, 124–126
Nasalization, 105
National Science Foundation, 147, 419
Nepal, 47, 67, 69, 70
Nepali, 57, 68
Nesting, *see* Embedding
Neutralization, 161–173
New Guinea, 44, 135, 308, 350, 357, 361, 372, 373
Newari, 57, 64, 68, 70
Newell, L., 300
Nida, E.A., 186, 195, 302
Nii, 350
Nomatsiguenga, 377, 389–418
Notation, 229
Noun phrase, 221, 247, 248, 424, 425
Nucleus, *see also* Peripherary, 17, 44, 62, 77, 123, 199, 251–282, 316

Observer, 42, 389, 400
Office of Education, U.S., 55, 162, 223, 307, 357
Oistakm, O.M., 11
Ojibwa, 144
Oksapmin, 11, 360, 371
Osgood, C., 5, 451, 452
Otomí, 361

Palmer, F.R., 270, 275, 277–280, 282
Pankratz, L., 82, 112, 133
Paradigm, 39, 235–249
Paragraph, 257–262, 385
Parker, G., 421, 440
Participant, 31, 32, 148

Particle, 5, 6, 45, 46, 79, 199
Passive-participle, 202–204
Pattern, 205
Paul, 7
Penn Warren, R., 1
Periphery, 17, 62, 251–282, 316
Perkins, M., 81
Perlmutter, D.M., 312, 355
Permutation, 135–144, 205–219, 226
Person, 135–146, 220
Peru, 42
Philippines, 44, 147, 235–249, 285, 307, 357, 369, 378
Phoneme, 4, 75–77, 99–103, 126–132
Phonological phrase, 104
Phonological word, 103, 104
Phonological word-phrase, 105, 122–126
Phonology, 4, 8, 11, 25, 44
Phonotagmeme, 78
Phrase, 13, 16, 24, 29, 31, 161, 166–167
Phrase structure, 223
Pickett, V.B., 29, 33, 34, 241, 301, 446, 452
Pike, E.G., 57
Pike, E.V., 37, 75, 81, 82, 106, 133
Pike, K.L., 1, 2, 5–8, 11, 23, 26, 28, 34, 35, 37–42, 44–46, 48, 53, 54, 57, 61, 66, 74, 75, 82, 106, 133, 134, 147, 161, 162, 173, 176, 179, 199, 203, 223, 226, 228–230, 251, 282, 310, 355, 377, 384–387, 391, 418, 441, 445, 451, 452
Pike, S., 52
Platt, J., 311, 355
Plot, 394–400
Postal, P.M., 11, 12
Potawatomi, 134–144
Predicate, 29
Price, R., 374, 375
Process, 228
Process phoneme, 105, 106
Pronouns, 46–52
Propp, V., 394, 418, 420
Props, 12

Quechua, 75, 78, 419–440
Quotation, 265–267

Rand, A., 373, 375
Rank, *see* Hierarchy, Level
Reading rules, 230
Recipient, 51
Recursiveness, 224–229

Redfield, R., 441, 452
Redundancy, 39, 56–58, 187, 236
Reid, A., 26, 34, 262, 282
Reid, L.A., 251, 256, 283, 300, 307, 310, 355, 375
Replacement, 226
Rhythm, 77
Robins, C., 375
Role, *see also* Case, 12, 35, 41–43, 58, 62–69, 147–160, 230, 285–309, 389–418, 442–452
Root, 197
Ross, J.R., 23, 282, 312, 355
Rule, 175–222, 225–229
Rule ordering, 186

Saito, Y., 200, 201
Sandburg, C., 365, 375
Saporta, S., 11
Schachter, P., 81, 106, 134
Schaeffer, F.A., 260, 261, 283
Schöttelndreyer, B., 57, 69, 74
Schulze, M., 57
Scott, E., 37
Scott, G., 41, 375
Semantic category, 135, 230–232
Semantics, 31, 56, 59, 60, 230
Sentence, 169, 170, 251–283, 308–354, 420–424
Serial construction, 161
Setting, 12
Shand, J., 300
Shaver, R., 390
Shephard, G., 57
Sherpa, 57, 68, 69, 72, 73
Shipibo, 301
Situation, 41, 148–160, 451
Slot, *see also* Function, 5, 11, 60, 148–160, 195, 197, 445
Small, P., 81
Smeall, C., 186
Snow, J.H., 145
Social space, 445–449
Social structure, 389–400, 441–452
Social time, 445–449
South America, 258
Spanish, 78, 133
Speech acts, 31
Spolsky, B., 230
Stem, 206
Stennes, L.H., 310, 355, 362, 375

Stevens, W.J., 200
Stoll, R.R., 355
Strahm, E., 57
Stratificational grammar, 7, 44
Stress, 37, 103, 104
String, *see also* Construction, 161, 168, 169
Structuralism, 13
Structure, 235
Stucky, A., 350
Subject, 5, 41, 42
Summer Institute of Linguistics, 52, 75, 135,
    147, 154, 251, 256, 285, 302, 308
Sunwar, 57, 68
Surface, 183
Surface structure, 23, 24, 33, 229–233,
    308–354
Syllable, 75–79, 103, 126
Syntagmeme, *see also* Construction, 17, 18, 21,
    25, 28, 29, 205–222, 231
Syntax, 235–249
System, 28, 59, 178, 262, 317
Systematization, 73

Taber, C.R., 310, 355, 372, 375
Tagmeme, 4, 11–13, 15, 17, 19, 20, 24, 33,
    37, 57–73, 147–152, 175–222,
    253–255, 445
Tamang, 57, 67, 68
Taxonomy, 312
Taylor, D., 57
Tense, 163–168
Terai, 67
Tereno, 125
Thatcher, G.W., 145
Thomas, D., 147, 148, 301, 303
Thrall, W.F., 365, 375
Time, 58
Tolkien, J.R.R., 257, 258, 283, 365, 376
Tone, 81–134
Tone sandhi, 91–99, 105, 111–122
Topic, 287, 425, 426
Totonac, 13
Trail, R.L., 34, 57, 74, 182
Transformation, 7, 20, 21, 246
Transformational grammar, 18, 56
Transitivity, 62–70, 147–160, 197, 198,
    236–242
Translation, 43
Trique, 13, 16, 19, 21, 26, 360
Truth, 31

Twaddell, W.F., 197
Twi, 81
Typology, 66–69
Tzotzil, 205–222

Unit, 28, 36, 43, 175, 176, 179, 199, 203
Universals, 52, 66
Uru, 75
Uru-Chipaya, 75

Van Haitsma, W., 367, 376
Variant, 12, 65, 66, 70–73, 84, 85, 101, 110
    111, 127–129, 276
Variation, 36
Verb, 65, 147–173, 424
Verb phrase, 175–204, 206–213
Voegelin, C.F., 451, 452
Voigtlander, K., 361, 376
Vološinov, 304
Vowel harmony, 163

Ward, R.G., 152
Watters, D., 57
Wave, 5, 6, 40, 44–46, 78, 199, 200
Weathers, N., 207
Weaver, D., 300
Wells, R.S., 14
Welmers, W.E., 81, 106, 134
West, D., 376
Wheeler, A., 311
Whitfield, F.J., 2
Whittle, C., 300
Whorf, B.L., 441
Williams, J.M., 57, 269, 283
Wise, M.R., 35, 42–44, 47, 54, 57, 74, 311,
    362, 376, 377, 380, 386, 390, 391,
    396, 418, 419, 440
Wistrand, K., 106, 133
Wojokeso, 373, 374
Wolfenden, E., 237, 248, 302
Women's speech, 132, 133
Woods, W.A., 187
Word, 161, 182, 183, 186, 206
Word order, 12
Wrigglesworth, H., 376

Young, R., 44, 53, 54, 385–387

Zapoteco, 19
Zoque, 21